D1246772

AWAKE, MY HEART

BOOKS BY DR. J. SIDLOW BAXTER . . . .

A New Call to Holiness
Awake My Heart
Divine Healing of the Body
Does God Still Guide?
Explore the Book
God So Loved
Going Deeper
His Deeper Work in Us
His Part and Ours
Mark These Men
Our High Calling
Rethinking Our Priorities
Strategic Grasp of the Bible
Studies in Problem Texts

AWAKE, MY HEART

Daily devotional and expository studies-in-brief based on a variety of Bible truths, and covering one complete year

by

J. SIDLOW BAXTER

ZONDERVAN PUBLISHING HOUSE
OF THE ZONDERVAN CORPORATION
GRAND RAPIDS, MICHIGAN 49506

AWAKE MY HEART

First published U.S.A. 1960

Twenty-fourth printing 1981
ISBN 0-310-20590-5

Printed in the United States of America

FOREWORD

Another book of daily readings? Yes, and why not? It may be that this one, like the others, will have its own distinctive usefulness to at least *some* readers. We do not expect for a moment that it will sell in hundreds of thousands; yet if it only exhausts its first edition of several thousands its ministry even within *those* limits will make its publication worth while. Besides, as so often happens with such books, in an indirect way its contents and influence may seep through to a far larger number than its actual readers. Again, it is to the point just to mention here that *this* book of daily readings really is a variant from others of its species. Its daily instalments are decidedly longer. That is because, in general, they are not only devotional, but expository and homiletical so far as space allows. Moreover, each article is one complete study-in-brief, or else one member in a pair or trio or quartette of such studies, and not merely a few devotional thoughts dovetailed together as in many other useful books of briefer daily readings. Well, here it is, dear reader; with the prayer that our gracious Lord may deign to use it to your profit and for His own honour.

J.S.B.

DEDICATION

To those many esteemed ministers and congregations of U.S.A. and Canada who, during our Bible-teaching itinerary of 1955 to 1960, received our ministry of the Word with unforgettable cordiality and responsiveness, this book of daily meditations is inscribed with ever-fresh remembrance.

AWAKE, MY HEART

Awake, my heart, in joyful lays
To Him who blesses all thy days.
His lovingkindness crowneth thee
With daily mercies rich and free.

Awake, to worship with the morn,
And consecrate the day new-born.
Again at eve in prayer be found,
As shadows curtain earth around.

Awake, thy watchful vigils keep!
For some neglect and idly sleep.
Lift up to God, in sacred tryst,
Thy priestly ministry in Christ.

Awake, His all-wise will to see
In all that He assigns for thee.
Whate'er His providence permits
Designs for thee fresh benefits.

Awake to trust and love and serve,
For can His mercies less deserve?
Till yonder, perfected in love,
Thy heart awakes in heaven above.

J.S.B.

New Year Peaks

"On the first day of the month were the tops of the mountains seen."—Gen. 8 : 5.

THIS verse has a unique applicability to the first day of a new year. The "tenth month" here corresponds with our January; so the "first day" is our January first. What an exhilarating discovery were those uncovered mountain-tops that first day! The flood was declining. God had not "forgotten to be gracious". Those mountain-tops speak to *us* on the first day of *this* year. What will the new year bring, of joy or sorrow, achievement or frustration, health or sickness, good or ill? We cannot foresee what darksome vales or verdant plains or surprise vistas the unfolding months may unveil. Yet if we are truly Christ's, we are not in total obscurity. Up from the unknown, misty morrows, certain grand securities stand out in advance view.

There are those reassuring mountain-tops, *the divine promises*; "exceeding great and precious promises" (2 Peter 1 : 4), pledging to us the divine presence, protection, provision, throughout the coming days. Oh, those sunbathed peaks, "the promises"!

There are the mountain-tops of *spiritual possibilities*. To all who have received Him our Lord gives "power to become" (Jn. 1 : 12). "Thou art . . . thou shalt be" (Jn. 1 : 42). Let us wrest our minds away from pathetic enchantment with "it might have been", and say afresh, "I can do all things through Christ who strengtheneth me" (Phil. 4 : 13).

There are the mountain-tops of our *Christian privileges*—of fellowship "with the Father and with His Son" (1 Jn. 1 : 3); of heavenly joy and peace and guidance imparted by the Holy Spirit; and many more.

There are the mountain tops of *challenging opportunities*. How they shine already in the new-year's sun! Forget the failures of the past, except to learn from them to trust Christ more and self less; and prayerfully resolve on godly conquest in this new year.

And there is that glory-capped peak, the hope of *our Lord's return*. The darker the times, the more resplendently it shines, gilding all the unknown tomorrows with its lovely guarantee of ultimate blessedness.

But note: (1) The mountain-tops were seen from the *ark*, which typified our Saviour. No such radiant peaks greet those who are out of Him. (2) They were seen from *Ararat*, which means "holy ground". Without true consecration there can be but hazy vision of the higher truths. (3) They were seen from *another* mountain top. We ourselves must be on a high altitude. Some of the Lord's people live, as it were, in the basement of the ark, in the twilight of a faith which is never quite sure. They lie against the ribs of the ship, hearing the thud of the waters, and nervously asking whether the ark can survive the strain, and whether or not salvation will last. This is a joy-killing suspense. Fellow-believer, as the new year comes in, climb the ark! Gaze out from the higher places, with "assurance of faith". Lo, the "tops of the mountains"!

Like sunlit peaks His mercies rise
Before my grateful, wondering eyes;
Then let me trust Him, and confess
His endless, glorious faithfulness.

A New Door Opens

"For a great door and effectual is opened unto me, and there are many adversaries."—1 Cor. 16:9.

THERE are open doors in every life, doors to high achievement and wide usefulness and spiritual discovery. Many of us, in moods which we allow too often, look upon our circumstances in life as barriers to attainment; but in our moments of truer perception we discern that the imagined prison bars are in reality open doors of opportunity. Our circumstances only look like barriers because the inward eye by which we recognise spiritual values is diseased.

But there are never open doors without opposition. "A great door and effectual is opened unto me, and there are many adversaries." There is an opportunity in every difficulty and a difficulty in every opportunity. That is why so many blessings are missed, so many heights left unscaled, so many fine chapters of service left unwritten. Some of the finest foreign missionaries are those who never went! They heard the call, they felt the urge, they were keen to go, they saw the open door and would have gone through; but there were adversaries, obstacles, discouragements; there was hesitation; the vision faded; and the grand vocation was never fulfilled.

Just here we are thinking specially about *the open door of this new year*. The last day of the old year is shut against us. However much we may wish to wrench it ajar again, we cannot. But the door of the new year, by the grace of God, now swings open. As we cannot go back to re-live the old year, let us not pine amid useless regrets, but turn our eyes to the great new door of opportunity which the new year sets before us. There are many who go blindly into the new year without a thought that it is a God-given door of opportunity. The "god of this world" blinds their minds. Let us not be like them. May we see the new year to be what it really is—a "great door" opened to us!

First and foremost it is a door to *richer fellowship with God*. Fellowship with God has no attraction for the unbeliever. But God has awakened a new nature in us who are Christ's, and that new nature has both the hunger and the capacity for spiritual joys. The purest joy this side heaven is fellowship with God. At the break of the new year our heavenly Father calls each of us to a closer fellowship with Himself.

But the new year is also an open door to *greater usefulness for Christ*. When at length we cross the river, and ascend yonder shining approach to the heavenly city, will some of us give wistful looks backward, wishing that we might have used our opportunities more faithfully to bring others to that fair place where the King reigns in His beauty? The pleasures and pursuits and concerns on which we spend so much time *now* may seem strangely small *then*. We ought always to view things as we shall view them *then*. How loyal and willing and active we ought to be, despite all discouragements, in the matter of daily bearing our witness for the Saviour! It has been said that a pessimist is one who sees a difficulty in every opportunity; whereas an optimist sees an opportunity in every difficulty. Let this be a year of seeing opportunities rather than difficulties. If we have eyes to see, there are "open doors" everywhere.

Good, Better, Best

"And it came to pass, that, while they communed together and reasoned, Jesus himself drew near, and went with them."—Luke 24: 15.

NEW Year! How appropriate are those words in the Emmaus story —"Jesus Himself drew near and went with them!" One of the earliest grammar lessons we learned at school was the comparison of adjectives—positive, comparative, superlative. The three degrees correspond very happily with this text. Here is something positively good—"Jesus Himself". Here is something comparatively better—"drew near". Here is something superlatively the best—"and went with them".

Reflect for a moment on the first of these. As those two crestfallen men sadly "communed together" on the Emmaus Road, it was none other than "Jesus *Himself*" who joined them. The reflexive, "Himself", is added to emphasize that it was the real, personal Jesus, the very subject of their conversation, who actually drew near, then and there, unchanged after His crucifixion and resurrection. Yes, "Jesus Himself". And oh, how precious it is to know that it is this same "Jesus Himself" who links up with us as we step forth into this new year! Few things grieve me more than to hear preachers speak of our dear Lord as though He were merely a figure of the bygone, with us now only as a benign influence, or in a vague, uncertain way. No, our dear Master Himself is really with us, invisibly yet none the less *personally*; "Jesus Himself".

But second, "Jesus Himself *drew near*". Yes, He drew near even though, paradoxically enough, He was "near" before He "*drew*" near. He was with them spiritually and invisibly before He now drew near observably. So is He always with *us*, while yet there are times when He draws near in some special way, making His presence a luminously conscious reality to us. We may well observe that it was while those two men were *conversing about Him* that He drew near. How often in our social converse with other Christians we let the time slip away without any mention of His dear Name! And what blessings we thereby forfeit! When Christ draws near it is always that He may make some further revelation of Himself, even as on that Emmaus road He "expounded unto them in all the Scriptures the things concerning Himself" and then made that rapturous Self-disclosure in the "breaking of bread". At the beginning of this year, He draws specially near to us. He would reveal Himself in some new and fuller way. Are we ready for this?

Third, and best: "Jesus Himself drew near *and went with them.*" Superlative inspiration at the opening of the new year! He who draws near on the first day of January will companion us to the last day of December. He goes with us as individual disciples, guiding, guarding, encouraging, renewing, and sharing the qualities of His own life with us. He loves His people's company. He delights to make our days a sunlit Emmaus walk. Oh that this may be for us a year of the burning heart, as He "talks with us by the way"!

"Jesus Himself"—inspiring word!
"Drew near"—their inmost thought He heard!
"Went with them"—oh, what truth they learned!
Their hearts, enrapt, within them burned.

Grace and Peace

"Grace to you, and peace, from God our Father, and the Lord Jesus Christ."—Rom. 1 : 7.

HAVE you noticed that every one of the nine "Christian Church Epistles" begins with the same invocation? *"Grace be to you, and peace, from God our Father and the Lord Jesus Christ."* From such a heart as Paul's it was no mere wish, but an earnest, loving prayer. It is always appropriate, and particularly so at the incoming of a new year. There are three great truths comprised in it, namely, the fatherhood of God, the lordship of Christ, and the true blessing of the Christian believer. It will mean much if we enter the new year with these great truths in mind.

We are living in such times as never were before. Awful convulsions have shaken the world. Millions have died in recent world wars. Thrones have fallen. Sweeping changes have come. Science has now put into men's hands powers of almost unlimited possibility either for racial good or racial destruction. The war-haunted world is a smouldering volcano. It is not strange that apprehensive feelings should cling around us as we peer into the future, and that we fall back with relief on the doctrine of the divine *sovereignty*. Yet somehow even that is not enough. We need the further truth that the God who is sovereign is also *"our Father"*. All our life will feel safer and gladder; the enigmas of human history will assume a kindlier aspect; and the big universe itself will become friendlier, if we go into the new year with this precious truth in mind, that the sovereign God is our *Father*, ever-loving, ever-present, compassionately interested in all our concerns, and ever pursuing through our changeful earthly vicissitudes His purposes for our ultimate good.

But see now the absolute lordship of Christ in this Pauline benediction. Admittedly, the Greek word *kurios* here translated "Lord" is used in the New Testament as a mere honorary title not unlike the English "Sir"; but it is also used as the equivalent of the Old Testament "Jehovah". It is in this latter sense that Christ is Lord—in the sense in which God alone can be Lord. If proof of this were needed, it is here in this very benediction. The "grace" and "peace" are to come from "God our Father *and the Lord Jesus Christ*". Such close association of our Lord's name with that of God, and such implied identity in the imparting of grace and peace, would be sheer blasphemy if Christ were not co-equal with the Father. May we never cease to marvel that our Saviour and Lord is the eternal Son of God Himself, in whom there is the perfect union of human sympathy and divine power! He is Lord of *history*. The vast turmoils and evolutions of our day are but the predicted precursors of His own return in kingly authority, to establish His worldwide millennial empire. We are thinking realistically—He may return *this* year!

Paul prays that "grace" and "peace" may be given to us. These are two lovely words. Grace here is the imparting to us of God's holy love.

That other word, "peace", here means well-being in general. How often we Christians misunderstand our real needs! How often we think that if only we had more money, higher position, greater gifts, or perhaps better health, we should be much better off! No, our real need is *"grace and peace."* Thank God, they can be ours through all the coming days.

Climb High

"He carried me away . . . to a great and high mountain."—Rev. 21 : 10.

It is understandable that in days like these we should tend to be preoccupied with the vast affairs of the times. Wide-sweeping ideologies contend against each other. Huge world-movements are taking shape. Never did the individual seem so dwarfed. Yet it is true today, as ever, that the individual is the crux of the whole situation. Moreover, the omniscient heavenly Father never deals with men and women on the *en masse* principle of the modern Dictator. After all, the biggest of the stars is small against a human being made in the image of God! The humblest believer, bought with the precious blood of Calvary, is more precious to the heart of the Creator than Orion and Pleiades! Let us go into this new year realising that the ever-watchful eye of God is upon us *individually*.

As Christians, we ought to see all the portentous developments of our time *from a high altitude*. Only when we stand high do we see far. Broad landscapes are never commanded from lowlands. It is elevation which gives wide vision. If we want greater latitudes and longitudes we must have higher altitudes. When John was to be shown the New Jerusalem descending out of heaven, he was carried away to "a great and high mountain". Before this he had stood down by the sea shore and seen a "beast" rise up out of the deep (13: 1). We see too many "beasts" today, rising up from our troubled modern world, and too few "New Jerusalems" coming down from the sovereign skies! There are too many of us living down at sea-level! There are many influences to keep us there. The average radio and television stuff will keep us there. So will the usual newspaper. So will the common run of magazines. So will the average conversation of the street and the place of daily business.

Christ's people were never meant to live at the world's sea-level. We are meant to have the mountain view, the long view, the wide view, the really understanding view. We are meant to see the happenings of our time in the light of inspired prophecy, through the eyes of the Holy Spirit, from the high view-point of the divine purpose, and with our gaze on the ultimate victory of Christ. The "beasts" which are arising from the sea in our day are unknowingly preparing for the "New Jerusalem". Even 666 will but prove the devil's herald of the Lord's final triumph.

But how shall we keep that high altitude of vision in our daily life? We must live near to the Scriptures. We must love the place of prayer. We must guard against easy-going toleration of things in our lives which grieve the Holy Spirit, and rob us of His inward witness. Many of us have been taught to distrust new-year resolves; but they can mean great blessing if they are made in dependence on the Holy Spirit. It could mean untold blessing to go into this new year having made the following covenant with our Lord: I WILL GIVE NOT LESS THAN THIRTY MINUTES EACH DAY TO PRAYER. I WILL COMMEND MY SAVIOUR IN EARNEST CONVERSATION TO AT LEAST ONE PERSON EACH WEEK. I WILL READ CONSECUTIVELY EACH DAY FROM BOTH OLD AND NEW TESTAMENTS. I WILL ALLOW NOTHING IN MY LIFE WHICH MIGHT IN ANY WAY COMPROMISE THE NAME OF JESUS. If we were thus to live through this incoming year, it could only prove a year of peaceful hope.

Our Ever-Present Lord

"Lo, I am with you alway."—Matt. 28:20.

BETWEEN our Lord's resurrection and His ascension there were forty days during which, to quote Acts 1:3, He "showed Himself alive" to His disciples "by many infallible proofs". A remarkable phenomenon of those forty days was that our Lord, instead of remaining continuously visible to the disciples, communicated with them in a series of sudden appearances separated by intervals of invisibility (look them up again). Why was this? It was to teach them that when He was not visible He was none-the-less present. In His sudden appearances He gave evidence that He had heard all their conversations during His invisibility, as when He suddenly appeared and tenderly chided doubting Thomas, thereby indicating that although unseen, He had heard Thomas's words. Then, He wound up those forty days with the culminating assurance, "Lo, I am with you alway, even unto the end of the age."

Those first disciples really *learned* the lesson that their risen Lord was with them though no longer visible; but I wonder whether you and I have equally learned it in relation to ourselves. We have often heard it said that our Lord's resurrection transformed those first disciples from weaklings and cowards into strong men and heroes. That, however, is not the *whole* truth. It was five things all in one which made them such joyful, constant, fearless testimonials to the saving-power of Christ; first, that He was really risen; second, that He was on the throne of heaven in complete control; third, that He was invisibly present with them everywhere; fourth, that He would eventually reappear in royal dominion; fifth, that if they died before His return, then to be "absent from the body" was to be "at home" with the Lord.

The centre-point of all was, that during those unforgettable forty days they had learned the transforming truth of His invisible presence with them. Indeed, they had grasped the precious fact that He was now more *closely* with them than when He was moving visibly before them in a physical body. He was with them now, not merely outwardly, but *inwardly*—invisibly all around them and also indwelling them by the Holy Spirit! Even so, our dear Lord is really with *us*. His presence is no mere vague, hazy, shadowy, vapoury, unreal idea. It is no mere figure of speech, or fond sentiment, or superstitious imagination of hoodwinked hero-worshippers. It is the real, personal presence of the ever-living, ever-loving, everlasting Saviour Himself.

His presence is meant to be *real* to us, all the time and everywhere, especially when we are bearing our witness to Him, or are suffering for His sake, or are in trouble of any kind. But with all too many of us the realisation of His presence is intermittent, fluctuating, indistinct, unsatisfying. What a pity is this! When we lack the consciousness of His presence we are easily disturbed, disheartened, nervous, ruffled, impatient, wrongly self-assertive; but when we live in the joyful comfort of His realised presence, we become optimistic amid discouragements, patient amid tribulation, brave amid danger, calm amid strife, cheerful amid monotony. The desert blossoms as the rose, and the parched ground becomes a garden. Christian, pause at these precious words again: "Lo, I am with you alway, even unto the end. . . ."!

Our Subconscious Mind—and Christ

"Lo, I am with you alway."—Matt. 28: 20.

But someone asks, "Is it *possible* for us to be *always conscious* of our Lord's presence with us?" Our own considered answer is: Yes. I do not think we can be always on the mountain-top of transfiguration, seeing heavenly visions, hearing heavenly voices, and experiencing supernatural ecstasies. Nay, too much of *that* would be a doubtful luxury, unnecessary to our present service for Christ, and a strain on our nervous system. Yet I *do* think we are meant to carry with us the unbroken awareness of His presence.

I am not supposing that our minds must always be riveted on religious subjects. Most of us have to give hours every day to mundane matters which require our undivided attention. We cannot always be in church, or on our knees in prayer, or reading the Bible. None the less, I believe we may carry the continuous awareness of our Lord's presence.

God has implanted in our human constitution a wonderful faculty which we call the *sub-conscious mind*. There is an upper and a lower consciousness in our minds. Besides the upper stratum of fully conscious thought and will and experience, there is this lower stratum of *sub*-conscious mental activity. We should be mentally poor without it. A large part of what we call memory is sub-conscious activity of the mind. For instance, we married persons may not at this moment be deliberately thinking back to our wedding day; yet the memory of that day is retained in our sub-conscious mind, and can be called up at will on to the higher level of fully conscious thought. In all of us there is this mental duality. Below the upper consciousness by which we voluntarily engage in thought, there is this undercurrent of non-volitional consciousness all the while continuing; and often when the upper consciousness lies dormant the sub-conscious pours its contents into the *upper* part of the mind—which largely accounts for dreams, and day-dreams, and mental wanderings over the sportsfield while the clerk is adding up the columns of his ledger.

Now the sub-conscious mind can be of immense value in the Christian life. It is by means of it that we may carry the continual awareness of our Lord's presence. We may be in a lovely garden of fragrant flowers and be sub-consciously appreciative of them even when our minds are not directly thinking of them. So is it with the clothes we wear, and the sunshine which we enjoy. We can carry the continued consciousness of things even when we are not directly thinking of them. In these days of speed and strain and tension, I would urge Christian believers: Develop a continual sub-conscious awareness of Christ. You will find that again and again the *sub*-conscious rises to the surface of the *fully*-conscious, to bless and sweeten it. Thus, besides the presence of Christ being *real*, it will be continually *realised*. Does someone ask *how* this may be developed? (1) Hand all the *keys* of your heart to Him. (2) Keep tryst with Him by regular daily prayer. (3) *Practice* His presence; for even in this, "practice makes perfect". (4) Remember ever that it is a special ministry of the Holy Spirit, as the "Paraclete", to make our Lord's presence inwardly real to us. Our Lord said so (see John 14: 20). I believe it is true to say that exactly in degree as we are yielded to and possessed by the Holy Spirit, so is our consciousness and *sub*-consciousness of Christ.

The Ever-Abiding Presence

"Lo, I am with you alway."—Matt. 28:20.

WHAT a difference it makes to our life when we *experience* that our dear Lord is really with us! What a transforming effect Jacob's discovery of the divine presence had upon him! When he fled from Isaac's tents he thought he had left his father's God behind. His exclamation was one of astonishment, "Surely the Lord is in *this* place, and I knew it not." It was a life-transforming discovery, as we see from the vow he there uttered.

There was a Hebrew prophet, once, who thought to sail beyond the reach of "the presence of the Lord". Had he only read certain verses from the Pentateuch for his Scripture reading that morning, or a few verses from Psalm 139, he would never have paid his fare! Later, he was grateful to find that even his strange submarine inside the "great fish" could not shut him off from God! What a comfort was the presence of the Lord to *Paul* as he took his trial before Nero!—"At my first defence no man stood with me, but all men forsook me: I pray God that it may not be laid to their charge. Notwithstanding, the Lord stood with me, and strengthened me."

And how real has the Lord's presence been to multitudes of others! One could fill books with testimonies. The danger is that in picking out examples we should give the impression that such realization of His presence is only for a favourite few. No, God is not a respecter of persons. The supporting consciousness of His presence may be known by the humblest among us. There is no good reason why the realisation of the divine presence should not be a cloudless experience with us.

We think of "Brother Lawrence", the seventeenth-century kitchen-servant: "The time of business does not with me differ from the time of prayer: and in the noise and clutter of my kitchen, while several persons are at the same time calling for different things, I possess God in as great tranquillity as if I were on my knees. . . . I make it my business only to persevere in His holy presence, wherein I keep myself by a simple attention, and an habitual, silent, and secret conversation of the soul with God, which often causes in me joys and raptures inwardly, and sometimes also outwardly, so great that I am forced to use means to moderate them, and prevent their appearance to others. . . . There is not in the world a kind of life more sweet and delightful than that of a continual conversation with God. Those only can comprehend it who practise and experience it; yet I do not advise you to do it from that motive; it is not pleasure which we ought to seek in this exercise; but let us do it from a principle of love, and because God would have us."

O believer, dear to the great Father, made unspeakably precious to Him by the redemption-price paid on Calvary, made sacred to Him by the indwelling of the Holy Spirit, think over this great truth, that God would hold fellowship with you every hour of the day. If we are conscientious and resolute to maintain times of prayer and Bible meditation each day, and are willing to put from us vain ways and questionable practices, determining to love God with all our heart, we may develop such a radiant realisation of His fellowship with us as shall keep us always "rejoicing with joy unspeakable".

"And as He prayed, the fashion of His countenance was altered."—Luke 9: 29.

WHEN we survey perspectively our Lord's life on earth, seven pre-eminent events stand out like successive mountain-pinnacles. Those seven are, His birth, His baptism, His temptation, His transfiguration, His crucifixion, His resurrection, His ascension.

Our Lord's transfiguration is the fourth and therefore the centre-point of the seven; and certainly it is a towering peak resplendent with significances. It is an arresting attestation of the Father's pleasure in the Son. It is equally an attestation of our Lord's superiority over Moses and Elijah. Also, in its circumstantial features, it is a remarkable fore-picturing of our Lord's future return in the glory of His kingdom.

But whatever other significances inhere in it, we miss the *spiritual challenge* of it if we overlook those three little words in Luke 9: 29—"*As He prayed*". We are distinctly told that our Lord went up that mountain "to pray", and that His transfiguration occurred "*as He prayed*". What happened to our Lord suddenly and objectively may happen in ourselves spiritually, gradually, progressively, if we are much in prayer. So then, with the transfigured Lord before our inward eyes, let us briefly reflect on the transfiguring power of prayer.

First, we put this, that prayer transfigures *our view of life*. Real prayer is an ascending of the soul to a spiritual summit. And just as high altitude transforms a landscape in the physical world, so does real prayer in the spiritual realm. When a man climbs to some mountain height, he sees the relative size and importance of things in a way which he never could from the plains below. That building which seems so massive to the town-dwellers down there now seems a mere dot. Even the big town is all but lost amid the spreading expanses. Other objects which were greatly underestimated through being seen only partly from a lower view now assume immense proportions and impressiveness.

So it is when by prayer we climb "the mount of God". From that hill-summit of communion with God we see things in broader view and truer relationship. We begin to distinguish between the *seemingly* great and the *really* great. Many of the seemingly big concerns which have surrounded us, and felt almost on top of us down there, shrink into surprising littleness as we now see them against the *really* big things which they prevented us from seeing while we were down there among them!

We often speak about getting "a bird's-eye view" of things, but as G. H. Knight says, "From the mountain-top of secret prayer we get a '*God's-eye view*' of everything; and it is marvellous how that makes many great things look small, and small things great; how all mere worldly ambitions look surprisingly poor, and heavenly ambitions the only ones worth having." "Many a false estimate is rectified there. Our ambitions, plans, labours, worries, vexations, sorrows, cares, fall into their true proportions."

Yes, that is what happens, especially if our times of secret prayer are regular and unhurried. In that secret tryst of communion with the Eternal we are lifted above the world in which we daily mix and move; we begin to see things as they appear to the eye of Heaven.

A True View of God

"Show me now Thy way, that I may know Thee."—Exod. 33 : 13.
"Moses, whom the Lord knew face to face."—Deut. 34 : 10.

REGULAR, unhurried daily prayer in secret not only transforms our view of life; it corrects and clarifies and vivifies our view of *God*. We may learn something of God from nature; and something more from history; and immeasurably more from Scripture; and culminatingly from His self-revelation through our Lord Jesus Christ. Yet wonderful as that varied revelation of God is, it is all necessarily objective, something outside of ourselves. Before we can see God luminously in nature, in history, in Scripture, or even in His incarnate Son, something needs to happen in ourselves—to our organ of spiritual vision.

In all persons truly converted to Christ the Holy Spirit has begotten a new spiritual nature, with faculties of spiritual seeing and hearing and understanding. Yet even that new nature needs the supernatural illumination of the Holy Spirit. It is that fact which Paul has in mind when he prays, in Ephesians 1 : 17, 18, "That the God of our Lord Jesus Christ, the Father of glory, may give unto you the Spirit of insight and unveiling in the knowledge of Himself; the eyes of your understanding *being enlightened, that ye may know. . . .*" Apart from this supernatural illumination of the Holy Spirit, the universe remains a riddle, and history an enigma, and the Bible a dead letter, and even Christ a lovely statue.

It is when we climb the mount of prayer that the Holy Spirit has His opportunity to prove Himself to us as "the Spirit of insight and unveiling" in the knowledge of God. Even the new nature cannot see God with full vision if continually denied the mountain-top of prayer, and forced to live entirely on lower levels.

You and I are living in an epoch when it is easy to get distorted views of God. We wonder why evils vast and vile are permitted to flourish on earth; why Christ-blaspheming despots, vain and vaunting, are allowed to gloat in triumphant trickery; and why a million agonies still daily scourge the bleeding body of mankind. And, quite apart from the days in which we are living, when severe sickness or intense pain or crushing sorrow lashes us individually, it is easy to inflict upon ourselves that added torture which comes from distorted views of God.

But such distortions never afflict those Christian men and women who daily climb the transfiguration-mount of secret communion with Heaven. Their view of God is transfigured. They come to know what Paul meant when he said, "He that is spiritual discerneth all things." They find that God has His own way of disclosing Himself to the spiritual mind, revealing His presence in the world and His purpose in history, and shedding the light of heaven over the mysteries of earth in a way which transcends explanation in words.

There are some things which God cannot tell us in words, any more than He could tell Job the reason and the purpose behind his grievous trial. There are some things which cannot be told; they have to be *seen*; and it is *there*, on that mount of secret prayer, that we *do* see them, and know them, and become radiant in their luminousness. It is there, on that prayer-summit, that we begin to see God everywhere in the *universe*, everywhere in *history*, and in all the happenings of *our own life*.

Prayer and Character

"When he came down from the mount, Moses wist not that his face shone. . . ."—Exod. 34:29.

IT is certainly true that there is no place like the mountain-height of prayer for bringing spiritual eye-openings to us concerning life and God. It is there that false estimates of earthly concerns are rectified; and it is there that we see God at work when others are blind to His presence. It is a true saying that they who climb highest see farthest. It is equally true that they who climb highest see clearest. In a spiritual sense it is correspondingly true that the mountain-top of secret prayer gives not only a *high* view, but a *far* view, and a *full* view, and a *clear* view. Above the mists of the plains and the vapours of the valleys, we begin to see both earthly and heavenly things in truer light, and our reaction is affected correspondingly.

Yes, it is all true; yet the greatest reflex influence of regular, unhurried, secret prayer is seen in the transfiguration of *character* which it invariably brings about in those who so pray.

Let me quote G. H. Knight. "The very countenance of a man of much prayer will often bear witness to his acquaintedness with the mountain height. It will show a softened spiritual beauty that in his prayerless days it never had. But whether the face bears witness to the mountain-top or not, the whole life and character will. There is sure to be seen in his whole tone an elevation of feeling showing clearly that he is accustomed to be often very near to God: and thus his high fellowship with God will bring about a high life before men. If any Christian finds that his soul is not sufficiently raised above the down-dragging influence of earthly things, and his life not transformed gradually but surely into the beauty of holiness, it is only because he does not often enough climb the hill of secret communion with God, nor linger long enough there to catch its heavenly glow."

We think of Moses, away back in the Old Testament, and how, after those forty days of unbroken communion with God on Mount Sinai, he came down among the people with the very skin of his face eradiating the contracted glory-light. We think of the seraphic Stephen, in the New Testament, the man of prayer, the man full of the Holy Spirit, and how the members of the hostile Jewish council, "saw his face as it had been the face of an angel". We think supremely of our dear Lord Himself, and how, on the mount of transfiguration, it was "as He prayed" that His transfiguration occurred.

These are but outward exhibitions and illustrations of that *inward heart-transfiguration* which prayer brings about. Think again of Moses—of all men on earth the meekest. Think again of Stephen—and his "Lord, lay not this sin to their charge". Think of our Lord Himself and His matchless character.

Psychologists speak about *intergrade.* They mean a certain process which operates in the minds of those who are often in each other's company, by which they tend to grow like each other. So, in the hearts and lives of those men and women who spend "much time in secret, with Jesus alone", there is always that growing more like the Lord, and a developing reflection of His beauty. Oh, for more of that transfiguration!

The Messianic Hope

"Behold, He shall come."—Mal. 3: 1.

THE Bible is Christocentric. Eliminate Christ from the Old Testament typology, psalmody, philosophy, prophecy, and the whole anticipative structure disintegrates into incohesive fragments. There is scarcely a more engaging or illuminating study than to trace the progressive unfolding of the Messianic idea right through the thirty-nine oracles of the Old Covenant. It moves forward in six stretches or stages.

First, there is the Sethite or *racial* period, from Adam to Noah. In Genesis 3: 15 the first promise is given, that the "seed of the woman" should crush the serpent; by which is implied that the Restorer should come from within the race itself. Thereafter, through the antediluvian centuries, the promise links down through a chain of chosen individuals, from Seth to Noah.

Second, there is the Shemitic or *ethnic* period, from Noah to Abraham. The great racial divisions of humanity branch down from Noah's three sons. The Shemite division is chosen; then, within that, the line of Arphaxad down to Abraham.

Third, there is the patriarchal or *tribal* period, from Abraham to Moses. Abram is separated as the first father of a promised seed from which Christ should come; then Isaac, to whom the covenant is renewed; then Jacob whose twelve sons become the patriarchs or fathers of the Israel tribes; and the promise of Shiloh is narrowed to the tribe of Judah (Gen. 49: 10).

Fourth, there is the national or *theocratic* period, from Moses to David. At Sinai the twelve tribes were welded into one nation. They were given laws, statutes, ordinances, directly from God, and were thereby constituted a theocracy. This was because the Messianic idea was now to be unfolded institutionally or typologically through the divinely designed system of Israel's priesthood and sacrifices.

Fifth, there is the royal or *family* period, from David to the Exile. David is told that the Messiah shall come of his own house or family (2 Sam. 7). Thus the stream narrows down from the race as a whole, to one ethnic division, then to the Hebrew tribes, then to the Israel theocracy, and now to David's household; and the promise is handed down, king after king, until the catastrophe of the Exile aborts the historic Davidic throne, and disperses the people through Babylonia.

Sixth, there is the final or *post-exilic* period, from the Exile to Christ Himself. What changes during Israel's 850 years' occupancy of Canaan!

It is wonderful to see how, as the stream narrows down from race to family, in another sense it grows wider and wider, until Messianic predictions reach flood-point. Psalms and Prophets foretell His birth of a virgin in Bethlehem; His character and ministry; His betrayal and crucifixion; His very words on the Cross; His ultimate kingdom; and a variety of other features. What does it all say to you and me? Why, this: the purposes of God are marching down the centuries with irresistible tread. Let us have no fear, God is in control. The first coming of Jesus as world-Saviour guarantees His second coming as world-Sovereign. And the golden daybreak must surely be upon us ere long.

"His mother saith unto the servants: Whatsoever He saith unto you, do it."—Jn. 2:5.

In my early teens I was a pleasure-loving young worldling. My spiritual desires were feeble. The pull of the world was strong. I must have been a keen disappointment to my dear mother, who, before ever I was born, had dedicated me to God, so far as *her* will was concerned, for the Christian ministry. She was patient with me, however, and wise. She did not try to force her religion on me, but took all the little opportunities which came her way to influence me favourably. When I was sixteen she gave me a nicely bound copy of the Bible for my birthday, though at that time I never read the Bible; and on the fly-leaf she inscribed it thus: "To my dear Son, on his sixteenth birthday", following which was a suggested motto for my life: "WHATSOEVER HE SAITH UNTO YOU, DO IT" (Jn. 2:5).

That same year I was truly converted; and that dear Bible thereupon was in constant requisition. I kept seeing that motto on the fly-leaf; yet nearly ten years passed (such was my mental obtusity!) before I suddenly realised the special point of it, as my *mother's* suggested life-motto for me. One morning the words fairly leapt upon me from the printed page: "His *mother* saith. . . ." Why, yes, of course; it was "His *mother*" who said the words, "Whatsoever He saith unto you, do it"; and it was *my* mother who was now saying it to *me*, on His behalf. Ever since then, that verse has really *been* my motto: "Whatsoever He saith unto you, do it."

Observe the three features in this motherly advice. First, our obedience is to be *entire*; for the scope and range are in that word "whatsoever". Second, our obedience is to be *exclusive*; for we are to do "whatsoever *He* saith", to the exclusion of all others, if they differ from Him. Third, our obedience is to be *specific*: "Whatsoever He saith unto you, do *it*"; not just something rather like it, or something part-way, or something supposedly equivalent; but "*it*".

Notice, also, the three features in the obedience of those Cana servants, They obeyed *immediately*, as verse 7 indicates. They obeyed *completely*. filling the waterpots "to the brim". They obeyed *successively* each new instruction as it came—to "fill", to "draw", to "bear".

And now notice the three main features of the outcome. In response to their obedience there was (1) a supernatural *intervention*, for the water was turned into wine; (2) a wonderful *transformation*, for the social catastrophe was given a glad climax; (3) a significant *revelation*, for it is written, "This beginning of miracles did Jesus in Cana of Galilee, and manifested forth his glory; and his disciples *believed on him*." Such surprise interventions, transformations, and revelations happen again and again where there is full obedience to Him.

How this should speak to the younger among us! Young friend, insofar as choice of career rests with yourself, let this be your governing motto: "Whatsoever He saith unto you, do it." Let that same motto govern love, courtship, wedlock. When Jesus is left out of the wedding, sooner or later, in a spiritual sense, the wine fails; but when He is the Guest of Honour, He turns the water into wine, sublimating our poor human love into a joy which is a very foretaste of heaven.

Our Holy Calling

"To all that be in Rome; beloved of God; called to be saints."—Rom. 1 : 7.

EVERY true Christian is called of God; and lying behind that call is divine foreknowledge and predestination (Rom. 8 : 29, 30). Behind our conversion is the electing will of God; and our regeneration by the Holy Spirit is the experiential evidence of it. The subject of predestination is one of vast mystery, but emerging from it are practical truths which the simplest of us can readily grasp. Here is one of them: "Called to be saints."

God would have us be reflectors of His own holiness because He has specially set His love upon us, as our text says. Am I truly born again of His Spirit? Am I washed from guilt before God, by the precious blood of Calvary? Do I really love the Lord Jesus? Then I am one of "God's loved ones" who are "called to be saints" This carries with it three weighty reflections.

The first of these is, that here is *the supreme glory* of the Christian life: we are "called to saints". Nowadays that word, "saint", is often used sarcastically as a poke at some sanctimonious person—"Oh, he's a saint". Or, if the word is used seriously, it is reserved for persons of specially distinguished piety. The Roman Catholic Church has sickeningly perverted it into meaning only outstanding Romanist believers of the past whom the pope and the cardinals have canonised as "saints". A little boy known to me, on being asked to define a saint, replied, "A saint is a dead Christian"; and that is a pretty common idea.

It is a pity the word has been so mishandled. We must not fight shy of it, for it is one of the great terms in our Christian vocabulary. Sainthood is the call of the New Testament to every Christian, as we see from the word, "all", in our text. Positionally, in Christ, *all* Christian believers are "saints" (1 Cor. 1 : 2; Eph. 1 : 18, etc.); and what we all are positionally is meant to have its practical counterpart in saintly character and conduct.

The meaning of the word "saint" is exactly the same as "sanctify". True sainthood is Christian sanctification or separatedness—separatedness *from* our unregenerate past, from worldliness, from all known sinful ways; and separatedness *to* an outward confession of Christ, and an inward fellowship with Christ, and a daily usableness by Christ. The first business of every Christian is this sanctification or separatedness, and the developing of holy character. This is not incompatible with legitimate employment in business, unless our occupation itself is wrong. We can make all our circumstances contribute, if we will, to the furtherance of real sainthood. This is the highest of all callings; and this is the supreme glory of the Christian life.

As has often been said, we are not all called to be preachers, teachers, missionaries, authors, hymn-writers, whole-time evangelists, or public Christian leaders; but we are *all* "called to be saints"; that is, we are all called to entire sanctification.

Sanctify me wholly, Sovereign Saviour mine;
Spirit, soul and body now make fully Thine.

"Called to be saints."—Rom. 1: 7.

IN this call to sainthood we see not only the supreme glory of the Christian life, but its supreme *difficulty*. We never know how really bad we are until we try to be really good. We never know how really selfish we are until we try to be really sacrificial. We never know how many vices there are in us until we really try to practise all the virtues. We never know what sinners we are until we really try to be saints. Yet there it is: "called to be *saints*".

It is comparatively easy to preach sermons, write books, compose hymns, conduct meetings, engage in active religious work; but practical, thorough sainthood is of all things the hardest. This New Testament insistence on sainthood is a broom which sweeps into every room and corner of the life, and refuses to leave any of the dust undisturbed. It is a flash-lamp which shines into every darksome niche of heart and mind, of motive and desire. Inwardly and outwardly, through and through, we are "called to be saints".

Christianity puts its first emphasis on character, not on service. We are "called to be saints". That is, we are called to "*be*" something before we try to "do" *any*thing. This cannot be stressed too often. We are not *saved* by our character; it is *Christ's* character which saves us, not ours. On the principle of imputed righteousness *His* character becomes legally *my* character, and in Him I therefore have a new judicial standing before God. But once having become saved through the sinless character and vicarious saviourhood of Christ, I am to become *transformed* in my own character. *My* character is to become like *His*, through consecration on my part, and impartation on His. We are not saved by good works; we are saved by grace alone on God's part, and faith alone on ours; yet neither can we be saved *without* good works, for as James 2: 17 says, "Faith, if it hath not works is dead"—and a dead faith is *no* faith.

"Called to be *saints*." A converted housemaid had learned her first lessons in practical sainthood when she said, "Before my conversion I swept *round* the mats; I now sweep *under* them as well." A padre, after a seemingly futile conversation to win a young soldier for Christ, suddenly thought to ask: "Was no one in your family ever converted to Christ?" The soldier replied, "Yes, my father." "And did your father's conversion make a difference at home?" the padre asked. "Yes," replied the soldier, "it made us all miserable." That father illustrated something which true sainthood is *not*. Instead of diffusing the fragrance of the rose, he was shooting out the spikes of a cactus plant. True sainthood requires us to be unbending in principle, but kindly and fragrant in disposition.

Thank God, true sainthood is *possible*. Look at the words again—"*Called* to be saints." All God's challenges are pledges. All His commands are enablings. If I *must* be, then I *may* be, whatever my circumstances. If I am meant to be a saint, then I myself must *mean* to be one, and my living Lord will *make* me one, by His indwelling of my heart. Do not try to live a holy *life*; live a holy *minute*!—sixty of them make a holy hour; and hours make days, weeks, years. This minute is yours. Live it for Him, in thought, desire, behaviour, speech. Yes, that is really possible. Christ Himself is within you. Hand over to Him; trust Him, *prove* Him.

Strange Reverse

"Why is it that Thou hast sent me?"—Exod. 5: 22.

MOSES is distinguishingly called, "the servant of the Lord", and he well merits the title. The Scripture record of his life is full of weighty lessons to all who would be the Lord's true servants. We are all familiar with his early history. By a singular providential interposition he was snatched from death as an infant, and actually reared among the Egyptian royalty. He became "learned in all the wisdom of the Egyptians", "mighty in words and in deeds" (Acts 7: 22).

His sympathies, however, remained with his own people, the enslaved and downtrodden Hebrews, and he was not ashamed to identify himself with them, which doubtless would be the covert talk of the royal court (Acts 7: 25). He believed that under God he was to emancipate his brethren, and he struck a first blow to that end. But it was based on a wrong assumption (Acts 7: 25) and it was by a wrong method, in the wisdom and strength of the flesh. It proved abortive, Moses had to flee for life; and thereupon for forty years he was in Midian.

Then, when he was eighty, the unexpected happened. From the burning bush of Horeb God called him to lead the exodus of Israel from Egypt. By this time, however, so thoroughly had those forty years done their work that not only had Moses' impulsive spirit died down, but he who had once run *before* God now lagged *behind*. Moses did not want to go. Was it that he dreaded the busy turmoil of those teeming hives of population? Was it that the pressure of years disinclined him from such exertion? Was it that he was loathe to leave the open solitudes and the companionship of the mountains? Or was it that he feared for the safety of his own person? We do not know; but God gave him such signs and tokens, that eventually Moses was constrained.

But now, instead of immediate success, there comes heart-rending reverse. Not only does Pharaoh disdainfully refuse to let the people go, he adds new rigours to the already pitiful lot of the slave-driven Israelites, so that the distraught Israelite captains bitterly accuse Moses and wish he had never shown his face again in Egypt (verse 21). It is after *this* that we read, "And Moses returned unto the Lord and said, Why is it that Thou has sent me?"

Have we not all had experiences of a like kind? We have felt the unmistakable urge of the Spirit to some new form of service, or to some special line of action, and have obediently pressed forward, confident that the inward urge itself was the guarantee of immediate success. Then, instead of success, opposition and disappointment and seeming failure have stunned us into bewildered despair, until we have even been ready to fling the charge of unfaithfulness in the face of God. What can we say about it? Well, the truth is that the irony of refusal and the agony of recoil were graciously preparing Moses for the greatest experience and mightiest service of his life. Immediate success *might* have been a cruelty rather than a kindness. God had called Moses to a position of unequalled greatness. He had given him miraculous powers and marvellous promises. As with all such elevations and privileges, these by themselves were a danger. *Moses must be taught to rely on God alone.* So must you and I; and God is gracious by whichever means He accomplishes this.

Baffled Yet Blessed

"And Moses returned unto the Lord, and said: Lord, wherefore hast Thou so evil entreated this people? Why is it Thou hast sent me? For since I came to Pharaoh to speak in Thy name, he hath done evil to this people; neither hast Thou delivered Thy people at all."—Exod. 5. 22, 23.

SEE here Moses' heart-rending *recoil*. Try to get into his mind. He had come with such impressive guarantees and such high hopes that any thought of such humiliating reverse had been far from his mind. And now, here he lay on the ground, alone before God, asking why? why? why? Yet as he lay there, baffled and humbled, something big and blessed was happening in this man's soul. He was learning to die an inward death to selfism. If God was to use him as He desired, then Moses must somehow be brought to the place of this death—death to self-regard, death to pride in his new miracle-working power, death to self-importance in leadership, death to any desire for the adulations of the multitude, death to everything self-inflatory. Yes, Moses must die. Such death is difficult to most of us, in the present condition of our human nature, but it is possible, and indeed it is the decisive necessity if God is greatly to use us for His own glory in bringing blessing to men. Moreover, such death to "self" brings wonderful peace. With pride and fear and envy and self-seeking gone—oh, what peace!

But though death is peaceful, *dying is painful*! Let me quote dear old F. B. Meyer. "It is not easy to forego one's own plans, to cease from one's own works, to renounce one's own reputation, to be despised and flouted by the very slaves you would save. What corn of wheat enjoys having its waterproof sheath torn from it, its elements disintegrated, its heart eaten into, as it lies helpless, exposed to the earth-forces, in the cold, damp, dark soil? Yet this is the necessary condition ere it can put forth the slender stalk, like a hand holding to the sun thirty, sixty, or a hundred grains like itself." Well, there it was, this heart-rending *recoil* of Moses; and this was the purpose behind its permission: death to "self". How graphically it preaches to you and me!

But now, beside Moses' recoil, see his *resort*: "And Moses returned unto the Lord." Oh, however ill may seem the stormy blast, it is a blessing if it drives us to that safest of refuges, the heart of God. That was Moses' resort in his critical dilemma and amid his anguish of perplexity; so must it be ours in all such straits. Panic visits to other human beings for interpretation or rescue are a poor substitute, and usually increase rather than cure our sore problem.

Finally, see Moses' *relief*. Chapter 6 begins: "And the Lord said unto Moses; Now shalt thou see. . . ." God gives a wonderful new assurance. Twice He says "I AM"; then seven times "I WILL" (2–8), pledging both His covenant faithfulness and His emancipating power. It was God's own word which brought His baffled servant relief. And Moses *did* "see" even greater things than he had dreamed. Let us learn it once for all: reverses and seeming frustrations do not necessarily mean that we are out of God's will; they often come because we are *in* His will. They are tests which God intends to overrule for our great blessing. Though He allows us to struggle through fire and flood, He will be with us, and crown us with victory bigger than our biggest prayers.

Fourfold Union with Christ

"So shall ye be My disciples."—Jn. 15: 8.

IN the early years of my Christian life, I developed a fascination for reading the biographies of the early Methodists. Oh, the rapturous flame of devotion, and the vivid experience of sanctification, which many of them possessed! It was wonderful. Would God there were more of it in evidence among us today! At the moment there flashes back to my mind a sentence from the diary of William Carvosso, a Cornish Wesleyan who could neither read nor write until he was over fifty: "Oh, the heartfelt blessedness arising from a conscious union with the Son of God!" I wonder how many of us today know it as vividly as *he* knew it—"the heartfelt blessedness arising from a conscious union with the Son of God"?

In this fifteenth chapter of John there are four verses all speaking of this union with Christ. See verses 5, 15, 20, 27. In verse 5 we are "branches"; in verse 15 "friends"; in verse 20 "servants"; in verse 27 "witnesses".

Do you catch the fourfold significance in these four aspects? We are "branches", so we *live* in Him. We are "friends", so we *joy* in Him. We are "servants", so we *work* for Him. We are "witnesses", so we *speak* for Him. Branches, friends, servants, witnesses; so He is our *life,* and our *joy,* and our *Lord,* and our *theme*!

Perhaps you may notice, now, that going with these four aspects are four special ideas. We are "branches"; that speaks of *fruit-bearing.* We are "friends"; that speaks of *fellowship.* We are "servants"; that, says Jesus, will occasion *persecution.* We are "witnesses"; and for that, He tells us, there is the provision of the *Paraclete,* the Holy Spirit.

These four seem to strike a level balance. The first two are *spiritual.* The other two are *practical.* Our relationship as "branches" and "friends" speaks of *union* and of *communion.* Our relationship as "servants" and "witnesses" speaks of *toiling* and *telling.*

Branches bearing fruit!—why, that speaks of spiritual *renewal.* Friends enjoying fellowship!—why, that speaks of spiritual *privilege.* Servants fulfilling His will!—why, that speaks of spiritual *endeavour.* Witnesses for Him to others!—why, that speaks of *responsibility.* So there are large and significant bearings in these four aspects of our union with Christ!

Now if we are sincere and thoughtful readers of God's Word, we can never find ourselves confronted by a great truth like this without finding our hearts both gladdened and *challenged* by it. With these four aspects before us, let us ask ourselves four questions: (1) Am I vitally united to Christ, as one of the branches? (2) Am I living closely and daily in fellowship with Him? (3) Am I faithfully serving Him, even though incurring the world's hostility? (4) Am I daily giving discreet witness for Him, as opportunity allows, and in the power of the heaven-sent Paraclete?

Oh, that you and I may experience more fully (to quote dear old William Carvosso again) the "heartfelt blessedness arising from a conscious union with the Son of God"! The *fact* of our union with Him means life eternal. The *consciousness* of it is heaven begun below!

"I am the Vine; ye are the branches."—Jn. 15 : 5.

With this metaphor of vine and branches before us, we do well to ask: Am *I* really, vitally, savingly united to Christ, as one of the spiritual *branches* in the living Vine? It is important to appreciate the force of the first sentence in this chapter. When our Lord said, "I am the true Vine", the emphasis was on that adjective "true", and with good reason. In the Old Testament, the nation Israel is spoken of again and again as the vine which Jehovah planted and nourished. The members of the nation Israel came to look upon themselves as the favoured branches in that vine of Jehovah. But the covenant nation had failed to realise God's "vine" ideal for it. *That* vine was blighted by apostasy and degeneracy. It was not enough to be a branch in *that* vine. There was no saving or regenerating power whatever in simply being a member of the nation Israel. *Christ* was the true Israel, the true "Vine", in whom all the ideals and longings and blessings of the elect nation found their fulfilment and expression.

Even so, today, Christendom is not the true vine. The Roman Catholic Church is certainly not the true vine. Protestantism is not the true vine. The various Protestant denominations look upon themselves as "branches" in the "true Vine", yet strictly speaking they are not so. A man may be an ardent Episcopalian, a sincere Presbyterian, or a so-called "good Baptist", and yet not be in Christ, the "true Vine". Being a member of this or that or the other church does not make us living members of Christ Himself. There must be a personal, individual, heart-to-heart union with the living Saviour. Am I in the "*true* Vine"? If I am, then am I daily "*abiding*" in Him? And am I "*bearing fruit*" for Him, in character, and in acts of service, and in answers to prayer?

In this metaphor of vine and branches, our Lord shows us that there are three prerequisites to fruit-bearing. First, there must be pruning or *cleansing*. See verse 2: "Every branch that beareth fruit He (the Father) purgeth it, that it may bring forth more fruit." Second, there must be *abiding*. See verse 4: "As the branch cannot bear fruit of itself, except it abide in the vine, no more can ye, except ye abide in Me." Third, there must be *obeying*. See verse 10: "If ye keep My commandments ye shall abide in my love." Yes, there must be this cleansing, abiding, obeying.

How, then, are we "cleansed"? Verse 3 tells us: "Now ye are cleansed (or pruned) through the *word* which I have spoken unto you." That word is now to us the Holy Scripture; and that Word, as we read it, and learn it, and respond to it, has a purifying power within us.

How do we "abide"? To abide is to allow nothing in the life which breaks our communion with Christ; to leave no known sin unconfessed, unjudged, unexpelled; and by prayerful faith to draw upon Him for all strength and wisdom needed to live a Christlike life.

How do I yield the required obedience? Well, to those of us who are already His, our Lord's one, all-inclusive requirement is: "This is my commandment, that ye love one another, as I have loved you" (verse 12). When we love our brethren as *He* did, with a love which seeks only their truest good, even to the point of self-sacrifice, we "fulfil the law of Christ"; we are "cleansed"; we "abide"; and there is "much fruit"

Three Test-Questions

"Friend" . . . "Servant" . . . "Witness."—Jn. 15: 15, 20, 27.

With our Lord's words before us, in verse 15, "I have called you *friends*," we may well ask ourselves: Is my friendship, my communion with Him, constant, sacredly familiar, rich and satisfying?

I wonder at times whether some of us, despite our Christian profession, will really know our Lord as "friend with friend" when we meet Him in heaven or at His return, we have so neglected getting to know Him here, through prayer-communion. Years ago, when King George the Fifth visited Edinburgh, I stood with a number of other persons on a pathway overlooking Holyrood Palace, where his majesty was staying. A talkative woman was telling a companion, "Oh yes, I know the king. I've often seen him. I'll point him out to you when he comes into the palace grounds." Soon afterward a military attaché came from some side egress and strode briskly toward the outer gateway. "There he is!" exclaimed the talkative woman, only to be corrected by another bystander who knew better. Later, when the king himself *did* appear, she did not recognize him, until the cheers of onlookers apprised her. She had *thought* that she knew the king, when actually she did not know him at all. May it *not* be so with ourselves! Let us count it our princeliest privilege to develop a close friendship with our heavenly King while we are here on earth. We cannot begin too early; nor, thank God, is it too late if we are now elderly. If we seek Him daily, regularly, frequently, with hearts which hunger for Him, we shall surely find that "He satisfieth the longing soul".

But now look at verse 20: "The servant is not greater than his lord." Jesus is my Lord, and I am His privileged "*servant*". Then let me ask myself: Am I faithfully living for Him? Am I bravely enduring the world's hostility? Am I willing to undergo suffering, or to part with *any*thing, for His dear sake, if necessary? Or does this seem too big a demand?

And must I part with all I have,
  Jesus, my Lord, for Thee?
Yes, this my joy, for Thou hast done
  Much more than that for me.
Yes, let it go. One smile from Thee
  Will more than make amends
For all the losses I sustain
  Of credit, riches, friends!

Finally, if as verse 27 says, I am His "*witness*", let me ask: Am I giving my daily witness for Him, in the power and under the guidance of the *Paraclete*, or Comforter? We cannot all be public preachers, but each one of us is constituted an individual witness-bearer. Such witnessing is not expounding a text, but the telling of an experience. It is giving first-hand testimony to the saving power of Christ as actually experienced in our own individual life. Notice, at the end of this fifteenth chapter, that it is really the Paraclete Himself who bears witness *through* us: "*He* shall . . . *ye* shall."

"There is joy in the presence of the angels of God over one sinner that repenteth."—Luke 15: 10.

THESE words are woven into the wonderful fabric of our Lord's threefold parable: the lost sheep, the lost coin, and the lost son—one of the best-known and best-loved passages in all the Bible. It is challenging to reflect on what is here implied concerning the unfallen angels.

To begin with, the words imply the *existence* of angels. Such is the present-day departure from the Word of God that multitudes of people, like the Sadducees of old, believe neither in angel nor demon, neither in heaven nor hell, neither in God nor devil. To speak about angels, in many an office or workshop today, is to invite sarcastic ridicule; and when the sacred truths of Christianity are thus made fun of, it is easy for younger Christians to be bluffed into doubting them. Let newer converts remember, therefore, that the truths of Christianity rest upon a well-tried foundation. The birth, life, teaching, miracles, death, resurrection, and ascension of our Lord Jesus, are all well-authenticated facts. Quite apart from supernatural inspiration, there is every reason to believe in the thorough trustworthiness of Matthew, Mark, Luke, and John. Here, in Luke 15, it is the infallible Son of God Himself who tells us about this joy among the angels over repenting sinners; and He prefaces His words with a weighty, "I say unto you."

But further, the words imply that the angels *observe us*. How can they rejoice over us when they see us turning to God if they cannot even see us do this? Surely it is artificial to suppose that they are completely screened off, and can only know about us what God deigns to tell them. That idea is out of keeping with the general tenor of Scripture. For instance, do we not read in Hebrews 1: 14, that they are "ministering spirits", sent forth to minister to the "heirs of salvation"? But how can they so minister to us if they cannot even see us?

Again, our Lord's words imply that the angels *feel concern for us*. If they have joy at our conversion, then obviously they feel concern beforehand. Living as they do in the spiritual and eternal realm, they know far more vividly than we do what it means for a soul to be lost, and what it means for a soul to be saved. They see in a sharper, clearer way than we do, the monstrous tragedy of human sin, the utter fiendishness of Satan's insurrection, the tremendous issues at stake in each human life, and the transcendent marvel of the Gospel. Yes, the angels are intensely concerned. That is why we read in 1 Peter 1: 12, "Which things the angels desire to look into."

Once more, our text implies that at the conversion of sinners the angels exult with an *extraordinary joy*. It surely must be extraordinary if it can bring added bliss to them in their already perfect felicity. Perhaps the most amazing thing of all is, that this special joy of the angels is "over *one* sinner that repenteth"—just "*one*"! What must have been their joy at Pentecost! What must be their joy in times of revival! And, mark it well, this joy of the angels is over "one *sinner*"—one drunkard, one down-and-out, one tramp, one impure evil-doer, who repents! Oh, what a rebuke in this are the angels to some of ourselves!

We May Learn from This

"There is joy in the presence of the angels of God over one sinner that repenteth."—Luke 15: 10.

If this is true of the angels, then it is full of reflex suggestions to ourselves. It may sound rather startling, yet it is true, that we may *augment the joy of heaven!* Those unfallen angels are there, amid the pure ecstasies and shadowless raptures of the glory-land, yet somehow all *that* joy is augmented when human sinners on earth are converted to Christ. Oh, what soulwinners we should prayerfully endeavour to be!—for if the winning of a soul to Jesus means such joy to the angels, what joy must it be to our Lord Jesus Himself!

Further, we should feel as the angels do *about impenitent sinners.* The angels evidently grieve over them. Do we? How unconcerned some of us are! How little we persevere in prayer for their conversion! How seldom we pluck up courage to warn them of "the wrath to come", or try to draw them to the Saviour with the silken cords of love!

Again, we should feel as the angels do *at the conversion of sinners.* There is "joy" among them; but how casual some of ourselves are! Oh, it is a mighty wonder when even "one" sinner becomes eternally saved in Christ! Early in the Second World War, when Paris fell, Hitler ordered all the flags to fly throughout Germany for seven days, and all the church bells to be rung non-stop for three days. How ought the flags to wave and the bells to ring in every Christian heart when sinners are saved through the precious blood of Christ and the regenerating power of the Holy Spirit!

Again, let us learn from the rejoicing of the angels over repenting sinners that *the conversion of a soul to Christ is an incomparably great thing.* I find no hint in Scripture that the angels exult over titanic battles, military conquests, political debates, huge commercial ventures, scientific discoveries; but the thermometer of even *their* pure joy immediately rises when souls are won to the Saviour. Every God-conscious human soul is a world in itself, with immeasurable possibilities for good or evil, in time and eternity. When a soul falls deeply away from God, demons beat the gongs of darkness. When a soul is saved through union with God's dear son, heaven sounds its trumpets in joyful fanfare; eager fingers pluck new strains of gladness from a thousand harps; and all the belfries peal out jubilation!

Finally, with the lovely encouragement of the angels before us, let us resolve that while we are spared on earth, we will endeavour so to witness for our dear Saviour that souls may be won, bringing joy, not only to the angels, but to the heart of God Himself.

After years of toiling and teaching and praying for the salvation of the heathen in the New Hebrides, John G. Paton saw the harvest of his sacrificial labour in a gracious work of conversion which broke out among the natives. There came a time when the first Communion Service was held, and John G. Paton speaks of it thus: "At that moment when I put the bread and wine into those dark hands, once stained with the blood of cannibalism, but now stretched out to receive and partake the emblems and seals of the Redeemer's love, I had a foretaste of the joy of glory that well nigh broke my heart to pieces. I shall never taste a deeper bliss till I gaze on the glorified face of Jesus Himself."

"And King Solomon gave unto the Queen of Sheba all her desire, whatsoever she asked, beside that which Solomon gave her of his royal bounty."—1 Kgs. 10: 13.

IN his personal character, Solomon is by no means a satisfying study, but in his royalty and riches and reign over a united Israel he is a remarkable type of our Lord Jesus Christ. It is instructive to remember this when we read of his liberality to the queen of Sheba.

We note a triple measure of his generosity. First, he gave her "whatsoever she *asked*". Second, he gave her "all her *desire*". Third, he gave her of his own "*royal bounty*".

As for her "*asking*", she would not ask, of course, without having been invited to do so; but once having been invited, she would see so many things of irresistible charm that she would doubtless ask much and often.

As for her "*desiring*", we may well suppose that a point came where she was ashamed to ask for more, yet could not successfully conceal her still-continuing desire. King Solomon detected her desires and gave accordingly.

As for Solomon's "*royal bounty*" to her, the Hebrew wording is, "according to the hand of King Solomon", indicating that his lavish overplus was commensurate with his unparalleled riches.

Now there is a parallel, almost too obvious to need pointing out, between this and Ephesians 3: 20—"Now unto Him that is able to do exceeding abundantly above all that we ask or think, according to the power that worketh in us."

Note the threefold measure here again: (1) "All that we *ask,*" (2) "All that we *think,*" (3) "*Exceeding abundantly above* all that we ask or think."

Make no mistake about it, we are to *ask*. Our Father knows what we have need of before ever we ask, for He is far wiser than the wise Solomon; yet it is both for our own good and for His glory that we should *ask*. Often the very act of asking forces us to be clear instead of vague, and makes the answers unmistakable when they come.

Yet praying must not be limited just to asking. There is a spiritual *desiring* which is bigger than words. We sense that some of our needs are deeper than we ourselves can understand, and cannot be put exactly into speech. Also, by a spiritual instinct we divine that God has enrichings and purposings for us, which we long to experience but do not understand clearly enough to put into words. We must keep on *desiring* all God's best for us, and not limit Him to our mere asking.

Finally we must look for God's overplus, His "royal bounty", His "*exceeding abundantly above*". We must not limit God even to our desirings. We must look to Him for His magnificent extras. A farmer sent his young son to gather fruit (gooseberries, I think), and made him promise not to eat any himself. When the boy returned with the fruit, the father asked him, "Did you eat any?" The laddie replied, "No, father." The father then said, "Very good; now you can take a *handful* for yourself." The lad hesitated. He looked at his own small hands, then at the big hands of his father, and then said, "Father, *you* give me a handful!" And *that* little story, too, can be a parable to us, if we will let it. Our biggest asking is never too big for God.

"Behold, waters issued from under the threshold of the house eastward."—Ezek. 47: 1.

WHATEVER these waters (Ezek. 47: 1–12) may refer to, either in the historical past or in the prophetical future, one thing is certain: in a latent sense they are a remarkable parable of spiritual possibilities in the Christian life. Again and again in the Holy Scriptures water is used as an emblem of the Holy Spirit; so these waters in Ezekiel 47 may well speak to us of His gracious outflowing toward the Lord's people.

Notice first the *SOURCE* of these waters: "from under the threshold of the house" (verse 1). Unlike many other ancient capitals, Jerusalem had no natural river; but here, in vision, a *super*natural river is seen proceeding from under the house of God. And does not the Holy Spirit now flow down to us as "rivers of living water" from the heavenly sanctuary, even from "the throne of God and of the Lamb" (Rev. 22: 1)? In John 7: 37, 38, our Lord says, "If any man thirst let him come unto *ME*; and the one believing on *ME*, let him drink. As the Scripture hath said, out of *HIM* (the Christ) shall flow rivers of living water." Then verse 39 adds, "This spake He of the Spirit which they that believe on Him should receive; for the Holy Spirit was not yet given, because Jesus was not yet glorified."

Notice, next, the *COURSE* of the waters. They issued "from under the threshold of the house *eastward*" (verse 1). Why was that? Verse 8 tells us: "These waters issue out toward the east country into the desert and into the sea, which (i.e. the Salt Sea, or Dead Sea) shall be *healed*." So these waters were directed toward two places of barrenness and bitterness, i.e. the "Wilderness of Judea" and the Salt Sea. Both were places of deadness; but the barren was to become fruitful and the bitter to be "healed" by these crystal waters from the sanctuary. Even so, those heavenly and spiritual waters which our glorified Lord has released through the sluice-gate of Pentecost are seeking to channel their course through consecrated believers, so as to communicate new life and verdure amid surrounding spiritual death and sterility.

And now notice the *FORCE* of the waters. First they were a mere "*trickle*" (see verse 2 in R.V. margin). Then, a "thousand cubits" further (1,500 feet), they were "to the ankles" (3). Next, another thousand cubits, and they were "to the knees" (4). Next, another thousand, and they were "to the loins" (4). Still one more thousand, and they were "waters to swim in" (5). All in just over a mile the "trickle" had become a "river" at least six or seven feet deep! This was no merely natural river! No river normally grows at that rate. This was the "river of *God*". This *certainly* speaks to us of the Holy Spirit. Young Christians whom I now address, do not think you must wait for years before the Holy Spirit may be to you as "waters to swim in". You may know His copiousness *now*. Older Christian, if you have been a believer for years, yet are still only "up to the ankles", the fulness is for *you*, just down-stream a little. In other words, the deeper you and I make the channel through our hearts and lives, the more deeply the Holy Spirit will flow through us.

"The Gladdening River"

"Everything shall live whither the river cometh."—Ezek. 47:9.

WE have seen (in yesterday's meditation) the *source* and the *course* and the *force* of these waters from the sanctuary; but now, what is the outcome of it all? Glance back at the last sentence of verse 9: "And everything shall *live* whither the river cometh." So there is transformation from death to life. See also verse 8: "At the bank of the river were very many trees on the one side and on the other." So there is transformation from barrenness to loveliness. See verse 9 again: "There shall be a very great multitude of fish because these waters shall come thither." So there is transformation from sterility to productivity.

And now see verse 12, which gives us the lovely final picture: "And by the river, on this side and on that side, shall grow all trees for *food*, whose leaf shall *not fade*; neither shall the fruit thereof be consumed, for it shall bring forth new fruit according to his months (i.e. month by month) because their waters issued out of the sanctuary; and the fruit shall be for food, and the leaf thereof for medicine." So there is transformation from dearth to fulness. From that sanctuary river there is new life and new beauty; new food and new fruit; new healing and new health; unfailing supply and unfading freshness! What a captivating picture of the Spirit-filled and Spirit-controlled Christian life!

All of us who love the Saviour want to live that kind of a life. We long to experience the deeper depths of the Holy Spirit's infilling. We cannot be satisfied with the waters merely "to the ankles" or even "to the loins"; it is those "waters to swim in" which we would fain know.

Yet, somehow, many of us seem to miss all but the meagre shallows. *Why?* In many cases it is because we confuse "claiming" with *yielding*. We think that the blessing will come through our praying, begging, claiming; whereas the truth is that when once we are really *yielded* to the Holy Spirit for His unobstructed possession, there is no need for all our asking, praying, begging or claiming. You and I cannot *commandeer* these waters; we need to let *them* have *their* way through *us*. There is no restraint on the part of the Holy Spirit. The heavenly waters have flowed forth to us once for all from the spiritual watershed of Pentecost. They are seeking channels through consecrated hearts.

This deeper and fuller experience of the Holy Spirit in our lives is not to be confused with either natural or spiritual *maturity*. No; for whereas maturity comes only by experience, this filling of the Holy Spirit is wholly a matter of *yieldedness* to Him. There are many older believers who find an entire yielding more difficult than younger believers do. They have evaded or postponed so long, or have become so set in their ways, or have become so sceptical of anything which seems like a doubtful experiment, that they find a complete abandonment of themselves to the invisible Spirit far more problematical than the younger believers do. But whether we are younger or older, the fresh-flowing, ever-deepening, heart-gladdening, life-transforming river is *there* for us. Oh, that we might go that further few "thousand cubits" and find those "waters to swim in" which not only fill our own hearts but flow through us to the renewing of others!

Brother, Fellow-Worker, Fellow-Soldier

"Epaphroditus my brother and fellow-worker and fellow-soldier."—Phil. 2 : 25 (R.V.).

WINSTON CHURCHILL once twitted a political opponent: "He has a genius for compressing a minimum of thought into a maximum of words." In contrast, word-artist Paul has a genius for concentrating the most telling pen-portraits of personalities in a few immortal lines. What sketches he has drawn of character-types like Ananias, Onesiphorus, Demas, Priscilla and Aquila, and others, each in a few vivid, impressionist strokes! Here and there we find them, in his epistles, like valuable miniatures in the niches of art galleries.

Paul first describes Epaphroditus as "my *brother*" (25), by which he means that the two of them were brothers in Christ. They had both been "born again" of the Holy Spirit; both possessed the same new spiritual life and nature; both were members in the family of the redeemed: both were children of God in Christ; and both had the same indwelling Saviour. That is the most wonderful brotherhood in the world. Some evangelical preachers are scared of the expression, "the brotherhood of man". Yet they need not be. Nay, they should welcome it; for there is a true, natural sense in which all men *are* brothers. Does not Scripture say that God hath "made of *one blood* all nations of men" (Acts 17: 26)? This Bible doctrine of natural, racial brotherhood is a bulwark against the evolution theory. We should not hesitate to support any movement which aims at having men and nations live more *like* brothers. But the new, spiritual brotherhood of believers, in Christ, is something far higher, truer, stronger, than mere racial kinship.

But Paul also describes Epaphroditus as a "*fellow-worker*" (25 R.V.). There are too many believers who are not workers. Zeal without knowledge is bad; but knowledge without zeal is worse. Without workers the Cause of Christ would drag to a full stop. Lazy visionaries are simply pious make-believes. We must witness as well as worship. We must work as well as wish. Mind you, spiritual work must be done by spiritual men; men in vital union with Christ; men filled with the Holy Spirit. Such a worker was Epaphroditus. Moreover, he was a "*fellow*-worker". He could work well with others, and others with him—a most commendable quality! Have we never heard it said, "He's a fine Christian; but nobody can work with him"? Such porcupine individualists can be a real hindrance. We should avoid domineering self-opinionativeness, and develop comradeship.

But again Paul describes Epaphroditus as a "*fellow-soldier*" (25), and in this connection, what a study he is! Note the following five points. First, the "messenger" (25) like a despatch-rider "not regarding his life" (30). Second, the willingness to be an ordinary "private" in the army, a "minister" to others (25). Third, his love for his comrades (26). Fourth, his concealment of his own suffering (26). Fifth, the willingness to "hazard" his life in service (30 R.V.). We cannot here develop comment on these five aspects of Epaphroditus as a "fellow-soldier", but they already stir the prayer within us—"Dear Captain, help *me* to be another Epaphroditus."

Power is the Answer

"In demonstration of the Spirit and power."—1 Cor. 2: 4.

SOME time ago, in the lounge of a swaying, storm-beset Atlantic liner, I sat reading the opening chapters of First Corinthians, and became so taken up with a certain feature in them that I even forgot the uncomfortable lungings of the vessel. It was the recurrence of that word, "power" (1: 18, 24; 2: 4, 5).

Why this emphasis on "power"? Well, it is clear that the preaching of the Cross was meeting with two forms of opposition; two antagonisms which in one guise or another have persisted to the present. There was the *intellectual* resentment of the cultured Greek. There was the *religious* resistance of the Judaistic Jew.

But *why* those two blocks of opposition? It was because the Cross offended the natural, sinful pride of both. It offended the intellectual pride of the Greek because it would not allow him to devise salvation by his own wisdom. It offended the religious pride of the Jew because it would not allow him to gain salvation by his own moral merit.

It has been the same ever since. Organised religion, when it assumes impressive outward dimensions, or adopts a philanthropic humanitarianism, or garbs itself in aesthetic culture and ceremonial pageantry, easily wins the world's homage. When it offers divine prizes to those who bow and scrape to its ceremonies, or to those who give large financial support, or to those who build up a supposed self-merit by religious devotedness, it flatters human vanity and often becomes popular.

But real Christianity is not merely a religion. It is the *only* divinely provided and authenticated way of redemption. The Christian Church was never put into this world just to provide an additional institution of worship, but to give *witness* to specific truth which saves. The Gospel makes available *God's* way of salvation, through the substitutionary sin-bearing of His crucified Son. All men *need* salvation. Most men *know* their need of salvation. But this way of salvation through that sin-expiating *Cross* has always been objectionable to the two large classes of people who are the present-day counterpart of those Greeks and Jews.

How did Paul meet these two antipathies? Well, the notable feature is that he does not argue to the Greek the profound *philosophy* of the Cross behind its seeming "foolishness"; nor to the Jew the moral *sublimity* of the Cross behind its outward ugliness. No, he appeals to the *power* of the Cross. It works! It really saves! (1: 18, 24; 2: 4).

So when Paul preached "Christ and Him crucified" there was the "demonstration of the Spirit and power". What does he mean? He means that the "power" was in the preacher, and the "demonstration" in the hearer. This was the best of all reply-arguments. It was living proof. The "power" and "demonstration" might be resisted, but they could not be refuted.

If we preachers today were as prayerful as Paul, the same "power" and "demonstration" would become operative again; and when the Cross is thereby applied to the human soul by the Holy Spirit, it becomes indeed "the power of God" to save—to reconcile and regenerate, to give peace, rest, victory, and to transform character. Oh, for more of that power! It is the greatest of all Christian apologetics.

How to Protect Your Nest

"It is written . . ."—Matt. 4: 4, 7, 10.

SOME years ago, a traveller who was hunting in South America was attracted by the startled cries of a bird which fluttered agitatedly over its nest, in which were the female and her tiny family. The cause of alarm soon appeared. Creeping slowly toward the tree was one of the most venomous snakes in South America, his small glittering eyes fixed on the nest, while his forked tongue darted out and in as though anticipating his prey. The traveller unslung his gun, but paused to watch for a moment or two. Then he saw a curious development. The startled male bird suddenly flew away from the nest, fluttering hither and thither, as though looking for something. A minute or two later it returned with a small leaf-covered twig which it laid carefully over the nest. Then, calmer and quieter, he perched on one of the upper branches, and watched the enemy. The snake twisted round and up the tree; then glided along the branch to the nest. He poised himself to strike; then, suddenly throwing his head back as if he had received a deadly blow, he recoiled and writhed away down the tree again as fast as possible, while the male bird now broke into rapturous song. The fascinated traveller climbed to the nest and secured the twig. Later he learned from the natives that it was from a bush which is a deadly poison to snakes, the very sight and odour of which causes them to flee. The helpless little bird knew this bush, and had plucked those covering leaves as a sure defence in the hour of danger.

We are reminded of another serpent, even more deadly, and of another tree, the leaves of which always drive this serpent away if we pluck them and use them. That other serpent is the devil; and the protecting leaves are the precious words and truths of our dear old Bible. How clearly did our Lord Jesus demonstrate the protective power of Scripture, during that first-recorded open onset of Satan upon Him, in Matthew 4! Three times the tempter approached with solicitations which seemed reasonable, complimentary, attractive; and three times our Lord repulsed him with, "It is written" (verses 4, 7, 10). Three times the serpent raised his hideous head and bared his venom-fang to strike; but three times he recoiled from that protective leaf which our Lord plucked from the tree of Holy Scripture—"It is written"; until, at the third approach, Jesus could say, "Get thee hence, Satan," and the serpent fled.

Ah, that is the way to protect our nests from "that old serpent which is the devil and Satan" (Rev. 20: 2). We should learn our Lord's secret and follow His example. We should be ready to pluck off an "It is written" in every time of temptation. To this end, like the godly man of the first Psalm, we should "meditate day and night" in God's word. We should follow out the injunction of Colossians 3: 16: "Let the word of Christ dwell in you richly"; and be able to say again with the Psalmist, "Thy word have I hid in my heart, that I might not sin against thee" (Ps. 119: 11).

For instance, when Satan comes in with his, "You are not equal to this," and I am tempted to defeatism, I should be ready with, "I can do all things through Christ which strengtheneth me" (Phil. 4: 13). When he tempts me to think that the Lord is not really with me or caring for me, I should be ready with, "I will never leave thee nor forsake thee" (Heb. 13: 5). There is a "leaf" in the Word to repulse every approach of Satan.

A Rainbow in the Cloud

"I will be with him in trouble."—Ps. 91 : 15.

WHAT "balm of Gilead" is this ninety-first psalm! Was ever a kindlier reassurance given from God in heaven to godly souls on earth! As to its human authorship, it was written by Moses, the man of the Law; yet from beginning to end it breathes the unmerited grace and favour of God. We may say that the psalm as a whole is the gracious response of God to the human heart which truly loves and trusts Him.

At the moment, however, it is that middle sentence of verse 15 which holds our attention: "I will be with him in trouble." It comes with something of surprise, for up to that point there is not a hint that trouble could ever swoop down upon the godly man envisaged in this psalm. He seems to live a charmed life. Angels are given special charge over him. No plague comes nigh his dwelling. Even if there are lions and dragons, he tramples them underfoot. Glance through the verses again, and see. Providence has all smiles and no frowns for him, so it seems, until we reach this fifteenth verse; and then we are gently jolted from our easy misunderstanding. God loves us too well and too wisely to leave us continually amid enchanted arbors and flowery beds of ease.

Yes, mark it well: trouble has a permitted place. All of us find it so as we pilgrimage to the heavenly summer-land. Often indeed does beaming-faced Joy meet us, with hands full of luscious fruits and lovely flowers. But from time to time, also, stern-eyed Duty accosts us, with hard challenges. Sometimes, too, black-draped Sorrow says, "Walk a mile with me," and we can only drag on with leaden footsteps.

Yet trouble not only has a permitted *place*; it has a precious *ministry* (think well over this); and, further, it often gives our Lord His timeliest opportunity to prove His sympathetic and protective *presence* with us. "When thou passest through the waters," He says, "I will be with thee, and through the rivers they shall not overflow thee. When thou walkest through the fire thou shalt not be burned, neither shall the flame kindle upon thee" (Isa. 43 : 2). It was when Shadrach, Meshach and Abed-nego were flung into the intensified furnace that they suddenly made their most thrilling discovery of the divine companionship. It is when the seas "roar" and the mountains "shake with the swelling thereof", that our heavenly Keeper shows Himself "a *very present* help in trouble" (Ps. 46). It is in "the fourth watch of the night", as the storm lashes most fiercely, that He tramples the billows and scatters the night, and comes to us with His "Be of good cheer; it is I".

How many married couples, happy in each other's love, will tell us that although they were truly one in heart on their wedding day, they never knew how deeply they loved, nor how much they meant to each other, until they had to go through *trouble* together! And how many of the choicest saints, whose hearts have found the secret of true repose in the Saviour's love, will tell us with radiant gratitude that it was when they were in *trouble* that they made their richest discovery of all that Christ can be to a human heart! Dear Christian, let it be your endeavour neither to *cause* trouble nor to *fear* it. Remember, Jesus says, "I *will be with him in trouble.*"

Jesus . . . and Jim

"I will be with him in trouble."—Ps. 91 : 15.

So, then, trouble is permitted even in the godliest lives; but our Lord pledges His companionship in it. Thus trouble is transformed. Our extremity becomes His opportunity. Amid our trial He comes closest to us, and whispers His choicest secrets. His presence paints a rainbow over every weeping sky, and shoots a golden sunshaft through every storm-cloud.

Remember, however, that the promise, "I will be with him in trouble", is given only to the really *godly* heart, not to the superficial "off-and-on" or "now-and-then" believer who lapses into wilful backslidings when things are going well, and only flies to God as a panic-resort in times of emergency. Our Lord is often very merciful to such fickle pilgrims; but they never taste that sweet companionship of Christ which makes every trouble a shining ladder up to heaven. As the first verse of our psalm makes clear, the one to whom this promise of the divine presence belongs is, "He that dwelleth (or habitually abideth) in the secret place of the Most High"—the man or woman whose sustained response to God is that of true faith and reverent love; of humble heart and sincere desire to please Him; of regular daily prayer and daily reliance upon Him.

Some time ago, in a southern English town, the clergyman of an Anglican church happened to be looking out through his vicarage window when he saw a rather rough-looking workman stroll past to the main door of the church, where he halted rather furtively, and then entered. The next day the clergyman noticed the same thing; and again a couple of days later, always about the same time, twelve-thirty noon. His suspicions became aroused, so he set the verger to spy. This is what the verger saw. The man entered, stuffed his cap into his jacket pocket, and walked down the main aisle, to the rail before the communion table. There, with bowed head, he stood in silence. Then, putting his hands on the communion rail, and looking over towards the communion table, he said in a low voice, "*Jesus . . . it's Jim.*"

Some days later there was a nasty accident in town, and Jim was carried to the local hospital. He was put in a men's ward which at that time was filled with the roughest mixture of men ever admitted. Such was their coarseness and crude ungratefulness that more than one of the nurses had shed tears. However, after Jim had been there a few days there was a marked change; and after two or three days more it was such that the sister and nurses simply could not conceal their happy surprise. One morning, just as the sister entered to start her round of the beds, the men were all enjoying a good-natured laugh at something. She could not help asking the first man what it was which had made such a change in them all. He replied: "Oh, it's that chap in the fifth bed. They call 'im Jim." So when the screen was round Jim's bed, she said to him: "Jim, you've made a wonderful change in this ward. Tell me how you've done it." With a tear glistening in his eyes, Jim replied: "Well, sister, I'm not sure you'd understand if I told you. But somehow, every day, just about twelve-thirty, I see Jesus coming toward the end o' my bed. He stands there for a minute; then he just puts His hands on the bed rail, an' leans over, an' says: '*Jim . . . it's Jesus*'."

"And God is able to make all grace abound toward you; that ye, always having all sufficiency in all things, may abound to every good work."—2 Cor. 9: 8.

THERE is a pressure about life today. Business men tell of the strain in modern commercial life; and all too often the strain "tells" on them. In the professional sphere things are keyed up to tension-point. Home life is beset with nerve-wearing problems such as the worry of children who, having been brought up amid unprecedented social conditions and godless psychological theories, refuse many of the healthy restraints which beneficially conditioned family and social life in the younger days of their parents.

Much of the pressure today is the product of *uncertainty*. There is uncertainty about the big things—international issues; and the repercussions from this tremble right down to the individual worker and housewife. Uncertainty engenders *anxiety*. Below the surface of many lives today there is a state of chronic suspense arising from a sustained chain of uncertainties. Life itself becomes anxious. Anxiety breeds worry. Worry means tension, strain, pressure. Paul has an expression, "pressed out of measure" (2 Cor. 1: 8). It is poignantly up-to-date!

To the *Christian*, these days are both exacting and challenging. The true Christian life never was easy. It is least easy perhaps just now. Crises of outward persecution often call forth spectacular heroism, but day after day of inward pressure tends to wear one down both nervously and spiritually. A non-Christian may become impatient or sour or sullen, and nothing be thought of it except the nuisance of it; but the spirit and temper of the *Christian* when under pressure always reflects upon the Christian *faith*. Does our Christian joy, peace, patience, survive under such strain? Does it merely struggle against it?—or does it *thrive* amid it? The prince of evil will make Christ's people his priority-target these days, seeking to wear out our patience, disturb our peace, smother our joy, undermine our spirituality, and silence our witness. His device is to preoccupy the mind with cares, and swerve the gaze away from Christ. "*Pressed* out of measure": take that word with its prefixes—*de*pressed, *sup*pressed, *re*pressed, *op*pressed; all these are states into which the adversary would bring us through *pressure*.

But over against all this is *the all-sufficiency of our triune God*; the Father above us, the Son beside us, the Spirit within us. "God is able to make ALL GRACE abound toward you, that ye ALWAYS having ALL-SUFFICIENCY in ALL THINGS may abound to every (or all) good work." Oh, those "all's"! Multiplied assurance! Our Lord is inexhaustibly adequate. He can keep us serene amid strain, and patient through trial, if only there is daily yieldedness and prayerfulness on our part. On the desk of a busy London editor, not so long ago, there stood a small clump of lavender. It had been sent, along with a cheery letter, by a poor and almost blind old lady living alone in a Northamptonshire village. Under its genial influence the office stuffiness gave way to fragrance. Attached to one of the little lavender branches was a scrawly note —"*Pressure brings out the perfume*". What a parable! Never forget, dear Christian, there is *always* grace all-sufficient to "bring out the perfume".

The Omniscient Psychologist

"Before I formed thee . . . I knew thee; and before thou camest forth . . . I sanctified thee, and ordained thee a prophet unto the nations."—Jer. 1: 5.

THESE words were spoken to Jeremiah, and he was led to record them with good purpose for *our* perusal who live all these centuries later. We may well halt at them, for they certainly speak to *us*, as they originally did to *him*. If, in reading the words again we listen inwardly, we hear God saying to each of us, "Before I formed *thee*, I knew *thee*; and before *thou* camest forth I set *thee* apart, and ordained *thee*." Here, then, are two tremendous concepts, namely, divine foreknowledge and divine foreordination in relation to individual human beings.

Reflect for a moment on the divine *knowledge* of us. God knows us better than the outer world knows us; better than our closest friends know us; better than our nearest relatives know us; better than we know ourselves. He knows us, every breath and every heart-beat, every thought, word and act, all our life through. He knew us anticipatively before we were, and before the world was; and He will know us omnisciently throughout the entire futurity in which we have thought and being. He knows us through and through. As the wondering psalmist says in contemplating this, "Thou understandest my thought afar off," i.e. even in its embryonic beginnings (Ps. 139: 2). In a word, God knows us *absolutely*. "Before I formed thee, I knew thee."

How foolish, therefore, to think of *concealing* anything from Him, or of *evading* Him! Listen to another of His words to us through Jeremiah: "Am I a God at hand, saith Jehovah, and not a God afar off? Can any hide himself in secret places that I shall not see him?" (23: 23, 24).

And how foolish it is to reject God's *verdict* upon us! See what God says through Jeremiah about the human heart: "The heart is deceitful above all things, and desperately wicked; who can know it?" (17: 9, 10). That is true of the best of men as well as the worst; and the best of men *know* it, as well as the worst. And it is not because God originally constituted man so, but because man has fallen, in Adam. Man needs saving not only from the damning guilt of his transgressions, but from a "stony" and a "wicked" heart. That is why, in Jeremiah 31 and Ezekiel 36, God speaks of making a "*new*" covenant to deal with this.

> "A new heart also will I give you, and a new spirit will I put within you: and I will take away the stony heart out of your flesh, and I will give you an heart of flesh. And I will put my Spirit within you, and cause you to walk in My statutes, and ye shall keep My judgments and do them."
>
> (Ezek. 36: 26, 27).

Yes, that is what we fallen members of Adam's race need—a "new heart" and a "new spirit"; and, thank God, that is just what the new covenant in our Lord Jesus Christ effects for us. Instead of the old "stony heart", we become "born anew" of the Holy Spirit, and a new nature is thereby implanted within us; a new nature which loves the things of God, and of Christ, the things which are upright, pure, and truly worthy.

"Before I formed thee . . . I knew thee; and before thou camest forth . . . I sanctified thee, and I ordained thee a prophet unto the nations."—Jer. 1: 5.

But pause, now, at that further word in our text: "And before thou camest forth I sanctified thee (i.e. set thee apart), and ordained thee." Yes, here is a preordaining divine *purpose*. Before ever the man is born, God has a previsualised role for him—"I ordained thee a prophet to the nations"! But is this pre-existent divine purpose something which pertains only to specials like Jeremiah—prophets, kings, apostles, or other outstanding figures? No, we believe it pertains to *all* human beings.

We believe this if for no other reason than that it is scarcely possible to think otherwise. If there is *no* such ante-natal purpose, then human life and human lives become merely accidental, fortuitous, and therefore largely meaningless; the hand of God becomes slack on things, and His heart does not greatly care. This surely seems out of keeping with what the Bible teaches us concerning God and human beings. We believe that David is speaking representatively for all of us when he says, in Psalm 139: 16, "In Thy book all my members were written."

Moreover, do we not read more than once or twice in our New Testament epistles that the redeemed who comprise the true Church, our Lord's mystic body, were "chosen in Him before the foundation of the world", and that those whom God "did foreknow" He also "did predestinate"? Is it not plainly revealed in those same inspired oracles that the eternity *before* time and the eternity *after* time are both linked by a divine purpose running right *through* time (Rom. 8: 38; Eph. 1: 9; 2 Tim. 1: 9; Titus 1: 2, etc.)? And does that purpose accidentally *overlook* any of us?

We realise, of course, that our race has fallen from the higher level of God's *directive* will to the lower level of His *permissive* will, and that in this intermediate succession of time-ages there is an accommodated *overruling* of permitted evils which God never *directly* purposed (for God cannot be the author of evil); nevertheless the Jeremiahs and the Davids and even the poor blind beggar of John 9: 3 are written in God's pre-cosmic "book", to fulfil predesigned intention. There is mystery about it all, yet enough is revealed to make these deductions firm.

But we may thwart the divine purpose for us. Human free-will is a fact. Sin is a fact. And God's *permissive* will is as much a fact in the lives of individuals as it is in the sweep of ages. Let us grasp these big truths then: (1) God has an advance purpose for each human life. (2) His purpose for us may be foiled by sin, as indeed occurs in millions of lives, over which the God of John 3: 16 grieves. (3) In Christ, the restored, re-generated, consecrated Christian believer may really and fully implement "the pattern in the mount": see again Ephesians 2: 10 and Philippians 2: 13. Let it be our deepest concern to get into line with that divinely drawn plan, by an entire yieldedness to Christ. If we are young, let us be grateful to do so early. If we are older, let us remember that the "high calling" stretches on into the Beyond. Let us each pray it meaningfully—"Dear God, who hast a special purpose and plan for *my* life, help me to get *into* it, to *keep* in it, and to *fulfil* it, both here and hereafter."

A Bondman of Jesus

"Paul a servant of Jesus Christ . . ."—Rom. 1 : 1.

THUS does the incomparable Paul designate himself in the first sentence of his greatest epistle. In modern parlance, however, that word "servant" scarcely reproduces the Greek original. The phrase should read: "Paul, a *bondman* of Jesus Christ." Those who know anything about the condition of bondmen in old Roman times will sense at once the keen edge of the phrase to those long-ago recipients of the epistle. "Paul a *bondman* of Jesus Christ." In no single word could Paul have bent lower or climbed higher.

See first how *low* he here stoops. A Roman slave or bondman had no legal rights of his own. He was another man's property. He did not even have a free-will of his own. He must fulfil another man's will. He must do just what he was told, and go just where he was sent. His very life was under another man's control. He must respect, obey, suffer, or even die, with no say of his own in the matter. Of course there were comparatively decent masters as well as bad; but that did not alter the basic status of the bondman, or rather his *lack* of status. His time, his will, his body, his life, were not his own.

Such was the bondman; and such was Paul in relation to his Lord Jesus. He was no longer the proprietor of his own personality. He was Another's property. His life, his mind, his will, his body, were under the control of this Master named Jesus, to render the most menial or humiliating service if called upon; to labour, to suffer, or even to die, at his Master's behest!

That is how low Paul stoops; but by lovely paradox the lower he gets, the higher he wings. Paul the self-abased slave at the feet of such a Master is Paul at his noblest and greatest. Whenever we really get down there, we find the sinless cherubim and seraphim worshipping with us; we are in the highest society of heaven!

How different, the willing bondage of Paul, from that of *other* slaves in the old Roman world! *They* were bondmen against their own will, and because they had no choice; and because they could not escape. Most of them hated their slavery, their service, and their masters. *Paul* was the bondman of Jesus by his own free-will, by a glad, free choice which was the product of gratitude, devotion, adoration and love.

"Paul, a *bondman* of Jesus Christ." Oh, how the word searches and rebukes many of us! How it exposes our insubordination to Him whom we glibly call "Lord"! Note: as soon as Paul has called himself a "bondman" he adds, "called to be an apostle"; but (mark it well) "bondman" comes before "apostle". Most of us prefer to invert the order. We want to be apostles; but we fail because we are not willing to be bondmen. Many a preacher is *only* a preacher, and not a prophet, because he will not give up being his own master and become a slave of Jesus. All of us believers want spiritual *liberty*; but thousands of us never experience it because we will not lose *self*-liberty in a loving, life-long slavery to our Lord Jesus.

Thus to know and love and serve Him
Let my high absorption be,
Finding, as His willing bondman,
Life, unfettered, radiant, free.

Apostolic Succession

"Paul . . . called to be an apostle of Jesus Christ."—Rom. 1 : 1.

No sooner has Paul introduced himself as a "*bondman* of Jesus Christ" than he adds, "called to be an *apostle*". To us Christian believers, that ancient word "apostle" has an *acquired* dignity by its connection with the "Twelve" whom our Lord specially appointed long ago; yet we ought not to forget the original meaning of the word itself.

The two words, "apostle" and "epistle" are twins. They are from the Greek *apostello* and *epistello*. They are both *stello*, which means, "I set apart" or "I send"; but they differ in their prepositionary prefixes. In the one case the prefix is *apo* (which means "from"), and in the other it is *epi* (which means "to"). When *stello* is prefixed by *apo* it has the meaning, "I send *from*"; and when it is prefixed by *epi* it means, "I send *to*". Thus, our word "apostle" is derived from *apostello*, and it means, "one who is sent *from*". That is the meaning of the word which would be uppermost in the minds of those long-ago Romans as they read the opening sentence of this great epistle: "Paul, a bondman of Jesus Christ; called to be an *apostle*."

The *first* apostles, of course, were a group of men in a category all by themselves. They were men specially endowed with miraculous gifts and supernatural prerogatives for a special purpose belonging to a special epoch. They were never *meant* to have "successors" in any ecclesiastical or sacerdotal sense such as the Roman Catholic Church fondly but vainly assumes. Israel *twice* rejected the kingdom of heaven—first as it was offered by our Lord Himself, second when it was again offered through the supernaturally accredited "apostles". When the renewed offer of the long-promised kingdom was again stubbornly refused, the suspense-period covered by the Acts gave place to the present age, the *Church* age. When the apostles died, the special prerogatives of that apostolic age died with them; and they will not reappear until the King Himself reappears in the glory of His second advent, to set up at last the long-deferred kingdom.

But there is a real sense, also, in which those original apostles were meant to be the first of thousands and millions. Just as all true believers are priests in Christ (1 Peter 2 : 5, 9; Rev. 1 : 6; 5 : 10) so are true believers *apostles* or "sent-ones". Was not our risen Lord speaking to *all* of us when He said, "As the Father hath sent Me, *so send I you*" (Jn. 20 : 21)? The ordination of Christ is upon *all* and upon *each* of His redeemed people. He covers the whole body of His followers when He says, "Ye shall be witnesses unto Me" (Acts. 1 : 8).

It would infuse a wonderful new dignity, quality, joy, and worthwhileness into life for many of us, if we reminded ourselves afresh every morning: I am one of my Lord's "sent-ones". I am His apostle. This day I am "On His Majesty's Service". I am to be Christ-communicative by what I *am*, by what I *do*, by what I *say*; also by what I *refrain* from being or doing or saying.

Paul realised that he was an apostle by a divine bidding. "Paul . . . *called* to be an apostle." You and I, also, are "called" and "sent".

Bondman, Apostle, Separated

"Paul, a bondman of Jesus Christ, called to be an apostle, separated unto the Gospel of God."—Rom. 1 : 1.

IT is that word, "separated", which now claims our attention. In this introductory description of himself, Paul is first a "bondman", next an "apostle", and now "*separated*". These are the three prerequisites for any Christian worker who is to be greatly used of God. Self-will must abdicate in favour of complete mastery by Christ, and the heart must become His affectionate "*bondman*". Then there must be a sense of divine commission, of being an apostle or "*sent-one*", whatever the God-ordained task or employ may be. And there must also be this third thing, this being "*separated*", as Paul was.

Whenever this trinity of spiritual essentials really and fully unite in a Christian believer, big and blessed results always follow; and this applies not only to ministers, missionaries, evangelists and other public servants of the Gospel, but to those who seldom if ever appear in the limelight.

There used to be a man known as "Praying Hyde", in whom these prerequisites blended. He seems to have been barely average as a preacher; but oh, what Jerichos were laid low and what Jerusalems were built up by that man's secret prayings! There was another man in whom these same three features were conspicuous, a sixteenth-century kitchen-servant, a man known as "Brother Lawrence". He was nothing publicly; but oh, how that bondman kitchen-apostle brought heavenly glory-rays among the servants by his prayerful separatedness! There was a woman in eighteenth-century England, the mother of a large family, who similarly blended these same three features. She lived in a day when any public ministry by women was frowned upon; yet she brought salvation to millions, and set millions singing the great truths of the Gospel, for she gave us John and Charles Wesley! Yes, these are the three decisive qualifications if we are to be much used by our Lord: (1) Self-surrender, (2) sense of vocation, (3) separatedness.

This matter of separatedness has two sides to it—the divine and the human. From his very birth, Paul was divinely "separated" for a special ministry (Gal. 1 : 15). Later, his conversion actualised this in his life (Acts 26 : 15–19). Was this exclusively peculiar to Paul? No. As human beings you and I are equally dear to God as Paul. We are chosen in Christ by the same electing grace. We are redeemed by the same precious blood. We are regenerated and sealed by the same Holy Spirit. God is no respecter of persons. He indulges no capricious favouritisms. Fundamentally, you and I are as dear to His boundless heart as all the Pauls and Johns and Peters. He has His particular plan for each of us, though, alas, it is possible for us to be "disobedient to the heavenly vision".

On the human side, separatedness has both a negative and a positive aspect. There is to be a separation *from*, and a separation *to*. As a product of our own devoted, determined choice we are to be self-separated from all that is sinful, worldly, unworthy, doubtful. We are also to be separated *to* our Master's will and use. This set-apartness is *sanctification*; and by it each of us may become "a vessel unto honour, sanctified and meet for the Master's use, and prepared unto every good work" (2 Tim. 2 : 21). Oh, to be His "bondman", His "apostle", and entirely "*separated*" to Him!

Holiness unto the Lord

"Ye shall be holy: for I the Lord your God am holy."—Lev. 19: 2.

THE first five books of the Bible are all from the pen of Moses. They form a complete group, and are known as the Pentateuch. In Genesis we see *ruin* through the sin of man; in Exodus *redemption* through the power of God; in Leviticus *fellowship* on the ground of atonement; in Numbers *guidance* during pilgrimage; in Deuteronomy *destination* after completed discipline. In Genesis we see the divine *sovereignty*; in Exodus the divine *power*; in Leviticus the divine *holiness*; in Numbers the divine "*goodness and severity*"; in Deuteronomy the divine *faithfulness*.

Leviticus, the middle book of the five, is the divine call to holiness. God insists on the sanctification of His people. The book falls into two main parts. In chapters 1 to 17 all relates to the *tabernacle*; in chapters 18 to 27 all pertains to *character and conduct*. Part one shows the *way* to God—by sacrifice; part two shows the *walk* with God—by sanctification. Part one teaches us the propitiatory *basis* of fellowship with God; part two teaches the personal *behaviour* which conditions fellowship with God. All the way through there rings the call to holiness. In part one the stipulation is *ceremonial and hygienic* purity; in part two it is *ethical and practical* sanctity in daily walk.

So then, the call to *practical* sanctification begins at chapter 18, and it speaks to God's people in every generation. It gives us the three basic reasons why we should be a holy people.

Reason number one is that *our God Himself is holy*. The chapter begins: "I am Jehovah your God. After the doings of the land of Egypt wherein ye dwelt ye shall not do; and after the doings of the land of Canaan whither I bring you shall ye not do. Ye shall do My judgments, and keep Mine ordinances, to walk therein: I am Jehovah your God."

Reason number two why we are to be a holy people is that *our High Priest is holy*. As the tabernacle was a threefold structure—outer court, holy place, and holy of holies, so the nation Israel was arranged in a threefold way which corresponded, i.e. the congregation, the priesthood, and the high priest. Israel's sanctification reached its culminative representation in the high priest, who wore the golden crown invested with the words, "Holiness unto Jehovah". (See Lev. 21: 12 with Exod. 28: 36 and 29: 6.) Even so, *our* dear and wonderful High Priest, the Lord Jesus, stands yonder in the *heavenly* temple, wearing the crown of perfect holiness, bearing our names as jewels upon His mighty shoulders and tender heart, the Representative of a spiritual Israel called to be "a peculiar people, zealous of good works". Oh, is not *that* a radiant, sacred challenge to us to cleanse our hands and separate ourselves from unholy ways?

Reason number three why we are to be a holy people is that *the Spirit who indwells us is holy*. As the shekinah light shone above the mercy seat and between the arching wings of the two cherubim in the holy of holies (Exod. 25: 22; Num. 7: 89), so the divine Spirit indwells each of us who are blood-bought, covenant members of Christ, making us "temples of the living God" (1 Cor. 3: 16; 6: 19). Must we not as human sanctuaries of the *Holy* Spirit allow Him so to possess us and control us and suffuse us that all our words and works and ways are holy?

How Trials Become Triumphs

"My grace is sufficient for thee."—2 Cor. 12:9.

EVEN thorns and trials are blessings if they bring the opportunity for the grace of Christ to perfect *our character*. Some flowers, as the rose, must be crushed before their full fragrance is released. Some fruit, as the sycamore, must be bruised before it will attain ripeness and sweetness. Some metals, as gold, must be flung into the furnace before they reach full value and purity. The old oak log must be laid on the fire, and the flames encircle it, before its imprisoned music is set free. So is it often with the saints. It is true with many of us that we must be laid low before we will look high. We must know God's smiting before we can appreciate His smiling. The potter must break the vessel ere he can make out of the same material a new and beautiful vase. Our hearts must be broken before their richest contents can leak out and flow forth to bless others.

But whenever God sends a trial with one hand, He gives grace with the other. Thus trials become triumphs. Burdens become wings. Affliction, instead of being a bed of thorns and a pathway of nettles, becomes a quilt of roses. The very things which seem to break us are the things which really make us. Euroclydon blows its tempests upon us! We shall be dashed in pieces on the rock-bound coast! We shall be strangled in the hidden reef! But nay, we are self-deceived. Lo, God is in the hurricane, and instead of driving the scared mariner to destruction, it beats him into that safest of all harbours, the encircling arms of the divine love. Yes, it is so; trials, tribulations, adversities, are often our biggest benedictions; blessings in disguise; angels garbed in black for a small moment; messengers from heaven, come to make us more like our Captain of salvation who Himself was made "perfect through sufferings". The thorny crown was in the plan for Jesus; but the thorns have given place to diadems! The Cross was the step to the throne. "It is God which worketh *in you* both to will and to do of His good pleasure." However jagged the "thorn", it is a blessing if it bleeds away our selfishness. And Jesus Himself has said, "*My grace is sufficient for thee.*"

His grace is great enough to meet the *great* things,
The crashing waves that overwhelm the soul,
The roaring winds that leave us stunned and breathless,
The sudden storms beyond our life's control.

His grace is great enough to meet the *small* things,
The little pin-prick troubles which annoy,
The insect worries, buzzing and persistent,
The squeaking wheels that grate upon our joy.

"*My grace is sufficient for thee.*" Oh, what a wondrous promise this is! The more one thinks upon it, the more glorious it becomes. We are such unutterably needy creatures that only God Himself can know the measure of our need; and God Himself, in Christ Jesus, pledges to meet us at every point of our need. The promise is in the present tense: "My grace *IS* sufficient." His grace is sufficient *now*.

"Speak ye unto the children of Israel, and bid them that they make them fringes in the borders of their garments throughout their generations, and that they put upon the fringe of the borders a ribband of blue: and it shall be unto you for a fringe, that ye may look upon it, and remember all the commandments of the Lord, and do them; and that ye seek not after your own heart and your own eyes, after which ye use to go a whoring: that ye may remember, and do all my commandments, and be holy unto your God."—Num. 15: 38–40.

THIS regulation concerning the apparel of the old-time Israelites is an item of interesting peculiarity, though if it were nothing *more* than that we might dismiss it with a cursory perusal. The fact is, however, that it has a divinely intended reference to ourselves, even though there is such a sweep of centuries between then and now; for it comes in that Mosaic narrative of which Paul specifically says, in 1 Corinthians 10: 6, 11, "Now all these things happened unto them as ensamples . . . for *our* admonition." That fringe of blue admonishes us in three ways.

First, it was an *aid to remembrance.* See verse 39: "That ye may look upon it, and remember. . . ." It recognised the weakness of human memory. Even those who are sincere can be forgetful. It reminded the wearers what good *reason* they had to remember the One who had wrought such deliverances for them (41). It also prompted them to remember things *heavenly,* for it was blue in colour.

Second, it was an *urge to obedience.* See verse 39 again: "That ye may look upon it, and remember all the commandments of the Lord, and *do* them." Their remembering was not to be merely sentimental, but practical. Heavenly-mindedness was to be linked with obedient godliness.

Third, it was a *mark of separation.* See verse 40: "That ye may remember . . . and be *holy unto your God.*" It is in this connection that the ribband of blue becomes most of all significant. A separation symbolised by a blue border on their apparel was evidently meant to be a separation obvious to all; yet not an odd or ugly kind of isolation; a separation clinging about them all the time, and meant to be specially observable both to wearer and watcher when the wearer bent to earthly activities.

How all this speaks to you and me as the people of Christ! *We* are a separated people. (See Titus 2: 14; 1 Peter 2: 9; Eph. 5: 25–27; Gal. 1: 4; 2 Cor. 6: 14–18.) He would have us ever to be *remembering* Himself who has so loved us and wrought such redemption for us (1 Cor. 11: 24; Jn. 14: 26; 2 Peter 1: 13; 2 Tim. 2: 8). And He would have our remembrance of Him express itself in real *obedience.* It must be no mere sickly relic-worship, no mere shouting of slogans, no mere exploding in pious expletives, no mere sanctimonious professionalism such as that which He rebuked in the Pharisees. "To obey is better (even) than sacrifice" (1 Sam. 15: 22). There must be thoroughgoing godliness. And all the while there must be the mark of *separatedness* about us—not that of cowled monks, but of everyday saints.

Yes, the mark of our separation is to cling about us all the time. That long-ago ribband of blue, being stitched hem-like to the very clothes of the Israelites, was *continually* with them, obvious wherever they went, and whatever they were doing. Read what John Bunyan says about Christian and Faithful at Vanity Fair. Then read 2 Corinthians 6: 14–18 again.

The Bank that Never Fails

"But my God shall supply all your need according to His riches in glory by Christ Jesus."—Phil. 4:19.

No Christian ever need beg bread with a promise like this in the Bible. We are unkind to ourselves and dishonouring to God when we tantalise ourselves with nervous fears.

Years ago, a dear old Christian woman who lived alone in a village cottage had used her last penny and her last loaf. She prayed God to supply her with a loaf. Some village youths who often teased her for her religion overheard the prayer, and decided to play a joke by quickly getting a loaf wrapped up and dropping it down the chimney. This they did; and as the dear old woman was rising from her knees, what should she hear and see but a brown parcel come down through the wide old-fashioned chimney! Upon opening the parcel, she lifted up her voice in praise to God; but the youths then opened the door and laughingly exclaimed, "Ah, it was we who sent the loaf, and not God at all!" The dear old saint quickly replied, "Dinna ye think it my laddies; God sent it, even if He let the devil bring it!" God may use a variety of agencies, but He will fulfil His promise.

The word "supply" means, literally, to fill full. It takes our minds back to 2 Kings 4, to the widow and her cruse of oil. The woman is in desperate need. The creditor has come to take her sons as bondmen. She has nothing in the house but a pot of oil. Elisha says, "Go, borrow thee vessels abroad of all thy neighbours, even empty vessels; borrow not a few." This is promptly done. Elisha's further word is, "Thou shalt pour out into all those vessels, and thou shalt set aside that which is full." The woman takes her solitary cruse of oil and begins to pour out. There are small jars, big jars—jars of all shapes and sizes. She comes to one very large container, and thinks, "*This* will never fill *that*". Yet as she pours, the more there is to pour!—until all the receptacles are filled, and she calls for yet another, only to find that the supply is greater than all that which needed filling. The oil is sold; the creditor is paid; the sons are freed, and the need is "filled full" even as were the oil-pots, and in a way which becomes for ever a type of how God "supplies" His peoples' needs.

Note that it is our "*needs*" which God pledges to supply. God could do nothing unkinder to some of us than to say yes to all our mere "wants". Sometimes, too, even things which we deem really needful are withholden that we may become more grateful for blessings which we already have, and that we may be led into closer leaning upon God. A heathen philosopher long ago went into the temple of his idol-god to complain because he had no shoes. As he rose he saw that the man next to him had *no feet*. Overcome with rebuke he kneeled down again to give thanks that he himself had feet.

See the *completeness* of the supply—"all", or "every" (R.V.). What a vast field this covers! The greatest tree of the forest, bending beneath its summer foliage, has not a thousandth part as many leaves as we have needs. But God knows *all*, and His supply is both commensurate and constant. This is no mere toying about with artificial platitudes; it is glorious truth. Would that the Lord's people more fully proved it!

Going Out in Faith

"So Abram departed, as the Lord had spoken."—Gen. 12 : 4.

ABRAHAM is not only one of the greatest names in history, he is one of the greatest of the great. No man ever marked a greater turning-point in history. No man ever became father to a greater posterity. No man ever received greater promises from God. What is more, besides being great as an historical figure, he is great in his personal character. Because of certain distinguishing qualities he is distinctively called "the friend of God".

But it is with the *spiritual* significance of Abraham that we are concerned just now. He moves before us in a typical and representative way as *the man of faith.* Whatever else he may or may not be, Abraham is outstandingly and representatively the man who "believed God". Some of the most precious and vital lessons of the faith-life are to be learned by studying his personal history.

For the moment, we turn only to the twelfth and thirteenth chapters of Genesis, where we have the *call* of Abraham (or "Abram" as he then was) and his first stepping forth into the walk of faith. There are three key verses in the narrative: 12 : 5—"Abram went *forth*"; 12 : 10—"Abram went *down*"; 13 : 1—"Abram went *up*".

In the first of these we see that Abram "went forth" *into Canaan.* In the second we are told that Abram "went down" *into Egypt.* In the third we are told that Abram "went up" *back to Canaan.*

Why was it that "Abram went forth into Canaan"? He went in response to a divine call. Why was it that "Abram went down into Egypt"? He went at the suggestion of his own mind. Why was it that "Abram went up out of Egypt", back to Canaan? He went back because he had learned that faith in God is better than trust in human reason.

Thus we here have three lessons in one. In the first movement, where we see that "Abram went forth into Canaan", we have *faith responding.* In the second movement, where we learn that "Abram went down into Egypt" (because of famine) we see *faith receding.* In the third movement, where we learn that "Abram went up out of Egypt", back to "the place of the altar which he had made there (in Canaan) at the first", we find *faith returning.*

Let us think for a moment about the first of these, i.e. FAITH RESPONDING. Chapter 12 : 4, reads, "So Abram departed, *as Jehovah had spoken.*" Faith is always a response to the word of God. Therefore, faith is not presumption, a believing *without* reason. Nor is it ever *against* reason, though it is sometimes *above* reason. Suppose someone now reading these lines has been aroused to a sense of sin and the need of salvation. The first thing for that someone to ask is, "Has God spoken any word for *me*?" Then, if convinced that the Bible is by clear credentials the Word of God, there is neither presumption nor risk if that someone accepts passages like Hebrews 1 : 1–3, John 5 : 24, and says, "I therefore believe that I am now saved." It is not presumption for me to accept the *assurances* of God's Word that through union with Christ I am now "a child of God". Nor is it presumption for me to accept and act upon the promises of God's Word, for that Word itself tells me that they are all "yea and amen" to me, in Christ.

Faith Responding then Receding

"Abram went down into Egypt."—Gen. 12 : 10.

YESTERDAY we pointed out that in Genesis 12 : 1—13 : 4, there are three aspects of faith, as follows:

12 : 5—"Abram went *forth*" (to Canaan)—faith responding.
12 : 10—"Abram went *down*" (into Egypt)—faith receding.
13 : 1—"Abram went *up*" (into Canaan)—faith returning.

Ponder these three in turn. First see *FAITH RESPONDING*: "So Abram departed, as the Lord had spoken . . . into the land of Canaan." Notice what Abram's faith *involved*, i.e. separation ("Get thee out"); obedience ("to a land which I will show thee"). Next notice what Abram's faith *inherited*, i.e. divine promises ("I will make of thee a great nation", etc.). Next notice what Abram's faith *enjoyed* (revelation, assurance, communion; 12 : 7).

How eloquent is all this to ourselves! God calls us to a life of faith. Here are its *elements*—separation and obedience. Here are its *endowments*—the divine promises. Here are its *enjoyments*—divine revelation, assurance, fellowship. You and I, as Christian believers, are called to a separation from sin, from self-will, from selfishness and from living merely by human reason. We are also called to a life of step-by-step obedience to the will of God. Many Christians trust Christ for final salvation, but prefer to manage their own affairs. Such Christians will certainly be saved from Gehenna, but they will miss the high rewards of God's Abrahams. Living by faith does not necessarily mean that we must immediately empty our banking accounts, give away all that we have, and then trust God to send in each meal and each penny by supernatural intervention; but it *does* mean that we are prepared to accept God's will and guidance in every detail of our life. To all who live that life God gives wonderful promises, gracious inward manifestations of His presence, rich assurances, and a heart-to-heart fellowship which the superficial never know.

Next, see *FAITH RECEDING*: "There was famine in the land, and Abram went down into Egypt." He did what the Bedouins have done ever since, under similar circumstances; but he acted in the absence of any such direction from Heaven, taking the matter into his own hands. Next, he has to compromise and prevaricate, ambiguously representing his wife Sarai as being only his sister. Next, the beautiful Sarai finds herself in Pharaoh's harem! So now, what? We well understand, of course, that Abram had not meant to endanger his dear one. His ambiguity had seemed the readiest means of guarding her honour, since if she were regarded as his "sister", her hand would be sought and certain formalities gone through which would give time for escape. Abram has still kept true in the "letter", but he has become false in spirit. Let us learn the lesson: directly we step aside from the divinely marked path, for reasons which appear politic, we begin to find ourselves obliged to take care of ourselves in ways other than we intended. God, in His faithfulness, intervened to rescue Abram, but Abram's testimony was gone to the winds, and he was even rebuked by a pagan king for his shambling and dissimulation.

Faith Returning

"And Abram went up out of Egypt . . . unto the place of the altar which he had made at the first."—Gen. 13: 1, 4.

As we noted in our yesterday's reflection, when Abram stepped aside from the faith-principle, taking things into his own hands, and going down into Egypt because of famine in Canaan, he not only acted without divine guidance, but pushed himself into a most disturbing situation. Through his equivocations, Sarai, his beautiful wife, the mother-to-be of the promised Messianic Seed, found herself in the harem of an Egyptian king!

In some way or other, however widely the circumstances may vary, that is always the kind of result when we slip away from the faith-life, and lapse into self-managing again. For the moment, we seem so busy and sensible and practical again, and this "getting on with things" seems so much more expeditious than waiting in prayer, that we enjoy an exhilarating self-assurance. Then we find ourselves involved and complicated. Something has gone wrong somewhere. Why have we lost the sense of God's presence? Why does He not intervene? How can we undo things, or get out of the tangle?

Yes, that is always what happens when we take things into our own hands. We cannot run the spiritual life by the wisdom of the flesh; the attempt to do so always ends in failure; and we find ourselves sighing, "God is not real to me." It is not that God has failed us, but that we ourselves have violated our fellowship with Him by the intrusion of self-will, or have wandered aside by neglectful disregard of prayer. If we are true Christian believers, we are called to a life of faith, and the faith-principle is meant to cover courtship, wedlock, married life, career, finance, Christian service, indeed everything. It never impoverishes our life; it enriches and transforms it.

But now, watching Abram again, let us see *FAITH RETURNING*: "And Abram went up out of Egypt . . . unto the place of the altar which he had made there (in Canaan) at the first" (13: 1–4). Thank God, if the man of faith can lapse he can also recover. Though he trip and stumble, he may steady himself and become the more firm-footed. Blessed are we if, having turned aside from the straight and narrow pathway of faith and obedience, we get back to our first altar, as Abram did.

It was a disillusioned and repentant, yet wiser Abram who now bowed again at that first altar. With a sense of failure and emphasized need, but with new dedication and assurance, he "called on the name of Jehovah". By special bond Jehovah was his God, and would restore him. God *did* restore him, and he will restore you and me, if we have been sidetracked but are back at that first altar again. In a war, there may be several incidental defeats or reverses without the loss of the whole campaign. Sometimes the severely repulsed have recovered and finally triumphed. It can be true of ourselves. Back to that first altar!—to the place of new dedication and renewal! The minute God sees us getting back there again, He is there to meet us. He is not there with glowering face of rebuke. No, He says, "I will heal their backsliding; I will love them freely" (Hosea 14: 4). Thus we may turn relapse into recovery and new victory.

The Supreme Ideal

"Walk worthy of the Lord . . ."—Col. 1 : 10.

IN these days, when all too many leaders in the organised church doubt or deny precious tenets of our historic Christian faith, there are others of us who by way of differentiation call ourselves "Evangelicals". By that term we indicate the following five persuasions: (1) That the Bible is the authoritatively inspired Word of God, and therefore the sole standard of Christian faith and practice. (2) That Christ and the Holy Spirit are personally and eternally one God with the Father. (3) That the Cross of Christ was a substitutionary atonement for sin, confirmed and vindicated by His bodily resurrection from death. (4) That the salvation offered to men in the Gospel is by grace alone on God's part, and through faith alone on man's part. (5) That all Christian doctrine has a practical end, namely, the promotion of character after the pattern of our Lord Jesus Christ.

Besides these, of course, there are other indispensable tenets in our creed; but these five are basic; and it is the fifth of them which here claims attention. All Christian doctrine has a practical aim in the development of Christian character.

The New Testament sets before us many incentives to the living of godly, noble, worthy lives. In Ephesians 4: 1, we read: "Walk worthy of the *vocation* wherewith ye are called." Philippians 1 : 27, says: "Let your manner of life be such as becometh the *Gospel*." 2 Thessalonians 1 : 5 speaks about being "worthy of *the kingdom of God*". These are just three out of many.

We who live in this later part of the Christian era have additional incentives. There is our precious old *Bible*. In the early days the canon of Scripture was not finalised; but *we* have the complete Bible, crowned, as it now is, by centuries of beneficent conquests. What other book can match its lofty ethics, spiritual ideals and noble record? Must we not strive to be worthy of *it*?

There are the exemplary lives of Christians in former times. Turn again through the pages of the Church's history, from the heroic ministries and martyrdoms of Paul and Peter onwards. To name them all would wear out the clock—saints, mystics, confessors, martyrs, devout characters, servants and lovers of Jesus who considered even torture and death for Him a high privilege. Do we not long to be worthy of *them*?

And there is the price beyond all telling which has been paid that the pure truth of the Gospel might continue with us. Oh, those tens of thousands of fiery, gory, agonising martyrdoms; those lonely, painful, costly missionary journeyings; those protracted, exacting hours of painstaking translation by candlelight in dungeon and cell! As we think of the thousands who have not only laboured sacrificially, but have paid the supreme price, to preserve the truth for us, do we not pray to be worthy of *them*?

Yet however stimulating all these incentives are, the *supreme* incentive is that which is worded in our text: "Walk worthy of *THE LORD*." Oh, to walk worthy of *Him*, the greatest and dearest and loveliest of all! Oh, to walk worthy of His *teaching*, and of His *example*, and of His *Cross*, and of His promised *return* for us!

Reassuring Compassion

"A bruised reed shall He not break, and the smoking flax shall He not quench."—Isa. 42 : 3.

THAT this passage refers supremely to Christ has been held by interpreters both ancient and modern. Those of us who believe in the divine inspiration of the New Testament can have no doubt about it in the light of Matthew 12 : 15–21.

So, then, think of our text as pre-describing our Lord Jesus. The chapter begins with, "Behold!"—an exclamation represented as uttered by God Himself. This is meant to rivet our attention on the wonderful One who, in contrast with a degenerate Israel, is Jehovah's perfect Servant. In verse 1, see His qualifications and ultimate achievement. In verse 2, see the temper and type of His ministry. In verse 3, see His gentle character as revealed in compassion toward the bruised reed and smoking flax. In verse 4, see His eventual conquest, in establishing righteousness throughout the earth.

"A bruised reed shall He not break, and the smoking flax shall He not quench." This is a captivating way of expressing our Lord's sympathetic *COMPASSION* for the weak. Isaiah's metaphors, in their aptness, colourfulness and variety, are a delight to the poetically minded. Look again at those in our text. What could more aptly set forth human *feebleness* than the figure of a bruised reed? A reed stands so straight and looks so strong, yet it is one of the weakest things which grow. It cannot endure the least rough usage. The passing storm, the windy blast, the tread of a small animal, will quickly bow and bruise it or bend and break it. Of all helpless things the crushed reed is perhaps the most helpless. And it is even so with us poor human, sinful creatures. We are "frail children of dust, and feeble as frail". There may be much self-confidence and seeming strength while life goes smoothly and skies are beaming; but let the clouds rain trouble, or life's burdens press heavily, or the rod of affliction smite us, and lo, the brave-looking reed suddenly wilts or even breaks!

And what could picture our human *faltering* more realistically than the "smoking flax"? Flax was used in the East to make wick for oil lamps. Unless the wicks were well cut and constantly trimmed they gave only a glimmering light, pothering thickly, and easily flickering out. Even so, what are our staunchest human resolvings but glimmering wicks? We appear so determined, but are so easily deceived, diverted, discouraged. The lovely wonder is that our dear Saviour, unlike the bland but impatient world and its dictators, does not break the bruised reed or quench the glimmering wick—you, me; but forgives, encourages, restores. Therefore, let our failures and weaknesses drive us not *from* Him, but *to* Him!

What a poor, bruised reed was Peter, after "the dark betrayal night" on which he denied His Lord with oaths and curses! What a weak and wilting reed was John Mark when he turned coward and retreated to Jerusalem, leaving Paul and Barnabas to go on alone! What pothery, fickle wicks were the fear-struck "apostles" when they all "forsook" Jesus and "fled", after the Gethsemane arrest! Yet did Jesus afterward break Peter or snuff-out the apostleship of those twelve? Has Jesus ***ever*** treated the sincere but weak in that way?

The Bruised Reed

"A bruised reed shall He not break, and the smoking flax shall He not quench."—Isa. 42 : 3.

FROM one cause or another, not a few among our Lord's disciples are weak in the spiritual life. They are aptly represented by these two metaphors, the crushed reed and the glimmering wick. They are easily offended, easily discouraged, easily prostrated. Their spirituality is an unequal struggle rather than a riding in triumph; a smoky glimmer rather than a steady flame. They are easily sent floundering in some "slough of despond", or tumbled into mazes of doubt. Perhaps, indeed, there are few of us who do not have times when we feel much too like bruised reeds or feebly glimmering wicks.

What comfort, then, our text brings! Take the first member in it: "*A bruised reed shall He not break.*" Our Lord Jesus came not to crush life, but to restore it; not to despise the weak, but to raise them up. In this He differs utterly from the Alexanders and the Caesars, the Hitlers and the Stalins, and others who have aspired after world dominion. *Their* policy has been to break the bruised reed, to tread down the nuisance minority. What are the feelings or the heartbreaks of one individual to a Hitler or a Soviet?

But Jesus does not crush the bruised reed; and in this He contrasts also with much that goes by the name of Christianity. How the Roman Church has crushed the broken reed! How it has crushed individual liberty of conscience, initiative, protest, by its deadly dogmas of exclusive authority and Papal infallibility, its inquisitions and racks and tortures! What intolerance there has been in the Greek Orthodox Church, and in the State Church of England! What wrong ideas of Christianity this has spread abroad! How many minds have inferred that Christianity is a system which crushes or cramps human life, instead of liberating and lifting it! Can we wonder at the resulting apathy or hostility?

But now, to give the text a more individual turn, our compassionate Saviour does not crush those of us who are bent down under *the bruisings of conscience.* Once we were unconcerned about our guilt before God, but we have now been awakened to our plight, and feel that God can only trample us down in deserved judgment. But the Son of God does not crush us; He comes with tender hand of pardon to raise us up.

Nor does He angrily crush us when we wilt under the *bruisings of doubt*; when we want to believe, but somehow cannot (Jn. 20: 27). Nor does He come to do anything but sympathetically lift us up again when we give way under *the bruisings of sorrow.* "For He knoweth our frame; He remembereth that we are dust" (Ps. 103 : 14), and He is "touched with the feeling of our infirmities" (Heb. 4: 15).

Nor does He trample us down even when we are bruised by our own *sinful fallings.* When we have yielded to temptation and given way to wrong—ah, then it is easiest of all to think that Jesus is disgusted, or that His brow is dark with thunder. Yet we are mistaken. If we ache with sorrow that we have grieved Him, He knows that underneath all else we love Him, and that what we have done does not really represent what we meant to be. He is the sympathetic Christ. He is on the spot, not to chide, but to restore us to the joy of His salvation.

The Smoking Flax

"A bruised reed shall He not break, and the smoking flax shall He not quench."—Isa. 42 : 3.

GLANCE at that second metaphor in our text: "The smoking flax shall He not quench." See in it encouragement for *the young convert.* Sometimes, older Christians have recommended new believers to wait until they were maturer before engaging in service for Christ. Our own advice is otherwise. We would say to the young convert: Serve Him right away, as best you know how, for He will not quench the glimmering wick. You want to speak to others about Jesus, but you know so little? Then speak what you know, and our Saviour will not disdain to use it. You say that owing to being so new in the way, you stumble and blunder? Keep on! Jesus looks far more at your loving motive than at your style or polish. Even a glimmering wick He will not quench!

But besides incentive for the young convert, here is comfort for *the obscure Christian.* To you who mourn because you lack talents or training or other advantages; to you who feel that social inferiority or obscurity debars you from serving Christ; and to you who feel that sickness or poverty or impediment or lack of personal charm foil and frustrate you, we would say: Be encouraged; speak for Jesus just as you are, just where you are, just whoever you are; for He loves you as dearly as if you were some silver-tongued Spurgeon of the modern pulpit; and because He so loves you, even *your* glimmering little wick He will trim to give light in surrounding darkness. Only recently when we asked a man why he was seeking conversion, he said that he could hold out no longer against the life and witness of a Christian workmate who could scarcely speak for stammering!

"The smoking flax shall He not quench." Here is compassionate encouragement for *the returning backslider.* What a feebly glimmering wick Simon Peter was after His grievous denial of our Lord! But did Jesus angrily extinguish the choking last flicker? No, He graciously revived it into bright flame again! Backslidden believer, return to Jesus; He will not despise the messy, smoky, almost expired flicker of your spiritual life. He loves you, as His own. He will receive you, and restore to you the joy of salvation. He will trim the wick of your faith and testimony again, making you once more "a burning and a shining light".

"The smoking flax shall He not quench." This is true of all our poor efforts to serve Him. It is true of our desires after holiness. It is true of our prayer life. Oh, it applies in so many ways. It is because He does not quench the glimmering wick that many an unpromising youth has become a mighty servant of God, and that many a glorious revival has sprung from obscure prayer-meetings. Let us pray on, in faith and hope and love!

Allow me slightly to re-word the translation of our text: "A *wilted* reed shall He not break, and the *flagging* wick shall He not quench". Look now at the verse which follows our text, where the very same words are used in a contrastive way of our Lord Jesus Himself: "HE shall not *flag*, nor become *wilted* till He shall have set justice in the earth"! Over against all *our* wilting and flagging is the ever-victorious, ever-persevering Saviour who *never* flags, and *never* fails.

Strength out of Weakness

"Out of weakness were made strong."—Heb. 11:34.

THE eleventh chapter of Hebrews has often and aptly been called the Westminster Abbey of the Bible. Here are the heroes and heroines of Old Testament times; men and women of faith who wrought exploits in the name of the Lord. Here are the monuments and epitaphs of illustrious worthies who were "great in the sight of the Lord". As we read the memorials of their darings and doings we are held and challenged. Yet at the same time there is a subtle suspicion sticks obstinately in our minds that they were different from ourselves, and that therefore *we* could never be like *them*. They were "specials", whereas we are just plain, average "ordinaries". Then we suddenly come across this revealing little clause in verse 34, "Out of weakness were made strong", and it gives a new complexion to the whole story. Here is comfort, urge, hope: "Out of weakness were made strong." Those men and women of long-ago faith-exploits were real flesh-and-blood heroes and heroines; men and women of "like passions" with ourselves. We must look at them again. If they were indeed weak humans like ourselves, then may not you and I become like them? Yes, we may; but *how*? Well, in all those Old Testament worthies we see the triumph of a certain principle, which must triumph also in you and me. It was the triumph of the faith principle. "Out of weakness were made strong"—by a faith which lifted them above the merely human. Is the writer thinking specially of Job and Hezekiah when he says, "Out of *weakness* were made strong"? or do the words cover a wider field—Moses, Gideon, Jeremiah, and others? Is not this the story of every human soul which has risen to a life of victorious godliness, and of every Christian worker signally blessed in service for Christ, and of every righteous cause which has won its way to victory—"Out of *weakness* were made strong"?

Think of this in relation to *character*. When I was but a youth I read the life story of Archbishop Tait, a former primate of the Church of England. It is abundantly true that never did a saintlier intellectual adorn that high office. Yet he had such continuous illness, weakness, weariness that all who knew him marvelled at his consistent brightness, patience, uncomplaining submission, and the amount of work he accomplished. Another such instance is the at-one-time wonderfully famous Robert Hall (1764–1831). Perhaps in all the history of preaching there has never been a more brilliant, electric, strangely stirring pulpiteer than he. Never for a moment through long years was he free from acute pain; yet he was never known to complain or become irascible. His presence and conversation were a benediction everywhere, and his preaching was characterised by such raptures that again and again his hearers rose and remained standing under the power of the heavenward spell. Or again, take Miss Frances Ridley Havergal, whom Spurgeon well described as "the sweetest of English religious poets". What a treasure of consecrated genius are her lovely hymns! Yet most were written in ill-health.

Are you a nervous person? Do you have ill-health? Is your complaint that you are not made of hero stuff? Then let these aforementioned victors file before you, all under the one banner—"Out of weakness were made strong." Do not seek power; it is *faith* which God honours.

Are You Weak Enough?

"Out of weakness were made strong."—Heb. 11: 34.

THINK of this in relation to Christian *service*. During the past century few biographies have influenced young Christians more than that of Hudson Taylor. What was his secret? Here it is, in his own words: "The Lord was looking for a man *weak* enough to use, and He found me." D. L. Moody aptly observed, "We may easily be too big for God to use, but never too small." Job 28 tells about the way of the wind and the water and the lightning. The way of the wind is that of easiest motion. The way of the water is that of easiest coursing. The way of the lightning is that of easiest yielding. In other words, the wind and the water and the lightning take the line of least resistance. Even so, in human lives the Spirit of God always seeks the line of least resistance to the will of God. It is the absence of such resistance which gives the Holy Spirit His opportunity, and transforms weakness into strength. That is why Paul writes in 1 Corinthians 1: 27, 28, "God hath chosen the foolish things of the world to confound the wise; and weak things of the world to confound the mighty; and base things . . . and things despised, yea and things which are not, to bring to nought things that are." You say that you are not made of the stuff for heroism and service? Then here is just the very army in which you can enlist!

The fact is that most of us are disqualified, not through weakness, but through a deep, subtle resistance in our human *ego* to the divine will. Before God can bless or use us as He wishes, He has somehow to break this resistance down. There are classic exemplifications of this in the Scriptures. See that strange Wrestler from the unseen world as He struggles with Jacob at the brook Jabbok. Through the years God has been trying to break down that *ego* resistance in Jacob, as in Abraham and Isaac, but now nothing will suffice but a crisis-wrestle in which Jacob is made a lame and limping man. See the resistance which had to be overcome in *Moses* before God could use him to evacuate the covenant people from Egypt. "Who am I, that I should go to Pharaoh, and that I should bring the children of Israel out of Egypt?" "They will not believe me, nor hearken unto my voice." "I am not eloquent, but I am slow of speech and of a slow tongue." "Oh my Lord, send by the hand [of someone else] Thou wilt send." Or see the resistance in *Gideon* before God could use him to deliver Israel from the iron oppression of the Midianites. When the Angel of the Lord appears to him he reacts with a protestation of "Oh!" "If", "Why?" "Where?" "But" and "Show me a sign". When once our resistance to the divine will is broken down, *then* what wonderful things God can do with the weak and the despised! Moses, what is that in thine hand?—a shepherd's rod, despised by the Egyptians. Yet that rod in the hand of a yielded Moses lays Egypt low, divides the sea, and leads Israel to liberty. Shamgar, what is that in thine hand?—an ox goad. Jael, what is that in thine hand?—a tent peg. Gideon, what is that in thine hand?—an earthen pitcher. Samson, what is that in thine hand?—the jawbone of an ass. David, what is that in thine hand?—a sling and five smooth stones. God never uses the unclean; but he *does* use the weak, the foolish, the despised. That opens the door wide to all of us—if "resistance" is gone.

Unexpected Wings

"Out of weakness were made strong."—Heb. 11: 34.

THINK of this in relation to *suffering*. Most of us think that suffering will break us; but the fact is that suffering trustfully submitted to, and sanctified by the Holy Spirit, is one of Heaven's surest means of lifting Christian believers from spiritual immaturity and instability into spiritual mellowness and strength. When the faith principle triumphs in us, then, so to speak, by the homœopathic process of "like curing like", our weakness, with God in it, becomes the very thing which *ends* our weakness. It is the same with fear. When our fear so drives us to God that we utterly hide in Him, then our very fear becomes the catalyst which *cures* fear by provoking its opposite. When the faith-principle so triumphs in us that we gratefully see God even in permitted suffering, and hand it over to Him to sanctify it to us, then suffering, instead of breaking us, lifts us up on eagle wings.

Some time ago, I was reading in a horticultural magazine that flowers are really the product of the plant's weakness. The main strength goes into making stems and stalks; then, out of its failing strength, or weakness, the plant can only produce the delicate but beautiful petals of flowers! In this light, think of the glorious triumph of the flowers, season after season, all the world round. What a victory of weakness issuing in loveliness and fragrance!

Several times, recently, in a western city, I have had the privilege of meeting a dear Christian brother who has been a helpless invalid for over fifteen years. He loves the house of God, and is brought to the services on a stretcher. There he lies and listens—flat, rigid, arms and legs paralysed, hands and feet twisted, both eyes now blind, but a brightness on his face which reminds one of a pleasant sunrise. One day a middle-aged lady told me that she had formerly been his nurse. She had not wanted to look after such a helpless case, but now she could never thank God enough that she had been given the privilege, for it was her dear invalid who had brought her to Christ. About the same time I learned that one hundred and sixty other persons had been converted to Christ through him, some by letter, some by interview, some by telephone. Again and again people call him by 'phone on spiritual matters. He "rejoices evermore" and is "always abounding in the work of the Lord". He has transformed his very helplessness into a vehicle of service for Christ. When once faith imports God into a matter, all is changed. Lazarus's sickness becomes "that the Son of God might be glorified thereby" (Jn. 11: 4). A bow drawn "at a venture" pierces the joints of an Ahab's armour (1 Kgs. 22: 34). We are all needing to learn this lesson afresh—"Out of weakness were made strong." We need to learn it again in relation to character and service and suffering. A shepherd's rod is a dead stick in Aaron's hand until God is in it; then it buds and blossoms and bears fruit (Num. 17: 8). Five little barley loaves and two little fishes are scarce enough for one little boy's appetite; but when they are handed over to Jesus they replenish a famishing multitude, and leave twelve baskets over for the Lord's own servants. If only our resentings and refusings and rebellings and resistings could be eliminated, then faith would prove it today as ever—"Out of weakness were made strong."

Salvation—Here and Now!

"Who hath saved us, and called us . . ."—2 Tim. 1: 9.

SOME time ago, when I was returning from a funeral, a lady who shared our car remarked, "You ministers must find preaching easy these days as compared with former times. There are so many new inventions, and so many interesting new magazines, and such great events taking place in the world, that you need never have any difficulty in finding something to talk about." As courteously as possible I tried to explain that a Christian minister is not a lecturer on current topics, but one to whom is entrusted a supremely vital message from God, a message which remains unchanging amid changing times, though with ever-new relevances to new developments; a message which the sinning, suffering, dying millions around us need today as much as ever; the Gospel message of salvation from sin and coming judgment and eternal consequences in the hereafter. I added that in my own judgment the multiplied mechanisms and journalisms and big movements of our times are, if anything, a *dis*advantage to the Christian minister in that they divert attention from that which is the *first* concern, namely, the salvation of the soul.

With this in mind, look at the first clause in our text: "Who hath saved us." Note that our salvation is here spoken of as an accomplished *fact.* It does not say merely that God *may* save us, or even *will* save us in the future, or in the hereafter; the fact is that God already *has* saved us, through the atoning blood of His incarnate Son and the regenerating power of the Holy Spirit. Certainly, now that we *are* saved, our salvation is a progressive thing in a moral and spiritual sense; but in the sense of reconciliation with God, and forgiveness by a gracious heavenly Father, and justification by faith, and cleansing from guilt, and rescue from Gehenna, and promise of heaven, and the testimony of God's Spirit in our hearts, in *that* sense we are saved here and now, and we know it by the clear pronouncement of inspired Scripture. We can only say, in the words of Paul, that we have "great heaviness and continual sorrow" for those many thousands who through link-up with modern unitarian cults such as the so-called Christian Scientists and the Jehovah's Witnesses never have the joy of this present certitude, this knowing here and now that we are saved for ever. What peace and rest and assurance they miss! What a lot they know! Yet how strangely blind they are to the *simplicity* of the Gospel! Even the Seventh Day Adventists, although they are clear as to the triunity of the Godhead, have so stressed the fourth commandment and the keeping of the moral law as to cover up this distinctive emphasis of the New Testament that we may *have* salvation, and know for *certain* that we have it *here and now,* without dependence on keeping the moral law, which not even Seventh Day Adventists are able to keep completely, any more than the zealous Paul could! Look again at verses like John 3: 36: "He that believeth on the Son hath [not merely *may* have, or *yet* will have, but *HATH* here and now] everlasting life." Oh, with what relief do we turn from mere theories to the plain statements of the Scriptures! It is there that we find absolute certainty written with unmistakable simplicity. Read our text again—"Who hath saved us." Yes, thank God, it is an accomplished *fact.* Let us give glory to God!

Saved—Now and for Ever!

"Who hath saved us, and called us . . ."—2 Tim. 1. 9.

THERE is good reason why we ought to look specially at that word, "saved", in this text. In the Greek original it is in the aorist tense of the verb, which denotes an act not only past but complete and final. In our text the force of it is that God has saved us *once for all.* Does that seem scarcely believable? Well, the context informs us that this saving of us is the expression of an eternal divine purpose which is inexorable and without revocation. Read verses 9 and 10 together: "Who hath saved us, and called us with a holy calling, not according to our works, but according to His own purpose and grace which was given us in Christ Jesus before the ages of time." Going with this inflexible divine purpose is the absolute finality of our Lord's work for us on the Cross. When Christ died as our Sinbearer on Calvary He drank the sinner's cup of punishment to the last dregs; He paid the sinner's debt to the last farthing; He bore the sinner's load of guilt to the last ounce; He endured the sinner's curse to the last stripe; He took the sinner's place to the last requirement of divine law and holiness. Then, after He had laid down His life as our Substitute, God raised Him from the grave in attestation that the perfect atonement was accepted, that the ransom-price was infinitely all-sufficient, that the vast debt was cancelled and redemption was achieved. The idea of adding anything to Christ's finished Calvary work, by supposed good works of our own, or by church sacraments, or by other religious ordinances, is like holding up a candle to help the sun to shine, or a flickering taper to augment the flaming brilliance of an alpha star. It is like taking a paint brush to add richer colour to the anemone, or trying to make a solid cube more symmetrical, or trying to make a perfect square into a better rectangle. If *GOD* has already accepted it as perfect, who am *I* to be vainly presuming to add to it? If Jesus on the Cross died exclaiming, "It is finished!" who am *I* to be insinuating that it is incomplete without additions of my own? Thank God, our Lord's atonement is complete, perfect, final, and for ever. As soon as I accept Him as my Saviour, I am forgiven, acquitted, justified, regenerated; my sin is "blotted out as a thick cloud".

But look again at our text. It does not say that God has saved all. It says, "Who hath saved *us*", that is, us Christian believers. It is we Christian believers, and we alone, who can unite in this glad testimony, "God hath saved us". We know it, we feel it, we daily prove it. Not only do we have certified history behind us that Jesus really rose, and the inspired word of Scripture before us with its written assurance of salvation, but the Holy Spirit has come to witness within us that we are indeed the regenerated children of God. We have new tastes, new desires, new spiritual perception, new moral power, new awareness of God; we are "new creatures" in Christ. The unbeliever may doubt it; the sceptic may deny it; the worldling may deride it; the earthly wiseacre may despise it; the "modern" preacher may dismiss it; but each of us born-again Christian believers can honestly affirm—"One thing I know, that whereas I was blind, now I see." It is *not* true of others; but it *is* true of us. Let us keep on giving our witness, praying that other eyes, too, may be opened to the truth which saves.

Christ Everything to Us

"Christ is all."—Col. 3: 11.

To the inner circle of His people Christ is everything. Those who know Him best love Him most. Those who make a clean break with sin and the world for His sake find in Him their all-in-all. They can truly say with Charles Wesley: "Thou, O Christ, art all I want; more than all in Thee I find." They can sing with Bernard of Clairvaux: "The love of Jesus, what it is, none but His loved ones know." Yes, Christ is everything to those who are truly His own; and, should it be asked *how* and *why* He is so, our answer is a very ready one.

First, Christ is everything to us *in our relationship with God*. Many topics fall within the orbit of Christian preaching. The Gospel has its social and political bearings, its national and even international aspects; but first and foremost the message of the Christian pulpit has to do with the relation of the individual soul to God. No question which can ever engage human thought can be more urgent or vital than that. On that, namely, on our individual relationship toward God, depends the salvation of our souls, and our eternal destiny.

Now Christ is everything to us, we repeat, in the matter of our relationship with God. There was a time with some of us when we thought that our own supposed uprightness would win us a saving acceptance with God; but later, when we knew our hearts better, we found ourselves saying with the disillusioned prophet of long ago, "All our righteousnesses are as filthy rags", and we realised that without Christ as our Saviour we must perish. Others of us imagined that salvation lay in conscientious church membership, in observance of the sacraments, or in striving to live out the Sermon on the Mount. But when we read the Scriptures under the illumination of the Holy Spirit we saw with terrifying clearness that we were undone sinners in danger of Gehenna fire, that no system or sacrament or ethic could save us, and that Christ alone, through His atoning work on our behalf, could be the answer before God for our sin.

Oh, how vital, how precious, how wonderful Christ became to us as soon as we saw Him thus! When, by the eye of faith, we beheld Him on the Cross, bleeding there as our atoning Substitute and Sin-bearer, we exclaimed in Isaiah's words, "His name shall be called Wonderful!" And now, in Him, we have found solution for our sin-problem, peace with God, rest of heart, and prospect of eternal joys. We have flung all other confidences to the moles and the bats. Christ is everything to us. We now say,

Upon a life I did not live,
Upon a death I did not die,
Upon *His* life,
Upon *His* death,
I stake my whole eternity.

The natural man may disbelieve, and the worldly man may scorn, when we preach the Gospel doctrine of salvation through the substitutionary work of Jesus on the Cross; but we who know Him have proved that only *there* is real solution and salvation to be found.

Yes, He is Everything to Us

"Christ is all."—Col. 3 : 11.

CONTINUING our meditation of yesterday, let us now gratefully reflect that Christ is everything to us *in our experience of life.* Especially is this so in times of great disappointment. There are some disappointments in life which leave human souls in what seems to be a very abyss of desolation. The one whom we love above all others on earth is suddenly taken from us. Life can never be the same again. The sun seems blotted out. The days drag. We wonder how the world can go on around us without pausing to share our grief. Or it may be that in younger years the one who has claimed our heart's supreme love is given to another, and we know that whatever future years may bring we shall always carry a grave in our heart. Or it maybe that sickness fells us, and at one stroke knocks the bottom out of our most cherished plans. Or it may be some gradual perception that our life's highest ambition can never be realised because of thwarting circumstances; or the heart-breaking discovery that a loved one has proved unfaithful; or some major business reverse which seems to shatter our happiest prospects at a blow; or it may be something else equally poignant and desolating. Oh, at such times Christ is wonderful to His own people.

Whenever my thoughts flow in this channel I think of Rev. Henry F. Lyte, composer of the immortal hymn "Abide With Me". At the very zenith of a brilliant career he was confronted with the information that he had only a matter of weeks to live. He was in the grip of fatal consumption. He returned home, went into his study, looked death squarely in the face, and then sat down to write the brave and beautiful words:

> I fear no foe with Thee at hand to bless,
> Ills have no weight, and tears no bitterness.
> Where is death's sting? Where, grave, thy victory?
> I triumph still, *if Thou abide with me*!

Ah, yes, Christ is everything to us amid life's disappointments, amid sickness and trial and trouble. So is He in every time of temptation, and most of all in the hour of death. Did the author of "Abide With Me" really find his hymn was true as he was passing from this world into the beyond? Just as he was passing he was heard to exclaim in a husky whisper, "Peace! Joy!" Frances Ridley Havergal crossed over with the full vision of Jesus before her eyes, and exclaiming, "My King! My King! My glorious King!" I have stood at the death-beds of ungodly men; I have seen the stark terror or the cold comfortlessness; and I have said, "Let me not die like that!" I have stood by Christ's people in the solemn hour: I have seen the peace and joy and assurance; and I have said, "Let me pass over like that!" Yes, Christ is everything to us in our experience of life, and especially so when we pass through the valley of the shadow.

> 'Tis Jesus who can give
>   Solid comforts while we live.
> 'Tis Jesus can supply
>   Solid comforts when we die.

Why He Means so Much to Us

"Christ is all."—Col. 3: 11.

YESTERDAY and the day before, our theme was *how* Christ is everything to us. Let us now follow that up by reflecting on *why* He is so. The one, all-inclusive reason, of course, is that He is our SAVIOUR; but it is good to break open that lovely word "Saviour" into its aspective meanings.

When we use the word in its stricter sense we mean that Jesus is our Saviour from *sin*. By his substitutionary sin-bearing on Calvary He saves us from the legal guilt and penalty of sin, providing imputed righteousness, justification, and reconciliation with God. By His present spiritual occupancy of our hearts He saves us from the enslaving tyranny of hereditary sin entrenched in our nature, both from the courser sins of the flesh and the more refined sins of the mind such as pride, fear, hate, and evil ambition. At His second coming He will be our Saviour even from the last lingering constitutional effects of sin in our nature, translating us with sinless hearts and perfected powers and amplified capacities to share His royal glory and heavenly blessedness.

But besides these more specific aspects of His Saviourhood, He sustains many other precious relationships to us, all included in His lovely name "Saviour". He is our constant Companion, Comforter, Counsellor, Confidant; our indwelling Sympathiser, Sustainer, Sanctifier, Satisfier; our never-failing Refuge in every crisis or disappointment or loss or trial; our secret source of strength and cheerfulness for day-to-day hum-drum routine and testings. He guides us and guards us. He shares our life with us through sunshine and shadow, lining every cloud of sorrow with heavenly gold and painting a rainbow of reassurance over every stormy sky. Through all our pilgrim way He is the "Friend that sticketh closer than a brother", with a glorious love surpassing that of Jonathan for David. And, oh, He is so much more which we can never outwardly express. He is *everything* to us; or as the text says, "Christ is *ALL*".

But besides all this that Jesus is *toward us*, He is everything to us because of what He is *in Himself*.

First, He is *both living and ever-present*. Some of us think a great deal of Paul, Peter, and John, but we cannot develop a friendship with *them* because although they are alive as disembodied spirits in the invisible realm, they are no longer present with us here. But Jesus is both living and present with us, so that He and we have direct contact in a constant, heart-to-heart friendship. No Mohammedan would ever dream such a friendship possible with Mohammed, nor a Buddhist with Buddha, nor a Confucian with Confucius. Mohammed is dead and gone. So is Buddha. So is Confucius. But the bodily risen Christ is ever-living and ever-present as our closest and dearest Friend.

Second, He is *both divine and human*. Because He is really divine He has a perfect understanding of us; and because He is really human He has a unique sympathy with us.

Third, He is *both loving and almighty*. There are those who are loving but not mighty; and there are others who are mighty but not loving; but Jesus is both. His is love "to the uttermost". And His is the power which upholds the very universe. Yes, "Christ is *ALL*"!

Are You in His Will?

"Whatsoever He saith unto you, do it."—Jn. 2 : 5.

THE more one considers it, the clearer it becomes, that there can be no worthwhile meaning in life apart from fulfilling the will of God, "in whom we live and move and have our being". Nothing that we do, whether religious or otherwise, can be truly called *service* unless it is inside that will by our own intelligent yieldedness. So far as our moral and spiritual obligations as human beings and as Christian believers are concerned, God has revealed His will for all of us alike in His written Word, and supremely in His incarnate Son, who comes to us as Teacher and Exemplar in the four Gospels, and then is redeemingly interpreted to us in the Epistles. If we receive the Saviour, and live according to the moral and spiritual teachings of God's Word, then, in a general sense, we live within the will of God, and are blessed accordingly.

But for those of us who would know "the *fulness* of the blessing of the Gospel of Christ" there are *further* reaches. There is an individualizing will of God, a plan and pattern and purpose for each one of us separately, especially in relation to Christian *service*. If only we saw the fundamental simplicities of life with undiseased vision, we should see that the highest of all success, and the truest of all self-fulfilment, is to know that will, and get into it, and stay in it to its complete outworking.

There is a compassionate *adaptability*, however, about God's will for us, in a way which many of us need to realise more clearly. Because we have not been in God's special will for us from the beginning, there is no reason why we should not get into it *now*. He can take up from where we get right. One of the dearest friends my wife and I ever had was a "mother in Israel" who in her younger years had received a distinct "call" to the overseas mission field, and had deliberately said "No" to God. She was much in love with a fine young man, and was not willing to forego marriage for the sake of the mission field. Marriage brought unexpected, heavy trials, including the husband's long-drawn-out suffering and death by cancer. But, most of all, she was now broken by a sense of the awful wrong she had committed in deliberately going out of the will of God. For a time there was blank despair. Then she realized that an all-foreknowing heavenly Father must surely have *alternative* avenues of service for such as herself who come back in deep contrition. She really got back into the will of God again; not into the original blueprint of overseas missionary service, but into an alternative design which was waiting for the rest of her time on earth. She gave herself up to Christ, to do His will as He should reveal it. Her master-motto was, "Whatsoever He saith unto you, do it". She became the greatest soul-winner I have ever known among women. Sunday after Sunday, during the Second World War, she would bring in a dozen or more soldiers, sailors, airmen, or service-women to our Gospel meetings. Scores of them she herself led to Christ. When she celebrated her eightieth birthday I was a guest speaker; and I am not exaggerating when I say that her face and personality eradiated the presence of Christ. The great thing is for you and me to get into the special plan and purpose of God for us *now*. It is not too late. Remember, this present life is only the beginning.

Obedience: the Costly Side

"Whatsoever He saith unto you, do it."—Jn. 2 : 5.

TO LIVE in intelligent obedience to God's will for us individually is life on the highest plane, and the gladdest of all self-fulfilment. Yet it has its costly side so far as the "flesh" is concerned. Such obedience to our divine Lord is a far bigger commitment than many Christians seem to realize.

To begin with, it requires deep and constant *communion with Christ*, and that in turn requires time. A soldier cannot obey his superior's orders until he knows what those orders are. A child cannot acquiesce in its parents' will until it knows what that will is. A disciple cannot do his master's bidding until he knows what that bidding is. Nor can a Christian follow the Lord's directing without first understanding what that directing is, about each matter concerned; therefore all who would know an intimate, daily, divine guidance must live a life of correspondingly regular waiting in His presence, for He only reveals His will in the more individual, heart-to-heart way to those who linger long enough in seasons of prayer. Others may *infer* His will from circumstances, but only the believer who develops a daily, deep communing has a secret, inward guidance every hour of the day.

Further, this full obedience of which we are speaking presupposes an unreserved *yieldedness to Christ*. There must be complete subduement to Him, with absolutely no controversy. Much as we love and adore our Saviour, which of us finds this utter "No" to self easy? Yet so it must be, not merely as the crisis-victory of a moment, but as the continual response of the heart. We must be perpetually on the altar of consecration; always at our Lord's disposal, whether we work at an office desk, or behind a counter, or in a school, or in the home; for the Lord adapts His secret communications to our individual circumstances, and He would have us always "on call".

Again, this out-and-out obedience obviously implies an acceptance of the *responsibilities* entailed in it. Whatever our Master's biddings, we must neither falter nor doubt; nor must we only half-do His good pleasure. In an adverse world like this, such outright obedience to Christ is bound to mean many a clash, and sometimes a jagged tearing of our natural susceptibilities. At times it may mean going contrary to the desires of our families and relatives and friends. Sometimes it rains tears and strews thorns along our pathway. Again and again such obedience means real self-sacrifice. Our Lord's full obedience to the Father meant the Cross. Paul's full obedience to Jesus meant self-abnegations such as few have known. However much this may discourage the faint-hearted, it has to be faced. It may mean loneliness, or being misunderstood, or being considered peculiar, or having to do the thing which hurts "the flesh". The obedience which *really* obeys is the only obedience which really *counts*; and that which really *counts* is usually that which really *costs*. After conversion to Christ, the greatest crisis-point is the tremendous moment when we say: "Lord Jesus, from now onwards my rule of life shall be, Thy will alone; nothing less, nothing more, at all costs." A great missionary made this his life-motto: "If Jesus died on Calvary to save *one*, then no sacrifice can ever be too great for one to make for Him."

Obedience: its Rich Rewards

"Whatsoever He saith unto you, do it."—Jn. 2 : 5.

YES, as we were remarking yesterday, a life of real obedience to Christ *costs*; but is that all? A thousand times, No! That is only the one aspect. Nothing else brings such rich rewards. A life of obedience to Christ brings the consolations of *a rich communion with Him.* The discomforts which such obedience sometimes occasions to the "flesh" become heavenward wings to the spirit. Surely that is what Paul had in mind when he wrote, "For as the sufferings of Christ abound in us, so our consolation also aboundeth through Christ" (2 Cor. 1 : 5). What are the trials which obedience to Christ brings, compared with the sorrows which sooner or later come to those who live only for this world? The sorrows which this world inflicts are sorrows which nothing in this world can heal. They are sorrows which all endeavour to shun, but cannot, whereas those trials to the "flesh" which we voluntarily endure through obedience to Christ bring a communion with Him which is "heaven begun below".

Next-door-neighbour to this is the fact that entire obedience to Christ brings *the purest kind of joy.* This joy is nothing so outwardly demonstrative as the worldlings vociferous jollity, but it is the inward reality of which the other is only an outward pretence. No hearts are so really free as those who are willing bondslaves to Jesus. No hearts have such joy as those who forego joy for His dear sake. He makes Himself so clear, so near, so dear, to those who live to obey Him, that the very *act* of obeying becomes a joyous privilege. Yet however much joy there is in the *act* of obeying, there is a very coronation of joy in the heart when some such act of obedience is *completed.* It is then that we experience lovely fulfilments of John 14 : 21, "He that hath my commandments and keepeth them shall be loved of my Father; and I will love him, and will *manifest* myself unto him."

He said that He would manifest
His presence with His own;
And oft today in trystings blest
He makes His visits known.

Again, a life of continual obedience to Christ brings *spiritual vision.* S. D. Gordon well commented, "Obedience is the eye of the spirit. Failure to obey dims and dulls the spiritual understanding." Our Lord Himself says, "If any man will *do.* . . . He shall *know*" (Jn. 7 : 17). As obedience continues, discernment develops, and knowledge of God expands. That inner, deeper understanding of divine things which some believers possess is always a by-product of obedience to Christ.

Finally, a life of obedience to Christ brings wonderful composure and confidence *in the hour of passing beyond.* Whether we depart from this present life by what is called "death", or are "caught up" in rapture to meet our returning Lord in the air, nothing can so enhance or augment the joy of meeting Him as to be able to say, "Master All-glorious, I always made Thy will my choice and my delight." It is specially to them that the Lord will say, "Well done, good and faithful servant. Enter thou into the joy of thy Lord." "They shall walk with the King in white" (Rev. 3 : 4).

"Jairus . . . fell at His feet, and besought Him greatly, saying: My little daughter lieth at the point of death . . ."—Mark 5: 22, 23.

A MERE glance is enough to show us that many of the incidents recorded in the Gospels fairly glow with spiritual significances. As pieces of wood washed up by the waves shine with a silvery light in the darkness, because of the phosphorous which they have absorbed, so these incidents in the Gospels are luminous with spiritual relevance. This is noticeably true in the Jairus episode. It is an interesting coincidence that the very name "Jairus" means *diffuser of light.* Certainly, the paragraph in which he figures coruscates with illuminating applicability. Three simple but telling features meet us in the account of his coming to Jesus: (1) The *reason* for his coming; (2) the *response* to his coming; (3) the *result* of his coming.

Just here, we reflect on one thing only, that is, the *reason* for his coming to Jesus. He came *because he was in trouble.* How often it takes trouble to bring people to Jesus! It is grim and desolate to face serious trouble without Him. While circumstances remain prosperous, many people forget Him, and live without Him. For that reason, just as an eagle stirs up the nest, and turns her young ones out into mid-air, compelling them to use their wings, so God allows many a human heart to be disturbed by troubles in order to beget an urgent sense of need for the Saviour. When we are in real, deep trouble, the world fails us. As Ella Wheeler Wilcox says,

> Laugh, and the world laughs with you;
> Weep, and you weep alone;
> For the sad old earth must borrow its mirth,
> It has trouble enough of its own.

But again, Jairus came to Jesus *because no other could help*: "My little daughter lieth at the point of death." That is the "point" to which we must all come. Our paths in life are various, but eventually they all meet at *that* point—"the point of death". It is a point concealed from mortal sight; but sooner or later each of us is there; sometimes sooner, like Jairus's little girl; sometimes later, amid weight of years. We never know! In one sense, we are *always* at that "point". A slip on the kerb, a traffic accident, a whiff of impure air, an unsuspected growth, and almost before we realise it, we are at "the point of death". Jairus knew that doctors were now no use; nor could his religion answer, even though he himself was a "ruler of the synagogue". Jesus was the one hope; and to Jesus He came, with urgent entreaty.

Once more, Jairus came to Jesus *because he believed in the power and willingness of Jesus.* Presumably Jairus had seen Jesus before this, and had heard His teachings and had witnessed some of the "mighty works". Perhaps he had professed doubts about Jesus; but now that he was in dire need, his real convictions came out. At heart, he knew that Jesus was the Messiah, "mighty to save"; and he acted accordingly. You and I have far *more* reason to believe in the power and willingness of Jesus. Are *we* really trusting Him?

"Talitha Cumi"!

"My little daughter lieth at the point of death . . . Come and lay Thy hands on her, that she may be healed."—Mark 5 : 23.

Did Jesus turn away from that distraught father! Did He *ever* turn away from deep need or sincere love or true faith? It would not have been Jesus at all, if He had.

Jesus never answered, Nay,
  When a sinner sought His aid;
Jesus never turned away,
  When request to Him was made.
No, each needy, weary one
Found a friend in God's dear Son.

That is what Jairus found when he came to Jesus. Yesterday we reflected on the *reason* for his coming. See now the *response* to his coming. At once Jesus "went with him" (verse 24). There was immediate *readiness* to meet the deep need and to honour sincere faith.

Besides readiness, however, there was discerning *wisdom*. Our Lord allowed Jairus's faith to undergo a test. He was delayed by the sick woman who came behind and touched the hem of His garment; and while He lingered with her, word came to poor Jairus, "Thy daughter is dead. Why troublest thou the Master any further?"

It must have seemed to Jairus that the response of Jesus was too slow; but now there came a lovely word of *reassurance*: "Be not afraid; only believe." As it was then, so is it now: Jesus is always immediately ready to save, to heal, to answer; but sometimes He allows faith to be tested with a view to an even bigger answer than we have dared to ask; and whenever He allows faith to be tested, we always have His word of reassurance: "Be not afraid; only believe."

As for Jairus, see now the *result* of His coming. First, Jesus entered his home (37, 39). Second, Jesus expelled all unreality—the groaning and wailings of the professional mourners (40). Third, Jesus proved Himself the prayer-answering wonder-worker. There, on a small bed, was the rigid little body, with the pallid, pretty face, and the eyes closed in death. There were just seven in the room—Jesus, Peter, James, John, the father and mother, and the dear little girlie now lying dead. What anguish in the hearts of those two parents! But what utter joy now breaks upon them! Jesus takes the little one's hand, bends over her, and says, "Talitha Cumi" ("Little girlie, get up"). The eyes open. The lips part in a lovely smile. She takes a deep breath, sits up, gets out of bed, and hurries into the fond embrace of her overwhelmed parents!

What pen could describe the joy of those parents? Let us be quick to learn that when Jesus seems to delay His answer to our urgent prayer, or to delay His response to our pressing need, it is always because He has some even bigger and better thing for us in prospect. Delay is never denial, but infinite love and wisdom planning an answer bigger than our biggest asking.

"Take heed therefore how ye hear."—Luke 8: 18.

THIS is not the only place where our Lord refers to the way people hear the preaching of the truth. Again and again He punctuates His teachings with "He that hath ears to hear, let him hear". He evidently realised with much concern that His biggest problem was not the subject of His preaching, but the way people heard it. Hence, in the parable of the Sower (His explanatory introduction to *all* the parables of the kingdom) He likens His hearers to different *soils*, and shows how the seed sown is largely at the mercy of the soils.

This matter of the way people *hear* is still the Bible preacher's nagging concern, and often his most disheartening problem. It has been a heart-break to prophets and apostles. When God sent Ezekiel, He said, "But the house of Israel will not hearken unto thee" (Ezek. 3: 7). Then why send him? Because the people *must* be given the *chance* to hear; for God never inflicts judgment until a fair chance to hear and respond has been given. In Acts 7 we have seraphic Stephen's address to the Jewish supreme council. Those Jewish leaders heard only too clearly what Stephen said, and had they responded the whole course of history would have been affected; but in another sense they did not hear at all; they *would* not hear. See verse 57, "Then they . . . stopped their ears, and ran upon him with one accord." Ah, the problem that day was not in the preacher, but in the hearers! When they "stopped their ears" they were symbolically acting what they had already done with their hearts. No people are so deaf as those who *will not* hear! In 2 Corinthians 2: 16, we find Paul realising how solemn is this matter of hearing, especially in relation to the Gospel; "To the one [kind of hearers] we are the savour of death, and to the other the savour of life."

Many a preacher goes home heavy-hearted, wondering why his preaching has failed, when it is not the preacher who has failed, but his hearers. It is a subject which has many tears in it. We often talk unworthily about preachers, but do not reflect seriously enough on our unworthy *hearing*. What is the use of preaching without hearers? And what the use of hearing if there be not a right response? Nay, it is even more serious than that: there is no higher privilege and no bigger responsibility than that of hearing the Gospel, the very Word of God. "Blessed . . . are your ears, for they hear", said Jesus to an inner group of true hearers; but to others He said, "Hearing ye shall hear and not understand" (Matt. 13: 14, 16). Well may we pray, "Lord, help me reverently to listen; and give me the ear which really hears to soul-saving, eternal profit."

There was a young man in Lancashire who used to be anxious about salvation as he heard the preachers in the local church. He had determined, however, that when he grew up he would somehow become owner of a cotton mill; and not even salvation must interfere with *that.* For years he worked inordinately, until, in his forties, he owned a big mill and much money. Then he became ill and lay dying. He died frantically muttering, "Over there . . . Jesus . . . saying something . . . but . . . *I cannot hear for the noise of the mill.*"

Caution and Reason

"Take heed therefore how ye hear; for whosoever hath, to him shall be given; and whosoever hath not, from him shall be taken even that which he seemeth to have."—Luke 8: 18.

HERE is a caution to all hearers of the divine Word. It is so to *undiscerning* hearers, who hear a sound preacher of the Word one Sunday, and an *un*sound preacher the next, yet in both instances say merely, "How interesting! Wasn't that good!"

It is a caution to *feverish* hearers, always, hankering after something new on prophecy, or blatant in controversy, or exciting on current issues, instead of steady, constructive Bible doctrine.

It is a caution to *Gospel-hardened* hearers, who by listening imperviously have built up a resistance. As soldiers gradually develop an ability to sleep through the noise of the battle zone, so these Gospel-hardened hearers sleep now through the most stirring warnings of coming judgment and the most moving recitals of redeeming love.

Again, our text is a caution to the *already-set* kind of hearers; those who are great "sermon-tasters", but have determined beforehand that they are not going to be really disturbed, or give up their pet ideas.

It is a caution to the *prejudiced*. A well-known minister was pale as he said, "Even as I start my sermon I know there are certain members here who will not respond to *any* truth which comes to them through *me*." A certain church member said about her pastor, "I don't like him, and nothing *he* can say will *ever* please *me*." Paul knew something of this. In 2 Corinthians 4: 1, he says, "Seeing we have received this ministry . . . we faint not." He wanted to say, "we exult", but so strong was prejudice against him, he could only say, "we faint not".

Most of all, perhaps, our Lord's caution should sting the *perpetually criticising* hearers. Recently I saw five or six sparrows all fighting each other away from a nice slice of bread. While they were fighting, a black Labrador dog came nosing in and gobbled it up! And how true it is that while the habitual criticisers are busy criticising the preacher's message, the simple-hearted go off with the blessing! How many Christian parents sour their children against Christianity by their criticising of the Lord's prophets! Constructive criticism is one thing; this criticising *attitude* is another; and God will not hold such hearers guiltless. "Take heed therefore how ye hear."

But now, see the *reason* behind the caution: "For whosoever hath [by hearing sincerely] to him shall be given; and whosoever hath not [by closed-heart hearing] from him shall be taken even that which he seemeth to have." Our Lord's own preaching ministry exemplifies this. This was why He resorted to parables in addressing the curious but unresponding crowds (Matt. 13: 10–17). See also John 8: 43, 47. Capernaum, Bethsaida, Jerusalem, all heard, yet would not; and from them was taken away even what they *seemed* to have. Those who keep rejecting lose the power to hear savingly. It is a striking fact that the parting word of the Bible is not to churches or preachers, but to hearers (Rev. 22: 18). "Take heed, therefore, how ye hear"—great blessings may hinge upon it, or painful chastisements, and even eternal destiny. "Faith cometh by *hearing*" (Rom. 10: 17), so does salvation—and *heaven*.

Veni, Vidi, Vici

"He touched her . . . the fever left her."—Matt. 4: 15.

WHEN I was in my 'teens, an older friend asked me if I had read the works of Charles Dickens. I had not; though I have since remedied the defect. My friend exclaimed, "Oh, I envy you the thrill of a first reading!" I have sometimes wished we could read these Gospel incidents as though for the first time. Would there not be wide-eyed wonder? Well, we cannot go back and read them for the first time, but however often we return to them, we find something new. The Scriptures often state the most amazing things with the most stringent verbal economy. In no other writings is so much said in so little, and with such wealth of latent new surprise. As I recently re-read the two short verses which record how Jesus healed Peter's mother-in-law my mind darted back to the Latin class, and Caesar's famous words, *Veni, Vidi, Vici*: "I came; I saw; I conquered." How truly the words describe what happened when our Lord entered Simon's house!

First, then, Jesus *came* into Peter's house (has He come into *ours*?). It is an interesting circumstance that Peter's home was *there* at that time. John 1: 44 tells us that he lived in Bethsaida, but here we find his home in Capernaum. There had been a removal. Why? Well, *Jesus* had now come to live in Capernaum (Matt. 4: 13). Mr. and Mrs. Peter had an earnest chat, and decided to remove there too. Whether the removal had been too much, or the heat was too humid, or there was an epidemic, we do not know; but they had not been very long in their new home before Simon's wife's mother was stricken with fever. Affliction comes even to those who follow Christ; but the compensation is that He is always easy of access. The more fully we follow Him, the more immediate is His help. Peter and his wife "besought Him" (Luke 4: 38) to heal the dear invalid, and at once He came.

Second, He *saw*. Luke (who was a doctor) tells us that it was a "*great* fever" (old-time physicians classified fevers into "great" and "small"). This patient's condition was serious. Her loved ones were deeply anxious. Jesus took in the situation at once. He "saw" with eyes such as no other diagnostician ever had.

Third, He *conquered*. "The fever left her." There was no slow, uncertain reducing of the fever, like the slow subjugating of an obstinate enemy. The cure was immediate and complete. "She arose and ministered to them." Luke adds a vivid touch: "He *rebuked* the fever"—as though there was an evil intelligence behind it. If there *was*, then both disease and demon fled at the omnipotent touch of that hand!

All this illustrates what happens or is meant to happen, when Jesus comes into a human heart. He comes. He sees. He conquers! The sin-fever, the passion-demon, the soul-sickness, the worry-prostration, give way before His wonder-working touch, if we really put Him in command; so that instead of *our* being ministered to all the while, we rise and "minister" to others in His Name! The big question for each of us is, "Has He really come, and seen, and conquered, in *my* heart and life? Am I *allowing* Him to do in my nature what He did in Peter's home?" Remember, His sympathy is equalled by His *invincibility*!

The Tempest Quelled

"He arose and rebuked the winds and the sea; and there was a great calm."—Matt. 8:26.

THERE are three theories concerning this long-ago storm: (1) that it came by purely natural causes; (2) that it came by special divine purpose; (3) that it came by Satanic interference.

Those who hold the first view point out that the physical features of the terrain around Galilee quite naturally explain such sudden squalls across the lake. Those who hold the second view claim that the storm was supernaturally occasioned to give our Lord opportunity of impressively demonstrating His power over the forces of Nature. Those who hold the third view believe that the storm was Satanically contrived to *destroy* our Lord. They point out that our Lord is said to have "*rebuked*" the wind and the waves, as though speaking to an evil spirit-power behind the boisterous elements.

As for ourselves, we incline to the first view, as being all that is necessary to an intelligent appreciation of the incident. We are *dis*inclined to the second, as being quite unnecessary. We definitely reject the third, as merely fanciful. To press that word "rebuked" unduly, as implying some evil mind behind the storm, is surely over-imaginative.

Coming to plain fact, the salient features of the story are (1) that the storm came; (2) that it was beyond human control; (3) that our Lord Jesus completely quelled it; (4) that it taught big lessons to the disciples. The whole episode thus becomes spiritually parabolic to us.

The storm came. And just as the Sea of Galilee was subject to such sudden disturbances, so are these hearts of ours. I have sometimes heard that Galilean storm compared to storms of persecution or adversity or temptation; but no, the comparison will not hold; for whereas our Lord *quelled* that storm on Galilee, He often does *not* quell storms of persecution, or adversity, or temptation. By strict comparison, that long-ago storm on Galilee speaks to us of those *inward* tossings and surgings which beset our minds and hearts. Persecution, adversity, temptation, may be the outward causes, but the storm itself, as represented by turbulent Galilee, is inward, mental, spiritual. After all, if persecution, adversity, temptation, did not inwardly disturb us, they would be no problem. The storm which we need Jesus to quell is that which persecution and adversity and temptation cause *inside* us. Persecution assails us; and inwardly there breaks a storm of fear, panic, or resentment. Adversity besets us; and inwardly there arises a storm of doubt, discouragement, or rebellion. Temptation allures us; and inwardly there starts up a storm of wrong desire, impure motive, or evil passion such as jealousy, hate, temper.

Many such storms we ourselves simply cannot quell. They seem beyond our control. But if Jesus is in control, He can change them into "a great calm". And what lessons we thus learn of His wisdom, power, and love! Let persecution, adversity, temptation beset us as they will, the Galilee of our inner life may be kept calm and even serene. Swellings of fear, resentment, doubt, evil passion, die away when Jesus really controls the heart. He rebukes the winds and the sea, and there is a "great calm".

Jesus "At Home"

"He reclined in the house."—Matt. 9: 10 (R.V. marg.).

OFTEN, in the Scriptures, there is a world in a word, in the colour of an adjective, the tense of a verb, the turn of a preposition. So it is with this little phrase, "in the house". In the Greek it is the usual idiom for "*at home*", and it sends the mind roving in pleasant reverie.

Jesus "at home". Yet it was not in His own house; it was the dwelling of Levi, the quisling Jew who had become a tax-collector for the hated Romans. Jesus "at home" *there*! But then He is somehow "at home" anywhere. He was a "land man", yet He was so "at home" on the water that He could sleep amid the frantic storm! He was a "rustic", yet He was "at home" in the city. He was "at home" amid the solitudes (Mark 1: 35) yet He was always genially "at home" among the crowds, where "the common people heard Him gladly" (12: 37). He was "at home" in the residences of the rich, and never fawned there. He was "at home" in the dwellings of the poor, with no artificial "condescending". He was "at home" with the *ones*, as willing to hear as to speak; and "at home" with *groups*, as willing to serve as to lead. He seemed significantly "at home" even at Caesar's judgment seat, where He stood bruised but disconcertingly dignified before the puzzled and ill-at-ease Pilate (Jn. 18: 33–38). He was "at home" in popularity, and somehow "at home" in adversity. We say it with awe: He somehow seemed "at home" even on the Cross!—He Himself said, "For this cause came I unto this hour" (Jn. 12: 27).

Yes, He was always "at home". But *why*? It was because to Him the heavenly *Father* was everywhere. This world was a part of God's great home. Because God was everywhere, love and good purpose were everywhere. It was because He was so sensitive to this that He wept the more feelingly over human sin and blindness. To Him, sin was not just a breaking of God's law, but a wounding of His heart. The Father was in everything; and thus, even in Gethsemane, Jesus could say, "Not my will, but Thine be done."

Should not we Christians be like Jesus in this sense of at-home-ness? To the sceptic, as someone has put it, this world may be no more than "the empty eye-socket of a dead deity"; but to the Christian the heavenly Father should be everywhere. Long ago, a scornful emperor asked a Christian, "Where is God?" The Christian replied, "Where is He not?" Should we not be like Jesus in our at-home-ness with *people*? Jesus was "holy, harmless, undefiled, and separate from sinners" (Heb. 7: 26), yet He was the best "mixer" who ever lived. And should we not be like Jesus in this, too, that no one ever called on Him, and found the notice, "Not at Home"?

My heavenly Father is so real,
  Wherever now I roam,
That always, everywhere I feel
  His universe is "home".

Yes, like Jesus, let us always feel "at home" in our Father's universe, and always be "at home" to human need.

The Best of Visitors

"And they came . . . into the country of the Gadarenes."—Mark 5 : 1.

MARK has a vivid way of telling things, and nowhere more so than in this account of our Lord's visit to the Gadarenes, where He set free the man possessed by demons. We observe, first, that when Jesus came to those people *He came to do good*. Everywhere, around those shores of Galilee, He had bestowed blessings such as had never been known before. He had healed the sick, cleansed the leper, cured the cripple, given sight to the blind, and speech to the dumb, and hearing to the deaf, along with other such works of gracious miracle. So is it always. Whenever Jesus comes to a locality or community or individual, He comes to do good; to make wrongs right, to supplant vices and implant virtues, to banish sadness and bring gladness. He comes to heal men's souls, to remedy their spiritual maladies, to cure the ugly sores of social life, to cleanse the moral leper, to set free the sin-enslaved, to expel the unclean spirit, to drive away the fever of unholy passion. He comes to enlighten the inwardly blind, to make the weak strong, to straighten the deformed. He comes to infuse new life, new fragrance, new wholesomeness everywhere. Yes, that is always what happens when He draws near through some season of revival, or through some chosen evangelist, or through some other approach. The pity in Mark 5 is that the Gadarenes were self-blinded to it; and the tragedy today is that most people are *still* blind to it.

But we observe, second, that when Jesus came to those Gadarenes, the first thing which He did was to *crush the power of the devil*. He was confronted by a demon-possessed prodigy; and immediately He set the devil's prisoner free. This was surely the worst case of demon-possession. Not only was the frantic demoniac too strong to be bound by chains; he was indwelt by a whole "*legion*" of demons! Jesus was the only One who could rout such a concentrated demon force. And Jesus is the only One who today can rout the evil spirits which plague our human society. Behind the evils which curse our race are Satanic powers (Eph. 2 : 2; 6 : 12). Behind the modern drink and dope traffic is Satan. Behind much of the deadly trash which the modern cinema industry puts over is the devil. Behind political systems such as Communism, and the veneered politico-religious intrigues of the Romish hierarchy, is the devil. Behind the superstitious evils of heathen idolatries is Satan. We never get far with spiritual enterprise until we recognise three things. (1) Behind all this world's wickedness is Satan. (2) Only the Lord Jesus can oust him. (3) The Lord Jesus actually *does* this whenever He is received. Hence the strategy of *prayer*. Hence the importance of *revival*. Real visitation of revival means Jesus on the scene, and the "legion" of demons cast out!

All the best blessings in our *own* country, we owe to the fact that Jesus came, in the days of our forefathers. All the noblest legacies of our social order come, either directly or indirectly, from the impact of the Christian faith upon our history. Our democracy, our public educational system, our universities, our philanthropic and healing institutions —trace them back to their origin, and what do you find? We owe them all to JESUS, the great Liberator of men and nations. It is *JESUS* who has always proved the supreme Benefactor.

Occupation by Demons

"There met Him out of the tombs a man with an unclean spirit."—Mark 5: 2.

LOOK at this poor creature in Mark 5, almost dehumanised under the tyranny of demon possession. "But was it *really* demon possession?" someone asks. "Was it not lunacy or epilepsy? When our Lord referred to it as demon activity, was He not simply condescending to current phraseology though He knew it to be a popular delusion?" We cannot think so. Our Lord's way was to expose error, not sanction it; and especially would that apply to such a sinister matter as demon invasion of human personality. Also, the many New Testament references to demons are too discriminating to allow any supposed confusion with mental disease (see Matt. 4: 24; 7: 22 with Scofield note).

Maybe someone asks, "Then why do we not see such demon possession *today*?" Many a Christian missionary will tell us that there certainly is such demon possession in non-Christian areas. I myself used to have tentative reservations on the subject until I travelled abroad. I have met at least two demonized men. One was a witch doctor in the Belgian Congo. The other was a mendicant "holy man" in India. In both cases, there was no mistaking it; the look through those eyes was no phenomenon of mental disorder; it was a demon looking out at us through those human windows. I could only shudder. The first of them clearly would have torn me, in wild frenzy, had circumstances permitted; the other just doddered there with a gaping gaze.

But why then do we not see such demon possession in the English-speaking and other Christianised parts of the earth? Well, there *are* cases of it, though in much restricted occurrence. Our large deliverance is due to the generations-long impact of Christianity, and to the constant stream of prayer which rises to the true God, and especially to the fact that since the atoning death and resurrection-victory of our Lord Jesus demon operations have been checked everywhere.

But why was there such a seeming *epidemic* of demon possession in Palestine when our Lord was on earth? Did it not seem as though the evil spirits of the invisible realm were apeing the incarnation of God's holy Son? Well, we believe it to be entirely feasible that the entering of the divine Christ into human flesh roused to intense excitement and activity the whole realm of these evil beings (as also of the unfallen angels) and that therefore demon upsurge was then at flood-point.

We can never touch on these matters without exclaiming again, "Thank God, for the mighty emancipations wrought through the redeeming intervention of God's dear Son!" The demons cowered before Him, and fled at His word! Dear Christian, ever remember, "Greater is He that is in you than He that is in the world" (1 Jn. 4: 4).

Oh, where is He that trod the sea?
  Oh, where is He that spake—
And demons from their victim flee,
  The dead their slumbers break?
Oh, where is He? Why, still today
  He quells the stormy wave,
And ousts the demon from his prey,
  Almighty still to save!

The Legion Routed

"And the unclean spirits went out."—Mark 5: 13.

THIS case of demon-possession was startling. As soon as Jesus entered the vicinity, the indwelling demons rushed their wild-eyed human victim to Jesus' feet, where he cried out, "What have I to do with Thee, Jesus, Son of the most high God?" Then when Jesus asked, "What is thy name?" there came the strange, awesome confession, "My name is Legion; for we are many." Think of it: "*My* [singular] name is Legion; for *we* [plural] are many." This combine of demons was a plurality in unity. Perhaps in the invisible realm there are personal pluralities in unity of which we have no concept in this physical world, and which may make perfectly intelligible to us the triunity of Father, Son, and Holy Spirit in the Godhead, the Three in One, which seems baffling to us at present.

But note further the staggering *number* of these associate demons: "My name is *Legion*; for we are *many*." The old-time Roman "legion" was a military unit varying from about 3,000 pedestrian and 300 equestrian soldiers in earlier times, to between 5,000 and 6,000 foot soldiers under the empire. Here were some 5,000 demon spirits, not only a vast plurality in unity, but organised into a principal military unit, or "legion", for the prosecuting of spirit-warfare! What an eye-opening glimpse this is, into that invisible realm! Oh, how glorious does our holy Lord Jesus become as we see Him there, with that host of evil spirits cowering before Him in that cringing demoniac! One word from Him, and they must quit their human prey.

Perhaps most astonishing of all is the behaviour of the demons when our Lord commanded them to quit. Their spokesman addressed Him as "Jesus, Son of God the Most High", and then said, "I adjure Thee, *God*, that Thou torment me not"! These demons were clearly regarding Him as *divine*, and were "trembling" (Jas. 2: 19) before Him. He could "torment" them if He chose. In Matthew's version they ask, "Art Thou come hither to torment us *before the time*?" Luke's account tells us that "they besought Him that He would not command them to go away into the *abyss*"—that is, into the deepest pit of Hades where Satan is to be interned during the millennium (Rev. 20: 1–3). Then they pleaded that Jesus would allow them to enter into a large, nearby herd of swine—as though they dreaded complete disembodiment again for some torturing reason. They knew He would not permit them to enter clean animals or another human being. But when Jesus (who knew in advance what would happen) gave them permission, and they entered the swine, the whole herd rushed into the sea and were drowned; so that the "legion" were dispersed in disembodiment after all!

Oh, this wonderful Lord Jesus of ours! The demons cringe and cower before Him! Let *us*, His redeemed loved-ones, be low at His feet in *worship*! If He could rout the legion of demons, He can rout my legion of temptations, and subdue every unholy appetite. Do the demons "believe and *tremble*", as James 2: 19 says? Then Christian believers may believe and *triumph*, as Philippians 4: 13 says. This Son of God, who "came to destroy the works of the devil", is to *them* the Foe unconquerable; but to *me* He is the Saviour-Friend who saves to the "uttermost".

"And they began to pray Him to depart out of their coasts."—Mark 5 : 17.

So that is how the episode ended. Jesus had come among those Gadarenes to do good; He had come to crush the tyranny of Satan among them; He had demonstrated His irresistible mastery and compassionate benevolence; yet they all (Luke 8: 37) urge Him to leave them, and the sooner the better.

But *why*? Well, they were awed at the strange, supernatural intervention which had suddenly freed the demoniac whom they now saw quietly "sitting, and clothed and in his right mind". They were also angry with the anger of *greed* at having lost the great herd of swine (14 with Luke 8: 36). The "means" (so they inferred) by which the demonized man had been transformed was the destruction of those swine. Not one word of gratitude that the dreaded prowler of the tombs was saved! They had lost those pigs! Jesus must go! To them, the material loss outweighed the spiritual gain. They preferred the swine to the Saviour; and they illustrate to us that the most outstanding miracle of mercy will not produce desire toward God, or faith toward Christ, in those who care more for their earthly possessions than their spiritual interests. John Oxenham has put it into striking lines:

Rabbi, begone! Thy powers
Bring loss to us and ours.
Our ways are not as Thine.
Thou lovest men, we, swine.
Oh, get you hence, Omnipotence,
And take this fool of Thine!
His soul? What care we for his soul?
What good to us that Thou hast made him whole,
Since we have lost our swine?

And Christ went sadly.
He had wrought for them a sign
Of love, and hope, and tenderness divine;
They wanted—swine!
Christ stands without our door and gently knocks;
But if our gold, or swine, the entrance blocks,
He forces no man's hold—He will depart,
And leave us to the meanness of our heart.

Yes, as it was then, so is it now. *That* is why Jesus is rejected. If *He* comes, the swine, the unclean, must go. But that hurts human flesh; and men say, "No, I must have the swine." The greatest hindrance to the spread of the Gospel is not Satanic power, but human selfishness. I know a church in which a whole body of members asked the minister to resign, because the socially uncouth were coming in and getting saved. I know another church in which influential members fought a real revival-work of the Holy Spirit, because it was "disturbing and undignified". One of our *daily* prayers should be that this poison-weed of selfishness may be torn completely from our hearts.

The Fragments

"Gather up the fragments that remain, that nothing be lost."—Jn. 6: 12.

HAD we not been told otherwise, we might have surmised that our Lord's motive here was that of tidiness. Alexander Whyte remarks, "Our Lord was a tidy Man." Probably His mother would teach her little wonder-boy from earliest years to be tidy. The general impression given by the Gospels is that He was tidy in dress and habits. Did He grow up with the habit of leaving His bedroom tidy in the morning? One could gather so from the way He left His garments when He rose from the grave. (Jn. 20: 7)!

However, His special motive after the feeding of the five thousand was *economy*—"that nothing be lost". It may be that our Lord, knowing how far many of His hearers had to go, would have them provided for. At any rate, His economy with "fragments" suggests a quite challenging line of thought. Some of us who lived in Britain during the Second World War will never forget how the government kept urging us to salvage food scraps and metal scraps. It was a pathetic echo of our Lord's words, "Gather up the fragments which remain, that nothing be lost." Reflect on some of life's "fragments" which are of much importance.

Take just one "fragment" here: *our leisure time.* I rather think that character is made more by our use of leisure than by work hours. Hitler realised this when he invented his "Strength through Joy" scheme for the German workers. He knew how vital it was to capitalise their leisure time. How then should we use ours? I would say first, *preserve it from unworthy things.* In these days of invasion by television, lewd magazines and low-down novels, this advice is the more pertinent. Bad as it is to *waste* our leisure time, it is far worse to turn it into moral poison! Let there be downright honest fun such as best suits our years. We Christians have found spiritual joy and peace; yet because we live in the consciousness of eternal issues we take life more seriously than others. Let there be times of relaxation (Mark 6: 31). Let Jesus be in it all, like the young Indian Christian in the football team who was heard to exclaim after a brilliant kick-away, "Ooh, look Lord Jesus; watch it travel!"

My second advice on leisure time is: *give place in it to sympathy.* We cannot follow Jesus long without finding ourselves among those who need our sympathy and help. Sympathy is a gracious balance to fun, and keeps it from becoming selfish. If we are always seeking to get pleasure without giving it, not only do we inwardly shrivel, but we find ourselves lonely as we grow older.

And my third advice on leisure time is: *take time to think.* The fateful tendency in recent times has been for men to hand over their thinking to others; hence the rise of dictatorships and totalitarianisms. If we don't do our own thinking, dictators will soon do it for us! Above all, we should take time to think on God, life, death, eternity, destiny. There used to be a famous book, Hervey's *Meditations Among the Tombs.* We suggest no such morbid scenery for leisure-time reflections, but we *would* suggest the judicious use of a superb classic like Thomas à Kempis's *Imitation of Christ*—not to gulp in pages, but to take two or three sayings only at a time, thinking right through them to the richest realities of the spiritual life. Such gathering up of fragments is not only economy but measureless enrichment.

"The Master is come, and calleth for thee."—Jn. 11:28.

ALTHOUGH Martha little guessed it, these words of hers to Mary are far bigger than their local context. They are wide as the world, and big as history. Proclaim it throughout the race; shout it through the centuries: "The MASTER has come!" The words may well stir us to active response, even as they were intended to rouse bereaved Mary from her brooding reverie. How much it meant to the two mourning sisters, that Jesus had at last come to Bethany! And how much it means to *us* that He ever came to our *world*! Did Martha and Mary think He had come too late? Lazarus had now been dead four days, even as, in the larger context, there were four long thousand-year days of racial sin and death before Jesus "brought life and immortality to light through the Gospel".

But it was of set purpose that Jesus came after those four days. Only thus could He give the crowning miracle-proof of His Messiahship, Saviourhood, and Deity. Moreover, only by that delay and super-exploit could He most deeply confirm the faith of the sisters, and make Lazarus all the dearer to them. So is it ever with divine delays: they lead to blessings bigger than our biggest prayers.

Pause, then, at these words, "The Master is come, and calleth for thee." More recent versions give the crisper, truer translation—"The Master is *here* and calleth *thee*." Christian, if these words speak at all, they speak to professed Christian believers of the present day.

Ponder it well: "The *MASTER* is here." Yes, Jesus is the Master. He is "*the* Master", in divine distinguishment from all merely human pedagogues. Yet how many professing Christians today want to call Him Saviour without acknowledging Him as Master! How many denominational leaders and church members with affected reverence call Him "Lord" who in much of their behaviour repudiate His real Lordship! Who do they think themselves to be, for instance, in belittling this or that or the other part of the Old Testament, when Jesus Himself accepts and endorses its inspiration as unique, entire, verbal? We are tired of their pseudo-intellectual evasions. We earnestly challenge them. They have no right to call Him Lord while they politely repudiate Him as "Master".

Let us remember that to the true believer our Lord Jesus will be Master *in things moral*. His ethics and standards and ideals, as revealed both in what He said and how He lived, will be the decisive rule of faith and conduct.

He must also be our Master *in questions intellectual*. If Jesus accepts the Genesis cosmogony, so must I. If He accepts the Jonah narrative as a factual record, so must I. If He believes in the effectuality of prayer amid a cosmos controlled by natural law, so must I.

So, too, He must be our Master *in things emotional*. Second in importance only to our true conversion is what we do with our love. It is here that "self" most resents interference. But if we are truly Christ's disciples we must acknowledge Him Master in all our choices pertaining to courtship, wedlock, friendships, and social groups.

Think again also of this: "The Master is *HERE*"—He has come to *stay*; and He "calleth *THEE*"!

The Privilege of the Three

"He was transfigured before them."—Mark 9: 2.

THERE were seven participants in this resplendent episode: the invisible Father, who spoke with audible voice from the excellent glory; and the six visible personages on the holy mount. In this brief meditation our eyes are on that group of six. They assume a threefold aspect: first, the privilege of the *three* (Peter, James and John); second, the testimony of the *two* (Moses and Elijah); third, the supremacy of the *One* (our Lord Jesus Christ).

Reflect again on *the privilege of the three.* The Scripture here informs us that Jesus was "transfigured before *them*". Their beholding the supernatural metamorphosis was not by chance. They were taken up the height for that set purpose. They had seen His miracles, heard His teaching, watched Him in public and in private, and had discerned His character, until, at length, they had just confessed, "Thou art the Christ, the Son of the living God" (Matt. 16: 16). And now, as the Galilee ministry draws to its close, they are actually given to see the outflashing glory of Him whose divinity they had just confessed. Up to this point His deity had been covered by His humanity; but now His humanity is iridescent with His deity.

What astonishment must have overspread the faces of those three disciples! We know that the dazzling spectacle made an indelible impression on their minds (2 Peter 1: 16–18; Jn. 1: 14). They were being given an advance picture of our Lord's future coming and kingdom (Matt. 16: 28). There, before them, was our Lord, suddenly appearing in glorified body; there were the three disciples, high on the mountain summit, representing our Lord's people taken up to meet Him; and there were Moses and Elijah, representing the sealed and saved of the earthly Israel who will be the centre of the kingdom.

Or were Moses and Elijah typical in another way? The Scripture calls attention to the fact that Moses "died" and was "buried" by none other than God Himself (Deut. 34: 5, 6). Elijah, on the other hand, had the notable distinguishment of being translated to heaven, and thus escaping the grave (2 Kgs. 2: 11). Does Moses, the buried of the Lord, typify those saints who will be "asleep in Jesus" when the advent call opens the graves? And does Elijah forepicture the saints then living on earth, who will be translated to meet the Lord in the air? It may well be so. Both the Rapture and the Kingdom are seen in advance miniature on that glory-lit mountain-top.

Those three disciples were seeing our dear Lord as *we* shall see Him when He comes again. Surely John had the transfiguration mount in mind when he later wrote: "When He shall appear, we shall be like Him, for we shall see Him *as He is*" (1 Jn. 3: 2). John had already seen Him "as He is", and could not forget it. We too are going to see Him, not just as He *was*, in the days of His first earthly sojourn, but *as He now is* since His glorifying ascension; even as He was on that mountain height, long ago. What a privilege indeed it was for Peter, James and John on that "holy mount"! And oh, what comforting, sanctifying, heart-thrilling challenge there is in the prospect that we too shall soon see Him as He is —"the King in His beauty"!

"And, behold, there appeared unto them Moses and Elijah."—Matt. 17: 3.

THE more one thinks about the appearance of those two Old Testament worthies on that mountain top, the more remarkable it becomes. Peter, James and John must have been staggered into inexpressible astonishment. From their boyhood days they had been taught about those two spectacular figures in their nation's history—Moses the venerable lawgiver, and Elijah the dramatic prophet-reformer. If anyone had suggested to Peter or James or John that they were actually about to see Moses and Elijah down here on earth, they would have laughed it off as fantastic, the more so since Moses had now been gone fourteen hundred years, and the fiery Elijah nine hundred. Yet there they now were, Moses and Elijah, on that hilly headland; and the three disciples were seeing them talk with the transfigured Jesus!

But did they come to draw attention to themselves? No; they came to bear witness to *HIM*, even our Lord Jesus. Moses represents the Law. Elijah represents the Prophets. In these two men the Law and the Prophets do fresh homage to Jesus, and point to Him as the fulfilment of both. He fulfils all that the Law demands, and all that the Prophets promise. "For Christ is the end of the Law for righteousness to everyone that believeth" (Rom. 10: 4.). "To Him give all the prophets witness, that through His name whosoever believeth in Him shall receive remission of sins" (Acts 10: 43).

Luke tells us that Moses and Elijah spoke to Jesus about "His *decease* which He should accomplish at Jerusalem". In the Greek, the word here translated as "decease" is *exodus*. That is why the word "accomplish" goes with it. One does not need to "accomplish" a mere "decease". Moses had "died" and Jehovah Himself had buried him in an unknown grave. Elijah had ascended to heaven in defiance of the grave. Our Lord Jesus was both to die and to ascend, and thereby to "accomplish" a mighty "exodus" for His people. Moses had led the exodus from Egypt. Elijah had headed up an exodus from apostasy. But Jesus was to "accomplish" the exodus of all His redeemed people from bondage to sin and death and Satan. It was *that* to which Moses and Elijah came to bear testimony.

The presence of Moses and Elijah on that summit not only bears witness to human survival beyond the grave, but to the continuity of personal individuality, and to reciprocal recognition among those who are now yonder. It shows also that the departed are still actuated by keen concern in the things which happen on this earth. But, supremely, we see that the eyes of that other world are upon our Lord Jesus and the great salvation which is accomplished in Him for us human beings.

Moses said not a single word about himself or Mount Sinai. Elijah said not a single word about himself or Mount Carmel. No; the one topic was "Christ and Him crucified". In those two visitors from the beyond, the entire Old Testament and the invisible world were focussed upon *HIM*. That is what the three wondering spectators, Peter and James and John, were meant to grasp, as indeed the awesome voice from heaven soon taught them. And that is what we ourselves must ever remember: we are to be continual *pointers to HIM*.

The Supremacy of the One

"And when they had lifted up their eyes, they saw no man save Jesus only."—Matt. 17:8.

How skilfully the Transfiguration narratives converge their emphasis, not on the privilege of the three, nor on the testimony of the two, but on *the supremacy of the One!* The sun arises; the stars retire; and we see "no man, save *Jesus only*".

It is noticeable in each account that as soon as Peter says, "Lord, let us make here three tabernacles—one for Thee, and one for Moses, and one for Elias," those two Old Testament worthies withdraw, and a cloud envelopes the three disciples. Even the majestic Moses and the extraordinary Elijah must never be associated on equal level with Jesus.

Our Lord's supremacy is that of divine finality; and it is seen here in three ways. First, there is His ultimacy as *Teacher.* The voice from the cloud says, "This is My beloved Son . . . hear *HIM.*" No longer are the Old Testament Law and Prophets the final court of appeal. One greater than all the prophets is here. He does not contradict any of them; for His own Spirit was in them all; but He crowns them with that completive word which they were not able to speak. His kingly "I say unto you" is the ultimate. His solemn "Verily, verily" is the signature of finality. All that the Law and the Prophets say must now be interpreted in the light of *His* culminating word.

Second, there is His finality as *Saviour.* Moses and Elijah pointed to His "*exodus*". What were Sinai and Carmel compared with Calvary? Moses and Elijah knew that all the typological sacrifices and prophetical expectations of the old dispensation were fulfilled in the first and second comings of Jesus as Sinbearer and Sovereign. "The Law was our schoolmaster to bring us to Christ, that we might be justified by faith" (Gal. 3: 24). All the voices of the prophets find focus in Malachi's parting cry, "Behold, *He* shall come!" (Mal. 3: 1). The Law could command but it could not save. The prophets could reform but they could not redeem. God's answer to the cry of the ages is here—Jesus the SAVIOUR.

Third, there is His finality as *the divine Son.* Hear again the august voice from the cloud: "This is my beloved SON." That title marks His infinite superiority to Moses and Elijah and all other merely human servants of Jehovah. Oh, this wonderful Jesus! In every aspect He is the *Ne Plus Ultra*; the solitarily supreme. With utter fitness the narrative ends, "They saw no man save JESUS ONLY." Do we address some unconverted person? Unsaved one, get your eyes away from all others, to Jesus. Moses, the Law, self-effort, self-merit, self-righteousness, cannot save you. When you have done your miserable best, you are still a fearful sinner, and your self-righteousnesses are as "filthy rags". Elijah, reform, ethics, religion, cannot save you. After your most rigorous reforms the heart itself remains "desperately wicked". You need a *Saviour.* Moses and Elijah both point to "JESUS ONLY". In Him alone is blood-bought pardon for the past; new life and power for the present; and pledge of heaven hereafter. As for those of us who know and love Him, it must be "JESUS ONLY" in all our living and serving, until at last we see Him in the heavenly glory which flashed out on that holy mount long ago.

"I have overcome the world."—Jn. 16: 33.

At a cursory glance, this claim might seem strangely out of keeping with the "meek and lowly" Jesus. We can more easily imagine it as the loud boast of a Caesar, or the proud presumption of a Hitler. Who is this Jesus who so speaks?—a Galilean in peasant garb, His friends the poor and the fallen, without rank or wealth (Matt. 8: 20). He is about to be charged with sedition, to be mocked by the brutal soldiery, and then put away by the most shameful form of public execution. Yet never did anyone speak more truly than Jesus when He said, "I have overcome the world." He spoke not after the manner of the flesh, but of victory over a moral and spiritual world of *evil*. When you and I see *through* the external to the internal and spiritual, we recognise Jesus as the greatest Conqueror in history.

The "world", in the sense which Jesus meant, is the present world-*system*, the order of things which prevails throughout the human race today, due to the sin of man and the powerful influence of Satan, who is the "prince of this world". The system of things which prevails on earth today is not that which God either originally instituted or ultimately purposes. The "world" is the sum of all the possessions, powers and pleasures which this earthly life offers, organised under the influence of Satan so as to leave God out, to oppose His sovereignty, and keep the heart of man bound to sublunary things. Satan has usurped a temporarily permitted power over men, and has organised the world of mankind upon the principles of force, greed, selfishness, ambition, pleasure. He has organised it so as to push God out, and to keep men's minds chained to mundane things. The present world-system, it has been truly said, is outwardly imposing and powerful, religious, scientific, cultured, elegant, but seething with national and commercial rivalries and ambitions.

So far as our individual attitude is concerned, the "world" is *anything that shuts God out*. If we would know whether a thing is "of the world" or not, we only need ask, "Does it shut God out?" To us as individuals the "world" is that present consistency of things which surrounds us with its customs, fashions, maxims, rules, modes, manners, and forces. There is much of good everywhere around us, but the world-system itself is the outward, visible expression of an invisible and controlling evil. This is the "world", in the morally evil sense, through which Satan seduces souls away from God. It is just as alluringly attractive as it is deceptively destructive. Millions are overcome by it. But there was One who, although tempted by it as no other, rode over it in absolute triumph, thereby breaking its power over all who become savingly united to Him. It is *HE* who says in our text, "I have overcome the world"! With Him indwelling us, we too may overcome; for "greater is He that is in you than he that is in the world" (1 Jn. 4: 4).

Our history books have told us that Alexander the Great overcame the world, and then sat down and "wept because there were no more worlds to conquer". Wrong! Alexander died prematurely, in a drunken debauch. He was overcome *by* the world. The true victor and hero is the man who overcomes *the world within himself*.

Victory in Review

"I have overcome the world."—Jn. 16: 33.

THIS calm assurance of Jesus at once raises the question: In what *ways* did He "overcome the world"? We may profit much by reviewing His victory, and then relating it to ourselves. To begin with, He overcame the world's *flatteries*. No one else ever had such magnetic spell or miraculous power, such consummate wisdom or matchless eloquence, such resistless might to subjugate either demons or humans. No other ever awed or moved the multitudes with such amazement. No other ever beheld such possibility of global conquest spread before him. It is not surprising that when Satan first ventured an undisguised meeting with Him, he began with flattery (Matt. 4: 3, 6). But no flattery of Satan or men (Jn. 6: 15) ever begot the faintest breath of pride in that "meek and lowly" One who "emptied Himself" and took "the form of a servant".

Equally decisively, our Lord overcame the world's *hostilities*. None was ever so venomously hated by religious hypocrites, political intriguers, and angered Mammon-worshippers. Like hounds they ran Him down to His death. Like beasts of prey they thirsted for His blood. Yet in the fiercest moment of their dastardly devilry, all they could wring from Him was, "Father, forgive them; they know not what they do"!

Again, He overcame the world's *principles*. He never used His power for selfish ends, or modified His message to avoid opposition. He never descended from absolute integrity to excusable expediency, or from utter honesty to accommodating diplomacy. With Him, instead of getting, it was all giving; instead of jealous rivalry, co-operative sympathy; instead of selfism, otherism. He was the embodiment of sheer love, transparency, purity, unselfishness.

Once more, He overcame the world's *prince*. From that first repulse in the wilderness, right on to the final wrestle in Gethsemane, the arch-fiend found that at last he was up against the guileless One who was stronger than the strong. As Jesus entered Gethsemane, He was able to say, "The prince of this world cometh, and hath nothing in Me" (Jn. 14: 30). In that garden agony, when Jesus cried out amid those falling blood-drops, "Father . . . not My will, but Thine be done", Lucifer, Diabolos. Apollyon, had met his Waterloo.

Are you and I overcoming the world?—its beguilings, its self-seeking, its prejudices, and its evil genius, as Jesus did? We should keep so close to Jesus and the written Word that the carnalising influence of the world is continually counteracted, and our minds overcome the material by spiritual vitality. The supreme wonder of Christian experience is that in the truly consecrated heart the mighty Victor Himself takes over, and shares His own victory with the believer by the infilling Holy Spirit.

Thus preserved from worldly guile,
  Safe from slavish care and fear,
Let me live beneath Thy smile,
  Finding Thou art always near,
Living every day and hour
  In Thine overcoming power.

Our Lord's Prayer for His Own

"I pray for them. . . ."—Jn. 17: 9.

We cannot read the seventeenth of John without being conscious that we are treading holy ground. Like Moses before the burning bush of Horeb, we must needs take off our shoes from our feet, for the place whereon we stand is holy ground. We are actually hearing the Son of God Himself at prayer. May God give us hearts to understand!

Every part of the sublime prayer repays careful consideration; but for the moment let us view it as a whole. As we do so, it speaks to us principally in three ways—(1) in the comfort it gives, (2) in the purpose it shows, (3) in the pattern it sets.

First, there is the COMFORT of it. There is comfort in the very *fact* that our Lord thus prayed for His own. It shows that His people were on His heart now that He was about to leave them and return to the Father. That, no doubt, is one of the reasons why the prayer was recorded. It could have occasioned no surprise if our Lord's mind had been too filled with His own suffering and death to be praying for others.

Yet there is even more comfort in the *nature* of the prayer. Throughout, it breathes the most tender concern and affection toward all the Saviour's disciples; and it reaches on through the years, right down to the present; for in verse 20 He continues, "Neither pray I for these alone, but for them also which shall believe on Me through their word."

But there is most comfort of all in the *significance* of this prayer. Remember, it comes right at the end of our Lord's ministry on earth, just before He goes to the Cross, and then returns to the Father in heaven. It is surely meant to be taken as a type of the High Priestly prayers which our Lord prays for us *now*, in heaven. What a comfort it often is to us, to know that other Christians are praying for us! But is not the sweetest and most cheering of all such comforts, to know that our dear Lord Himself now and always prays for us before the very presence of the Father amid the excellent glory?

See now the *PURPOSE* revealed in our Lord's prayer. In verses 11 and 15 He prays for our *preservation*; in verse 17 our *sanctification*; in verse 21 our *unification*; in verse 24 our *glorification*. Think of all the things which our Lord *might* have prayed for on our behalf, but did not. We soon see what *He* considers most important!

The preservation which our Lord asks on our behalf is no mere preservation from physical trouble, but from *moral* evil. The sanctification He wants for us is no mere monastic reclusion, but a separatedness to the Divine *will and service* (see 18). The unification He prays for is no mere external uniformity of organisation, but an inward and *spiritual* oneness.

Think finally of the *PATTERN* which this prayer sets for us. If it is indeed an intended specimen of the prayers which our Lord prays for us in heaven, then what an example it becomes for us! His present ministry in heaven is one of *intercession*—a praying for *others*. How much earnest, unselfish "otherism" is there in my own praying? Am I really functioning as a priest and intercessor? We cannot do a more Christlike thing than interceding. Note in our Lord's prayer (1) its catholicity, (2) its spirituality, (3) its motive, i.e. the glory of God (see verses 1, 4, 26).

Satan's Sieve

"Simon, Simon, behold Satan hath desired to have you, that he may sift you as wheat. . . ."—Luke 22: 31.

OUR Lord uttered this awesome forewarning during those intense hours which headed up in His betrayal and crucifixion. The words are indeed startling, for they suddenly expose a sinister activity of Satan against the Lord's people. Just before this, our Lord had said to the disciples, "Ye are they which have continued with me in my temptations; and I appoint you a kingdom . . ." (28–30). *Now* He warns them that they were also to be the fearful tempter's special prey; and a little later, as they apprehensively accompany Him into Gethsemane, He counsels them again, "Pray, lest *ye* enter into temptation."

Our Lord knew, as no other, how crafty, cruel, powerful, was the archfiend, and He warned the disciples with a corresponding intensity. His twice-uttering of the apostle's name—"Simon, Simon", as He now addressed him, indicated this intensity. Always, in Scripture, this form of double appellation indicates intensity: "Abraham, Abraham" (Gen. 22: 11); "Moses, Moses" (Exod. 3: 4); "Samuel, Samuel" (1 Sam. 3: 10); "Jerusalem, Jerusalem" (Luke 13: 34); "Saul, Saul" (Acts 9: 4). When our Lord said, "Simon, Simon", there was concentrated concern; for He knew what a serious thing it was to be in Satan's sieve.

Note that word, "sift". One of the striking contrasts between our Lord and Satan is that our Lord has a "fan" (Luke 3: 17), whereas Satan has a sieve (22: 31). The difference between the fan and the sieve is that the fan winnows or wafts away the chaff and retains the good grain, whereas the sieve lets the grain fall through and retains only the chaff!

But the most startling thing of all is that in the Greek our Lord's solemn words read, not merely, "Satan hath desired you . . ." but, "Simon, Simon, behold Satan *hath obtained you,* by asking that he might sift you as wheat"! There had actually been a permission from God in response to a request by Satan! Does it seem hardly believable? Nay, on the contrary, it is most revealing, and we may well be grateful for this sudden, illuminating glimpse into the beyond. The fact is, our Lord's words to Peter mark an exact New Testament parallel with the Old Testament case of *Job.* Satan challenged God concerning Job, and *obtained permission* to test him by excessive afflictions. Job was allowed to be in Satan's sieve. The same thing was now permitted in the case of the apostles! It was not just Peter who was to be "sifted", but *all* the apostles; for our Lord, although He directly addressed Simon, said, "Satan hath obtained *you* [plural] that he may sift *you* [all of you] as wheat."

Now, however, there was one big difference; for our Lord added, "*But, I have prayed for thee* that thy faith fail not . . ." Our great Saviour had got there first!—and had prevailed!—and Satan was thwarted! Christian, beware of Satan's sieve! But be comforted; we have a wonderful Interposer whose victorious solicitations always provide advance coverage if we trust Him. See 1 John 2: 1 again: "If any man sin, we have a Paraclete with the Father: Jesus Christ the righteous." In every temptation, remember that He is there, continually praying for *you.* As Hebrews 7:25 says, "He ever liveth to make *intercession*" for us.

"Then took Mary a pound of ointment of spikenard, very costly, and anointed the feet of Jesus, and wiped His feet with her hair; and the house was filled with the odour of the ointment."—Jn. 12 : 3.

THIS lovely little episode illustrates the meaning of consecration to Christ more appealingly perhaps than any other in the New Testament. Mary's spikenard not only pervaded that long-ago Bethany homestead with its fragrance; its sweet savour ascended to the very angels in heaven; and it lingers on through the centuries; for "wheresoever this Gospel is preached" its aroma breaks forth afresh.

We are left in no doubt that Mary's "alabaster box" (as Matthew and Mark identify it) was of most expensive quality. As its name indicates, it was from Alabastron in Egypt, famous for its manufacturing of such vessels and perfumes. Our first two evangelists tell us that this particular spikenard confection was "very precious", while John adds that it was one "pound" in weight, and "very costly". Whether Mary had procured it through a merchant or it had been bequeathed by her mother; whether she had treasured it for a longer or a shorter time, we do not know; but it may have been "very precious" for sentimental reasons as well as "very costly" in terms of purchase.

There were *four choices* open to Mary in her use of it. First, she could have used it entirely on herself—which is what many do with the alabaster boxes of their hearts and lives. Second, she could have poured it on some loved one or loved ones other than Jesus. Third, she could have distributed it between herself and others, either including or excluding Jesus as a part-sharer. Fourth, there was the choice which she actually made, namely, the devoting of it exclusively to Jesus her Lord. And when she gently unsealed it upon His head and feet, she therewith outpoured the supreme love and devotion of her heart.

There were *four motives* behind Mary's lovely impulse. First there was *reverence*. Hers was no mere sentimental adoration of an idol. In that sublime Manhood she had recognised incarnate Godhead, and must worship. Second, there was *gratitude*. While others seemed blind, her tear-clarified eyes had seen that the way to the throne was via the Cross (verse 7). Third, there was *faith*—convinced faith in Him as Son of God, Saviour, King. Fourth, there was *love*, a love which, having been begotten of the other motives—reverence, gratitude, faith, had become strongest of all.

There are also *four traits* here which illustrate all true consecration to Christ. (1) Lip-worship was not enough; she must *give*. (2) The cheap was not enough; she must give the *very costly*. (3) A part was not enough; she must give *all*. (4) The unbroken was not enough; it must be actually *outpoured*, and Mary must fall at His feet—the respected Mary of all people—and linger there like the lowest slave!

Well; how do you and I compare with *that*? The same four choices are open to each of us today, with these alabaster boxes of our *lives*. The first choice, i.e. ego-devotion, self-gratification always turns fragrance to sourness in the end. The second and third choices affect us for good or ill according to the worthiness of the objects on which we spend ourselves. May ours be the *highest* choice of pouring our best at *HIS* feet!

Consecration to Christ

"Then took Mary a pound of ointment of spikenard, very costly, and anointed the feet of Jesus, and wiped his feet with her hair; and the house was filled with the odour of the ointment."—Jn. 12 : 3.

As we remarked in yesterday's meditation, this incident strikingly illustrates consecration to Christ. Ought we not now to press home its application to our own hearts and lives?

This matter of consecration is of tenderest concern to all of us who love the Name. Its importance is beyond exaggeration. It is the golden door which alone admits us into "the *fulness* of the blessing" (Rom. 15 : 29). It is the crucial hinge on which all true Christian service turns. It is the one and only secret of inward rest and of victory over sin. Exactly in proportion as we are self-governed instead of Christ-governed our hearts lack poise and quietness, our lives lack fragrance, and our testimony lacks persuasiveness.

True consecration to Christ *simplifies* life, for it leaves the management to HIM. It also *unifies* life, for it blends all our motives and activities in one all-controlling aim to please HIM. It *purifies* life, for it expels all that is disapproved by HIM. It *amplifies* life, for it gives the divine will spacious fulfilment through us to uplift HIM. And it *glorifies* life, for it makes us a blessing to others and a praise to HIM.

Our entire consecration is that which our Lord Himself desires for us above all else—far more than our service, our money, our time, or even our prayers. He never really sees the "travail of His soul" in us so as to become "satisfied" until our conversion has crowned itself in total self-committal to Him. There can be no substitute for this, simply because there is no equivalent. How incalculably important, also, is our consecration to Christ when we think of the unsaved all around us, and of the low spiritual average among believers today, and of our Lord's nearing return!

Are not *all* Christians thus consecrated? No; far from it. But do they not all *desire* it? Yes, I think they all do. Why then are so few *actually* consecrated? It is because consecration, although in one sense a simple "handing over" followed by a simple "hands off", is the hardest of *all* capitulations to the self-centred *ego* in us. To give up this or that or the other sin is comparatively tolerable, but to give up self-management, self-motives, grudges, plans, and self-everything, is utterly unbearable to our hereditary Adam-nature, which is supported in its resistance by Satan and the world, and perhaps unintentionally by other Christians.

Oh, it is a super-crisis of the soul, to give up your claim to every bit of merit, your desires for the present, and if necessary your plans for the future, your first claim on every penny you possess, your own ideas, your everything—not just for a year or a decade, but for ever! One of the most powerful deterrents is our fear of being misunderstood by loved ones, and the loneliness which may be thus occasioned. There is only one thing which can make this complete hand-over easy. It is to have such a trustful, grateful, adoring *love* for Jesus that all else seems "dross" compared with His dearness and excellency. Such consecration is indeed the gateway to "*fulness* of blessing", but it is also *the supreme test of our love.*

It is only when we make this unreserved surrender, that Jesus sees in us "the travail of His soul", and is "satisfied" (Isa. 53 : 11).

The Vital Focus-Point

"Behold, the Lamb of God, which taketh away the sin of the world!"—Jn. 1:29.

If ever Christian believers needed to echo and re-echo these words of John the Baptist, they do today. We are not fond of flinging aspersions; yet we cannot help openly lamenting that many so-called Christian pulpits and churches are doing anything except exhorting men and women to behold Jesus as "the Lamb of God which taketh away the sin of the world". In many places Jesus is preached merely as an idealist, a standard-bearer of high morals; or as a kind of pioneer in things spiritual. His significance is ethical rather than redemptive. His death on the Cross is either left out, or else its true nature as a substitutionary sacrifice for human sin is hidden under the drapery of aesthetic adulations of His pathetic heroism. His death is exemplary rather than expiatory. The inner glory of the Cross is missed, because its outer ugliness is shunned. The lingering presence of Jesus in His church is a mystical vagary rather than the actual personal presence of the Living One who rose bodily from the grave. Meanwhile, new-fangled unitarian cults are everywhere around us, preaching a spurious demi-god Christ stripped of His real deity. It is the sacred business of every true Christian to help uplift the real Jesus again as "the Lamb of God which taketh away the sin of the world"!

Let these words of John the forerunner remind us that whatever other offices belong to our Lord Jesus, He is first and foremost "*the Lamb of God*". We do not forget that He is the "Lion of Judah"; the "Star of David"; the "True Vine"; the "Wonderful Counsellor"; not to mention His many other illustrious titles; but before everything else He is "the *Lamb*". He is Prophet, Priest, and King; yet even before these He is "the *Lamb*". He did not become incarnate merely as Prophet to teach, or as Priest to pray, or as King to rule. Nay, before all else, He became incarnate as "the Lamb" to *save* us. His first significance is not ethical or religious, but *redemptive*—as He Himself taught (Matt. 18:11; 20:28; 26:28).

Undoubtedly, when He is called "the Lamb", there is a reference to His *character*. In His meekness, guilelessness, innocence, gentleness, harmlessness, purity, simplicity, He is indeed the "Lamb". There is nothing harsh or haughty or retaliative about Him. Nor is there the slightest blemish in His nature. His character is that of the Lamb.

Yet though this is so, the fact remains that when He is called "the Lamb of God", the first reference is not to His character, but to His *substitutionary sacrifice* as the race's Sinbearer. Everything is subordinate to that. John the Baptist flings his emphasis on the words, "Taketh away the sin of the world". That is the supreme feature: Jesus is the Saviour. That is why John pointed to Him. That is why *we* must point to Him. He is the substitutionary guilt-bearer. He took *our* place. He bore *our* sentence. He was offered for *our* sakes. "He is the propitiation for *our* sins", yea even for "the whole world" (1 Jn. 2:2). A doubter once said to a Christian worker, "I cannot believe in the virgin birth of Jesus; there has never been any other such birth in all history." The Christian replied, "That is quite true: there is no other such in all history, simply because there is *only the one Saviour.*"

The Great Sin-Bearer

"Behold, the Lamb of God, which taketh away the sin of the world."—Jn. 1:29.

How startled those long-ago crowds must have been when the cynosure dervish prophet actually pointed to Jesus, and shouted from the edge of the Jordan, "Behold the Lamb of God"! Remember, they were Jews. The Old Testament Scriptures were read to them in their synagogues every Sabbath. Almost as quickly as John the Baptist's electric syllables struck their ears they would think of Abel and his propitiatory lamb; of Abraham and his memorable word, "God will provide Himself a lamb; of the Passover lamb in Egypt; of the Levitical lamb and the Tabernacle"; and of the great prophecy in Isaiah, "He was wounded for our transgressions . . . He is brought as a lamb to the slaughter . . . He bare the sin of many". Yes, they would immediately think of these things; and then they would grasp that John was identifying Jesus as the antitype and fulfilment.

How their hearts would stir with awed wonder at that phrase, "the Lamb of God"! And well may we ourselves be stirred to a like wonder. Our Lord Jesus is "the Lamb of God" in the sense that He is the Lamb *provided* by God. The Jews were used to providing their own lambs for the temple sacrifices; but here is the Lamb of Jehovah's own providing—not just for one individual, or for one family, or even for the covenant nation, but for the whole world!

And, further, our Lord Jesus is "the Lamb of God" in the sense that He is the Lamb who *incarnated* God. No less than eight titles of our Lord are used in this opening chapter of the fourth Gospel, all implying His messiahship and deity: "The Word", "The Life", "The Light", "The Son", "The Lamb", "The Messiah", "The King", "The Son of Man". Our Lord Jesus Christ is the *divine* Lamb. The very fact that He could bear "the sin of the world" implies His absolute Godhead. Frankly, it is an enigma to my own mind how anyone claiming to be rationally minded can believe that Jesus bore "the sin of the world" if He was a mere creature. How could *any* mere creature make atonement for our race's sin? As Psalm 49:7 says, "None can by any means redeem his brother, nor give to God a ransom for him." How then shall any mere creature-Christ bear a whole universe's guilt, and make infinite expiation?

Furthermore, our Lord is "the Lamb of God" in the sense that He substitutionally *satisfies* God. Away back in Isaiah 42, Jehovah says through the prophet, "Behold My Servant whom I uphold; Mine Elect *in whom My soul delighteth.*" And now, eight centuries later, at our Lord's Jordan baptism, that prophecy finds its historical echo in the voice which now calls down from the opened heaven, "This is My beloved Son, *in whom I am well pleased.*" From first to last our Lord's life on earth "magnified the Law, and made it honourable" (Isa. 42:21); so that when He offered Himself up as our vicarious propitiation on Calvary, His sinless humanity in union with His boundless divinity made an atonement well-pleasing to God, and infinitely meritorious for man. Oh, the marvel of that Cross! Nothing can be more profitable, even for the advanced believer, than continually to "behold the Lamb of God, which taketh away the sin of the world".

"Behold, the Lamb of God, which taketh away the sin of the world."—Jn. 1 : 29.

But why was it *necessary* that the Prince of Glory should become that Lamb of sacrifice, and undergo the fearful ordeal of Calvary? Was there no other way?

Well, if the Bible is truly the Word of God, and if our Lord Jesus is truly the incarnate Son of God, then according to their clear teaching there certainly was *no* other way. The Cross was a necessity if man was to be saved. We are not merely arguing in a circle when we say that the very fact of its being divinely ordained proves its necessity. God would never have indulged the prodigal agony of that awful Cross as a theatrical superfluity, to display a love which was not needed redemptively. If damnation were not a reality then redemption would not have been a necessity. But death and judgment and Gehenna are fearsome realities; and only the vicarious agonies of Gethsemane, Gabbatha, and Golgotha could achieve rescue.

Those paltry thinkers who glibly aver that God could easily have forgiven men's sins if He wanted, without any need for the Cross, know not whereof they affirm. They do not adequately estimate either the holiness of God or the sinfulness of man.

It is inconceivable that the all-holy God should govern His universe with even the slightest moral laxity. If the principles of absolute righteousness were not strictly upheld, there could be no true heaven; the universe would become a moral chaos, if not an inferno. The very safety of the universe depends upon the inflexible righteousness of the divine administration. Sin, whether in Satan and his angel-confederates, or in the human race, is not only moral leprosy, it is ugly enmity against Him who is pure light and love.

If God is to save man, it must be in a way which is in harmony with the divine holiness and which honours the necessities of the divine government. It must be in a way which demonstrates to an onlooking universe the awful sacredness with which God Himself looks upon His holy law. It must be in a way which shows God's hatred of sin; and nowhere else was there ever such a revelation of divine wrath against sin as on Calvary. One has only to ponder carefully these and other aspects of the case to see how necessary was the Cross of Christ if God was to save us. It was not that God "required blood" (as we heard one preacher vulgarly say), but that sin necessitated an infinite substitutionary expiation if man was to be saved according to the principles of eternal righteousness. And who could make that infinite expiation but the infinite God Himself? No less a marvel was required than that a member of the divine Triunity should assume our manhood, live our life, conquer our foe, and yield Himself an atoning Substitute to "take away the sin of the world".

This the Son of God actually did. There was no binding incumbency that He should do so. He did it of purest love for us. "God so *loved* the world that He gave . . ." "The Son of God *loved* me, and gave Himself for me." "Behold the Lamb of God which taketh away the sin of the world." Thank God, He bore it "*away*"! Once for all, and One for all, with an eternal finality!

The Victim is the Victor!

"And I, if I be lifted up from the earth, will draw all men unto Me."—Jn. 12 : 32.

HERE is one of the most remarkable utterances which ever fell from the lips of our Lord Jesus. That expression, "lifted up", seems to have been understood (or misunderstood!) in more ways than one. Some have held it to mean our Lord's *resurrection*, because it says "lifted up from the earth". Others have taken it to mean His *ascension*, claiming that the words, "from the earth", mean up from the earth to heaven. Pope Urban the Sixth gave it a characteristically presumptuous Roman Catholic slant: the words, "Give unto Caesar the things that are Caesar's" were abolished when Christ was lifted up from the earth in His ascension, for He then drew all kingdoms to the Pope's empire, thus making the Pope "King of Kings and Lord of Lords"!

Now it is patent that our Lord meant neither His resurrection nor His ascension when He said, "If I be lifted up", for the very next verse tells us explicitly that He meant His death by crucifixion: "This He said, signifying *by what death He should die.*" In face of such a clear comment by the Gospel writer himself, it is surely strange of expositors to make the words mean anything else.

So, then, our Lord's words, "I, if I be lifted up", refer exclusively to His Cross. This immediately gives them a captivating significance, for the Greek word here translated as "lifted up" is one which in other places is used of our Lord's heavenly *exaltation* (see Acts 2 : 33; 5 : 31, etc.). Do you catch the gleam of new light? Our Lord uses a word to describe that awful Cross which at once transfigures it. He looks beyond the revolting externals, to the inner glory and ultimate triumph of it. With one word He suddenly releases its imprisoned glory-light, bathing all the ugly exterior with a heavenly sublimity. Thus we see Calvary transfigured.

That Cross gives Christ a higher glory than even the throne of heaven, apart from it, could ever give Him! Little did His murderers suspect it, but in crucifying Him they were glorifying Him. He was being "lifted up" indeed, but not merely in the way which *they* intended! His crucifixion was a coronation! He was there crowned as the King of Love. To the perceiving eyes of His redeemed people, the thorns on His brow become eternal diadems, and His wounds the divinest gems in the universe. No beings in all the creation can ever love Him quite like that "multitude which no man could number, of all nations and kindreds and tongues" who have "washed their robes in the blood of the Lamb", and are saved for evermore. Think what Calvary means to every single soul which understandingly and adoringly exclaims with Paul, "The Son of God loved *me*, and gave Himself for *me*!" With what wonder and worship do all the millions of the saved unite in grateful chorus, "We love Him because He first loved us"! Yes, Calvary is transfigured. Redeeming grace transforms the Cross into a throne. Love reigns supreme.

O love of God, O sin of man,
   In this dread act your strength is tried;
And victory remains with Love;
   For He, our Lord, is crucified.

"And I, if I be lifted up from the earth, will draw all men unto Me."—Jn. 12 : 32.

YES, our Saviour transforms that evil Cross by calling it an exaltation or being "lifted up". He also thereby utters a caution against preoccupation with the merely outward. The outward is ever to be seen in sharp contrast with the inward.

Outwardly, you see a nailed-up Victim expiring in agony and weakness. You see the pinioned hands and feet, the utter helplessness of the Sufferer, the few sympathisers and their powerlessness to do anything but weep brokenheartedly. You hear the mocking taunts of His crucifiers. You hear the heart-rending gasp, "I thirst!" from the burning throat of the pain-racked figure suspended there. You see the bruised face, the scarred brow, the ugly wounds, the dripping blood, and the head as it jolts forward in death.

Ah, but take a deeper look, and you see the Cross transfigured like a dark cloud on which the sun has suddenly poured a flood of gold. In a flash, that transfixed Sufferer could have summoned legions of angels to annihilate His murderers. One release of His concealed power, and He who stilled the stormy waves, cast out demons, healed the sick, and raised the dead, could have swept down from that Cross and obliterated His Satan-inspired enemies. It was not the nails which held Jesus there, but *love*. That which outwardly looks like weakness in its most pitiful form, is in reality love at its loveliest, love stronger than death, love which all the floods of hatred cannot drown. Through His dying He shows His *un*dying love. It is in His being helplessly there that His love demonstrates its omnipotence. Sin has done its worst, yet He dies saying, "Father, forgive them. . . ." Oh, sublime paradox of Calvary! See love's victory: because it cannot do anything to save itself it can do everything to save others!

Outwardly we see the deepest tragedy of human sin: inwardly we see the highest triumph of divine grace. Outwardly we see a hideous crime; inwardly we see the sublimest expression of the Son's perfect obedience to the Father. Outwardly we see a shocking miscarriage of justice; inwardly we see the all-controlling, overruling sovereignty of the divine purpose. Outwardly we see frustration, for He is prematurely "cut off" from the land of the living; inwardly we see completion, for He dies exclaiming, "It is finished", and provides an eternal salvation. Outwardly we see an apparent victory by the powers of evil, for it seems as though the Messianic promises and prophecies concerning the reign of David's Son over a regenerate Israel have crashed in failure; inwardly we see the very opposite, for on the ruins of Jewish unbelief and Christ-rejection, God builds the Church of His dear Son, and brings in the Gospel age of grace to Jew and Gentile alike. When Jesus is "lifted up", Satan is cast down. When heaven bleeds on that Cross, hell is defeated by its own stratagems. Calvary is transformed; and Jesus, knowing all things, calls it His being "*lifted up*"! That which showed how much He was hated, is that for which He is now most loved. That Cross of stark desertion is the very magnet which "draws all men" to Him.

The Transfiguring Cross

"And I, if I be lifted up from the earth, will draw all men unto Me."—Jn. 12 : 32.

When our Lord thus calls His Cross a being "lifted up" or exalted, not only is Calvary transfigured, but by its sympathetic outreach Calvary now transfigures *other* sorrows.

To begin with, it transfigures human *suffering*, especially the suffering of the godly. Outwardly Calvary seemed entirely a coincidence of human wickedness and merely natural circumstances. But no; it was foreknown and overruled as the master-stroke of divine grace, wisdom and power in the saving of a lost world! Troubled sufferer, pause and ponder that! In *His* suffering there was mysterious but gracious *purpose*: may there not be the same in yours? That Cross ultimately led to a joy which even the Son of God had never known before. Could it not be the same with you? But besides this, Calvary means that *God Himself has suffered*. He suffered not only *for* us, redeemingly, but *with* us, sympathetically. He still has the same human nature, and is "touched with the feeling of our infirmities". Does not that transfigure suffering?

Then again, Calvary transfigures life's *enigmas*. How is it that the young Christian student who offers his life for overseas missionary service, and slogs at study to become a qualified doctor, is suddenly afflicted with illness the very year he qualifies, and is informed that he can *never* go out as a missionary? Is God mocking him? Oh, there are these ironic enigmas which wring many an agonising "Why?" from our baffled minds and frustrated longings. Look at Calvary again. It seemed a mocking frustration indeed. The godly wept that it was so. The wicked gloated that it was so. Both were wrong. As Samson's bees gave honey from the carcase of the lion, so have the sweetest of all joys come from Calvary; and so it is with many another enigma. William Cowper had a strange enigma in his life, but he learned to write, "Behind a frowning providence, God hides a smiling face."

That young medical graduate, also, who could not go out as a missionary after all, learned the same thing later; for he was used to influence and train *hundreds* for the overseas fields; and today there is a large missionary memorial hospital erected to his venerated memory! Puzzled, frustrated, disappointed Christian, try to believe it: there is a golden lining to the cloud, and a hidden good purpose in that which seems cruel.

Once again, Calvary transfigures the *sin-problem*. Look at Jesus on that Cross again. Yes, He is Man; but He is *God*-Man. God is the ultimate target of sin. Whatever be the sin I commit, in its final meaning it is a wound inflicted upon God. Sin is not just a breaking of His *law*, but a wounding of His *heart*. That is why He was there, as that broken-hearted Sufferer on Calvary. And now the resultant fact is, not that you and I have been born into a lost world, but that we have been born into a lost world which has been potentially saved! It is for you and me to enter into the wonderful legacy which Calvary has made ours. In the person of His dear Son, God Himself took our place, and became reckoned as the criminal. Wonderful Calvary! Love transfigures Calvary; then Calvary transfigures everything else!

EASTER READINGS

NOTE: If Easter Sunday occurs earlier than April 22nd., use the Easter week readings in the immediately following pages (i.e. pages 97 to 102) after which resume the daily readings at the appropriate date.

An Easter Week Longing

"That I may know Him." Ah, I long to know
Not just a Christ of far-gone years ago;
Nor even reigning on a heavenly throne,
Too high and distant to be really known.
I long to know Him closely; this is how—
Alive—and in this ever-pressing "now";
Communicating His all-conquering power,
A living One, within my heart this hour,
Who now no longer lives from me apart,
But shares His resurrection in my heart.

J.S.B.

"The Lord is Risen Indeed"

"But now is Christ risen from the dead."—1 Cor. 15 : 20.

THIS is the morning of mornings! Christ is risen! Thanks be to God! Amid a world blinded by Satan and blighted by sin and blasted by war, amid the crash of armies and amid the crash of wrecked hopes, amid the pathetic breakdown of human nature and the ironic failure of proud, little, twentieth-century man to work out his own salvation—amid all this, and amid the gloomy problems which beset the immediate future, the one great fact which gives solid comfort and hope and promise is the fact that nineteen hundred and some years ago, on the sixteenth day of the month Nisan, A.D. 32, God raised up the crucified Jesus Christ from the grave. That empty tomb means Diabolos vanquished and Christ victorious. It means that in the next chapter of human history God's kingdom shall come, and His will be done on earth as it is in heaven. The biggest of problems to the natural man in this present age is the silence of God. "Why does not God speak?" he asks. "Let God speak, so that we may hear Him and know that He really *is*." The resurrection of Christ proclaims that God *has* spoken already, and that the God who spoke yesterday will speak again in a soon-coming tomorrow. As truly as He rose Christ will come again to this world of ours. His resurrection tolls the knell on evil's dark kingdom, and rings the glad bell of God-given hope for the travailing earth. The present age (we verily believe) is rushing on with accentuated momentum to the world's Friday night; the morning of the Millennial seventh-day thousand-year Sabbath is soon to break, when the Christ of the Easter morn shall become the Christ of the Davidic throne; when swords shall become ploughshares, and spears become pruning hooks, and the nations shall learn war no more.

Such is the significance of our Lord's resurrection for human history; and it is well that we should gratefully keep it in mind during days like these. But besides this, let all of us who know the cleansing efficacy of our Saviour's precious blood, and the regenerating reality of the Holy Spirit, pray that the "Spirit of wisdom and of revelation" may vivify it all afresh to us, causing it to grip us and thrill us and impel us onward in the train of our Lord's triumph. Let us pray that the historical *fact* of it may become more and more corroborated by the *power* of it in our daily experience; and that the risen Jesus who reappeared *bodily* to His disciples may be the indwelling Christ who becomes *spiritually* luminous to our minds. Let us pray that we may know the *subduing* power of our Lord's resurrection over self and sin and Satan—its power to subdue evil tempers, unruly tongues, flaming passions, enslaving desires, inordinate ambitions, fear, pride, hate, jealousy, temptation, circumstance, and innate proclivities to sin. Let us pray that we may know its *transforming* power in heart and disposition and character—its power to lift us above earthiness and littleness into refining fellowship with God and spacious consciousness of things divine. Let us pray that we may know its *vitalizing* power in Christian service, in our preaching or writing or witness-bearing or organising—its power to infuse an inward glow and a communicative vitality and a soul-winning *telling-power*. Yes, thank God, "Now is Christ risen from the dead". On this Easter day, may you and I prove His resurrection afresh *in our hearts*!

Vistas of the Super-Victory

"The power of His resurrection."—Phil. 3 : 10.

WHAT infinitudes in one short phrase—"the power of His resurrection"! What vistas the super-victory of that vacated sepulchre opens up! You and I are meant to know "the power of His resurrection" in its various aspects toward ourselves. How vital is its *evidential* power! The classic Corinthian passage on the subject makes it the prime apologetic of the Christian religion: "If Christ be not raised, your faith is vain." How complete is its *justifying* power! "He was raised for our justification" (Rom. 4: 25). "Who is he that condemneth? Christ died, yea rather is risen again" (Rom. 8: 33, 34). How wonderful is its *quickening* power! We are "raised up together" with Him in spiritual union. We "walk in newness of life" and "sit together with Him" in the "heavenlies" (Eph. 2: 5, 6). How reassuring is its *certifying* power! "God hath given assurance unto all men in that He hath raised Him from the dead" (Acts 17: 31). What greater public proof could there be that the atonement is accepted?—that Satan is defeated?—that the power of death is broken? (Rom. 5: 10; 2 Tim. 2: 14). How unmistakable is its *demonstrative* power! "Destroy this temple," says our Lord Jesus, "and in three days I will raise it up" (Jn. 2: 19–21). He said it; and His resurrection demonstrates it. (Jn. 10: 17). How precious is its *consolatory* power! The risen Victor is the tender-hearted Saviour who not only "ever liveth to make intercession" for us, but is "touched with the feeling of our infirmities", and is our constant Companion "even unto the end of the age" (Heb. 7: 25; 4: 15; Matt. 28: 20). How titanic in prospect is its *reanimating* power! "Now is Christ risen from the dead, and become the firstfruits of them that are fallen asleep" (1 Cor. 15: 20). He is the pledge and specimen of the mighty resurrection-harvest yet to be.

Especially, how wonderful is its *liberating* power in the minds and hearts and experience of His blood-bought people! It was this which Paul longed to prove more and more when he wrote the words of our text—"That I may know Him, and the power of His resurrection".

Think how "the power of His resurrection" is exhibited in our Lord Himself. First, it crowns His victory over *self*. From first to last He had answered a firm "No" to every movement of His human nature which would have infringed upon His utter loyalty to the Father's will—"even to the death of the Cross"; and now, that emptied sepulchre culminatively testifies His complete victory over the human self. Second, it proclaims His victory over *sin*. Had there been sin, death could have held Him; but the Father now gives crowning attestation that there is *no* sin in His incarnate Son. Third, it manifests His victory over *death*. "Death hath no more dominion over Him" (Rom. 6: 9). Fourth, it signalises His victory over *Satan*. At last, One stronger than the strong has come to the rescue. He has broken the power of Satan over mankind, and wrenched from him the "keys of hades and death". And now, "the power of His resurrection" is given availability to us Christian believers. A crowned Christ in a consecrated, prayerful heart makes it all real again today—victory over self, and sin, and Satan, and even death.

"Our Saviour, Jesus Christ, hath abolished death and hath brought life and immortality to light through the Gospel."—2 Tim. 1 : 10.

IF Jesus has really done this (and He *has*!) then He is the greatest Figure of history; and the most important thing is to know Him as Saviour. Are the two words "life" and "immortality" tautologous here? No; they mark a scientific distinction between things which differ. The word "life" refers to that new *spiritual* life which Christ brings to us; whereas the word "immortality" relates to the *body*.

He has "brought life and immortality *to light*". Gross darkness enwrapped these subjects until then. Among the ancient philosophers there was only dark groping, while even among the prophets of the covenant nation there was comparatively little more than a flickering of tapers. None of Israel's teachers had lived in the invisible sphere before being born, and therefore none knew anything by experience of that spirit-realm which hovers invisibly all around this visible earthly scene. But our Lord *had* lived before He was born in Bethlehem. His birth was not His beginning; it was His incarnation as Man. He was not only "born"; He "*came*" (1 Tim. 1: 15). He knew all about the world beyond, and therefore spoke about it as no other ever had. Then, He actually underwent the experience of death, the dissolution of soul and body; and as a disembodied Ego He went from the Cross into Hades, and "preached" to the departed human spirits there; after which He arose, both spiritually (from Hades) and physically (from the sepulchre), for He now reoccupied the temporarily discarded corpse, reanimating it, not with blood again as a *mortal* body, but with *spiritual* life-force which made it supernal and immortal.

If, then, someone asks *how* Jesus has "abolished death, and brought life and immortality to light", we answer in a two-fold way.

First. He has done so *in Himself*. Death is the offspring of sin (Rom. 5: 12). Christ overcame that which is the *cause* of death. He was "tempted in all points like as we are". He was tempted more fiercely than any other, for He was Satan's prize-target. He "suffered" being tempted (Heb. 2: 18; 5: 7). Yet he sinned not. Therefore it was "not possible" (Acts 2: 24) that He should be held by death. Of moral necessity the sinless Sinbearer rose, and by so doing He stripped death of its power.

Second. He effects "life and immortality" *in His people*. After man's fall in Adam, death was imposed not only as a judgment, but as a salvage measure. Mark that word in Genesis 3: 22, "*Lest* he . . . live for ever." Immortality would have put fallen man beyond redemption. Our present wrecked nature must be taken down in death, and a new human nature erected, if we are to be saved. Our Lord Jesus has removed the sin-barrier between man and God, releasing the life-giving Holy Spirit who effects within us a new spiritual nature. The redemption of the body is included in our Lord's Calvary-work, though the body is not yet *actually* redeemed (Rom. 8: 23); but at the return of Christ, eternal life in the soul and immortality of the body shall go together in lovely consummation.

My Redeemer Liveth

"I know that my Redeemer liveth."—Job 19: 25.

EASTER has come again. It has broken upon a world of problems, enigmas and disquieting circumstances. Turn again to the immortal words of Job 19: 25–27. "I know that my Redeemer liveth, and that He shall stand at the latter day upon the earth: and though after my skin this body be destroyed, yet in my flesh shall I see God."

The occurrence of the word "Redeemer" here is striking in the extreme. When we reflect that the Book of Job is probably the earliest written book of our Scriptures, we realize that so far as we have any record this is the first time that a human soul called God "Redeemer".

Job has at last found solution and satisfaction in the great fact that over against problem and pain in the present there is a sovereign Vindicator of the righteous, who is Himself the pledge of restitution yet to be.

And is not that the great fact upon which we ourselves must rest today? We cannot explain the enigmas, the problems, the sufferings, the mysteries, of our present lot. Considered by itself this present life often seems bitterly unfair and hopelessly baffling. Here is a man who would do service for God and for his fellow-men, but he is stricken down with some fell disease which holds him bedfast for weary years: while here is another whose every thought is selfishness and vice, and he walks abroad in unimpaired health. Here is a young man conscious of gifts and powers, and of an inward urge to some noble vocation; but he is without due social prestige, without monetary reserves, and is frustrated while others without either the gifts or the urge are pushed before him. Here is a man of wisdom, integrity, and benevolent heart, who would have been a benefactor to thousands had he possessed material means; while here is another of grovelling mind who possesses more than he can count, and wastes his substance in riotous living. Oh, how endlessly could one multiply such instances! All over the world there are men and women good and true who are mercilessly thwarted and beaten back by ironic inequalities. All through the churches there are saints longing to do some big and noble thing for their Lord, yet they are dashed back panting and breathless, crushed and seemingly mocked, by wave after wave of frustrating circumstances. Is not this true of all of us in some way? What we would do! . . . but that incurable illness lays us low, that crushing blow falls and smashes our hopes, that gnawing trouble wastes our strength, that irretrievable disappointment plunges us into darkness, that life-long poverty, that adversity, that impediment, that affliction, cuts us off from serving Christ as we would.

What can we say about it all?—and about the wars which curse the race, the devilish cruelties which are perpetrated, the colossal evils which breathe across the earth? We can say what Job said, and say it with the confirmatory evidence of an historical background which Job never had. There is a Living One on high, the sovereign Vindicator of the righteous; and in the Person of our Lord Jesus Christ He will certainly stand up, upon the earth, in a day of restitution which is the goal of Biblical prediction. Christian, be comforted. God accepts the will for the deed. Those who are thwarted *now*, shall be given full opportunity *then*!

". . . and Peter"

"But go your way, tell His disciples and Peter that He goeth before you into Galilee."—Mark 16:7.

"*And Peter.*" This particular mention of Peter by the angel, on the morning of our Lord's resurrection, is retained for us only in Mark's Gospel. It is one of those incidental touches which indicate the influence of Peter on this second of the four accounts. Peter was John Mark's father in the faith (1 Peter 5:13). The two of them had spent years together in Jerusalem. There is a tradition going right back to sub-Apostolic days that this second Gospel was written by Mark as the *amanuensis* of Peter, or else as a translation and compilation of original memorabilia written by Peter in Aramaic.

"*And Peter.*" This final touch of Peter's hand in the story is rich with significance and appeal. To begin with, it holds a pledge of *restoring grace* to backsliders. Death almost invariably brings sorrow; but in some cases the sorrow is much keener than in others. Grief is always accentuated when the one whom death has taken from us was a leader of outstanding goodness; a friend or relative deeply beloved; or someone in whom high hopes were centred. Sometimes, too, the sorrow of bereavement becomes almost unbearably cutting when the one whom death has snatched away was cruelly offended by some mourner who is now cheated of any chance to make amends.

Poor Peter's grief was accentuated on all those four counts when our Lord expired on the Cross. But most of all would be his stinging torture and futile grief as memory kept dragging him back to his base and cowardly denial of Christ with oaths and curses.

Even when the resurrection morning brought its stunning gladness of glad surprise, Peter would find a gloomy cloud quenching the new sunrise. Even if Jesus *had* miraculously come back to life, could He ever again reckon such a cursing traitor as His disciple?

But now the women break on the disciples with the message from the angel in the tomb; and one of them, noticing Peter's strange look, excitedly exclaims that the angel had said, "Tell His disciples *and Peter* . . ." Oh, what those two little words must have meant to broken-spirited Peter! Tongue could never tell!

Yes, the fearful backslider was in the Saviour's first thoughts on that resurrection morning, and a special word was left for him with that angel-sentinel in the tomb. Even so does the risen Saviour think and feel toward all those other Peters, those backsliders whose love for Him has given way; those who have slipped back into worldliness; even those who have basely denied Him. Listen, backslidden Christian, He sends a special word to *you*, just now. He calls you back, and assures you of His restoring forgiveness. See His word again in 1 John 1:9. Kneel in prayer before Him. Dare to look into His face again. Read there again the love that is unchanged toward you. Then believe that according to his promise He receives you, and restores you, and recommissions you for service, even as He forgave and reinstated and re-empowered Peter.

Did you never hear *these* words before?—"I will heal their backsliding; I will love them freely" (Hos. 14:4). Yes, tell His disciples—"and *Peter*"!

A Meaningful Addendum

" . . . and Peter."—Mark 16: 7.

THIS significant little addendum, "*and Peter*", not only contains a pledge of restoring love to backsliders (as we commented yesterday), but also an assurance of *victorious love to the Church.* Not long before, remember, Jesus had asked His disciples, "Whom say ye that I am?" to which Peter had replied, "Thou art the Christ, the Son of the living God." Thereupon, our Lord had declared, "Thou art Peter (*Petros,* a stone or piece of rock); and upon this Rock (this *Petra,* this mighty Rock, i.e. Christ Himself) I will build my Church (*ecclesia*), and the gates of Hades shall not prevail against it."

Our Lord certainly did not say that He would found His Church on Peter (a mere *petros*) but upon Himself (the great *Petra*) the "Rock of Ages". Yet Peter, none the less, was at that time significantly representative of the Church. His natural forcefulness made him spokesman among the apostles.

The Church, historically, did not come into existence until after the descent of the Holy Spirit at Pentecost; but Peter and that little group of men were the advance nucleus of it. Redemptively and dispensationally they were now of strategic importance. They had in their mental possession the most stupendous of all secrets, the incarnation of the Godhead, and the soon-coming inception of the *Ecclesia,* or fellowship of called-out-ones. No sooner has our Lord mentioned the Church than He now speaks of His death (Matt. 16: 21). With the first mention of the *Church* comes the first mention of the *Cross.* Our Lord never died for the "kingdom"; nay, that is His by Davidic pedigree; but "Christ loved the *Church,* and gave Himself for *it*" (Eph. 5: 25).

Moreover, immediately after this, Peter and the other apostles are in Satan's sieve. Our Lord has to say even to Peter, "Get thee behind Me, Satan: thou art an offence unto Me; for thou savourest not the things that be of God, but those that be of men." And in Luke 22: 31, 32, He says, "Simon, Simon, behold Satan hath desired you (i.e. *all* of you) that he may sift you as wheat. But I have prayed for thee, that thy faith fail not." Oh, how Peter and the others were sifted in Satan's sieve! What a lot of chaff was found in them! When Peter denied Jesus with oaths, and the other apostles fled, it looked as though his faith and theirs *had* failed; but no; our Saviour's intercessions had already covered the crisis. Satan's sieve was allowed to get without a lot of chaff, but the real wheat was preserved. And now, on the resurrection morn, our Lord's first message is, "Tell my disciples *and Peter* . . ."! Satan's assault, except for our Lord's anticipative intercession, would have destroyed the Church before ever it was historically founded; but Apollyon's assault was defeated. Our Lord's, "Tell my disciples, *and Peter*", proclaims the indestructibility of the true Church. It is founded on Christ, the Son of the living God, the risen Christ, the ever-living Rock of Ages. Have no fear, dear Christian believer; you are in that true Church; and it is indestructibly founded on that eternal Rock. Have no fear, either, that the gates of Hades will ever imprison you. Jesus now has "the keys of Hades" (Rev. 1: 18); and so far as *you* are concerned, to be "absent from the body" is to be "present with the Lord" (2 Cor. 5: 8).

"Christ died for us."—Rom. 5: 8.

HERE is a simple sentence of four words. The first two words state an historical act: "*Christ died.*" The second two add the theological significance: "*for us.*" The full four form the crux of the Gospel: "*Christ died for us.*" Never did four short words hold bigger or better message.

Isaac Watts, in his immortal hymn, "When I survey the wondrous Cross", could not have chosen a truer adjective than "wondrous". From every aspect our Lord's death on Calvary is "wondrous". Most of all is it so, in its intermingling of tragedy and sublimity, ugliness and loveliness. Think back, just now, to the *historical act*: "Christ died."

Think again of the *fact* that He died. That in itself is a strange marvel. Remember, He was God the Son. He had to become human in order to be even capable of death (Heb. 2: 9, 14). It is a mysterious wonder that God the Son *could* die; still more that He *should* die; still more that He *would* die; and most of all that He *did* die.

Think again of the *place* where He died. We ourselves all hope to die in our own homes surrounded by our loved ones; but our Lord was led out to Calvary, the very atmosphere of which was permeated with a gruesome eeriness. Many a crime-stained felon had been torturously done to death there, with foul language and wild shrieks and blasphemous oaths pouring from his lips. "And sitting down they watched Him *there*" (Matt. 27: 36). Think of it: "*HIM . . . there*"!

Think again of the *death* that He died. He was crucified—the most lingering and torturously excruciating of all legally inflicted killings; and not only so, but the most shameful, exposed, humiliating, infamous and accursed of all executions. It was the lowest, hardest, and most degrading of all deaths. "There they *crucified* Him" (Luke 23: 33).

Think again, now, with *whom* He died. It was not with a group of noble martyrs, giving themselves for a lofty cause, and bravely sealing their godly testimony with undishonoured blood. No, it was between two ruffians, two gangsters, two foul-mouthed murderers, who reviled Him. There He was, propped up between the two, as though worse than either! —suspended between earth and heaven, as though fit for neither!

Think again of the *way* he died. Although He had been treacherously betrayed, unjustly condemned, brutally bullied, whipped, mocked, and nailed there in agony, without one single crime that could be laid against Him, His first cry was, "Father, forgive them; for they know not what they do"! Even the sarcastic, gloating Pharisees confessed, when once they had Him nailed up there, "He saved others . . ." (Mark 15: 31). To eyes that can really see things, His birth at Bethlehem was all the lovelier because it was in the rough stable; and his loveliness in death was all the sublimer because of the very ugliness which surrounded it on Calvary.

Yes, think of it all again: "Christ died." It really happened, on that stark hillock outside old Jerusalem: the most startling event of all the ages, the most incomprehensible mystery of the Godhead. He who built the pillars of the universe hung there, a disfigured corpse, on that wooden beam and transom! Must we not "pour contempt on all our pride"?

"The Wondrous Cross"

"Christ died for us."—Rom. 5: 8.

WELL may we marvel at the *historical fact* recorded in the two words, "Christ died"; yet even more to be wondered at is the resultant *theological truth* in those other two little words, "for us". Here is the Gospel message in focus-point: "Christ died *for us*."

The first meaning of the Greek preposition here translated as "for" is, *for the sake of*. Christ died for our *sake*. He died *because* of us. He was not just a martyr, sealing his testimony with his own blood. Nor was He just a leader, setting an heroic example to his followers. He died for *our* sake, just as directly as a certain mother in a famine-stricken city suffered starvation for the sake of her infant son to whom she gave up her own scanty rations. He died for *our* sake, just as truly as a father has sometimes suffered for the sake of his son, to provide him with a better chance in life. Yes, just as directly, Jesus died *for us*, because He loved us—loved us in a far higher and sublimer sense than any earthly mother or father ever loved.

But this Greek word translated as "for" also means *in behalf of*. Our Lord's death was vicarious. He not only died for our sake; He did something on our *behalf* which we could never have done for ourselves. He made an appeasing offering to the infinitely good and holy Creator, against whom the sin of mankind is a measureless outrage. As our sinless, self-sacrificing Representative, He propitiated the offended divine righteousness; thus magnifying the divine law, and honouring it on our behalf (Isa. 42: 21).

Still further, this Greek particle translated as "for" means *instead of*. Yes, the incarnate Son of God was there in my place. He was not only my Representative who died on my behalf; He was my *Substitute* who died in my very *stead*. The stripes which should have fallen on me fell on Him. All the punishment due to me, *He* bore in my place. So fully did He become my Substitute that He somehow bore both my punishment and my *guilt*; for "He was numbered with the transgressors" (Isa. 53: 12), and "God reckoned Him to be sin who knew no sin . . ." (2 Cor. 5: 21). Oh, the wonder of it—"Christ died *for us*"; for our *sake*; and in our *behalf*; and even in our very *place*!

Look again now at that word, "died". It is not merely that Christ was *put to death* for us. He "*died*", that is, He voluntarily and deliberately yielded Himself up to it for us. His death was not merely an execution inflicted upon Him, or a savage injustice which just happened; it was an eternally significant ordeal which He himself purposefully underwent with a view to our redemption. Humans and demons were permitted to combine in the perpetration of the nefarious crime, but the omniscient Triunity foreknew it, and anticipated it, and overruled it, so that Sin's foulest revolt became Love's sublimest victory. Yes, He "*died*". What it cost Him we can never know, except in distant dimness; but the enormity of anguish involved in bearing the damning weight of human sin, from the beginning to the end of time, He knowingly determined to bear. Such was His love for us. Oh, how *we* should love *Him*!

"Father, forgive them; for they know not what they do."—Luke 23:34.

THE spectacle of that awful Cross on which the very Son of God was publicly humiliated is so subduing that any merely sermonic analysing of His seven utterances while hanging there seems almost an irreverence. Yet the crucifixion narratives evidently intend us to devote our earnest attention to them; and the more sympathetically we do so, the more affecting and revealing they become. Those seven sayings are like seven windows into our Saviour's mind as He hung there, "despised and rejected of men".

First of the seven was, "Father, forgive them; for they know not what they do". Even the hardened soldiers must have been taken aback. Before all else, it was the expression of quenchless *love*. Presumably, our Lord would be nailed to His Cross while it was still lying on the ground. Then strong hands would upraise the impaled Victim and lunge the perpendicular stake into a deep hole already prepared. As the Prisoner was hoisted upright, the whole weight of His body became suspended entirely by the nails; and that first, excruciating jolt into the ground would send shuddering spasms of pain through His frame, turning every nerve into a strand of fire, and every vein into a river of anguish. What shrieks of frantic blasphemy and impotent rage those soldiers had often heard from crucified criminals in that moment of convulsive torture! But now, for the first time, they hear, "Father, forgive them . . ."! Our Lord's whole life had expressed divine love; but this crowned it with sublimest splendour. They had taken away everything He had; yet even crucifixion torture could not take away His *love*. This was the love which fiercest flames could not quench, and many waters could not drown.

"Father, forgive them . . ." Oh, the *selflessness* of it! Acute suffering often contracts the mind, so that the sufferer can think only of himself; but the sublime "otherism" of Jesus came out even more in His crucifixion than ever before.

"Father, forgive them." Oh, how *characteristic*! He seized on the one thing which could lessen their guilt—"they know not what they do". Even that was only a *negative*; yet He turned it into an intercession.

"Father, forgive them . . ." How full of *concern* His plea was! He Himself needed no forgiveness; but *they* did. They were hurting themselves far more than their Victim. More than ever, now, they would *need* forgiveness; and He knew that through His atoning suffering they could *have* forgiveness. Oh, that you and I may know that dearly bought forgiveness! Oh, that you and I may show the same forgiving love!

Seven times He calls, suspended there,
  As sinning mortals do their worst;
Seven calls of gracious love and care,
  "Father, forgive them," is the first.
The very Cross where thus He pleads
  Becomes the answer to His call;
For as He there redeeming bleeds,
  He makes forgiveness free to all!

A Plea of Ignorance

"Father, forgive them, for they know not what they do."—Luke 23: 34.

THESE words are startling as they relate to *Israel.* Our Lord pleaded ignorance for them. Somehow, as we read the accounts, we cannot shake off the feeling that many of Israel's prejudiced leaders *did* know what they were doing. Their hypocrisy betrayed itself when once they had Him on that Cross (Matt. 27: 40, 42, 63, etc). Doubtless, though, *some* among the intelligentsia could honestly say, as Paul did, years later, "I did it ignorantly, in unbelief" (1 Tim. 1: 13). As for the mob, incited by the slandering priests, it certainly was true, "they know not what they do".

Our Lord's plea, "They know not what they do", immediately became a momentous factor in the divine dealing with Israel. Could it be said with any measure of truth that Israel perpetrated the Calvary outrage in ignorance, then retribution must be stayed. God will not inflict judgment until guilt is clearly and fully proved. But for that intercessory plea of ignorance, the judgment of God must have broken loose at once upon Israel; for leaders and people alike had shouted with gloating bravado, "His blood be on us, and on our children!" (Matt. 27: 25). When Israel's pinioned Messiah prayed, "Father, forgive them, for they know not what they do", the hand of judgment was stayed. The nation must be given a *further* opportunity to accept Jesus as Messiah King—a renewed opportunity of such a character that any further refusal on the ground of ignorance will be out of the question! As a matter of historical fact, that further opportunity was given during the suspense-period covered by the Acts; given with the added message of individual salvation through the crucified, risen, ascended Lord Jesus, and attested by the unmistakable miracle-signs of Pentecost. The apostolic message is focalised in Acts 3: 19, 20, "Repent ye therefore and be converted, that your sins may be blotted out, so that there may come the times of refreshing [i.e. the promised reign of blessing under the Messiah] from the presence of the Lord; and that He may send back to you Jesus Christ who before was preached unto you."

Alas, Israel again said, "We will not have this man to reign over us" (Luke 19: 14), sealing the further refusal in the martyrdom of Stephen and the attempted lynching of Paul. In A.D. 70 judgment fell. After a bitter siege, Jerusalem capitulated to the Roman general Titus, and amid such tribulation as exceeded all before it, the Jews in their thousands were butchered or scattered. Their fateful cry, "His blood be on us and on our children", has haunted them down the centuries. But the time is nigh when "they shall look on Him whom they pierced, and shall mourn for Him . . ." (Zech. 12: 10). Then shall the Calvary prayer, "Father, forgive them", have full and glorious answer.

After an historical hiatus of 2,000 years, without king or country or city, and in which they have been peeled and persecuted as no other people in history, the Jews are back in Palestine as a self-governing State, with their own parliament, currency, language and institutions! It is without parallel in world history. It is the prelude to a consummation of predicted splendour. It is a sign that soon, now, Messiah Jesus shall reign in the very city where He was crucified!

"Father, forgive them, for they know not what they do."—Luke 23: 34.

LINGER over these words again, and reflect how tenderly challenging they are to each of us *individually* as Christian believers. Do we call ourselves disciples of Jesus? Then do we have the same kind of forgiving love? Being able to pass a test in theology, or being wonderfully sound in doctrine, or being able to "speak in tongues", or being able to work miracles of healing, is a poor compensation for lack of this forgiving love. Let us test ourselves. Do we have the forgiving love which Jesus showed?

These words of Jesus on the Cross are echoed by Peter in Acts 3: 17, "And now, brethren, I know that through *ignorance* ye did it . . ." There is a further echo by Stephen in Acts 7: 60, "Lord, lay not this sin to their charge." Even so, there ought to be a gracious echo of it in every Christian heart: "Father, forgive them . . ." Oh, how unlike Jesus many of us are! How unforgiving! How resentful! How hard! How retaliative! How self-justifying! How big we seem in our self-imagined right to hold a grudge! How petty, how ugly, how pigmy-little we *really* are, in our unforgiving snobbery! Lord, melt our icy hearts by Thine own example! Shame us by Thy Calvary prayer. If we cannot cure our own wretched unlikeness to Thee, may we surrender ourselves to the inflow of Thine own love, so that pride and hate may be completely expelled.

"Father, forgive them," help me pray it,
Tho' they hate without a cause;
"Father, forgive them," help me say it,
Tho' they tear with fang and claws.
"Father, forgive them," Jesus save them,
For they "know not what they do".
Help them learn through *my* forgiveness
Of Thine *own* forgiveness too.

"Father, forgive them, for they *know not* what they do." So even sins of ignorance need forgiveness! How much more then do we need forgiveness for all our wilful, *knowing* sins! It is almost unbearable to think of all those sinnings in which we have indulged knowing all the time how wrong they were, yet pretending otherwise! What forgiveness *we* need!

"Father, forgive *them* . . ." Mark this well: if He prayed for "them"—His murderers on Calvary—then He will not turn a deaf ear to you and me, if we *ask* for His forgiveness!

"Father, *forgive* them." Oh, the forgiveness of sin must be a big, big thing, if it took that Cross to effect it! But, thank God, *no* sin is too big to be forgiven *there*!

NOTE: IF EASTER SUNDAY OCCURS EARLIER THAN APRIL 22nd, USE THE EASTER WEEK READINGS FROM PAGE 97 TO PAGE 102, AFTER WHICH RESUME THE DAILY READINGS AT THE APPROPRIATE DATE.

The Monster Exposed

"Away with Him!"—Jn. 19: 15.
"One died for all."—2 Cor. 5: 14.

THE first of these texts photographs the Cross on the manward side: "Away with Him!" The other interprets it from the God-ward side: "One died for all." Of two things supremely the Cross is a revelation. It is a revelation of human *sin*. It is a revelation of divine *love*.

Ponder the first of these. The Cross is *an exposure of human sin*. On that mound outside old Jerusalem the real ugliness of sin was once for all unmasked. There is an eastern story floats down from those times, about a false prophet who by big pretensions and swelling words deceived many hundreds into allegiance. He always wore a veil, on the pretext that he was too sacred to be looked upon without it. One day, however, a suspicious member of his guard suddenly ripped the veil away, exposing a sinister, repulsive face. So does the Cross tear away the deceptive veil from sin, uncovering its stark hideousness.

Think of it: Jesus was the purest, holiest, manliest, gentlest human being who ever lived. He was the most guileless, gracious, virtuous, inoffensive, generous-hearted Man who ever breathed. He was the meekest, lowliest, truest, wisest Teacher, Healer, Exemplar, who ever offered His friendship. He was the most sympathetic, self-sacrificing philanthropist who ever wept over human woes. In Him the sublime *ideal* became incarnated into the visible *actual*. That highest good after which the world professes to seek, was *here*, manifest and unmistakable! Yet how did men treat Him? They were jealous. They hated Him. They stripped Him. They mocked and murdered Him! They could find no fault; but they could not endure Him because by very contrast His utter genuineness exposed their own hypocrisy. "Away with Him!"

Think of this, also, that the representative men who perpetrated the monstrous deed were the highly pious, the fanatically "godly"! They did it in the name of religion, and gloated over it! Think of the three representative nations involved. The indictment was written over His cross "in Hebrew and Greek and Latin". The Hebrews, despite their boast of God-given religion, intensely *hated* Him. The Greeks, despite their boast of philosophy, blindly *laughed* at Him. The Romans, despite their boast of iron justice, publicly *executed* Him without fair trial.

In all this, see the veil ripped away. See the human heart laid bare. See the real ugliness of sin exposed. The silken-skinned, gorgeous-coloured creature is a savage tiger. The "serpent" which beguiled Eve was not the writhing reptile of today. In its Edenic form, it was probably the most beautiful of all the creatures. That was why Satan entered and used it. Eve's surprise that it now spoke with a human voice only increased her admiration of it. But the murderous sin inside that elegant form was that same evil thing which nailed Jesus to the Cross. Oh, let me see and learn! Let me watch and pray against this monster, however attractive it may seem, whether in the world outside or in my own heart. Let me ever remember that though sin should assume the innocence of a cherub, it is still the ugly horror which spiked the guileless Jesus to that awful Cross.

"Away with Him!"—Jn. 19:15.
"One died for all."—2 Cor. 5:14.

Ah, but we would never crucify Jesus today! Oh, then why does the world in general, despite its twentieth-century civilization, philosophy, science and enlightenment, push Him out of its commerce, society, pleasures, politics, and even its religions? Sin in human nature is still the same. It still cries, "Away with Him!" And the Cross *still* exposes sin in its real, devilish ugliness. When I see sin gloating in that dastardly deed, driving the nails through those healing hands, mocking the one perfectly lovely character, and pinioning the very Son of God to that shocking Cross, then I see sin as it *really* is. Let me recognise it, hate it, loathe it, and seek cleansing from it!

Thank God, there *is* cleansing from it; the very Cross which exposes the sin of man supremely reveals the saving love of God. Yes, let us see in that Cross again *the supreme expression of divine love*: "One died for all." To say that He was "crucified" is only one side of the truth. The other side is that He voluntarily "died". Not all the combined strength of humans and demons could have held Him on that Cross if He had willed otherwise. Never were wicked men more fantastically self-deluded than when those top politico-religious cliques congratulated each other on having tricked Him into their clutches. Their power was simply the slackened leash of divine permission. They were unknowingly illustrating our Lord's words to Pilate, "Thou couldest have no power against Me, except it were given thee from above."

No, in the deeper sense, it was not iron spikes, but *love* which held Jesus to the Cross. "One died for all." Oh, the wonderful love of God in Christ! Again and again the New Testament expounds it, yet nowhere defines it. It defies definition. You must *see* it to know it; and you only really see it in that mysterious Cross. Even John can only say, "*Herein* is love. . . . He sent His Son to be the propitiation for our sins" (1 Jn. 4:10).

"One died for all"; then He died for *me*! The sin-penalty of all and each was omnisciently gathered up in that Cross, from the first sin away, back in Eden, to the anticipated multi-million aggregate in the yet future day of general judgment. *My* sin, in all its immensity, was anticipated in that Cross. In His infinite capacity to suffer, the Son of God exhausted all of *my* sin-penalty. And when I realise that *my* sins somehow helped to nail Him there, and that *my* sins somehow added conscious weight to His expiatory suffering, I am melted and broken. He loved *me*! He died for *me*! It is said that however far inland you may be, if you hold a sea-shell to your ear, you can hear the sound of the far-away ocean. So in the Cross, we may hear the mighty deeps of a divine love which is far bigger than man's biggest sin.

God's thoughts are love, and Jesus is
The loving voice they find;
His life lights up the vast abyss
Of the Eternal Mind.

This is the love "uncomprehended and unbought, beyond all knowledge and all thought"—a mystery to the intellect, but heaven to the heart.

The Sixth Cry from Calvary

"It is finished."—Jn. 19: 30.

It is a paradoxical singularity of our Lord Jesus that He was *born to die*. All others were born to live; but the sinless Jesus, the solitary One on whom disease had no hold and death had no claim, was born in order to be capable of dying. His death on Calvary was the supreme purpose of His birth at Bethlehem. It is affirmed that Jesus came to restore the lost knowledge of the true God; to give new revelation of the divine nature; to erect new ethical standards; to incarnate new and loftier ideals; to become the race's supreme moral Exemplar. All these are true, but they are not the supreme thing: they are the lesser lights of the firmament. The central sun is that Cross outside the walls of old Jerusalem "where the dear Lord was crucified who died to save us all".

Undoubtedly, our Lord had more than one reference in mind when He cried, "It is finished." First of all, as we can sympathetically appreciate, He referred to His own *unfathomable sufferings*. What sufferings they were! None ever suffered as He, for no other had such exquisite sensativeness or profound capacity for suffering. Think on the sufferings of His *body*. In dark Gethsemane great drops of blood-red sweat ooze through His pores. Then, with the betrayer's kiss upon Him, He is hurried through the night to the palace of Caiaphas, the high priest, to undergo the false trial, the spitting, the cuffing, the smiting. In the grey dawn, tired, bruised, empty, bound with cords, He is pushed before Pilate, then hurried before Herod who allows the men at arms to mock Him; then He is back again before Pilate, for the scourging, the stripping, the scarlet robe, the cutting thorn-crown, the reed-sceptre, the buffeting. Then comes the shouldering of the cross; the weary drag to Calvary; the iron spikes driven through the quivering flesh, the propping up, nail-suspended and bleeding, in utter torture. Oh, see Him there, hung up between heaven and earth as though fit for neither; pinioned naked beneath the pelting rays of the sun; every movement a pang, every vein a channel of suffering.

But the soul of His sufferings was the suffering of His *soul*. How awful must have been that inward agony which made Him sweat blood, so that He needed an angel to strengthen Him! How fearful must have been the pressure of that stupendous weight, "the sin of the world", which He was now allowed consciously to bear! How deep must have been the darkness of that loneliness into which He now passed as the race's Sin-bearer! Who shall ever sound the depths of that utter woe when, out of that mid-day darkness on Golgotha, the Sufferer cried, "My God, my God, why hast *Thou* forsaken Me?" Many a martyr has died amid the flames, exulting in imparted grace which lifted him above all his sufferings; but Christ became even *God*-forsaken as he bore our sin on the Cross! Oh, the love which would suffer so, for our sakes! Can we ever thank Him, praise Him, or love Him half enough?

Think of it all again—those hands which had mixed the eye-salve and given blind ones sight, now nailed to that cross; those feet which had hasted on errands of healing mercy, spiked through with that cruel iron; those lips which had poured forth such gracious wisdom, closed in death; that heart through which the very love of God beat toward poor human sinners, thrust through with a spear!

"It is finished."—Jn. 19: 30.

We cannot doubt that when our Lord thus cried, He referred to His vicarious *achievement of redemption.* The redemptive stupendousness of that Cross is beyond all measure. Many supernatural abnormalities are reported in the Bible, but the Cross utterly outclasses them all. We think of spectacular miracles such as the dividing of the Red Sea for the transit of two million Israelites, the sudden gushing of streams out of the flinty rock, the walking of the three Hebrews unharmed amid the "burning fiery furnace"; and we include all such under the category of "miracle". But the Cross is in the realm of *super*-miracle. Marvel of marvels that the eternal God *could* die! Still more that He *would* die! And most of all that he actually *did* die, as our vicarious Sinbearer on Calvary! He had to be born into our humanity to be even capable of dying. Having become Man, He had no *need* to die, for He had a deathless humanhood. When human martyrs have laid down their lives, they have merely antedated their death by a few years; for if they had not been martyred, death would have cut them off later. But when our Lord died on Calvary, He yielded up a life with *eternal* value in it.

What is more, on that Cross, He bore not only our punishment, but our *guilt.* There is a big difference between bearing the penalty of sin, and bearing its guilt. Suppose the law of our land allowed some good man to take the place of a man condemned for murder. Imagine yourself visiting the substitute in the prison cell, and saying to him, "I am so sorry you are convicted of murder." What would he reply? Why, he would exclaim, "Oh no; *I* am not the murderer; I am bearing his *penalty,* but I cannot bear his *guilt*!" On the Cross, however, the Lord Jesus somehow bore our very *guilt.* That is why the Father must needs turn away from Him, and leave the Son to exclaim, "My God, my God, why hast Thou *forsaken* Me?"

Thank God, if as our Saviour said, "It is finished", then there is *nothing more to add.* His Calvary work for our salvation was all-sufficient and final. The Roman church's doctrine that we can add merit of our own to the Calvary work of Christ, is a flagrant denial of plain Scripture teaching, and an insult to the Saviour who cried, "It is *finished.*" Somebody once asked a Christian believer, "How is it that *you* seem to have such peace, while I, although I go to church, do *not* have peace?" The Christian replied, "I think it is because yours is a religion of '*do*', mine is a religion of 'done'—done once for all in my place by Jesus on Calvary." Real peace with God comes when we really believe on Christ in the sense of accepting His finished work of atonement for us; when we can truly say, "I have flung away every other confidence; I am trusting Jesus only, Jesus wholly, now and forever."

Upon a life I did not live,
Upon a death I did not die;
Upon *His* life,
Upon *His* death,
I stake my whole eternity.

The Focus of Prophecy

"It is finished."—Jn. 19: 30.

JESUS was the only One who in the strict sense could say, "It is finished." Incompleteness, fragmentariness mar the works of all others. The pen falls from the author's hand; the brush, the chisel, slips from the artist's grasp. How many have died sighing, "Oh, that I might have completed!" Our Lord's parting cry was, "It is finished!" It was a mark of His super-humanity.

Our Lord's death on the Cross was a *real* death, but it was no mere accidental catastrophe. It was a fulfilment of prophecy. See the verse but one preceding our text: "After this, Jesus knowing that all things were now accomplished, *that the Scripture might be fulfilled*, saith, I thirst." As He hung there, His omniscient mind surveyed all the Old Testament prophecies on His death, and He knew that all were now fulfilled, save the remark about His thirsting, in Psalm 22: 15. Therefore He now said, "I thirst." After *that* He cried, "It is finished", then bowed His head, and dismissed His spirit.

So, when our Lord cried, "It is finished", He evidently alluded to that long line of *prophecies on Messiah's death.* All the Old Testament prophets are finger-posts pointing to the Messiah-Redeemer. Whether it be Moses the lawgiver-prophet, or David the psalmist-prophet, or Isaiah the excelsior writing-prophet, or Jeremiah the broken-hearted prophet, or Ezekiel the visions-prophet, or any of the other prophets, all point to *HIM.* Indeed, so many and varied are the predictions all converging on the Messiah, and so exactly are they fulfilled in Jesus, that if He be not the Messiah, then Old Testament prophecy is an inexplicable medley of non-fulfilment. Apart from the Christ of Calvary, the Old Testament is a book of unexplained ceremonies, unachieved purposes, unappeased longings, and unfulfilled prophecies: it becomes revelation without *destination.*

Remember, the coming One must be a second Adam, a prophet like Moses, a priest like Aaron and Melchizedek, a champion like Joshua, an offering like Isaac, a king like David, a wise counsellor like Solomon, a beloved, rejected, exalted son and world's bread-supplier like Joseph, and other typical personages, all in one! He must be the ark of the covenant, the sacrifice on the brazen altar, the mercy seat in the sanctuary, the water from the rock, the manna from the sky, the brazen serpent lifted up, the passover lamb, the scapegoat, the lion of Judah, the good shepherd, the lily of the valley, the "root out of a dry ground" yet the "fruitful branch"; "without form or comeliness", yet the "altogether lovely", not to mention other type-aspects! The endless marvel is that all are perfectly fulfilled in Jesus. Take away Jesus, and Messianic prophecy becomes flat, dead, a road leading nowhere. See *Him* as the glorious *Antitype,* and it all becomes luminously alive (Luke 24: 27). Oh, what a mighty fulfilment is the Christ of Calvary! All the enigmas of prophecy are resolved at the Cross. The hieroglyphics of the types are all deciphered at the Cross. The serpent's head is crushed at the Cross. The door of heaven is opened at the Cross. The fountain of salvation is unsealed at the Cross. Yes, Calvary is the tragic, triumphant, tremendous focus-point of fulfilment. "It is *finished*"!

"It is finished."—Jn. 19: 30.

LOOK again at this sixth word from the Cross. Surely when our Lord exclaimed, "It is finished", He meant that He had now finished *the work which the Father had given Him to do*. The cry, "It is finished", was the rejoicing, even amid anguish, of the perfect Servant. Glance back to His earlier public ministry. In John 4: 34, He says, "My meat is to do the will of Him that sent Me." That was His master-passion. Later on, in chapter 12: 27, 28, as He contemplates His crucifixion, He says, "Now is My soul troubled; and what shall I say? . . . Father glorify Thy Name." It is said that the ruling passion is strongest in death. So it was with our dear Lord. On His way to Gethsemane and Calvary we find Him saying in prayer to the Father, "I have glorified Thee on the earth. I have *finished the work* which Thou gavest Me to do" (17: 4).

Once more, our Lord's cry, "It is finished", was the shout of a Conqueror exulting in His costly but victorious *conquest over the powers of darkness*. The late Dr. A. C. Dixon tells how one day when he was in his garden, he heard the yelping of hunting hounds near by, and went to look over the hedge to see what might be happening. Rushing wildly toward him was a beautiful young fawn, with panting sides, and terror in its eyes, as the hounds raced after it. For a split second it hesitated, gave one despairing look to the right and to the left, then, taking its one and only chance, it leapt into the preacher's arms. All in a flash, he saw hunting in a new light, and grabbed a knobbed stick to defend the poor creature. On came the dogs, and for nearly twenty minutes Dr. Dixon fought them off, until the last one skulked away whining from his blows. Afterwards the fawn would never leave him. It became the best-loved pet of the household. Even so, in His Gethsemane wrestle and Calvary death, the Lord Jesus as our Champion fought off the hounds of hell which were bent on our eternal ruin. And now, "Who is he that condemneth? Christ died; yea rather is risen again" (Rom. 8: 34, and see Col. 2: 14).

Finished! hear the cry victorious!
  Love's redeeming deed is done!
Now the Cross becomes all-glorious;
  Now is wondrous triumph won!
Heaven's atonement is completed
  In redemption's mighty plan!
Powers of darkness flee defeated!
  Now salvation comes to man!

NOTE: IF EASTER SUNDAY OCCURS EARLIER THAN APRIL 22nd., USE THE EASTER WEEK READINGS FROM PAGE 97 TO PAGE 102, AFTER WHICH RESUME THE DAILY READINGS AT THE APPROPRIATE DATE.

The Venom of the Viper

"He saved others; Himself He cannot save."—Mark 15: 31.

THIS taunt came from *a surprising quarter*: not from the soldiers, not from the crucified robbers, not from the common bystanders, but from the chief priests and scribes—the religious leaders and doctors of divinity. However raw their jealousy of the pure-souled Nazarene, they ought at least to have been subdued now that He was hanging unretaliative on that torturing cross. He had committed no crime. His character was unimpeached. The very fact that He was willing to die in such agony for His claim to be their Messiah should have sobered them! Even their knowledge that the people looked up to them as religious examples should have begotten restraint in them. But no; not only did they fling away all reserve and dignity, they led the chorus of ribald mockery. "He saved others; Himself He could not save!" Let us learn: sarcastic ridicule and vitriolic resistance often come from those who should be the readiest supporters of true Christianity. Turn through the pages of your Church History; again and again organized Christianity (so called), especially the Roman Catholic Church (so called), has been, through its dignitaries, the bitterest persecutor and assassin of our Lord's noblest representatives on earth!—and this is still true in many connections today.

Furthermore, this taunt, "He saved others; Himself He cannot save", expressed *intensest hatred*. Had it been the disciples who were the speakers, it would have vented their bewildering disappointment and broken-hearted sympathy; but from those Satan-perverted priests and scribes the words were flung at the pinioned Sufferer as a raucous jibe of gloating malice. It is strange, but there is no hatred like religious hatred. It is awful to have to say it, but there are those who in the name of religion can laugh fiendishly over the fall and shame of others. Oh, let us beware of any such hatred in ourselves toward those who are holier than we are, or who have gifts which we do not possess, or whose views differ from ours in religious matters. However much we may hate heresies, let us love the heretics! *God* loves them! Christ *died* for them! And when we ourselves are persecuted for righteousness' sake, let us pray for grace always to be able to say, with that pain-racked, humiliated, sublime Sufferer on the Cross, "Father, forgive them . . ."

Once again, that mocking taunt, "He saved others; Himself He cannot save", *unmasked despicable hypocrisy*. Those priests and scribes had charged that our Lord's miracles were fakes, that He had a demon, and that His supernatural cures were activities of Beelzebub (Jn. 8: 48; Matt. 12: 24). Yet as soon as they had Him fastened up there in ignominious execution, they confessed what they had known deep down in their hearts all the time—"He saved others." Let us pray that *we* may never give way to such hypocrisy. Most of us need to guard against it, for we are human. I have known otherwise venerable lives disfigured by this hypocritical jealousy of prestige and position. It can exist among workers in a small mission as well as among dignitaries in a cathedral. God save us from it, for it is the venom of the viper!

"He saved others; Himself He cannot save."—Mark 15:31.

WHEN those gloating chief priests and scribes thus jeered, they were unwittingly uttering a profound *truth.* I wonder if we ourselves have grasped it.

Here is *the master principle of redemption*: "He saved others; Himself He cannot save." In the very nature of things, if He would save others, He dare not save Himself. If He had saved Himself (as He easily could have done) He could not have saved others. The self-blinded priests and scribes mistakenly supposed that His apparent inability to save *Himself* proved that He could not be a Saviour of *others*, whereas the very opposite was the case: His becoming the Saviour of others depended on His not saving Himself.

That, indeed, is *the binding law of all true service.* As our Lord Jesus says elsewhere: "Whosoever will save his life shall lose it, and whosoever will lose his life for My sake shall find it" (Matt. 16:25). That which counts is always that which costs. We must bleed if we would bless. We must lose ourselves if we would save others. Jesus did; and so must we, in our lesser way. What we selfishly retain we lose. What we sacrificially give up we gain. We conquer by yielding. We get by giving. We win by losing. We live by dying. We save others only when self-absorption gives place to compassionate otherism. A contemporary novel describes a certain female thus: "Edith was a little country bounded on the north, south, east, and west by Edith." To this we may add, "And, behold, the country of Edith was desert." See our Lord, again, on that Cross; then recall His words, "Except a seed of wheat fall into the ground, and *die*, it abideth alone; but if it die, it bringeth forth much fruit." If our Lord had saved Himself, He could not have saved *us*. To save us, Himself He could not save. How like or unlike Him are you and I, who call ourselves His followers? All around us are Christless souls. What are we doing to win them? Is it inconvenient? Does it bring rebuff? Does it hurt? Does it cost? Is it tiring? Well, listen again to those priests and scribes: "He saved others; *Himself He cannot save*"!

And now, finally, in that spiteful sneer—so strangely wicked yet so strangely true—see *the supreme meaning of our Lord's life and death.* It was His crucifiers themselves who confessed it—"He saved others", or, to translate it more exactly, "He *has* saved others". Yes, He *has*, in their millions. It was in order to save that He lived and died and rose again. Had Israel's priests and scribes only realised it, even as they were sarcastically admitting that He had saved others, His very dying was to save *them*! But, alas, those hard-hearted leaders, by their own use of that word, "others", placed themselves outside His saving reach. What they were really saying was, "He saved *others*, but He has not saved *us*". By that word, "others", they excluded themselves. And it is still true that the only ones excluded are the *self*-excluded. "He saved others." He *still* saves others. If He has saved you and me, let us be out to tell them!

Is it costly? Is it hurtful? Easier far be dumb than brave?
Then remember, "*He* saved others, But Himself He would not save."

"Christ Died for our Sins"

"I delivered unto you first of all . . . how that Christ died for our sins according to the Scriptures; and that He was buried, and that He rose again the third day, according to the Scriptures."—1 Cor. 15: 3, 4.

We have here three categorical affirmations: (1) "Christ died"; (2) "He was buried"; (3) "He rose". These were the first three planks in the apostle's platform, for he says, "I delivered unto you *first of all* . . . that Christ died . . . that He was buried . . . and that He rose again the third day." These three are a trinity of truths absolutely basal and vital to the Gospel which we preach. They are a trinity in unity. They belong together as the three component parts of the one supreme event, the profoundest event of all time.

All three are true. All three have been assailed by critics ancient and modern. Some have said He never really died, He only swooned. Some have said the body was stolen from the burial. Some have said He never bodily rose again. But all three have been repeatedly proved genuine against successive forms of attack. They have weathered the fiercest blasts of nineteenth- and twentieth-century religious scepticism; and they *are true today*. Amid the swirling currents of changeful human speculation, this rock of redemptive truth remains immovably secure. The Christian believer is no mere mystic visionary fondly doting on castles in the air. We ground our faith on the solid bedrock of authenticated fact: "Christ died . . . He was buried . . . He rose again the third day."

Just here, we concentrate on the first of the three: "Christ died for our sins according to the Scriptures." This breaks into three obvious parts. First there is the *statement* of the fact: "Christ died." Second there is the *meaning* of the fact: "For our sins." Third, there is the *background* of the fact: "According to the Scriptures." The first ("Christ died") is an event of *history*. The second ("For our sins") is its issue in *doctrine*. The third ("According to the Scriptures") is the attestation of *prophecy*. Or, to put it in different words, first we have an *avouchment* ("Christ died"), which implies an *atonement* ("For our sins"), which is a foreseen *fulfilment* ("According to the Scriptures").

This trinity of truth is the very centre-point of the Gospel, i.e. a *crucifixion* ("Christ died") which is a *substitution* ("For our sins") by divine *revelation* ("According to the Scriptures").

"Christ died for our sins": Paul *started* his Gospel where many modern preachers seem to *end* theirs. Those who espouse the ideas of the so-called "liberal" theology, or the Neo-orthodoxy, start with the human birth and boyhood of Jesus (viewed as merely natural rather than supernatural), and make much of the exemplary human character. In *their* preaching, Jesus is the great Teacher, the high Exemplar, the religious Pathfinder. They make much of His manhood but little of His saviourhood. The Cross seems to be viewed as a pathetic end, whereas with Paul it was the vital beginning—"I delivered unto you *first of all* . . . how that Christ died for our sins." That indeed *is* the beginning of the Gospel. What we sinners need is not merely a pattern, but a *pardon*; not merely a Pathfinder, but a *Sinbearer*; not merely instruction, *but salvation*!

Though boundless, timeless, in its reach, is this dear Gospel which we preach; its *heart* is in His wounded side who on the Cross for sinners died.

"I delivered unto you first of all . . . how that Christ died for our sins according to the Scriptures; and that He was buried, and that He rose again the third day, according to the Scriptures."—1 Cor. 15: 3, 4.

OBSERVE the background of prophecy here: "according to the Scriptures". We ought to realise how pertinent this is to us today. One of the things which urgently needs reasserting among our Protestant churches is the divine inspiration of the Old Testament; for the redeeming revelation which we have in the *New* Testament has its life-giving roots in the inspiration of the *Old* Testament.

Reflect how true this is. The statement here that "Christ died" needs no special *revelation* from God to prove it. It is a statement of fact so well accredited that we can verify it for ourselves, each of us, if we are so minded, without any need for a direct unveiling of it from heaven. But the further truth, that "Christ died *for our sins*" is something which we could never know apart from divine revelation. It is a reality in the realm of the metaphysical which only God Himself could reveal.

How then do we know that when Paul says, "Christ died *for our sins*", he is uttering divine revelation, and not just human opinion? It is because it was "*according to the Scriptures*", the fulfilment of scores and scores of prophecies written hundreds and hundreds of years beforehand; and such prophecy is proof absolute of divine inspiration. Yes, it is proof *absolute*; we are using that word "absolute" in its exact and scientific sense, not in the loose and commoner way. *One* such prophecy, written in detail centuries before its designed consummation, and then fulfilled in point-by-point counterpart, is proof positive of divine intervention and supervention, for the only one who knows the future for centuries ahead is the One who *determines* the future, that is, *GOD*.

Do we not see, then, how solid is the rock beneath our feet? First we have the historical fact—"Christ died". Then we have the revelation of its meaning—"For our sins". Then both the fact and its meaning are authenticated and guaranteed to us by a seal which can be no other than the seal of God Himself.

Now it is fashionable today to doubt or to deny the inspiration of the Old Testament. Yet this is always harmful if not fatal to Christian faith; for the greatest authentication of New Testament *revelation* springs from Old Testament *inspiration*. The other day I picked up a book by the late Sir Robert Anderson in which he observes how noticeable it is that those who give up belief in inspiration generally end by giving up belief in the Atonement. Surely, to minds which are honest as well as logical, the two things go together—inspiration and revelation; and from the two together we have the supernaturally homologated Gospel doctrines of Atonement and Salvation. In fact, the Old Testament and the New Testament are necessary *to each other*. The inspiration of the Old authenticates the revelation of the New; and the fulfilments which we find in the New prove the inspiration of the Old.

A Universal Language

"The Son of Man came, not to be ministered unto, but to minister, and to give His life a ransom for many."—Matt. 20: 28.

In recent times there has been a desire to find a universal language. There have been three competitors: Esperanto, English, French. Quite apart from the language of the lips, however, there are languages which already *are* universal.

There is the universal language of *natural beauty* (Ps. 19: 1–4). This is a language which speaks to people of all colours and climes. I stood with a German, a Frenchman, and an Italian, on one of the heights of Haute Savoy in France. We looked out, in spell-bound admiration, over the magnificent vista of those French and Italian Alps. Each of my three companions knew only his own language. None of them could understand what any other commented. But there was one language which was speaking with equal clearness to us all: the language of that wonderful beauty before our eyes.

There is the universal language of *human art.* I turned on my radio, the other day, and found a quick succession of languages, German, Dutch, Russian, not one of which I could understand. Then, suddenly, there came a burst of glorious music, and no matter *what* country it came from, immediately it was a language which I understood. Some years ago, an acquaintance of mine was at an Exhibition of Chinese Art, in London. The exhibits were of a very different style from our traditional English, yet again there was a language speaking through them which was universal; and the beholders would exclaim, "How perfectly lovely!" We have talked about British art, European art, Asiatic art. Perhaps the time is nearing when we shall speak about "*world* art".

Most of all, there is the universal language of *self-sacrifice.* I heard a Scot telling about the history lessons at school when he was a boy. All the heroes whom they were taught to admire were Scots—Robert Bruce, William Wallace, John Knox, and so on. Those who lived down beyond the border, or in other lands, were foreigners and a bad lot. How different is the teaching of today! We have found that whichever country it comes from, the language of heroism and sacrifice speaks to us all. Joan of Arc could not speak English, but she spoke a language which all the world understands. During the First World War, even when bitter feelings were strongest, a British airman, telling his radio listeners about a German who sacrificed himself for others, said, "My! he was a brave chap, that German!" Yes, there is something in vicarious self-sacrifice which talks to us all.

The greatest of *all* vicarious self-sacrifice, and the highest expression of *all* moral beauty, is the sacrifice of our Lord Jesus, the incarnate Son of God, on Calvary. Why? Because it was the most utter self-sacrifice for others, by the loveliest of all characters, under the costliest of all circumstances, with the loftiest of all motives, for the sublimest of all purposes. The appeal of that Cross is universal. It appeals to the heart as light to the eye, as truth to the conscience, and as beauty to the aesthetic sense. A cultured Brahman said to a Christian missionary, "I don't like the Christ of your creeds and churches; but the story of Jesus in your Book is the most appealing I ever read." Calvary is a universal language!

What is Your Reaction?

"The Son of Man came, not to be ministered unto, but to minister, and to give His life a ransom for many."—Matt. 20: 28.

In these words our Lord Himself interprets for us the central meaning of His life and death. He came to "minister" or serve; and in that, we see Him as our *Example*. He came to give His life a "ransom for many"; and in that, we see Him as our *Saviour*. With what eager gratitude we should seek to relate ourselves worthily to both these aspects!

What is our reaction, as Christian believers, to His life as our *example*? The distinctive messages of the world's various religions and philosophies have been epitomised as follows. Greece said, "Be wise; know yourself." Rome said, "Be strong; acquit yourself." Confucianism says, "Be superior; correct yourself." Shintoism says, "Be loyal; suppress yourself." Buddhism says, "Be disillusioned; annihilate yourself." Hinduism says, "Be absorbed; merge yourself." Mohammedanism says, "Be submissive; yield yourself." Judaism says, "Be holy; conform yourself." Modern Psychology says, "Be self-confident; fulfil yourself." Modern materialism says, "Be acquisitive; enjoy yourself." Modern Communism says, "Be collective; secure yourself." But in characteristic contrast to all these, Christianity says, "BE CHRISTLIKE; GIVE YOURSELF FOR OTHERS."

If we Christian believers would have our lives and lips really *tell* for Jesus, we need to speak the language of a Christlike, self-forgetting "otherism". It has an appeal which nothing else has. Unconverted people will often admire a religiously upright character in just about the same way that they admire beautiful, dumb statuary. Often they listen to our spoken witness with distant politeness. But when they see our Christianity expressing itself in glad self-sacrifice for them, they break down, or begin to melt like ice under a powerful sun. "The Son of Man came not to be served, but to *serve*, and to *give* . . ." Dear Christian, how much of that is there in *your* life? It is your greatest argument with *any*body. It almost always wins where everything else fails.

But now, what is our reaction to the second part of our Lord's words—"And to give His life a *ransom for many*"? Beyond a doubt, our Lord here teaches that His death was a voluntary, vicarious sacrifice for the redeeming of human sinners. That, He says, was *the* purpose of His coming. One day, in an ornate Hindu temple near Calcutta, I chatted with a charming-mannered Hindu priest, as we stood before the images of his gods. I noticed there an effigy representing our Lord Jesus; so I said, "You have no right to demote Jesus to their level. Did any of those others make the claims that Jesus made, or rise from the dead, as Jesus did?" He replied, "Ah, sir, the resurrection was merely a miracle. The important thing is the *teaching* of Jesus." "Did you ever read the teaching of Jesus?" I asked. "Yes, I have read it all," he claimed. I could only reply, "If you had read the teaching of Jesus as carefully as you claim, you would have seen that Jesus Himself plainly says that His teaching is *not* the main thing, but His redeeming *death*. All those other philosophers and demi-gods lived to teach. Jesus died to save. All those others taught and then died. Jesus died and then rose. All those others are gone. Jesus ever abides." Yes, He is both Example and *Saviour*!

The Common Salvation

"The common salvation."—Jude 3.

THE Gospel of Christ has absolutely nothing of the clandestine about it. Blazoned on its escutcheon the heraldic sign-word is, "WHOSOEVER". It has nothing whatever in common with secret societies. It is the utter antipodes of anything cloistered, shadowy or recluse. The fellowship of Christian believers, while it is the deepest of all human fellowships, is the most open and inviting; its *ethos*, or distinguishing characteristic, is the indiscriminateness of its welcome. Such thoughts leap afresh to mind as we glance again at this little phrase in Jude 3: "The common salvation." Think again on some of the ways in which it is "the common salvation".

It is the "common salvation" in the sense of *Testamental oneness*. Our Bible is in two main parts, the Old Testament and the New Testament, but both Testaments are one in their testimony to the same Gospel. It is not true to say, as some do, that the whole Bible is the Gospel. There are broad dispensational divisions which only the self-blinded do not see. The Law of Moses is not the Gospel. The Sinai Covenant is not the Gospel. Even the lofty ethic of the Prophets is not the Gospel. The Old Testament has to do distinctively with the *old* covenant. The New Testament has to do distinctively with the *new* covenant. Yet both the Old Testament and the New are united in their *testimony* to the one Gospel of our Lord and Saviour, Jesus Christ. As Peter says, in Acts 10: 43, "To Him give all the prophets witness, that through His name whosoever believeth on Him shall receive remission of sins." He is the one Saviour. There is one "common salvation". That which is anticipation in the Old is accomplishment in the New. Isaiah was preaching the Gospel in advance in his chapters 53: 4–10; 55: 6–13, not to mention many other places in the Prophets. Yes, in the united testimony of both Testaments, the salvation which comes to us in Christ is "the *common* salvation".

It is also the "common salvation" in the sense of *Apostolic unanimity*. There is as much difference of style, vocabulary, disposition, idiosyncrasy among the New Testament apostles as there is among the Old Testament prophets; but they are unanimous as to the basic facts and cardinal truths of the Gospel. The one doctrine of salvation is common to them all. One gets rather tired of hearing that Peter and James disagreed with Paul doctrinally, when the very passage which is supposed to placard their disagreement (Gal. 2: 11–18) is the one which emphasises more strikingly than any other their doctrinal *unity*, and the basic unanimity of *all* the apostles. The disagreement was not on doctrine, but about a certain *behaviour*; and Paul, in correcting that, appeals to their *doctrinal* unity in "the common salvation". To see how really one they were, we have only to compare such verses as Romans 4: 22–25; James 2: 22, 23; Titus 2: 13—3: 8; James 5: 7, 8; 2 Peter 3: 15.

The Scofield Bible note on Romans 4: 2 versus James 2: 24 is much to the point. "Paul speaks of that which justifies man before *God*, viz., faith alone, wholly apart from works; James of the proof before *men*, that he who professes to have justifying faith really has it. Paul speaks of what *God* sees—faith; James of what *men* see—works, as the visible *evidence* of faith." Both are true aspects of the "common salvation".

The One Gospel

"The common salvation."—Jude 3.

Yes, it is the "common" salvation. It is so in the sense of *intellectual agreement.* The salvation which we Evangelicals preach is not one which is merely sectarian, partisan, or peculiar to any one denomination. It is common to us all, when we are true to our respective denominational positions. It is the genuinely *traditional* Gospel of salvation—and we need not be afraid of that word, "tradition", for there is good tradition as well as bad. Presbyterian Chalmers and Salvation Army Booth had sharp differences as to propriety of methods, but they were completely one in their preaching of "the common salvation". The Victorian pulpit genius, Spurgeon, detested "State Churchism", while the silver-tongued Episcopalean, Canon Liddon, looked down his nose at "Dissenters"; yet Spurgeon at the Tabernacle and Liddon at St. Paul's were gloriously one in their proclamation of "the common salvation". Up to the time of the Dark Ages, and since the Protestant Reformation, all the great Bible loyalists have been one as to the essential substance of the Gospel and its way of salvation. There may be imperfection, error, prejudices for or against particular names and sects, yet we can truly sing with all the members of the true church, irrespective of denomination, "We are not divided; all one body we; one in faith and doctrine, one in charity."

Again, it is "the common salvation" in *spiritual experience.* The sense of forgiveness and reconciliation; of justification and peace with God; the experience of new life by regeneration, and the Saviour's indwelling; of fellowship with the Father and the Son through the Holy Spirit; the joy of answered prayer, and the new wonder of the divine promises; all these are "common" to Christian believers. We are all one in a common experience of present salvation, in a common enjoyment of spiritual privileges, and in common hopes for the future.

Furthermore, it is "the common salvation" in its *applicability and appropriability*. The Gospel is not like a river which branches out into different streams—one for the rich, another for the intellectual, and others for the poor and the illiterate and the nobodies. Nor is it like a hospital with superior wards for the well-to-do where aristocratic disease can be treated with aristocratic medicines, and inferior wards for others. No, as all of us are one in our common need as sinners, so there is one "common salvation" which avails for us all. It is not only the Newtons and Ruskins and Gladstones and Lord Kelvins and others of the élite who find it applicable and appropriable, but the "rags and tags and bobtails", and the "broken earthenware" of Skid Row.

The "common" salvation is not only a common *privilege*; it is a common *responsibility*! It is our responsibility, as Christians, to preserve and propagate it. Or, if we are yet unconverted, it is our responsibility to appropriate at once this unspeakable provision of "the common salvation".

Now spread the tidings far and wide,
The Saviour—One for *all*, has died!

Obverse Aspects

"So great salvation."—Heb. 2 : 3.

AFTER looking long at a picture of the crucifixion, by one of the great artists, the famous John Ruskin wrote, "We must leave it to work its will on the spectator; for it is beyond all analysis, and above all praise." If that is how we feel about a *picture* of the crucifixion, what are our thoughts and feelings when we deeply contemplate the Cross *itself*? It is the utterly and transcendently incomparable revelation of that which is deepest and most glorious even in God! It is also that which procures and provides everlasting salvation for human sinners who penitently and believingly appropriate it.

It always seems to my own mind that there are two opposite yet mutually complementary ways of estimating that "so great salvation" which comes to us through the Cross. First, a salvation which necessitated the incarnation and humiliation, the hungering and thirsting, the testing and tempting, the tears and groans, the shame and outpoured blood of the divine Son, *must* be a "great salvation"; for if there had been any other way, God would never have effected it at such awful, unspeakable *cost*.

Second, a salvation which brings to me, and to millions of others, rescue from sinnership, both legally and morally; a salvation which in its judicial provisions delivers me from the guilt and penalty of multiplied transgressions against God's holy law, from "the wrath to come", from the judgment at "the great white throne", and from the fearful flame of Gehenna; a salvation which in its moral provisions brings me regeneration by the divine Spirit, reconciliation with God, inward cleansing and sanctification, fellowship with God, present victory over hereditary perversity, and eventual deliverance from every trace of it, the promise of heaven at last, and perfect rapture in the presence of God through endless ages; surely a salvation which brings all that to millions and millions of us could have been procured by *nothing less* than the infinite cost of Calvary.

Oh, this "so great salvation"! Oh, this dear and glorious Saviour! Oh, this precious Gospel! Can we ever hear it without deep emotions of awed wonder and adoring gratitude? As for those of us who by simple but vital faith in Christ have come into the present experiencing of this salvation, can we make any less response than to "glorify God" in thought, word, life and service? "One died for all"; then must we not say with Paul, "the love of Christ constraineth us"—to live for Him, to serve Him, to sacrifice for Him, and, if need be, to die for Him? Or can it be that we now address someone who has never accepted the Saviour? Oh, foolish procrastinator, be warned. Sin is *really* sin, and hell is no fiction! Let the terrible nature of sin, and its eternal consequences alarm you! Yea, rather, let the mighty, tender, marvellous love of God's dear Son cause you to open your heart to Him this very moment.

O Love, Thou bottomless abyss!
  My sins are swallowed up in thee!
Covered is my unrighteousness,
  Nor spot of guilt remains in me!
While Jesus' blood, in earth and skies,
Mercy, free, boundless mercy cries!

The Christian's Altar

"We have an altar."—Heb. 13: 10.

IN Biblical symbolism the altar is ever the meeting-place between God and man. It proclaims that God and man may meet, even though God is holy and man is sinful; yet at the same time it emphasises that the holy God and sinful man can come together only through an atoning sacrifice—for the altar is the place of sacrifice. There must be a sacrifice which, on the one hand, propitiates God, whom sin has monstrously wronged, and which, on the other hand, reconciles alienated man to his condescending God. Nothing in the universe is more important to us human beings than the altar, the place where God and men meet.

Notice in our text an emphasis on the pronoun, "*We*". Yes, we Christians, as well as the ancient Jewish temple and ritual, have our altar, but it is an altar different from and superior to that of Judaism. That is what our text was saying to Christians of the first days; and that is what it says to us today. Yet Israel's altar was a *type* of the Christian's, as this Hebrews epistle makes plain.

Turn back to Leviticus 17. No thoughtful reader can fail to be impressed by the solemnly emphatic language of that chapter concerning the one place of sacrifice. Five times, with insistent explicitness, the one place of sacrifice is prescribed, while all other places are interdicted. (Read 17: 3–9.) The meaning for ourselves is clear. There is one place, and only one, where God in sovereign grace has elected to meet with penitent sinners, and that is the Cross—of which the altar at the door of the tabernacle was a type. None other sacrifice! None other altar! "None other name under heaven given among men whereby we must be saved." There, and there alone, is the one perfect sacrifice for our race's sin. There, alone, have the requirements of the divine law and holiness been vicariously honoured on behalf of man. To reject that one-and-only meeting-place is to exclude oneself from the only possible reconciliation, and to presume a right to life which all of us as sinners have forfeited. Nor must we invent other altars such as the Roman Mass. There is absolute finality in the Cross. Other altars are superseded. There is *endless* continuity of efficacy from that once-for-all, *ended* offering of Christ on Calvary. To make the offering *itself* continuous, as in the Mass, is to deny both its completeness and its efficacy; for if it is still continuing, it is incomplete; and if it is incomplete it is without saving efficacy; for it is only as a *completed* atonement that it *begins* to have efficacy. The New Testament emphasis is that Calvary is a completed, once-for-all offering. *That* is our altar: Calvary alone; but Calvary all-sufficient to save us for evermore!

None other Lamb, none other Name,
None other hope in heav'n or earth or sea;
None other hiding-place from guilt and shame,
None beside Thee!

Lord, Thou art life, though I be dead;
Love's fire Thou art, however cold I be;
Nor heav'n have I, nor place to lay my head,
Nor home, but Thee.

The Blood on the Altar

"It is the blood that maketh atonement for the soul."—Lev. 17: 11.

LOOK again at this seventeenth chapter of Leviticus. After the emphasis on only one place of sacrifice (3–9) the remaining verses (10–16) explain the sanctity of blood, and the meaning of blood sacrifices. See especially verse 11: "For the life of the flesh is in the blood; and I have given it to you upon the altar to make an atonement [lit. a covering] for your souls; for it is the blood that maketh a covering for your souls."

Mark well: it is the *blood* which gives such vital meaning to that *altar*; and, conversely, it is the *altar* which gives such vital meaning to the *blood*. The two must go together. The altar without the blood is no meeting-place for God and sinful man. The blood apart from the altar has no covering value. It must be the blood; and upon the one altar.

The Scofield note on this verse aptly says: "The meaning of all sacrifice is here explained. Every offering was an execution of the sentence of the law upon a substitute for the offender, and every such offering pointed forward to that substitutional death of Christ which alone vindicated the righteousness of God in passing over the sins of those who offered the typical sacrifices" (Rom. 3: 24, 25). And again: "The value of the 'life' is the measure of the value of the 'blood'. This gives the blood of Christ its inconceivable value. When it was shed the sinless God-man gave His life." The shed blood is the basis of all. It is through the shed blood of Calvary's Lamb, nothing more, nothing less, nothing else, that we have our reconciliation and salvation.

No book of the Bible is more methodically progressive than Leviticus. It divides into two main parts. Part one (1–17) shows the *way to* God—by sacrifice. Part two (18–27) shows the *walk with* God—by separation. Part one breaks up thus: Chapters 1–7, the offerings (absolution); chapters 8–10, the priesthood (mediation); chapters 11–16, the people (purification); chapter 17, the altar (reconciliation).

It is all immensely significant. In Genesis we see God's remedy for man's ruin—the promised Seed of the woman. In Exodus we see God's answer to man's cry—the blood of the Lamb. In Leviticus we see God's provision for man's need of heavenward fellowship—a sacrifice, a priest, an altar. The first part of Leviticus answers four big questions: Why cannot I choose my *own* sacrifice? (1–7). Why cannot *I* offer my own sacrifice? (8–10). Why cannot I choose my own *place* of sacrifice? (17: 1–9). Why must the sacrifice be one of bloodshedding? (17: 10–16).

Conan Doyle, author of the famous Sherlock Holmes stories, turned from the evangelical faith, saying that he could not believe in a God who demanded blood before He would forgive. Yet surely that was unworthily superficial. As any fair reading of the Bible shows, it is not that God demands blood, but that sin necessitates atonement. How then shall atonement be effected? As we ponder the holiness of God, the enormity of sin, the innate perversity of fallen man, must we not confess?

There was no other good enough
  To pay the price of sin.
He only could unlock the gate
  Of heav'n, and let us in.

We Need a Priest

"We have . . . an high priest."—Heb. 8: 1.

THERE is accentuated need today for doctrinal preaching. Our Protestant congregations need to hear the great doctrines of the Bible again. It is mainly due to a lack of grounding in New Testament doctrine among our Protestant churches that the Roman church makes strident advance. To this also is due the present-day degrading of national politics to the inferior level of expediency rather than that of moral principle. I still believe that the destiny of the great democracies is in the hands of the Protestant pulpits, if only they will recapture the passion to teach the great evangelical doctrines of the New Testament again. Apropos of this is our text, which focus-points one such great doctrine in the four short words: "We have a priest." This simple sentence, so brief, so big, advertises three great truths concerning us human beings in our relationship with God. (1) We *need* a priest. (2) We *have* a priest. (3) We need *no other* priest.

Reflect on our *need* of a priest. The Hebrews epistle is one of the two main theological treatises in our New Testament. Its main argument is based on the assumption that we need a priest, and that we need a priest such as only Jesus can be for us. Yet we do not hear much today about the priesthood of Christ. Do some of us wonder why? I think that probably one reason is our nervous reaction away from priesthood such as we see in the Church of Rome. The corrupt Romish doctrine of priesthood has maybe soured our minds against the very idea of a mediating priest. Yet we ought not to let the false priest-craft of Rome keep us from the true doctrine of priesthood as taught in the Word of God.

Then, also, the comparatively scant reference to our Lord's priesthood may be due to our present-day neglect of emphasis on the divine *holiness*. Our need of a priest to mediate between God and ourselves arises from the difference between what *God* is, and what *we* are. In His utter, awful, glorious holiness, God can only be as "a consuming fire" to us fallen, defiled human sinners, unless there is an atoning sacrifice and a sinless, qualified, mediating priest. Even after we have found a full and forever forgiveness through the finished work of Calvary, we are still sinners; so the further problem remains: how can even *forgiven* sinners who are *still* sinners hold fellowship with the inviolably holy God? That is just where the high priestly ministry of Jesus comes in. By His finished work on the Cross we have a full, free, final and forever *forgiveness* from God; by His intercessory priesthood we are kept in continuous *fellowship* with God.

What was the first high-priestly request our Lord made when He returned to heaven? He told in advance: "I will pray the Father, and He shall give you another Paraclete . . ." (Jn. 14: 16). It was in response thereto that the Holy Spirit was given at Pentecost (Acts 2: 27). "God hath sent forth the Spirit of His Son into our hearts, crying, Abba Father" (Gal. 4: 6). Yes, the Spirit begets a yearning for fellowship with God as our *Father*; yet it is that which also wakens us to our need of Jesus as High Priest; for the divine holiness is a "consuming fire", whereas we who fain would draw near as "sons" are still *sinners*. How then *can* we hold "fellowship with the Father"? See the answer in Hebrews 4: 16, Ephesians 1: 17, and 1 John 2: 1.

We Need, and We Have

"We have . . . an high priest."—Heb. 8 : 1.

Yes, we *need* a priest such as Jesus is, to represent us in heaven. Although we are so completely absolved from guilt, and so fully "accepted in the beloved", yet in ourselves, while down here, we are still erring, sinning, feeble, needy creatures, exposed to trials and temptations, liable to stumble, and encompassed by infirmities. How we need the high priestly mediation of our dear heavenly Advocate, whose presence yonder keeps us in all the benefits of the New Covenant, maintains our standing in grace, and releases to us the paraclete ministries of the Holy Spirit. It has been well said, "We could not stand for a moment down here, if *He* were not living for us up there."

Thank God, "we *have* such an high priest"! This is the "sum" of the argument mid-way in this Hebrews epistle. Read the full verse in which our text occurs: "Now of the things which we have spoken this is the sum: We have such an high priest, who is set on the right hand of the throne of the Majesty in the heavens."

And what perfection of qualification stamps every aspect of His priesthood! There is the all-glorious perfection of His *person* (1 : 3; 4 : 14; 8 : 1). There is the utter perfection of His *character* (4 : 15; 7 : 26). Then there is perfection of *sphere*—no mere earthly sanctuary, but the heavenly (8 : 2; 9 : 24). There is also perfection of *basis*—an accomplished redemption (9 : 12, 25, 26). So, too, there is the perfection of *perpetuity* (7 : 24, 25). What perfections are these—of person, of character, of sphere, of basis, of duration!

Such, then, is our "Great High Priest". Into this heavenly priesthood He entered when He had "offered Himself without spot to God". Our Lord Jesus never was a priest on earth. Whenever He went to the temple, it was as a prophet to teach, not as a priest to sacrifice or burn incense. By human descent He was neither in the tribe of Levi nor in the family of Aaron, but of Judah (7 : 14; 8 : 4). The only priesthood God ever appointed on earth was the Aaronic; therefore, to go back to an earthly priest-class, as the Romanists do, is to retrogress to Old Testament concepts which are now abrogated and superseded. Earthly priesthood is done away in Christ, except in the sense that *all* believers are priests (1 Peter 2 : 5, 9; Rev. 1 : 6; 5 : 10).

Jesus, my Great High Priest,
   Offered His blood and died;
My guilty conscience needs
   No sacrifice beside.
For He whose blood did once atone
Now stands for me before the Throne.

To God I'm reconciled,
   His pardoning voice I hear;
He owns me for His child,
   I need no longer fear.
With confidence I now draw nigh,
And "Father, Abba Father", cry!

We Need No Other

"We have . . . an high priest."—Heb. 8: 1.

WITH Jesus as our all-sufficient High Priest we need no other; nor can we tolerate it that self-deluded, fictitious *clerical* priests should ever intrude between Him and us. Certainly, no other priest is needed *in heaven*, for Jesus has passed "into heaven itself, now to appear in the presence of God for us" (Heb. 9: 24) and His priesthood there has the all-sufficiency of perfection in every aspect.

Equally definitely no other priest is needed *on earth*. The old-time sacrifices are all done away in the one perfect sin-offering on Calvary. This is where the Romanists go fundamentally wrong. They are self-blinded to the fact that if priests are still offering sacrifice, then redemption is not completed. Hebrews 8: 3 says, "Every high priest is ordained to offer sacrifices." Therefore, if the Roman church insists that its clerics are "priests", they must needs have a sacrifice to offer. This requires changing the Lord's Supper into their "Mass", which turns the Cross into a *still-continuing* offering instead of a *once-completed* offering. Thus Christ is kept on the Cross; and the Romanists miss the central truth and glory of the Gospel, namely, a once-for-all completed work of redemption on Calvary. The whole emphasis in this Hebrews epistle is upon the once-for-all finality of that Calvary sacrifice. The efficacy of it is ever-continuing, but the offering itself was once-for-all. Therefore the spurious priests of Rome are a contradictory superfluity. One only is our all-sufficient priest, even Jesus Himself.

This also is utterly true: no other priest was ever *intended*. Here, most of all, we see the sad error in the Roman doctrine of so-called "Apostolical Succession". Quite apart from lineal gaps which break the historical succession, the apostles themselves were *not* priests, but laymen; nor did they ever *become* priests; nor did they ever *appoint* priests to succeed them! There is no such thing as an apostolic succession in priesthood; the very idea is an exotic contradiction. If the Roman hierarchy insists on priesthood by descent, then obviously it must go back *beyond* the apostles, to the *Aaronic* priesthood; and if so, what then? Why this: the *only* priesthood which *God* ever appointed on earth He has Himself done away in Christ!

Most significant of all, perhaps, is the statement in Hebrews 7: 24, "But this Priest [Christ], because He continueth ever, hath an unchangeable priesthood." The Greek word here translated as "unchangeable" (*aparabatos*) really means *intransmissible*, untransferable. That priesthood was never transmitted even to the apostles. It is solitary, inviolable, exclusive, incommunicable. No pope, cardinal, cleric, or any other religious dignitary on earth, is a priest *of* Christ; but in a subordinate way, all true believers are priests *in* Christ. *HIS* priesthood is solitary but absolutely ALL-SUFFICIENT. Thank God, *we need no other*.

No other priest in heaven I need,
No other priest on earth to plead.
His wounded hands and feet and side
Exclude all need of priests beside.
Thus I enjoy, through Him alone,
Glad fellowship with yonder throne!

What is the Upshot?

"We have . . . an high priest."—Heb. 8 : 1.

In the preceding three meditations we have reflected on three aspects of our Lord's heavenly priesthood: (1) we *need* such a priest; (2) we *have* such a priest; (3) we need *no other* priest.

But now, what is the upshot of all this? Well, see Hebrews 4: 14 again: "Seeing then that we have a great high priest who is passed through the heavens, Jesus the Son of God, *let us hold fast our confession*." And what is "our confession"? See chapter 10: 23, "Let us hold fast the confession of our *hope*" (not "faith" as in A.V.). What then is this "confession of our hope"? The answer is in chapter 9. See first, verse 26, "But now, once in this end-era of the ages He [Christ] hath APPEARED to put away sin by the sacrifice of Himself." Next see verse 24, "For Christ is entered . . . into heaven itself, now to *APPEAR* in the presence of God for us." Finally see verse 28, "And unto them that look for Him He shall *APPEAR* the second time, apart from sin, unto salvation."

Note those three "appearings" of our Lord. First, He *did* appear, on earth, to put away sin. Second, He *does* appear, now, in the presence of God for us. Third, He *shall* appear, the second time, with completive salvation to them that look for Him.

That is the "confession of our *hope*". It is the glorious hope that He who once appeared on earth as our Sinbearer, and now appears in heaven as our all-perfect Priest, will ere long appear again, in His garments of heavenly glory and beauty, to bring us the *consummating* benedictions of the new covenant in His blood. Meanwhile, our glory-robed, sympathetic High Priest and Advocate and Intercessor ministers representatively for us yonder in the heavenly Holy of Holies, bearing our names like jewels on His mighty shoulders and on His gentle bosom.

Beyond the clouds that drape the sky,
Beyond the stellar worlds on high,
There gleams a heavenly temple fair,
And Jesus, my High Priest, is there.

Yes, there for me He intercedes,
And all His Calvary merit pleads;
And represents before the Throne
My needs as if they were His own.

"Seeing then that we have a great high priest, that is passed into the heavens, Jesus the Son of God, let us hold fast our confession. For we have not an high priest which cannot be touched with the feeling of our infirmities; but was in all points tempted like as we are, yet without sin. Let us therefore come boldly unto the throne of grace, that we may obtain mercy, and find grace to help in time of need." (Heb. 4: 14–16). Notice the four things in that sixteenth verse: (1) *where* to come—"the throne of grace"; (2) *how* to come—"boldly" or confidently; (3) *why* to come—to "obtain mercy and find grace"; (4) *when* to come—"in every time of need", that is, *continually*.

Tear-Blinded Mourning

"But Mary stood without at the sepulchre, weeping."—Jn. 20: 11.

THE incident is one of the most touching in the Gospels. To the perceiving eye, it is also full of spiritual lessons.

See Mary's pathetic *mourning*. She was a woman for whom Christ had "done great things". Having been forgiven much, she loved much. Her attachment was deep, womanly, constant, reverent. She ministered to Him during His itinerating; lingered with Him through His crucifixion; stayed to ascertain His tomb; and was the first there at His resurrection. It was she who found the stone rolled away, then ran to bring Peter and John.

Observe her *lingering*, after Peter and John had gone away. She was disturbed as to what had happened to that precious corpse. Meanwhile she felt nearest to Him just there, and could not tear herself away. How constant was her devotion! Though how helpless it now seemed! How *we* should love Him, who owe our eternal salvation to Him! However much He had done for Mary, He has done far more for us.

Notice again that as she lingered she was *weeping*. Tears are sometimes more eloquent than words. What *cause* she had to weep! She wept for a lost Saviour. Ah, those who lose Christ have cause to weep! What is loss of money, loss of earthly comforts, loss of friends, compared with that? Of course, had Mary only known it, she had not *really* lost Him. That opened sepulchre meant that He was coming back in a new way. Even so today, when we who are the Lord's lovers sometimes lose the sense of His presence, it is not that He has really left us; He has merely withdrawn the *sense* of His presence, that He may break upon our consciousness again with new brightness.

Notice also that Mary was *seeking*. She "stooped down" and peered "into the sepulchre". There she saw two angels; yet apparently she was not diverted in the least by surprise. What were angels compared with *Him*? When once Jesus has been possessed by a human heart, none but He can satisfy.

Mary, however, fell prey to erroneous "*supposing*". "She turned herself back, and saw Jesus standing, but knew not that it was Jesus." Whether she turned because she saw the angels do obeisance we do not know; but she turned and saw Him, "*supposing* Him to be the gardener". How could she fail to recognise Him? Had He not foretold His disciples that He would rise? Yes, yet somehow the word had not sunk in. The seeming impossibility of it had cheated them. Had they only realised it, Jesus was speaking His biggest word through that awful cross and grave. As for Mary, she was so blinded by her grief that when He came she failed to recognise Him.

Let *us* be quick to learn from this. Often through our biggest sorrow Jesus speaks His loveliest word to us; but we can be so obsessed and self-blinded by our very tears that we do not recognise Him. Let us wipe away the mist of doubtful supposings, and see Him really *there*, amid the tear-bedewed lilies of sorrow's garden—risen, ever-present, sympathetic, never-failing! Out of their deepest suffering, Job, Jacob, Jeremiah, Mary, and many others, have made their supreme discovery of God. Thrice blest are they whose spiritual vision sees Christ when He is least visible to the senses.

The Revealing Voice

"Jesus saith unto her, Mary."—Jn. 20: 16.

REFLECT again on the way Jesus revealed Himself to Mary Magdalene on that resurrection morning. It was by *voice.* This, perhaps more than anything else, would reveal that it was really Jesus Himself, unchanged after His death and burial and resurrection. Mary knew it by its tone, which circumstance is of much interest. After His resurrection, our Lord's body, although in structure and appearance the same as before, was different in its essential substance. It was now a supernalised body, fitted for heavenly as well as earthly activity. It was no longer bound by the law of physical gravitation, nor its travel conditioned by geographical mileage. It could be visible or invisible; on or off the earth; here or there or anywhere, in an instant. Yes, His body was changed; yet His *voice* remained the same. Of course, He can make His voice awesome "as the sound of many waters" whenever He so wills (Rev. 1: 15, etc.), but His conversing voice is just the same as when He tramped Galilee with His disciples. Mary knew it, and knew *Him* by it. We ourselves shall hear that very same voice one day soon!

But further, when Jesus revealed Himself to Mary Magdalene, it was by more than voice alone; it was by *word.* Besides the well-loved tone and accent there was speech and message. The voice had something to *say.* So does Jesus speak to *us,* if we will hear. "My sheep hear my *voice,*" He says, in one place; but He also says, "He that heareth my *word. . . .*" "Faith cometh by hearing, and hearing by the *word*" (Rom. 10: 17). He has His own way of speaking to us, if we love Him, through His written word, and by His Holy Spirit within us. Ah, if only we have an ear for Him as Mary Magdalene had, we know not only the voice, but the meaning.

Furthermore, our text tells us that when Jesus disclosed His presence to Mary, it was not only by voice and word, but by *name.* At first He had addressed her as "Woman", but now, with a never-to-be-forgotten tone, and in a way which at once brought rapturous recognition, He said, "*Mary*". Oh, the utter, almost painful joy of Mary in that moment, as she flung herself at His feet, clinging there and exclaiming, "Master!" It was not simply that *she* now knew *Him*; she knew also that *He* still knew *her,* as in the days before His crucifixion. He was verily alive again! He remembered her! He had called her "*Mary*" again! Yes! and so does He know and love *each* of us by name; for each one of us means something unique and precious to His boundless heart.

Note: on that resurrection morning our Lord was *revealed,* not discovered. It is ever so. He must reveal Himself to us if we are truly to know Him. But always He *does* reveal Himself, if we seek Him with the same longing as Mary.

Note again: there was a purposeful *delay* before the revealing. The seeking and waiting was good for Mary. It made Him even more precious afterward. Such delays are always compassionate and educative.

Note once more: Mary became the first *evangelist* of the risen Lord (18)! Even so, as our risen Master reveals Himself to you and me, *we* must become voices for Him to others. With what eagerness Mary hastened to break the news! Should our eagerness be less?

Jesus Present but Unknown

"She, supposing Him to be the gardener . . ."—Jn. 20: 15.

HAD Mary only known, Jesus was standing there with her, as she wept at the tomb on that wonderful morn. Truly, "The Lord is nigh unto them that are of a broken heart" (Ps. 34: 18). Alas, the broken-hearted often fail to recognise His presence because they are blinded by their own tears.

Reflect, then, on *WHY MARY DID NOT KNOW HIM.* To begin with, she was *not expecting Him,* any more than the disciples were when Jesus walked over the tossing waves during the stormy night. How often *we* forfeit Him by not expecting Him!

Next, Mary was *dazed by despair.* Someone had opened the sepulchre. The body was gone. She was too numbed by these seeming further catastrophes to grasp their real meaning. Is it not often so with ourselves? Things which seem like further troubles are our Lord's way of coming to us in new surprise, but we allow preoccupation with *them* to dull our perception of *Him*!

But again, Mary was *blinded by her own tears.* See the abject grief on her ashen face. Hear her wail, "They have taken away my Lord, and I know not where they have laid Him." Even when the risen Lord comes right to her, and actually speaks, she is too bowed with grief and blinded by weeping to recognise Him. Have there not been many others like her? The grief which should make Him more than ever real to us, we allow to blur our vision of Him!

Still further, poor Mary was *disinclined to believe.* Verse 14, "She turned herself back, and saw Jesus standing, and knew not that it was Jesus." Even when He asked, "Woman, why weepest thou?" she failed to detect Him. So incredulous was she of His ever coming back to her in an after-death reappearance that she could even see Him and hear Him, yet take Him for someone else! Oh, how doubt dulls ear and eye to Christ!

Once more, Mary was *prone to misconstruction.* She "supposed" Him to have been "the gardener". Deep grief or acute trial often lays us open to wrong suppositions concerning our Lord. "All these things are against me!" exclaimed aged Jacob (Gen. 42: 36) when in fact they were leading to the loveliest of consummations!

We can add but a word on *HOW CHRIST REVEALED HIMSELF.* It was to Mary *first*; not to Peter or John or His mother, lest it should seem there was favouritism according to relationship; but to her who lingered longest looking for Him. It was in such a way, also, as let her know how He *appreciated her devotion.* And it was in a way which showed that whatever changes death may make, *love survives it.*

Finally, a word on *WHY HE THUS REVEALED HIMSELF.* It was to transform her grief to joy. It was to give her new faith and hope in Himself. And it was to make her the earliest human messenger of His resurrection. How all this speaks to you and me, if we have minds which understand!

Has Jesus risen from the grave?
  And can we silent bide?
Out! out! and tell His power to save
  To sinners far and wide!

Angels in the Tomb

"Two angels in white sitting, the one at the head, and the other at the feet, where the body of Jesus had lain."—Jn. 20: 12.

So intense was Mary's preoccupation with her grief at finding the Lord's body gone from the sepulchre, that apparently even the presence of angels did not strike her either with astonishment or fear. What were even angels, compared with *Him*? Yet we may well turn back and observe again those two shining visitors from the unseen realm. The very idea of angels in a tomb is arresting.

As to their identity, they are definitely called "*angels*"; and, whether in the Old Testament or the New, the original word so translated means primarily a messenger. There is no heredity among the angels, and no death such as pertains to man. We have no idea how many ages those two angels may have lived, but we do know that never before in all their existence had they been dispatched on such a triumphant errand.

As to their *number*, notice that there were but *two* of them; not a quartet or a group. Two is the number of witness. They had not come to join in chorus as on the night when our Lord was born in Bethlehem. They were in the tomb to give *witness* that Jesus had "risen indeed".

Notice also their *posture*: they were "*sitting*", one at the head, the other at the feet. They were not standing on guard; they were sitting at rest. They were now there, not with flaming swords to protect a sacred corpse, but with folded wings of repose in the victory of One who had risen. Their very recumbency seemed to express the rest of heart which the redeemed were now to find in the vicarious victory of Christ. Their reclining in that vault immediately gave death a new aspect. Our Lord's resurrection has transformed it, and brought angels into it. Now, as dear old Matthew Henry quaintly observes, "The grave is not much out of our way to heaven"!

Next, notice again the *attire* of those two angels: "Two angels in *white*." They came from a world of light. Those white garments indicated heavenly holiness. They also must have been of a whiteness which shone, otherwise they could scarcely have been seen in the darkness of the windowless cave. And their outshining whiteness betokened the glory of that realm into which Christ had now risen, and into which we ourselves shall enter when He calls!

And again, notice the *position* of the two angels. They were sitting "one at the head, and the other at the feet, where the body of Jesus had lain"—as though they had been on guard all the while between the entombment and the resurrection, lest there should be interference either human or demon. Though now in repose after the vigil, they lingered at their stations as evidence of what the angels think about that body and that Saviour.

Once more, reflect that those two angels must have been *luminous*, otherwise Mary could not have seen in the dark tomb (see how verse 11 says she had to "stoop down" into it). Yet their luminousness must have been a soft, beaming, friendly epiphany, for it did not frighten Mary, but reassured her. The same angels can be a flaming terror to others (see Matt. 28: 2–4 and 2 Thess. 1: 7, 8). One of the joys of heaven will be our fellowship with the angels.

The Question of the Angels

"Woman, why weepest thou?"—Jn. 20: 13.

To those angels in the tomb it must have seemed a poignant irony that Mary should grope there weeping when the One for whom she wept had risen, and was walking toward her amid the shadowy garden. It must have been with concentrated tenderness that they asked, "Woman, why weepest thou?" And is there not considerable significance in their question?

Let it represent to us, right away, the *interest* which the angels feel toward us. Although they are non-human and apparently bodiless beings, they are not impassive toward us. On the contrary they display keen interest in the concerns of our race, as many verses of Scripture attest. Our text expresses their compassionate interest in just one individual woman.

But their question also expresses *sympathy*. One can almost hear the solicitous tone in which they addressed Mary. Perhaps the sinless angels cannot enter too understandingly into our sorrows as *sinners*; yet the pure love in their hearts gives them an outreach of sorrowful emotion toward us, especially as they see us in our times of grief.

Almost certainly, too, in the angels' question to Mary, there was a touch of kindly *rebuke*. The sense of it was: "Dear woman, why do you continue weeping when you ought now to be rejoicing?" Perhaps Mary suddenly detected the thrilling suggestion which was latent in their sympathetic rebuke, for immediately thereupon she looked round and saw Jesus.

Then, of course, the angels' question also expressed their special *knowledge*. Before ever our Lord's resurrection became known to men, it was known to the angels. Doubtless they had already surrounded their crucified but risen and glorified King with angelic hosannas and adoring congratulations. Maybe many other things are known to them which are not yet revealed to us, and that this is a main reason why they are intensely concerned in our salvation (1 Peter 1: 12).

Once more, the question of the angels articulated their *great joy* in the resurrection of earth's Saviour and heaven's King. They and we are one in that; though we have even more cause to exult in it than they. Jesus is risen! He is our ever-living Saviour, from whom, now, neither death nor any other foe shall ever separate us.

Remember, it was our Lord Himself who posted those angels in that tomb; and *that* tomb has thus become symbolic of every other Christian repository. Bereaved believer, reflect again: there are angels in the tomb! Their presence fills it with light. They have guarded your loved one through it into the very presence of the Lord on high! There are angels in *other* kinds of graves too—the grave of disappointed hopes, of thwarted ambitions, of unrequited love, of departed youth, of broken health, of frustrating trials and denials. They tenderly ask: "Why weepest thou?" By their question they would turn us to that dear, risen Saviour who comes to companion us amid the tear-bedewed garden of our sorrows. As the dear old hymn says, the "dews of sorrow" are always "lustred with His love". And as experience proves, His companionship is dearest of all, amid the shadowy bowers of human heartbreak.

Angels Eclipsed

"Rabboni, which is to say, Master."—Jn. 20: 16.

THIS is our sixth day with Mary Magdalene and her day-break discoveries at the sepulchre. We have picked our way with her through the shadowy garden, and peered into the rocky vault, and seen the two shining ones there. We have wondered at their *presence*, and reflected on their *question*, and cannot but notice now their *eclipse*. Mary turns and sees Jesus Himself. After momentary failure to recognise Him, she knows Him, and instantly is at His feet in a rapture of adoring worship. The angels are never so much as noticed after that! The sun has risen; the stars retire!

The apostle John narrates the incident with deft artistry, but who shall describe the tumult of glad emotion in Mary's heart? Did ever brightest sun-burst through blackest clouds compare? In one electric moment she is transported from abysmal grief to utter joy. The stark enigma, the baffling mystery of His awful death is suddenly luminous. The body has *not* been stolen from the sepulchre! It has somehow come alive again! The Master has crowned all His miracles by coming back to life! Swift as lightning, her mind flashes back over the bygone. His faultless character, guileless life, profound wisdom, incomparable teachings, and amazing miracles, had convinced them that He was Israel's Messiah, and in some mysterious way the very Son of God. Then, suddenly, on being seized, He had seemed strangely helpless against His evil persecutors. They had rudely shamed Him, and crucified Him on Golgotha, a place reeking with the blood of executed criminals! Oh, the agony of it! But now, oh, ecstasy, He really lives again! Verily, it is His voice that Mary now hears! It is His form which she now sees. He is there before her in the garden, with the dawnlight reflected in His radiant eyes! Yes, one splendid instant of rapturous recognition, then Mary is at His feet, exclaiming "*Rabboni!*"

Our Lord's reply, "Touch me not, for I am not yet ascended", has seemed strange to many. Three explanations are suggested. First, Jesus as high priest, having offered the sacrifice, has now withdrawn and is on His way to present the blood of atonement in the heavenly sanctuary, as typified in Leviticus 16. We have looked up Leviticus, however, and there is *no* parallel. Besides, why should Jesus side-step to tarry in the garden and appear to Mary, only to forbid her to "touch" Him? Second, it is supposed that Jesus meant Mary now to know Him no longer "after the flesh" but in the sense of 2 Corinthians 5: 16. This, however, is contradicted by Matthew 28: 9, "They held Him by the feet, and worshipped Him." Surely the simplest explanation is the true one, that our Lord meant sympathetically, "You need not cling, dear Mary, as though I were about to elude you. Have no fear; I am not yet ascended to My Father ..." The Greek word translated "touch" would be better rendered in our text as "cling". For forty days yet Jesus was to "eat and drink" with them (Acts 10: 41). Moreover, although He now *has* ascended, He still lingers in *our* gardens of sorrow and prayer, outwardly unseen but inwardly real, transforming them into gardens of sanctifying discovery. "He that loveth Me shall be loved of My Father; and I will love him, and will *manifest* Myself to him" (Jn. 14: 21).

Fact Versus Fiction

"God . . . hath raised up Jesus."—Acts 13:33.

As Saul was head and shoulders above all the other sons of Israel, so is Easter morning above all the other mornings of the year. It is so for three reasons mainly: (1) The resurrection of Christ is the basic evidential event upon which the Christian faith is built; (2) in conjunction with the death of Christ it is the most significant act of God in history; (3) it is the most vital of all assurances to the Christian believer.

Think here about the first of these: it is *the basic evidential event upon which the Christian faith is built.* Nowadays, the so-called "Neo-Orthodoxy" rides the saddle in no small way among the seminaries and churches of our Protestant denominations. Yet of all the schools and schemes which have successively appeared, it is surely the fuzziest. Even the utmost personal respect for its progenitors cannot repress our astonishment that specialist theologians can lose themselves in such cloudy ambiguities. According to the neo-orthodoxy the Bible is *not* the Word of God in the clear-cut older meaning; yet it *is* the Word of God in the sense that it *becomes* the Word of God by spiritual impact; though even then it is full of mistakes and "unhistoriographical" myths! Some of us may be impossibly slow, but to us it sounds rather like saying, "What isn't is, yet all the same what is isn't."

Again, according to the neo-orthodoxy, the cross of Jesus is indeed the atonement, yet its significance is not in the historical Jesus, nor in the actual blood; for (according to Karl Barth) the historical Jesus is an elusive figure about whom it is difficult to get information; and although Jesus died "for us", it is scarcely in the clear-cut older sense that He died in our stead and for our sins (see his *Epistle to the Romans*, p. 160).

As for our Lord's resurrection, what happened historically at the tomb is quite unimportant (says neo-orthodoxy). To believe in a bodily resurrection of Jesus is beside the point for Christian faith; the important thing is that in Jesus we can *believe* in resurrection. In Him humanity was taken up into God, and thus the way was opened to Him. To some of us this is an incomparable blend of casuistry and naïveté. It is saying: We have the *doctrine*; why bother about the *fact* on which it is built? Apparently, this wonderful house of neo-orthodoxy does not need actual foundations: it can float in the air! It tells us we can retain the *truths* of the Gospels even though we cannot believe the *records*! But what if the body of Jesus is still in the tomb somewhere? I will tell you what: despite the neo-orthodoxy, the whole Christian faith becomes a delusion, and falls to the ground. Let neo-orthodoxy deny *that*! What a relief it is to get back to the down-to-earth realism and objectivism of the New Testament! Listen to Paul again: "God . . . hath raised up Jesus. . . . He whom God raised again saw no corruption." "Be it known unto you therefore, men and brethren, that through this Man is preached unto you the forgiveness of sins." *That* is the message which shook the synagogues and "turned the world upside down"! That is the message which could shake the *twentieth* century. There is the same human heart-need and heart-cry; and today, as ever, the one, unchanging, all-sufficient answer is the risen Christ, mighty to save.

The Mighty Attestation

"God . . . hath raised up Jesus."—Acts 13 : 33.

TESTED by the sound canons of historical enquiry, the bodily resurrection of the crucified, dead and buried Jesus really happened. In conjunction with what happened on Calvary, it becomes the most significant act of God in history.

It is *the decisive divine testimony to Jesus Christ.* It proclaims with finality the absolute virtue of His life, and the absolute value of His death as an atonement for sin. Moreover, when God raised Jesus from the dead, He thereby declared to the human race that Jesus is His standard for human life. Jesus is the Man God accepts; and God's acceptance of Jesus as the standard means His repudiation of all others as such. Jesus Christ is the One in whom the divine ideal for man is embodied. Jesus Christ is the One in whom the divine purposes are perfectly realised. His resurrection proclaims this. It proclaims Him God's ideal Man, the representative Man of God's new order which shall ultimately cover the whole earth. It proclaims Him the One who alone is accepted of God as true King of our human race. The Alexanders and Caesars of old, the Napoleons and Hitlers and Stalins of modern times, have envisaged world-conquest. They have all failed—inevitably so, for they themselves were conquered by sin and by death. All other such are bound to fail and perish, for Jesus Christ is God's appointed World-Ruler, attested by resurrection as the One who has conquered both sin and death.

It was not simply the might of opposing armies and navies and airfleets which defeated Hitler and his frightful Nazi war-machine in the Second World War, but the purpose of God in the risen Christ. Because Christ was raised from the dead, the Nazi swastika could never wave over the world; and for that same reason the Communist hammer-and-sickle will never wave in world domination. Proud little Hitler, with his jack-boot on the neck of capitulated France, looked across the English Channel and said with mock sorrow, "I am sorry Fate has 'decreed' that I should end the British Empire." But the blaspheming dictator misread the "decree". If he had turned to Psalm 2 he would have read the *real* decree:

> I will declare the decree:
> Jehovah hath said unto Me,
> Thou art my Son, this day I begot Thee,
> Ask of Me, and I shall give unto Thee
> The nations for Thine inheritance,
> Earth's utmost bounds Thy possession.

So Jehovah has pre-covenanted world dominion to *Him!* Meanwhile His resurrection *pledges* it. That is why Hitler licked the dust. That is why the Kremlin must fail. In Acts 13 : 33, from which our text is taken, Paul tells us that the words, "Thou art my Son; this day have I begotten Thee", refer to His *resurrection.* His resurrection yesterday guarantees His world dominion tomorrow. Between the yesterday of resurrection and the tomorrow of world dominion He is the living Saviour of today to all who call upon Him. Yes, "God hath raised up Jesus". This is the one big fact of the *past* which gives the one big hope for the *future.*

Unmistakable Assurance

"God . . . hath raised up Jesus."—Acts 13: 33.

THE resurrection of the Lord Jesus is the most conclusive and satisfying of all assurances to the Christian believer. All the redemptive values of the Gospel come to us from the Cross of Calvary; but they would never come to us at all were it not for our Lord's resurrection. A dead Christ could be no Mediator.

Remember, again, His resurrection is the divine declaration that *atonement on our behalf is accepted*. It is good that you and I should be satisfied with Christ; that you and I should accept Him; but that is not the thing of first importance. The question of first importance is *God's* attitude to Him. Is *God* satisfied with Jesus? Does *God* accept Him? Are the virtue of His life and the value of His death perfect and accepted as an atonement for human sin? His resurrection is God's demonstration that the life which Christ lived out and then laid down is indeed a complete and accepted satisfaction.

But further, in His resurrection Jesus objectifies *our wonderful new union with God through redemption*. By His incarnation He has linked God with our human nature. By His resurrection He has linked our human nature with God. He has carried that risen manhood up to the very throne of God, as the Representative of the new humanity, the "sons of God", who shall one day share His glory, and repeople a renewed earth.

Then, of course, our Lord's resurrection means that for Christian believers *death is disarmed and transformed*.

No longer must the mourners weep
  And call departed Christians dead;
For death is hallowed into sleep,
  And every grave becomes a bed.
To fall asleep is not to die!—
  To sleep, yet wake in larger life!
Instead of exile, rest on high!
  Instead of struggle, peace from strife!
Now once more, Eden's door
  Open stands to mortal eyes!
Now at last, old things past,
  Christ is risen! We too shall rise!

Again, the resurrection of Christ symbolises the Christian believer's present *spiritual* resurrection "in newness of life" (Rom. 6: 4). It also pledges the believer's coming bodily resurrection in deathless physical perfection as a glorious replica of Christ Himself (1 Jn. 3: 2). It also assures us of a consummating *reunion* with our departed Christian loved ones in the beyond. It is the certain guarantee that the Christ who came to earth a first time as the world's Saviour will come to earth a *second* time as the world's Ruler. It is the sign and warning, also, that He is God's appointed *Judge* of the world (Acts 17: 31). And it is also the sure prophecy of a *new order* yet to be when this same, dear, risen Christ shall be King over "a new heaven and a new earth" in which sin shall be no more.

Lo, the Rainbow!

"My bow in the cloud."—Gen. 9: 13.

THE rainbow is a picturesque phenomenon of nature, easily explainable in terms of modern science. What our text explains is the divine *significance* with which God invested it. Whether there had been storms or rainbows during the antediluvian age may remain indeterminate, but it must not dull our appreciation of the rainbow as God explained it to Noah.

First, the rainbow is a *symbol*; God's symbol that "behind a frowning providence, He hides a smiling face". Life's darkest episodes are overruled to contrive our richest blessing. The rainbow genius is that the very cloud which glowers becomes a chariot beaming with divine reassurance and salvation. The rainbow is formed by sunshafts falling on raindrops which break up the rays into seven colours, and so paint on the opposite sky an arch of sevenfold hue. The cloud only needs the sun on it, and lo, the rainbow!

There is a rainbow in *every* cloud permitted to overhang God's people. Christian, those ominous clouds which affright or dismay you, if only faced bravely and discerningly, will disclose heavenly goodness. I can imagine Noah's perturbation when, soon after the Deluge, great buffalo clouds came tumbling and rumbling over the sky. "Alas, is there further destruction?" But no; the showers fling a lovely archway-sign across the expanse. *God* is in the cloud, as well as in the sunshine. His bow is the symbol!

God's rainbow is in every cloud of *trouble*. Did it seem a dark cloud, that Paul was imprisoned just when most needed? Read the prison epistles, and see the rainbow! Was it an ugly cloud, that John Bunyan was unjustly incarcerated in Bedford jail? Read *Pilgrim's Progress*, which he indited there, and see the rainbow! An aged minister told me how all through his life he had been plagued with ill-health and adversities; but now, on looking back, he could see a whole arcade of rainbows, for his troubles had kept him prayerful, and made him more widely usable by Christ.

The rainbow is in every cloud of *sorrow*. A dear friend of mine, who did not marry until in his forties, lost his dear one only five years later, when they had become all-in-all to each other. In his abysmal sorrow he besought God for some sustaining promise, and was strangely guided to Revelation 3: 8. Soon after, God used him as leader in a spiritual revival which lasted teens of years; hundreds were blessed, and as a result I myself am in the ministry. Years later my friend said, "Yes, there was a rainbow even in *that* cloud. I could never have done all this if my dear one had lived."

There is a rainbow in the dark cloud of *death*. Philippians 1: 21 enrings it with, "To die is gain"! And even the dread cloud of coming age-end tribulation is over-arched with the rainbow promise, "I will come again, and receive you to Myself, that where I am, there ye may be also" (Jn. 14: 3).

When the days are hard or dreary
Till you scarce know what to do,
Lift your eyes, and see the rainbow,
With the promise shining through.

A Token and a Type

"I do set my bow in the cloud."—Gen. 9: 13.

THE rainbow is a *token*: "A token of the covenant between Me and the earth." For the first time since sun and rain had known each other, the seven-hued arc was now "set" in the cloud for that purpose.

It betokens the gracious *kindness* of God, that He should condescend to contract a covenant with ill-deserving mankind, and bind Himself to it for ever. Yet it also betokens the *severity* of God, for it ever recalls that at least once God loosed "the foundations of the great deep" upon human sinners. It also betokens the *goodness* of God. It is a pledge to all who live beneath its glistening semi-sphere, that no such water-engulfment shall ever again destroy our race. Further, after lapse of millenniums, the rainbow is now a witness to the *faithfulness* of God; for the covenant which He articulated to Noah, He has honoured these five thousand years. Nevertheless, the rainbow may well be a warning, now, that the future will yet bring *another* all-destroying intervention of God, far bigger than the Noachian Flood (see 2 Peter 3: 7–13).

But further, the rainbow is a *type*. It is not *statedly* so, and we therefore have no warrant for *dogmatically* asserting its typical nature; yet in point of fact there are striking parallels between that rainbow-sign in the dark cloud and the Cross of our Lord Jesus on that dark hill of Calvary.

The rainbow speaks of the Cross inasmuch as it is *the seal of a great covenant*; a covenant of salvation (Gen. 9: 11); which is everlasting (12); and world-embracing (10). The Cross is the crimson seal of a covenant bringing world-embracing, everlasting salvation to men.

The rainbow further parallels with the Cross as it displays *the permanent amid the transient*. The dark cloud blots out the sun! Nay, see that beaming rainbow!—there can be no rainbow unless the sun still shines! The clouds are passing; the sun is abiding. So the Cross tells of a life, a love, a good purpose, which outlive the sins of men and the vanities of time.

Again, the rainbow corresponds with the Cross in its being *a perfect light-prism*. By its exquisite prismatic refraction of the sun's rays, it breaks up the constituent colours and inner beauties of light into their sevenfold differentiation—red, orange, yellow, green, blue, indigo, violet. So, in the Cross of Christ do we see a sevenfold refraction of the truth that "God is light". All in one, yet all distinguished, we see the infinite righteousness, omnipotence, truth, immutability, holiness, wisdom, and love of God.

Finally, the rainbow speaks of the Cross as *the great sign of mercy after judgment*. Ezekiel saw that rainbow above and beyond the judgments which were falling on his nation (Ezek. 1: 28). John saw it, too, above and beyond all the judgments which are yet to strike our earth (Rev. 4: 3). We, too, must see that rainbow. The Dyaks of Borneo call the rainbow "The King's Son". In their Bible, Revelation 4: 3 has, "And round about the throne there was, as it were, the King's Son in the sky."

"Oh, see God's lovely rainbow!" said Daddy to his tiny daughter. "Yes, Daddy, He must have done it with His left hand." "Whatever do you mean?" asked Daddy. "Well, Daddy, *Jesus* is on His *right* hand!" Amusing? Yet how true!—it is indeed because Jesus is *there* that the rainbow is *here*!

Crestfallen Doubters

"But we trusted that it had been He which should have redeemed Israel . . ."—Luke 24: 21.

THE account of the Emmaus walk is one of those gems of literature from which the lustre never pales. There is such an artless simplicity and transparent sincerity about it, and it so mirrors the experience of many among us who have passed through the gloom of doubt to the clear shining of faith, that its appeal is unwaning.

Certainly, those two crestfallen men, treading with leaden steps those three-score furlongs north-west of Judah's capital, picture to us *the sadness of doubt*. The first words of the risen but unrecognised Jesus, as He linked up with them, were, "What manner of communications are these that ye have one to another, as ye walk, and are *sad*?"

Those two men were *honest* doubters. Their doubt had nothing in it akin to the pooh-poohing oscillations of many present-day intellectual pedants. Nor did it have in it the headstrong stupidity of those who "doubt for doubting's sake". They would have been only too glad to believe; but in the sudden, shameful crucifixion of the One who had inspired their highest hopes, they had suffered a stunning reversal. There seemed no longer a foundation for their faith or hope; and because they were honest doubters they were sad men.

Such doubt is *always* sad. The sadness may be disguised (and people are clever at disguising it) but it is there. Those men and women who are in real doubt about God, about Christianity, and about the vital concerns of the soul, are seldom if ever happy people. Doubt may have other gloomy by-products, such as dumbness, moroseness, irresoluteness; but its most general pathos is sadness.

This sadness of doubt *is not surprising*. Faith is the very life of man's spiritual nature. What blood is to the body, faith is to the soul. We are so constituted that until the mind can rest itself by faith in guaranteed certainties there is no real joy for us. Apart from an intelligent faith in God, in the fundamental goodness and ultimate rightness of things, deep peace and bounding gladness are impossible to us; for life in its present scheme is full of distressful enigmas which obstinately baffle disentanglement.

There is a difference, of course, between doubt and unbelief. Doubt is a state of *suspense* in which the mind is not made up either to believe or reject. Unbelief is a definite attitude of *negation*. There are many who think to escape the sad suspense of doubt by deciding definitely not to believe; but unbelief is as unsatisfying as doubt, for it is a negative blank, and therefore *sterile*. Oh, had those two men known it—Jesus was risen and with them! Doubt was needless. Nor need *we* doubt Him today. He is just as really with you and me.

The walls of Jericho fell flat
  At Israel's mighty shout;
But no one ever shouts like that
  While paralysed by doubt.
Lord, turn our doubt and leaden tread
To leaping, joyous faith instead!

"Did not our heart burn within us as He talked with us by the way?"—Luke 24:32.

TAKE another look at those two Emmaus wayfarers. We can sympathetically enter into their sadness. They had "followed the gleam". They had learned at the lips of One who was "mighty in deed and word before God and all the people" (19) and who had seemed to augur wonderful things for the future. Yet now, He who was the object of their implicit trust had been shamefully crucified, and their dearest hopes were buried in His grave. What though certain of the women had supposedly seen a vision of angels which said He was risen? Who could believe such an idea, even though some of the men had later found the grave empty? The one stark fact remained that "*Him* they saw not" (24). There was an "aching void" in those two men as they trudged to Emmaus.

But oh, what a transformation came to them ere that day expired! They were lifted right over from the sadness of doubt to *the gladness of faith* (read verses 30 to 35 again). Get the picture of those two men as they hurry back to Jerusalem to break the news there, that Jesus was really risen and had appeared to them. See the light of new confidence gleaming in their eyes. See the radiant eagerness of men who bear superlative good-tidings. The mist of doubt has been wiped from their eyes. Limping doubt has become leaping faith. The wilderness has blossomed as the rose. Instead of the thorn has come the fir tree. The oil of joy has banished mourning, and the garment of praise replaces heaviness!

Theirs was now the gladness of *certainty*. They had seen and known and communed with their Lord. There was not the shadow of a doubt: the Lord was risen; they had met Him, and they *knew*.

Theirs was also the gladness of *fellowship*. On arriving at Jerusalem they found all the others rejoicing in *their* proofs that the Lord was "risen indeed". It is wonderful to us, when we come into the joy of faith in Christ, to find this bond of glad understanding with others who know Him.

Finally, note how the *transition* from sad doubt to glad faith came about. First, it was through the testimony of *Scripture* (27). Our Lord did not scatter their doubt by one transporting word. He "expounded" the Scriptures so that they might see the Cross in the whole sweep of the divine purpose. He knew that in a fuller apprehension of the Scriptures doubt would fly. Second, it was through their *welcoming* Him (29). Third, it was through a direct revealing of our Lord Himself, so that "they knew Him" (30, 31). It was *that* which crowned the proof and gave them "joy unspeakable". Did you ever read William Cowper's poem on *Conversation*? He thus describes the end of that Emmaus walk:

The humble Stranger soon became their guest,
And, made so welcome at their simple feast,
He blessed the bread, but vanished at the word,
And left them both exclaiming, "'Twas the Lord!
Did not our hearts feel all He deigned to say?
Did not they burn within us by the way?"

The Sadness of Doubt

"Not all men have faith."—2 Thess. 3 : 2.

YESTERDAY we were speaking about the sadness of doubt. May we add further notes here? A couple of generations ago, no one man disturbed general faith in the Christian religion more than the renowned philosopher-author, David Hume. After years of supposedly scientific doubting and denying, what comfort did his sceptical philosophy afford him? Here are his own words: "I am appalled at the forlorn solitude in which I am placed by my philosophy; and I begin to fancy myself in the most deplorable condition imaginable, environed by the deepest darkness." Poor, brilliant Hume! A writer, quoting this confession of Hume, well says, "Any man who, like Hume, regards himself as nothing but a bundle of natural forces and impressions which is to be unbound and scattered to the winds by death, who denies that there is any evidence for the existence of the soul after death, or for the existence of God, must abide in a solitude which is indeed forlorn."

Many of us, in the philosophy class, had to encounter the brilliant mind of John Stuart Mill. Was there ever a keener logician or more intellectual reasoner? Yet as regards Christianity, God, the soul, the beyond, he aligned his "much learning" with the unbelievers. A regretful commentator on him sadly writes, "The talent and success of John Stuart Mill make more distressing the periods of despondency in his early manhood, and the loneliness of his later years. His wife dies, and he tells his heart this is the end. He buries her, not her body only, but herself. She has ceased to be. He has no religion but his memory of her; no hope but of annihilation."

Some years ago, a well-known, avowed atheist wrote: "I am not ashamed to confess that with this virtual negation of God, the universe to me has lost its soul of loveliness. Moreover, when I think, as at times I must, of the appalling contrast between the hallowed glory of that creed which once was mine, and the lonely mystery of existence as now I find it, at such times I shall ever feel it impossible to avoid the sharpest pang of which my nature is susceptible."

Yes, doubt, scepticism, unbelief, are false refuges. We have spoken truly in saying that doubt is *sad*. The late F. W. Robertson described the final misery of the doubter as that of "one who has felt the ice cracking beneath his feet, and finds himself on a single ice-block, severed, alone, and drifting out into freezing darkness". In view of the repeatedly vindicated bases of our Christian faith, it is puzzling to us that such deep doubt can be; but we must accept the fact of it, and should daily pray for the spiritual enlightenment of those who doubt or deny.

The late R. A. Torrey did not believe there was any *real* atheism, despite all outward profession of it. He used to say, "The truth is, men hope, by denying God's existence, to shield themselves from the discomfort of His acknowledged presence." I wish I could concur; but of this I *am* sure, that atheism never made anyone really *happy*. Many have thought that atheism would give them mental freedom from a binding idea. The real motive has been selfish rebellion against a sense of accountability. Always they have found atheism a *false* freedom—freedom from truth, to slavedom in darkness. Their palace has proved a dungeon. Yes, we may well pray for such!

Those Two Men

"And, behold, there talked with Him two men, which were Moses and Elias."—Luke 9: 30.

THE sudden appearance of Moses and Elijah, on the mount, is full of informing surprise. First, here is "proof by demonstration" of *life after death*. Years ago, in studying historical philosophy, I could not help being depressed by the fog of incoherence concerning the Beyond. In contrast, the Bible gives divinely guided and guarded teaching on life after death, not only by stating it, but by *showing* it, as in this sudden reappearance of Moses and Elijah.

Second, Moses and Elijah were alive as *individuals*. There is nothing here of Hindu "karma" issuing in a "nirvana" of self-extinction by absorption into infinite, impersonal Brahma. Nor is there anything of Buddhist "karma" gradually achieving a far-off emancipation in beatific oblivion. Nor is there anything akin to the unbiblical illusions of misnamed "Christian Science". Moses and Elijah are alive yonder as separate individuals.

Third, they appeared on that summit as continuing *personalities*. Moses was still Moses; and Elijah was still Elijah. There was personal identity and recognisable differentiation, so that Peter, James and John immediately knew which was which.

Fourth, Moses and Elijah were still alive as *human beings*. They did not have wings. They had not become cherubim or angels! They had evidently remained human. So did our Lord Himself, after *His* death and resurrection, as evidenced in His post-resurrection appearances to the disciples.

Fifth, they were alive *consciously*. Nothing here of soul-sleep, unless the two Old Testament worthies were walking and talking in their sleep! If they *were*, it is strange that they both walked on to that mountain top at the same moment, and both were talking in their sleep about the same subject! The soul-sleep theory just cannot live in the light of that transfiguration mount.

Sixth, Moses and Elijah appeared in *glorified bodies*; bodies which could suddenly appear or disappear; bodies similar to, yet different from, those which Moses and Elijah had possessed on earth; similar in structure, yet different in texture. They were bodies such as *we* shall have in the coming "first resurrection".

Seventh, Moses and Elijah, in their life beyond this, evidently enjoyed *fellowship*. The subject on which they now conversed with Jesus they must have discussed beforehand; and they thus indicate that similarly *all* our departed Christian loved ones are in fellowship with each other yonder.

Eighth, Moses and Elijah were intelligently *in touch with earth*. On that mount they talked with Jesus of "His decease which He should accomplish at Jerusalem". Heaven as well as earth awaited the Cross. And are not *all* the departed in Christ alive to concerns on earth, especially matters of salvation? Do they not pray for us? Is their ministry as priests in Christ aborted at death? Is there a thick cloud of ignorance flung between them and us? Moses and Elijah seem to imply the very opposite! Perhaps, in the consummation yet to be, we shall be astonished at what we owe to the prayers of departed Christian loved ones.

More about the Two Men

"And, behold, there talked with Him two men, which were Moses and Elias."—Luke 9: 30.

THE supreme thing about the sudden appearance of Moses and Elijah on that transfiguration mount was *their testimony to our Lord Jesus*. Among the outstanding figures of Israelite history, Moses was the most venerable, and Elijah the most dramatic. The two main parts of the Jewish Scriptures were the Law and the Prophets. Moses, the law-giver, represented the Law. Elijah, the prophet-reformer, represented the Prophets. In Moses and Elijah, Jewish history and Scripture unite in bearing witness to Jesus as the Lamb-Lion of Messianic prediction. Moreover, suddenly emerging from the invisible realm, on that mountain top, they unite all the godly departed in the Beyond with all the godly still on earth, in gratefully bearing witness to the Saviour's Cross which accomplishes eternal salvation for us all.

Note again (verse 31) that Moses and Elijah "spake" with Jesus "of His *decease* which He should accomplish at Jerusalem". The word "decease" here is, literally, *exodus*. Moses had led the great exodus from Egypt. Elijah had led a great exodus from apostasy. But the supreme exodus was that spiritual and eternal exodus from the guilt and power of sin which Jesus was to "accomplish" for millions by His Calvary death and triumphant resurrection.

See now how remarkable is this testimony of Moses and Elijah to Jesus when linked up with other New Testament references. Travel on to Luke's account of our Lord's resurrection. When the women found the stone rolled away, and entered the sepulchre, "Behold, *two men* stood by them in shining garments . . . and said, Why seek ye the living among the dead? He is not here, but is risen . . ." (Luke 24: 4–7). Travel on now to the ascension narrative in Acts. "And while they looked stedfastly toward heaven as He went up, behold, *two men* stood by them in white apparel, which also said, 'Ye men of Galilee, why stand ye gazing up into heaven? This same Jesus shall so come again in like manner as ye have seen Him go into heaven'." And now travel on to Revelation 11: 1–12, "And I will give power unto My *two witnesses*, and they shall prophesy a thousand two hundred and threescore days, clothed in sackcloth. . . . If any man will hurt them, fire proceedeth out of their mouth and devoureth their enemies. . . . These have power to shut heaven, that it rain not in the days of their prophecy [Elijah]; and have power over waters to turn them to blood, and to smite the earth with plagues" [Moses].

Here then is a wonderful link-up. Those "two men", Moses and Elijah, bear witness on the mount to our Saviour's redeeming *death* on the Cross. They bear witness in the sepulchre to His *resurrection*. On the brow of Olivet they attest His *ascension* and bear advance-testimony to His personal, visible, and still future *second-coming*. In Revelation 11 they testify amid the "great tribulation" immediately before the actual, overwhelming *descent* of our Lord to Armageddon and millennial empire. Above all, let this witness of Moses and Elijah to Jesus graphically exhibit how concerned are all the intelligences of heaven in the vast subject of human salvation. See also 1 Peter 1: 12. Can we ourselves be less concerned? Like Moses and Elijah, let us keep pointing to "Jesus only".

"In such an hour as ye think not, the Son of Man cometh."—Matt. 24 : 44.

THESE words refer to our Lord's still-future second coming, and are a warning against presumption. The warning is only too necessary, for the human heart seems incurably prone to this folly of presuming in such matters. The unconverted are forever presuming that they can be saved at their own time and in their own way, instead of in God's time and way; and at this very hour the dark vaults of Hades are full of remorseful souls who perished by such presuming. Nor are believers immune from it. We allow wrong thoughts, words, habits, secretly indulging the idea: "Well, I'm saved; a few doubtful things don't matter. All will be well in the end." Thus we presume to "sin that grace may abound".

However, although our text refers specifically to the Second Advent, it also exemplifies a general characteristic of our Lord's dealings with us; and viewed in that light it is full of *comfort*. There are trial-worn Christian hearts fearing what a day may bring forth. To all such our text says, "In such an hour as ye think not, the Son of Man cometh."

We find a commentary on this in *the record of the past*. Examine the narratives of God's dealings with His people. Again and again, just when the battle has seemed lost, just when the situation has seemed hopeless, just when the worst has seemed inevitable, and God the least concerned, the Lord has come, the tables have been turned, defeat has given place to victory, the saints have been saved, and God glorified! How vividly we see this as Moses stands electrified before that unexpected Voice from the flaming bush of Horeb; and again in the Esther drama, with Hitler-Haman the Jew-baiter dangling on the very gallows he has prepared for Mordecai! How clearly we see it again in the Lord's raising of Lazarus after four days entombment, and in His walking the waves to the storm-exhausted disciples in the fourth watch of the night!

We find further illustration of this in our *experience of the present*. There are seasons when we lose the sense of our Saviour's presence. We wander in the gloom of a spiritual eclipse. We mourn sore like lonely doves. Or like Solomon's Shulamith we wearily sigh, "Where is my Beloved?" Or like desolate Job we groan, "Oh, that I knew where I might find Him!" We long to hear His voice again, and to feel His strong arms around us. But even the Bible seems strangely dumb, and prayer seems only to echo our mournings in empty space. We wonder why. But just when it seems we are deserted, the clouds break, the sun bursts through, the mists evaporate, the flowers appear on the earth, and the time of the singing-birds has come.

It is the same sometimes in relation to things temporal and material. Hard circumstances hem us in until, like poor, distracted Jacob, we can only moan, "All these things are against me." The wolf of poverty licks his hungry lips at our door. Sickness flings its gaunt shadows over the home. Testings fall on us like the strokes of a scourge. We are in dire straits: the sea lies before us, the Egyptians are behind. Just *then*, the unexpected happens: the sea divides; adversaries are drowned; we break into song. "In such an hour as ye think not, the Son of Man cometh"!

In Such an Hour

"In such an hour as ye think not, the Son of Man cometh."—Matt. 24:44.

YES, as we were saying yesterday, it happens again and again, in both spiritual and material concerns: "In such an hour as ye think not, the Son of Man cometh." Troubled, tried and tested believer, take comfort. God not only answers prayers, He guides lives, and often educates His saints in strange-seeming ways.

Almost insensibly we fall into thinking of Him as "the God of the dead" (Matt. 22:32) who did great things for the saints of long ago, but is now "resting from His labours". No, He is also "the God of the living". Our Lord is the living Contemporary of this twentieth century. He mingles with us in our crowded thoroughfares, and speaks to us in life's solitudes. He sees, He knows, He loves, He cares, He plans. His eye is still on the sparrow. He still lights the evening star. He still paints the wayside flower. He still keeps vigilant watch over us, especially in our temptations and tribulations, our quandaries and dilemmas; and "in such an hour as we think not, the Son of Man cometh".

He never fails the soul that trusts in Him.
  He never fails.
Tho' disappointments come, and hope burns dim,
  He never fails.
Tho' trials surge like angry seas around,
And testings fierce, like ambushed foes abound,
Yet this my soul with millions more has found,
  He never fails.

But of course our text looks specially *to the future*. It is both a promise and a warning: "In such an hour as ye think not, the Son of Man cometh." There have always been the date-fixers and scaremongers who have said, "He will certainly come by such and such a day"; but the day has come and gone without the advent trumpet sounding; and the prognosticators have been exposed as presuming false prophets. There are those who say He *must* come within the next five years, or the next ten years, or the next twenty years. There are those who say He *cannot* come this year, next year, or until certain prophesied signs have appeared. Both groups are presuming. "In such an hour as *ye think not*, the Son of Man cometh."

What a blessing it is that we do not know the day! If we knew, what different reactions there would be by different types of persons! Some would take it as a license for sinning with safety up to a day or two beforehand. Others perhaps would feel it scarcely worth while continuing to work or to live normally. The fact is, we just do not know either "the day or the hour" of His sudden descent. Let us keep our lamps trimmed and burning. Let us stand as men who watch for the dawn. Let us be faithful stewards, ever remembering our Master's words, "Occupy till I come." Let us think nothing, say nothing, do nothing, which we would not like to be thinking or saying or doing when He comes. Let us go to no place where we would not like to be found when He comes. "In such an hour as ye think not, the Son of Man cometh."

"Lovest thou Me? . . . Feed My sheep . . . Follow Me."—Jn. 21 : 15, 17, 19.

LIVING or dying, if we are Christ's, what is the deepest desire of our hearts? Is it not to please Him and to serve Him? And is not this our loveliest incentive to serve Him, that He who lives to be our King once died to be our Saviour? What then are the fundamental qualifications for serving Him? Well, there may be many qualifications which are incidental, ornamental, or subsidiarily useful, but there are three which are indispensable and prior to all others. They are the three which stand out in our Lord's heart-to-heart talk with Peter, in John 21.

First comes, "*Lovest thou Me?*" Three times the risen Master asks Simon, "Lovest thou Me?" Everything hinged on the answer to that. Everything hinges on *our* answer to it. Everything is determined by the degree to which we really love our Lord Jesus. The first thing which makes a true Christian minister or missionary or evangelist or preacher or Sunday School teacher, or leader or Christian worker of any kind, is not learning, not eloquence, not wisdom, not organising ability, not pleasing personality, not even a "passion for souls", but a love-passion for Jesus Himself. Nothing, *nothing*, *NOTHING*, can take the place of that. All else without that is like withered flowers.

The second thing which makes a true servant of the Lord is a sense of *ordination by Christ*. Three times our Lord responded to Peter's avowal of love: "Feed my lambs"; "Tend my sheep"; "Feed my sheep". Did you ever read *Down in Water Street*, the story of the Water Street Rescue Mission, New York? One night, years ago, there staggered into that mission a drunken criminal named Sam Hadley, who there and then became truly converted and morally revolutionised. Later, that same Sam Hadley became the Leader of the Water Street Mission, where he did a simply amazing work for Christ. Hundreds of sotted drunkards and blackened criminals were saved and transformed; and when Sam Hadley died, he had one of the biggest funerals ever seen in America. Let me tell you what he says about his ordination to Christian service. On the night when he was converted, he had just suffered his third bout of delirium tremens. He had one hundred and twenty-five forgeries against his name on one firm alone, and a list of crimes enough to put him in prison for the rest of his life. But at his conversion he became so wonderfully saved, that the very taste for drink and the lust for crime were plucked right out of his nature in one tremendous deliverance. That very night Christ gave him his commission to preach. Sam Hadley's own words shall tell it:

"I went out into the street, and looked up to the sky. I don't believe I had looked up for ten years. A drunken man never looks up; he always looks down. It was a glorious, star-lit night, and it seemed to me that I could see Jesus looking at me out of a million eyes. . . . That night, right on the corner of Broadway and Thirty-Second Street, I was ordained to preach the everlasting Gospel, and have never doubted it for an instant. I have never stood before an audience without that vision inspiring me." It is a great thing to have a sense of direct commission from Christ Himself, to have "the ordination of the pierced Hand". We should seek to know it; and a waiting on Him in prayer will surely bring it, if we are in the line of His will.

Are You Following?

"Lovest thou Me? . . . Feed My sheep . . . Follow Me."—Jn. 21 : 15, 17, 19.

CONTINUING our meditation of yesterday, we point out that the third thing which makes a true servant of our Lord is an obedient *following* of Him, wherever He leads us. After our Lord had asked Peter that question three times, "Lovest thou Me?" and had spoken that re-ordination three times, He added, "*Follow Me*". Peter then asked (and how Peter-like it was!) "Lord, what shall *this* man (i.e. John) do?" To which our Lord replied, "What is that to thee? *Follow thou Me.*"

How meaningful it all seems! Three times, "Lovest thou Me?"; then three times a new ordination; then twice, "*Follow Me*". Yes, this obedient following, prayerfully, willingly, lovingly, daily, is the third of these vital prerequisites to true Christian service. It is the servant who thus "follows" who receives the daily anointing with heavenly unction, and is "endued with the power from on high" for special exploits. Closely following is not always easy. Sometimes it is hard indeed to the "flesh", for there are crucifixions come to us in the wake of those beloved sandal-prints. But its rewards utterly outweigh all else; and the fellowship which it brings with our Lord is a sweet foretaste of heaven.

For many of us, this willingness to follow *utterly* is the centre-point, the sensitive nerve of our love to Christ. The "self" in us will yield up anything else—money, time, comforts, yes *any*thing else, if only it can dodge yielding up self-management and self-direction. There is no substitute, however, for this utter yielding and following, because there is no equivalent; nor is there anything which brings such a heartfelt realisation of oneness with our dear Lord.

"Wilt thou follow Me?" the Saviour asked.
The road looked bright and fair,
And aflame with eager hope and zeal,
I replied, "Yes; anywhere!"

"Wilt thou follow Me?" I almost blanched,
The road now fearsome grew;
But I felt His love-grip on my hand;
And I answered, "Yes, right through."

"Dost thou follow still?" His tender tone,
Mid the storm-clash thrilled my heart;
And I knew in a way before unknown,
We should never, never part!

Note that the first time Jesus exhorts Peter to follow Him He uses only the two words, "Follow Me", whereas the second time He adds a further word, "Follow *thou* Me". Peter had expressed curiosity about the future of John. There is gentle but firm rebuke as our Lord now adds, "What is that to thee? Follow *thou* Me". It is easy to let curiosity concerning other servants of the Lord divert us from closely following Him ourselves. Our first concern must ever be our own individual obedience.

The Determining Factor

"Lovest thou Me? . . . Feed My sheep . . . Follow Me."—Jn. 21 : 15, 17, 19.

WELL, there it is: "Lovest thou Me?" . . . "Feed My sheep" . . . "Follow Me." But "Lovest thou Me?" comes first, for it determines all else. When our love to Christ is what it should be, everything else falls into just its right place.

This is true in the matter of our *separation*. When we really love Him, do we allow worldly pleasures, unworthy practices, social compromises, in our lives? When we really love Him, as the first and dearest love of our hearts, does the renunciation of *any*thing unworthy or questionable greatly pain us? However hard any such renunciation may be to "the flesh", if our love to Christ is the supreme thing in us, it so overrides "the flesh" as to make even the hard easy. To have to live the separated life because we *must*, as a Christian obligation, is always irksome; but to live the separated life because we *may*, as an expression of love to our heavenly Bridegroom, transforms duty into joyous privilege.

The same is true as regards our *consecration*. When we really love Him above all else, is there anything we would knowingly keep from Him? Could we ever say, "Lord Jesus, Son of God, who lovedst me, and gavest Thyself for me, I love Thee more than I love any other on earth or in heaven; but I am not prepared to give myself unreservedly to Thee"? No, we want the entire territory of our personalities to be under the sway of His sceptre. He must have the throne, and wear the crown!

And the same is true as regards our *sanctification*. Whatever may be our theory of sanctification or holiness, it is practically spurious unless it floods and sways the heart with love to *Him*. On the other hand, even though we know nothing of such theories as "eradication" or "counter-action", if our hearts love Him so dearly as to yield Him everything, then without our struggling and "claiming the blessing", He fills us with His sanctifying Holy Spirit; "perfect love casteth out fear" (1 Jn. 4: 18); we are in the promised land, and we find ourselves singing,

> I've reached the land of corn and wine.
> Its riches all are freely mine!

Oh, yes, our *love* to Him is the really determining thing. Let us pause to hear again His searching but heart-drawing question, deep in our consciousness: "Lovest thou Me?" Then, let us linger again over the lovely mystery of *His* unquenchable, exquisite love for *us*. Then, let us pray again with utter meaning,

> Break through my nature, mighty, heavenly love;
> Clear every avenue of thought and brain.
> Flood my affections, purify my will;
> Let nothing but Thine own pure life remain.
>
> Thus, wholly mastered, and by Thee possessed,
> Forth from my life, spontaneous and free,
> Shall flow a stream of tenderness and grace,
> Loving because *Thy* love now lives in *me*.

Grapes of Eshcol!

"If ye then be risen (lit. were raised) with Christ, seek those things which are above, where Christ sitteth on the right hand of God. Set your affection on things above, not on things on the earth. For ye are dead, and your life is hid with Christ in God. When Christ who is our life shall appear, then shall ye also appear with Him in glory."—Col. 3: 1–4.

HAVE you heard of the grapes of Eshcol, rich and red with the wine of Canaan? Well, here is a choice cluster from the vintage of our *spiritual* Canaan in Christ. See here the three *tenses* of our union with God's dear Son:

Past — "Ye were raised with Christ."
Present — "Your life is hid with Christ in God."
Future — "Ye shall appear with Him in glory."

Do you notice that in each case it is "with Christ"? All comes through union with Him. And do you observe the three *aspects* of this union?—"*raised*" from death; "*hid*" in God; "*revealed*" in glory. Did ever a more staggering wonder flow through pen and ink? It is a heart-moving epitome of the true Christian life: its origin—"raised with Christ"; its source—"in God"; its consummation—"glory"!

Think for a moment of the past tense: "Ye were raised with Christ." This spiritual resurrection is a positive *fact*, and no mere theory, in the experience of every true Christian. Every genuine conversion to Christ is a spiritual resurrection. See John 5: 25.

This spiritual resurrection is the *primary* fact of our new life. There is no living before rising. Too many people are in church membership and service today who have no real qualification for either, because they are still spiritually dead. Natural goodness and religious sincerity are mistaken for spiritual life. What delusion is thus fostered! Classes are held to "educate" persons for church membership. But without conversion such classes are a deceptive superfluity. You cannot educate the dead to life!

Again, this spiritual resurrection is an *abiding* fact. "Christ, being raised from the dead, dieth no more" (Rom. 6: 9). Neither do we! Even though natural life ebbs from our bodies at our demise, our spiritual life is not aborted; it continues in heaven; and at our Lord's Parousia even the disintegrated body shall be reassembled to share our unquenchable resurrection-life in Christ.

Dear believer, is not this more to you than riches of earth or treasures of ocean, or garlands of temporal popularity? Think again of all it means to you. Let it give wings of rejoicing to your spirit, whatever your present circumstances may be. It is a big and blessed thing indeed to be saved, and to be in such indissoluble union with the Son of God. We have already had *one* resurrection morning: *another* is coming by and by!

From the glory-lit skies will the Saviour descend!
Sleeping bodies arise, and, transfigured, ascend!
Oh, the utter surprise! oh, the joy without end!
When the Saviour returns for His own!

Two Prepositions

"For ye are dead, and your life is hid with Christ in God."—Col. 3 : 3.

IN this Colossian epistle, we may well linger over the two little prepositions, "with" and "in", as they express our union with Christ. The former always expresses our union with Christ in the sense of *identification* with Him. The latter seems to express it in the sense of *position and possession* in Him.

"Dead"	*with* Christ.
"Buried"	*with* Christ.
"Quickened"	*with* Christ.
"Risen"	*with* Christ.
"Hid"	*with* Christ.
"Appear"	*with* Christ.

Did *He* die? So did we by identification with Him. Was He buried? So have *we* been, and the old way of life is gone. Was He quickened again from death? So are we quickened to newness of life through our identification with Him. Was He raised? So are we. Is He now hidden and invisible? So are we, insofar as our true life is concerned. Will He yet "appear in glory"? So shall we, "*with* Him". All these experiences which we see objectively in Him have their counterpart subjectively in ourselves through our identification with Him.

On the other hand, that preposition, "in", expresses our *position and possession* in Christ. The believer is

a "saint"	*in* Christ (1 : 2)
has "faith"	*in* Christ (1 : 4)
is "reconciled"	*in* Christ (1 : 22)
has "redemption"	*in* Christ (1 : 14)
is to "walk"	*in* Christ (2 : 6)
is "complete"	*in* Christ (2 : 10)

Oh, this Christ-believer union is wonderful! In varying aspect and metaphor it recurs throughout the New Testament, and gives us joy beyond telling. It is everlastingly indissoluble. Our Beloved is ours and we are His for ever. Heaven's undying rapture will consist in the consummation and continuity of this oneness with Him. Oh, to give Him, here and now, the full revenue of His blood-bought estate in us!—our uttermost devotion as expressed by separatedness to Him, communion in prayer, and humble serving. And all the while let us remember that our *true* life is "*hid*" with Him *in God*!

Our joint-possession with Christ is a doctrine at which we can only marvel perpetually. It could never have been invented; and it is too amazing not to be true. A young woman in New York once wrote: "Yesterday, I was worth fifty dollars. Today I am worth millions." She had married a millionaire, and they had a common purse. She continued, "But what are all our millions, compared with my beloved himself?" Finally, she added, "What was *my* bit to *him*? Yet he said it meant more than all his millions, *if my heart came with it*."

The Hidden Life

"Your life is hid with Christ in God."—Col. 3: 3.

It is a remarkable circumstance that those things which are most prized seem most hidden. This is so in the *physical* world. Gold, that metal most coveted and alluring, hides deep in the bosom of the earth. The diamond, most valuable of precious stones, lies hidden in the alluvial deposit. The emerald hides deep in the granite vein. The pearl lies down below the tropical waters of Madagascar and Mexico, and sometimes in the very body of the pearl-oyster.

The same is true of the *mental* realm. The deepest and purest emotions are hidden, inasmuch as outward action ever falls short of thought. The faith, the love, the richest virtues of a noble soul are never fully disclosed in speech or conduct. The more profound the emotion, the more hidden it is, so that the deepest love can sometimes only "love and be silent".

This is also true of the *spiritual* sphere. There is something deeper in man than the mental. Besides the *pseuchē*, or mind, there is the *pneuma*, or spirit. Fundamentally, the basis of human personality is spiritual, and because of this it is a mystery which eludes the inmost penetration of psychological enquiry and defies ultimate definition.

But pre-eminently this hiddenness is true of that *new life* which we Christian believers possess in Christ—that new spiritual life which the Holy Spirit imparted to us when by faith we became savingly united to the Son of God. It is the hidden life of Christ Himself which is introduced into our being. It is a life with motives other than those of this world; with heavenly aspirings and affinities unintelligible to earthly minds; a life replenished by hidden manna and secret springs; a life which in all its sources and resources is "hid with Christ in God".

This new life is our most precious secret. It is neither understood nor recognised by the world. "The world knoweth us not" (1 Jn. 3: 1). "He that is spiritual . . . is discerned of no man" (1 Cor. 2: 15). But those of us who possess it know its reality. It is not something which we merely carry *about* us, as one may carry *religion*; it is hidden within us, beyond any possibility of being destroyed by the sword of any earthly slayer.

Once when looking round a museum in the north of England, I saw an imitation of the Sanci diamond. That diamond was named after Sanci, a French nobleman. He sent the gem by a messenger to Henri IV of France; but the messenger was assassinated while on his journey. The corpse, however, was afterward found, and opened, whereupon the diamond was discovered in the stomach, having been swallowed by the faithful servant! Mere religion is like carrying a gem simply on one's person—and there are many robbers! But those who possess the inliving Christ have the glorious Jewel of the ages actually within them! The life is hid *within* us; it is also "hid with Christ *in God*"; so we are doubly safe!

Long ago, a royal despot tried to terrify a Christian who was dragged before him. "Do you not know I can take your life away?" With calm respect the Christian replied, "O king, you are wrong. You may kill my body; my true life you cannot touch; it is hid with Christ in God." Did not our Lord say, "Fear them not which kill the body?" Did He not say, "Where your treasure is, there will your heart be also"? And is not our treasure *there*—"with Christ in God"?

"Your life is hid with Christ in God."—Col. 3: 3.

THE tense of the verb here repays observation. It says much more in the original than our English present tense. To bring out its full import would require the rather cumbersome translation, "Your life *has been* and *still is* hid with Christ in God". It is the Greek "perfect" tense, which indicates a completed action with a resultant condition. "Your life has been"—there is the definite act. "And still is"—there is the resultant condition or abiding effect.

Think first, then, about the definite *act* whereby our true life as Christian believers has been "hid in God".

We are "hid in God" by the eternal will of the *Father*. It is the product of His electing love toward us "from before the foundation of the world". Ephesians 3 tells us that the spiritual Church was a "mystery" or sacred secret which "from the beginning of the world hath been *hid* in God". Each member of it was hidden there, locked in the undivulged counsels and purposes of Heaven. The first Adam's unparadised posterity could not cleave their way back to the Eden of communion with God, but by act of eternal covenant God has elected to Himself the redeemed in Christ, hiding them in the mystery of His predestinating will, and in the love-life of His own boundless bosom.

Second, we are hid in God by the redeeming work of the *Son*. The first Adam dragged his descendants into sin and ruin; but in the miracle of the Incarnation the Son of God took our human nature to Himself in order to become the Second Adam, and redeem us from our wreckage in the first. Behold the mighty marvel! He takes our place, overcomes in our behalf, makes atonement for our sin, thus making possible the impartation of the Holy Spirit whereby He is able to share His own life and victory with believing men and women. He thus becomes the Author of a new line, a *re*generation, the "sons of God", who are made "new creatures" in Him. And now the new Man has ascended to the Father, as the Progenitor and Life-giver of His people, bearing with Him his glorified human nature and the true life of His regenerate people; so that our true life is *there*—"with Christ in God".

Third, we are hid in God by the renewing work of the *Holy Spirit*. That which is eternal in the will of the Father, and potential in the work of the Son, the Spirit makes actual in the soul of the believer. It is the Spirit who regeneratingly incorporates us into that true spiritual Church in which all the individual members receive their life from Christ the Head. Even the will of the Father and the work of the Son remain ineffective apart from the executive operation of the Spirit whereby we are united to Christ. Thus we are "hid with Christ in God" by the co-operative activity of the entire Trinity.

What dignity, grandeur, sacredness does this give to the Christian life! With what significance and deep preciousness does it invest it! How we ought to prize and treasure the work of grace which has been wrought within us! How we ought to nurture and attend the new life and nature which have been imparted to us by regeneration! God save us from cramped and little views of the Christian life! "Now are we the sons of God." His *life* is "in" us here. *Our* life is "in Him" *there*.

Hidden in Light

"Your life is hid with Christ in God."—Col. 3 : 3.

THERE is a peerless splendour in the concept of Christ, as the Life-bearer of His people, ascending up through the heavenly spheres, far above all principalities and powers, even to the throne and the very heart of God. But besides this there is the precious mystery of our *abiding* hiddenness with Christ in God. This is the inner secret of the believer's true life; and it is good to let our minds linger upon it, for its implications are gladdening and challenging in highest degree.

This being "hid with Christ in God" is no hiddenness in *darkness*. We are accustomed to associate hiddenness with darkness. We think of the "treasure hid in the field"; of the lazy servant's talent hidden underground; of the fugitives in the Apocalypse who endeavour to hide themselves "in the dens and rocks of the mountains"; and it is easy to connect the thought of hiddenness with darkness. Yet darkness is not indispensable to hiddenness, and certainly when we think of being hid "*in God*" it is utterly foreign. Not as the gold in the dark earth, or the diamond in the alluvial deposit, or the emerald in the thick granite, or the pearl in the ocean bed, is our true life hidden with Christ in God.

We are hidden *in light*. Light hides as well as darkness. The sun, that great ball of flaming gases which gives our solar system its coherence, cannot be properly seen because of its own flaming brilliance. Even so the glory of God is such that no man can see Him and live. Christ is hidden in "the light to which no man can approach". The glory-blaze envelops Him.

Some time ago, when hiking among the English Pennines, I climbed a high hill on which stands an old stone tower known as Hartshead Pike. The view, which usually repays the climb, was disappointing that day because of the dull, damp weather. A haze hung about the hills and obscured the view so that only a short distance could be seen before the landscape lost itself in the drizzly grey void. The tower—a landmark for miles around—seemed unusually high that day, standing up in the monotonous grey overhead; but on descending the hill a little way and looking round, I was surprised to see how quickly it was becoming obscured in the heavy atmosphere. Soon it was completely lost. So really *there*, yet so completely *hidden*, it seemed strikingly to illustrate the reality of our life "hid with Christ in God". But the comparison quickly broke down! That stone tower, indistinct and blurred and finally lost in the chill haze, was no parallel with the ascended Christ bearing our life into the noon-tide splendour of the third Heaven! The Christ who is "our life" did not become vaporized away into some dark void! He is engulfed in the glory of the heaven of heavens; and our life is hid with Him *there*, in that splendour ineffable.

But if this life is *in* us here, how can it be away yonder? Let our solar system illustrate. The sun is 93,000,000 miles away. It is there, not here. Yet see that wayside flower. The same sun is in that flower, and in all the myriad flowers around the earth; or, rather, the sun's *life* is in them, without which they could not bloom. Even so, the heaven-imparted new life is in all Christian believers, yet in its derivation and sustenance it is "with Christ in God".

"When Christ who is our life shall appear, then shall ye also appear with Him in glory."—Col. 3 : 4.

THIS is our supreme hope. It will publicly consummate our identification with Christ. As we were "raised" with Him, and are now "hid" with Him, so eventually, at the glad trumpet-sounding, we shall "appear" with Him "in glory".

Two of the sorest complaints with many today are the silence of God and the non-appearance of Christ. "Let God speak; let Christ show Himself; then we will believe." Perhaps they *would* "believe" then, but it would be the mere believing of convinced reason, not the grateful faith of sin-burdened souls who accept Christ as Saviour and then sympathetically ally themselves with Him.

Many intellects will be confounded when Christ actually does appear according to promise; they will no longer be able to disbelieve in Him; yet will they therefore love and welcome Him? Nay, if they do not desire and love Him now, as the Saviour who bled for them on Calvary, will they do so when He comes to "rule them with a rod of iron"? "The demons also believe and tremble" (Jas. 2 : 19), but that is not saving faith!

It is to those of us who prize Him *now* that our Lord's reappearance is such a precious pledge. Already, as the text says, He is our very "life"; but when He suddenly re-emerges from invisibility, the true splendour of that life already in us will flame out from rapture of soul through supernalised bodies, suffusing us with a heavenly sheen, and transforming us into living replicas of our Lord Himself. It is good to compare Paul and John on this:

Colossians 3 : 1–4	*First John* 3 : 2
1. "Ye be risen with Christ."	"Now are we the sons of God."
2. "Your life is hid with Christ."	"It doth not yet appear what we shall be."
3. "When Christ who is our life shall appear, then shall ye also appear with Him in glory."	"When He shall appear, we shall be like Him."

Oh, for His appearing! We have already known the thirtyfold and sixtyfold of His lovingkindness in our present experience; but *then* there shall be the never-fading hundredfold of perfect fruition. The sun of our joy will be at endless meridian. The bride shall make herself ready, and the heavenly Bridegroom shall receive her, all-glorious, to Himself. His life within us will shine out with unhindered loveliness. "We shall appear with Him in glory." Oh, this triune marvel of our union with Christ!—"*Raised*" with Him, from the depths; and now "*hid*" with Him, in the heights; and ere long to "*appear*" with Him in "glory"!

As a flash of lightning, sudden, vivid, clear,
Robed in utter splendour, will our Lord appear.
One electric second! Lo, the saints are *there*—
Caught away to greet Him, in the shining air!
Instantly we "see" Him, "like Him" we shall be;
Then, our joy unending—His dear face to see!

Israel: Past, Present, Future

"Thus saith Jehovah, which giveth the sun for a light by day, and the ordinances of the moon and of the stars for a light by night. . . . If those ordinances depart from before Me, then the seed of Israel shall cease from being a nation before Me."—Jer. 31 : 35, 36.

Of all the stories ever written, the most wonderful are the story of the Jewish race, and the story of the Christian church. Both these stories are *true*; both are yet unfinished; both are filled with alternating triumph and tragedy; and both are to have a final chapter of glorious consummation.

What a story is that of the Covenant People, from Abraham, Isaac and Jacob onwards! Is there anything to match it in all the records of kingdoms and nations? Never was there such high calling with such deep sinning. Never was there such a covenant with such violation of it. Never was there such a theocracy dishonoured by such apostasy. Never was there such unique privilege with such big responsibility. Never was there such a divinely ordained national ministry and destiny, seemingly frustrated, but persevering through slowly unfolding millenniums, and divinely predetermined even yet to issue in a golden age of final realisation.

Never has any race or nation suffered such recurrent slaughterings and scatterings without becoming finally disintegrated into extinction. If they could have retained at least some small territorial foothold *somewhere* on earth, they might have had some semblance of a reason for their continuing survival; but for over two thousand years they have had no throne, no kingdom, no colony, no land, no city, no laws of their own. *Yet they are still here!* They have been hated, deprived, peeled, persecuted, suppressed, massacred, driven as helpless fugitives to the four winds. *Yet they are still here!* From the time of Xerxes (Ahasuerus) in 500 B.C., down to the demon-possessed Adolph Hitler of present times, maddened Jew-haters have determined to stamp them out completely. *Yet they are still here!*

And now, in this second half of the twentieth century, they are not only still here, but a large part of the world's financial wealth is in their hands; they are back in their own land—"Eretz Yizrael", with their own government, their own laws, their own coins, their own language, and their own preserved institutions. They have had no king of their own, nor have they had any self-government since the long-ago days of the Maccabees; yet now, after an historical hiatus of 2,300 years, they are again acknowledged by all the other nations of the earth as an independent, self-governing Jewish state! There has never been anything like it in all history. It is amazing—*amazing*.

And what does it say to you and me? It says that God is supreme in history—just as much so today as ever. It says that however much God may allow to happen in His present, *permissive* will, He overrules all permitted happenings so as ultimately to fulfil His *purposive* will. It says that God does not violate the free-will of men and nations, but allows them to learn even through self-incurred suffering, while at the same time He overrules all to a good end. Nothing can ultimately defeat God. His purpose always triumphs in the end. Meanwhile, "The goodness of God endureth continually" (Ps. 52 : 1). Even "if we are unfaithful, He abideth faithful" (2 Tim. 2 : 13). "This God is our God for ever and ever; He will be our guide even unto death" (Ps. 48 : 14).

The Church Through the Centuries

"The Church of the living God."—1 Tim. 3: 15.

WHAT a story is that of the organised, historical Christian church! Is there anywhere a comparable romance of truth stranger than fiction? What a contiguity of opposites—of heavenly minded exploit and carnal drama; of noble adventure and ignoble lapses; of orthodoxy and heterodoxy; of selfless spirituality and clerical avarice; of heroic martyrdoms and surreptitious manœuvrings; of triumph and tragedy; of periodic decline and glorious resurgence!

For sheer fascination I know nothing to excel it. Every Christian should read it, and know it in at least a general way. Yet how few there are who trouble to acquire more than vague snatches of the critical periods and dominating personalities between apostolic times and today!

The story runs in three main periods: (1) the *early* period, i.e. the first five centuries A.D.; (2) the *middle* period, i.e. A.D. 500 to 1600; (3) the *later* period, i.e. 1600 to the present.

Take the first of these, that is, the first five hundred years. Up to A.D. 300 Christianity was *on trial*. Its political environment was the Roman Empire. Its intellectual environment was the Greek hand-down from Socrates, Plato, and others. Its religious environment was Judaism and the "Mystery" religions. During this period the Christian faith withstood fiery trial, propagated itself irrepressibly, and triumphantly overcame.

Then, from 300 to 500, we see Christianity freely *at work*. The decree of Constantine ended all official persecution. Early Christian missions spread abroad, as represented by Gregory and his work in Armenia; Martin's going to the inhabitants of Gaul; Patrick's crossing to Britain and Ireland; and Columba's work in Iona.

From 500 to 900 we see Christianity *at bay*. There came the deadly heresy of the Nestorians in India, and the influence of Boniface in Germany; the rise and spread of Islam which pretty well obliterated a decadent Christianity in Africa, and threatened it everywhere.

From 900 to 1300 we see Christianity *compromised*. In Europe the "dark ages" set in, under the supremacy, political ambition, corruption and tyranny of the Roman church. Spread through two hundred years of this period we see the seven "Crusades", which attempted to conquer for Christianity by the sword, and ended in a failure which led to the rise of the Jesuits.

Then, from 1300 to 1600 we begin to see Christianity *revived*. The very corruptions of Rome at length provoked a shock of reaction which, under the fiery Luther and his fellow-reformers, accomplished what all the intellectualism of Erasmus failed to do, and brought the glorious Protestant Reformation.

And now, in this *later* period of the Church's history, we have seen and are still seeing all these phases re-enacted *under different circumstances*—Christianity on trial, at work, at bay, compromised, revived. But in a way heretofore unrealised, the process of expansion now sees the Christian Church encircle the globe. Of course the *real* church is a minority *within* the outward, organised church, and will continue indestructibly until the Lord Himself returns. Then the true Church will be the "Church Triumphant".

Forty Days and Ten

"Being seen of them forty days."—Acts 1 : 3.

THE Old Testament finds its fulfilments in the New, not only in the bigger, broader senses, but in many an incidental way too. Away back in Leviticus 23, we find that between the annual offering of the "firstfruits" and the later offering of the harvest wave-loaves, "seven sabbaths", or "fifty days", were to elapse; and both those offerings were to be made "on the morrow after the sabbath". The offering of the "firstfruits" found New Testament fulfilment in our Lord's resurrection (1 Cor. 15 : 20). That of the harvest wave-loaves found fulfilment at Pentecost. Our Lord's resurrection and the Spirit's coming at Pentecost both occurred on the first day of the week, the "morrow after the sabbath", with exactly "fifty days" between them. Those fifty days are highly significant; forty from our Lord's resurrection to His ascension; then ten more to Pentecost.

There seems to have been a sixfold purpose in those forty days between the resurrection and the ascension. Obviously our Lord's first intention was to *convince* the disciples that He was really alive again. Two or three sudden appearances, only, might have left room for later doubt; but to be "seen of them forty days", and daily to be "speaking" with them, destroyed the last vestige of doubt (Acts 10: 41).

Another intention of those forty days was to *instruct*. Our Lord was with them "speaking of the kingdom of God". Not only did He instruct them, He "opened their understanding" (Luke 24: 45).

Again, those forty days were used to *prepare* the disciples for intelligent witnessing, for team fellowship, for public leadership; and especially for our Lord's invisible control in the Church after His ascension.

Yet another purpose of those forty days was to *assure* the disciples that His presence was still with them even when they could not see Him. That is why He kept suddenly appearing and disappearing. It was to educate them in the realisation that He was with them always, even though unseen.

Another intention of those forty days was to *inspire* the disciples with missionary zeal. It was not for them "to know times or seasons", but they were to receive the power of the Spirit in order to their being witnesses "to the uttermost part of the earth".

Once more, those forty days were meant to *unite* them in holy purpose to "wait for the promise of the Father", even the "baptism in the Holy Spirit not many days hence".

Then, after our Lord's ascension, there followed the ten days of "one accord in prayer" (1 : 14); *and then the power fell!* Oh, how these things still speak to us! Look again at those first disciples—convinced of His resurrection; instructed in the Word; prepared for the Lord's control; assured of His real presence; inspired with missionary zeal; united in purpose; and now continuing "with one accord" in prayer. That is how Pentecost came; and that is how it still repeats itself in Christian fellowship today. Yes, the power fell on a prepared and praying group, and then "turned the world upside down". Let me say to myself again, "Jesus is really alive, and invisibly with me." Also, what about *my* being in a prayer-group, to pray *until* that power falls again?

The Mystic Marriage Union

"A great mystery . . . Christ and the church."—Eph. 5: 32.

THE New Testament uses various metaphors to express the union of Christ and the Church, but the most sacred is that of marriage. In a mystical sense, Christ is the Bridegroom and the Church His bride. Over against certain hyper-dispensationalists, we insist that Ephesians 5: 25–32 clearly teaches this. Verses 28–31 latently allude to Eve, the first of human wives. Taken from Adam's body, Eve was verily "of his flesh and of his bones" (30), but she was also "his wife" (31), which two facts together comprise a "mystery" expressing the union of Christ and the Church (32). The Old Testament furnishes illuminating type-aspects of the Church's mystical bridal relationship, in Eve, Rebecca, Asenath, Zipporah, and Shulamith.

How full of meaning is the metaphor as applied to the union between Christ and His people! In wedlock, husband and wife are one in *law*. As soon as both parties have subscribed to the marriage contract, the voice of special authority says, "I now pronounce them husband and wife". Similarly, in the eyes of the divine law, believers are "married to . . . Him who is raised from the dead" (Rom. 7: 4).

Next, in wedlock husband and wife become one in *name*. The bride foregoes her maiden name for the privilege of assuming her husband's. Even so, James 2: 7 reminds believers of "that worthy Name by which ye are called". Every true wife glories in her husband's name, if it is worthy, even when it is ill-used.

Again, in wedlock husband and wife are one in *love*. They are all to each other. "Christ loved the church, and gave Himself for it." "My Beloved is mine, and I am His." If the husband has done great things for his wife, her love is the more increased. Christ "gave *Himself*" to save and win *me*! How *I* ought to love *Him*!

But further, in ideal wedlock husband and wife are one in *service*. So is it with our Lord and His people: "Go into all the world . . . lo, I am with you."

Moreover, in ideal wedlock, husband and wife are one in *possessions*. So is it with the heavenly Bridegroom and ourselves (Jn. 17: 22; 1 Cor. 3: 21, 22; Eph. 1: 11).

Also, it is a remarkable fact, that in loving wedlock husband and wife often become one in *likeness*. There is "intergrade" in disposition and even in facial appearance. So is it, or should be, with us believers and our glorious Lord (2 Cor. 3: 18) until perfected in His likeness (1 Jn. 3: 2).

Last but not least, husband and wife are one in *home*. And our heavenly Bridegroom is even now preparing ours for us with Himself (Jn. 14: 3).

Meanwhile, what is the bride's true attitude? It is to be devoted to His interests; to delight in His will; to have no secret from Him; to long for His coming and the joys of that heavenly home.

And when my Saviour face to face I see,
When at His lofty throne I bow the knee,
Then of His love in all its breadth and length,
Its height and depth and everlasting strength,
My soul shall sing.

The Spirit is Speaking

"He that hath an ear, let him hear what the Spirit saith unto the churches."—Rev. 3 : 22.

AMONG the various New Testament injunctions to Christian believers concerning the Holy Spirit, not the least arresting is this one. It ends each of the seven letters to the seven churches of the Apocalypse, acquiring thereby a sevenfold solemnity. Let us here notice three things about it.

First, observe who is to *hear*: "He that hath ears." Not every one can hear. The unsaved, the unregenerate, cannot hear; they are spiritually deaf. They can no more hear this special speaking of the Spirit to the churches than a disconnected radio set can pick up the sound-waves from a broadcasting station. A further sad fact, however, is that even among Christian believers, not every one who *can* listen to the Spirit *does* listen to Him. That is why the injunction runs, "He that hath an ear, *let* him hear . . ." In this connection, many Christians are like radio or television sets which are tuned in but not turned on. One of our biggest needs today is that those who have "ears to hear" shall practice "listening in" again to the Spirit. That is how God-given initiative and direction come to organised Christian activity—without which much so-called religious effort is merely a "beating the air". Again and again it has been proved that those who kneel lowest and longest see clearest and farthest.

Second, observe who is to be *heard*: "the Spirit saith . . ." This is the one divine Spirit, coequal of the Father and the Son in the eternal Triunity. He is to be heard because He is *God*, and because He communicates the *will* of the Father and the Son. His voice is heard in the Scriptures, as in the seven letters to these seven churches; also directly in the soul, as it was by John who therefore penned those seven letters. The Scriptures are now completed. This present age is not that of further *inspiration*, but of Spirit-given *illumination* to those who "hear what the Spirit saith . . ."

Third, observe *what* is to be heard: "what the Spirit saith unto the churches". He speaks not to the world, but to believer-fellowships of New Testament pattern. He speaks to the "churches" (plural) not only to any one denomination. But He speaks through *individuals* in the "churches", for the injunction runs, "He that hath ears, let *him* hear . . ." Moreover, He is *still* speaking, and speaking *continually*, for the verb "saith" is in the present continuous tense. Doubtless, also, John meant in our text, "Let him hear [i.e. *heed*] what the Spirit saith through *me* . . ." None of ourselves today can claim inspiration in that *apostolic* sense; yet I shall not hesitate to claim in a subordinate way that the Spirit speaks through *me* as I now call *you*, dear reader, more than ever before to *"listen in" to the Spirit.*

In my opinion, the two worst breakdowns in modern Protestant Christendom are (1) the breakdown denominationally in attitude to the Bible; and (2) the breakdown individually in the practice of prayer. Intellectually, this is the age of uncertainty. Individually, this is the age of activity, hurry, and nervous tension. The strong current is *against* prayerfulness; yet the *need* for prayer is more urgent than ever.

The Heaven-sent Paraclete

"When the Comforter is come. . . ."—Jn. 15: 26.

WHEN our Lord began to apprise His disciples that His ministry on earth was nearing its end, and that soon He must leave them, their hearts were deeply disturbed. He consoled them, however, by revealing that after His own departure, "another Comforter" should come to them, even the Holy Spirit. What strange wonderings were evoked in their minds we do not know, but they would be impressed that our Lord used the most meaningful title for the soon-coming Holy Spirit. It was the word, *Paraklētos,* translated "Comforter". It means "One called alongside to help". What a significant name for the Holy Spirit!

Yes the Spirit is the Paraclete. He comes to "*abide*" with us (Jn. 14: 16); to *indwell* us (17). By Him our Lord indwells us (20). So does the Father (23). He comes to "teach" us (26); to bear witness in and through us (15: 27); to "convict" the world through us (16: 7, 8); and to "comfort" us in many other ways.

Because the Holy Spirit is God, equally with the Father and the Son, He is to be *worshipped* equally with them, and *prayed to* equally with them; for though the three Persons of the Triunity are distinguishable they are inseparable, co-eternal, co-equal. Any subordination of the Son to the Father, or of the Spirit to the Father and to the Son, is purely expedient in the plan of redemption, not fundamental.

Oh, this wonderful, ever-indwelling Paraclete! Obviously we are meant to pray to Him, listen to Him, commune with Him, be guided, taught, strengthened and comforted by Him, every hour, every moment. Ought we not make the very most of His wonderful companionship? If we are trustfully yielded, He will make His presence real and His voice heard deep in our consciousness. He will hear each reverent whisper of our minds.

In these later chapters of John, where our Lord unfolds His new teaching on the coming Paraclete, have you underscored the four "Ye shalls" which indicate the transforming effects which the Spirit's coming was to have for the disciples? The first comes in chapter 14: 19: "Because I live, *ye shall live also.*" Connect from verse 16—"Another Paraclete . . . He shall be *in* you . . . I will come to you . . . Because I live ye shall live also."

The second "Ye shall" comes in chapter 14: 20: "At that day *ye shall know* . . ." Know what? "That I am in the Father, and ye in Me, and I in you."

The third comes in chapter 15: 27: "*Ye shall bear witness.*" Take it with the preceding verse—"He shall bear witness of Me; and ye also (i.e. by His imparted power) shall bear witness."

The fourth comes in chapter 16: 26: "At that day *ye shall ask in my name.*" With opened understandings (25) access to the Father (27).

Wonderful! Look up the four "Ye shalls", and prayerfully linger over them in their connections. "Ye shall live", "Ye shall know", "Ye shall bear witness", "Ye shall ask in my Name". Are you *filled* by that life? Do you enjoy that vivid, inward certainty? Are you bearing that witness? Are you praying enough in the Name?

Experiential Christianity

"The love of God is shed abroad in our hearts by the Holy Spirit. . . ."—Rom. 5 : 5.

THESE words teach the *inwardness* of true, Christian religion. Christianity is not only something believed; it is something experienced. Whatever Godward bearings Pentecost may have, this is its first meaning for *us*. Christian conversion is nothing less than a supernatural impartation to the soul. Christianity was never meant to be a religion of elaborate rituals and draperies, such as Romanists and other sacerdotalists have made it. It is the love of God in the heart.

Moreover, our text teaches the *immediateness* of true Christian religion. Our experience of God is not mediate, through priests or sacraments, but a direct infusion by the divine Spirit. At Pentecost, where did the effusion of the Spirit occur? In the temple? No. Temple, priests, altars, all were passed by. Christianity is God, no longer in temples of man's building, but *immediately* known and possessed in the human heart through direct invasion by the Holy Spirit.

Notice also *where* it is imparted, "in our *hearts*"; not just to our reason or intellect, but to the very centre of desire, emotion, and responsive capacity.

Notice further *how* it is imparted: "by the Holy Spirit"; not by some impersonal influence, but by One who is as personal as the Father and the Son. That is surely the most wonderful fact of all. See the little word, "shed", indicating *copiousness*. Notice also the word, "abroad", which implies wide *inclusiveness*—for all of us, not just some clerical class.

Well, such was apostolic Christianity. Do we measure up to it today? It seems beyond doubt that Paul was referring to something which was a *conscious* reality to those early believers. There are some things in our Christian life and faith which are *not* matters of emotional experience. Election, predestination, and other great divine activities in our salvation, are quite outside us, and utterly beyond us. But this inflooding of God's love is surely, necessarily, intendedly a *conscious* possession in mind and heart. Indeed, it has been so, all through the centuries, among evangelical, sanctified, prayerful believers.

Dear Christian, let me ask you: Are *you* living in this heart-enrapturing experience? Do you at least enjoy recurrences of it, when released from nagging work-day obligations? Note three things about those first disciples: First, they loved the place of prayer (Acts 1 : 14). Second, they were in "one accord" (14)—no grudges, place-seeking, or cruel gossip! Third, they really believed the promise, "Ye shall be immersed in the Holy Spirit" (5).

I take no pleasure in making my next remark, but wide observation has convinced me that nowadays comparatively few Christian believers are living in the vivid experience of those early days. The continually luminous inward *glow* of the suffusing heavenly Spirit seems a rare feature among our church members. It was the *general* experience in those long-ago days. It always flames forth again in visitations of revival. Is it not time that we gave ourselves to prayer—to long and earnest secret prayer, until, in sanctifying power and joyful reality, "the love of God is shed abroad in our hearts by the Holy Spirit"?

Invasion from Heaven!

"Suddenly there came a sound from heaven as of a rushing mighty wind."—Acts 2 : 2.

NONE who lived in war-battered Britain when the Nazi and Fascist enemies at last capitulated, will ever forget with what stirred emotions victory was celebrated. Many could only express their relief and reaction in tears; and all over the land large gatherings in the churches expressed deep gratitude to God. Yet even greater than the greatest physical victory ever celebrated is the wonderful event which claims our grateful remembrance at this present time.

We are at that period of the year, up to seven weeks after Easter, when we remember more particularly the down-shedding of the Holy Spirit on that historic "day of Pentecost", two thousand years ago. All Christendom looks back to that "new thing" in history as the organic beginning of the Christian Church, and the present "age of grace". In England, where annual religious observances have largely followed the calendar of the Anglican Church, the special Sunday of commemoration is known as "Whit Sunday", and the season as "Whitsuntide" ("whit" being short for "white") because formerly it was the custom on that Sunday for all the children and many of the grown-ups to dress all in white. In America the season seems little observed. But whether the annual "season" be observed or not, it is specially important for us, in these days, to remember and reconsider that long ago Pentecost and its abiding meanings for us. We do not think nearly as much as we ought about the coming and the person and the work of the Holy Spirit. So, then, in this and the next two of these daily meditations, let us prayerfully reflect again on that historic Pentecost when in revolutionising fulness the Holy Spirit came upon that first band of Christians as they lingered on in united prayer, away back yonder in old Jerusalem.

The first captivating fact is that it was an invasion of earth by a power from heaven. It was the coming of the Holy Spirit to operate among men in a new and fuller way. He came to be the dynamic life, vitalizing and empowering the true church, that church which consists of all the spiritu ally reborn. He came to be the power to convert and regenerate men, and sanctify Christian believers, and to curb the powers of evil, and to make Christian prayer the mightiest weapon on earth. That power is still with us, and still operating on the earth. Why did Hitler fail and perish, when outwardly it seemed as though he must surely go on "conquering and to conquer"? It was because behind armies, navies, airfleets, and other outward factors, the far mightier Christian, spiritual, invisible forces energised by the Holy Spirit proved in the end too strong for him. Why must Communism fail, and perish in the same way? Because Jesus rose, lives, reigns, controls; and because He has sent forth the Holy Spirit whose descent in fulness was signalised on that long-ago "day of Pentecost".

We are living in days when the desire is very strong for some big reunion of the religious denominations in Christendom. The idea is that such an imposing super-church would wield an influence which we do not now have. But let us never forget that the only *real* power of Christianity is the flame of Pentecost which burns through it.

"Write the Name of the Day"

"And when the day of Pentecost was fully come . . ."—Acts. 2: 1.

THE story of that historic Pentecost is written in Acts 2. As we review it, we cannot but be impressed by three sets of meaningful singularities: (1) the significant *circumstances*; (2) the significant *characteristics*; (3) the significant *consequences*.

There was a notable peculiarity in the *day*: the day of "Pentecost". There were five annual religious celebrations in Israel's calendar: Passover; Pentecost; Trumpets; Day of Atonement; Tabernacles. The first of these, i.e. Passover, commemorated Israel's exodus from Egypt. It began at evening, the second sabbath of the year (our own mid-April). On the "*morrow after* the sabbath", the Israelites were to offer before the Lord "a sheaf of the *firstfruits*" (Lev. 23: 9–14). As the lamb of the Passover typified our Lord in His death, so the sheaf of "firstfruits" offered on the first day of the week, typified Him in His resurrection. "Now is Christ risen from the dead . . . the *firstfruits* of them that sleep" (1 Cor. 15: 20).

From that first day of the week the Israelites were to count fifty days, and on "the morrow after the seventh sabbath" (first day of the week) they were to observe *Pentecost*. The very name, "Pentecost", is the Greek numeral for *fiftieth*. On that fiftieth day two *loaves* ("bread of firstfruits") were to be presented. In Pentecost, the "firstfruits" had now become the "bread" of life to men, to be received inwardly. Correspondently, it was exactly fifty days after our Lord's resurrection as the "firstfruits" that the glorious fulness of His life and power came down in the Holy Spirit of Pentecost, on that first day of the week, two thousand years ago.

But there is an even more notable parallel. God brought Israel out of Egypt on the 14th of Abib or Nisan (Exod. 12: 2, 6, 18, 41). They went by night, halting next day at "Etham" (13: 20). Next they moved to the Red Sea (14: 2, 3). Meanwhile Pharaoh, apprised that they had gone, pursued, and "overtook" them there. The following night (14: 21) Israel crossed the Red Sea, so that by the third morning their exodus was complete. That crossing of the Red Sea, three days after the Passover, was a wonderful picture of resurrection—to new life and freedom after deadly servitude. Just forty days later, on the first day of the third month, they were at Mount Sinai (19: 1). Then three days after that, in cloud and glory, "Jehovah descended" (16) for "six days" (24: 16), and on the "seventh day" (50 days after the Red Sea crossing) God called Moses alone to Him, to give the pattern for the tabernacle. Thus, *fifty days exactly* from that Red Sea resurrection-exodus, God brought in the new dispensation and commenced the pattern of the tabernacle which He was to indwell. Even so, just forty days and ten from our Lord's resurrection, Pentecost brought in the new dispensation of the Spirit, and God began to form on earth the new, *spiritual* sanctuary which He was to indwell, even the *Church*! Yes, that "day of Pentecost" was indeed a significant day!

I would not seem over-dogmatic on this, but I think it true that our individual *experience* of the Spirit's infilling usually begins with a "day of Pentecost" in the *soul*, when, in utter yieldedness to Christ, by faith we appropriate it. This is usually some time after conversion. Dear Christian, have you had *your* "day of Pentecost"?

Significant Circumstances

"With one accord in one place."—Acts 2: 1.

NOT only was there vivid force in the *day* on which the effusion of the Spirit occurred; all the other salient facets flash with suggestion. Think of the *group* on whom the fire and fulness fell. They were a band of *praying* Christians. "These all continued with one accord in prayer . . ." (1: 14). The praying was a never-to-be-forgotten feature of that transforming Pentecost. It was prayer which made the human vessels ready to receive the divine infilling. As it was then, so is it now; waiting on God in lowly, tenacious, believing prayer is that which Heaven honours, and on which the blessing falls.

Moreover, that continued praying together had ridded those disciples of all discord. There had been strifes and competitive ambition before, but all that was now gone; they were all down before God in unifying humility, adoration, and intercession. Twice the record says that they were all "with one accord" (1: 14; 2: 1). It was the prayer and the oneness, both together, which made them ready for the big thing which happened.

Still further, they were pleading a clear *promise*, the Master's promise of the immersing Spirit (1: 5, 8). This gave their prayer concentration and anticipation.

Also, for the first time in history, they were practising the unique kind of praying which Jesus had taught them, i.e. prayer "*in the Name*" (Jn. 16: 24). They had seen Jesus ascend. They now felt a new and holy familiarity with heaven. God was no longer just a vast, baffling infinity. As they now looked up to heaven they saw God looking down on them through a human face (2 Cor. 4: 6). The new era of praying "in My Name" had begun. They were on covenant ground with God through the blood of Calvary and the ascended Mediator.

But now, think of the *place* where the big and blessed wonder burst into occurrence. "It filled all the *house* where they were sitting." So it was in a private house, as the Greek word indicates, not in the temple, where, as in chapter 3: 1, they were wont to go at the set seasons of devotion (see Luke 24: 53; Acts 2: 46). Perhaps it was the house of rendezvous mentioned in chapter 1: 13, 14. The magnificent temple, with its ordinances and appointments all speaking of the *old* covenant, was by-passed. The *new* temple of the *new* covenant was to be *spiritual*, not material, a spiritual temple in human hearts; in human hearts both individually and collectively; instead of consecrated buildings, consecrated and Spirit-filled human beings.

Note, also, the *time* when the heavenly invasion came. It was on the tenth day of their continual praying. In Scripture numerology, ten marks a complete round. Perseverance in prayer was given a full round of testing. One wonders if Peter's impetuous nature found the eighth and ninth days rather taxing to faith. Had something gone wrong? Why did the promised enduing not come? But no, there is not a fleck of suggestion that there was anything but quiet determination to wait on God until the window of heaven opened, and the promised power came. Oh, how all these things challenge you and me today! How many of us miss the big blessing because we cannot wait out the "ten days"!

How the Spirit Came

"A rushing mighty wind . . . cloven tongues like as of fire . . ."—Acts 2: 2, 3.

EVERY time we read Luke's graphic sketch of that long-ago Pentecost we are arrested again by the signs and symbols which characterised it. When the big thing happened, it happened suddenly. First there was the rushing "sound *from heaven*". There was no gale sweeping the city that early morning or swirling noisily around house corners. This was something directly downwards, from God. And it was the sound as of a "*rushing, mighty wind*". What could more aptly symbolise the boundless, resistless, sweeping, overwhelming almightiness of the Spirit to envelop believers in power, and to overthrow the citadels of evil? The air of the room was still; but the sound awful as a hurricane.

Next, "there appeared unto them cloven tongues like as of *fire*". Yes, besides the wind, for volume and power, there was the fire, for intensity; the fire to search and purify and refine. And mark it well: the fire was not a shapeless flame; it came in "cloven *tongues*". The symbol of the new dispensation was a tongue of fire; human speech aflame with divine presence. This was to be the Church's great weapon, and the individual believer's power in witnessing. Notice that the fire "sat on *each* of them". No exceptions were made, even as no exceptions are made today, where the conditions are fulfilled. It "sat on each of *them*", not merely as a collective unit, but as individual human beings, fusing them into spiritual oneness, yet emphasizing individual separateness. "It *sat* upon each of them"—indication that it came to stay!

And now observe the significant *consequences*, the realities behind the symbols. The first thing is that "they were *filled with the Holy Spirit*". What heavenly love, joy, peace must have flooded their souls! What rapture of fellowship with God must have been theirs! Next, "they began to speak with other *tongues*, as the Spirit gave them utterance". What power with men this gave them—even when they were speaking in their *own* tongue, as Peter in his great address to the "men of Israel"! The Spirit "gave them utterance"! Next, they *went out to tell*, and the thing was "*noised abroad*". Yet these were the men who, only weeks earlier, had retreated furtively behind closed doors "for fear of the Jews". Their timidity has now become radiant audacity to make Jesus known. Doubts and jitters have been ousted by certainty that Jesus is risen, is alive, is ascended, is in control; and nervous shrinkings have been submerged in this tidal wave of Pentecostal infilling.

Finally, see the *evangelistic impact*. The same Peter who quailed before a servant girl on the crucifixion eve, now faces the congregated thousands on that Pentecostal morn; "And the same day there were added unto them about three thousand souls"! How it all *still* preaches! Why are things *so* different today? Well, where are those ten-day prayer meetings?

When our God beholds us there,
Pleading in the place of prayer,
Then the flag of truth prevails,
Foes slink back, and Satan quails.
Bring us, Lord, yea *keep* us there,
Where we learn prevailing prayer.

"And they were all filled with the Holy Spirit."—Acts 2 : 4.

IN that historic Pentecost there is a fivefold outreach of mighty meaning.

(1) *As regards God.* That effusion was a culmination. In the Old Testament we find intermittent Self-revealings of God to men. Also, after the welding of the Israelite tribes into the theocracy, Jehovah came to "dwell among" His convenant people, in the Shekinah which flashed in the holy of holies. Again, the Spirit of God "came *upon*" certain individuals for prophetic utterance. But at Pentecost God came down to indwell continuously all His people in Christ, making each one a "temple" of the Holy Spirit!

(2) *As regards Christ.* In verse 16, Peter explains: "This is that which was spoken by the prophet Joel: It shall come to pass in the last days, saith God, I will pour out my Spirit . . ." Then, in verse 33, "*He* (Christ) hath poured out this." The implication is obvious: the ascended Lord Jesus has done that which *God* was to do; He has exercised an exclusively divine prerogative; He has poured forth the divine Spirit; therefore Christ is God.

(3) *As regards Israel.* See Peter's "This is that" (16). Does that Joel prophecy predict the Church? No. It relates to our Lord's Messianic kingdom, which is to centre in the throne of David. It should ever be recognised that the first import of the Acts is the renewed offer of the long-promised "kingdom of heaven" to Israel, with the now-added message of personal salvation through the crucified but risen and exalted Lord Jesus. Only as Israel's further refusal becomes deep-fixed do we see that in the all-anticipating super-control of God those first groups of believers, scattered over the Roman world, are the first components of that "*Church*" which is the mystic body of God's dear Son.

(4) *As regards the Church.* Owing to Israel's further rejection of Jesus, the ultimate fulfilment of the Joel prophecy awaits the millennial reign of Christ. Meanwhile, that long-ago outpouring at Pentecost fused all true believers into one spiritual organism, and thus historically originated the Church. As Israel more and more fixedly rejected Jesus, the miracle "signs" were withdrawn from Israel; but the effusion itself was *never* withdrawn from the *Church.* Pentecost is the Church's power all through this present dispensation.

(5) *As regards the individual.* See verse 38. "Ye shall receive the gift of the Holy Spirit." What the Holy Spirit was to mean to the individual believer, our Lord foretold in John 14 to 16. Especially in 14 : 20; 16 : 23; 16 : 26, see (a) the divine indwelling, (b) spiritual understanding, (c) answer to prayer. Remember, "the promise is unto *you*" (Acts 2: 39). Was ever a more wonderful promise given?

Dear Christian believer, are *you* living daily in the fulness of the Spirit? It is your redemptive right, your blood-bought prerogative. But as it was in the beginning, so is it today—there must be abdication of self-government, a complete abandonment to Christ, and a simple-hearted "laying hold" on the pledged infilling. At Pentecost the Spirit was poured out potentially upon the whole Church; but the fulness only becomes *experience* in those who thus appropriate it.

Pentecostal Preaching

"But Peter . . . lifted up his voice."—Acts. 2: 14.

HAVE you ever reflected what forbidding difficulties Peter was up against when he preached his first open-air message on that historic day? I have no doubt that Peter was a well-built, bonny-faced, ruddy-complexioned man, with a round, pleasant, sonorous voice. Those characteristics would be prepossessing for the moment; but they were quite outweighed by the *dis*advantages which beset him. Let me mention four.

(1) He was *charging home an awful guilt.* There could be no wily trimmings of flattery, no "beating about the bush"; those proud Israelites had murdered their Messiah, the very Son of God. The blood of the most shocking crime in history was upon them; and Peter must convict them of it.

(2) He was *championing a new faith*; a new doctrine, a new "sect", a new religion, without a history, without a college, without prominent patron or figurehead; the new religion (so it seemed) of a murdered "blasphemer".

(3) He was *challenging the most deep-set prejudice.* All that was most ancient, venerable, fanatical in Judaism would rise up in fearsome opposition. The religious leaders, the political power-cliques, the theories of the learned, the passion of the mob, like swelling waves of an incoming tide, were ready to sweep the poor little preacher away for ever; and Peter knew it.

(4) In the eyes of leaders and learned, Peter would seem to *cheapen his message* by the fact that he was uncultivated, according to academic standards. He wore no college tie. He spoke with no rhetorical finesse. He had the up-country accent. He smacked of the homely fisherman. Who was *this* unlettered yokel, to be declaiming in the crowded capital?

Yet see the outcome: "They were pricked in their heart." "What shall we do?" "The same day there were added unto them about three thousand souls" (37, 41). What a preaching exploit! All disadvantages were more than offset by the singular power operating through that country preacher and his Galilean brogue.

Why was it so? Well, for one thing, Peter had just emerged from a ten-day prayer meeting. Prevailing with God is always the best preparation for prevailing on men. As Peter stood there preaching, the glow of communion with God was on his face. He was God-conscious and God-atmosphered. Besides this, Peter and his prayer-comrades had just come into a transforming spiritual blessing. "Cloven tongues like as of fire" had "sat upon each of them". The unction of the Holy Spirit was upon Peter. He had become "endued with the power from on high". All the way through his address he stuck to the Scriptures. All the way through He focussed upon Christ. All the way through he was "filled with the Spirit". *That* was Pentecostal preaching.

What does this say to ourselves? The symbol of the new dispensation is a "tongue of fire". The great weapon of Christ's witnesses is to be Spirit-filled utterance. Not military might, nor political pressure, nor any other way of worldly warring, but a "tongue of fire"—the human organ transmitting divine power.

The Purpose of the Paraclete

"He shall glorify Me."—Jn. 16: 14.

IN THESE later chapters of John, our Lord's teachings about the Holy Spirit are full of surprise and comfort. The coming Comforter would be to the disciples all that Jesus had been—Teacher, Guide, Friend, Consoler, with the added wonder that besides being *with* them, as Jesus had been, He would be *in* them, and never leave them as Jesus must now do. Moreover, Jesus Himself was somehow coming back to them in this soon-coming Paraclete. These and other precious features our Lord pre-delineated and then crowned them all with this finalising word: "*He shall glorify Me.*" The incarnate Son had glorified the Father. The Holy Spirit comes now to glorify the Son, that is, to focus attention upon Him in the perfections of His character and redeeming work, and to exalt Him in human esteem. The context indicates three spheres in which He does this: (1) in the world, (2) in the Church, (3) in the believer.

In verses 8 to 11, we are told how the Spirit glorifies Jesus *in the world*: "He will reprove the world of sin, and of righteousness, and of judgment: of sin because they believe not on Me; of righteousness because I go to the Father; of judgment because the prince of this world is judged." The Holy Spirit does not convict merely of crime (wrong between man and man) but of *sin* (wrong between man and God). The world itself shows far more interest in crime than in sin, as watching T.V. any day will show. Moreover, the average T.V. or radio or magazine presentation of crime feeds morbid appetite for crime-*thrills* rather than stirring healthy moral *concern.* I seldom watch the programmes; but if I should ever wish to turn criminal, I have learned far more how to go about it from T.V. than I ever knew before! The Holy Spirit comes to convict of sin in a most significant way, i.e. "of sin *because they believe not on Me*". He exposes the sin of the human heart by a new and decisive test, namely, attitude to Christ. Sin is no longer merely transgression of a law, but *refusal of a Saviour.* A man may admit himself a sinner through transgressing God's law, yet he may excuse himself that he could not help it because of inherited tendencies; but he can give *no* excuse for refusing a *Saviour.* To reject that dear Saviour is the sin of all sins which damns the soul.

The Spirit comes also to convince the world "*of righteousness because I go to the Father*". Where Jesus leaves off, the Spirit takes on. He comes to attest the *personal* righteousness of Jesus, now ascended to God as the ideal Man; and the *vicarious* righteousness of Jesus, now accepted of God as man's Saviour.

Again, the Spirit comes to convince "*of judgment because the prince of this world is judged*"—not just "*going* to be judged", but already "*is judged*". The world's condemnation of God's holy Son to that awful Cross boomerangs back as the most awful condemnation of the world which did it. Sentence is already passed on this world and its prince. Why then is not the sentence executed? It is because God would not allow His Son to be rejected and crucified with no response or reward from the world for which He died. God puts Christ on the throne of heaven, and sends the Holy Spirit to call out a people to be a special treasure to His dear Son—even the *Church.*

The Holy Spirit in the Church

"He shall glorify Me."—Jn. 16: 14.

As we have noted (yesterday) in verses 8 to 11, the Holy Spirit comes to "glorify" Jesus in the *world*; but now, in verses 12 to 15, He comes (as the wording clearly predicts) to "glorify" Jesus among believers, i.e. *in the Church.* Some glorify church buildings, sacraments, ministers, human leaders, cardinals, popes; but the Holy Spirit comes to glorify "Jesus only". Science glorifies knowledge. Philosophy glorifies reason. History glorifies great men. Society glorifies its dollar kings and big-hit artists and movie stars. But the Holy Spirit comes to glorify "Jesus only". Especially does He do this in the Church, in the true Church consisting of all the blood-washed and Spirit-born.

He comes to complement and amplify our Lord's own teachings. That is what our Lord indicated when He said, "I have yet many things to say unto you, but ye cannot bear them now . . ." He knew that the Spirit would teach them all those further truths which they needed to learn. Also, when Jesus said about those further truths, "Ye cannot bear them now", He knew that the Holy Spirit would expand their capacity to apprehend.

Notice now the two things here which our Lord said that the coming Paraclete would do. First, "*He shall guide you into all the truth*". Which truth? Astronomical? Geological? Chemical? Biological? No, the Holy Spirit by-passes all such matters pertaining to the physical universe. The discovery that our earth is spherical, that the sun is the centre of our planetary system, that the constitution of matter is atomical, He leaves to the exploratory genius of Galilei and Copernicus and our modern atom-splitters. It is to "guide" us into "all the truth" about *Jesus* that the Holy Spirit comes. That is *His* big concern. That is why Jesus said, "He shall glorify *Me*". If we would know how wonderfully the Holy Spirit *has* "guided into all the truth" concerning the Saviour, we need only to consult the New Testament Gospels and Epistles, and study those writings under the *illumination* of the Spirit.

The second thing is this: "*And He shall show you things to come.*" Turn to 1 and 2 Thessalonians and the Book of Revelation to see how He has done this. See the ending of the present age in the translation of the Church, the return of Christ, Armageddon, and the internment of Satan. See the millennial worldrule of Messiah-Emperor Jesus; then the final abolition of sin, the general judgment of mankind at the great white throne, and the bringing in of the new order, with its new queen city, the New Jerusalem, in which the eternal King is the glorified Lamb! In and through it all, the Holy Spirit has glorified Jesus. There is nothing to gratify mere prurient curiosity. Everything centres in Jesus. In all things He has the pre-eminence. In the Holy Spirit's unveiling of the future, nothing is more noticeable than the way He has made Jesus the focus-point and crown of everything. In the Book of Revelation we see Jesus first on the throne of heaven (chapter 5), then on the throne of earth (20: 4–6), and then on the throne of the New Jerusalem through eternal ages (22: 3–5). Yes, that is ever the occupation of the Holy Spirit in the Church—to glorify Jesus. Should not *we* always do the same? There is never any obtruding of "self" when we are filled by the Spirit.

Is Jesus Glorified through Me?

"He shall glorify Me."—Jn. 16: 14.

THE Holy Spirit comes to glorify Jesus in and through every individual believer. Mark those two prepositions, "in" and "through", for they represent two distinct aspects. He comes to glorify Jesus *in* the believer. That is what our Lord Jesus referred to when He said, along with our text, "He shall receive of Mine, and shall show it unto you". One by one the Holy Spirit takes the different relationships which Jesus sustains to us, and makes them inwardly real to us. Truths which we could never decipher by natural reasoning He makes luminous to our minds, especially illumining the spiritual treasures of our *union* with Christ, and all the while inwardly flash-lighting the excellencies of our heavenly Bridegroom to us. See verse 15: "All things that the Father hath are Mine; therefore said I that He shall take of Mine and shall show it unto you." Do you perceive the parallel between that verse and the immortal story in Genesis 24? Away back in that Genesis story, the "father" is Abraham. The "son" who can say, "All things that the father hath are mine" is Isaac (verse 36). The "servant" who goes forth to find a bride for thc father's son, and "takes of the things" of Isaac to show them to the chosen bride (53) represents the Holy Spirit who now does that selfsame thing to the members of our Lord's mystic bride, the Church. It is the Holy Spirit who reveals to us all that we have in Christ, making Him real to us as Saviour, Friend, Sovereign, Bridegroom, Sanctifier, Enduer, Indweller, and, oh, so much more. Yes, He "glorifies" Jesus *in* us.

But He comes, also, to glorify Jesus *through* us, to others. If we would know to what degree we are filled or controlled by the Holy Spirit, the surest of all tests is to ask, "To what degree is Jesus seen and known and glorified through me?" Not speaking in tongues, performing miracles, or preaching persuasively, but how much like my Master am I?—that is the vital test. During the brilliant Victorian days in England, when those two great preachers were at their zenith—Parker at the City Temple, and Spurgeon at the Metropolitan Tabernacle, the fashion for visitors to London was to hear Parker on Sunday morning and Spurgeon at night. An American visitor followed this procedure. His morning comment was, "My! what wonderful oratory!" His evening comment was, "Oh, what a wonderful Saviour!" Dear Spurgeon!—with him it was Jesus, *Jesus*, *JESUS*, all the time. And that is *always* the distinguishing trait when the Holy Spirit is filling a person or a ministry. The saintly old Dr. F. B. Meyer used to say, "In all real believers Jesus is *present*. In some He is not only present, but *prominent*. In others (all to few) He is not only present and prominent, *He* is *pre-eminent*." I wonder which of those three categories you and I belong to—present? or prominent? or pre-eminent? A man may "speak in tongues" all day; he may perform supernatural feats of healing; he may preach with captivating versatility; but if He is not Christlike, I shall judge him superficial or even hypocritical. I wish to be judged in the same way myself. The really decisive test of being filled with the Spirit is just this: Is the life Christlike? Dear Holy Spirit, imprint the likeness of Jesus upon our whole personality.

Living in the Spirit

"If we live in the Spirit . . ." —Gal. 5: 25.

ONE of the most remarkable developments of the past century has been the accumulating confirmation of the Bible by the comparatively new science of archæology. Our discoverers and decipherers have gone forth into Bible lands, and such have been their disclosures that now, almost as by the waving of a magician's wand, much of the ancient Orient is made to relive before us. Many of those Scripture records upon which rationalistic criticism has poured the most scorn have been most decisively substantiated, so that if ever there was sound reason to believe in the thorough integrity of the Scripture documents, there is so today.

But besides the evidential value of the findings, there is their *topographical* illumination. In these days topography is generally confused with geography; but strictly the two are different. Geography has to do with location, whereas topography has to do with *description*. Much new light has come to us about those early Galatians, or Galatai. They lived in Asia Minor. They were almost entirely rural. Most of them were common farm-labourers, and many were slaves. They were largely illiterate, and of an excitable temperament. Yet they were a people of quick intelligence and impulse, whose descendants later surged westward through Europe to found the kingdoms of the Gauls.

In the final part of his epistle, Paul talks to them of living in the Spirit, and it is captivating to see how he pictures it in just those metaphors which would be most readily appreciated by them, in their agricultural surroundings. As farm-workers and slaves, those Galatians knew a good deal about four kinds of *bearing:* (1) fruit-bearing, (2) burden-bearing, (3) seed-bearing, (4) brand-bearing.

See now how Paul talks their language. First, in chapter 5: 22, 23, there is *fruit*-bearing: "But the fruit of the Spirit is love, joy, peace, longsuffering, gentleness, goodness, faith, meekness, godly self-control." Second, in chapter 6: 2, there is *burden*-bearing: "Bear ye one another's burdens, and so fulfil the law of Christ." Third, in chapter 6: 7, there is *seed*-bearing: "Whatsoever a man soweth, that shall he also reap. For he that soweth to his flesh shall of the flesh reap corruption, but he that soweth to the Spirit shall of the Spirit reap life everlasting. . . ." Fourth, in chapter 6: 17, there is *brand*-bearing: "I bear in my body the brands of the Lord Jesus."

It draws a highly challenging fourfold picture of living in the Spirit. First, there is to be *fruit*-bearing. Most of us think that fruit-bearing is service, but we are mistaken. Look again at this ninefold cluster, and mark well that every item has to do with *character and behaviour*. Let us never, never forget that "the fruit of the Spirit" is Christlikeness of character.

Next there is *burden*-bearing. Before their conversion many of those Galatian slaves and toilers shirked a burden, or shifted it to others whenever they could; but now they were to be burden-*sharers* for Jesus' sake. Am *I* a willing burden-sharer?

Next there was to be *seed*-bearing. Am *I* sowing to the Spirit? Or do I become "weary" in well doing? Last there was to be *brand*-bearing. Am *I* willing, if need be, to bear brands for Him even in my body?

"Christ in you, the hope of glory."—Col. 1 : 27.

How wonderful is this truth, that our Lord actually indwells the hearts of His people! In the Messianic prophecies of the Old Testament many and varied aspects of the coming Christ are pre-envisaged, but nowhere are we told that He would *indwell* His people. As Paul tells us in the verse preceding our text, *that* was part of a divine "mystery", or sacred secret, "*hid* from ages and generations". But now the secret is divulged, and, as verse 27 says, "God would make known what is the riches of the glory of this mystery among the nations, which is *Christ in you*, the hope of glory."

These words, "Christ in you", remind us that if our Christian experience is to be rich in quality and alive with communicativeness, we need to know Christ in three ways. Putting it in the first person singular, I need to know Christ *for* me; Christ *in* me; Christ *through* me.

Christ "for" me is Christ *dying* on the Cross. Christ "in" me is Christ *living* in my heart. Christ "through" me is Christ *speaking* by my life.

Christ "for" me is my substitution and sacrifice. Christ "in" me is my sanctification and satisfaction. Christ "through" me is my service and sufficiency.

Christ "for" me is my only acceptable standing before God. Christ "in" me is my only true victory over sin. Christ "through" me is my only real power for spiritual ministry.

As a corollary to this prepositionary trio—this "for" and "in" and "through", I am to sustain a threefold relation to Christ, represented by the three words, purchased, possessed, permeated.

His dying for me means that I am Christ-*purchased*. His living in me means that I am Christ-*possessed*. His working through me means my being Christ-*permeated*.

He died *for* me: I am to *take* Him. He lives *in* me: I am to *prove* Him. He moves *through* me: I am to *transmit* Him.

Oh, that all of us who call Him Saviour might be fully possessed and permeated by His life and love and grace and peace and power! Dear old Dr. F. B. Meyer used to say: "In all His people Christ is *present*. In some He is *prominent*. In a few He is *pre-eminent*." Dear fellow-believer, to which of these classifications do you and I belong?

Those who are indwelt and controlled by Christ, find in Him their all-in-all. He is Saviour, Sanctifier, Healer, for spirit, soul and body. We may say with A. B. Simpson,

I take salvation full and free,
Through Him who gave His life for me,
He undertakes my all to be:
    I take—He undertakes.

I take Him for this mortal frame,
I take my healing through His name;
And all His risen life I claim:
    I take—He undertakes.

Is This Your Supreme Desire?

"That I may know Him."—Phil. 3: 10.

THE supreme longing of the Christian heart should be to know Christ; to know "*Him*" personally and intimately; to know Him experientially in "the power of His resurrection"; to know Him in that deepest and closest of all ways, in the oneness of a sympathetic, heart-to-heart fellowship in His sufferings over a world with its back turned on God.

But I can only know Him thus when I make Him truly "MY LORD", counting all things loss for His dear sake, living wholly for Him, and keeping daily tryst with Him in the quiet place. This is open to all of us, even though we must give hours of each day to mundane things; and who shall tell the rich, deep, spiritual joys which come to those who know the Lord Jesus thus?

I sometimes fear that despite all our busy Christian service, our attending meetings and conventions, our singing of hymns, and our outward Christian activities, some of us, even though we are truly trusting on the finished work of Calvary for our salvation, may find, when we pass into the Beyond, that we do not know *Jesus Himself*—having so neglected the secret tryst with Christ down here that we find ourselves strangers to Him there.

"That I may know Him." Are some of us so full of ourselves and our busy servings that we cannot see Christ in all His beauty? Some years ago a certain lady and her little daughter were staying at the home of a friend. On the bedroom wall, just over the head of the bed in which they slept, there was a picture of the Lord Jesus, which was reflected in the large mirror of the dressing-table standing in the bay of the window. When the little girl woke on her first morning there, she saw the picture reflected in the mirror while she still lay in bed, and exclaimed, "Oh, mommy, I can see Jesus!" Then she quickly kneeled up to take a better look, but in doing so brought her own body between the picture and the mirror, so that instead of seeing the picture of Jesus reflected she now saw herself. So she lay down again, and then again saw the picture of Jesus. She was up and down several times after that, with her eye fixed on the mirror. Then she said, "Mommy, when I can't see myself I can see Jesus; but every time I see myself I don't see Him."

That is the trouble with many of us. We block our own vision of Him. We are in the way of our own eyes. We must first get ourselves away from obstructing the soul's gaze. We must get to where Paul was when he said, "I count all things loss for the excellency of the knowledge of Christ Jesus my Lord."

"That I may know Him." When Paul wrote this he had already known Christ thirty years! His longing was to know the mind and heart and love and friendship of Christ in ever-developing degree. We say that Columbus discovered America; but not all America is even yet discovered. There are a thousand still-unnamed lakes in northern Canada. There are mineral and other treasures not yet guessed at. So it is, in an infinitely sublimer way, with our exploration of Christ. We are to be continually discovering new treasures in Him. Well may this be our life-long motto: "*That I may know Him.*"

"Ye are complete (or filled full) in Him."—Col. 2: 10.

IN imagination, travel back to the beginning of our Christian era, and visualise yourself in the old prison-house at Rome, where the now elderly apostle Paul is incarcerated awaiting further trial before Nero. His imprisonment is not of the more rigorous sort, for he is not a criminal of the lawless type. He is under guard, but is allowed to have visitors, hold consultations, read scrolls, and write letters. One of his most interesting visitors is Epaphras, who has travelled all the way from Colosse, away yonder in the Roman proconsular "Province of Asia" (modern Asia Minor). He has some good things to report, but Paul quickly detects that there is something seriously wrong underlying the visit of his beloved comrade. Alas, the unhappy tidings are that certain eloquent and influential heresiarchs are propagating a specious false doctrine. It is a semi-Judaistic mysticism with a false cosmogony, angel-worship, and supposedly penetrative insight into spiritual secrets. One of its bases was the common Eastern concept that matter is evil, and the source of evil. To preserve the idea of divine *holiness*, therefore, God must be removed as far as possible from matter, which is evil; yet the bond between God and matter dare not be entirely broken, for that would deny the divine *creatorship*. So the measureless vast between God and matter must be bridged by a long, misty file of intermediate beings, each one from God downwards approximating a bit more to the material until at last the visible world of matter is reached. Fantastic as these notions may be, they are playing havoc at Colosse. Christ Jesus, instead of being the one glorious GOD-MAN whose incarnation flings its all-sufficient, divine-human archway right from God to man, is reduced to merely one of the highest of these intermediate angel-beings!

With apprehensive heart the apostle now dictates and despatches this "Epistle to the Colossians", in which he champions and exhibits again the incomparable Christ of the Gospel; His all-supremacy as Lord, and His all-sufficiency as Saviour. "In Him dwelleth all the fulness of the Godhead bodily" (2: 9); who then are the poverty-stricken fantasies which the Gnostic pedlars would dare to put beside *Him*? (2: 8, 10, 18). He is the fulness of God in *creation* (1: 15–18). He is the fulness of God in *redemption* (1: 19–23). He is the fulness of God to the *Church* (1: 24—2: 7). He is the fulness of God over against all that the fine-feathered pseudo-intellectualists are offering in their illusive compound of Gnostic theosophy and Judaistic asceticism (2: 8–23). Whatever supposed superiorities the new sophists were insinuating for their subtle new cultus, they were *inferiorities* compared with the transcendent Christ of the Gospel.

In union with such a Christ and Saviour, the Christian believer has "*all*"—all that can ever be needed or desired or explored. "For in Him dwelleth all the fulness of the Godhead bodily; and *ye are filled full in Him*." Oh, what a Saviour! Let us never forget that in Him is all fulness *for us*—whatever our need! In Him is fulness of wisdom, love, power; fulness of grace, patience, forbearance; fulness of all those qualities which you and I need, to make our lives rich, and our character noble, and our service effective. Daily prayer, simple trust, and browsing in the written Word, keep the supply lines open between Him and us.

Hidden Treasure

"In whom are hid all the treasures of wisdom and knowledge."—Col. 2: 3.

THOSE long-ago Gnostic cultists who troubled the little church at Colosse were probably as well-meaning as they were self-deluded. Likely enough, they were as sincere as many another heretical group since then. Doubtless it was their sincerity and seeming superiority which made them so beguiling, and such a threat to the soundness and simplicity of the fellowship. That they should be so philosophical, speculative and mystical (2: 8, 18, 23) yet so ritualistic and ascetic (2: 16, 20–23), may seem a strange wedlock of contradictory opposites. Yet is it so strange after all? Do we not find the same in Hinduism and Buddhism: at the one end heads in the mists, at the other end feet in the mire? Do we not see it in the Roman church, with its sentimental superstitions and mysticisms on the one hand, yet its vulgar, mediæval penance-works and flesh-mortifications on the other?

Those old-time Gnostic errorists strained the spirituality of God into an *ultra*-spirituality which made it impossible to conceive of Him as having contact with matter. This led to the viewing of matter, including the human body, as evil. Thus they conjoined ethereal speculations with punishings of the flesh. Now one of their subtle insinuations was that their cult gave its initiates a secret insight into hidden mysteries; it had a hidden wisdom which made them superior. Paul counters this with the resplendent declaration, "*IN HIM (CHRIST) ARE HID ALL THE TREASURES OF WISDOM AND KNOWLEDGE.*" In Him, not only is there union of the spiritual with the material, and of the heavenly with the earthly, but of the divine with the human, of the eternal with the historical. Not only is there the simple, blessed reality on which faith can lay hold for salvation, but hidden treasures of divine wisdom and knowledge to challenge endless exploration.

But our text, beside having this original relation to the Colossians, has its independent significance for ourselves. "*IN HIM ARE HID ALL THE TREASURES OF WISDOM AND KNOWLEDGE.*" Yes, the deeper riches are "hidden". There must be searching, studying, praying, communing, trusting, yielding, obeying, proving.

In this we may see a *principle.* God never casts His pearls to the spiritually indolent. "They that seek shall find." He does not do the needless for us. That would stultify our spiritual development. We must pursue; we must persist with determination which matches that of the old gold-prospectors of Kalgoorlie or the Klondyke.

In this we may see also a *criterion.* God always employs this method of challenging us to explore for ourselves. It is so with the Bible; we must study it for ourselves. It is the same with prayer, with providence, and will be so in heaven (Eph. 2: 7).

Once again we may see here an *incentive.* As we have said elsewhere, these riches are "hid" in Christ for us so that we may have the joy of continual new discovery and surprise. (See Deut. 28: 12; Jn. 16: 15.)

Then let me gratefully explore
These boundless riches evermore—
The fulness of the Christ divine,
That precious Jesus who is mine!

"For our light affliction, which is but for a moment, worketh for us a far more exceeding and eternal weight of glory."—2 Cor. 4: 17.

THIS verse draws a quadruple contrast between present tribulations and future compensations; between troubles here and triumphs hereafter. You and I know not what a day may bring forth, and we are very fragile creatures. Sooner than we think, perhaps, heavy weather may beat upon us. Some of us, maybe, are already struggling with the billows. It is well for us to take a steady look at 2 Corinthians 4: 17.

First, view it in its context, as the second member in a series of striking contrasts. In verse 16 there is a contrast between the *outward* and the *inward*: "Though our outward man perish, yet our inward man is renewed day by day." In verse 17 there is a contrast between the *present* and the *future*: "Our light affliction, which is but for a moment, worketh for us a far more exceeding and eternal weight of glory." In verse 18 there is a contrast between the *seen* and the *unseen*: "We look not at the things which are seen, but at the things which are not seen; for the things which are seen are temporal, but the things which are not seen are eternal." Next, in chapter 5: 1, there is a contrast between the *earthly* and the *heavenly*: "If our earthly tent-house be dissolved, we have a building of God, a house not made with hands, eternal in the heavens." Next, in verse 4, there is a contrast between the *mortal* and the *immortal*: "We that are in this tent-house groan, being burdened; not that we would be unclothed, but clothed upon, that mortality might be swallowed up of life." Finally, in verses 6–8, there is a contrast between being *in* the body and *out* of the body: "Whilst we are at home in the body, we are absent from the Lord. We are willing rather to be absent from the body, and to be present with the Lord."

Dear Christian, you and I should live with these contrasts ever before our minds. They help us to put a true evaluation on things. They set off the merely outward and present and seen and earthly and mortal and bodily, against the spiritual and the ultimate, and the unseen and the heavenly and the immortal and the being "at home with the Lord".

But look now, in particular, at chapter 4: 17: "For our light affliction, which is but for a moment, worketh for us a far more exceeding and eternal weight of glory." Our present troubles are here described comparatively in fourfold aspect. (1) As to their *nature*, they are "affliction". (2) As to their *weight*, they are "light". (3) As to their *duration*, they are "but for a moment". (4) As to their *utility*, they "work for us" eternal glory. Sometimes, when we are undergoing seemingly interminable adversity, the cry is wrung from us, "How long, O Lord?" Let suffering Paul show us that the victory of faith is to see the transient present against the everlasting glory which is yet to be.

Yes, let suffering Paul show us. . . . Theory is one thing; demonstration is another. Paul not only preaches; he practises—and *proves* to us. How he endured! Here was a man who, although still amid the physical, was living in the spiritual; although still amid the temporal, was living in the eternal; although still amid the earthly, was living in the heavenly. He was not waiting to shout, "Glory!" *then*. Despite all setbacks, he was saying it *now*!

Troubles Now: Triumphs Then

"For our light affliction, which is but for a moment, worketh for us a far more exceeding and eternal weight of glory."—2 Cor. 4 : 17.

So, then, this verse describes our present troubles in fourfold aspect. First, as to their *nature* they are "afflictions". It is part of the present pathos that "afflictions are the common lot". The older among us have proved it so. The younger must acquiesce in its being so. But the afflictions which befall Christians assume a supernatural significance. They are never merely accidental; they are divinely permitted with a purpose, and overruled to our eternal good, if we bear them devoutly. Let us always view our present troubles as "afflictions" in that sense.

Second, as to their *weight*, Paul calls them "our *light* affliction". Some of his own sufferings he discloses in chapter 11 : 23–28. What sufferings! Yet even those are all "light" compared with the coming reward. So is it with our own. Sickness, infirmity, blindness, deafness, impediment, bereavement, business losses, domestic anxieties, disappointments, loneliness, fears, temptations—how they weigh upon us! Yet they are indeed "light" compared with that "weight" of glory in the yet-to-be.

Third, as to their *duration*, Paul says our afflictions are "but for a moment". Do I hear the sigh, "A long moment!" from someone whose cup of trouble has been filled to the brim? Perhaps at times we suffer more from the length than the strength of our trials. There seems no end to them. Every day brings new waves, and we are sure our little barque must flounder. Yet in comparison with those rolling ages yet to be, our longest trials here are "but for a moment".

Fourth, as to their *utility*, Paul says "our light affliction . . . *worketh for us*". Yes, our afflictions work both *for* us and *in* us. They give scope for the exercise and development of faith. They stabilise and mature us. They lead us to self-examination and purification. They wean us from the world. They call Christian graces into activity. They drive us closer to Christ. They promote separation and holiness. They quicken our desires toward heaven; and they accumulate for us a corresponding reward, as we undergo them faithfully.

And now look back over our verse again, observing the fourfold contrast. (1) Over against present "*affliction*", is future "*glory*". (2) Over against "light" affliction, is a "*weight* of glory". (3) Over against that which is "but for a moment", is that which is "*eternal*". (4) Over against affliction which "worketh" for us now, is a "*far more exceeding*" compensation then! A widely-used servant of Christ was asked, "What have you found to be the most helpful practice in your Christian life?" He replied, "To view everything in the light of eternity."

Brief life is here our portion,
  Brief sorrow, short-lived care;
The life that knows no ending,
  The tearless life is *there*.
Oh, happy retribution—
  Short toil, unending rest!
Eternal consolation!
  A mansion with the blest!

"For our light affliction, which is but for a moment, worketh for us a far more exceeding and eternal weight of glory."—2. Cor. 4: 17.

THIS matter of "affliction", then, is one to which we ought to relate ourselves thoughtfully and prayerfully. We belong to the present "bundle of life", which means for most of us a full share of those afflictions which come by *natural processes*. Some persons seem to think that the godly have more afflictions than the ungodly; but my own observations convince me otherwise. The ungodly bring upon themselves afflictions which we Christians are spared, and for which there is neither comfort nor remedy. Moreover, the desolateness of the ungodly when severe afflictions lay them low is sometimes awful to see.

From time to time, however, we Christian believers may also have to bear those afflictions which come by way of *human persecution*. The Greek word translated "affliction" in our text means, first of all, *pressure*. A strange new pressure and intensity have come to human life in this twentieth century. On the European continent, and in other places, we have seen highly educated, scientifically intensified persecution of Jews and Christians alike. In other parts there is a slow, grim, determined pressure against all forms of religion. Crises of outward persecution often call forth spectacular heroism, but long-drawn-out "pressure" is often more than flesh and blood can endure. But whether afflictions come to us by natural processes or by way of human persecution, let us seek to bear them after the pattern of Paul as exhibited in our text.

Mrs. C. H. Spurgeon, wife of the famous Victorian preacher, was for many years afflicted with illness which at times was acutely distressing. One wintry evening, as the deeper darkness drew on, she lay on her couch, much discouraged, and wondered again why such lingering affliction should be allowed to frustrate the service she would fain have been rendering to the Lord's servants. Suddenly, she heard a clear, musical sound like the trill of a robin; but no, surely no robin could be singing out there in such wintry darkness. Again the plaintive, melodious notes stole into the room; and then she found to her surprise that they came from the fire-place. The fire was letting loose the imprisoned music from the heart of an old oak log which was burning there. The old oak had garnered up that song in the days when all went well with him, when birds twittered merrily on his branches, and the soft sunlight flecked his leaves with gold. But since then he had grown old and hardened; ring after ring of knotted growth had sealed up the long-forgotten melody, until at last the fierce tongues of the flames consumed his callousness, and enabled him to sing his sweetest song even amid self-sacrifice. "Singing in the fire"! Says Mrs. Spurgeon, "If that is the only way to get a song of praise from these apathetic hearts, then let the furnace be heated seven times hotter than before!" "For our light affliction, which is but for a moment, worketh for us a far more exceeding and eternal weight of glory."

In Revelation 7: 9, 10, John writes, "I beheld, and lo, a great multitude which no man could number . . . stood before the throne . . . clothed with white robes, and palms in their hands." It will be wonderful to wave our palm of final victory *then*; but that which prepares us for it is our learning here and *now* to say "Hallelujah!" *through our tears*!

Bitter Stem but Sweet Fruit

"Tribulation worketh patience."—Rom. 5 : 3.

TRIBULATION is a thorny tree, but it yields sweet fruit. Usually, given the proper soil, the thornier the tree, the sweeter the fruit. Mark well: our text is not just the expression of a *hope* that tribulation may work patience; it is the statement of a *fact*, that tribulation actually does so in the true Christian character. Moreover, in these words and their context, Paul is photographing his *own* experience. His having borne excessive tribulations was no empty boast (see again 2 Cor. 11 : 23–28) and even in *his* impetuous nature tribulation had developed this virtue of mellow maturity, "patience".

It is a good, practical test-question to ask ourselves, "How do *I* behave under tribulation? Does it engender patience within me?—or its opposite?" You and I have not been called to go through tribulations such as beat upon Paul, but in any lesser way that we have incurred tribulation for Christ's sake, how have we borne it? Could we truthfully exult with Paul, "We *glory* in tribulations also; knowing that tribulation worketh patience"?—or have we been resentful, squeamish, panicky? Our text raises two aspects which it is well to ponder. First, here is the true Christian *attitude*: "We glory in tribulations also." Second, here is a good spiritual *reason* for it: "Tribulation worketh patience."

So, then, the true Christian *attitude* is to "glory in tribulations also". This is the *Christlike* attitude; for in John 12 : 32 our Lord calls His very cross a being "lifted up", or exalted. It is also the only *worthy* attitude. See the other things in which we glory: "justified" (verse 1); "peace with God" (1); "access into grace" (2); "hope of the glory of God" (2). Shall we glory in these superlative wonders of our salvation, yet unworthily shirk temporary tribulations on earth? Nay, glorying in tribulation should be the *accepted* attitude, as it was long ago with the apostles, who "rejoiced that they were counted worthy to suffer shame for His name" (Acts 5 : 41). Present trends seem to suggest that before long many of us may be called to endure tribulations who have hitherto escaped. We should never aggravate needless hostility; but if tribulation should come, let us count it an honour to suffer for the Name. Of course, the word "tribulation" in our text may well include cares, troubles, sorrows, bereavements, bodily sufferings, but it especially covers all those penalties and persecutions which come upon us because we are Christians.

Finally, let us never forget the good spiritual *reason* why we should "glory in tribulation", namely, that "tribulation worketh *patience*", and patience is a God-like virtue. Patience has been defined as the capacity to endure calmly, confidently, and without complaint. That is surely a mark of rich spiritual maturity; and if tribulation begets it within us, then even tribulation is a blessing. Ought we to hate the flames which purify the gold? Dear Lord, help us even to "glory in tribulations"!

When tribulations jag and irk,
Let Patience do her perfect work.
The very Captain of salvation
Was "perfected" by tribulation,
And turned the thorns to diadems!

From Darkness to Light

"Show forth the praises of Him who hath called you out of darkness into His marvellous light."—1 Peter 2 : 9.

THE Christian life begins with conversion to Christ. In conversion there are always two sides. On the human side there is the act of receiving Christ as Saviour. On the divine side there is a supernatural intervention by which regeneration is wrought. In our New Testament we find a fascinating variety of metaphors to express conversion. One of these occurs in our text. Peter was an outdoor man, with an inbred aptitude for culling metaphors from Nature. So, here, when he speaks of conversion, he says, "Show forth the praises of Him who hath called you *out of darkness into His marvellous light.*" Conversion is a transition; a coming "out of" and "into". In Peter's metaphor there are four aspects of this which indicate what a wonderful thing conversion is.

First, see the *vividness* of it: "Out of darkness into His marvellous light." Few things stand in acuter contrast than darkness and light. Yet Peter was not indulging hyperbole when he used his metaphor. *Every* true conversion is such a transition. Whether it happens with volcanic suddenness or as the result of some dawn-like process, it is a coming "out of darkness into His marvellous light". Some of us, in our pre-conversion days, thought we knew everything about the Christian religion; but *after* conversion, we wondered that for so long we could have groped in such stupid conceit and darkness.

Second, see the *supernaturalness* of this transition: "Show forth the praises of *HIM*. . . ." Yes, this is the work of God just as truly as His bringing Israel out of Egypt (which Peter maybe had in mind: see context). However great *that* exodus was, this *spiritual* exodus from darkness to light is greater. Darkness binds. We know not what is on our right or our left, what is before or behind. We are bound by fear, ignorance, superstition. In the light we are free; free to see and know, to move and act. Conversion is a *supernatural* exodus from darkness to light. We gratefully acknowledge the usefulness of modern psychology, but when it "explains" conversion on merely natural grounds it only advertises that it can be just as blind spiritually as it is awake mentally. Real conversion is nothing less than a gracious divine interference in the very basis of human personality.

Third, see its *marvellousness*. The Greek word translated "marvellous" means, literally, "to be wondered at". Could Peter have used a more fitting word? Well may we wonder at the new light into which we have been brought. By natural light and reason we can see only natural objects and truths; but in this new light of regeneration we see and understand things spiritual and divine.

Fourth, see its *definiteness*: "Show forth the praises of Him who hath *called* you. . . ." There is a divine call and a human response. The two together result in conversion. The call comes through the written Word and the inward voice of the Spirit. The response is a grateful opening of the heart to receive Christ. Then, the noble obligation is to "show forth" His "praises". Lord Jesus, help us to do so! Thou hast saved us by Thy precious blood; Thou hast given us new life by Thine indwelling; Thou hast bought us, and we are Thine. May all that we are, and say, and do, always advertise *Thee*.

Show Forth His Praises

"Show forth the praises of Him who hath called you out of darkness into His marvellous light."—1 Peter 2 : 9.

WELL, if God has wrought for us such a soul-saving exodus from darkness to light, should we not esteem it our radiant *obligation* to "show forth" His praises? The Greek word here translated as "praises" more properly means virtues or excellences. The moral beauties of our gracious God, as incarnated in the Lord Jesus Christ, are now to be exhibited in *us* who live in the wonderful new light of saving truth and communion with Heaven. In the words of an Old Testament phrase, our lives are to show forth "the beauty of holiness". Upon all our character and conduct, in all our business practices and leisure diversions, there is to be the stamp of reverent worship, godly sincerity, and spiritual joy. Whatever differences of disposition and personality there are among us Christian believers, the impress of our Saviour should be so uniformly observable that men "take knowledge" of us that we have "been with Jesus".

It is specially noteworthy that our text calls us to "*show* forth" His virtues. That word, "show", here flames with *challenge*. What we preach by lip we must show by life. Our religion must be real Christianity, not mere churchianity. Perhaps most of us know the pleasant little comedy of the two bachelor brothers named Robertson, one of whom was a Doctor of Divinity, and the other a Doctor of Medicine. They lived together, and not infrequently were mistaken for each other. One day a person who needed medical attention telephoned: "Are you the doctor who preaches, or the doctor who practises? I want the one who *practises*, please." Yes, we want the one who practises, please. That is just what our text insists on when it tells us to "*show* forth" his virtues.

But that word, "show", also brims with *comfort*. Not many of us can be ministers, evangelists, missionaries, preachers, but we can all "*show* forth His praises". If we cannot address the brethren, we may "adorn the doctrine". If we cannot command attention in public, we may commend the Saviour in private. If we cannot expound the truth from a pulpit, we may express the truth in our conduct. If we cannot shout, we can shine! Lighthouses blow no horns, they only shine; but they save thousands every year from a watery grave. Some years ago, at a conference of Christian girls in Japan, the theme was, "How to glorify God in our lives". One of the girls made the following contribution. "Early in the spring my mother bought some flower seeds, rather ugly little things, and planted them in our garden. Presently they grew and bloomed forth most beautifully. A neighbour coming round and seeing them exclaimed, 'How delightful are your flowers! Will you please give me some of the seeds?' Now if that neighbour had seen only the flower seeds, and not the flowers themselves, she would never have asked for them. It was only when she saw the flowers that she wanted the seeds from which they came. Even so, the truths of Christianity may not in themselves appeal at first to certain kinds of people. They may seem hard to grasp, or unlikely to work. But when people see those truths blossoming out in beautiful, fragrant lives, sacrificial service, kindly doings and speakings, they begin to long after the truths which have wrought such lives."

What the Flower Said

"Show forth the praises of Him who hath called you out of darkness into His marvellous light."—1 Peter 2 : 9.

At one time my home was in a semi-rural area, several miles out from the city church where I ministered. When the weather permitted, I used to enjoy the long walk in, on a Sunday morning, to the church service. One Sunday morning, as I walked by a field, soon after starting, I heard a pleasant little voice say, "Good morning, sir," but on looking round I could see no one anywhere. Thinking myself mistaken, I was about to resume my walk when out piped the little voice again, so I said, "I cannot see you. Who are you?" To my utter surprise the sweet little voice replied, "Why, of course you can see me, sir. I'm the little flower nearest the pathway." I could scarce believe it—a flower talking! "Well, well!" I exclaimed. "I never knew flowers could talk"; to which the pretty bloom replied again, "Nor did I until this morning; but, you see, *God* told me to speak to you." This was really too much for me. "What!" I gasped. "*God* told you to speak to me?" "Yes, He told me to tell you to preach this morning on 1 Peter 2 : 9: 'Show forth the praises of Him who hath called you out of darkness into His marvellous light'."

By this time I was spellbound; so after nodding gracefully in the morning breeze, and giving a grateful smile to the morning sun, the demure little pinky-white flower continued, "You see, sir, I was not always a pretty flower like this. I used to be an ugly brown seed, and it seemed as though nothing beautiful or worthwhile could ever come of ugly little *me*. What was worse, I was in utter darkness, under the soil, though I did not know then that its name was darkness. All I knew was that I was down there, an ugly little seed, and could not see, and seemed to be dying without ever discovering why I was there at all. I don't know just how long I was there, but I began to feel a strange influence pulling me upwards. There was a power working in me which I could not explain. I felt that somehow there must be something above me to which I must reach up. Then, one morning when the sun had been shining for some time after rain-showers, I felt a wonderful power lift me right up; and suddenly I found myself in the light of a wonderful new world up here! After that I grew into the lovely flower at which you are looking; and now I gratefully bloom just for one thing—to 'show forth the praises of Him who called me out of darkness into His marvellous light'." I was just going to ask the dear little flower a question when it added, "And now, sir, I am not allowed to speak any more; I can only *show* forth His praises by what I *am*. Good-bye, sir. Don't be late for church." Then all was silent again. But I have never forgotten that morning walk; and some of my people said they would never forget my sermon on 1 Peter 2 : 9. Dear God, help us to learn from the flowers, that there is nothing higher or lovelier than to "show forth" Thy virtues who hast called to us "out of darkness" into Thy "marvellous light".

God make my life a fragrant flower,
   Diffusing joy to all;
Content to bloom in native bower,
   Although the place be small.

Cure for Depression

"Why art thou cast down, O my soul? and why art thou disquieted within me? hope thou in God: for I shall yet praise Him, who is the health of my countenance, and my God."—Ps. 42:11.

Most of us know something about seasons of depression. They can be a sore trial; and how to deal with them can be a wearying problem. Notice the words which the psalmist uses of himself—"cast down" and "disquieted". The first looks backward, the second looks forward. The godly man had been "cast down" by what had already occurred. He was "disquieted" by what might yet be.

Once or twice in recent air travel I have been with the pilot in the nozzle of the plane, and have had him tell me of the various factors in the safe piloting of aircraft through unfavourable weather. Similarly, as we sit with the writer of these two psalms we find him telling us much about piloting our *hearts* through squalls of depression.

In the earlier part of the psalm, see his SELF-INTERROGATION. He turns in upon himself with, "*Why* art thou cast down, O my soul?" In times of depression it is wise to make our emotions give account of their behaviour before the united board of reason, judgment and conscience. This usually lays bare certain causes which can be counteracted. In the first strophe of this psalm we note three.

First, there was *interrupted communion with God*. "My soul thirsteth for God, for the living God: when shall I come and appear before God?" This devout habitué at Jehovah's sanctuary was driven beyond Jordan, and ached to be back for his set times of devotion in Jerusalem. Even so, if you and I are really born again, we shall be the prey of depressions if the new nature in us is denied communion with God.

Another source of the psalmist's gloom was *misunderstanding by others*. "They continually say to me: Where is thy God?" Such misunderstanding, especially by those who are dear to us, can be dejectingly disconcerting, most of all when it concerns God's dealings with us.

The third contributor to this good man's depression was *unhelpful brooding over the past*. See verse 4. It is a strange characteristic of our human nature that we find a tempting deliciousness in dwelling hopelessly on departed joys. Almost always when we become broody we become moody.

But now see the psalmist's SELF-EXHORTATION. "Hope thou in God. . . ." Self-interrogation leads to self-*exhortation*. But is this self-exhortation as intelligent as it is brave? It is. The trouble-beset writer has found the true sources of hope. First, he resolves that instead of merely remembering the past, he will fixedly remember *God*—"My soul is cast down within me; therefore will I remember THEE. . . ." Next, there is new confidence in *God's sympathy, faithfulness and presence*. "The Lord will command His lovingkindness in the daytime, and in the night His song shall be with me." This is wonderful improvement: even in the night, a *song*! Finally, there is *the resolve to pray it through*. "I will say unto God, my Rock . . ." To know his prayer, read psalm 43.

Thus this godly man rose above his cloudy depression into clear shining —"I SHALL YET PRAISE HIM"! His circumstances were not yet changed, but *he himself was*. Does this speak to you and me?

"Those which had been carried away unto Babylon . . . came again unto Jerusalem and Judah."—Ezra 2 : 1.

TAKEN as a whole, the eight hundred years' occupancy of Canaan by the covenant people is a woeful story. Towards the end it becomes the most tragic national record ever written. In it we see high calling and deep sinning; transcendent privilege and grovelling abuse of it; until deportation into exile was the only answer. That banishment cured Israel of idolatry once for all. A new chapter began when in 536 B.C. the "Remnant" (some 50,000) returned to Judea.

Try to get into the thoughts and feelings of the parents among those fifty thousand. When carried away captive, fifty-one years earlier, they were but children or youths; they are now advanced in years. What strange thrill of emotion must have been theirs, to be back again in the homeland! What memories! What gratitude to God! What discouragement at the silted débris of cities, and the unkempt entanglements of weeds where once had been fields of waving grain! Jerusalem was in ruins. The temple was destroyed. The Davidic throne was gone.

What was there left? Well, first, there was the teaching of the *past.* They had really learned, specially of God's faithfulness. Second, there was promise for the *future.* Although the Davidic throne was no more, the Davidic *line* was, from which the Messiah should come. Third, there was the presence of Jehovah among them in the *present.* The edict of Cyrus had just given new evidence. Fourth, they had the Holy Scriptures.

Does not all this speak to ourselves today? Does not the story of that long-ago sinning and tragic exile and later restoration objectify what happens widely in individual human experience?

We go on, year after year, living our lives in our own way, pushing God out of our thoughts, loving our idols, fondling our sins, choosing darkness rather than light because our deeds are evil; or else we go on in proud self-righteousness, disdaining any need of a Saviour.

Then something happens which corresponds with that awful exile of long ago. Our fair city is laid low. We had thought it so strong, so safe, so lasting; but its walls are battered down, its palaces flung to the ground, its gates twisted in the fire. That which has meant so much to us is suddenly struck down in ruin, and we are dragged into an exile of grief, disillusionment, wretchedness, remorse. It may come upon us through sickness, accident, reverses, bereavement, and pitiful is our desolation.

In our exile we begin to think about God; the way we have neglected Him, dishonoured Him, wronged Him. We begin to reflect how patient He has been; how awful is His anger; how sovereign His power. We begin to fear Him; to be troubled about our sin, and to sense that all this calamity has come upon us because of it. We are convicted. We begin to know our need of God, of forgiveness, of salvation. Like the returning exiles of long ago, we come back to look at our life through new eyes, eyes which are sadder and older but wiser. We see the wreckage of what was once so brave and bright and buxom; and we ask, "What is left?"

And it is then that we find God in a new way. We are done with idols. *HE* is left, faithful, compassionate, all-sufficient as ever. He becomes our *all*; and at last we find the joy which is deeper than all others.

What is there Left?

"My Spirit remaineth among you: fear ye not."—Hag. 2:5.

IN our reading yesterday we imagined ourselves with the long-ago Jewish "Remnant", returning to Judea after the fifty-one years of exile in Babylonia. We sat down with them amid the heart-breaking ruins of Jerusalem. We tried to look through their weeping eyes at the weed-tangled fields outside. The Jerusalem of their younger days was no more. The glorious temple was no more. The Davidic throne was no more. No city, no temple, no king! *What was there left?*

Oh, there are experiences in life when we find that question wrung from our destitute hearts—"*What is there left?*" After long and deep sinning, when we would fain come back to God, but feel we have sinned away the last chance; when we would give anything to blot out the past, but cannot; when we would give our very life-blood to undo the bitter consequences, but are helpless; when we would recapture the many wantonly wasted years, and despair that they are gone forever; *then,* in our agony, we find ourselves asking, "What is there left?"

For the remorseful, repentant, returning prodigal or backslider there is *the precious Gospel* which tells of a heavenly Father whose love is bigger than our biggest sinning; of a Saviour whose atoning death for us wipes out all the black guilt of the past; of a sympathetic, patient, mighty Holy Spirit who comes into the heart to renew it with power to live a new life. Even though the past cannot be undone, it can be forgiven. Even its consequences can be overruled if sincerely committed to God.

And for all other desolate hearts, remember, there are the *divine promises* which are given to us in our dear old Bible. There was a business-man in New York who returned home one day and threw himself on the couch, saying, "Well, everything's gone." Those at home asked him, "Whatever do you mean?" "Oh," he replied, "we have had to suspend payments. Our house has gone to pieces. *There's nothing left.*" His little child bounded from the other side of the room, and said, "Papa, you have *me* left." Then his wife, who had been very sympathetic, came up and said, "My dear, you have *me* left." And the dear old grandmother, seated in a corner of the room, put up her spectacles on her wrinkled forehead, and said, "My son, you have *all the promises of God left.*" Then the merchant burst into tears, exclaiming, "What an ingrate I am! How many precious things are left! God forgive me!"

Then again, there is a *living Saviour,* who loves us dearly and deeply, and who says to us in Hebrews 13:5, "I will *never* leave thee."

Then again there is *the Advent hope.* Just as the long-ago Jewish "Remnant" had the promise of their Messiah's eventual coming, when they started the mammoth task of rebuilding Judea, so there is still left to *us* the promise of that golden daybreak which will bring Him back the second time as the Church's rapturing Bridegroom. (Rom. 8:18.)

Finally there is left to us *the challenge of a new task.* As the fifty thousand returned to Judea to rebuild the *theocracy,* so each of us today is meant to be a living theocracy among our neighbours. The divine kingship is to be seen in our lives; and through us His kingdom is to be built up in *other* lives. Yes, thank God, there are *many* precious things left to us!

Wanted: Palm Trees!

"The righteous shall flourish like the palm tree."—Ps. 92 : 12.

YES, there is need for palm-tree Christians! Let me here mention seven characteristics of the palm-tree which are well worth considering. First, there is its featuristic *uprightness*. In this it is markedly unlike many of our European and North American trees, with their curved and bending trunks and arms. Whether you see it on the flat or on the slope it grows uniformly upright. The prophet Jeremiah has this in mind when he says, "They are upright as the palm tree" (Jer. 10: 5). Oh, that the same might be said of all Christians!

Second, there is its *overcoming power*. It grows, it even "flourishes" amid the dearth and drought of the desert. Where most other trees would find survival impossible, it lifts its fronds in kindly victory. Oh, for more of this flourishing despite circumstances! (See Exod. 1 : 12.) There is much emphasis today on improving environment, education, working conditions, and recreational amenities. It is all good; but there is something even better, and that is a change in people themselves. In the long view, it is not environment which changes the man, but the man who makes his environment reflect himself. A Spirit-filled Christian will live a holy life amid the unholiest surroundings. (See 1 Thess. 1 : 6, 7.)

Third, the palm tree is peculiar in its *way of growth*. Unlike most other trees, instead of adding a new outer ring to the trunk every year, it grows inwardly, from the centre. So, indeed, is it with true Christian life. Vital Christianity is an inward renewal by the Holy Spirit, an inward sanctification of heart, and an inward development of character, which then outwardly manifests itself in uprightness, beauty, and fruitfulness.

Fourth, the palm tree is *not amenable to grafting*. Many other trees may be, but not the palm. Nor is the true Christian life. "Having begun in the Spirit," we cannot now be "made perfect by the flesh" (Gal. 3 : 3). We cannot graft law into grace; flesh into spirit; Moses into Christ; salvation by works into salvation by faith.

Fifth, the palm tree is an *evergreen*. It knows no autumn brownness or winter bareness. Oh, for a similar all-the-year-round "beauty of holiness" among us believers!

Sixth, the palm tree is outstanding in *the height of its foliage and fruit*. It is as though it would fain bear its beauty and fruit before the eyes of heaven, rather than just to be "seen of men". Does not that, also, speak to us?

Seventh, it is notable for its *beauty of stature*. Each kind of palm has its own beauty, but I can recall how my wife and I, on our first visit to Florida, admired the stately *royal* palms there. The regal lover, Solomon, must have had such palms in mind when he said, "Thy stature is like to a palm tree" (Song. 7 : 7). See also 1 Kgs. 6 : 29. Oh, for more palm-tree beauty of stature in a *moral and spiritual sense*!

Finally, mark the *usefulness* of the palm tree. (1) Strong and "goodly" (Lev. 23 : 40). (2) Yields palm sugar and wine. (3) Fruit to refresh the weary traveller. (4) The older the tree, the sweeter its fruit. (5) Gives welcome shade. (6) Points to where there is water, as we Christians should be pointers. (7) It is the symbol of rejoicing and victory (Rev. 7 : 9). Fellow-believer, are you a palm-tree Christian?

Something to Talk About

"Make known His deeds among the people."—Ps. 105: 1.

ONE thing which often impresses me in the Old Testament, especially in the psalms, is that godly hearts in old-time Israel had a much tenderer concept of God, and a much more affectionate fellowship with Him, than many present-day critics of Old Testament religion are disposed to acknowledge. Besides religious awe, there was a sense of *filial* relationship toward God, and a truly *loving* exultation in His graciousness. It is revealing and uplifting to travel through the psalms picking out the warm-hearted responses toward a Jehovah who is as condescending and compassionate as He is ineffable in holiness. Here are a few: "Oh, how I love Thy law!" "Thy lovingkindness is better than life"; "Jehovah God is a sun and a shield"; "I love Jehovah"; "He crowneth thee with lovingkindness and tender mercies"; "How precious are Thy thoughts unto me, O God!" "Whom have I in heaven but Thee? and there is none on earth I desire beside Thee."

See how the psalm begins from which we take our text: "O give thanks unto Jehovah! Call upon His name. *Make known His deeds among the people.* Sing unto Him. Talk ye of all His wondrous works." Is not that a delightful, eager enthusiasm?—and does it not challenge us Christian believers who have become eternally saved at the infinite cost of Calvary? Should *we* not continually "give thanks", and "call upon His name", and "make known His deeds among the people"?

How, then, are we to "make known His deeds among the people"? The psalmist gives us seven ways. First, he says, "*Sing unto Him*" (verse 2). Yes, even if you have a weak throat or a cracked voice, sing your grateful testimony and let others hear. A religion which saves should be a religion which sings! Second, "*Talk of all His wondrous works*" (2). Tell especially His wondrous works in redemption. Tell how He converted and saved your soul. That which is vital should be vocal! Third, the psalmist says, "*Glory in His holy Name*" (3). Instead of keeping your Christian enthusiasm severely under lock and key, let it be evident that you glory in the God who has saved you—far more than the rich man glories in his riches or the worldling glories in his godless absorptions. Fourth, the psalmist adds, "*Let the heart of them rejoice that seek Jehovah*" (3). Grumblers and grousers never attract anybody to their philosophy, nor do grumpy religionists attract souls to Christ. New Testament Christianity is a rejoicing religion—that was the secret of its original contagiousness. Fifth, the psalmist counsels us, "*Seek Jehovah and His strength*" (4). From Him will come the joy and strength for our witnessing and singing and speaking and glorying and rejoicing. Sixth, "*Seek His face evermore*" (4)—that is, linger often in the secret trysting-place of communion with Him. Seventh, "*Remember His marvellous works that He hath done*" (5). Few things are more stimulating than to keep remembering what He has already done in behalf of His faithful people. Every backward glance of memory reminds us that "God hath done great things for us, whereof we are glad"! Is it not an obligation of sanctified gratitude, to "make known His deeds among the people"? Dumb statues, however beautiful, can never substitute for speaking witnesses.

The Homeopathic Prophet

"Elias was a man subject to like passions as we are, and he prayed earnestly . . ."—Jas. 5 : 17.

THE greatest blessing which can come to an unconverted man is for him to become savingly united to Christ; but when once we are saved, the highest honour which can ever be ours is to become used of Christ in the saving and blessing of others. Now it is a fact, exemplified both in the Scriptures and in Christian experience, that the men and women whom God most uses are men and women of prayer. We may not be able to grasp all the divine philosophy of prayer, but this we *do* know, that in the providential government of this world, and in the administration of redemption, prayer creates an opportunity for the working of divine grace and power in men which otherwise there would not be. Not that there is any power inherent in prayer itself, any more than it is faith itself which saves the soul; but prayer is the coupling-link between human need and divine omnipotence. With this in mind, think again of Elijah. The brief reference to him in this Epistle of James tells us three things: (1) he was "a man"; (2) he "prayed"; (3) he "prayed again".

So first, then, "Elias was a *man* . . ." We tend to overlook this. Distance wraps those long-ago Old Testament heroes in garments of fire, until we scarcely think of them as being human like ourselves. Especially is this so in the case of the startling, rugged, fiery prophet, Elijah. Ask a dozen people who Elijah was, and probably eleven of them, if not all twelve, will reply that he was "a prophet". In the case of this sinewy-armed, dervish-looking challenger of wicked Ahab, it is easiest of all, perhaps, so to see the *prophet* that we lose sight of the *man*.

But to bring home to us that Elijah was as human as we ourselves are, James says, "Elias was a man *subject to like passions as we are*." This, of course, does not mean that Elijah was subject to human passions in the sense of being a morally defeated man. Nay, we know him to have been a strong, austere man of the ascetic mould. James simply means that Elijah had just the same "raw material" of human nature as ourselves; the same human susceptibilities, dispositions, and infirmities. He was human with all those sensations, temptations, fears, hopes, reactions, which are our common human accompaniments. To quote James literally, "Elias was a man homeopathic" (*homoiopathes*). Never do we see it so clearly as when the overwrought champion sinks down under the juniper bush and requests to die. That which made this very human man so mighty was the supernatural power which flamed through him.

Despite all his rugged qualities and self-denying austerities, if Elijah had not been a man of prayer we should never have heard of him. Probably there were many equally gifted or far more gifted men than Elijah in the "schools of the prophets" during that long-ago religious apostasy; yet we do not hear of them. Elijah was a man "very jealous for the Lord of Hosts", not only in spectacular public exploits like that on Mount Carmel, but behind the scenes, in lonely, persevering *prayer*. Many ministers today are so anxious to be *preachers* that they fail to be *prophets*. It is prayer which makes prophets. The man of prayer is the man of power. It was so in Elijah's day; and it is so still.

Prayer . . . Drought . . . Rain

He prayed earnestly that it might not rain . . . and he prayed again, and the heaven gave rain."—Jas. 5 : 17, 18.

"*And he prayed earnestly.*" This lets out a secret. Away back in the First Book of Kings, where we have the account of the long, dreary drought, we are simply told that Elijah warned the wicked King Ahab of its approach, and that it then came. Now, however, the New Testament penman tells us that behind the drought was a praying man!

"And he prayed earnestly *that it might not rain.*" Note here the operativeness of prayer in relation to natural forces. He who quelled the winds and waves of Galilee at the entreaty of His distraught disciples still controls the forces of Nature, and still commands them to do His special bidding if that is necessary to the answering of His people's prayers.

"And he prayed earnestly *that it might not rain.*" So here was a prayer that God should inflict judgment. Shame on you, Elijah! How dare you pray such a prayer? Think of the innocent women and children! Think of the poor animals! Think of *all* the sufferings which will be entailed in such a drought! Well, Elijah *does* think of it all; and he has the spiritual insight to perceive that even the worst of merely physical calamities is a blessing if it saves a nation and people from *spiritual* suicide.

"*And he prayed again . . .*" Yes, mark it well; he prayed "*again*". Earlier answer to prayer now became the basis of further prayer. If God had answered prayer to inflict drought—a drought which had eventually served its purpose, bringing king and people to a religious crisis-point on Mount Carmel, surely God would now hear further prayer—prayer to send rain. Let us lay it well to heart: if God answers prayer to inflict judgment (and He does), how much more will He hear it to send blessing!

Well, there it is; read it again: "Elijah was a man subject to like passions as we are, and he prayed earnestly that it might not rain; and it rained not on the earth for the space of three years and six months. And he prayed again, and the heaven gave rain, and the earth brought forth her fruit." However dramatic, arresting, commanding Elijah may be as a public figure in the Israel story, he assumes a new significance for us in the light of this New Testament comment. He suddenly becomes very close to us as a human brother with sensitive human susceptibilities like our own; and behind the fiery, public champion of the Jehovah religion we see the humble intercessor, on his face before God, pleading in lonely prayer "with strong crying and tears" (Heb. 5 : 7) for his apostate countrymen. In many a rocky cavern, in many a secret ravine, this son of the hilly solitudes poured out his soul to God. He is a great challenge to us today. God knows we need a new generation of praying Elijahs. Were times ever more urgent or ominous? Were the issues ever immenser or more desperate? Our ministers need to pray more. Our church leaders need to pray more. All of us Christian believers need to pray more. Prayer operates not only individually, but nationally and internationally. We claim to believe this, but do we implement it by practice? We should daily spread the modern situation before God in prayer. Why, the very reason James refers to Elijah is to illustrate his statement in verse 16, "*The effectual, fervent prayer of a righteous man availeth much.*"

"The effectual fervent prayer of a righteous man availeth much."—Jas. 5: 16.

IF the effectual fervent prayer of a righteous man availed much under the *old* covenant, how much more does it under the *new* covenant! And if prayer operates in the *natural* realm, as in Elijah's praying for drought and then for rain, how much more in the *spiritual* realm, as we pray for the release of divine power to save men and nations from the tyranny of sin! And how vital is such prayer in the prosecution of our "holy war" against evil; against anti-God ideologies outside the organised church, and subversive heresies inside it!

Observation for a long period and over a wide area has convinced me that few Christians, comparatively, maintain what could honestly be called prayer *warfare*; yet that is what we should all be doing. We have listened too easily to the materialistic scientist and his confident opinion that prayer cannot affect the fixed operations of natural law. There are many realities in the universe which cannot be seen through telescopes or decided by mathematics. Of all ideas, the most inane is that God is a prisoner behind His own laws.

It is time we Christians "believed our beliefs" again in this matter of prayer. We must resolutely believe again that God answers prayer, *whatever* it may involve in relation to cosmic laws. The evolution of events on this earth is controlled by God as the all-sovereign First Cause; and prayer occupies as real a place in His administration as all other second causes. Divine power is called into operation by the prayers of Christ's people. They may be a minority, but this apparatus of prayer makes them the vital factor on earth, if they will to be so. Praying is thus far more than a wholesome spiritual discipline.

We must recognise the difference, of course, between prayer concerning things inanimate, such as weather or circumstances, and prayer concerning living intelligences, such as human beings. It was one thing for Elijah to pray for a chastising drought; it was another thing praying for impenitent human rebels like Ahab and backslidden Israel. The elements, or forces of Nature, do not have consciousness, intelligence, or volition; and therefore they may be immediately manipulated in answer to prayer, if God so wills; but with prayer for *human* individuals it is different. God will not violate the freedom of the human will. He *could* do. He could bring the stoutest rebel cringing in terror to His feet. But there would be no *moral* victory in *that*; nor would there be regeneration effected in the human rebel. That is why prayer for human beings is often a longer process. We are praying for free-willed intelligences. God seeks the voluntary co-operation of free-willed intercessors to bring about the free-willed response of *other* human beings; and if the intercessor continues in earnest prayer, there comes a point when God can say in all righteousness against the powers of evil, "Should not this much-prayed-for soul be released?"—and the constraining power of the Holy Spirit becomes victorious in the soul of the one for whom we have prayed. Mystery? Yes, of course there is mystery; but that is what happens, and seemingly that is the "how" of it! "The effectual, fervent prayer of a righteous man availeth much"!

The Golden Prospect

"The hope which is laid up for you in heaven."—Col. 1: 5.

IN the ancient world of Greece and Rome, that word, "hope", had become opprobrious. To the people of that era, hope was an empty bubble, a will-o'-the-wisp, a mocking mirage, a delusive irony. When Christianity came, it rescued the word, and crowned it with glory. Just as Nature, by one of her master-strokes, brings the exquisite butterfly out of the ugly worm, so, by the miracle-stroke of His resurrection, our Lord Jesus transfigured that despised word, "hope", into radiance and beauty; for He "abolished death, and brought life and immortality to light through the Gospel". "Hope" is now one of the dearest words in our Christian vocabulary.

Hope always has a twofold reference. It has both an objective and a subjective meaning. Hope must always have an object outside ourselves on which it fixes, and in that sense is *objective*. Yet hope is also a reaction within our own minds, and in that sense is *subjective*. Hope always has these two aspects. On the one hand it is a prospect of the future; on the other hand it is a possession of the present.

Undoubtedly, a hope grounded in truth and focussed on a noble goal is one of the greatest influences in human life, fashioning character, stimulating endeavour, sweetening the disposition, and fostering patient endurance. It is the soul's anchor amid many a storm; the gleam of dawn in the fourth watch of many a dark night; the snowdrop peeping through the winter snow as the delicate but determined prophet of the coming Spring. It was hope which kept William Carey at it through those early years of heavy setbacks in India, and rewarded him at last. It was hope which kept Adonirah Judson at it, preaching every day for fourteen years in a Burma bazaar without seeing a single convert, and then saying, "The future is as bright as the promises of God." After one of the worst bombings of London, during the Second World War, a notice was seen in the wrecked premises of a businessman, "*Everything lost here, but hope*"!

Think again, for a minute, of our hope in its *objective* sense. Our text speaks of it as "*the hope which is laid up for you in heaven*". Let it be both admitted and claimed, then, that our Christian hope is one which looks above this world, and beyond this present age. We shall always vigorously rebutt the charge that we Christians are too set upon the future life to do much good in the present. The history of Christian philanthropy gives the lie to that allegation. Yet we have no high hopes of any man-made utopia down here. We shall do all we can to improve the world while we are in it; but the hope which our New Testament sets before us is above and beyond "this present world", and we are not ashamed to say so.

The psalmist said, "I will lift up mine eyes unto the hills" (Ps. 121: 1), but we Christian believers are to lift up our eyes above and beyond the hills of earth, to that land which is "fairer than day", where our heavenly Bridegroom has gone to prepare us a place. *Our* hope is, "the hope which is laid up for us in *heaven*". Not in any dreamy, monastic, or absent-minded sense, but in the sense of real, practical godliness, you and I are meant to be *heavenly minded*. Our Lord, who is our dearest treasure, is there; and as He Himself said, "Where your treasure is, there will your heart be also." Yes, our hope is *there*. Let us *live* for it.

"Beyond the Stars"

"The hope which is laid up for you in heaven."—Col. 1: 5.

So, then, our hope is *there*. "Far beyond the clouds, and beyond the stars, it is *there*"—the heavenly glory-land, the Father's house, the place of "many mansions"!

It will be the place of *utter sinlessness*. The last lingering effects of sin in our human nature will have been for ever obliterated. With sinless hearts and perfected powers we shall gather in ecstatic felicity amid that bliss ineffable.

Oh, for a heart that never sins!
Oh, for the robe of white!
Oh, for a voice to praise my King,
Nor weary day nor night!

It will all come true *there*! We shall be as sinless as the unfallen angels and the flaming seraphs!

It will also be the place of *perfect rest*. In Revelation 14: 13 the Spirit's voice says to John, "Blessed are the dead which die in the Lord . . . they *rest*". Many of the saints down here are so wearied with burdens and so spent with toil that one of heaven's loveliest aspects to them is its perfect rest. Yonder is the land where the heat and the burden, the sweat and the dust, the weight and the worry of toil are no more; the land where service itself is exhilaration, in the fadeless bloom and untiring freshness of perennial youth. And besides rest from toil, burden, worry, weariness, there will be rest from *battle*; rest from the continuous battle against temptation; rest from the unrelaxing treachery, ambushments, and frontal attacks of the world, the flesh and the devil.

This reminds us that heaven will also be the place of *consummated victory*. There the sword will be sheathed, and the clanking armour discarded. There we shall lay down our battlearms at the feet of a greater than Alexander or Caesar. There we shall wear the white robes, and wave the palms of victory, with that mighty multitude which no man can number! There the overcomers shall enter into the joy of their lord. The King shall bring them into His banqueting house, and His banner over them shall be love.

Heaven will also be the place of *perfect joy*. Our present natural senses give us no clue to the pure bliss of that celestial spirit-realm. We shall "hunger no more, neither thirst any more". The Lord Himself shall lead us to "fountains of living waters". Our sun of joy shall never set. The roses will never fade. No withering blight or wintry blast shall ever disfigure that fair paradise. Sickness shall never invade. Death shall never divide. There we shall have superior powers and faculties; amplified opportunities and facilities; enlarged capacities and capabilities, for service, for fellowship, and for the vision of the heavenly Throne. There we shall be re-united with our Christian loved ones—a meeting without a parting! There we shall see them all again, beautified into perfect replicas of Christ, yet retaining those distinctive traits of character and personality which made them peculiarly dear to us here on earth. There they and we shall mingle among the sinless immortals, and all the highest we ever longed to be, we *shall* be!

Our Hope Reflexively

"The hope which is laid up for you in heaven."—Col. 1 : 5.

It is good that we should reflect upon this hope in its *subjective* aspect, that is, in its present, experiential value to us. The goal of this hope lies away up yonder in heaven, and away out yonder in futurity; but the hope itself is a present possession and experience. Such a high-soaring, far-reaching hope should have a deep-going influence in heart and life.

First, and obviously, such a hope for the future should *sanctify the present*. Both hopelessness and hopefulness deeply affect the mind. Find a man who is hopeless concerning the future, and you have a picture of present wretchedness. Find a man who is hopeful concerning the future, and you see a heart that is vivacious and buoyant. There is an old saying, "While there's life there's hope." It is equally true to say, "While there's hope there's life." And the bigger, the stronger, the higher, the nobler a hope is, so the more benign and uplifting is its influence.

Now of all hopes, our Christian hope is the loftiest and loveliest, and it should have a corresponding reflex upon us. With such hope of high destiny before us, can we grovel among the mean and unworthy things? Can we live like those whose hope has no terminus beyond the grave or the crematorium? Nay, as the apostle John says, "When He (Christ) shall appear, we shall be like Him, for we shall see Him as He is. . . . And every man that hath this hope set upon *HIM* (Christ), *purifieth himself* even as He (Christ) is pure" (1 Jn. 3: 2, 3). As we shall be like Him then, in consummation, must we not grow like Him now, in character? Oh, Christian brethren, "partakers of the heavenly calling" (Heb. 3: 1), must we not live as befits that coming coronation day?

But further, such a hope should be a fountain of *joyous effort*. Can we pilgrimage to that heavenly summerland without endeavouring to win others for the Saviour? Must we not say, as Moses said to Hobab, "We are journeying into the place of which the Lord said, I will give it to you. *Come thou with us, and we will do thee good*"? The very glory of our hope should increase our pity for those who are without it. We should seek to save them because of the dread alternative to this hope, even the "wrath to come", and the "Great White Throne" of final judgment. Even the blessedness of heaven will be augmented to us if we see those there whom *we* recommended to the Saviour.

And, just once again, such a hope should keep us contentedly *labouring without present reward*. Look at the text again: it says that this hope is "laid up", or safely secured for us, "in heaven". No thieves can break through and steal it. It is inviolably guarded for us, so that neither men nor demons can ever cheat us of it. The inheritance is kept for *us*; and *we* are kept for the inheritance. It will be a hundredfold-sufficient reward for all our present labours, to hear our names read out at the great Roll-Call in the sweet by-and-by.

Then let me sanctify each day
By prayerful service while I may;
Until at last I share with Thee
The hope "laid up in heaven" for me.

"Deep calleth unto deep at the noise of Thy waterspouts: all Thy waves and Thy billows are gone over me."—Ps. 42:7.

ALTHOUGH David is not said to be the author of this psalm, we cannot doubt that it is from his pen. It bears the marks of David's style and experience in every sentence. Evidently, too, it refers to one of the most trying crises in his eventful life. It may well allude to the time when he had to flee the country from the insurrection movement of traitorous Absolom. In his whelming trouble David imagined that all God's waves and billows had gone over him, and that every conceivable calamity had engulfed him. He was wrong. There has been only One who ever could truly say, "All Thy waves and billows are gone over Me", and He was the Man of Calvary. All the waves and billows of suffering, indignation and wrath *did* break over *Him* as He bore "the curse of the Law" in our stead.

David's grief, however, was excessive enough. Not only did it seem as though all God's "waves and billows" had gone over him, he felt that the great deep of the sky above and the great deep of the sea beneath were calling to each other in some dread conspiracy against him—"deep calleth unto deep", just as they unite with each other in a terrifying waterspout! I have never seen a waterspout, but reports leave no doubt that they are strange and frightening phenomena. They are fairly frequent along the coast of the land where David lived. Apparently they are caused by palls of cloud overhanging the sea in windy or boisterous weather. Long funnels of black vapour are drawn down to the sea by the whirling of the wind; then, as these are driven whirling along by the wind, the swirling water beneath is caught up in sudden spiral motion, and rushes along with the vapour-spout above it. Dr. Thompson (*The Land and the Book*) says he often saw the water and the vapour actually unite in mid-air, then rush with loud noise toward the mountains, writhing, twisting, bending "like a huge serpent with its head in the clouds and its tail in the deep".

It certainly was a vivid metaphor which David used: "Deep calleth unto deep at the noise of Thy waterspouts." Yet I think, none the less, that David was also suspecting a most *comforting* lesson in those answering deeps of sea and sky. He was realising that the deep of his own sorrow was calling to the replying deep of God's sympathy, as the verse following our text shows. Those are two deeps which are *ever* calling to each other—the deep of our human *suffering*, and the deep of the divine *compassion*. Sorrow-stricken Christian, think not that there is no answering sympathy from heaven. Calvary pledges that there *is*. The God who there suffered *for* us, still suffers *with* us. Now read the psalm right through, especially noting verses 8 and 11. "Why art thou cast down, O my soul? And why art thou disquieted within me? Hope thou in God; for I shall yet praise Him, who is the health of my countenance, and my God."

Why did the eternal Son of God leave the glories of heaven for the ignominy of that felon's Cross? Why did He bleed to redeem us? It was because the deep of our human need called to the deep of His divine compassion. And does not the deep of each *individual* anguish find answering call in the deep of His loving sympathy?

Answering Depths

"Deep calleth unto deep."—Ps. 42 : 7.

THOSE answering deeps of the sky above and the sea beneath remind us of other great deeps which call to each other. *The deep of God's work in creation calls to the deep of the human intellect.* Ever since the beginning of human history, God's voice in the universe has been calling to the soul of man, and has awakened an answering call. We open our eyes on this wonderful world, its mountains, oceans, forests, rivers, and as we look we hear a voice calling to something deep within us. Surely all these material phenomena are not the products of a blank void! It is unthinkable that everything came from nothing and leads nowhere. These vast and verifiable realities of the physical universe *must* be the work of God. If we are true to the deepest and most native within us, must we not say with Jacob, "This is the house of God"?

Amid the bright light of the morning we lift our gaze to the heavens, to the draping clouds, the vast blue, the flashing sun; or amid the awing hush of night we look up to the friendly moon, the neighbour planets, the mysterious stars hung out like silver lamps in the dark vastness; and that same voice calls from the baffling deep out yonder to the inquisitive deep of our own minds, "Lo, God is here!"

Even more, as man's ability to explore and apprehend increases, so does the universe increase in its magnitudinousness and wonder. We sweep the heavens with our telescopes, and see constellation after constellation, profuse thoroughfares of stellar systems; or we take the microscope, and see the perfection of a snowflake, the exquisite beauty of a wayside flower, or the explosive universe concentrated inside an atom; everywhere we see the touch of a master hand; and everywhere we hear a voice from the deep of creation to an answering deep in our own being.

If we will simply listen as "deep calleth unto deep", we shall know that God is. If we are honest with ourselves we shall admit that atheism is madness. Men's unbelief in God is a matter of their *opinions*, not of their *intuitions*; that is why atheists pray when in trouble or in the solemn crisis of death. Intellectually warped by prejudice, the atheist says, "God is nowhere", but the innate instinct of his soul splits the word "nowhere" into "now here". The deep of God's work in creation calls to the deep within man's own intellect, and evokes an answering call despite all speculative evasions. When we are true to our own nature, we hear and sense and *know* that God is; that He is almighty, all-wise, all-seeing, all-knowing, omnipresent, beautiful in His thoughts, good in His purpose, and all-covering in His care.

Years ago, now, the *Watchman Examiner* reproduced the remarkable testimony of Lady Hope concerning Charles Darwin's return to the Christian faith in the later months of his life. I wish everybody *knew* that the father of the modern theory of organic evolution had thus returned. He wistfully reflected, "I was a young man with unformed ideas. I threw out queries, suggestions; and to my astonishment the ideas took like wildfire." He asked Lady Hope would she address the servants, tenants, and some neighbours, at a little meeting the next day. "What shall I speak about?" He replied, "Christ Jesus—and His salvation." In the end, convictions overcame opinions.

"Deep calleth unto deep."—Ps. 92 : 7.

Yes, "deep calleth unto deep". The *deep of God's Word in the Scriptures calls to the deep of human intuition.* Wonderful as is the reasoning faculty in man, there is something deeper and profounder than that in our human nature. Mind, soul, reason, intellect, all these terms are distinctively expressive of elements in the spiritual nature of man; but there is that which, in contradistinction to all else, we call the "*spirit*". Paul marks this distinction when he says, "The psychic man receiveth not the things of the Spirit of God . . . because they are spiritually discerned." There is that in human nature which gives a certain intuitive knowledge of what is true in things moral and spiritual. It may be abused and blurred; but it is there, and without it we should not be human at all. Indeed, this faculty of moral and spiritual intuition is the inmost reality of our being. However socially refined or vulgarized a man may be, there is at the centre of his being an innate response to that which is spiritually true when it is made known. Now the Bible addresses itself not only to the reasoning faculty, but to the *spirit;* and therefore it may be *tested* spiritually. I know that there are people who stumble over certain things in the Bible, but in most cases this is due to misunderstanding of the thing in question. We cannot deal here with such instances one by one. All of us are familiar with the type of cavilling to which I refer. Speaking here of the Bible comprehensively, does it evoke that intuitive recognition of spiritual truth which trembles sensitively in the deep of our moral and spiritual consciousness? Who can honestly deny that the answer is "YES"? That which is inmost and deepest in men all over the world responds to the spiritual truth of the Bible.

There is that old story of King Richard the First of England, and his minstrel. The king, you may recall, was imprisoned in the dungeon of an Austrian nobleman, and for some time Britain could not discover what had happened to him. Richard's minstrel went through Europe, visiting the great prisons, playing on his guitar outside each prison, an air which only the king and he himself knew. At length he came to the place where Richard was imprisoned. When he played and sang the familiar piece, he heard the king's deep voice responding from the dungeon. Thus the king was found and his release secured. Is it not even so with the Bible and the spiritual nature of man? As these divine strains penetrate to the inmost spirit, is there not that within us which instinctively responds in deep-down recognition? Give yourself time to meditate quietly, thoughtfully, prayerfully on this Book, and it will speak to you about itself far more impressively than any preacher can. As you reverently meditate on it you will find yourself inwardly recognising the voice of the Eternal; and there is no belief in the inspiration of the Bible which is so profoundly satisfying as that which springs from this certainty of spiritual intuition.

"Your Bible has no proofs that it is inspired," said a sceptic to a godly farmer. "Maybe," replied the happy rustic, "but it and me gets along fine without 'em." "But how, then, do you know it is the Word of God?" rejoined the sceptic. "I don't know *how* I know," said the farmer; "I just *know*. That Bible o' mine *talks*."

Divine Love and Human Need

"Deep calleth unto deep."—Ps. 42 : 7.

WITH these words before us, reflect how *the deep of God's love in the Gospel calls to the deep of our human need.* Wherever we follow the footprints of man we find not only ineradicable God-consciousness but an equally ineradicable sin-consciousness. There may be many subterfuges of evasion or camouflage, but these cannot obliterate man's disturbing consciousness of a God above and of wrong within. It is these two things together which oppress us with a weary sense of *need.*

Even the voice which calls to us from the "deep" of the creation has a tragic note. There is the destructive lightning, the erupting volcano, the earthquake, the blasting tornado, the savagery of the beasts, the jungle law of tooth and claw, the fearsome scourge of disease, the dire agony of war. There is a jarring discord in the music of things. There is something grievously wrong; the more so because there is a counterpart to it deep in the human soul. We are conscious that there is something painfully wrong within our own nature, something which somehow has a relatedness to that poignant suffering in the outer world. Thus we have a deep sense of wrong, of sin, of mystery, of fear, of *need*; and we cry out for God—cry out for Him in the pathetic wail of Job, "Oh, that I knew where I might find Him!"

The testimony of Scripture confirms and explains this witness of nature. The present groanings of the creation are the result of *sin*—a rebel movement which existed in God's universe even before the appearance of man; a moral corruption injected by Satanic guile into the blood-stream of the human race, away back in Eden. We human beings now find the excruciating contradiction within ourselves of wanting to escape God yet at the same time desperately needing to find Him. Conscious of inward estrangement from Him, we are terrified at the consuming fire of His holiness; yet oh, if we could only find Him a God of compassion . . .! Is there none can tell us?

Yes, there is One who comes to tell us! His name is Jesus. In Him, God looks on us through human eyes, beckons to us with human hands, feels with us through human emotions, weeps for us with human tears, and undertakes to be our Rescuer. Inasmuch as the holy law of God must be upheld for the moral safety of the universe, He voluntarily assumes representative responsibility for our total human guilt, and makes judicial reparation by His atoning Self-sacrifice, thereby releasing full and free forgiveness to us from the boundless father-heart of God. That is the very centre-truth of the Bible. That is the glorious Gospel, in which the great deep of God's redeeming love calls to the deep of our human need as sinners. Read again John 3: 16, and Matthew 11: 28. Does not the deepest depth within us call back in grateful reply?

Enveloping me everywhere—the God I ache to find,
Yet cannot find Him anywhere—above, before, behind;
Nay, miracle of miracles—in human form He stands!
He calls me with a human voice, and sympathetic hands!
In Jesus the eternal One has come from heaven above,
To answer all my aching cry, with everlasting love!

Antidote to Discouragement

"Looking unto Jesus."—Heb. 12 : 2.

THIS little participle clause often appears on motto cards, but how many of us catch the special meaning which glints from it in the light of its context? In these opening verses of Hebrews 12 the focal exhortation is, "Let us run with patience the race"; and the emphasis is on that word "patience". The supplemental clause, "Looking unto Jesus", gets its particular slant from that word "patience". We are to "run with patience . . . looking unto Jesus" as the supreme *example* of such patience.

The Greek word translated "patience" has the fuller meaning of patient *endurance*, which connects it with the surrounding territory. Chapter 10 : 36 says, "For ye have need of patient *endurance*. . . ." Then follows chapter 11, which is all about the patient enduring of faith. Then comes chapter 12 : 1, "Let us run with *patient endurance*. . . ." Then 12 : 2, "Who for the joy that was set before Him *patiently endured* the Cross. . . ." Then 12 : 3, "For consider Him that *patiently endured* such contradiction of sinners." Then 12 : 7, "If ye *patiently endure* chastening, God dealeth with you as sons." So this stretch of the epistle is all about patient enduring; and when our text urges us to run the race "looking unto Jesus", it is telling us the best antidote to discouragement.

"Looking unto Jesus." This should be our fixed mental habit, especially in days like ours. These are the age-end times. Iniquity abounds in a multiplicity of new expressions. The world was never more glamorous or seductive. International affairs move on an immense scale hitherto unparalled. Atomic research and invention have keyed life up to new tension and sensitivity. In all the human story there were never distractions of louder gaiety on the one hand, and of deeper gravity on the other. Life was never so fast or complex. Politics, finance, cliques, slogans, were never so clever, complicated, or deceptive. The status quo never seemed more shakily susceptible to violent disruption. This is the age of mental and nervous disorders, of druggists shops, sleeping pills and psychiatry. This is the twentieth-century apostasy of Christendom from the evangelical faith; of moral breakdown, of repudiated sanctions, of adolescent unchastity, of increased divorce, of tyrannical trade-unionisms, of totalitarianisms, and syndicated crime. There have never been such changes in *any* preceding century.

With all this, and the kaleidoscopic changefulness of the international situation, and the seemingly overwhelming odds against evangelical Christianity, and the temptations to compromise, and the plentiful discouragements to those who would be out-and-out Christians, it is easy to get our eyes diverted from Christ to the disturbing developments and discouraging doings all around us. "Looking unto Jesus": the words might have been written for this very hour; for the full force of the Greek word is, "Looking *off*, unto Jesus". By an act of intelligent determination we must "look *off*" to *JESUS*, the perfect example of patient endurance and the now-enthroned Forerunner who is the pledge of our own heavenly glorification. Our Lord foretold us, "Because iniquity shall abound, the love of many shall wax cold; but he that shall *endure* unto the end, the same shall be saved" (Matt. 24: 12, 13). And the best secret of enduring is, "Looking unto Jesus".

Keep Looking!

"Looking unto Jesus."—Heb. 12 : 2.

YES, we are to "run with *endurance* . . . looking unto Jesus". The danger of discouragement was much in the mind of the inspired penman. See chapter 10 : 23, "Let us hold fast the confession of our hope *without wavering.*" See 10 : 35, "*Cast not away* therefore your confidence. . . ." See 12 : 3, "Consider Him that endured such contradiction of sinners against Himself, *lest ye be wearied* and faint in your minds." See 12 : 12, "Wherefore lift up the limp-hanging hands, and the failing knees. . . ."

The peril of discouragement arose from two troublesome factors. First, there was the problem arising from present experience of human persecution. Second, there was the problem arising from delayed fulfilment of divine *promise* (see how "promise" recurs in 10 : 23, 36; 11 : 9, 13, 17, 39). What *was* the promise? It was three in one. There was the promise of our Lord's return (10 : 23–25; 10 : 37); the promise of the believer's resurrection (11 : 35); the promise of the New Jerusalem (11 : 10, 16). With persecutions pressing, and the promised consummations painfully delayed, those early converts from Judaism were sorely tempted to discouragement.

It is to *them*, and through them to *us*, that the texts say, "Let us run with patient endurance . . . *looking unto Jesus.*" Moreover, this "looking unto Jesus" has a threefold aspect. We are to look to Him, first, because of *who He is*—"Author and Finisher of our faith"; second, because of *what He did*—"endured the Cross"; third, because of *where He reigns*—"the right hand of God".

That word, "Author", in the Greek is "File-leader". We say to a rank of soldiers, "Right turn", and as every man turns right, the rank becomes a file with a leader. The people of Christ are here viewed as a long file with Christ Himself as the leader. Christian disciple, look ahead of you along the far-stretching file. Jesus, the File-leader, has passed beyond, and one after another the earlier figures in the file have followed after Him into the beyond. We ourselves, who bring up the rear of the long train, are stepping forward, keeping line, still following the great File-leader, and in the Apostolic succession. It is a great picture, the more so because Jesus is both the File-leader and the "*Finaliser*" of our faith. In Him the whole faith-life of the Christian is seen visibly objectified from start to finish; from earth to heaven; from time to eternity; from blood and shame to crown and throne!

But see what this File-leader and Finaliser *did*: "Who *instead of* [not "for"] the joy that was set before Him [and which He might have gone on uninterruptedly enjoying] endured the Cross, despising the shame"! And see where He now *reigns*: "at the right hand of the throne of God"—as the sovereign pledge that *we* shall one day share heaven's glory! Yes, yes; we must keep on "looking unto Jesus"!

And here the bright immensities
  Received our risen Lord,
Where light-years frame the Pleiades,
  And point Orion's sword?

Yes, and even more: He is in the very *throne* of the universe!

The Riches of His Goodness

"The riches of His goodness."—Rom. 2 : 4.

Most men reckon their riches in terms of the American dollar or the sterling pound, or some other national monetary unit; and in most countries there have been three metals of coinage—copper, silver, gold. We scarcely ever see gold coinage today, but the older among us can remember when it was common currency. There is an interesting parallel between those coinage-metals, copper, silver, gold, and the "riches" of *God* towards mankind, as revealed in the Bible.

First, we read about the "riches of His *goodness*". Romans 2 : 4, asks, "Despisest thou the riches of His *goodness* . . .?" These "riches of His goodness" are, so to speak, the *copper* coinage of the divine treasury. The goodness of God is no new idea. It is as old as the rainbow and the seasons of the year. When the Anglo-Saxon ancestors of the English-speaking peoples wanted a name for the Supreme Being, they called Him "God", their word for *good*.

The "riches of His goodness" *all* of us enjoy. God is good to all His creatures without partiality or favouritism. He is no respecter of persons, except that He respects us all alike. "He maketh His sun to rise on the evil and the good, and sendeth rain on the just and on the unjust." The psalmist had every reason to exclaim, "Thou crownest the year with Thy goodness." And all of us, if we have seeing eyes, can say, "Goodness and mercy follow me all the days of my life."

There is no meagreness in God's goodness. Romans 2 : 4 calls it "the *riches* of His goodness". 1 Timothy 6 : 17 says, "The living God giveth us richly all things to enjoy." And James 1 : 5 echoes, "God giveth to all men liberally, and upbraideth not." The vast majority of us have good reason to be thanking God all the time for food and clothing, friends and loved ones, home and shelter, sunshine and rain, singing birds and lovely flowers, sympathetic trees and restful green countryside; health of mind and body, use of limb and muscle, eyesight and hearing, individual liberty and many social comforts.

But "the riches of His goodness" are most meaningful of all in their *spiritual* intention. Read Romans 2 : 4 in full: "Despisest thou the riches of His goodness and forbearance and longsuffering; not knowing that *the goodness of God leadeth thee to repentance*?" What influence is so likely to make us repent of wrong which we have done to some person, than that person's heart-melting retaliation of kindness in return? Even so, the munificent, undeserved, continuous goodness of God is meant to beget within us a turning away from evil, to uprightness and godliness. "He hath not dealt with us after our sins; nor rewarded us according to our iniquities" (Ps. 103 : 10). Oh, to repent at His goodness, rather than at last tremble before His righteous wrath!

How oft have my footsteps
  To ruin drawn near,
In quicksands deceiving,
  By precipice sheer!
Yet there, in the shadows,
  My Watcher has cared;
My soul has been rescued,
  My life has been spared.

The Riches of His Grace

"The riches of His grace."—Eph. 1 : 7.

YESTERDAY we were thinking about the riches of God's *goodness*, which we likened to the *copper* coinage of the divine treasury. But now reflect on "the riches of His *grace*", which we may liken to the *silver* coinage of His kingdom. The *goodness* of God has to do with us as *creatures*, whereas the *grace* of God has to do with us as *sinners*. As we noted in Romans 2 : 4, the *goodness* of God would lead us to *repentance*; but following upon that, the *grace* of God seeks to bring us into *redemption*.

Is there a lovelier phrase in all the Scriptures than "the riches of His grace"? We have heard and read various definitions of God's "grace", but those definitions of it which we like best are the actual words of the New Testament. In Ephesians 2 : 4, it is called, "His great love wherewith He loved us"; and in verse 7, "His kindness toward us through Christ Jesus". In Titus 3 : 4, it is described as "the kindness and love of our Saviour-God toward man". God's grace, then, is His unmerited favour expressing itself in redeeming love. In this we see a further distinction between the "riches of His *goodness*" and the "riches of His *grace*". His providential goodness comes to us through *nature*. His redeeming grace comes to us through *Christ*.

Observe now that this redeeming "grace" which comes to us through Christ, comes to us in "*riches*". It is "the *riches* of His grace"! Read the whole verse in which the phrase occurs: "In whom (Christ) we have redemption through (at the cost of!) His blood; the forgiveness of sins according to the riches of His grace." Even God could not pay a vaster, costlier, more awful or glorious price for our redemption than that of His own incarnation in human nature, and His own sin-bearing, substitutionary Self-sacrifice on Calvary. It cost even the outpoured blood of incarnate deity! And because of this, the grace of God now pours to us in "riches". There is nothing hesitant or stinted about the forgiveness which comes to us through Christ. Notice the gauge, the measure, the "according to" in our text—"the forgiveness of sins *according to* the RICHES OF HIS GRACE"! As John Bunyan would say, this is "grace abounding"; big pardon for big sinners. None can out-sin such "riches" of grace, except by refusing the dear Saviour Himself, through whom the riches come to us.

If we have been inwardly awakened to our sinful state before God, and our ruinous plight as members of Adam's fallen race, surely there can only be the following reaction to this "forgiveness of sins according to the riches of His grace". First, we desperately *need* it; for only such riches of gracious forgiveness can cover the enormity of our sinning. Second, in Christ we *have* it; for as Romans 5 : 20 says, "Where sin abounded, grace did much more abound." Third, we love and adore the wonderful Saviour-God by whose "riches of grace" we are forgiven and eternally saved.

It passeth praises, that dear love of Thine,
My Saviour, Jesus, yet this heart of mine,
Would sing that love, so full, so rich, so free,
Which brings a guilty, rebel soul like me
Nigh unto God.

The Riches of His Glory

"The riches of His glory."—Rom. 9: 23.

HAVING briefly contemplated (in the two meditations preceding this one) the "riches of His goodness" and the "riches of His grace", let us now complete a trio by thinking on the "riches of His *glory*". If the "riches of His goodness" are the *copper* coinage, and the "riches of His grace" are the *silver* coinage, then the "riches of His glory" are the *golden* coinage of His infinite treasury. The everlasting surprise is that He shares all these "riches" with you and me. The riches of His goodness come to us through *nature*. The riches of His grace come to us through *Christ*. The riches of His glory wait for us in *heaven*. In Acts 7: 2 He is called "the God of glory", and in Ephesians 1: 17 "the Father of glory". Such epithets are used not only descriptively but distinguishingly. Over against all the figment gods and godlings and demiurgi of the Greeks and Romans, this God revealed in Jesus was, and evermore is, in the absolute sense, the one Divine Reality; distinguishingly and exclusively, "the God of *glory*".

But our text speaks about "the *riches* of His glory". What bewildering vastnesses such a phrase opens up! Think of the glory-riches in His *nature and attributes*: the "glory of His grace" (Eph. 1: 6), the "riches of His wisdom and knowledge" (Rom. 11: 33), the riches of His compassion (Rom. 10: 12), the "glory of His power" (2 Thess. 1: 9), the "glory of His majesty" (Isa. 2: 10). Try to imagine the glory of His *heaven* (Jn. 17: 5, 24; Acts 7: 55). The very word "glory" is used as a *name* for heaven in Philippians 4: 19 and 1 Timothy 3: 16.

The crowning wonder, however, is that these "riches of His glory" become *our* inheritance as "the redeemed of the Lord"! As Romans 8: 17 says, we are "heirs of God, and joint-heirs with Christ"! See John 17: 22: "And the *glory* which Thou hast given Me, I have given *them*." See Colossians 1: 27, "Christ in you, the hope of *glory*." See 1 Thessalonians 2: 12, "God hath called us unto His kingdom and *glory*." See 2 Corinthians 4: 17, "Our light affliction, which is but for a moment, worketh for us a far more exceeding and *eternal weight of glory*." See 1 Peter 5: 10, "The God of all grace . . . hath called us unto *His eternal glory*."

Oh, the "riches of His goodness"!
  Oh, the "riches of His grace"!
Oh, the "riches of His glory",
  Inexhaustible as space!
Oh, the love beyond all measure
  Which for me would suffer so,
That a heav'n of glory-treasure
  Through the ages I might know!

What the glories of heaven will be, who shall describe? Our physical senses give no clue. The glories of the spiritual sphere must be indescribably superior to merely material glories. All earthly symbols which Scripture uses to represent them are *only* symbols. The heavenly *realities* must utterly transcend them. "Earth's joys grow dim; its glories pass away." The heavenly joys and glories to which God has called us in Christ *never* grow dim or pass away.

If We But Knew

"If thou (Jerusalem) hadst known. . . ."—Luke 19: 42.
"If thou knewest the gift of God. . . ."—Jn. 4: 10.

As we read these two plaintive "ifs" what wide areas of human pathos, wistful regret, and poignant warning, open out before our minds! How often do we hear the sad, useless excuse, "If only I had known. . . ."! It is one of those helpless pleas which always come too late. Yet have we not all indulged it far too frequently? Early rashness can never be mended by later remorse. What cruel risks we take! What grievous wounds we inflict! What bitter hurt we cause! Then we apologetically endeavour to ameliorate it with, "If only I had known"! Yes, many a time, if only we had stopped to think; if only we had known; if only we had perceived the real instead of the merely seeming, the inward instead of the merely outward, how different would our feelings and words and actions have been!

We may well ponder this in relation to life's short-lived *opportunities*. One morning just before leaving for business, a husband offered his wife a kiss of reconciliation after a domestic misunderstanding. She coldly refused it. At noon he was brought home dead. "Oh, God forgive me!" exclaimed the suddenly widowed woman. "If only I had spoken to him as I should have done! If only I had known . . .!" Yes, if only she had known! But that is just it: we none of us know, and therefore should not presume. Let the law of kindness rule our hearts and our tongues.

If we but knew that through the closing door
Someone we love would enter never more,
Would we not hasten with our richest store?
    If we but knew!

If we but knew some heart beside our own
Had walked some dark Gethsemane alone,
Oh, in what bounty would our love be shown!
    If we but knew!

A dear old grandfather breathed his last on earth. His grandchild, a sweet little girl, took his big hand in hers and said, "Dear grandpa, you know that I was always good to you while you were alive." What a world it is worth to be able to speak like that! Most of us, perhaps, as we look back over the years, wish we could expunge unkind words and deeds to loved ones. Let us seize opportunities of being kind while they are here.

Most of all, let us seize opportunities of winning souls for Christ while we may. D. L. Moody tells how he gave an evangelistic address to a large Chicago audience, and then told them to go home and think carefully about accepting Jesus as Saviour. Before the next Sunday came, the great Chicago fire occurred. Many of those people were burned to death, and many others Moody never saw again. After that, whenever he preached the Gospel, he always pleaded for immediate decision. Opportunities are often here just for a day, an hour, a moment, and then are gone for ever! That is why Galatians 6: 10 says, "As we have *opportunity*, therefore, let us do good unto all."

Yes, If We But Knew

"If thou (Jerusalem) hadst known. . . ."—Luke 19: 42.
"If thou knewest the gift of God. . . ."—Jn. 4: 10.

CONTINUING our reflections on "If we but knew", we may apply this to life's perplexing *trials*. If we knew how gracious are the divine purposes in many of the trials which are permitted to come to us on earth, how resigned and praiseful we should be! In Genesis 42: 36 we find old Jacob groaning, "All these things are against me"; yet the very transpirings he was bemoaning, if only he had known it, were leading up to the loveliest of climaxes; for soon afterwards he was exclaiming, "Joseph my son is yet alive!"

Outside an Anglican church, a man looked up at the beautiful artistry of a stained-glass window, and noticed, high up, strange lettering which he could not read. He then entered the church, and read the letters from the inside: *GOD IS LOVE*. Many a time, if we only saw the enigmatical hieroglyphics of trouble and trial the right way round, and with the light of heaven shining through them, we should read *GOD IS LOVE*.

Ill that He blesses is our good
And unblessed good is ill;
And all is right that seems most wrong
If it be His sweet will.

"If we but knew." We may apply this to our daily *speech and conduct*. If we only knew what would be the results of certain words and deeds which we say and do, how differently would we speak and act! When I was a boy, one of the commonest items of sage warning which used to appear in autograph albums went something like this:

When the boys fly kites in play,
They haul in their white-winged birds;
But you cannot do that way
When you fly, not kites, but *words*!

In a crowded night train most of the passengers were trying to doze off to sleep, but a baby kept crying fitfully. Suddenly a man's voice called out angrily, "Won't that child's mother for goodness' sake keep it quiet so that we can get some sleep?" Another man's voice replied with a sob in it, "She can't; she's in her coffin in the guard's van; and I've been trying these two nights to pacify the baby." There was a hurried movement down the carriage, and presently the first speaker returned carrying the baby. Eventually the little mite whimpered itself to sleep. Next morning the baby was handed back to the bereaved father, with the words, "I'm sorry I spoke so harshly last night; *but I did not know. . . .*"

Harsh and hasty words are not always so easily counteracted or forgiven as on that railway train. If we but knew what irreparable damage is often caused by idle gossip, cruel criticisms, wicked exaggerations, or jealous sarcasm, how stunned we should be! On the other hand, if we knew what lovely harvests of blessing often grow from seeds of good, kind, wise words and deeds, how eager should we be to sow only the good seed!

But We Do Not Know

"If thou hadst known."—Luke 19: 42.

STILL continuing our animadversions on, "If we but knew", we may also relate it to *our ignorance of tomorrow*. Again and again, if we knew what tomorrow is bringing, how differently would we live today! Only last week a colleague was telling me of a minister who went playing golf with a man whom he was anxious to win for Christ. This minister felt strangely constrained to raise again the matter of salvation as the two of them played golf. They sat down to rest at one point, and the golf companion said, "I have known for some time that I ought to accept Christ as my Saviour, but I'll tell you what: as soon as this game of golf is over, I'll seriously think of doing it." So saying, he rose to resume the game: but just as he did so, a misdirected golf ball came whizzing through the air and struck him right on the temple, killing him instantly! Oh, if only he had known!

I am no lover of melodramatic incidents; yet how foolhardy it is to treat such warnings indifferently! Somewhere, every day, something of that kind happens. At the funeral of a young woman, the pastor asked her sorrowing friend, "Was Mary converted?" With a pained look the friend replied, "Three weeks ago I felt a strong impulse to speak to Mary about her soul; but my courage failed." Later, the pastor asked the girl's Sunday School teacher, who replied, "Two weeks ago in class a voice within me said, 'Speak to Mary about it', but somehow I got diverted." Still later, the pastor asked Mary's mother, who sadly admitted, "Several times lately I have felt urged to tell Mary of my concern . . . but you know she was snatched away so unexpectedly." Oh, if they had known what the morrow was bringing!

What of you and me? Shall we listen and learn? If only we knew what tomorrow is bringing!—but we do *not* know. Let us not laughingly say, "Oh, *that* simply could *not* happen." We just do not know. Tomorrow may bring some unexpected bereavement. It may bring death to us. It may bring the second advent of our Lord. It may *not*; but it *may*.

"If we but knew." We may apply this finally to *the hereafter*. If we knew all the immense issues of eternity, how differently would many of us use time! If we could pierce the veil of futurity, so as to see the glories of the saved and the miseries of the lost, in that never-ending Beyond, oh, what a mighty difference it would make to our conduct here! After the last speech prime minister Gladstone ever made in the English House of Commons, when the House had emptied someone saw him go and stand alone behind the Speaker's chair, and, shading his failing vision as he looked out over the arena of his battles, he lingered reflectively, then quietly slipped out of the House for ever. It was the *last* look. Some day it must be so with us. We must take our last look down here. Eternity will open before us, and time with its unrecallable opportunities slip behind. Should we not view things now as we shall then? The greatest regrets in that solemn hour will be (1) to have known the Gospel yet rejected the Saviour. (2) To have known the Saviour yet never have sought to win another to Him.

His Part and Ours

"If ye shall ask anything in my name, I will do it."—Jn. 14: 14.

WHAT a regal promise this is! What a scintillating diamond in the rich jewel-case of the divine promises! Let it slowly revolve before the eyes of the mind. Catch the flash of each eradiating facet. Then remember again: the precious jewel is *ours*! It was really given to us.

"If ye ask . . . I will do." How appositely the "If ye ask" is matched by the "I will do"! The two little trios should always be seen over against each other. The only "if" is on our side, not His: "*If ye* . . ." On His part there is the kingly "*I will*".

The promise is, "If ye *ask*"; not "If ye think", nor "If ye desire". We may go about all day merely thinking or desiring in relation to spiritual blessings, yet those blessings will not be ours; for the promise is made to *asking*. Our Lord well knew the importance of actually asking. Very often, until there is specific asking, our thoughts and desires remain inchoate, vague, unorganized. Asking focuses and crystallises them into intelligent definiteness. We must *ask*. We must take *time* to ask; for although actual withdrawment in secret prayer is not fundamentally indispensable to asking, yet if we are to ask concentratedly, it is often circumstantially necessary that we get alone with Jesus.

The promise is, "If ye shall ask anything *in my name*." So this is prayer by a special approach, on a special basis, under a special aegis, and with special guarantees. This kind of asking is not just an asking by *any*body for general mercies; it is an asking by Christian believers on *covenant* ground. It is only after our conversion to Christ that we can truly pray in His name. God may or may not answer the prayer of others, entirely as He pleases; but in Christ He has condescended to bind Himself by covenant pledge to the redeemed people of His dear Son.

But of course this asking in His name means prayers *in the interests of His cause on earth*. The expression, "in my name" is equivalent to "for my sake". Obviously then we cannot pray in His name for something which is not in accord with His will or for His work. The promise is primarily for His co-workers. "In my name" is not just a handle by which to turn things our own way. It is our Saviour's all-inclusive equipment for the needs of His own work as carried on by His own people.

Within this *obvious* limit to the scope of the promise, there are *no* limits, for the promise says, "If ye shall ask *anything* in my name, I will do it." There is not a thing which I really need for His work, or for myself in the prosecution of it, which He will withhold. See how definite He is: "I will do it." How can the One who makes such a universal promise be less than God? Indeed, He *is* God; even God the Son; and He here pledges His infinite plenitude as our ever-available supply. Oh, why is there not among us more asking and receiving, more praying and proving? In these days of crazy rush and restlessness, of radio and television, of sensational newspapers and endless periodicals, we are in danger of becoming pathetically incapacitated for quiet seasons of lingering in prayer. There is vast challenge everywhere around us, but our Lord has matched it by this kingly promise: "If ye ask . . . I will do."

Clank, Clank, Clank!

"He had been often bound . . . and the chains had been plucked asunder by him."—Mark 5:4.

CLANK, clank, snap! Look at those chains, and listen to them. To begin with, they represent *the utmost that man can do against human depravity*. Those chains were a substitute for sanity. We may think them a poor substitute, but I imagine that if you and I had lived in that vicinity at that time we might have slept better at nights for the knowledge that those chains were there! We have to resort to the same kind of substitutes today. We put the madman in an asylum. We put the criminal in a prison. Internationally, we disarm and bind the aggressor nation, as in the case of Germany after the two world wars. Many individuals, also, try to deal similarly with what we call the "lower nature". Chains, however, only bind; they do not cure.

Next, those chains illustrate *the basic weakness in man's way of dealing with human depravity*. No doubt the townsmen got the stoutest chains available. The blacksmith would say, "There, now, he'll never break *that* one!" Then they would entice the demoniac, in one of his quieter moods, and suddenly hold him down while they chained him. But nothing proved strong enough. When the demoniacal frenzy seized him, with a supernatural strength he broke loose and broke out again. So is it with the madman and the asylum, the criminal and the prison, the aggressor nation and disarmament, the "lower self" and repression. The basic weakness is that such chains are not as strong as the nature which they seek to bind.

Third, those chains strike a pathetic contrast with *the way in which Christ deals with human depravity*. Our Lord diagnosed the fearful abnormality at once as an extreme case of inward invasion by demon spirits. The central citadel of the will had been battered down, and there was an almost complete usurpation of control over the human personality. Our Lord, who had just commanded the winds to retire, and the waves to subside, now commanded the regiment of demons, "Come out of the man"; and the unclean intruders were immediately expelled. Instead of an outward *chain*, there was inward *change*. When the local inhabitants came around, they now found the demoniac "*sitting*" (restfulness after restlessness) and "*clothed*" (decency after degradation) and in his "*right mind*" (harmony after wild confusion). During the last world war it was estimated that Britain was spending £18,000,000 a day, trying to put chains on the monster again! And now the demon, whose name is "Legion", haunts us as Communism, and glares at us through the eyes of the Russian bear! Oh, if only Britain and other nations had spent their millions on spreading the true Gospel of Christ throughout the world, what a different story there would have been to tell!

But let us individualise this. Friend, the Lord Jesus can change *you*. That is a big thing to say, but it is true. There is an old proverb which says, "You can change many things, but you can never change nature." It is time the old proverb itself was changed, for in the light of the Gospel it is wrong. The Lord Jesus changes our very nature. He does even more: He gives us a *new* nature. Ah, that is the kind of Saviour we need; and that is the kind of Saviour Jesus *is*!

The Old Song and the New

"The LORD is my strength and song; and He is become my salvation."—Exod. 15 : 2.

WHAT a salvation was Israel's exodus from Egypt! What a scene was that vast gathering of nearly two million redeemed Israelites on the further bank of the Red Sea! What a song it was which broke forth on that never-to-be-forgotten day! (Read it again: Exod. 15: 1–18, ending with "Jehovah shall reign for ever and ever".)

Note the order of the wording in our text. First, "The Lord is my strength and song", and then "He is become my salvation". In other words, when by faith I make Him my "strength" amid trial, and my "song" even before deliverance has come, as Israel did before the exodus, then He proves Himself *worthy* of my boast in His strength, and furnishes me with good *cause* for song.

Note, also, that the word "LORD" is in capitals, indicating that in the Hebrew original it is *Jehovah*, which is distinctively His redemptive and covenant name. The etymology of the name indicates its literal meaning as "the self-existent One who makes Himself known". In His incarnate Son He has revealed Himself to me as Jehovah-Jesus, and in the most glorious of all ways has "become my salvation". As my Redeemer He has actually condescended to bind Himself to me by *covenant*—a covenant sealed and ratified by the shed blood and bodily resurrection of the Eternal Son—so as to give me inviolable guarantee that He has "become my salvation" *for all eternity*. Oh, what abundant cause have I to exclaim, "Jehovah is my strength and song; and He is become my salvation"!

It is a remarkable fact that these words of our texts occur, in exactly the same order, three times in Scripture. First, in Exodus 15 : 2; second, in Psalm 118 : 14; third, in Isaiah 12 : 2. In the first of these it is salvation from Egyptian slavery. In the second it would seem to be restoration from the Babylonian exile. In the third it is final regathering from world-wide scattering at the end of this present age. In the first, salvation is effected under the leadership of Moses the *prophet*. In the second, restoration is effected under Ezra the *priest*. In the third, final regathering is to be effected by Messiah Jesus the *King*.

Thus, that "song of Moses" by the brink of the Red Sea over 3,000 years ago echoes and re-echoes through the centuries in Israel's history. But most notable of all is, that away on, after the yet future "great tribulation", and after the "wrath to come" which is to destroy the Beast whose number is 666, with his wicked accomplices, the redeemed of Israel are seen standing by the "sea of glass" having "harps of God", and singing once again that "song of Moses"; only now there is a wonderful addition to it. Look it up in Revelation 15: 3: "They sing the song of Moses, the servant of God, *and the song of the LAMB*"! At long last Israel recognises Jesus as Messiah, Redeemer, and "King of Saints"!

Israel's eyes shall be opened at last; but, thank God, ours have been opened *now*. Already *we* are singing "the song of Moses *and of the Lamb*". What singers we Christian believers ought to be! What songs God gives us—all of them belonging to the one great "song of the Lamb".

What Greater Honour?

"But rather rejoice because your names are written in heaven."—Luke 10: 20.

Of all the miracles which our Lord performed, His greatest was the distribution of His own miracle-working power to the twelve apostles, and later to seventy others. It was the multiple transfusion of a supernatural healing-energy; many miracles in one. Thereby the disciples were equipped with attesting seals when our Lord sent them forth as auxiliary evangelists.

Those first evangelists must have marvelled again and again at the "mighty works" which Jesus wrought; but even greater must have been their wonder when they found themselves doing the same exploits—cleansing lepers, curing paralytics, straightening cripples, healing diseases, and even expelling demons. We are not surprised that they "returned with joy, saying, Lord, even the demons are subject to us through Thy name".

Jesus rejoiced with them, but at the same time uttered this cautionary word which set all such spectacular miracle-workings in true perspective, and guarded the disciples against an exaggerated estimate of them: "*Rather* rejoice because your names are written in heaven." The words at once suggest a threefold application to ourselves.

First; they are a *corrective* to those who have outstanding powers and gifts. How easy it is for those who have popular public abilities to glory in them as though they were evidences of divine favouritism rather than solemn responsibilities! How easy it is to over-appraise such oratorical gifts as the more-important things, when in fact they are nothing compared with those spiritual and eternal privileges which belong even to the humblest of Christ's people!

Second; our Lord's words are a *consolation* to the untalented. How easy it is to feel resentful when others seem overloaded with charms and gifts while we ourselves seem comparatively destitute! Let us remember that our Lord's love to us individually is never to be measured solely by the natural or spiritual gifts which He here assigns to us. Some of the least gifted have received the sweetest manifestations of His love.

Third; our Lord's words are an *incentive* to each of His people. Mark these three points: (1) Our names are written in heaven *individually*, for our Lord uses the plural, "names". (2) They are written *appreciatively*, recording our service, see Philippians third chapter, third verse. (3) They are written there *indelibly*. Not all eternity can erase them.

Alone I walked the ocean strand,
A pearly shell within my hand;
I stopped and wrote upon the sand
My name, the year the day.
As onward from that spot I passed
One lingering look behind I cast;
A wave came rolling high and fast,
And washed my lines away.

All names written merely in the earth are like that; but the names written in heaven are there for ever!

Let Not Your Heart be Troubled

"Believe also in Me."—Jn. 14: 1.

In its ultimate meaning faith is not just believing for the pardon of our sins or the answering of our prayers, but faith in *Jesus Himself*, because of what He is, even when our problems remain unsolved and our prayers seem unanswered. Away back in the Book of Job we are given to see that behind the patriarch's sore trial there was a supernatural reason and a planned epilogue of lovely recompense, though Job did not know it. The point, however, is not merely that Job did not know, but that he was *not meant* to know. If he *had* known, the very purpose of the trial would have been frustrated. So is it with ourselves. If our Lord were always explaining our trials, and showing beforehand the "nevertheless afterward", there would be no schooling of faith, and the whole educative purpose of trials would be lost. Our Lord wants us to trust *Himself*; to rest in His fidelity even when we are baffled by what He permits. In Him have we not "seen the Father"? Have we found one shadow of falsity in Him? Can the love which bled on Calvary for us ever mock or fail us?

One of the most revealing comments Jesus ever made on human suffering was in connection with the "man born blind". (Jn. 9). The disciples asked, "Master, who did sin, this man, or his parents, that he was born blind?" Jesus answered, "Neither hath this man sinned, nor his parents: but that the works of God should be made manifest in him." Think of it—that unknown beggar, blind and *there* just at that time to fulfil a predesigned purpose in the permissive but all-anticipating will of God! Not only was his affliction overruled to the saving of his soul, but he became one of the most monumental credentials of our Lord's divine mission. And he objectifies to us the profound fact that *all* such permitted suffering is overruled by high divine purpose. In many cases the explanation cannot be given in *this* life; but our Lord's comment shows assuredly that there will be corresponding solutions and fulfillings of gracious purpose in that larger life beyond.

Dear friend—you who suffer by lifelong, physical incapacity, Jesus would have you relate your wearying, mystifying frustration to that high destiny beyond. He says, "Believe in *Me*." Even Jesus Himself once exclaimed, "My God, *why* . . .?" And *His* agonised question sanctifies *yours*, so long as yours is not rebellious. He *thoroughly* understands. The love which *bled* for you is overruling. Your present, dragging affliction is a tuition—if responded to resignedly, prayerfully, believingly—for a unique service which none but *you* can render in the palace of the King!

Thou, Lord, art Love, and everywhere
Thy name is brightly shown;
On earth beneath, Thy footstool fair,
In heaven above, Thy throne.

Thy chastisements are love; more deep
They stamp the seal divine;
And by a sweet compulsion keep
Our spirits nearer Thine.

New Light on a Dark Subject

"Blind from birth."—Jn. 9:1.

THE disciples asked, "Master, who did sin, this man or his parents, that he was born blind?" Jesus replied, "Neither hath this man sinned nor his parents; but that the works of God should be made manifest in him." This was new light on a dark subject. The disciples held the common view that every such evil was the direct penalty of sin—a notion as old as the philosophizings of Eliphaz, Bildad and Zophar. In one brief comment our Lord tears away this veil of error, and sheds a transfiguring light on bodily affliction. *Some* ailments are directly due to the fault of those who suffer them; but more generally it is otherwise. There are accidents, germ-diseases, and various contributory factors all blending in hereditary transmission from one generation to another. The big surprise is our Lord's disclosure that running through all the dark-seeming mysteries of God's permissive will is an all-anticipating good purpose—a purpose which takes in even the blindness of an obscure beggar!—"that the works of God should be made manifest in *him*'!'

So all is foreknown. Even beggars are dear to God. All such affliction is overruled. If only those of us who suffer with dragging, hurting maladies may win the faith-victory of relating our present strickenness to that ultimate destiny for which *this* life is but a preparation, what heart-rest and character-refinement it can mean! All our Lord's true people will at last be "presented faultless" before the heavenly throne; but do we thereby conclude that all will be alike in *traits of character*? No; the experiences of this present life effect in our character something which persists in the Beyond. It may well be that the hardest suffering *here* is leading to the highest ministry *there*. Mrs. Martha Snell Nicholson, after years of painful illness, tells a big secret in her little book, *Wings and Sky*:

In far-off lands is a pathetic thing
A child is being trained to be a king.
His teacher, looking far ahead, can see
What things a king will need to know. So he
Must put his cherished toys away,
And study when he longs to run and play.
But one day, looking back, remembering,
He will be glad he learned to be a king.

So I, through all my sorrow, yet can sing,
I too am being trained to be a king!
For if with Him we suffer we shall reign,
Co-heirs with Him our Lord! I need this pain;
Unfit am I, unlearned and knowing nought
Of how to reign, and so I must be taught.
And if, because of this my blindness here,
It sometimes seems that kingly lore comes dear,
Yet well I know, the blessed day will come
When I, from pain and sorrow free, at Home
At last, will be so glad that God would deign,
So patiently, to teach me how to reign.

Discipleship—Secret or Open?

"A disciple of Jesus, but secretly for fear of the Jews."—Jn. 19:38.

DURING our recent travels in Mohammedan areas a Christian missionary introduced me to a well-dressed Moslem young man, a day-school teacher; one of the finest-looking young Moslem intellectuals one could meet anywhere. In his spare time he was helping the missionary with translation work.

When I asked the missionary if this young man was a Christian, the answer was a regretful shake of the head; but the young Moslem then divulged that deep in his heart he believed on the Lord Jesus, and had accepted Him as Saviour almost a year earlier. He then went on to explain that he simply had to keep it secret or else lose everything. When his people had found out his interest in Christianity they had threatened him with expulsion and disgrace. He had been taken before high officials who guaranteed him a brilliant future for his superior gifts if he remained a Moslem, but warned him of sinister consequences if he became a Christian.

"What can I do?" he asked me. "I have good qualifications and can command high position; but if it leaked out that I had become a Christian I should lose everything, and they would secretly put poison in my food to kill me. So I think it best to be a believer on Jesus secretly."

That young Moslem and I looked steadily into each other's eyes. Then I said to him: "I am thankful to know that you are a believer upon the Lord Jesus. As for confessing Him openly, you understand your own circumstances better than anyone else. It is not for me or anyone else to dictate to you. That matter is between yourself and Christ alone. But I would ask you one question: 'When our Lord returns, or when you pass into the beyond to meet Him, and you tell Him why you remained a secret disciple, how will you feel when HE and you look into each other's eyes, and He reminds you that *He* went even to the Cross for *you*?'"

If the look which spread over that young Moslem's face truly indicated his mind, he had found himself suddenly plunged into disturbing reflections. I did not stay. I thought it better to leave him alone, to "struggle it out" on his knees before his Lord. I hope he took the brave way, the costly way, the really Christian way.

I hope he did so *for his own sake*. The only Christian discipleship which really overjoys the heart is that which is open, public, unashamed. On one mission field after another we found evidence of that. Some of the most radiant, Christ-conscious believers we ever met were dark-skinned Christian brothers and sisters in other lands, who, like Paul, had "suffered the loss of all things", with expulsion and physical tribulations as well. Did they regret the open stand they had taken? A thousand times, No! On the other hand, we were told of those who had withheld open confession, and who for that reason had never known the true joy of the Christian life, but had remained spiritually feeble, or else had gradually drifted back to their former darkness.

For his own sake, then, I hope that the young Mohammedan teacher took the way of brave, open confession. I hope, also, that he did so *for others' sake*. And supremely I hope that he did so *for the Lord's sake*. Circumstances are different perhaps in our own case; but the need for public confession was never greater than today. What about you and me?

It Costs to be a Christian

"Yea, and all that will live godly in Christ Jesus shall suffer persecution."—2 Tim. 3 : 12.

FROM that day when seraphic Stephen the protomartyr fell beneath the stones, crying, "Lord, lay not this sin to their charge", the story of the Christian Church has corroborated this Pauline prophecy. Our Lord Himself foresaw what was coming, when He said, "Blessed are ye when men shall revile you, and persecute you, and shall say all manner of evil against you falsely, for My sake."

Let us settle it in mind that if we are really living "godly in Christ Jesus", if we are living the out-and-out Christian life, we shall be in the world's bad books! A young man came to D. L. Moody and said, "Mr. Moody, I want to be a Christian; but must I give up the world?" Moody characteristically replied, "Young man, if you live the out-and-out Christian life, the world will soon give *you* up." If we are popular with the crowd of worldlings, or if we are not penalised in some way for our attachment to Christ, we have good cause to inspect our discipleship.

We would say to all young Christians: Do not provoke needless hostility; but, on the other hand, do not expect to be popular with the world now that you have become Christ's. Do not shun persecution; and do not fear it when it comes. Be like the early Christians of whom we read: "They departed from the presence of the council, rejoicing that they were counted worthy to suffer shame for His name."

The world varies its ways of persecuting us. Sometimes it uses the sword, and sometimes the lip of scorn. Most of us can stand the sword far better than derision or sarcasm. Henry Martyn, that prince among missionaries, was exposed both to peril and insult among Mohammedans in Persia; but he said that he found "sneers were more difficult to bear than brickbats". Let us be ready, and take the world's sneer with cheerful heart; for the Lord is ever at our hand to give grace; and one day He will return in glory to confess us before all men.

Let us remember, also, that there is another side to this being penalised for Christian godliness. It is equally true that all who live *ungodly*, and persecute God's people, shall suffer punishment. Old Testament incidents, as Paul tells us, were recorded for our admonition, as warnings and examples to us. Under the old dispensation God frequently visited punishment upon persons immediately after their committing of wrongs, so that the connection between the sin and the punishment might be clearly seen. In this present age, the judgment of the ungodly may be deferred; but it is none the less certain, and will be awful when at last it falls.

This present age is distinctively the age of divine grace, in which a patient God forbears with human sin; but let not boastful worldlings presume. If such heavy penalties are threatened in God's Word against those who flout the moral Law, what penalties are in store for those who "do despite to the Spirit of grace"!

Take heart, fellow Christian. It must needs be that offences come; but ere long the Lord Himself shall "descend from heaven with a shout . . . the dead in Christ shall rise first; then we which are alive and remain shall be caught up together with them." Wherefore "comfort one another with these words."

"And they anointed David king over Israel."—2 Sam. 5 : 3.

WHEN David was thus anointed king over all Israel, he had already reigned for seven years over Judah. The other tribes, under the influence of the powerful Abner, had not received him—probably because he had lived among Israel's enemies, the Philistines, for some while after fleeing from the murderous spite of king Saul. Now, at length, he is made king over *all* Israel; and the paragraph (2 Sam. 5 : 1–5) which tells how "all the tribes of Israel" now came "to David in Hebron" and anointed him king, is both touching and instructive. There were three grounds on which the tribes of Israel now acknowledged David's right to the kingship.

First, there was his racial *kinship* with them. See verse 1: "We are thy bone and thy flesh." It was not because he was a foreigner that they had hesitated to give him the crown; for he was the son of Jesse and great-grandson of the honourable Boaz. Nor were they now coming to him only because he was a brave and brilliant soldier, but primarily because of his Israelite pedigree.

Second, there was his *proven merit.* See verse 2: "Also in time past, when Saul was king over us, thou wast he that leddest out and broughtest in Israel." He had captained them in battle—and always to victory, never to a defeat. They now openly acknowledged it.

Third, there was his *divine warrant.* See how in verse 2 the elders of Israel now gladly admit this: "And the Lord said to thee, Thou shalt feed my people Israel, and thou shalt be captain over Israel." David was indeed the anointed of Jehovah Himself; and his countrymen knew it.

Is not this a threefold sermon, preaching to you and me the threefold right of our Lord Jesus to kingship over *our lives*? If through faith in Him we have found pardon for the past, and peace with God, and promise of "good things to come", we may well be profoundly thankful; but have we yet become grateful enough to crown Jesus *King* over the entire territory of our personalities?

Does someone ask what are His qualifications for such lordship of our lives? They are the very three which David had when the men of Israel chose to crown him king. First, there is His *human kinship.* In His incarnation He became linked by blood-relationship to each of us. In "all things" He was "made like unto His brethren" (Heb. 2: 17). In Him the love of heaven comes to us through a human heart-beat and the fellow-feeling of One who was "tempted in all points like as we are". Second, there is His *proven merit.* He is the Saviour-Champion who espoused our cause, fought our foe, and wrought our deliverance from the tyranny of sin. Third, He is King by *divine warrant.* It is of Him that the inspired pen writes: "The government shall be upon his shoulder." Rightly does He wear the crown and wield the sceptre. Is, then, the government of *my life* gratefully entrusted to Him?

See what happened when David was fully king. There was victory over the indwelling enemy. He overthrew the citadel of the Jebusites at Jebus, and turned Jebus into Jerusalem. There was also great feasting and joy (1 Chron. 12: 38–40). That is always what happens when *Jesus* is really crowned king—victory at the centre, and joy throughout all our borders!

Mysteries Versus Certainties

"The secret things belong unto the Lord our God; but those which are revealed belong unto us and to our children for ever, that we may do all the words of this law."—Deut. 29: 29.

THERE are two classes of realities mentioned here—the "secret" and the "revealed". Evidently there are some things which we are *not meant* to know yet. They are withheld from us for the purpose of discipline and development. The Word of God is as wise in its *reservations* as it is wonderful in its *revelations*. Enough is revealed to make faith intelligent. Enough is reserved to give faith scope for development.

Let us admit what we cannot deny, namely, that despite the Biblical revelation we are surrounded by many baffling *mysteries*.

Birth is a mystery. How and when the pre-natal embryo becomes imbued with the life-principle which constitutes a living, self-conscious *ego* is a mystery beyond the ken of the cleverest obstetrician or gynæcologist.

Life is a mystery. None can explain the mysterious cohesion by which spirit and soul remain in the body, for spirit and matter have nothing in common. None can explain how the sensations of the body become the experiences of the mind. We have our names for it, such as "psycho-physical parallelism", but we cannot unravel it.

Personality is a mystery. Stand before a mirror. Look at yourself. Then realise that you are not looking at yourself at all. Your body is not "you". Your name is an accidental tag. Those eyes are the windows of a thinking entity which is not the body.

Human experience is a mystery, with its tantalisingly unequal and seemingly unfair distribution of hereditary evil and disease, of affliction, adversity, frustration, and suffering. Much of the suffering may be traced directly to sin, or to the violation of hygienic safeguards; but a large margin of misery still remains which is agonisingly mystifying.

And so we might go on. *Death* is a mystery. The *universe* is a mystery. *Satan* is a mystery. *Eternity* is a mystery. *God* is a mystery.

What shall we say in the presence of all these mysteries? Let us fear. Let us be reverent. Let us be thoughtful. But let us also rejoice exceedingly because, breaking into all this mystery comes a glorious, transfiguring fact which not all of these problems can discount: it is *THE FACT OF CHRIST*. He is a certified *historical* fact; a supremely *significant* fact; an experientially *realised* fact. He really came, lived, taught, wrought, died, rose, and will return. So God really and infinitely loves; and perfect restitution is really on the way. I can never forget the wise words of an old Puritan: "Never let what you *don't* know disturb your faith in what you *do* know." What is, *IS*. Jesus Christ is a *fact*. Ponder Him carefully again—and you will conclude that Romans 8: 28 is true as well as verse 22. What about war, accidents, bereavements, and a thousand other tantalising ironies? Let us offer no cheap solution, but admit that they *are* mysteries. Yet not all of them can do away with the fact of Christ, or the divine love which pledged itself to us in His redeeming death and resurrection, and the promise of His return. Mysteries? Agonies? Tears? Yes. But also John 3: 16 and Romans 8: 38, 39, *YES*!

"Cast thy burden on the Lord, and He shall sustain thee."—Ps. 55 : 22.

THE psalmist, of course, was referring to burdens on the heart, not on the back. He knew that mental burdens are worse than physical, and that there is only one resort where true relief is found. His words open up whole continents of thought, but here we mention just three considerations which are suggested by them.

The first fact which we are reminded of is the *inescapableness* of burdens. This burdened psalmist, remember, was David. His words take on a more vivid colour from that circumstance. He was a king. He was wealthy. He was also godly. And he was now aged. Those four particulars remind us that burdens come to high as well as low, to rich as well as poor, to saints as well as sinners, and to old as well as young. There is always a tendency for us to think that our own burdens are heavier than those of others, or that we should escape if we were in somebody else's shoes. But we are wrong. Burdens are our common lot in the present scheme of things; and we can no more dodge them than Atlas could heave the globe from his bending frame.

The second reminder in David's words is that burdens bring *temptations.* Sometimes the strings of temptations which tie up the parcel of trouble are an acuter problem than the load itself. We find some of these temptations exhibited in the psalm. There is the temptation to think that *God is unconcerned*: see verse 1, "Give ear to my prayer, O God; and hide not Thyself." There is the temptation to seek *escape from life*: see verses 6–8, "Oh that I had wings like a dove! for then would I fly away, and be at rest." There is the temptation to become *broodily self-occupied*: see verses 12, 14, 21, "It was not an enemy that reproached me; then could I have borne it," etc. There is the temptation to become *bitter toward life and people*: see verse 15, "Let death seize upon them, and let them go down quick to hell!"

David's advice is, "Cast thy burden on the Lord." But someone sighs, "Ah, that is the very thing I long to do, but somehow cannot. If my burden were an outward and physical one, I could do so; but how to roll this inward and mental burden on to the Lord I do not know."

Well, the first thing to do is to realise that the words, "Cast thy burden on the Lord", do not stand alone; they are coupled with a promise, namely, "And He shall sustain thee". Now that promise in the second half of the verse is a key to the meaning of the advice in the first half. The promise says, "He shall sustain thee"—not just the burden *without* you. You cannot simply detach your burden from yourself, and heave it away, saying, "There!—that's that done with!" But what you *can* do is to hand over *yourself* to God along *with* your burden, and you will find that He sustains both you *and* your burden. The burden may still be there, but the weight, the drag, the bitterness, will be gone.

Remember that the words of our text are a Divine promise through a human medium. What a revelation of Divine *sympathy* the words are! God feels for you as you carry your burden. He desires to carry not only your burden, but *you.* What *is* your special burden? Or are there many, all pressing on you at once? Can you not slip away somewhere to a quiet place, and really, *really* this time, hand over to Jehovah-Jesus?

The Canaan Borderers

"Let this land be given unto thy servants for a possession, and bring us not over Jordan."—Num. 32 : 5.

ALTHOUGH not apparent at a glance, this request of Reuben, Gad, and Manasseh, to settle in territory recently captured on the *eastern* side of Jordan, was really a form of *compromise*. The basis of the appeal was the evident suitability of the Gilead area for their "very great multitude" of cattle. The request sounded reasonable, like most of the arguments which excuse compromise; but all the same it *was* compromise. Israel's place was inside Canaan, not just outside. But the three tribes wished the compromise for self-advantage, and so they were content with their portion partly adjoining Canaan and partly adjoining the outer world. In this they are a type of so-called "worldly Christians" today.

Note first, then, the OUTER GARB of compromise. It certainly had the appearance of *reasonableness*. Each new victory over the border nations had added more cattle to Israel. Especially had the latest conquest done so (i.e. Midian: Chap. 31), for the booty was 675,000 sheep, 72,000 beeves, and 61,000 asses. Moreover, Rueben and Gad seem distinguishingly to have been shepherd tribes (verse 1). Thus it seemed advantageous to stay east of Jordan amid the good pasturages of Gilead.

But it was an *eye-sight choice*: "When they saw . . ." (verse 1). It was choosing "after the flesh" instead of staying strictly in the will of God. Not far from here, long before, Lot had made the same kind of eyesight choice (Gen. 13); and we know the result.

Yet it was apparently *well-intentioned* (16–18). Superficial Christians will do all sorts of good things, if only they may be allowed just a bit of seemingly harmless compromise. They will go to meetings, conduct services, help by generous gifts and other active co-operation; and they think that "giving way" just a bit is useful diplomacy.

But note now the INNER TRUTH about compromise. In reality it was a *despising of the inheritance*. Gilead was so tempting that they said, "Bring us not over Jordan" (5). So is it with those believers of today who do not "wholly follow the Lord" (12) in separation. Their patronising of worldly amusements, and fraternising with ungodly social groups, is a despising of the inheritance in Christ.

This long-ago compromise, also, was a *discouraging of the brethren*. "Wherefore discourage ye the heart of the children of Israel . . .?" (7). So is it today with that worldly hobnobbing of professed believers in the name of Christian liberty (1 Cor. 8 : 9).

And again, it was a *disobeying of God* which risked the divine promise of protection (10, 14, 15). The place of promised victory and security was "over Jordan" and "into the land" (9). As it was then, so is it still.

Finally, note the AFTER-EFFECTS of compromise. There are three which later emerge for our warning from this Gilead compromise of Reuben, Gad, and Manasseh: (1) These tribes were the first to succumb to idolatry. (2) They were the first to be swept into captivity: see 2 Kings 15 : 29. (3) The utterly degenerate state of the stragglers who remained there may be seen in the Gadarenes of Mark 5 : 1–17. Fellow-Christian, our true place is across the Jordan!

"Speaking the truth in love. . . ."—Eph. 4: 15.

My Bible has a marginal note that the word "speaking" in this text would be better translated as "holding"—"*holding* the truth in love"; and I find that most of the newer translations change it accordingly. In the Greek, however, Paul's word here (*alētheuontes*) literally means *being* the truth, that is, being in ourselves embodiments of the Christian truth which we represent. None-the-less, perhaps the context requires some such word as "holding" or even "speaking" to bring out the associated meaning; and thus the text becomes highly salutary; for the "being" and the "holding" and the "speaking" of the truth are all to be "*in love*".

First, we are to "*be* the truth", or, as more in keeping with English idiom, we are to *be truthful*. No amount of religious fervour or service, or courtesy or pleasant disposition, can be a substitute for downright honesty, genuineness, truthfulness. We all say a ready "Amen" to that, but does all our behaviour conform to it? How much pious phraseology and profession there is which has no solid, underlying base in truthfulness of character? And how our witness suffers thereby!

Second, we are to "*hold* the truth in love". Even the truth, without love, can be hard and cold. What is worse, even evangelical truth can become the tool of narrow bigotry and petty hatreds and denominational animosities, if it is not held "in love". This, alas, has all too often actually happened. How earnestly and frequently do we need to pray that strong convictions may be steeped in a true love of our brethren!

Lord, try us, lest our holy creed
We hold in word, but not in deed;
Or hold mere "forms" of godliness,
Without a Christlike holiness.

Lord, halt us, lest with bigot tread,
We live a name and yet are dead;
Or lest, in fighting error's pen,
We smirch, not heresies, but men.

Lord, keep us true, but ever kind,
With Thine own gentleness of mind,
With Thine own "wisdom from above",
Whose strongest argument is *LOVE*.

Third, we must "*speak* the truth in love". We cannot remain dumb in face of heresies, perversions, misrepresentations, which imperil our Christian faith; yet even in speaking out against errors which we deeply deplore, we must "speak the truth in *love*". Vitriolic denunciation may serve the turn in secular politics, but our best weapon in *Christian* debate is truth dripping with the tears of loving concern. We are out to win souls rather than arguments. Let us never forget that most heretics have been sincere men. By all means let our loosened tongues "*speak the truth*"—frankly, firmly, fearlessly; but if we would be really like our Master, it must always be "speaking the truth *in love*".

Crying Turned to Singing

"Hear my cry, O God; attend unto my prayer."—Ps. 61 : 1.

THIS psalm begins with crying and ends with singing. "Hear my cry", David dolefully commences. "I will sing", he enthusiastically concludes. Night is turned to day; darkness to light; sorrow to joy; gloom to sunshine. Instead of the thorn comes the fir tree, and instead of the brier comes the myrtle tree. The oil of joy banishes mourning, and the garment of praise does away with heaviness.

How did the delightful transformation come about? The secret of turning sorrow to joy is surely coveted by us all. Look at this psalm, and learn the formula. Before David's crying was turned to singing, it was turned to *praying*. Scarcely has David begun with "Hear my *cry*, O God", before he adds, "Attend unto my *prayer*". His crying turned instinctively to praying. He spilt his tears in the lap of Jehovah. He felt he could not praise, but he could pray. Sorrows are angels in disguise when they cause us to pray. Troubles, instead of being millstones round our necks, can be Jacob's ladders up to God. Trials may be stepping-stones to blessing. Nothing is really ill which brings us nearer to God. It is always a good wind which blows the sailor into the desired harbour.

We may learn much from David's example here. In this brief ode from his pen, we see the *how* and the *when* and the *where* and the *why* of prayer.

See first, HOW: "From the end of the earth will I *cry* unto Thee." So David's praying here was quite *elementary in form*. There is nothing grandiloquent about crying. James Montgomery's lovely hymn says:

> Prayer is the simplest form of speech
> That infant lips can try.

But "crying" is even more elementary than that! It is not even "the simplest form of speech"; it is only an infantile substitute for it. Yet God understands the cry of His child even better than the most knowing mother understands the cries of her bairn.

David's prayer, also, was evidently very *earnest in character*; for usually such a "cry" indicates affrightedness, sudden extremity, or intense emotion. Many a stricken conscience, many a mourning penitent, many a harassed saint, has found relief in "cries" to God when the mind was too overwrought to devise ordered sentences. There can be a cloudburst in a sob; a whirlwind in a sigh; an ocean in a tear; a world in a word; a heaven or hell in one cry!

What is more, David's prayer seems to have been *repeated in occurrence*. Notice how that word "cry" in verse 1 reappears in verse 2. On the heels of the first cry comes a second. In the original, the word "cry" in verse 2 is not the same as in verse 1, but they are both cries. There is need for importunity. He who hears "the young ravens which cry", hears every cry of His saints, whichever kind of cry it may be.

A mother was telling me recently how easily she had become able to interpret the different cries of her little one—whether of pain, or hunger, or discomfort, or petulence. How much more does our heavenly Father understand the cries of His children! Christian believer, never doubt it: every cry of your heart is perfectly understood and interpreted in heaven.

"From the end of the earth will I cry unto Thee; when my heart is overwhelmed; lead me to the rock that is higher than I."—Ps. 61:2.

In our meditation yesterday we were noticing *how* David prays in this short sixty-first psalm. Observe now *where* and *when* and *why* he prays.

See first *where*: "From the end of the earth." To the Israelite of olden time, the ark and the temple and Jerusalem were the centre of things, where Jehovah's special dwelling-place on earth was, above the mercy-seat and between the golden cherubim in the Holy of Holies. To be away beyond Jordan, as David was when he now fled to escape the Absolom insurrection, seemed like "the end of the earth". Let us note well (1) that prayer is never invalidated by geographical position; (2) that prayer is never invalidated by extremity of circumstance, as when, like David, we are cut off from the usual means of grace; (3) that prayer in some circumstances needs firm resolve: see David's "I will".

Further, see *when*: "When my heart is overwhelmed." David is not only at "the end of the earth", he is in the deeps of the sea, "overwhelmed" like a storm-engulfed mariner. It is bad enough when one is removed in *body* to "the end of the earth"; it is worse when the "*heart*" suffers too. It is bad enough when ordinary sorrows sadden the heart; it is far worse when sorrows or trials "like sea-billows roll" until the heart is "*overwhelmed*". But that of all times is the time to pray.

Again, see *why*: "Lead me to the Rock that is higher than I." This is remarkable language. Undoubtedly David implies that the Rock is Jehovah; and oh, how wonderfully has God become the Rock and Refuge of His people in Christ! Let us learn well the three great lessons here: (1) God in Christ is our immovable Rock of Refuge, cleft to be our hiding-place; (2) this Rock is "higher" than we are, and high above all the storms; (3) we need to be "led" there—and that is just what the Holy Spirit does for us in every stormy trial.

Remember who David *was*. He was "the Lord's anointed". Does it seem strange that trouble should have come to such as he? Might we not have expected that Jehovah would exempt His chosen one from trouble? —especially from such trouble as "overwhelmed" him? Well, God did not. We Christian believers, also, are the Lord's "anointed" ones (2 Cor. 1:21; 1 Jn. 2:20, 27). May we therefore expect immunity? No, not even from those which seem to "overwhelm" us. David's troubles were from his own *family*: so may it be with ours. David's troubles were *national*; and we too may be involved with all others in such troubles. Indeed, David's troubles were the result of his own ill-doing; and so may ours often be. Yet even amid permitted adversity God remains faithful—the abiding Rock of refuge. It was in 1948 that I first heard the old hymn, "Thou art my Rock, O blessed Redeemer". Thereafter, it became a favourite in our Sunday evening gatherings during the troublous post-war years in Britain. The last verse goes like this:

Thou art my Rock; when kingdom and nation,
Ruler and crown, have crumbled to dust;
Thou shalt remain my Rock of salvation,
Rock everlasting, Thee will I trust.

Let Us Pray for Victory

"Rest . . . from all his enemies."—2 Sam. 7: 1.

It is a most desirable state of affairs, to be at rest from all *physical* enemies, as David was, at the height of his kingdom. It is even better to have the rest which comes from subduement of those *spiritual* foes which are entrenched in our very nature as members of Adam's fallen race. It is rest indeed to be saved from fear, pride, jealousy, hate, doubt, care, and from "fleshly lusts which war against the soul" (1 Peter 2: 11). But how many of us are living in such victorious spiritual rest? Would it not be good to turn this into earnest prayer?

Dear Saviour, give me complete victory over *fear*—fear of sickness; fear of accident; fear of poverty; fear of persecution; fear of ridicule; fear of loneliness; fear of trials; fear of old age; fear of whatever may be coming on the earth; fear of dying; fear of death itself; fear of the Beyond.

Dear Saviour, give me complete victory over *pride*—pride in natural gifts; pride in possessions; pride of family; pride in the merely physical; pride in dress; pride of intellect; pride in how I may have excelled others. Dislodge all such vain pride, and instead give me humble gratitude to Thee.

Dear Saviour, give me complete victory over *envy*—envy of another's physical appearance, gifts, possessions, advantages; envy of those who seem more blessed or used of Thee than I. Help me be content with what Thou hast purposed or permitted me to be, knowing that in Thee I have all things, and that heaven will perfect all my holiest ambitions.

Dear Saviour, give me complete victory over *hatred*—hatred of those who wrong me; hatred of those whose nature is offensive; hatred of those who seem to obstruct my progress; hatred of so-called foreigners; hatred of those linked with heretical sects or non-Christian religions. Give me a true, discreet love for all, a love like Thine, who when the nails were driven through Thy flesh couldst only say, "Father, forgive them. . . ."

Dear Saviour, give me complete victory over *doubt*—doubt of my eternal salvation when I am emotionally cold; doubt of Thy promises in Scripture when circumstances seem to negate them; doubt of Thy goodness in permitted sickness or other adversity; doubt of Thy faithfulness if all I have done for Thee seems overthrown by the enemy; doubt of the Gospel when it seems powerless to arrest and save people; doubt of Thy fairness when ironic trouble breaks over Thy sincere people; doubt of Thy sovereignty when evil things happen. May I never forget that the rainbow ever arches Thy throne, and that the God who bled on Calvary can never mock us.

Dear Saviour, give me complete victory over "*the flesh*"—over physical desires; over extravagant appetites; over habit-forming ill-tendencies; over every kind of lust; over laziness, self-indulgence, and every form of intemperateness; over headstrong assertiveness; unconsecrated ambition; misuse of the tongue in exaggeration, insinuation, idle gossip, tale-bearing.

Dear Saviour, give me complete victory over *anxiety*—anxiety over yesterday's consequences and tomorrow's omens; over domestic, business, financial, and all other problems, knowing that in Thee all is fundamentally well with me for ever. May my one concern be continual yieldedness to Thee. Then may Thy Holy Spirit so shed Thy love within me that I shall have rest indeed from all these foes.

"The Lord shall preserve thee from all evil."—Ps. 121: 7.

THIS is one of many precious promises in which God pledges special providential protection and preservation to the godly.

But at once we encounter an objection. Are there not thousands who have trusted God, yet have suffered hurt despite their faith? What about those who, although their faith in God has been even like Daniel's, have suffered martyrdom? What about Christian missionaries who have gone forth in faith, yet have succumbed to fever and other maladies in tropical climates? What about Christian businessmen who, despite their integrity, have been allowed to suffer bankruptcy?

The answer to this objection is twofold. First, God has not promised always to give protection either from physical or mental adversity. There is a higher form of protection than that. Very often, strange though it may sound, the physical and mental adversity are necessary to make real this higher form of protection. Which was the greater triumph of faith in God, David's slaying of Goliath, with a sling, or martyred Stephen's crying out, as he sank beneath the pelting stones, "Lord, lay not this sin to their charge"? In the one case physical victory and deliverance were given. In the other case the victory and deliverance were spiritual.

And what was true in the case of Stephen is true of all those others who, through good and ill, through laughter and tears, in living and dying believe in their God. No sickness, no adversity, no enemy can do them real harm; and when at last they rise to their inheritance in heaven, the angels crowd around them, rejoicing that the Lord has indeed delivered them from all evil.

But the greatest demonstration of the fact that no evil ever really harms any of God's Stephens is that which will be seen in the consummation yet to be. When the Lord Jesus returns in glory, to set up His millennial kingdom, those who have suffered for Him will reign with Him; and then it will be seen by all, that "no manner of hurt" is found on them. "I saw thrones, and them that sat upon them, and judgment was given unto them. And I saw the souls of them that were beheaded for the witness of Jesus and for the word of God . . . and they lived and reigned with Christ the thousand years"! (Rev. 20: 4.)

That consecrated young man who went out to be a missionary, and was martyred at the age of thirty, thus cutting his life on earth short by forty or even fifty years, is thus compensated by twenty times the forfeited years; for he "lives and reigns" on earth with Christ, throughout the Millennium! Those worldly-wise men and women who said he was throwing his life and gifts away in becoming a poor missionary, now stand confounded as they see him in his resurrection beauty and splendour. He lives again! That poor body which was battered to the grave has now come forth a glorious body, fashioned after the likeness of Christ Himself; an immortal, incorruptible body which eradiates a supernal glory.

How clearly and fully will God's promise of preservation then be seen to have been fulfilled! Surely it was on this, the *ultimate* demonstration of God's promise, that Paul had his mind when he said, "And the Lord shall deliver me from every evil work, and will preserve me unto *His heavenly kingdom*" (2 Tim. 4: 18).

On His Majesty's Service

"In the service of the king."—1 Chron. 26: 30.

MOST people in Britain receive periodic mail in envelopes which display four capital letters printed across them—O.H.M.S. Those same four letters should be written large across the life of all true Christians—O.H.M.S. He who died to be our Saviour, rose and lives to be our King. All of us who own Him as Saviour-King are "On His Majesty's Service"; and we should never forget it.

No professor at Edinburgh University was ever more beloved than the late Henry Drummond. When he was younger, Queen Victoria was still on the throne; and he tells this story about those days. There was a royal celebration of some kind, and where Henry lived the village hall was being decorated with colourful paper streamers in honour of the occasion. Soon there was a shortage of these, and Henry, who was then ten years of age, was asked to run to the local shop for more. Young Henry, however, refused—until a young man came down a ladder, looked him steadily in the eyes, and exclaimed, "Don't yer know?—it's O.H.M.S." That settled it for Henry; and he tells us that when he was returning with the big bundle, he felt ten feet high because he was "On Her Majesty's Service".

We must fling away the common error of thinking that we are only O.H.M.S. when we are engaged in some specifically religious activity. We are to wear the King's uniform every minute of every day. Very often we may be serving Him best when we are farthest away from church premises or public Christian occupation. If we are truly Christ's, then whoever and whatever and wherever we may be, we are HIS, to be used by Him in all we *are* and in all we *say* and all we *do*. The Bible is no mere record of religious services, evangelistic campaigns, revival gatherings and prayer-meetings. It has much to tell us about persons and things not directly connected with religion at all. Think of great figures like Moses, Joseph, Daniel. They were men of affairs. Their hands were full of administrative responsibilities. Joseph and Daniel were both prime ministers, next to the very throne, in two of history's greatest empires. They had jealous rivals, and lived amid circumstances which at times must have made it delicately difficult to give witness of their faith in Jehovah as the one true God. Yet amid all their exacting duties and responsibilities they had the fear of God before their eyes and the love of God in their hearts; and even to this day their influence lives on in thousands of minds which admire their godly loyalty.

We often divide things into "sacred" and "secular"; but to the real Christian all the secular become sacred because of this being O.H.M.S. Paul designated himself, "An apostle . . . by the will of God." I believe that just as truly many a Christian today may be "a grocer by the will of God", "a railwayman by the will of God", "a housewife by the will of God", and so on. John Wesley said, "Give me one hundred men who fear nothing but God, and hate nothing but sin, and I will shake the gates of hell." He got his hundred, and even if the gates of hell were not actually shaken, the whole of Britain was, with repercussions right round the globe. Oh, those early Methodists!—not only the preachers, but the rank and file! Their consecrated personalities were torches aflame with love for Christ by the kindling of the Holy Spirit. *They* knew the meaning of O.H.M.S.! Lord, kindle *me* afresh by a "live coal" from the heavenly altar!

We are His Witnesses

"Ye shall be witnesses unto Me."—Acts 1 : 8.

THE high service to which our royal Master specially calls us is that of being witnesses to Him as Saviour and Lord. Witnessing is not necessarily preaching. Most of the preaching in our churches is (or should be) the exposition and application of God's written Word, whereas witnessing has to do with what we ourselves, subjectively, have proved and experienced. The indispensable qualification and prime importance of a witness is *first-hand experience.* It is not cleverness or learnedness or preaching ability which constitutes a witness, but first-hand experience of whatever it is to which he is testifying. In our law courts, a witness is not asked what he *thinks*, but what he actually *knows* by direct contact with the case under trial.

So then, if you and I are to be true witnesses to Christ, we must have a first-hand experience of His saving power in our lives. Without that, we may preach, teach, lecture, we may hold ecclesiastical office, or take leadership in religious organisations, but we cannot be His witnesses.

That prince of the pulpit, the late J. H. Jowett, tells how his gifted preacher-friend, Dr. Charles Berry, first came into a saving experience of Christ after being in the ministry for years without really knowing Him as Saviour. Late one night a Lancashire girl with a shawl over her head, and clogs on her feet, called at Dr. Berry's home. "Are you a minister?" she asked. "Then I want you to come and get my mother in." Thinking she referred to some drunken brawl, Dr. Berry said, "You had better call a policeman to get your mother in." "No, no, sir; my mother is dying, and I want you to get her into salvation." Dr. Berry then enquired where she lived, and suggested that there might be another minister who lived nearer; but it was no use; she clung on determinedly. He wondered what the members of his fashionable church would say if they should see their minister out late at night with a girl of *her* appearance; but he just had to go. The house where she took him was one of ill-fame. In the lower rooms they were drinking and indulging in lewd conversation, but upstairs was the poor dying woman. Dr. Berry sat down and knew he must somehow talk about Jesus; so he told about His beautiful life and teachings, until, with an awful look in her deathly eyes, the dying woman interrupted, "Mister, that's no good for the likes o' me. I'm a sinner." Dr. Berry was dumb-struck, suddenly realising that he had no message for that poor, dying sinner. Then he recalled what his mother had taught him years before; and he began to tell the old, old story of God's love in Christ who died to be the Saviour of sinners. Soon the dying woman spoke again: "Now you're getting at it. That's what I want." In relating the incident afterward, Dr. Berry added, "And so I 'got her in'—and at the same time *I got in myself.*"

Ah, yes, we ourselves must have a real experience of Christ as Saviour before we can be His witnesses to others. We must "get in" ourselves before we can get others in. When we witness for Him to others, we must always point to Him as *SAVIOUR*. It is not Christ merely as Teacher or Example who gives relief and rest and peace to the awakened, conscience-stricken sinner, but Christ the *SAVIOUR*. Even among those many all around us who are still asleep in their undisturbed guilt and unrealised peril, we must keep witnessing to Jesus as the *SAVIOUR*.

Believe it. Live it. Say it

"We are His witnesses."—Acts 5 : 32.

If we are to be effective witnesses for Christ, we must have not only a first-hand experience of His saving power in our own lives, but a sense of *certainty* about our salvation. There are many people who are really saved, but are not sure of it. One day they think they are; another day they fear they are not. They lack what D. L. Moody used to call, "the *assurance* of faith". Sometimes trusting, sometimes doubting, they never know real "joy and peace" in Christ such as we read of in Romans 15 : 13. There used to be a saying, "The Blood makes me *safe*: the Word makes me *sure*." How true that is!

A wonderful spiritual revival once broke out in a large theological seminary. The head tutor in describing it said that its influence could be seen in the striking difference between the hymns which the students used to sing *before* the revival, and those which they sang *after* it. Before the revival they used to sing dismal dirges such as this:

'Tis a point I long to know;
Oft it causeth anxious thought;
Do I love the Lord, or no?
Am I saved, or am I not?

But when the revival had swept through their midst they started singing exultations such as:

'Tis done, the great transaction's done!
I am my Lord's, and He is mine.
He drew me, and I followed on,
Charmed to confess the voice divine.

It is always the note of ringing certitude which makes effective witnesses for Christ. If we are among the doubting Thomases, let us beg the dear Lord to help us fling our doubts to the moles and the bats.

We are to witness for Christ by our *lives*. Our words must be backed by our ways. One morning, centuries ago, the famous St. Francis of Assisi said to a brother monk, "Let us go down into the town and preach." The two of them walked slowly along the road, and eventually reached the town. Francis, however, did not stop anywhere for a preaching appointment, but gradually guided the way back from the town towards the monastery again. Presently his companion asked if he had forgotten the preaching. Francis replied: "My brother, it is no use walking to preach unless we preach as we walk."

But although this witness of the life is basic to all else, there must also be the witness of the *lips*. Without vocal witness, the life, however beautiful, remains dumb statuary. However full and deep the river, what is its navigable use if, like the arctic rivers, it is frozen at the mouth! There must be an overflow of heart which unlooses the tongue in eager, earnest, discreet speech. Let us pray with the psalmist: "O Lord, open Thou my lips" (Ps. 51 : 15). And let us say with the apostles, "We cannot but speak the things which we have seen and heard" (Acts 4 : 20).

"Let your conversation be without covetousness; and be content with such things as ye have; for He hath said, I will never leave thee, nor forsake thee."—Heb. 13 : 5.

TRANSLATED rather more literally than in the Authorised Version, this reads: "Let your turn of mind (your disposition), be free from the love of money; and be content with your present circumstances; for He hath said: I will never never fail thee, and never, never forsake thee."

There now, what say we to that? It is a straight, deep-cutting sword-thrust to those in our churches who bow and scrape to wealth or social position. It is a stinging rebuke to those in our churches who play for position and prestige. It is a smiting hand on the mouths of the unreasonable and incessant grumblers among us. As with the impact of an avalanche it sweeps away the wood, hay, stubble, on which we have been standing. Men, money, circumstances—are these things to which the Christian or the churches must look? Never! We are ever to say boldly: "The LORD is my helper," because He has said: "I will never, never fail thee; and never, never forsake thee."

Big terms these—"disposition", "money", "present circumstances". Why, these are things which lie at the very heart of the problem of life for men and women. A right attitude to money, a right adjustment to circumstances, a right attunement of disposition—these are the things which bring stable comfort to human hearts, build up strong, noble character, save men and women from crushing disappointments and life-souring embitterments; these are the things which light up the soul with the unclouded shinings of heaven.

Oh, that evil-eyed reptile, Covetousness! How it cuts its fangs into human hearts! How it fevers and poisons life with its venom! How its trail of slime makes ugly many an otherwise beautiful character! God save us from it!

Mind you, being content with our present circumstances does not mean that we are to be supinely unconcerned about present evils which we can help to remedy: but it does mean that we are to accept cheerfully those circumstances which are providentially permitted to surround us.

Nor does being content with our present circumstances mean a sluggard indifference to self-improvement. Let us remember, however, that true self-improvement does not mean merely an increase of income, a higher position, a larger house, but a greater love to God, a clearer perception of His will and ways, a truer likeness to the character of Christ, a more generous love to our brother, a truer fulfilling of just that place and purpose in this present life which God has in His heart for us to fill.

The Hebrew Christians to whom the words of our text were addressed had undergone fierce persecutions in which their worldly goods had been confiscated. See how they are spoken of in the tenth chapter of Hebrews.

O how easily some of us give way to bitter discontent! How we smart because we do not have the possessions, the advantages, the successes of another! How seemingly incurably we forget that each one of us is inexpressibly precious to Him Who redeemed us by His blood and tears and that He has said "I will never, never fail *thee*".

The Two Sauls—A Contrast

"I have played the fool."—1 Sam. 26: 21.
"I have fought the good fight."—2 Tim. 4: 7.

THERE are two Sauls in the Bible, one in the Old Testament, the other in the New. The one was Saul the first king of Israel. The other was Saul who became the apostle Paul. The one stood head and shoulders above his fellows *physically*. The other stood head and shoulders above his fellows *spiritually*. These two Sauls make a striking and instructive contrast. The one said at the end of his life, "I have played the fool." The other died saying, "I have fought the good fight . . . henceforth the crown!"

Look back again over the story of Saul the king. A man "plays the fool" when he neglects his godly friends, as Saul neglected Samuel. A man plays the fool when he goes on enterprises for God before God has sent him, as Saul did. A man plays the fool when he disobeys God even in seemingly small matters, as Saul first did; for such disobedience nearly always leads on to worse default. A man plays the fool when he tries to cover up his disobedience to God by religious excuses, as Saul did. "To *obey* is better than sacrifice." A man plays the fool when he tries to persuade himself he is doing God's will when in his heart he knows otherwise. A man plays the fool when he allows some jealousy or hatred to master and enslave and deprave him, as Saul did toward David. A man plays the fool when he knowingly fights against God, as Saul did in hunting David, to save his own face. A man plays the fool when he turns from the God he has grieved, and seeks an alternative in traffic with spirits in the Beyond. We can only finish any such down-grade course with the pathetic groan, "I have played the fool."

By way of sharp relief, look now at that other Saul, the Saul of the New Testament. Here, too, is a man of uncommon powers and advantages, with a call from God to a vital ministry, though a ministry involving many hazards, and having none of those outward conducements which king Saul's elevation had. What a contrast these two Saul's make! With the Saul of the Old Testament there is progressive downgrade. With the Saul of the New Testament there is progressive upgrade, for the "prize of the upward calling of God in Christ Jesus". With the Saul of the Old Testament "self" more and more gets the upper hand. With the Saul of the New Testament there is a progressive displacement of self-ism in favour of monopoly by Christ. With the self-centred Saul of the Old Testament the personality becomes more and more emaciated. With the Saul of the New Testament the personality becomes more and more sublimated. Instead of being egocentric, the Saul of the New Testament becomes Christocentric.

Oh, the contrast! For Saul to live was "self". For Paul to live was "Christ". For Saul to die was shame and gloom. For Paul to die was "gain" and "glory". Saul's heart-rending requiem is, "I have played the fool." Paul's martydom song is, "I have fought the good fight, I have finished the course, I have kept the faith. Henceforth there is laid up for me the crown . . .!" The Saul of the Old Testament, who lived for self, threw his crown away. The Saul of the New Testament, who lived for Christ gained a crown which will never lose its lustre through all the ages! Let us read, mark, learn!

Jesus Overhearing

"Jesus heard the word that was spoken."—Mark 5: 36.

When our Lord was on His way to heal the young daughter of Jairus the synagogue-ruler, He was delayed, and meanwhile word was sent from the house to Jairus, "Thy daughter is dead; why troublest thou the Master any further?" But (says Mark 5: 36) "As soon as Jesus heard the word that was spoken, He saith unto the ruler of the synagogue, Be not afraid, only believe".

I like the marginal rendering: "Jesus *overhearing* that word, said to the synagogue-ruler, Fear not, simply have faith." There is something quite taking in those words, "Jesus overhearing". They are purely incidental, yet they suddenly photograph one of our Lord's abiding attitudes toward His people.

"Jesus overhearing"!—the idea is captivating. He is *always* overhearing. Why, when we reflect on it, those sudden appearings and disappearings during the forty days between His resurrection and His ascension were meant to teach us this very thing, that Jesus is really present and overhearing, even though invisible.

It says, "Jesus overhearing *that* word . . ." What then was "*that*" word? It was not something spoken by Jairus himself; it was something said *to* him by others. Jesus not only overhears all that *we* say to others, but all that others say to *us*. What comfort there is in that thought, especially when *adverse* things are being said to us, like "*that*" word which was spoken to Jairus long ago! Glance again at "that word" which Jesus then overheard, and notice three unhappy characteristics in it.

First, it was a word of *discouragement*—"Thy daughter is dead". Oh, they might have broken it to him more gently! Must they needs rush into the street and push through the crowd to impart the news like a dagger-thrust? There are always discouragers. If you would be a soulwinner they will tell you these are not the Moody and Sankey days. If you would agonise for revival they will tell you that there can be no big revival before the Lord returns. And so on, in a thousand ways. Discouraged Christian, ever remember that Jesus is overhearing.

Second, here was a word of *misdirection*—"Why troublest thou the Master any further?" To human understanding the circumstances now seemed hopeless. It was taken for granted that although Jesus had healed the sick He could not raise the dead. Christian believer, beware of those who would persuade you that there is no more hope! Remember, Jesus is overhearing!

And it was a word of keen *hurtfulness*. It was meant to draw Jairus away from Jesus. It was just the thing to break his faith. Indeed, it was put in such a way as to make him seem rather ridiculous—"Thy daughter is *dead*; why troublest thou the Master any *further*?" Jesus overheard *that* word. He always does overhear such words.

But is that all? Oh, no. We move on, in the story, from Jesus *overhearing* to Jesus *OVERRULING*! See Him enter Jairus's house and transform weeping into singing! Even death is overruled to God's glory and man's blessing! How it all speaks to you and me!—for Jesus *still* overhears and overrules! However discouraging the reports and the setbacks, always remember, Jesus overhears, and Jesus can overrule.

Transforming the Commonplace

"Poor, yet making many rich."—2 Cor. 6: 10.

THE ordinary life is generally the most difficult to live beautifully. It has the fewest outward stimulants, and therefore requires a deeper and steadier faith within the heart. We need Christians who will live the ordinary life in a really out-of-the-ordinary way. Our lord has a special pleasure, as He Himself has said, in those of His servants who are "faithful over a few things". We should beware of mis-appreciating or undervaluing the so-called commonplace. It is the aggregate of commonplace things which constitutes the greatest of all influences in the social life and unfolding history of mankind. There is wholesome philosophy in the following lines:

"A commonplace life," we say, and we sigh;
Yet why should we sigh as we say?
The commonplace sun in the commonplace sky
Makes lovely the commonplace day.
The moon and the stars, they are commonplace things,
The flower that blooms, and the robin that sings;
Yet sad were the world, and unhappy our lot,
If flowers all failed and the sunshine came not!
And God, who considers each separate soul,
From commonplace lives makes a beautiful whole.

It is not only the front line of organ pipes which give forth music. Some of those out of sight are just as musical and sometimes are more important. A rose need not be seen before its fragrance can be appreciated. The longer I live, the more do I perceive the power and value of those lives which, although they never find mention in newspaper columns, transmit the love and life and grace of Christ among neighbours and workmates and friends.

Publicity is not essential either to faithfulness or true success. Service in secret often has "house-top" results, even though the connection may not always be detected. We may feel out of sight, but we are never out of *God's* sight. His love-look is ever on us. He is watching, to see whether we are faithful in our present circumstances.

What sort of a vessel should we ourselves use in an emergency? A draught of water is needed immediately for some unexpectedly ailing person. There are two vessels at hand. One is a beautifully wrought silver goblet; the other is a plain earthenware cup with the handle broken off. Outwardly there is no comparison. The costly silver goblet at once takes the eye. But on being picked up and quickly examined, it is found to be unclean inside from its use the night before; and there is not time to give it the thorough cleansing which it needs. The plain earthenware cup is picked up instead. It is beautifully clean, not a suggestion of dirt or defilement; and at once it fulfils the purpose, because it is ready for use just when wanted.

Christian disciple, seek no longer the elaborate and spectacular forms of service for Christ. Seek sanctification, purity of heart, humility of spirit, preparedness for any and every sudden call of our heavenly Master.

"He hath said: I will never leave thee, nor forsake thee. So that we may boldly say: The Lord is my helper, and I will not fear what man shall do unto me."—Heb. 13:5, 6.

THANK God, here is something we may say "boldly". In these days, when the knees of theological doctors bend beneath a burden of doubts, and orthodox creeds are bashfully apologised for in the hesitating syllables of uncertainty, this breath of healthful dogmatism comes as a refresher to wearied spirits.

"We may boldly say." No, no, we are warned, we must *not* "boldly say". We must on no account be dogmatic lest we offend the aesthetic sensitiveness of these cultured doubting Thomases around us. If by dogmatism were meant strong-headed self-opinionativeness we would surely join issue in decrying it; but this genteel plea for polite indefiniteness is nothing but disguised scepticism.

"We may boldly say." Thank God, here is something well *worthy* of being said boldly. "We may boldly say: The Lord is my helper." What comfort there is here! It brings a sympathetic divine Friend to stand with us right down amid the homeliest as well as the largest concerns of our earthly life. It comes to us as a promise of God, to strengthen the weak hands, to confirm the feeble knees, and to say to them that are fearful "Be strong; fear not!"

Note the argument here—"He hath said . . . we may say". This is the logic, the authority, the sheet-anchor, of faith. Thus faith is not mere presumption. It grounds every "We may say" in a "He hath said". It is the characteristic of doubt to turn affirmations into interrogations. It turns every "He hath said" into "Hath He said?" and every "We may say" into "May we say?" Doubt, therefore, by its very nature, is both dishonouring to God and dissatisfying to man. Faith, on the other hand, having duly ascertained by reasonable proof that God has indeed spoken, plants its feet unfalteringly on the firm foundation of the faithful divine Word.

Ponder the *graciousness* of this assurance. It is a double pledge. Our Lord will neither "leave" us nor "forsake" us. That word "leave", in common usage, means to depart from; but the Greek word here must not be thus limited. Weymouth renders it "I will never *let you go*", which keeps close to the literal sense. The Revised Version has it "I will in no wise *fail* thee", which perhaps best gives the inclusive idea. Then the second word, "forsake", means that God will never abandon or desert us. Thus God pledges that He will never let us go, and never give us up.

See, also, the remarkable emphasis here. No less than five negatives are heaped together in the Greek, to confirm the gracious pledge, and to give us strong consolation from God Who cannot lie. A literal translation is scarcely possible. It would run in this way, "No, not will I fail thee; nor, no, not will I forsake thee." A more emphatic, energetic guarantee could not be given. One can only struggle to bring out the full force of it by translating with a double negative in each line,

I will never, *never* fail thee;
I will never, *never* forsake thee.

A Strange-Sounding Election

"God hath chosen the foolish . . . the weak . . . base things . . . things despised . . . and things which are not (i.e. nonentities) . . ."
—1 Cor. 1 : 27, 28.

HERE is a strange-sounding election. What does it mean? Certainly not that the *Gospel itself* is foolish, weak, base; for in its ethics and doctrines, in its divine philosophy and redeeming power, the Gospel transcends all other systems ever known. Nor can it imply that the *ministers* of the Gospel are foolish, weak, base; for they have ever included first-rank scholars and thinkers and men of notable public gifts. It means that in many respects the Gospel is associated with persons and agencies which are *conventionally* poor, i.e. according to the artificial differentiations of worldly society. The Founder of Christianity was but a carpenter in the woodwork store at Nazareth; its first preachers were mostly humble fishermen or the like, displaying no college ties, wearing no royal purple, bearing no plumage of aristocracy, waving no proud banners of nobility, boasting no emblazoned coats of arms, and having no financial affluence; and the first spectacular conquests of Christianity were mainly among the "common people".

Yes, it means *that*, when it says that God has chosen the foolish, the weak, the base, the despised, the nonentities; but it also means it in a most deliberate and elective manner. God has "gone out of His way", so to speak, to *choose* just those very persons and agencies which could not but seem the most of all incapable and unlikely in the eyes of men. He has done this in such a way as to advertise it. And it has been according to a uniform principle, namely, "that no flesh should glory in His presence".

This same principle and purpose, says Paul, persists in the Gospel dispensation. God saves by a *cross*! Could anything seem more foolish or more to be despised? The famous Cicero said: "Not only let the cross be absent from the person of Roman citizens, but its very name from their thoughts, eyes, and ears!" Now hear Paul again: "The preaching of the Cross is to them that perish foolishness, but unto us which are saved it is the power of God." Could anything or anyone seem *weaker* than a cross and a supposed Christ who was *crucified*? Yet Paul says, "We preach Christ *crucified . . . the power of God.*"

Paul the preacher is a classic example of the same feature. Read his description of himself in chapter 2 : 1–5. He says, "I came not with excellency of speech or of wisdom"—so he was one of the *foolish* things. He says, "I was with you in weakness, and in fear, and in much trembling"—so he was one of the *weak* things. He says, "I determined not to know anything among you save Jesus Christ and Him crucified"—so he was one of the *base* things. Then he adds, "And my speech and my preaching was not with persuasive words of man's wisdom"—he was one of the *despised* things. He put himself completely out of the picture that Christ might be on full view—he was one of God's "nothings"!

But did God use this "foolish", "weak", "base", "despised", "nobody"? Listen to him again—"My speech and my preaching was . . . *IN DEMONSTRATION OF THE SPIRIT AND POWER*". This unimposing little Paul has moved men by the million—and still does! You and I can easily be too big for God to use, but never too little!

"Not many wise men after the flesh, not many mighty, not many noble, are called. But God hath chosen the foolish things of the world to confound the wise . . ."—1 Cor. 1 : 26–31.

THERE is a threefold divine activity indicated here: a "calling", and a "choosing", and a "confounding". It is one thing to be "called" at our *conversion* to Christ. It is another thing to be "chosen" through our *consecration* to Christ—chosen, that is, to give some special manifestation of Him to others. Not all who are called respond and become united to Christ by a Spirit-wrought conversion. Nor do all who become converted respond fully enough for special manifestation of Christ.

But the outstanding phenomenon of these Corinthian verses is what they tell us about the *discriminating selectivity* of God's calling and choosing and confounding. There are two aspects—the negative and the positive, i.e. those whom God does *not* call or choose, and those whom He *does*.

Look at the surprising negative here. Mark you, it says, "Not *many* wise men . . . not *many* mighty". It does not say, "not *any*"! Thank God, there have always been those among the earth's wise men and mighty men and noblemen who have been among the elect of God. One only needs to look among our city monuments or to explore the various avenues of scholarship, administrative influence, and social aristocracy, to know that God has never left Himself unrepresented there. Yet the general statement remains unaffected—"not *many* . . ."

We see this in *our Lord's choice of His disciples*. They were chosen from the little fishing towns which dotted the lake of Gennesaret. There, where many a hardy fisherman earned his livelihood, and among those humbler folk of Galilee, our Lord looked for His first co-workers. He did not choose men distinguished by conventional nobility.

We see the same thing in the *first spread of Christianity*. Few influential names are associated with the Christianity of that first century A.D. This was in marked contrast with the proselytising from heathenism to Judaism which the Jews were successfully carrying on. The Jews could boast big names among their converts to Judaism—Flavius Clemens, uncle of the Emperor Domitian, the Empress Helena, and the royal family of Adiebent, and Poppæa, the wife of Nero, not to name others. But apparently it was otherwise with Christianity.

And we find the same thing *persisting right down to our own times*. In many places of the earth today there are no longer the rigid distinctions which there used to be, between rich and poor, educated and uneducated, aristocracy and commonalty; yet it seems still true that the larger number of those who enlist under the banner of Calvary are not from among the wise and the mighty and the high-up of this world.

Let the humble among us be grateful; and let the superior be humble. The social distinctions which are big among men are nothing with God. Let not the affluent or the educationally polished among the Lord's people despise their poorer or duller-looking brethren, for they are thereby indirectly despising the divine election. Let us all get our eyes away from merely earthly distinctions of big and little, to the God who is sovereign over all. He who *called* us despite our sinfulness can also *use* us despite our littleness—if we will only let him.

Whom God Chooses—and Why

"Not many wise men after the flesh, not many mighty, not many noble, are called; but God hath chosen the foolish things . . ." —1 Cor. 1: 26.

WHY are the wise and the mighty and the noble of this world passed by? It certainly is not because the glorious Gospel of our Lord Jesus is inferior. Then why? There seem to be three underlying reasons.

The first of these is *worldly absorption.* Go back to our Lord's time again. The great and mighty men of Judaea were too much absorbed with this world's affairs and this world's gains to leave them for the service of One who had so little outwardly to attract them. The Pharisees, Sadducees, scribes and priests, the wise men and doctors of the law, were too absorbed with the forms and rituals, the minutiæ and politico-religious issues of Judaism, the state religion, to see any beauty in Jesus, that they should desire Him. So it has been ever since, in varying circumstances.

A second reason why "not many wise men after the flesh, not many mighty, not many noble are called", is their proneness to *natural conceit.* Remember our Lord's words in Matthew 11, "I thank Thee O Father, Lord of heaven and earth, that Thou hast hid these things from the wise and the prudent, and hast revealed them unto babes". Does that seem strange? Nay, it is most understandable and gracious, for few can become "wise", whereas all may become "babes"—*if they will.* Paul speaks about "the offence of the Cross". It is most of all offensive to the self-wise and mighty and exalted, for it means giving up all pride of human learning and standing, and coming as guilty, hell-deserving sinners to be saved by One who bled for them in public shame.

But look at our Corinthian paragraph again. Verse 29 tells us that this by-passing of the wise and the mighty and the noble is according to a *divine purpose,* namely, "that no flesh should glory in His presence". Fallen Adamic human nature is innately corrupt; but in the wise and mighty and noble after the flesh the very sin which should humble them inflates them with pride. God can no more tolerate their glorying than He would countenance the outwardly attractive garlands which Cain offered in lieu of the slain lamb. Indeed, as Paul says, God's purpose is to "bring to nought" all fleshly wisdom and glorying. My mind reverts to a certain proud young university graduate who returned to his hometown and met a young woman with whom he used to play very happily when she and he were just tiny children. She was now wearing Salvation Army uniform. "Goodness gracious, girl," he exclaimed, "we don't believe in that sort of thing nowadays! Why, if you'd been to the university, as I have, it would have knocked all that sort of nonsense out of your noddle. Why, if it came to it, do you know I could say the Lord's Prayer in five languages!" The Salvation Army lass replied, "Well, I certainly cannot say the Lord's Prayer in five languages; but, thank God, *I can say I'm saved in English!*"

Let there be no misunderstanding: the fact that "not many wise . . . mighty . . . noble, are called" is no reflection on Christianity, for Christianity is CHRIST—and equally might evening blush to own a star as Christianity be ashamed of HIM. His saved ones are *God's* aristocracy.

"Then took Mary a pound of ointment of spikenard, very costly, and anointed the feet of Jesus, and wiped His feet with her hair; and the house was filled with the odour of the ointment."—Jn. 12: 3.

THREE times in the Gospel records we come across Mary of Bethany, and each time she is at the Master's feet. We first meet her in Luke 10: 38, 39, "It came to pass that He entered into a certain village, and a certain woman named Martha received Him into her house. And she had a sister called Mary, which also sat *at Jesus' feet*, and heard (was listening to) His word."

Next, in John 11, we see her mourning her brother Lazarus's death, and she carries her grief to the feet of Jesus: "She fell down *at His feet*, saying, Lord, if Thou hadst been here my brother had not died."

The third and last time we see her is in John 12, where, six days before our Lord's crucifixion, she breaks that precious "alabastron" adoringly at His feet: "Then took Mary a pound of ointment of spikenard, very costly, and *anointed the feet of Jesus*, and wiped His feet with her hair; and the house was filled with the odour of the ointment."

From these three fleeting glimpses of Mary, we see a three-fold example from which we may learn much, if we will.

She sat at His feet to *learn* (Luke 10: 39).
She took to His feet her *grief* (Jn. 11: 32).
She gave at His feet her *best* (Jn. 12: 3).

It is about the third of these that we are thinking again just now. In that twelfth chapter of John, where we see Mary bending with her costly gift at the Lord's feet, we have an exquisite illustration of consecration to Christ. There are five prominent figures in the story: Martha, Lazarus, Mary, Judas, and the Lord Jesus. Busy Martha typifies service; Lazarus (feasting) communion; Mary consecration; Judas the world's attitude to consecration; while our Lord represents the divine attitude.

Mary's bringing of that precious ointment to our Lord's feet illustrates consecration in the following ways: (1) It was "very costly". (2) It involved a being "broken". (3) It shed fragrance. (4) It was discerning—see our Lord's comment. (5) It was misunderstood by others. (6) It was prized and blessed by our Lord.

Judas represents the *world's* attitude. It was the attitude of condemnation—"Why this waste?" (Mark 14: 4). The objection was plausible—"Why not sold and given to the poor?" Yet it was false and hypocritical—John 12: 6. The world as represented by Judas stands condemned by history, as well as by Christ; for consecration to Christ has done more for the poor and the suffering than any worldly treasurer's bag ever did. All our poverty-alleviating movements have had a Christian origin.

Our Lord represents the *divine* attitude. By Him Mary's lovely sacrifice was *praised*—a "good work" (Matt. 26: 10); and it was *prized*—"Verily I say unto you, Wheresoever this Gospel shall be preached in the whole world, there shall also this, that this woman hath done, be told for a memorial of her." Think those words over again. Do they not indicate that Mary's lovely act of devotion meant something inexpressibly precious to Christ? So is it when *our hearts* are truly His.

The King with the Golden Touch

"Jesus put forth His hand and touched him."—Matt. 8 : 3.

AMONG the old Greek legends there is the story of a king who did some act of kindness to one of the gods, and was told that as a reward he could ask for any favour he would. The foolish king, too excited to think soberly, begged that everything he touched might become gold. At first everything went splendidly. If he touched a stone it became a solid block of gold. If he picked up a twig it was immediately a stick of gold. His very throne became solid gold beneath him. But alas, his new power worked in other ways too. As he picked up his food it became lumps of gold before it reached his mouth. Water became gold as it touched him, and he could not drink. He kissed his daughter, and in an instant she became a statue of gold. At last he fled to the god and implored that he might be delivered from his cursed choice.

Such is the fable of an earthly king with a golden touch. But there is another King who, in all the lovelier moral and spiritual senses, is in very truth "the King with the golden touch". Whatever His nail-scarred hand touches, it blesses and transfigures. It brings forgiveness, restoration, healing. It transforms atrophy, paralysis and moral leprosy into health, vitality, and wholeness. It awakens hope, faith, love, joy, goodwill. It dissolves fetters, and frees prisoners, and communicates power to live victoriously. And who in this privileged land of ours needs to be told that this King with the golden touch" is JESUS?

In the Gospel records there are four places where we read of persons whom Jesus blessed by His miracle-working touch: (1) the leper whom He touched and cleansed from leprosy. (2) Peter's mother-in-law whom he touched and healed of fever. (3) The two blind men whom He touched and gave their sight. (4) The widow's dead son, whose funeral bier He touched as He raised him to life again.

In these four instances we see four *aspects* of His gracious, vital, transforming touch on human lives. In the case of the unclean leper, we see His *cleansing* touch. In the case of Peter's fever-stricken mother-in-law, we see His *healing* touch. In the two blind men, we see His *enlightening* touch. In the raising of the widow's son, we see His *life-giving* touch.

Think of it: cleansing, healing, new sight, new life! Why, in a spiritual sense, these are our four deepest needs. All our Lord's physical miracles were parables of the *spiritual* miracles which He works in human lives. What He did for men's bodies illustrates what He does for men's souls. And that wonder-working *touch*, by which He communicated His supernatural power, symbolises His cleansing, healing, enlightening, vitalising touch upon our inward nature. Moreover, He who has this power to cure and renew us is just as gracious and willing as He is powerful. His touch "has still its ancient power"; and His understanding heart still melts with compassion. Today, as ever, He is both able and willing. This dear "King with the golden touch" is also the "Friend of sinners", who brings cleansing through His atoning blood; healing and restoration to the sin-sick and fallen; new light and hope, new life and victory to those who receive Him. Dear Saviour-King, let thy touch be this moment upon *me*, to cleanse and heal and illumine and renew.

Self-Abhorrence—and Why

"Wherefore I abhor myself, and repent in dust and ashes."—Job 42 : 6.

HAVE you ever abhorred yourself? Then you will sympathise with the man in our text. This man's self-abhorrence, however, is astonishing because of who he was. See how he is introduced to us. He was "perfect and upright". He "feared God". He "eschewed evil". He was "the greatest of all the men of the East". He "offered burnt-offerings continually". And to crown it all, there was "*none like him in all the earth*" (Job 1 : 1, 3, 5, 8).

It is hard to think of any higher testimony that could be borne to a man. The most that the majority dare hope for is distinguishment among a few, but to be distinguished above all the dwellers of the earth, as Job was, is beyond any man's wildest dreams. Think, too, by whom this testimony was given. Had it been given by his friends, we might have discounted it as biased eulogy. But it is none other than *GOD* who thus testifies to Job!

Who can scan Job's character without admiration? His reproach and suffering only brought out in brighter lustre his inextinguishable hope and trust in God. In the presence of the most baffling enigma he held fast his confidence and sincerely maintained his integrity. Amid his desolating calamities he was able with clear conscience to rebut the charge of hypocrisy. When the first devastating waves swept away all his possessions and even his family, he "fell down upon the ground and *worshipped*"! "Jehovah gave; and Jehovah hath taken away. Blessed be the name of Jehovah"! Even when his wife, wringing her hands at the sight of his disfiguring disease, exclaimed, "Curse God, and die," he replied, "Shall we receive good at the hand of God, and shall we not receive evil?"

And this is the man who exclaims, "I abhor myself in dust and ashes"! We might well have expected self-congratulation rather than such utter self-abhorrence. If any man ever had a right to use the Pharisee's words, Job had—"God, I thank Thee that I am not as other men are"; yet instead there is this groan, "I abhor myself, and repent in dust and ashes"!

Why? It was because Job had seen God in a new way; and when he did so, he saw *himself* in a new way. "I had heard of Thee by the hearing of the ear, but now mine eye seeth Thee; *wherefore* I abhor myself, and repent in dust and ashes." That is always what happens when we see ourselves in the sight of God. We talk no more of our own supposed goodness. The loathsome leprosy of our innate sinfulness stands out stark and ugly; we see that "all our righteousnesses are as filthy rags".

Job was in no sense a hypocrite. He had sincerely lived up to the best he knew. But he had been self-righteous. He now saw his real condition as a member of Adam's fallen race, and his need of redemption, not only in the sense of atonement and forgiveness, but of *inward cleansing*.

Friend, do *you* know anything of such self-abhorrence? Do *you* know and feel your need of cleansing? Or do you meet the question with an impatient shrug? Do you flush with indignation? Pardon me; you must be better even than Job! But if you *repent* as Job did, listen to this: "THE BLOOD OF JESUS CHRIST, GOD'S SON, CLEANSETH US FROM ALL SIN" (1. Jn. 1: 7).

Tether's End

"They are at their wit's end."—Ps. 107: 27.

One can scarcely repress a sympathising smile at the words of a hot and bothered elderly washerwoman who became so desperately discouraged with household worries, and having to stick over the old wash-tub, that she cried, "When *I* get to heaven, I'll just have one big lie down and rest for ever!" It is a twentieth-century wash-tub version of royal David's sigh, "Oh, that I had wings like a dove! for then would I fly away and be at rest." There is a coloquial expression about "coming to the end of your tether". The overwrought washerwoman found herself there. So did David. When we get there we easily succumb to desperate depressions.

The exigencies of modern life tend to engender this "end-of-your-tether" extremity. The pressure of present-day business and domestic problems wears thousands of people down both nervously and spiritually. There are more neurotics and druggists today in this tense, complex, speed-mad, competitive western civilisation of ours than ever before. Our forefathers lived by the calendar; today we live by the clock. With measured tread, our grandsires used to go an hour before time for a railway train: today their grandchildren are impatient if a revolving door swings round too slowly.

Well, for better or for worse, such is our modern world; and there are many in it who know the "tether's end" experience. Worry, overwork, strain, ill-health, frustration; some dragging defeat by an evil habit; being misunderstood or shunned; these are some of the things which bring people to tether's end. It is really a coming to the end of one's resources with a sense of sickening helplessness and heart-breaking destitution.

What about *Christians* and this getting to "the end of your tether"? Our adversary strives to drag us there, and uses all his stratagems to that end, so as to smother our joy and silence our testimony. He sometimes oversteps himself, however, for when our overwhelmed hearts cast themselves on God, our cruel enemy has defeated his own purpose. Some time ago I saw a couple of lines which have lingered in my mind ever since:

WHEN YOU FEEL AT THE END OF YOUR TETHER,
REMEMBER THAT CHRIST IS AT THE OTHER END!

A friend came to me quite recently with the "tether's end" experience. There was hunger for God; but merciless circumstances caused a continuous recoil of hopeless self-frustration. Hard study for career-determining examinations took so much time and so tired the mind that somehow there could be little prayer. There were other difficulties too. There was a gnawing bondage to the thought that Christ was offended. In brief, my counsel was to look to a *sympathetic Christ.* He is no Egyptian slave-driver with a whip curled over us! We do not pray or serve because we *must*, but because we *may*! As soon as we introduce "must" we are under law, not grace. I am sure it wounds our Saviour when we suspect Him of anger while all the time His heart overflows with understanding sympathy. Dear fellow-believer, let us learn it well: you and I are dealing with a *sympathetic* Christ—especially when we seem at "tether's end".

"I was brought low; and He helped me."—Ps. 116:6.

YESTERDAY we were thinking about the "tether's end" experience. Most of us know something about it. Even an apostle speaks of being "pressed out of measure, above strength" and having "the sentence of death" in himself (2 Cor. 1: 8).

Sometimes this "tether's end" or "wit's end" extremity is brought on by circumstances over which we have no control. Sometimes we bring it on through our own wilfulness, injudiciousness, foolish risks, mishandling or misunderstanding. But whichever way it comes, it sweeps the heart with a feeling of being helplessly, hopelessly stranded. What we each need to learn, if we are sincere lovers of our Lord Jesus, is that especially at such times we are dealing with a *sympathetic* Christ.

Never could I express in words all that it has meant in my own life, amid spiritual ups and downs, amid quandaries and adversities, to know that I could count on a *sympathetic* Christ. This was first made comfortingly real to me through a self-inflicted "tether's end" crisis in the early years of my pastoral ministry. I used to make out an advance plan for each day: so much time for the Bible; so much time for prayer; so much time for this, for that, for the other. But early next morn, Mrs. So-and-So would ring me up in some deep distress and asking my help. What could I do? Could I say to her, "I'm awfully sorry, but I cannot call round; my plan for the day doesn't include it"? No, not if I would have a heart like my Master's. Thus, hours of the day would go in unexpected ways. My plan, with its Bible period, its prayer period, and so on, would be a shattered wreck by bedtime; and a gloomy sense of defeat would overhang my mind, taking away appetite for prayer. When this happened several days in succession, not only was there a mood of gloomy frustration, but I used to fear that I had offended Christ, and that perhaps He was glowering at me for my repeated breakdown in prayer and Bible study. One day, as I kneeled in miserable prayer, once again confessing and repenting, Jesus came and asked me: "Sid, did *I* make out that day's plan for you? Did *I* put you into this bondage? Must you thus put yourself under *law* again, when I have brought you into *grace*? And don't you understand that when you fail or fall, I am there, not to glower, but to sympathise, to lift you, and be your understanding Companion?"

Oh, I have never forgotten it. I have always known since then that I am in union with a *sympathetic* Christ who prizes every feeling of my poor heart towards Him, and every service I try to do for Him; a Christ who sympathetically understands that when I stumble or fall, even perhaps wilfully at times, it is still true that the deepest and truest part of me loves Him more than any other being on earth or in heaven.

What comfort indeed for sincere Christian hearts, to know that amid thwarting circumstances there is a sympathetic Christ who looks on us, not with gloomy blame because our aspirations have been frustrated, but with a compassionating sympathy which "takes the will for the deed". Most of all, when we are baffled, stunned, beaten down, weary, dispirited, and at the "end of our tether", let us lean on His sympathy. Let us remember Hebrews 4: 15 and 1 Peter 5: 7.

Spiritual Paradoxes

"For whosoever shall save his life shall lose it."—Matt. 16: 25.

THE above paradox reminds us that there are endless paradoxes in life. A paradox, says the dictionary, is "an assertion seemingly self-contradictory which nevertheless may be true to fact". In this present meditation we halt at certain paradoxes of the Christian life which we do well to ponder carefully.

Paradox one: *We are weakest where we are strongest, and strongest where we are weakest.* "When I am weak, then am I strong" (2 Cor. 12: 10). A middle-aged man was urged to drink just one "sociable" glass of beer. His refusal was adamant. "My father and mother were wretched drunkards," he said, "and they passed the craving on to me. It's in my system; and I know it; so I'll *never* take that 'first drink'." He had set his strongest guard at his weakest point. Another man, brought up by godly parents, was induced in youth to quaff some whisky. He became one of the most pitiable sots who ever staggered through Skid Row. After years of wretchedness he found salvation in Christ, and later wrote his life-story. He had taken that first draught of whisky inwardly saying, "I'm safe; there are no drunkards in *our* family." It was his strongest point, so he set no watch there. Yet to quote his own words, "Those first fateful gulps let loose a demon in my brain and stomach which made hell within me for twenty years." He was weakest where he was strongest. The same is true in countless other connections; especially so in the Christian life. When we are living in entire dependence on Christ we are strongest where we are weakest, for at our weakest point the strength of Christ has its fullest opportunity (2 Cor. 12: 9); but when we are living the *self*-sufficient life we are weakest where we are strongest, for there we are most liable to surprise attack (1 Cor. 10: 12). Christian, mark well this double paradox: in ourselves we are weak even where we are strong; in Christ we are strong even where we are weak.

Paradox two: *We climb highest when we stoop lowest.* How high floats the balloon of pride! Yet nothing is baser. Pride is the sin by which Satan fell from heaven to sheol. On the other hand, nothing stoops so low as humility, yet nothing soars so high. Our Lord Jesus "humbled Himself . . . even to the death of the Cross", and was lifted to the very throne of God, bearing "the Name which is above every name". What could be higher or lower than the pride of Lucifer: "I will exalt my throne above the stars of God; I will be like the Most High"? What could be lowlier or loftier than the humility of Jesus when He kneeled with basin and towel to wash His disciples' feet, or when He stooped to the depthless abasement of the Cross to redeem us? Oh, let us learn that the lower we are at the feet of Jesus, the higher we rise. When we stoop to apologise, to ask forgiveness of someone, or to bear cruel ill-treatment unresentingly, we are rising to lovely heights. Could we but realise it: when we "ride the high horse" of unforgiving pride, we are crawling in the dust with the serpent. Humility only *seems* to cripple us; in reality it gives us *wings*! The way up is down! The way to the throne is the cross! "Whosoever shall save his life shall lose it"; and "he that humbleth himself shall be exalted" (Luke 14: 11). Most of us do not scale the heights because we cannot stoop low enough.

A Further Paradox

"For whosoever shall save his life shall lose it."—Matt. 16: 25.

YESTERDAY we reflected on two of the spiritual paradoxes which belong to the Christian life. Here is another, equally strange-sounding yet equally true.

Paradox three: *That which is hardest is easiest, and that which is easiest is hardest.* How true this is in relation to *prayer*! Many people say they find prayer hard. God seems unreal. Their minds wander. If they fix a time for it each day, their hearts feel disinclined when the time comes round. So after a few days they give up. Yet the fault is in themselves, not in God. If only they had the will to persevere, instead of allowing their prayer-snatches to be at the mercy of their moods, they would find, as thousands of others have found, that after some days of patient faith and perseverance there comes a moment when with indescribable ease the mind slips into the luminous realisation that God is *there*, that heaven is *open*, that prayer is wonderful, and that communion with God is the purest luxury of the soul. That moment always comes to those who persevere; and from then onwards that which has been hardest becomes easiest. There is a holy impatience for the next prayer-tryst.

The same is true in other connections. How hard it is for most of us to love those who wrong us; to ask forgiveness of those who will only gloat over it; to repay cruelty with kindness; to rejoice in the advancement of others while we ourselves are held back; to resist those tit-bits of hurtful gossip; to give up our pet grudges; to overcome temper, impatience, irascibility, over-talkativeness, broodiness, selfishness, and so on! Yet it is true that what is hardest is easiest. It all depends which level we are living on. A bridge is a huge problem to a snail: but what problem is it to an eagle? When we are "living in the flesh" (Rom. 7: 18), how weary at times is the unequal struggle against these hereditary propensities and weaknesses in our nature! But when we really "live in the Spirit" (Gal. 5: 25); when we live for the new nature imparted to us at our conversion (Eph. 4: 24), yielding to its upward pull for fellowship with God through the Word and prayer, we are lifted to a higher level of living which Paul describes as "heavenly places in Christ" (Eph. 2: 6). The same old hereditary appetites and weaknesses may still be in our nature, but now, instead of *fighting* them down there on their own level, we are living *above* them; and what is *hard* down there on the lower level is *easy* on the higher! It is victory, not by suppression or eradication, but by *supersession.* The power of those lower-level temptations is broken because the mind is living on a plane where they have no force. Let him that readeth understand!

Moreover, just as the hard becomes easy, so the easy becomes hard (strange as this may seem). How easy it was for handsome young Joseph to yield to those prolonged solicitations in Potiphar's house! Yet what did he say?—"How *can* I do this great wickedness, and sin against God?" That which was *easy* to fall into on the lower plane was hard on the higher plane where Joseph's mind was living! Yes, it is possible to live on a plane where evil thinking and desiring and behaving are abhorrent and hard to give way to! But we need the eagle-wings which only prayer and absorption by Christ can give. Oh, to live always "in the Spirit".

Playing into the Enemy's Hand

"My brethren, these things ought not so to be."—Jas. 3 : 10.

SOMEWHERE among the hundreds of sermons published by the famous C. H. Spurgeon there is one entitled, "How Saints May Help the Devil". I have no idea what his text was, or what is in the sermon; but I remember seeing the title as I glanced through one of his volumes. Alas, saints often *do* help the adversary. I could write a sad book of portly size, telling of instances which have come to my own notice during my years as a minister of the Gospel.

Once we had a fine, strong man of about thirty years old attend our services and become truly converted. He made good spiritual progress, becoming a valuable asset to our young people's work, especially to our out-door Gospel meetings. Moreover, as he had been an athlete and sportsman, he now had a telling testimony among the men at the big depot where he worked. He became devoted to a Christian young woman who had been converted about the same time as himself. It was pleasant to see their interest together in the things of Christ. Then one of our older members, a woman who used to pray in most pious phrases at every prayer meeting, unearthed that thirteen years earlier, as a misguided youth, he had fallen into a certain sin (I later found he had been lured into it); and she gossiped it round the membership. Now if that young man had never come among Christians, that earlier fall would never have been raked up against him any more, for the other person concerned was now dead, and the incident was buried along with her. But now, when he came to church he found a touch of aloofness and a whispering. His friendship with the Christian young woman was broken. All his new-found joy was damped. Not all the apologising of that sanctimonious gossiper could undo the fatal consequences.

I remember, too, a wealthy, worldly lady who became converted, and then found further joy in witnessing for Christ by public baptism along with other believers. It was her way of testifying to all who had known her that she had now broken with the past, and was living for Christ. What joy was on her face as she went through the baptismal pool! A few days later she was in deep distress of mind. One of our members had passed on to her the nasty tattle of another couple who were saying that she had "cut *such* a figure" at her baptism, and that her profession was just make-believe. I cannot describe her suffering. She shrank from ever entering the church again. Oh, those wicked tongues!

I once lingered interestedly watching three large buses filled with eager-faced women, just as they were about to leave on the annual picnic of their women's meeting. The owner of a nearby butcher's shop happened to pause there too; and this is what he said to me: "Ah, they looks a fine lot o' Christians; but half of 'em owes me and the grocer pots o' money, and they wilna' pay us; but they can spend on picnics even while they stick in debt!" Oh, how such inconsistencies give "occasion to the enemies of the Lord to blaspheme" (2 Sam. 12 : 14).

This may seem a strange theme for a devotional meditation; but what is far stranger is that so many of us have cause enough to give it special attention. There can be a profession which is a living lie! "He that saith he abideth in HIM, ought also to walk even as HE walked" (1 Jn. 2 : 6).

Saints Assisting Satan

"Neither give place to the devil."—Eph. 4: 27.

I THINK it might be good today if we had a further dose from yesterday's bottle. One of the saddest sights on earth, to angel eyes in heaven, is to see the Lord's servants doing Satan's work. Far too many of us, at one time or another, either knowingly or unknowingly, become Satan's assistants!

In the early times of Roman history, when the common people were oppressed by knights and nobles, there arose a man named Caius Gracchus who strove for the welfare of the people, and very cleverly set the knights and nobles quarrelling among themselves. He then said that he had "thrown down a dagger with which the enemies of the people should stab each other". Oh, how clever is *Satan* in throwing *his* daggers among *Christians!*—and how cruelly Christians use them.

For instance, there is such a thing as sincere, constructive criticism; but what deadly harm is caused through the wicked criticising of godly ministers by church members! Two youths were going to a Sunday afternoon class. One of them was telling what a fine carving of turkey his father had given him at the mid-day meal. The other gloomily replied, "At *our* house we had carved *minister*". Oh, those wicked-tongued vivisectors of ministers! Is it surprising that in many cases their children grow up to deal in the same way with their parents?

I was with an evangelical leader some time ago, when he said of a certain Christian group in the same town, "We wouldn't touch *them* with a barge pole; they believe that the Church will go through the 'great tribulation'!" His words were a knife-thrust into the heart of Christ. Oh, the unlovely snobberies and snubbings between those who profess to love and follow the same meek and lowly Jesus! What does it matter whether the little fraction of the Church which will then be on earth may or may not go through the so-called "great tribulation", compared with whether we *love* each other here and now?

An earnest evangelical minister turned his back on several remunerative invitations in order to help a dwindling church in an unattractive locality. He flung himself body and soul into the work, but alas, the chariot wheels dragged heavily. After some time a prominent politician asked him, "How many members have you?" "Eighty," came the reply. "But how many of them are *active* members?" the politician asked. "Eighty," came the reply again. "Forty are active *for* me; and the other forty are active *against* me." Churches, like individuals, acquire characteristic complexes. Some of them are heart-breaks and death-traps to godly ministers. In the words of Revelation 3: 9 they have become "synagogues of Satan".

One of the most awful daggers which Christians ever use is the tongue of slander. Churches have been wrecked, loved ones estranged, and lives blighted by it.

Oh, let us beware lest we become helpers of Satan and wounders of the Lord whom we profess to love! I sometimes wonder whether some of us who glibly *say* we are "saved", yet use our tongues as Satan's daggers, are really saved at all. Well may we heed Paul's word in 2 Corinthians 13: 5, "Examine yourselves, whether ye be in the faith."

The Joy-Secret of "Otherism"

"Let us do good unto all."—Gal. 6: 10.

IN one of the bedrooms of a certain Christian home there hangs a little card which bears the words: THE SECRET OF JOY—God first, others next, Self last. Is this indeed the secret of joy? Then most of us are sadly wrong. We think that joy comes by the reverse order; and it is this mistake which lies behind the worship of wealth, the passion for power, and the pursuit of pleasure. Verily we are wrong, as we surely discover sooner or later. The first secret of joy lies in *otherism*—a going out of one's heart toward others. Egoism is the supreme enemy of true joy. By many providences God seeks to break our egoism down. Indeed, the very relationships which condition human family life are designed to that end. John Oxenham thus beautifully puts it:

> I, Thou, We, They,
> Small words, but mighty, in their span
> Are bound the life and hopes of man.
> For first his thoughts of his own self are full,
> Until another comes his heart to rule;
> For them life's best is centred round their love
> Till younger lives come all their love to prove.

The parental relationships of life are meant to break our egoism down. Henry Drummond says, "A man cannot be a member of a family, and remain an utter egoist." "No greater day ever dawned than that on which the first human child was born." Certainly the mother teaches the child; but in a far deeper way, *is it not the child who teaches the mother?*—and the little one teaches nothing sublimer than just this very thing—*otherism.*

OTHERISM! The supreme transition in a human heart is that from "selfism" to "otherism". "One man," says an old Latin proverb, "is no man at all." A Wayside Pulpit has it: "A man wrapped up in himself makes a very small parcel"! A life which is always getting and never giving is a Dead Sea. The Lord Jesus says: "Except a corn of wheat fall into the ground and die, it abideth alone"—self-preservation the cause of *loneliness*! Then He adds, "But if it die it bringeth forth much fruit"—self-sacrifice the *cure* of loneliness!

OTHERISM! Let the word burn into the mind. Like a flame shot into a dark room it suddenly exposes our fundamental error. Like the white flame of a forge let it strike into the thick rust of our selfishness. Oh, if we could but *believe* it, if we would but *receive* it, the first secret of true joy lies just here. We miss joy because we seek it! Is not the very seeking of joy for its own sake a subtle form of selfishness?—and is not selfishness the very thing that kills joy? Joy is a will-o'-the-wisp to those who run after it; but in some self-forgetting hour when we are touched by another's need, and we sacrifice to give succour, we suddenly find our hearts aflame with a glorious joy that has come unsought! It is thus that we come to know a like joy to that of our dear Lord. In self-sacrificing service for others we discern the marks of His sandals, and follow in the steps of His example, and share His joy. Must we roam afar to find glory? Nay, the secret of pure joy lies behind our own doors, in *otherism.*

"Peter therefore was kept in prison: but prayer was made without ceasing of the church unto God for him."—Acts 12:5.

THOSE two little words, "but prayer", arrest the eye, so suddenly do they mark the turning-point in a critical situation. Writers of fiction have made much of the "eternal triangle". Here, in Acts 12, is another sort of triangle. On the one hand there is a hostile world attacking the church. On the other is a beleagured church praying without ceasing. Above them both is a prayer-answering God who intervenes, and overrules.

In a representative sense the whole might of the natural man was arrayed against that early church. There was the power of Imperial Rome, the sinister violence of King Herod, the civil authority, the military, and the sharp edge of the royal sword, still dripping with the blood of the apostle James; while Peter, the human leader of the church, was at that very hour in prison, fastened with chains which none could break, held behind doors which none could open, due for trial the next morning.

Over against all that was just this: "*But prayer.*" The result?—angels to the rescue, chains unloosed, prison doors opened, Peter delivered, Herod struck dead, while "*the word of God grew and multiplied*"!

What all of us are needing to learn afresh today, as individual Christians, is that our secret daily prayer-audience with God has a "potential" which surpasses even the round-table deliberations of international diplomats. That secret daily session alone with God is greater than all merely human deliberations because it brings GOD into things. We are far too much under the spell cast by mere material bigness. We judge things by their outward bulk or noise—a big building, a big crowd, a big headline, big social names or governmental figures, and so on.

It may seem difficult to think that one humble Christian believer, kneeling in a small room in secret prayer, can wield an influence outmatching that of ostentatious state councils. There is nothing of outward impressiveness or dimensional grandeur. Yet once we grasp the real significance of that kneeling intercessor, pleading there the name of Jesus, and persevering in prayer under the compulsion of the Holy Spirit, our sense of values is revolutionised. The decisions of deliberative bodies, and the whole course of events, can be effected by such praying.

In recent times there has been a big battle between evolutionary scientists and theologians as to the existence of a personal "First Cause". Science has been defeated in that battle, not so much by the theologians as by its own further discoveries. So far as I know, most front-row scientists in the geology and biology classes today would gladly admit a First Cause, even in the sense of a personal God. The battle today is rather in the realm of *second* causes, between a mechanical and a spiritual interpretation of the universe. In a mechanical interpretation of the universe there is no place for prayer. But the mechanical theory is wrong, if for no other reason than that the Lord Jesus is necessarily right. His is the voice not merely of science, but of *omni*science. And He has shown us that prayer is the greatest of all the second causes which operate in the running of this world.

The voice of the hour to you and me is PRAY! PRAY! PRAY!

Prayer Changes Things

"Peter therefore was kept in prison: but prayer was made without ceasing of the church unto God for him."—Acts. 12: 5.

SEE what happens through united prayer like that in Acts 12. First, it brings *angels to the rescue* (read verse 7). The angels may not always make themselves visible as *that* one did to Peter; but in answer to believing prayer heavenly presences are on the spot—not only angels, but the Holy Spirit and our Lord Himself, to rescue souls and repulse the powers of evil.

Second, it *looses men from chains* (read verse 7). It snaps fetters and sets prisoners free. Oh, how Susannah Wesley prayed for her children! And how powerfully were they converted in consequence! Hear again what Charles Wesley sings about his own deliverance from sin's bondage:

Long my imprisoned spirit lay—
Fast bound in sin and nature's night,
Thine eye diffused a quickening ray;
I woke: my dungeon flamed with light.
My chains fell off; my heart was free,
I rose, went forth, and followed Thee.

What all the science and psychology and philosophy and humanistic religions in the world fail to do, our Lord Jesus can do; and in the economy of the Gospel the releasing of His invincible energy is somehow facilitated by the voluntary, co-operative praying of His regenerated people. Yes, indeed, prayer breaks chains, and sets the long-bound, helpless, despairing sinner free.

Third, it *opens iron-gates* (read verse 10). It brings men out of mental and spiritual dungeons. It brings them out into liberty and larger life again. That iron gate which had held Peter inside his prison made escape humanly impossible. But in answer to prayer even *that* gate swung open under the pull of an invisible hand; and Peter was out! The most impassable barriers give way before earnest, protracted, believing prayer in the name of Jesus. It not only opens iron gates, it penetrates iron "curtains"!

Next, it *guides men through dark cities.* See in verse 10 how the prayer-answering angel guided the surprised Peter through the dark part of the city. He put him right on the way to "John Mark's mother's house". How dark can cities be today—not only at nights! Ask Christian business-men. What problems cities create—not only commercial, but moral! How easy it is to get lost—not just in business, but lost to God! Oh, cities can be dark!—and those who must live and work in them need a guiding, guarding hand from heaven upon them. Prayer can bring this very thing to happen.

Again, it *restores men to fellowship with the Lord's people.* Read again verses 12 to 17. What joy there was at Peter's restoration! What a heart-thrilling climax it made to the answering of their prayer when Peter himself joined them at their very prayer-meeting! Well, what happened physically in Acts 12 can still happen, and *does* still happen, both physically and spiritually in answer to believing prayer. All the way through the account we are seeing the effectuality of prayer in the name of Jesus.

An Old Time Prayer-Meeting

"But prayer was made without ceasing of the church unto God for him."—Acts 12 : 5.

Yes, that prayer-meeting had big results; but we need to observe carefully its main features if our own praying is to be similarly effective.

First, it was a prayer-*meeting*. The believers had been called together for that purpose. However rich may be the blessings attending private prayer by separate individuals, there is a special place for *united* prayer in the fellowship and warfare of the Church. It lifts prayer above isolated individual asking and receiving, and encompasses the Church's concerns as a whole. The prayer "meeting" is the highest point of the Church's corporate fellowship, and the most vital focus-point of the Church's warfare. It concentrates all minds simultaneously on the same objectives, and unites them in wielding the Church's supreme weapon. There never was a time when prayer-meetings were more needed than today. They are the spearhead of all true spiritual attack. They are the vital cells in all true Christian expansion.

But, further, that prayer-meeting in Acts 12 was in very truth a meeting for *prayer*. Many so-called prayer-meetings today are scarcely worthy the name. There is so much of preliminary singing, and so much of addressing the meeting, that the actual time for addressing God is a mere apology for what it *should* be. In any prayer-meeting lasting one hour and a quarter, at least one full hour should be used in actual praying.

Besides this, we notice that the prayer-meeting in Acts 12 was a *well-attended* gathering. "*Many* were gathered together praying" (12). There is no sadder feature in organised Protestant Christianity today than the neglect of the prayer-meeting. In all too many places neglect has become total desertion. I agree that the power of a prayer-meeting is not determined by the number of heads; but in these age-end days, when the powers of evil are besieging Christendom with anti-Christian philosophies on a scale and with an intensity unprecedented, there is need to match it with a vast volume of united praying. If the "fervent prayer" of *one* "righteous man" can mean so much (Jas. 5: 16), how much more the similar praying of a hundred, a thousand, a million! We need thousands of prayer-pockets all over the nation.

But look at Acts 12 again, and see that the praying was *earnest and persevering*. Peter had been arrested during "the days of unleavened bread", and imprisoned until "after the Passover" (4) to be executed thereupon. James was already killed, and Peter's fate seemed hopelessly sealed. Three days, four days, more days, passed in which Heaven seemed deaf to the entreaties of the praying band; but they stuck at it with steady tenacity.

Finally, in Acts 12, the praying was *specific and concentrated*. It was for Peter's deliverance; for the repulse of hostile powers; for special guidance, courage, victory in a crisis-hour. They kept on at that one thing, using, no doubt, all kinds of holy arguments with God. What a lot of undirected propelling through cloudy space there is in some of the long-winded prayers which nullify prayer-meetings today! Men of Israel, help! We must rescue our prayer-meetings from this!—and really *pray*.

"Here is Wisdom"

"He that winneth souls is wise."—Prov. 11 : 30.

EVERY Christian should be ambitious, above all else, to please Christ. The very thought of pleasing Him ought to be a continual inspiration to us. It should govern all our desires. If, then, we would please Him, there are two essentials which we must keep ever-vigilantly in mind: first, our own practical sanctification, and second, the bringing of others into saving union with Him.

Speaking of these two things, David Brainerd, that saintly missionary to the American Indians, wrote: "There appeared to be nothing of any importance to me but holiness of heart and life, and the conversion of the heathen to God." These are the two concerns of supreme importance.

With this in mind, it is good to reflect again on Proverbs 11: 30, "He that winneth souls is wise." These words, of course, as they appear in the ancient proverb of Solomon, do not refer to soulwinning in the New Testament sense; yet they fitly express a New Testament viewpoint; and in that sense they challenge us every time they catch our eye.

It is instructive to compare the Authorised Version translation of our text with that of the English Revised Version. The Authorised Version reads, "He that winneth souls is wise." The Revised Version inverts the order, and reads, "He that is wise winneth souls." Both are true. The *Authorised* Version, which says, "He that winneth souls is wise", tells us that soulwinning *reveals* wisdom. The *Revised* Version, which reads, "He that is wise winneth souls", tells us that soulwinning *requires* wisdom. We do well to reflect on both aspects.

So, then, as the Authorised Version tells us, soulwinning *reveals* wisdom. When we give ourselves earnestly to soulwinning, we are becoming truly wise because we are seeing that spiritual and eternal concerns transcend merely material and temporal things. When we seek to rescue the perishing by bringing them to the Saviour, we are exhibiting a practical wisdom than which none can be wiser. Soulwinning is highest wisdom for the following three reasons. First, it fulfils the highest of all functions to our fellow-creatures, for we cannot possibly do any greater service to them than to bring about their eternal salvation in Christ. Second, it obeys the last and tenderest of our Lord's commands: "Go ye into all the world, and preach the Gospel to every creature" (Mark 16: 15). "Ye shall be witnesses unto Me" (Acts 1: 8). Third, it receives the highest of all rewards: "They that be wise shall shine as the brightness of the firmament; and they that turn many to righteousness *as the stars for ever and ever*" (Dan. 12: 3). Far better be that kind of star, than the brightest "social star"!

I suppose it is understandable that those of us who feel deficient in natural gifts should find ourselves longing, at times, for that ampler life which is promised to us in the Beyond. There we shall have superior powers as well as more spacious capacities; and we like to think of ourselves as then being able to serve our heavenly King in a way which we cannot while here on earth. Yet it is well to reflect that whatever forms of elevated service may open up to us in heaven, *nothing* that we can ever do there can possibly exceed in importance the winning of a soul to the Saviour; and *that* is something which we can only do *here*! He that hath ears to hear, let him hear!

"A Word to the Wise"

"He that winneth souls is wise."—Prov. 11 : 30.

WELL, that is how the Authorised Version gives it; but look now at the inverted translation of it in the Revised Version: *"He that is wise winneth souls."* Solomon's proverb means, of course, that the wise man wins souls, or people, to *himself*, as his friends. And the old proverb is just as true today as it was when it was first written, a thousand years B.C.

We Christian believers are not trying to wins souls merely to *ourselves*, yet we may learn, from this revised translation of the proverb, that we ought to cultivate personal winsomeness in ourselves as a connecting-link between the unsaved and Christ. We should seek to win people to ourselves with a view to winning them for *Him*. There is such a thing as being attractive for Christ. What I am in *myself* will give flavour to all I say about *Him*. Our Lord calls His disciples "the salt of the earth", but some Christians seem set on being mustard and pepper. They are keen, but it is a keenness which cuts rather than draws. They are zealous, but not considerate. They are repellents rather than emolients! They are just about as attractive to the outsider as ammonia to a fly, or as a moth-ball to a moth! They are hornets rather than magnets!

"He that is *wise* winneth souls." Soulwinning for Christ requires other qualities as well as wisdom. It requires courage, earnestness, patience, humility, prayerfulness, perseverence, and some knowledge of the Scriptures; but all these will go for little, if unaccompanied by wisdom. Obviously, for instance, we should seek to gain immediate decision for Christ; yet equally obviously we can do incalculable harm by trying to force a premature and unreal decision. We need sympathetic sensitiveness.

Soulwinning requires three kinds of wisdom. First, it requires *natural* wisdom. It calls for practical common sense. Many of us are limited both in available time and in opportunity. We should sit down and carefully plan our approach; what to say and what to do. Too much attempted soulwinning is like spasmodic guerilla warfare or hit-and-run tactics. Each of us should always have some one particular soul whom we are trying to win; and we should pray, plan, speak, work, until that one is won. In the main, men should seek to win men; and women should seek to win women. We should try to get them hearing faithful Gospel preaching, and reading useful evangelistic tracts, and mixing among Christian groups. And when we are trying to win those with whom we continually live or work, we should always remember that how we *live* determines the effectiveness of what we *say*.

Second, soulwinning requires *spiritual* wisdom. We need discernment as to the spiritual problems which perplex those whom we are trying to win; the subtle ensnarements of Satan which trip them; the fears and doubts which deter them. Such wisdom will be ours if we are prayerful. See James 1 : 5, with 3 : 17.

Third, soulwinning requires *divine* wisdom. We need the wisdom of the Holy Spirit Himself; and, thank God, we may have it, according to the degree of our consecration to Christ. What wisdom was given to Stephen (Acts 6 : 10)! The same Spirit of wisdom and power may be ours. See Luke 24 : 49, "Tarry ye . . . until ye be endued. . . ."

Christ Precious

"Unto you therefore which believe He is precious."—1 Peter 2 : 7.

THE Revised Version gives it, "For you therefore which believe is the preciousness"; and another renders it, "To you therefore who believe is *His* preciousness"; but whichever way we word it, the essential meaning is the same; it is *Christ Himself* who is precious—more precious to us than anything or anyone else.

(1) *THE PEOPLE TO WHOM HE IS PRECIOUS.* "Unto you therefore which believe." Unbelief is blind to His loveliness and insensitive to His preciousness; but to the opened eyes of faith He is "the chiefest among ten thousand" and the "altogether lovely".

He is precious to believers *as distinct from angels.* Up yonder the hosts of unfallen angels worship and wonder before the Lamb-Lion-King, yet He can never be so tenderly precious to them as to us. "They know not Christ as Saviour; but worship Him as King."

He is precious to believers *as distinct from worldlings.* One of the big shocks for young Christians is to find others coldly apathetic toward Him. It was so in my own case. My heart was so full that my lips could not help talking of Him; and I naïvely supposed that everyone else would sympathetically respond. What crushing disillusionment I underwent!

Again, He is precious to us believers *as distinct from our former selves.* There was a time when Christ meant little or nothing to us. He was "a root out of a dry ground". He had "no form or comeliness".

(2) *THE REASON FOR WHICH HE IS PRECIOUS.* The text says, "Unto you *therefore*. . . ." which connects it with what goes before: "Behold, I lay in Zion a chief corner stone, elect, precious: and he that believeth on Him shall not be confounded." So Jesus is nothing less than the divinely elected foundation or "corner stone" of our eternal salvation.

Then, when once we have come to know Him as such, we see in Him *many* precious things all in the *one.* He is precious to us in His birth, which sanctifies motherhood and childhood; precious in His guileless boyhood, youth, adulthood, which lift up the loveliest of all ideals for our emulation; precious in His carpentering, which sublimates our daily toil; precious in His poverty, which allies Him to the poor, and dignifies the vexing struggle against penury; precious in His teaching and healing ministry, which gives us authoritative sanction for faith and conduct, and reveals the sympathy of the divine Heart for those who suffer; precious in His atoning death and justifying resurrection and all-commanding exaltation and heavenly intercession; precious in His indwelling of our hearts; in His gracious promises; in the prospect of His glorious return.

(3) *THE WAY WE SHOW THAT HE IS PRECIOUS.* We should show forth His preciousness in the following ways: (1) By eagerly recommending Him to the unsaved. (2) By consistently preferring Him to the things of the world. (3) By choosing the society of His people. (4) By delighting in prayer and in His written Word. (5) By uncomplainingly suffering for Him if need be. (6) By daily praying and longing for His coming. Lord Jesus, help me show Thy preciousness this day, and every day until I see Thee in glory.

The Earthy Man and his Thoughts

"The man of the earth."—Ps. 10: 18.

One of the most remarkable things about the Psalms is that although they become older and older as human history lengthens out, they are seen to be truer and truer in their exposure of fallen human nature. Although this expression, "The man of the earth", does not occur until the last verse in this tenth Psalm, the whole composition is about him, his vain thoughts and vicious ways. It is like an X-ray photograph of his mental and moral interior.

Ever since Cain and Abel there have been the two types of men—the carnal and the spiritual, the earthy and the godly. The latter continually suffer from the former, and cry to God for help. From time to time God intervenes—sometimes supernaturally, more often providentially; but again and again He does not intervene at all; though whenever He permits the godly to be victimised, He gives them grace to bear it, and overrules it to their ultimate good. If God were forever interrupting human behaviour and society by direct interventions, it would negate the necessary process which disciplines godliness, develops faith, matures character, and separates "the precious from the vile" (Jer. 15: 19).

Meanwhile, the invisibility, silence, and seeming unconcern of God, create a sore problem for the innocent, and seem to give license to the gloating wicked-doer. The godly weep, and the wicked laugh. That is what this tenth Psalm is all about; though at the end the psalmist realises, as we all ought to realise, that it is better to go weeping to heaven than laughing to hell. In this psalm there are three verses which expose the three root-errors in the earthy man's thinking. They are three fatal mistakes about God, which he gratuitously supposes give him a free hand to do as he pleases, without any fear of consequences.

The first of these is in verse 4: "All his thoughts are, *God is not.*" In other words, the earthy man persuades himself that there is *no* God. He brags that he is an atheist, and lives like one.

Second, in verse 11, the earthy man says in his heart, "God hath forgotten; He hideth His face; He will never see it." If he cannot convince himself that there is *no* God, He persuades himself that God is too distant to observe what we infinitesimal human insects do.

Third, in verse 13, "Thou (God) *wilt not require it.*" Even if the earthy man cannot persuade himself that there is *no* God, or that God does not *see,* he dares to flaunt God under the illusion that God *does not requite.* He thinks that he can dodge God as he has tricked men.

And how do the earthy man's thoughts *affect his life*? First, there is *vain pride* (3, 4). Next there is *evil speech* (7). Then there are *cruel ways* (8).

And what does *God* do about it all? Mark verses 14–18: God *does* see; God *does* requite; and the earthy man is *doomed.* And what are *we* to do about it, who love the name of the Lord? Let us commit the "keeping of our souls" to God as unto "a faithful Creator" (1 Peter 4: 19), knowing that God sees and hears and knows and gives grace, with everlasting compensations by and by. A godless farmer said to a godly neighbour, "You've spent *your* Sundays at church; I've spent *mine* in my fields; and my crops equal yours." The godly neighbour replied, "Maybe, but God don't settle all His accounts in October."

The Good Fight

"Fight the good fight of the faith."—1 Tim. 6: 12.

SOME time ago we had the pleasure of hearing a distinguished preacher discourse on this text. There were many excellent touches in the sermon, but we had the unsatisfying feeling that the real meaning of the text was altogether overlooked. The address mainly concerned itself with "situations" in which it is a fight to maintain one's faith; a graveside where every tear is a question-mark; a prostrating illness in which providence seems to mock us; a seemingly needless handicap or business reverse or severe frustration; or the apparent deterioration of things from bad to worse in the world around us; all these, so the gifted preacher told us, are situations in which it is often a fight to maintain one's faith.

But the text does not refer to faith in *that* sense at all. Paul is not thinking here of faith in the sense of individual *believing*. He uses the definite article, and speaks of "*the* faith", by which he means the whole body of Christian truth, the Gospel, or the Christian *religion*. We are to "fight the good fight of *the* faith"—of that truth, that message, that holy religion which is the sum and substance of all that true Christians believe.

The very call to this "fight" implies the existence of foes. There are foes of the faith in the outside world, and in the organised church, and in our own fallen nature. We are to "fight the good fight of the faith" against error and evil in human society; against declension and apostasy in the professing church; against temptation and sin in our own hearts and lives.

Oh, how many and how strong are the foes of the faith in *our modern world*!—godless politics, economics, and commercial methods; anti-Christian schools of science, philosophy, psychology and education; the flood of vicious novels and magazines inciting to voluptuousness and violence; the connivance of our law-courts at unchastity and the dishonouring of marriage vows; the modern cinema and theatre, with much that comes through television; the deadly drink traffic; the huge gambling firms; the atheist clubs and pleasure rings determined on Sunday desecration; not to mention others.

What subtle foes, also, there are in the *present-day church*!—religious rationalism disguised as up-to-date Biblical scholarship; the resurgence of sacerdotal ritualism; denominational bigotry; over-organisation at the expense of spirituality; a cheap, noisy pseudo-evangelism with its catch-the-crowd tricks, high-pressure methods, and misleading superficiality; heretical unitarian sects which beguile the untaught, and lead many astray.

And what foes there are in *our own nature*!—ambushments of doubts and fears, hereditary weaknesses and proclivities; subtle tendencies to ulterior motive; lurking Judases ever ready to betray the citadel of "Mansoul" to invading temptations; and so on. Oh, how many and how mighty, how subtle and how scheming, how incessant and how insurgent are the foes of the faith! How can stripling Davids with their slings and stones meet Goliaths like these? How can little Israel's armed bands meet this seven-fold league of fearsome Canaanites? How shall gentle Esthers and despised Mordecais overcome such powerful Hamans and Xerxes as these? Let Romans 8: 37 answer: "We are more than conquerors, through HIM . . ."

"Fight the good fight of the faith."—1 Tim. 6: 12.

We return to our text of yesterday. Does someone ask *how* we are to "fight the good fight of the faith"? Paul tells us in the context. Our first weapon is that of *godly living*. In verse 11, Paul says, "But thou, O man of God, flee these things" (envy, strife, love of money) "and follow after righteousness, godliness, faith, love, patience, meekness." The most convincing apologetic of our Christian faith is its life-changing power. Pretentious talk without godly walk is an arrow with pretty feathers but blunted point. It may be as high-blown as a balloon, but it is just as empty, and bursts just as quickly when pricked. Let us never forget: our first weapon is Christlike behaviour.

Our next weapon is *witness-bearing* by word and pen, in public and private, as opportunity allows. See verse 12, "Lay hold on the life eternal, whereunto thou wast called and didst confess the good confession in the sight of many witnesses." Even Christian character, without spoken confession, remains to the unconverted merely like noble statuary—beautiful but dumb. Our joy and peace and victory in Christ must become vocal if they are to be intelligible advertisements of Jesus.

Another telling weapon of the faith is our expression of it in *good works* toward others. Verse 18 urges this, especially to those who are well-to-do in worldly goods. "That they be rich in good works, ready to distribute, willing to communicate." How many have been first influenced for Christ, not by eloquent sermons, but by practical help amid adversity!

Besides these weapons, there is a *de*fensive aspect of the good fight. In verse 20 Paul writes, "O Timothy, *guard the deposit*." By the "deposit" he means that body of precious, soul-saving truth which is committed to us in the Gospel. We are to "guard" the pure doctrines of the faith against heresies and perversions by all honourable means at our disposal.

But supremely, there is the weapon of *prayer*. That is the weapon which Paul himself places first (see chapter 2, 1–8). To the fight, then, sons and daughters of Israel! These weapons are such as even the poorest and humblest of us can use.

Does the fight sometimes seem hopeless? Are we tempted to give up the unequal struggle? Then read the following Scriptures slowly and thoughtfully: 2 Chronicles 14: 9–14; 20: 12–16, 22–29; Judges 7: 2–7, 20–22; Luke 10: 17–19; Romans 8: 31, 37; 1 John 4: 4.

In the First World War, when hard-pressed on the Western Front, General Foch sent this report to General Joffre: "My right is broken; my left is shattered; my centre is in retreat. The situation is excellent: I shall attack." Later when the battle had reached its height, he commented, "When you have faith, you do not retire, you stop the enemy wherever you find him." Fellow-soldiers, to the attack! Let there be no wilting in discouragement! God loves us too well to give us a continually easy time. He is preparing heroes for heaven, and gems for His crown. We are soldiers of the Cross; and shall we think of being carried to heaven on "flowery beds of ease" when our glorious Founder and His martyred first-followers "climbed the steep ascent through peril, toil, and pain"? Let us count it an honour to fight under such a Captain, and to be soldiers in such a holy war. Let our motto ever be, "For *His* sake."

"Always Abounding"!

"And this I pray, that your love may abound yet more and more. . . ."—Phil. 1 : 9.

THIS is one of Paul's prison prayers. Prison may cut a man off from men, but not from God. What a prayer from a man in prison! Paul's prison privations did not damp his faith, nor dull his hope, nor dim his love. By prayer-fellowship with Christ, he turned the clanking of his prison-chains into music. Just here it is that word, "abound", which captures us. It seems to open up three vistas of truth, as follows.

First, the Christian faith originates in God's *"abounding" attitude.* See Exodus 34 : 6 : "The Lord God, merciful and gracious, longsuffering, and *abundant* in goodness and truth." See Isaiah 55 : 7 : "He will *abundantly* pardon." See 1 Peter 1 : 3 : "According to His *abundant* mercy He hath begotten us again unto a living hope." See Titus 3 : 4–6 : "The kindness and love of God . . . which He shed on us *abundantly* through Jesus Christ our Saviour." See Ephesians 1 : 7, 8 : "The riches of His grace, wherein He hath *abounded* toward us." All this, this magnanimous compassion and benevolence of God toward us, is concentrated in that big, little, indefinite particle, "so", in John 3 : 16 : "God *so* loved. . . ." Apart from this abounding generosity in the bosom of God, there would have been no "wondrous Cross", no Saviour of sinners, no ringing of Gospel bells, no salvation, and no Christian faith.

But now, second, the Christian life consists in receiving *God's "abounding" blessings.* See John 10 : 10. Jesus says, "I am come that they might have life, and that they might have it more *abundantly.*" See Romans 15 : 13 : "Now the God of hope fill you with all joy and peace in believing, that ye may *abound* in hope through the power of the Holy Spirit." See 2 Corinthians 1 : 5 : "Our consolation also *aboundeth* in Chirst." See 2 Corinthians 9 : 8 : "God is able to make all grace *abound* toward you; that ye, always having all sufficiency in all things, may *abound* to every good work." See now our text again, Philippians 1 : 9 : "That your love may *abound* yet more and more." What a picture of the Christian life! Think of it : abounding in life; abounding in hope and the power of the Holy Spirit; abounding in consolation; abounding in grace; abounding in love! *That* is New Testament Christianity! How many of us today are living in the spiritual realization of it?

And now, third, the supreme elevation of Christian experience is *"abounding" in love.* Look again at our text : "This I pray" (see how specific he is), "that your love may abound" (this is the *first* item in his prayer), "yet more and more" (there must be no limits!) "in knowledge and in all judgment" (the more abounding it is, the more discerning it will be, if it is real love, and not just sentimental softness). Thank God, if we are *exhorted* to have this abounding love, we *may* have it. The Father's own love, the Saviour's own compassion, the Spirit's own yearning, may fill heart and mind!

Now look at 1 Thessalonians 3 : 12 : "And the Lord make you to increase and *abound* in love one toward another, and toward all men . . . to the end that He may stablish your hearts *unblameable in holiness.*" So this abounding in love is the true experience of *holiness* to which God calls us!

"Nevertheless death reigned between Adam and Moses, even over them that had not sinned after the similitude of Adam's transgression, who is the figure of Him that was to come."—Rom. 5 : 14.

WHY are we here told that death reigned between Adam and Moses? Is it not something to be taken for granted? Well, it may be taken for granted historically, but not providentially. Adam sinned against a specific command, "Thou shalt not." Moses brought in a *new* "Thou shalt not" which we call the Mosaic law. But *between* Adam and Moses there was not a specific "command" or "law". Therefore, those who lived between Adam and Moses did not transgress a specific command as Adam had done. As our text says, they did *not* sin "after the similitude of Adam's *transgression*". Thus, those who lived between Adam and Moses were not "*transgressors*" as Adam was, or like those who lived after Moses; for as Romans 4: 15 says, "Where no law is, there is no transgression"; and as the verse preceding our text says, "Sin is not imputed where there is no law."

But if they were not "transgressors", and if sin was not judicially "imputed" to them, they were not legally guilty. Why then did *death*, the penalty of Adam's transgression, reign "over *them*"? The answer is indicated in the first word of our text—"nevertheless". The sense is: although those who lived between Adam and Moses were not transgressors of a given command, and although the *sentence* of death was therefore not inflicted on them as legal transgressors, yet "*nevertheless*" death reigned over them as well, because they were sinners in their very *nature*; and as hereditary inheritors of a sin-corrupted nature they *inherited* death as part of that corruption. In other words, death reigned over them, not as a judicial sentence, but as an hereditarily transmitted consequence of sin. Although death was primarily a judgment on the *first* man, he, as the *father* of our race, handed death on to his posterity, and death became hereditary in humanity.

Now our text says that Adam, the first man, was a "figure of Him who was to come", i.e., of Christ. That is arresting. It is the first time in the New Testament that the racially representative character of Christ is mentioned; and it is mentioned in connection with this circumstance that "death reigned from Adam to Moses". It is remarkable. He by whom death comes (Adam) is made to forefigure Him by whom life comes (Christ). Through Adam death passed on to those whose sinnership was hereditary and therefore partly *involuntary*. Similarly, the atonement of the "*Second* Adam", Christ, covers hereditary and involuntary sinnership. No man will ever perish for Adam's sin alone. What we are by heredity is not our fault; and no man will be finally condemned on that ground, but on the basis of his own wrong-doing. Twice over we are told, in John's solemn forepicture of the final judgment, that it is "according to their works" (Rev. 20). The atonement of Christ covers all infants and others who are unresponsible.

Let us learn: (1) The sin of all sins, now, is to spurn the provided atonement. (2) As in Adam we fell, so in Christ we rise; but the wonder of the Gospel is that in Christ we rise infinitely higher than the level from which our forefather fell!

The "I Can" Life

"I can do all things through Christ which strengtheneth me."—Phil. 4 : 13.

I LIKE the glow of moral vigour and virility in those two little monosyllables, "I can". There is all the difference in the world between the "I can" life and the "I can't". One is the life of victory and gladness: the other is the life of depressing inadequacy. It is the difference between plus and minus. It is grand to feel thoroughly equal to things, physically, mentally, morally, spiritually. Of course, the physical, the mental, the moral and spiritual interact upon each other. Many Christians would find their spiritual life more vigorous and satisfying if they would watch their *physical* health, and rest their nervous system more. Many others would find their physical and nervous health much better if they enjoyed *mental and spiritual* rest. When we are living the "I can" life of spiritual victory, our whole nature benefits. And the secret of the "I can" life lies in the two words, "*through Christ*".

There, indeed, is *the secret of spiritual victory*: "through Christ". I heard of an old man who was converted late in life, and was recommended to read the four Gospels, the Acts, Romans, and Philippians. He read them through, up to Philippians 4: 13, which occurred at the foot of a right-hand page, part of the verse running over to the next page. The old man read, "I can do all things," then said, "Paul, that's wrong; you've gone a bit *too* far this time." He read it again: "I can do all things," and again looked up, saying, "No, Paul; you're getting conceited." Then he turned overleaf and found, "through Christ which strengtheneth me". "Ah," he said, "that changes everything. You're right after all!"

Nothing is more pathetic than wishful thinking. Quite recently I heard a friend exclaim, "Oh, if only I were a millionaire, what things I would do!" I heard a poorly woman moan, "Oh, if only I had health, then I should be on top of the world!" I heard a young man protest, "Oh, if only I had *his* opportunities, wouldn't I strike top level!" I heard another sigh, "Oh, if only I had the gifts, what wouldn't I accomplish!" Yet experience has shown that when such coveted possessions become ours, we often find that what we had thought would be golden advantages are difficulties, and what we had thought were our own disadvantages were in reality disguised opportunities. The true Christian position is to accept that which God appoints, and to say, "I can do all things *through Christ.*"

If this were not so, I can imagine Paul writing, "Oh, if only I were the Emperor of Rome, how quickly I would issue a decree enforcing the universal acceptance of Christianity!" I can imagine Peter writing, "Oh, if only I were a doctor of the Law, a learned philosopher, how I would startle the wicked old wiseacres of the Sanhedrin! How I would convert all the sophisticated Athenians by profound oratory from Mars Hill!" I can imagine John saying, "Oh, if only I were a leading statesman, I would institute the law of love in every legal code on earth!" Such plaintive sighs and wishing-spasms are absent from the New Testament. The whole attitude may be summed up in Paul's words, "I can . . . *through Christ.*"

Now I can imagine someone saying, "*I* want to live the 'I can' life, but my perplexity is to know how this thing works." Well, this is how: I can do all things through Christ, when I allow *Him* to do all things *through me.*

"I Can" or "I Can't"?

"I can do all things through Christ which strengtheneth me."—Phil. 4: 13.

"I *can* . . . through Christ." Here is true *enablement for Christian service.* All of us who know and love the Saviour long to "do" something for Him. Many of us are already engaged in Christian work of some form or another. If we are *not*, why? Are we saying, "I *can't*"? Or if we are already serving, are we in the winning or in the losing class? Are we seeing the results which we long to see and ought to see? If not, are we tolerating the disappointing sterility with a wearied sigh, "I just *can't* do any more"? Or have we still the spiritual vivacity to write over the obstinate challenge, "I *can*"?

Everything depends on whether we have truly learned the secret in our text: "I can . . . *through Christ.*" Again and again, if we look at things purely on the human level, the difficulties seem so big, and our own insufficiency so obvious, that we are easily dazed with dismay. In dull, grey letters we begin to write, "I can't".

We need to see burning before us in letters of inextinguishable fire, "I *CAN . . . through Christ.*" He who made the little slave-baby the strong champion of the Exodus; and the shepherd-lad the slayer of Goliath; and the captive Daniel prime minister of mighty Babylon; He who transformed Simon into Cephas, and Saul into Paul, and has made thousands of His humble followers spiritual giants, can enable you and me to "do all things" if we live in the secret of that little phrase, "through Christ". The flicker of my little candle can become a very sunshaft if Christ is in it. My simple word of witness can be a two-edged sword if Christ is in it. The commonest desert bush can glow with the Shekinah fire if Christ is in it. The one vital condition is that we guard against anything which interrupts our fellowship with Christ. The moment we lose contact, the spiritual electricity ceases to course through us. We become dead wires. The great thing is to "keep the contact", so that the life-current may flow through us continually. We *make* the contact by yielding ourselves completely to Him. We *keep* the contact by daily living in communion with Him. It is not necessary that you and I should always *feel* the current flowing through us; but it certainly *will* flow through us if we "keep the contact".

"I can do all things through Christ which strengtheneth me." Here is true *enablement for burden-bearing*. The text may júst as well be translated, "I can *bear* all things . . . " Indeed, the word "bear" fits the immediate context better. I met a cultured lady in Essex who told me that for years she had prayed for some special work to "*do*" for Christ. Eventually, there came a grievous trial into her life, which cut her off from "doing" anything. At first she was rebellious; but later, when she accepted the trial as the heavenly Master's will, she made one of her life's loveliest discoveries. It was a trial with a ministry in it. Grace and love and peace and joy flooded her soul. She became radiant amid her trial, and a wonderful testimony to many needy hearts. Hundreds were blessed by her sympathy and testimony. She said to me: "I prayed that God would give me something to 'do', but He has given me something to '*bear*'." That word, "strengtheneth", in our text is the present continuous tense—"strengthens and *goes on strengthening*". Yes, "I can . . . through Christ!"

True Encouragement

"But David encouraged himself in the Lord his God."—1 Sam. 30: 6.

THAT which makes these words meaningful to ourselves is the point at which they occur in the personal history of David. Twelve or more years earlier, Samuel had anointed David to be king after Saul. Thereafter, for a time, circumstances had seemed to be providentially paving the way. David had become Saul's harpist and armour-bearer. Then he had slain Goliath, causing the daughters of Israel to sing, "Saul hath slain his thousands, and David his ten thousands." But from that time there seemed to be only strange reverses. Twice Saul tried to slay David, with a javelin. Then he tried in other ways. Soon David was compelled to flee. Then mad Saul hunted him like a partridge on the mountains, and poor David had a pretty hazardous time. Eventually, in an eclipse of faith, David and the warrior band who had gathered round him, evacuated to the land of the Philistines. King Achish gave them the little city of Ziklag, where David and his followers lived for sixteen months. Then came crowning tragedy. The Philistines warred against Israel again, and David felt obliged, at least outwardly, to go with them. On the eve of the encounter, however, the Philistines insisted that David and his men return to Ziklag. Thus David was saved from a most awkward situation. But, oh, what an agonising shock awaited them back at Ziklag! Instead of wives and children to wave a welcome, the little city was burned to the ground; wives, little ones and goods all carried away captive by looting Amalekites!

Yet the very extremity of this blow became the turning-point for good in David's affairs. In his dire plight he was flung to one or the other of two alternatives—either to give up faith in God altogether, or to give up *himself* to God entirely, in utter trust. Now read the whole of the text: "And David was greatly distressed: for the people spake of stoning him, because the soul of all the people was grieved, every man for his sons and for his daughters: *but David encouraged himself in Jehovah his God.*" Yes, that became the turning-point. God gave David a new promise. Wives, children, goods were quickly recovered. Saul was slain in battle. David was welcomed as king in Judah. All this speaks, by parallel, of God's dealings with ourselves. Afflictions and trials are sometimes allowed to accumulate without intermission, until it seems as though one more ounce of pressure, and our spirit will snap. Then, just at what seems to be the last minute, providential intervention transforms the whole picture; and oh, what lessons in trust we learn! Human help is vain. Heart and flesh fail. The one resort is the flight of the lonely heart to *God.*

Do we not all have such experiences? How can we meet with ten thousand him that cometh against us with twenty thousand? How can we escape our prison of trials when iron gates shut us in and the keepers stand by with drawn swords? How can we struggle on any longer now that the last handful has been scraped from the barrel? Then, in such an hour as we think not, the Son of Man cometh! Over against bereavement, failure of cherished plans, loss of material possessions, unfaithfulness of dear ones, let us do what David did. "David encouraged himself in Jehovah his God." Let *us* find unfailing refuge in (1) His righteousness, (2) His faithfulness, (3) His love, (4) His promises.

In-Shining and Out-Shining

"For God who commanded the light to shine out of darkness, hath shined in our hearts, to *give* the light of the knowledge of the glory of God in the face of Christ Jesus."—2 Cor. 4:6.

THIS verse does not mean only that God has shined in our hearts to give this wonderful new light to *us*. What it teaches is that He has shined into our hearts with the purpose of transmitting this light *through* us to *others*. In our Authorised Version the word, "give", is in italics, which indicates that it does not occur in the Greek original. As with other italicised words, its insertion is designed to facilitate a ready understanding of the verse in the English, but it rather tends to *obscure* the real meaning. Delete the word "give" and the verse equals: "It is the God who told light to shine out of darkness who has shined into our hearts, with a view to (our) shining forth (to others) the light of the knowledge of the glory of God in the face of Jesus Christ."

So, then, the intention is that what God shines *in*, we are to shine *out*. The *receivers* of the light are to be *reflectors* of the light. That is the radiant obligation of the regenerate. Going with our reception of the light must be our radiation of it to others. There is no higher form of service, and it is open to us all. The moon makes no noise as it reflects the sun, but its effects are great and wonderful. D. L. Moody used to have a saying, "Many a lighthouse blows no horn, it only shines; but it saves thousands." Psalm 96:2 says, "Show forth His salvation from day to day." Mark, it does not say "Declare", or "Sing"; it leaves those to the other verses; but it says "Show"—"*Show* forth His salvation." If we cannot *shout* with mighty voice, we can *shine* with saintly life. If we cannot *trumpet the truth* in men's ears, we can *transmit its light* to men's eyes. If we cannot all be *orators*, we can all be *reflectors*.

See what it is which we are to reflect: "*The glory of God in the face of Jesus Christ.*" In the context (2 Cor. 3 and 4) a striking contrast is drawn between the face of Christ and the face of Moses, who represents the Law. Both faces shone, but how different the two shinings! The shining of Moses' face was purely a *contracted* light, from his forty days with God on the mount; but the glory-rays from the face of Christ are the effulgence of inherent deity. The shining of Moses' face was *intermittent*, and he wore a veil so that his kinsmen should not see its periodic disappearance; but the glory-light on the face of Jesus is unwaning and unchanging. The shining of Moses' face was merely *transitory*, symbolising the transitoriness of the old covenant; but the splendour of the "glory that excelleth" in the face of Jesus is eternally abiding. Moses represents the Law; but "the glory of God" which shines in the face of Jesus Christ is the love-light of the Gospel; the glory-light of redeeming *grace*; the intense light of the divine holiness, softened by the gentle rays of Calvary compassion. The very heart of God shines out through the face of Jesus.

That is the face, the light, the glory, which we are to reflect! Some time ago, a golden, almost dazzling light, struck my eyes, from something in the middle of the country lane where I was walking. It continued so until I was within several feet of it; then I saw plainly what it was—just a pool of water, which recent rain had left in a straggly hole; but the setting sun had transformed it into liquid glory! Could even that pool be a parable?

Handed Over

"Our beloved Barnabas and Paul: men that have hazarded their lives for the name of our Lord Jesus Christ."—Acts. 15: 26.

If we would know how Barnabas, and especially Paul, hazarded their lives, we only need to read the second half of the Acts. But that word, "hazarded", may well catch our eye for another reason. More strictly translated from the Greek, it should read, "Men who have handed over their souls", or "Men who have *handed themselves over*". The hazards were simply incidental to the one big hand-over to Christ. And the outstanding result was that their costly handing over of themselves to Christ covered them with glory. Their names "shine as the stars for ever".

"Men who have *handed themselves over.*" The expression notably describes what real consecration to Christ is. It is a complete handing of ourselves over to Him; nothing else, nothing less, nothing more, at all costs, and for evermore. Dear old F. B. Meyer used to speak of consecration as a handing over of the keys. For years, so he tells us, he lived with the whole bunch of keys handed over, except for just one key, which he was unwilling to give up even to Christ. Just what it was, he never said; but it was something intensely personal and precious to him. He felt it unfair that he should even be expected to relinquish *that* key, which unlocked his most private room. Yet so long as he withheld it, he did not have the fulness of spiritual joy and peace, or the liberty and power which he craved to experience in his ministry. Then one day he cast himself before the Lord with this prayer: "Dear Lord, I am not really willing to yield this thing to Thee; but I am willing to be *made* willing, by whichever means Thou mayest choose." The Lord answered that prayer, until presently F. B. Meyer was *made* willing; and from that time he became one of the greatest men of God in his generation.

Have you and I fully handed over the keys? Are we in the Paul and Barnabas and F. B. Meyer succession? Henry Drummond, author of the one-time famous book, *Natural Law in the Spiritual World*, speaks much of "a saved life". The more usual expression is "a saved soul"; but Drummond's emphasis was on "a saved *life*". I once heard a preacher remark, "It is possible to have a saved soul and a lost life"! That is because there are those who believe on Christ for the salvation of the soul from damnation in eternity, yet never hand over their *life* to Him, thus failing to render Spirit-filled service here, and to receive reward hereafter.

It is regrettable to have to say it, but this complete handing over to Christ is deadly difficult, because the "flesh" in us resists it desperately. The "flesh" resists it for various reasons. One reason is *fear*—fear of sarcasm, or of persecution, or of other consequences. Another reason is *selfishness*—the selfish disinclination to live without certain pleasant gratifications. But, as we have often said before, the *root* reason why the "flesh" resists is its utter abhorence of handing over *self-management*. It will hand over gifts, time, service, almost anything, if only it is allowed to retain self-government. Yet that is the very hand-over which vital consecration *is*, and which our Lord demands, so that instead of being egocentric, or self-centred, we become Christocentric, or Christ-centred. The one thing which defeats the "flesh" is *love*. When we love Christ dearly enough, we "hand over" to Him, however much it hurts the "flesh".

Christ the Rock

"And a man shall be . . . as the shadow of a great rock in a weary land."—Isa. 32 : 2.

THAT this prophecy points to our Lord Jesus is uniformly agreed among evangelical expositors. It is wonderfully photographic: "And a man shall be as an hiding place from the wind, and a covert from the tempest; as rivers of water in a dry place; as the shadow of a great rock in a weary land." Our Saviour is all those four things in one, and much more beside; but just here let us halt at that simile of the "great rock in a weary land." It reminds us that in six different aspects the Scriptures reveal our Lord Jesus as the "Rock".

First, as our text indicates, He is the *rock of shelter* for the weary. Great rocks meant much to dwellers in Palestine long ago. They gave the best of all foundations for dwellings. They made fortresses for protection. They provided caves of refuge, and points of elevation. By no means least, they also gave shade from the scorching sun to many a weary body of man and beast. During travels in the Middle East I myself have seen the sheep and goats with panting sides making for the welcome shadow of a great rock. Even so, our Lord Jesus is such a rock of shadow to the minds and hearts of His people. What a relief it is to get away from the glare and heat of public, social, commercial life into the restful shade of His presence! Better still is it, in a spiritual sense, to "abide" under His shadow (Ps. 91 : 1)—the shadow of His never-failing love and power and wisdom, His ever-faithful care and safe-keeping. What restful shelter we find in the shadow of His Calvary atonement! What rest indeed from the burning rays of awakened conscience, from the wearisome burden of sin, and the heat of remorse! What restful resort in the gentle shadow of His ever-abiding presence! What shelter from the relentless burning of temptation! Yes, our dear Saviour is to us "as the shadow of a great rock in a weary land".

But, second, He is the *rock of refuge* from the storm. See the Song of Solomon 2 : 14, where Solomon's beloved Shulamith is likened to "a dove . . . in the cleft of the rock". The dove is the gentlest of birds. It is not built to battle with fierce storms. Yet even the nervous dove is far safer in the cleft of the mighty rock than yonder imperial eagle in its aerie high aloft. Equally safe is the Christian believer in the cleft rock of Calvary. No swelling wave of persecution can touch our spirits there, whatever it may do to our bodies. It is beyond even Satan's power to pluck us thence. Even from the fearful storm of the "wrath to come" we are safe there. Many years ago, in an art gallery, I stood fascinated before the large picture of a fearful storm. I never saw anything more realistic. But rising up from the wild billows was a giant rock, majestic and immovable; and there, high up in a cleft of the rock, were two doves, perfectly safe, and nesting peacefully together. To me that work of art was more than a picture, it was a parable.

Oh, safe and happy shelter!
Oh, refuge tried and sweet!

Christian believer, reflect again how safe you are in that Rock of refuge, despite all your own unworthiness. You are safe there *for ever*.

The Rock of Ages

"The Lord is my rock."—Ps. 18 : 2.

BESIDES being a rock of shelter for the weary, and a rock of refuge from the storm (as we reflected yesterday) our Lord Jesus is the *rock of Horeb* giving water to the thirsty. In Exodus 17 : 1–7 we see the thousands of Israel thirst-plagued in the wilderness. God says to Moses: "Behold, I will stand before thee there upon the rock in Horeb; and thou shalt smite the rock, and there shall come water out of it, that the people may drink." The seven-fold type-teaching in the incident is capitivating. (1) The rock typifies Christ, as is stated in 1. Corinthians 10 : 4. (2) The smiting typifies Calvary. (3) Moses, who struck the rock, represents the Law, the stroke of which fell on Christ as our Sinbearer. (4) The rod with which Moses struck the rock is here, as elsewhere, the symbol of the divine presence. (5) The command to "strike the rock" points to the *necessity* of the Cross. Until the rock in Horeb was smitten, the water remained pent up, and the people's thirst unslaked. Similarly, Christ as Teacher or Exemplar only, cannot save from sin, or satisfy the soul's thirst. It is the Christ of *Calvary* who releases the "water of life". (6) God's word to Moses, "I will stand before thee there, upon the rock", anticipates the great New Testament truth that "*God* was *in* Christ, reconciling the world unto Himself". (7) The water which flowed from the smitten rock is a type of the Holy Spirit, as is clear from John 7 : 37–39.

Then, next, our Lord Jesus is the *rock of foundation* to the Church. See Matthew 16 : 18, again, where Jesus says, "Thou art Peter [*Petros*] and upon this rock [*Petra*] will I build my church; and the gates of hades shall not prevail against it." Our Lord here taught that He would found His church, not upon Peter [*Petros* a mere stone or rock-fragment] but upon Himself [*PETRA*, the mighty rock itself] whose deity the disciples had just confessed in the words, "Thou art the Christ, the Son of the living God." It is a pity our English translation does not transmit this clearly, for this verse which the Romanists make their proof text that the church was founded on Peter is that which most strikingly teaches otherwise, in the contrast between *Petros* and *Petra*. We are built on Christ, not on any mere creature!

Alas, our Lord is also a "*Rock of offence*" to unbelievers. See Isaiah 28 : 16 and Psalm 118 : 22 with Romans 9 : 33, 1 Corinthians, 1 : 23, 1 Peter 2 : 6–8: "A rock of offence, to them which stumble at the word, being disobedient." The Greeks were too wise; the Jews were too religious; and many moderns are too educated to tolerate salvation by the Cross. "The Cross is foolishness *to them that are perishing*"!

Finally, our Lord is the "*Rock of Ages*". See Isaiah 26 : 4: "Trust ye in the Lord for ever; for the Lord JEHOVAH is everlasting strength." The Hebrew phrase translated "everlasting strength" is "THE ROCK OF AGES". None who trust in Him can ever be ashamed!

How wonderful, then, is our Lord Jesus!—rock of shelter for the weary; rock of refuge from the storm; rock of Horeb for the thirsting; rock of security for the Church; rock of offence to the unbelieving; "Rock of Ages" to all who trust Him. Our twentieth century has shown us drastically the instability of everything merely human. Thrones, kingdoms, old-established institutions, have collapsed. JESUS IS THE "ROCK OF AGES". When we really trust Him we get real peace.

"And the Lord turned the captivity of Job when he prayed for his friends."—Job 42: 10.

POOR Job, what a *captivity* was his! There was captivity to Satan, for the evil accuser had been permitted to test him by malicious oppression. There was captivity to adversity, bereavement, and repulsive disease. There was captivity to the ironic verbosity of intended comforters who became unbending condemners. There was captivity to mental suffering, doubt, fears, depression, despair.

But what compensating *release* eventually came! The Lord "turned" his captivity into an abounding reward which was far more than restitution. The exonerated patriarch had more godly renoun, more material wealth and domestic happiness than ever before.

Notice specially the *agency* through which release came: "The Lord turned the captivity of Job *when he prayed* . . ." Although it was the Lord Himself, and no other, who turned Job's captivity, even as it is invariably He who turns all such captivities of His people, yet He made prayer the means. See here the indispensability of prayer in the affairs of the soul. Job's release did not come while he was argumentatively protesting his integrity against the cruel innuendoes and hostile bigotry of Eliphaz, Bildad and Zophar. It was prayer which wrought the miracle. Intercession was the invisible hinge on which the golden gate of deliverance swung open. Even so, prayer is the vital axis in the spiritual life of *any* Christian individual or church. There can be no genuine spiritual revival in any Christian individual or group where there is failure in prayer. The smallest mission hall with a ring of praying workers can be a victorious Gideon's band putting the alien army to flight; but the largest church in the land, if it has a prayerless membership, is a Samson shorn of his strength.

Most of all, however, observe the real *factor* in Job's praying which ended his captivity. "The Lord turned the captivity of Job when he prayed *for his friends*." That is immensely meaningful: It was not when Job prayed for *himself* that his liberation came, though that might have seemed the normal thing; but when he prayed for *others*! In this let us see at once the *reflexive* power of prayer. One of the high values of prayer is that when I earnestly pray for others, my intercession not only brings blessing to *them*, it boomerangs back in blessing upon myself. I do not mean merely a therapeutic soothing reaction on nerves, organism, and mind, though that is usually included. Prayer for *others* has a liberating reflex *spiritually* upon ourselves. If we spent more time in intercession we should discover that our prayers for others were opening the gates of freedom from many a bondage in our own lives.

How many of us have unconverted friends and relatives! What would we not do for them! Yet do we neglect to do the *greatest* thing for them? Are we too nervous to speak to them about their souls? If we were really roused to spend hours in prayer for them, we should soon find ourselves moved to plead with them—and in a way which could only prove blessed of God, both to them and our own liberation. Any psychologist will tell us that the surest way to get tied up in knotty bondage is to be continually thinking about one's own self. Even prayer must be rescued from making circles around "self", or it will become sterile.

David's Capture of Zion

"Nevertheless David took the stronghold of Zion."—2 Sam. 5 : 7.

MANY Old Testament incidents are illustrative of *New* Testament truths. So is it with David's conquest of Zion. It pictorially illustrates our Lord Jesus as the *heavenly* David, and His capturing the citadel of the human heart.

Take the incident *in its setting*. David had now been accepted by all Israel as king (5 : 1). His right to the kingship was acknowledged as threefold: (1) human kinship: "We are thy bone and thy flesh"; (2) proven merit: "Thou leddest out and broughtest in Israel"; (3) divine warrant: "Jehovah said . . . thou shalt be captain over Israel." By common consent David's rule was now gladly accepted; but right in the midst of the land, just where David wished to put his throne, was a stronghold of Jebusites whom the men of Israel had never been able to dislodge. There they were, those alien Jebusites, in Zion, the rocky southwest eminence of Jerusalem (which city at that time was called Jebus, after the Jebusites). The Jebusites defied David to take their citadel (6), for in an age when guns and bombs were unknown, its natural defences were considered impregnable. "Nevertheless," as our text says, "David took the stronghold of Zion."

Observe what followed. First, the Jebusites were permanently subdued, as the later Scriptures show. Second, Zion now became David's home (9). Third, David now commenced a programme of building, developing and improving.

And now take the incident *as a parallel*. You and I have made *Jesus* our King, on the same threefold basis as Israel made *David* king. So far as our higher desire is concerned, we have accepted His rule and lordship. Alas, however, there now comes a big obstacle. Our dear King would set up His *throne* in the heart, just as David desired to put his throne in Jerusalem; but firmly resisting Him there, and operating through the central citadel of the will, is our natural "*self*" which determinedly opposes the new King, just as the long-established Jebusites defied David. When our Lord captures the citadel of the *will*, as David captured Zion, the same three results follow. First, the old "self" is subdued. Second, our true King now reigns in the heart. Third, He begins to work wonderful renovation, development, reconstruction, in heart and life.

But there is one point at which the parallel breaks down. David captured that old-time Zion by *force*; but our heavenly King never subdues a human *heart* in that way. Thank God, there is that within you and me which *can* yield, if it *will*; and once we let Him capture and control us, then we begin to know "the *fulness* of the blessing", and the joy of practical sanctification.

The central *fact* is that David really got the citadel, and transformed it. Jebus became Jerusalem; and "if walls could talk" it might well have said, in Pauline phraseology, "I live, yet not I, but David liveth in me, and the new life which I now live as the transformed Zion, I live by the rule of royal David who now indwells me." Thus did "Jebus" (*trodden down*) become "Jerusalem" (*made peaceful*). Behold, a parable! It is a great day when Jesus is acknowledged as Saviour and Lord. After that, the greatest of all crises is when He really captures the will, and reigns supreme in the heart. Then only it becomes true of a human heart, as of Jerusalem—"Jehovah delighteth in thee" (Isa. 62 : 4).

Slay that Babe!

"Every son that is born ye shall cast into the river."—Exod. 1 : 22.

THERE are two classes who have been persecuted more than any other: the Jews and Christians. This first chapter of Exodus shows us anti-Semitic persecution in full swing four thousand years ago! —and it has been exceeded only by the inhuman anti-Jewish brutalities perpetrated by European powers of today. But Pharaoh-Hitler of long-ago found his persecution of Israel a boomerang which swung back and smote himself; so have others ever since.

This account in Exodus is genuine history; but we sense, also, a latent *typical* meaning in it. Old-time Egypt is a type of "this world". Pharaoh is a type of Satan. Many things which happened to Israel were adapted as types. We need not apologise, therefore, for spiritualising the narrative somewhat. When we do so, it utters weighty lessons. Pharaoh's persecution reached a new climax in his edict that all Hebrew baby-boys must be destroyed. Perhaps hundreds were drowned. Whenever the Egyptian Gestapo found a new-born Hebrew male, they ordered, "In the name of Pharaoh, SLAY THAT BABE!" It was an awful time; but with no lack of restrospective sympathy, may we give the incident a *spiritual* turn?

"Slay that babe!" Surely that is Satan's word about *the new convert.* The "god of this age" blinds the minds of "them which believe not". It is this Satanic opposition, in addition to the natural indifference of the human heart, which makes soul-winning so hard. Yet souls become saved! Then, when Satan cannot prevent conversion, he seeks to slay the new-born convert. As Pharaoh flung those new-born sons into the Nile, so would Satan fling the infant Christian into the swirling current of "this present evil world". Young believer, beware! Satan seeks to cut short the work of grace in your heart! He knows, perhaps even more than you yourself yet do, what a great thing conversion to Christ is. As the fowler spreads his net to catch the unwary bird, so Satan will spread his net to catch *you.* He will try to sow weeds to choke the "good seed" in your mind. He will come as an "angel of light" to deceive you; or as a "roaring lion" to scare you. He will try by his subtlest wiles to intrigue you, and by his cleverest snares to entangle you. He will try to *deny you food.* If he cannot at once fling you back into the river of Egypt, he will try to starve you to death by keeping you from the written Word. Or he will try to *discourage you into unbelief.* Young Christian, be warned; though at the same time be comforted, for "greater is He that is in you than he that is in the world" (1 Jn. 4: 4). Read your Bible regularly. Maintain fellowship with other believers. Make time for daily prayer. *Then* you will really prove that Jesus both saves and *keeps.*

"Slay that babe!" Just as surely, that is what Satan says about the intending *soulwinner.* If there is anything the devil hates and fights, it is our endeavour to win other souls to Jesus by faithful witness-bearing. He may let us get away with committees and organisations galore, so long as they keep us busy *inside* church; but the resolve to "go out into the highways and hedges" and bring the unsaved to Jesus—that infuriates the evil old Pharaoh. Do not be surprised, soulwinner, if discouragements come. The enemy will drown your high resolve if he can. Keep on! Your witness-bearing is a "goodly child", like Moses; and God will certainly use it.

Pharaoh's Deadly Edict

"Every son that is born ye shall cast into the river."—Exod. 1: 22.

"SLAY that babe!" In effect, that is what Satan always says about *the habit of prayer*. If there is one spiritual child which that evil Pharaoh would like to strangle at birth, it is the heaven-born resolve of a Christian believer to make time for regular, earnest, daily prayer. The evil one knows that all greatly used servants of our Lord have been men and women of prayer. He knows that nothing so develops and empowers a Christian as habitual prayer; that nothing so takes away worldly desires and increases wisdom; and that nothing is so dangerous to his own dark kingdom. He knows that nothing brings such blessing to churches, and nothing so mightily equips overseas missionaries, as prayer. John Gilmour, noble missionary to Mongolia, once wrote home, "Unprayed for, I feel like a diver at the bottom of a river, with no air to breathe; or like a fireman on a blazing building, with an empty hose." Many are the Christians of these days who say, "I have too many other things to do", or "I am too old now to develop the habit", or "It is not suitable to my present circumstances", or "Would not other people think me odd if I spent so much time in prayer?" Behind all these, and all other such useful excuses is Satan, saying, "Slay that babe!" Alas, what casualties there are!

"Slay that babe!" Why, of course, that is what Satan says also about *the hunger for holiness*. Our New Testament, all the way through, calls us to holiness of heart and life; not only to righteousness imputed, but to holiness *imparted*; not only to sanctification theoretically, but to sanctification *experientially*, through practical consecration to Christ and continual infilling by the Holy Spirit. But when Satan sees in us the new-born desire or determination to seek the blessing of holiness, he cries in fury, "Slay that babe!" The famous C. H. Spurgeon told his students for the ministry, "A holy minister is an awful weapon in the hand of God." He never said a truer thing, though it applies not only to ministers, but to *all* believers. Satan knows how true it is, and he uses deadliest discouragements. He tells us it is an impossible standard; the blessing is only imaginary; it will make us religious oddities; it will bring misunderstanding and loneliness. How often he succeeds!

"Slay that babe!" Satan always says that, when he sees *the beginning of revival*. Once the members of a church become spiritually aflame, hundreds may make exodus from his dark rule; so he tunes up the older grumblers, "This disturbs things"; and the younger grumblers, "This sort of thing is not for today"; then he sets the confidential gossips, criticisers and talebearers busy. He aborts revival far oftener by whispers *inside* than by scoffers *outside*. Yet Satan is not *always* successful. Both at the beginning and the ending of Scripture a man-child escapes (Exod. 2; Rev. 12). See with what mighty results!

"Slay that babe!" Yes, Satan seeks to slay the eager faith of the new convert; the high resolve of the soulwinner; the habit of prayer; the hunger for holiness; and the beginning of revival. But, as 2 Corinthians 2: 11 says, "We are not ignorant of his devices." If we "resist the devil", in the name of the Lord, he must "flee" from us (Jas. 4: 7). Through the power of Jesus, even babes shall be conquerors.

"Let us draw near . . . in full assurance of faith."—Heb. 10: 22.

In our New Testament there are two ninefold sets of writings: (1) the nine Christian Church Epistles, i.e. Romans to 2 Thessalonians; (2) the nine Hebrew Christian Epistles, i.e. Hebrews to Revelation. Romans, the leader of the first nine, shows us how a sinner may be given a new standing before God, even justification through imputed righteousness (Rom. 5: 1). Hebrews, the leader of the second nine, teaches the yet deeper and even more amazing truth that the justified sinner may *approach* this God of awful holiness.

One of the prominent ideas in this Hebrews epistle is that of "*drawing near*". See chapter 10: 22, "Let us draw near with a true heart, in full assurance of faith." See also 4: 16, 7: 25, 11: 6, 12: 18, 22, in which our word, "come" represents the same Greek word for "drawing near".

Nor is that all. The runner-up idea all through is that we may "draw near" *boldly*. See chapter 4: 16 again, "Let us therefore draw near boldly unto the throne of grace . . ." See also 10: 19; then 3: 6, 14; 10: 35, in which the word "confidence" translates the same Greek word.

Can you imagine how such teaching as this would sound to an old-time Jew, brought up under the ruling concept of Jehovah as the awesomely holy, flaming, unapproachable God of Mount Sinai (12: 18–27)? Can you imagine how it sounds to a deeply convicted sinner, terrified at the very mention of God? Can you imagine how it sounds to a starchy, politely conventional, or highly "religious" man, convinced that God may be approached only through clerics and rituals and ceremonies? How is it even *possible* to "draw near" to God so "boldly"?

Yes, how is it *possible*? Well, as this great epistle makes very clear, the Christian's boldness to draw near does not arise from a conceited false estimate of the dignity of *man*; nor does it arise from a deteriorated conception of the majesty of *God*. This Christian boldness is just as reverent as it is unhesitating. It arises from knowing a glorious, divine-human Sin-bearer, Saviour, Mediator, who has wrought atonement, reconciliation, and eternal redemption for us. Read our text in its context: "Having therefore, brethren, boldness to enter into the holiest by the blood of Jesus, by a new and living way which He hath consecrated for us, through the veil, that is to say, his flesh; and having such a High Priest over the house of God, *let us draw near with a true heart, in full assurance of faith.*"

Oh, what a dear and all-glorious Saviour Jesus is! Every aspect of His saviourhood is of surpassing preciousness to us; but this opening up of direct and ever-open access to the infinitely holy God Himself is one of the supremes of His redeeming accomplishments for us. Alas, one of the strangest incongruities is that so many of us leave this blood-purchased "new and living way" largely neglected! Daily let us seize the unspeakable privilege! "Let us draw near with a true heart, in full assurance of faith."

My crimson guilt is washed away;
My Saviour's wounds atone;
And by the "new and living way"
I now approach the Throne.

The New and Living Way

"Let us draw near . . . in full assurance of faith."—Heb. 10:22.

WELL, there it is: holy as God is, and sinful as we are, we may "draw near" to Him through the Lord Jesus, "in full assurance of faith". Does it seem almost unbelievably wonderful? Then examine the facts again. Verse 20 explains that our drawing near is "by a new and living way which He [our Lord Jesus] hath consecrated for us through the *veil*, that is to say, His *flesh*".

Away back in the old Israelite tabernacle, and later in the temple, the "veil" into the "holy of holies" both *gave* entrance, and at the same time *barred* entrance, into that inviolable, inmost sanctuary. It said, in effect, "God is in here! Sinner, keep out, or be consumed." Our Saviour's *body*, or "flesh", is likened to that veil. As God was behind the veil in the sanctuary, so "God was in Christ". But as the veil kept sinners out from God, so even Christ, the incarnate Son of God, the Word embodied in flesh, the One who revealed divine truth and holiness and goodness as they had never been revealed before—even Jesus could not, in His yet uncrucified body, open up a way of access for repentant sinners to our holy God. The veil must be rent. That life must be laid down. That body must be crucified. When Christ hung on Calvary, the veil of His flesh was "rent"; and at the very moment He expired, the veil of the temple in Jerusalem was rent from top to bottom by an invisible hand from heaven! The two things happened at the same moment so that we might not miss their significant connection with each other.

That rent body and that rent veil are tremendous in their meaning. First, they signify that all religion merely of material objects, of types and symbols and rituals, is now done away in Christ. The types are fulfilled. The symbols are no more needed. The rituals are superseded by the realities. All the spiritual realities prefigured in the Old Testament economy have now come into actuality.

Second, the rent body and veil signify that now access to God, not behind the veil of an earthly sanctuary, but spiritually and directly, is made open to all who would worship God "in spirit and in truth".

Yet even so, who will even now *dare* approach Him? The answer is supplied in the context. See verse 14, "For by one offering He hath perfected for ever them that are sanctified." That is *how God sees us* in Christ. Now, verse 15, "The Holy Spirit also is a witness to us . . ." *inwardly urging us* to "draw nigh". Next, verse 17, "Their sins and iniquities [God says] will I remember no more." So *the big barrier is removed.* Finally, see verse 19: "Having therefore, brethren, boldness to enter in even to the holiest by the blood of Jesus, by a new and living way which He hath consecrated for us . . ." There is the *blood* which transforms the judgment throne into a mercy seat; and there is the new *High Priest* (21) and the ever-living risen One who keeps the way of access ever open! Oh, brethren, "Let us draw near with a true heart, in full assurance of faith"!

Nor need I be deterred by fear,
My access is complete;
Within the veil I may draw near
The heavenly Mercy Seat.

"What man of you, having an hundred sheep, if he lose one of them, doth not . . . go after that which is lost, until he find it?"—Luke 15 : 4.

By this illustration of shepherd and sheep Jesus answered the Pharisees who criticised Him for ministering among people of ill-repute. It was an appeal to the human instinct of pity. If a man will feel pity for a sheep, and be at pains to save it, how much more toward those *human* sheep who are astray from God, and lost in sin? The difference of attitude between those Pharisees and our Lord Jesus was that *they* stood for a form of *religion*, whereas Jesus had come to show the way of *salvation*. Religion of itself never yet saved any man's soul. Not even Christianity, considered as a system, can save a single soul. What men need is not religion merely, but redemption; not some new ideology merely, but regeneration; not a new ethic only, but a new life; not just some new system, but a Saviour.

So, then, this illustration of the seeking shepherd is an appeal to the instinct of pity, and a defence against self-righteous critics; but it is much more; it is a *parable*. Under this figure of the seeking shepherd we are shown the Son of God Himself, seeking the lost souls of men. *We* are the perishing sheep; and Jesus is the Shepherd who comes to seek and to save us. It is this which gives the little parable-cameo its mighty meaning and abiding appeal. There are various viewpoints from which it may be considered; but here we limit ourselves to noticing again certain things which it teaches about the *Shepherd*, bearing in mind that the Shepherd is none other than the very Son of God Himself. The Shepherd is here pictured in three activities: (1) seeking, (2) finding, (3) rejoicing.

Reflect on the first of these, i.e. the Shepherd *seeking*. Mark well again that fourth verse: "What man of you having an hundred sheep, if he lose one of them, doth not leave the ninety and nine in the wilderness, and go after that which is lost, until he find it?" In the way that it is worded, who can miss seeing the divine *compassion* here betokened? The very numbers "ninety-nine" versus "one" make it plain that the motive of the Shepherd's seeking is compassion. If the sheep had been one out of twenty or fifty, the loss would have been such as to cause the sheep-owner to seek the lost sheep on account of the material loss to himself, without overmuch concern for the suffering of the sheep. But here is a man with ninety-nine left, and maybe the strayed one is now too broken to be of value much longer. The loss of merely that *one* from a hundred would be no serious matter. Yet away this Shepherd goes, amid the gathering night and the hazards of the hills, to rescue the one stray sheep because it is *dear* to Him, and He is moved by compassion. Oh, the compassion of this heavenly Shepherd who comes seeking us! Can we ever respond too gratefully to Him? Oh, the love that sought us! Oh, the blood that bought us!

"Lord, whence are those blood-marks all the way,
Which mark out the mountain track?"
"They were shed for one who had gone astray,
Ere the Shepherd could bring him back."
"Lord, whence are Thy hands so rent and torn?"
"They are piercèd and bleeding by many a thorn."

Seeking, Finding, Rejoicing

"And when he hath found it, he layeth it on his shoulders, rejoicing."—Luke 15:5.

THE lost sheep is said to be just one out of a hundred to show us that the seeking Shepherd's motive is compassion, not merely self-interest. It is just one out of a hundred so that in His seeking it we may see the value of one human soul to God. It is just one out of a hundred so that we may see the love of Christ for each one of us individually.

Observe the *perseverance* of the Shepherd. "Doth he not . . . go after that which is lost, *until he find it?*" In that word, "until", there is a hint of the difficulties and dangers which old-time Palestinian shepherds used to encounter in seeking lost sheep. But this seeking shepherd in the little parable goes forth undeterred by the difficulties and distances and dangers, to search and suffer "until he finds". What a picture of the Saviour! With what gracious persistence does He follow after the perverse and straying soul! Year after year He tracks after some of us, when all we deserve is to be left to our own obstinate folly and final ruin. Most of us, unless He had sought and sought and sought us again, would never have been saved. Oh, those thorn-pierced feet which have trodden the ragged rocks and swirling gorges to reach us!

But now see the Shepherd *finding*. "And when he hath found it, he layeth it on his shoulders, rejoicing." It might well have read, with many a shepherd, "And when he hath found it, he flingeth oaths at it, saying, Thou cursed sheep, why didst thou cause me trouble?" Or it might have read, "And when he hath found it, he smiteth it with his rod, to vent his wrath upon it." But no; this Shepherd in the parable behaves not so. When He finds the sheep, compassion beats in His heart as He sees the poor creature bleeding and panting on the ground.

He finds the sheep *helpless*, so "He layeth it upon His shoulders". That is how He finds you and me—spiritually helpless, broken, perishing. Then, with His mighty arm *He lifts us*, and bears us on His shoulders. Ah, poor, lost, bruised sheep, are you afraid of bleating to let the Shepherd know you want Him to save you? Are you afraid, thinking He will be angry with you? Are you afraid, thinking you may stray again? Do you not understand that He will carry you on His mighty shoulder?

See the Shepherd's *rejoicing*. He has a rejoicing which is *His alone*: "He layeth it on His shoulders, rejoicing." That rescued sheep means more to Him than to anyone else. He "sees the travail of His soul, and is satisfied". But He also rejoices over it *with others*: "He calleth together friends and neighbours . . . Rejoice with me, for I have found my sheep which was lost!" Lovely picture of our Lord Jesus! The angels rejoice with Him (7)! How *we* ought to rejoice with Him too!

> And all through the mountains thunder-riven,
> And up from the rocky steep,
> There arose a cry to the gate of heaven,
> "Rejoice, I have found My sheep!"
> And the angels echoed around the throne,
> "Rejoice, for the Lord brings back His own!"

"But speaking (or holding) the truth in love, grow up into Him in all things."—Eph. 4 : 15.

A TENEMENT was on fire. A frightened child gesticulated from a top-floor window. The firemen swung up a frail-looking ladder. One of them ventured the ascent. A strong wind was blowing. We watched him—clinging, then climbing, then claiming his quest. What an embrace! It was his own child!

See that ivy plant; how tiny against the giant oak! But look again after twenty years. Month by month it has been clinging; and steadily climbing; until now it is claiming the whole of the trunk and main branches.

I watched a cherub-faced little girlie clinging to her daddy's knee; then, with struggles and chuckles, climbing on to his lap; then, with bonny rapture, claiming the dear, whiskery face. Yes, I watched—this clinging, and climbing, and claiming.

Well, that is what we have in our verse. First there is *clinging*, for it says, "holding the truth . . ." Then there is *climbing*, for it adds, "grow up . . ." Then there is *claiming*, for it tells us to grow up appropriatingly "into *HIM*" in all things.

How vital that what we cling to is *strong*! If the ivy clings to a tottery wall it embraces its own downfall. The Scriptures warn us not to cling to Mammon, worldly-wise philosophies, the arm of flesh (see Ps. 144: 3, 4; 39: 6; Matt. 6: 19).

How important to cling to what is *worthy*! I once saw some rambler roses clinging round an ugly pig-sty. A friend of mine found his innocent sweet-peas bedraggled in the mire, because their gossamer fibres had twined round a pretty-looking but inwardly rotted trellis which collapsed when a storm came. The Bible warns us against clinging to attractive but unworthy things (Rom. 12: 9; 1 Thess. 5: 21, 22). Beware of any friendship or pleasure or pursuit which lessens desire toward Christ.

Again, how important to cling to what is *lasting*! Our hearts are foolish to twine too fondly round *any*thing earthly, for all is quickly passing. Some of those with tender hearts need to watch carefully. We invite eventual heartbreak when we cling inordinately even to our dearest loved-ones. We need not love them less, but only more wisely. Our affection must never be an idolatrous clinging.

Where then can we cling to the strong, worthy, lasting? "Thou shalt fear Jehovah thy God . . . unto Him shalt thou cleave" (Deut. 10: 20). "Trust ye in the Lord for ever, for in the Lord JEHOVAH is the Rock of Ages" (Isa. 26: 4). This glorious Jehovah has come to us visibly in Jesus; and is there not in Jesus everything to attract us—boundless love, purest sympathy, gentlest care for the weakest? These hearts of ours are ever sending out their wistful, eager tendrils. Oh, to let them fasten round Him who is loveliest and worthiest of all!

Then let the tendrils of my heart
Round *His* great heart entwine,
For then my Saviour will impart
His own pure life to mine.

More About Climbing

"But speaking (or holding) the truth in love, grow up into Him in all things."—Eph. 4 : 15.

YESTERDAY we were speaking about clinging, climbing, and claiming, as indicated in this verse. Let us ever remember that besides clinging there is to be *climbing*. We are to "grow up" into Christ "in all things". We may well learn from our favourite Virginia creeper or the climbing honeysuckle to cling only to that which draws us upward. May we never be like a certain kind of buttercup weed which only sprawls and spreads along the ground, with never a look heavenward! Nay, we must "grow *up*" into HIM.

Of course, it is easier just to cling without climbing than to cling and climb at the same time. It is one thing for the ivy to cling round the gnarled roots of the oak; it is a different thing to climb steadily up to where the great branches stretch themselves aloft in the glorious sunshine. It is one thing merely to believe on Jesus as the One who brings pardon for sin and promise of heaven. It is a different thing to climb daily upwards into spiritual-mindedness, Christlikeness of character, and heart-to-heart fellowship with God. This latter requires godly resolution. The apostle exhorts us in Colossians 3 : 2, "Set your affection on things above, not on things on the earth"; and if someone should complain that the affections are such variable, elusive things as to make it almost impossible to round them up and methodise them, we point out that Paul's injunction is better translated, "Set your *mind* on things above"—and we certainly can do *that*. By daily prayings, daily lingerings over God's Word, daily denials of selfism, daily words of witness for Jesus as opportunity discreetly allows, daily acts of thoughtful kindness, and daily practising the presence of God, we may climb up into the lovely sunshine of continuous fellowship with Him whom having not seen, as yet, we love.

There is nowhere else worth climbing. One afternoon a certain preacher sat in his garden and became much interested in the climbing of a caterpillar. Slowly this caterpillar climbed to the top of a painted stick which had been stuck into the ground as a decoration; then it reared itself, feeling out this way and that for some means of further progress, or for some juicy twig on which to feed, only to find nothing but space; whereupon, after several gropings, it slowly descended to the ground, crawled along to another painted stick, and did the same thing all over again. Oh, there are many such "painted sticks" in the world! Glamorous pleasures, colourful popularity, gay-looking luxuries which wealth can buy, the florid-painted satisfactions which social careering, high position, and pride of learning seem to offer—all these call to men, and say, "Climb me, and you will find the desire of your heart, the self-realisation which really satisfies." But they are only "painted sticks". Those who climb them, instead of finding satisfaction, find nothing but emptiness, till wearily they drop into the grave. Let us not expect too much from anyone or anything in this fallen world—money, marriage, business, houses, children, honours. Here is the one sure way to satisfaction—"GROW UP INTO HIM." Let me daily, hourly practise living by a faith which draws upon His sufficiency, and a love which blends all my motives in living to please Him. What rich quality, peace, and joy this always brings!

"But speaking (or holding) the truth in love, grow up into Him in all things."—Eph. 4 : 15.

THIS is our third day on this verse. We have spoken about clinging ("holding the truth"), and about climbing ("grow up"); but now think about *claiming*, that is, this "growing up" appropriatingly "into *HIM* in all things". This thought of claiming while climbing, or appropriating while growing, is certainly in the text. In the immediate context Christ and the Church are represented by the metaphor of head and body, in which the life of Christ the Head is in all the members. See verse 16: "From Whom (Christ) the whole body . . . maketh increase (i.e. growth) unto the building up of itself in love." The members are to *appropriate* His life for the purpose of upgrowing and upbuilding.

That metaphor of the "body" represents the Church collectively; but there is also to be an *individual* "growing up" into Christ, and an individual *appropriation* of Him; for the words of our text are addressed to individuals as such. Let us learn thoroughly that there can be neither life nor increase apart from HIM. There can be no growing without appropriating.

Mark it well then: we climb by *claiming*; the two things go together. Look again at the ivy or the mistletoe; they do not climb by their unaided strength; but all the while they are nourishing themselves from the life of the tree up which they are growing. Because of this they are somewhat unpleasantly termed "parasites"; but that in no wise detracts from their usefulness as illustrating this necessary union of climbing and claiming. It is indeed *blessed* parasitism which daily feeds on our life-giving Lord!

This claiming, however, is not only a necessity; it is a *privilege*. Christian believer, marvel at this afresh: you are *meant* to appropriate the life and strength of your Lord Jesus! He is graciously at your disposal—His grace, His peace, His strength, His guidance, His patience, His joy, His Spirit! Not only in our times of prayer and Bible-reading, but by silent prayer-communion and inward absorption we may appropriate His life all through the hours of the day. And there is one *special* way of thus "claiming" Him which we would mention here, namely our appropriating *the promises of His Word*, by which we become "partakers of the Divine nature" (2 Peter 1 : 4). Oh, may we learn this threefold process of clinging, climbing and claiming!

As the flow'r upon the trellis,
  Or the ivy on the tree,
May my heart its wistful tendrils
  Ever twine, O Lord, round Thee.

Clinging, climbing, upward going,
  Like the ivy, or the flower,
Keep me daily heav'nward growing
  In Thine own imparted power.

Ever clinging, daily climbing,
  Growing up in truth and love,
And for all my weakness claiming,
  Thine own fulness from above.

A Basket of Summer Fruit

"Behold, a basket of Summer fruit."—Amos 8: 1.

IN olden times, when God would impress important truths upon His people, He often used picture language. Kingdoms were likened to mountains; evil ruling-powers to beasts of prey; and so on. Such picture language makes truth vivid, and causes it to linger in mind like a living thing. One such instance is our text. Amos is shown "a basket of Summer fruit" which God compares to Israel. What a sad comparison it was, the subsequent verses unfold. Just here, however, that "basket of Summer fruit" may serve as a singularly apt emblem of the *Gospel*.

First, Summer fruit is *beautiful*, and in this it is like the *influences* of the Gospel. None of earth's products are more beautiful than Summer fruits. They have a "Benjamin's portion" of mild, sunny, balmy weather, and they blush their glad gratitude on a thousand hill-slopes and in a thousand verdant valleys. Whether hanging from the orchard boughs, or heaped in colourful conglomeration on the garner floor, or nicely arranged in fruit dishes, their red and yellow, their tender green and pink, their deeper hues and tints, give them a loveliness all their own. And is not the Gospel of Christ similarly beautiful in its effects and influences?

Summer fruit is also *bountiful*, and in this it is like the *blessings* of the Gospel. What a contrast there is between the full-orbed glory of Summer and the bleak barrenness of Winter, the pale slenderness of early Spring and the disrobed look of later Autumn! From the equatorial regions, sweltering beneath tropical suns, to the cooler hemispheres, a million plantations, fields, groves, orchards, labour under their picturesque burden of luscious fruitage. Thus copious are the blessings of the Gospel (Eph. 1: 3; Rom. 5: 5).

Again, Summer fruit is *attractive*, and in this it is like the *invitations* of the Gospel. There is an endless appeal about Summer fruit, not only to the eyes of the young, but throughout life's later years. There have never lacked great artists who have found special pleasure in painting fruits, even though the canvas cannot reproduce that favourite *aroma* which enhances the appeal of Summer fruits. And, correspondingly, how attractive are the invitations of the Gospel! Read again Matthew 11: 28; Isaiah 1: 18; 55: 1, 6, 7; Revelation 22: 17.

Further, Summer fruits are *healthful*, and in this they are like the *doctrines* of the Gospel. The failing of the orchards gives inroads to all kinds of disease. Plenty fruit in one's diet is a pleasant and powerful contribution to health. Similarly, of all moral forces in the world the Gospel is the most health-bringing. We only need to contrast the Bible doctrine of God, man, morals, origins, destiny, with those of the non-Biblical systems to know how vital they are to human well-being. Most of all the Gospel doctrine of the Cross lifts man from deepest depths to highest heights.

Finally, Summer fruits are *perishable*, and in this they are like the *opportunities* of the Gospel. It is this quickly perishable nature of Summer fruit which is referred to in Amos 8: 2. "Amos, what seest thou? A basket of Summer fruit. . . . The end is come upon my people." So is it with the opportunities of the Gospel. "*Now* is the accepted time" (2 Cor. 6: 2).

Ripe Fruit

"My soul desired the firstripe fruit."—Mic. 7 : 1.

AUTUMN is a beautiful season of the year, with its golden fields and laden orchards. Surrounded by rustic charms the reaper bands go forth amid the corn, and the ingatherers of fruit among the avenues of bending boughs. Autumn is also full of spiritual lessons. Again and again the Bible goes into the harvest fields and among the fruit groves, to gather ripe illustrations of spiritual realities. Our text is an instance. God says to His people Israel, "My soul desired the firstripe fruit." The words equally apply to you and me as Christian believers. Our Lord desires "firstripe fruit" in our lives.

To begin with, the firstripe fruit is *beautiful to the eye*. In the early months when the fruit is hard and small, it is not so inviting to the eye. But when Summer has exercised her final charms, when old Sol, that magic artist of the sky, has put his finishing touches to the face of the orchards, and the fruits have blushed amid the kisses of the latter rain, what a picture of loveliness captivates us! Even so, if there is a *spiritual* ripeness about you and me, there will be a beauty of character and demeanour. There will be what the Scripture calls "the beauty of holiness". No cosmetics could produce it; they could only spoil it. It is a lovely maturity which shows itself in consistent praisefulness and peacefulness.

Next, the ripened fruit is *sweet to the taste*. When the fruit is young and undeveloped, it is tart, even bitter; but when it is plumped out by the nutritious sap, and tempered by the elements, and sugared by that patent process which is known only inside the laboratory of the tree trunk, it becomes luscious and sweet. Just so, another mark of *spiritual* ripeness is sweetness of disposition and temper. What sour Christians one meets now and then! They are as tarty as young crab apples! Do not get your teeth into them or you will get a blistered tongue! There are those with strong doctrinal beliefs, who cannot stand to be disagreed with even on minor points. There is the junior who simply will not tolerate the slightest word of advice from a senior. There is the minister who resents even well-meaning criticism, and the member who is awfully offended because she was not visited after her first sneeze of influenza. There is the music leader who considers even the kindest suggestion as a reflection upon his ability; and worst of all, the nasty, anonymous letter-writer. Ah, what a sad, sad disappointment must such unpalatable immaturity be to the heavenly Husbandman who "desires the firstripe fruit".

Again, ripe fruit has a *delightful fragrance*. Go into a room where two or three dishes of tempting-ripe apples, pears, plums, have been left, and oh, what a luscious-scented freshness they have diffused! Equally so, fragrance of character is a mark of *spiritual* ripeness. There should cling about us what Paul calls a "sweet savour of Christ". Some time ago a man said to me about a Christian neighbour, "I always feel better when he's been around." That is the kind of fragrance which spiritual maturity engenders. One Sunday a rather rough-looking man came asking how to be converted. When we enquired what had awakened his desire to become a Christian, he replied, "The fragrance of my wife's life at home." Lord, give *me* the fragrance of spiritual ripeness.

More About Ripe Fruit

"My soul desired the firstripe fruit."—Mic. 7: 1.

BESIDES being beautiful to the eye, and sweet to the taste, and having a *delightsome fragrance*, ripe fruit is *tender to the touch*. In the earlier months the unripe fruit is hard—much too hard for our teeth to bite; but when it has mellowed to full ripeness it is pulpy, juicy, and yields to the pressure of our fingers. Even so, another mark of *spiritual* ripeness is tenderness, sympathy, easiness to be approached. How hard some of us are! How preoccupied with self, and unsympathetic toward others! How piously curious and gossipy we are about another's fall, instead of being genuinely compassionate and restorative! A pretty young woman once came to me seeking spiritual help. Her story was one of deep sin. A supposed lover had beguiled her, and from then she had gone deep into the mire. I suggested she should rather talk with certain of our lady members, but her eyes swam with tears and her lips quivered as she replied, "Oh, no, no, sir! They just wouldn't understand. I know them. Outwardly they would be ever so 'shocked', but inwardly as hard as rock!" We must never be tender toward *sin*. We must hate it. Yet tenderness, understanding, sympathy, compassion, is what many a remorseful defaulter is needing. Lord, give us tenderness—toward the young, the aged, the sick, the fallen, the needy.

Again, ripe fruit *hangs downwards*. Like the full-ripe corn in the golden harvest-fields which hangs its head down as though in humble worship, so in the colourful orchards the ripened apples and other fruits hang modestly downwards. In the Spring and early Summer how different! The stalk is like a stiff neck which holds a most obstinate little head. Then, as the fruit ripens it bends over, until laden with luscious goodness it hangs down as though in humble contrition that it was ever so stiff and proud. And in the same way humility is a mark of *spiritual* ripeness in the Christian life. Pride, egotism, boasting, and fondness for talking about one's own self, are always indications of spiritual under-development.

Still further, ripe fruit has a *loose hold*. In the earlier months you could shake the tree till you tore it up from the roots, but the hard unripe fruit would cling defiantly to the branches. Only wait till the fruit is dead ripe, however, and the slightest shake will bring it down. So is it with *spiritual* ripeness. We have a loose hold on the things of earth. We are ready to go at a moment's call.

Just once more, ripe fruit *often comes from young trees*. Any fruit-grower will tell you that. Even so, we must not confuse *spiritual* ripeness with merely *natural* seniority. I have known seventy-year-olds among Christians who were not near so ripe and sweet as twenty-year-olds; and I have known those who had been converted *forty* years earlier who had not matured to the ripeness of some who had been converted only *four* years ago. Our Lord desires the "firstripe fruit" in *all* of us—younger as well as older. "The fruit of the Spirit is love, joy, peace, longsuffering, gentleness, goodness, faith, meekness, godly self-control" (Gal. 5: 22, 23). This is *not* the fruit of experience, or elderliness, but of the *Spirit*; and it may be seen in *all* believers—*if they will.*

Essentials to Spiritual Ripeness

"My soul desired the firstripe fruit."—Mic. 7: 1.

So our Lord desires the "firstripe fruit". He would have you and me develop a *spiritual* ripeness as His disciples. How, then, do we mature to spiritual ripeness?

Well, the first requirement is that the fruit be *nurtured from a good soil*. Everything depends on where the tree grows. If the soil is poor the fruit suffers. If the soil is rich, you have the first big likelihood that the fruit will attain rich ripeness. What is in the soil determines the quality and flavour of the fruit. Around Clearwater, Florida, there is much sulphur in the soil. You taste it in the drinking water; and, what is more, you can taste it in some of the lovely big grapefruit and oranges from the groves there. Now the soil from which we Christians need to get the sap which makes for spiritual richness and ripeness is the written Word of God. Bible neglecters never become spiritually mature. Those who feed continually upon it find the most wonderful of all spiritual nurture.

But besides this, if there is to be ripe fruit, the tree must enjoy *the ministries of Nature*. It must get its full share of the Spring and Summer rains. It must be tempered by the varying seasons. It must be where the air is congenial. It must enjoy the evening kisses of the dew. Last but not least, it must have its full and generous share of glorious sunshine. If the tree is plagued by drought, or has to struggle against the fumes and polluted air of a smoky, gritty, industrial city, or if surrounding buildings cheat it of sunshine, then the fruit will greatly suffer. So, in the case of *spiritual* maturity, there must be the ministries of grace. There must be times of quiet communing with God, when the early and the latter rains can come to our souls from the presence of the Lord. There must be a tempering of our character through the ministry of trial, testing, temptation, responsibilities, and disappointments, and perhaps some windy blasts of persecution. We must give scope to the heavenly Comforter, the Holy Spirit, to sweeten us with the dews of heaven. We must be regular in attendance on the public ministry of the Word in some sanctuary where they really teach the Bible as the Word of God. We must find congenial fellowship with other evangelical believers. Last, but not least, by separation from all doubtful practices, we must keep our hearts open to the Saviour's love.

Next, if there is to be sound, ripe fruit, it must be *guarded against blight and pest*. Many of the most dangerous heretics have been sincere men, and often the most blighting heresies have an intriguing plausibility. We must test everything prayerfully by the written Word. We must shun *any* teaching which denies the deity of our Lord, the personality of the Holy Spirit, the real atonement of the Cross, the bodily resurrection of Jesus, or other cardinal truths of our evangelical faith. We must also guard against extravagances such as we find in movements which make much ado about "speaking in tongues" and bodily healings, under the plea of going "all the way" with God. First Corinthians shows that such extremes may go with very poor spirituality. We must guard also against pest-habits, and friendships which retard spiritual development. These are *some* ways, at least, whereby we may attain real spiritual ripeness.

A Harvest Exclamation

"O Jehovah, our Lord, how excellent is Thy name in all the earth!"—Ps. 8: 1.

It is suggested that this psalm was probably intended as a song for the winepress, a joyful hymn for the treaders of grapes during the time of harvest and the ingathering of the fruits. The golden sheaves and the luscious grape-clusters and all the other pleasant splendours of the old-time Palestinian reaping season are around us.

David looks round on it all again—this annual miracle of divine providence. He sees it as only a poet and godly man *can* see it. He wonders at it all again with a deep and reverent wonder. As he muses, the fire burns. He must sing! Where is his harp? He must write! Where is his pen? He can only begin with an exclamation, an exclamation addressed to God Himself: "O Jehovah, our Lord, how excellent is thy name in all the earth!"

Yet the very lifting of his eyes Godwards confronts him with immenser wonders, and he must needs add, "When I consider Thy heavens, the work of Thy fingers, the moon and the stars . . ." (verse 3). This in turn makes little man seem so *very* little that David with new surprise asks, "What is man, that Thou art mindful of *him?*" (4). Yet God is not only "mindful" of man, He "crowns him with glory and honour"; He commits to man the earth with all its creatures (5–8). The harvest now becomes one big, eloquent speech of God, and David can only end his ode by repeating the exclamation with which he began—"O Jehovah, our God, how excellent is Thy name in all the earth!"

Well, it is harvest season again. Is not the annual harvest a time for reverent and grateful *exclamation* such as David's? See the plenty and variety of produce from the good brown earth. Human labourers have ploughed and planted, nurtured and tended, reaped the fields and gathered the fruits, but it is God who "gave the increase".

At the end of this present age our Lord Jesus will reap a great harvest. The angel reapers will spread abroad. The saved ones will be garnered home. The ransomed of the Lord will gather to the heavenly Zion. The "innumerable company" who have been redeemed by the precious blood of Christ will be harvested to heaven. What a time of exclamation *that* will be!

Similarly, "in the sweet by and by", every true Christian labourer will reap a harvest. Our heavenly Master will bestow rewards for faithful service. They who have sown in tears shall reap in joy. Those who have had scanty results here will have lavish rewards there. What a time of exclamation *that* will be, with its culminating recognition of our poor service, "Well done, good and faithful servant."

The impenitent Christ-rejector, also, will reap a harvest by and by. Those who have lived for the flesh will reap a harvest of corruption. Those who have known the Gospel but have lightly neglected it will reap a harvest of confusion and damnation. "God is not mocked; for whatsoever a man soweth, that shall he also reap." What a time of dolorous exclamation *that* will be—to hear the awful words, "Depart from me ye cursed, into everlasting fire!" Yes, harvest is a time of exclamation, and a time to make us thoughtful about the really big things.

"Harvest is come."—Mark 4: 29.

HERE, in our northern hemisphere, harvest season has come round again. The fields are glorious with waving corn or golden sheaves. The valleys laugh and sing. The orchards blush with bashful ripeness. Nature is bestowing her bounties with wide-open arms upon the sons of men. Once again, also, harvest is preaching its annual sermon to us. It is one of the most telling preachers among the seasons of the year. "He that hath ears to hear, let him hear." In the Bible there are *seven* great harvests mentioned.

(1) There is the annual harvest of *the good brown earth.* This natural harvest preaches year by year that God is a covenant-keeping God. He put the rainbow in the sky as the fidelity-token of His covenant with the sons of men through patriarch Noah: "While the earth remaineth, seed-time and harvest, and cold and heat, and Summer and Winter, and day and night shall not cease." Four thousand annual harvests have implemented that pledge.

(2) There is the harvest of *a carnal life.* See Galatians 6: 7, 8: "He that soweth to his flesh shall of the flesh reap *corruption.*" The worldly, fleshly man often seems to have a gay old time of it, here on earth, especially if he has ample means; but in the end he perishes. When at death he passes as a disembodied spirit into hades, he is seen in his nakedness as a shrivelled, diseased, cankered, leprous, worm-eaten, ugly, tormented thing.

(3) There is the harvest of the *spiritual life*: "He that soweth to the Spirit shall of the Spirit reap life everlasting" (Gal. 6: 8). How do we sow to the Spirit? By following His leading; by cultivating obedience to His voice in the Holy Scriptures and in our hearts; by yielding ourselves to His control; and by going on unwearily in well-doing (Gal. 6: 9).

(4) There is the harvest of *present opportunities.* If we have eyes to see, there is always a harvest of opportunities to ingather. "Say not ye there are yet four months, and then cometh harvest? Look on the fields, for they are *white already* unto harvest" (Jn. 4: 35). The labourers are few; the loiterers are many! "As we have opportunity, therefore, let us do good . . ." (Gal. 6: 10).

(5) There is the harvest of *reward for Christian service.* "In due season we shall reap, if we faint not" (Gal. 6: 9). "He that goeth forth and weepeth, bearing precious seed, shall doubtless come again with rejoicing, bringing his sheaves with him" (Ps. 126: 6). See also Matthew 10: 42; 25: 21.

(6) There is the harvest of *the resurrection.* "Now is Christ risen from the dead, and become the firstfruits of them that sleep." The firstfruits are always the pledge and specimen of the full harvest by and by. "Christ the firstfruits; afterward they that are Christ's at His coming" (1 Cor. 15: 20, 23). What a glorious harvest *that* will be!

(7) There is the harvest at the *end of the age.* See Matthew 13: 38–43 again: "The field is the world. The good seed are the children of the kingdom; but the tares are the children of the wicked one. The harvest is the end of the age; and the reapers are the angels. As therefore the tares are gathered and burned in the fire, so shall it be in the end of this age . . ."

"He Faileth Not"

"He faileth not."—Zeph. 3 : 5.

PRICELESS gems have often been found in unlikely places. Many a choice flower has been found blooming in a rocky crevice. Rainbow artistries have suddenly lit up the drabbest skies. Beauty spots have charmed the traveller at surprise turns on the least-promising road. It is even so with this word in Zephaniah 3: 5: *"He faileth not."* In a context laden with rebukes to a perverse people, this expression of the divine faithfulness shines like a solitary star on a dark night. "He faileth not." How much this assurance means to the Lord's own! It suggests a comforting threefold homily.

First, "He faileth not" in His *power*—which is pledged in Christ to work on our behalf. Child of God, what is that big thing which thou wouldst have Him do for thee? Has faith begun to fail? Has the heart been looking at circumstances instead of to God? Think on this again, that if answer seems unduly delayed, it is not through any collapse of His "power to usward". Perhaps faith is being tested for the sake of your spiritual profit and progress.

Unanswered yet, the prayer your lips have uttered
In agony of heart these many years?
Does faith begin to fail, is hope departed?
And think you that in vain are all your tears?
Say not the Father hath not heard your prayer;
Your prayer shall answered be, sometime, somewhere.

But further, "He faileth not" in His *wisdom*. What comfort is this for the perplexed believer! Why is this disappointment, this loneliness, this dark experience permitted? Why is that thing for which the heart has yearned still left ungranted? We do not know—not *yet*; but we *do* know that our Father's wisdom never errs.

I know not by what methods rare,
But this I know, God answers prayer.
I know He gives His pledgèd word
Which tells me prayer is always heard,
And will be answered soon or late,
Though often it is hard to wait.
I know not if the blessing sought
Will come in just the way I thought;
I leave my prayer with Him alone,
Whose will is wiser than my own,
Assured that He will grant my quest,
Or send an answer far more blest.

Best of all, "He faileth not" in His *love*. Did He not love us, His power and wisdom would mean little to us, but to know they are employed in the service of His unfailing love gives us a triple guarantee of His faithfulness. "Love never faileth." "God is love." Tried and troubled believer, take heart! "He faileth not"!

"And when Abram was ninety years old and nine, the Lord appeared to Abram and said unto Him: I am the Almighty God; walk before Me and be thou perfect."—Gen. 17: 1.

WE wonder if among those who read this meditation there is some elderly friend plaintively sighing, "Ah, me; the bloom of youth and vigour of maturity are gone. My life has reached its Autumn. I am too old now to expect any further outstanding crisis of spiritual blessing." To any such we would say: See what happened to Abram when he was "ninety years old and nine"! Are you as old as *that*? My dear elderly friend, it may be that God has the biggest spiritual experience of your life yet to give you, if you will let Him. I am inclined to think that in these days we make too much of youth and too little of age; and the elderly themselves tend much to underrate their own usefulness and attractiveness. Let me ask both the younger and the older to reflect on one or two considerations which bear on this.

To begin with; did you know that as a general rule the elderly have the *best-quality abilities*? There are statistics which show that the richest productivity lies in the decade between the sixtieth and seventieth birthdays. I read recently that some four hundred names of the most noted men in all times were selected—statesmen, soldiers, painters, poets, authors. Opposite each name was placed what was considered to be his greatest achievement. Then the list was submitted to competent critics, to make thoroughly sure that the achievement put against each man's name really *was* his masterpiece. The following remarkable percentages were then abstracted: 35 per cent belonged between the ages of sixty and seventy; 23 per cent between seventy and eighty; 6 per cent over eighty. In other words, 64 per cent of the greatest masterpieces or achievements belong to those over sixty years old.

I know, of course, that someone will immediately ask, "Did not Alexander the Great conquer the world when he was only thirty-three? Did not Beethoven compose his immortal Ninth Symphony when he was only very young? And did not Handel produce his supreme oratorio, "The Messiah", when he was still youthful? Yes, true; but all of these were included in the statistics just given; and they are "exceptions which prove the rule". So, there it is: that as a general rule the elderly have the best-quality abilities.

Is it not true also that the elderly can render *richest-quality Christian service*? Who can give such mature testimony as they? Who can pray with such understanding? Who can sympathise with such seasoned fellow-feeling? Who can counsel with such gathered prudence? What youth has in alacrity, age more than counterbalances by sagacity. Oh, I am sure we need to come with new challenge to the elderly among us. Read Genesis 17 again. See what happened to Abram when he was "ninety years old and nine"—a new call to sanctification (verse 1); a new revelation of God as *El Shaddai*, i.e. "God All-sufficient" (1); the changing of his name from Abram to Abraham in token of fruitfulness (5); a further elaborating of the Divine covenant with him (7); and the crowning new promise—of Isaac (19).

Spring Versus Autumn

"I have been young, and now am old. . . ."—Ps. 37 : 25.

HERE is something that all the elderly can say equally truly as David, though not all of them say it with the same ungrudging contentedness. Yet age need never envy youth, any more than sunset need envy sunrise. Call the poets, ask the artists, which is lovelier, sunrise or sunset. "Be of good cheer" dear elderly friend. Life's best is not confined to immature youth. Have not the elderly the *truest-quality attractiveness*? Youth, like Spring, has its own charm; yet would many of us seriously disagree with the following double-sonnet? (which formed itself in my mind some time ago in tribute to a saintly elderly friend):

Yes, Spring has charm. Arrayed in unspoilt green,
Bedecked with blossoms—like a fairy queen,
Her magic wand grey Winter's spell transforms
To laughing loveliness in sprightliest forms,
And wakes the merry songsters in the trees,
And scents with dew-kissed petals every breeze.
Yes, Spring has charm. Yet none the less I hold
That lovelier still is Autumn's mellowed gold.
Tho' not with livelier, yet with kindlier eyes,
She smiles upon us from soft-dappled skies.
Her deeper crimsons and her wistful brown,
With russet hues weave Nature's richest crown.
Her laden boughs and glorious waving corn—
It was for *these* that Spring was ever born!

Yes, Youth has charm. Who doubts it or denies?
Unfurrowed brow, undimmed and questing eyes;
Lithe figure, supple limb and graceful poise,
And brave horizons bright with promised joys;
And merry heart all full of gleeful play,
And life and love and laughter all so gay.
Yes, Youth has charm. Yet none the less I hold
That fairer halos cling around the old.
The mellowed lustre of the long-lived wise
Beams out from kindlier if less lively eyes;
The ripened fruit, and gold of harvest field,
And softer hues which weathered seasons yield,
And milder charms which now the brow enring—
It was for *THESE* that youth awaked in Spring!

Few things more offend my own esteem for elderly womanhood than to see it self-lowered in the pathetic pretence of a sham youth plastered on by cosmetics, and the wearing of garments which, if they were ever really suitable even for youth, are quite unbecoming for elderly ladies. Oh, why must the grown and gracious tree ape the less-lovely sapling? The best of all cosmetics is the dear Saviour Himself so filling the heart that the very face of the elderly saint radiates the indwelling Shekinah!

The Moon and the Church

"He appointed the moon. . . ."—Ps. 104: 19.

A SCOFFER who was as empty of truth as he was full of bluff derisively remarked, "Religion is all moonshine." Unwittingly he came close to uttering a remarkable similitude. The moon and the Christian Church have much in common! What the one is to the physical world the other is to the spiritual; and we should be dark indeed without either! Trace the parallel.

The moon *shines with reflected light*. It has no light in itself. It shines with the reflected light of the sun. So the Church reflects the light of Christ. Apart from Him it has no light to give. In these days when the ecumenical movement gives large prominence to the so-called "world church", and sometimes talks more about *it* than about *HIM*, it is well to remember that the Church was never put into the world to witness to itself. It can only give light as it forgets itself in reflecting Christ.

The moon is *a part of the earth which broke off*. It is part yet no longer part. So is the true Church a people taken out of this world in a spiritual sense. When the moon broke off, ages ago, it was of irregular shape, a hot mass, and still close to the earth. See the early Church: organisation irregular, but glorious fire of loyalty to Christ; burning urgency in the rescue of souls; close contact with men by individual evangelism. The moon today is rounded off, much cooled, and farther from the earth.

The moon is *bigger than it looks*. So is the true Church. There are more regenerate souls on earth than perhaps we think. See the final issue—"a multitude which no man could number, of all nations . . ." (Rev. 7: 9).

The moon is of all the heavenly bodies *the most useful to us*, except the sun. Even so, the greatest blessings which have come to the human race have come by the precious Gospel which the Church has spread abroad.

The moon is "the lesser light to *rule the night*". So is the Church. Not by the sword, as Mohammed; not by a fear-instigating false authoritarianism, as papal Rome; but by the light of truth, the "light of the knowledge of the glory of God in the face of Jesus Christ" (2 Cor. 4: 6).

The moon *affects the earth greatly but silently*, influencing winds, tides, and weather. So does the true Church, unostentatiously, but spiritually, morally, purifyingly, affect human society.

The moon has *different phases*. The extent of it which *we* see is determined by the moon's position to the sun. Equally so, the degree of divine light which men find in the Church is always determined by its relation to Christ.

The moon has its *eclipses*. Alas, so has the Church! When the moon comes between sun and earth, the earth is darkened. So is it when a self-important Church comes between Christ and men. Sometimes earth has come between moon and sun, and the moon itself has been darkened. So is the Church darkened whenever the "world" comes between it and Christ.

All this speaks to us. Some people need saving from Churcholatry just as much as from moon worship! The Church is nothing apart from Christ. Let us pray that the organised Church may become again the unclouded luminary of Christ in a sin-darkened world.

My Lean Olive Tree

"Two or three berries in the top of the uppermost bough."—Isa. 17: 6.

THE whole verse reads: "Yet gleanings shall be left in it, as the shaking of an olive tree, two or three berries in the top of the uppermost bough, four or five in the outmost fruitful branches thereof, saith Jehovah, God of Israel." The prophet is foretelling a sorrowful day of leanness which was surely coming upon those idolatrous apostates who had treated Jehovah with perverse thanklessness. It should be with them as with an olive tree after its crop of berries had been removed by the beating of its boughs and branches; just "two or three berries in the top of the uppermost bough" where the sticks of the beaters had not reached, and only "four or five on the outmost branches".

Alas, for the lean olive tree! Alas, when it becomes symbolic of *my own spiritual life*! Can it be that even now some of us are in such a bereft condition spiritually, with faith and hope and love and joy and peace and strength and prayer and testimony and service lean and languishing? If so, why should it be? and what can we do about it?

See verse 10: "Because thou hast forgotten the God of thy salvation..." Ah, there has been *forgetfulness of God*. I have allowed myself to become inordinately immersed in mundane things, in business, in pleasure, in domestic absorptions, in social affairs, in getting and spending, in working and playing, in much "coming and going" (Mark. 6: 31). My life has become so full that I now find it empty! I have been so busy remembering the *many* things that I have forgotten the *one* thing which is really needful. I have become a cumbered Martha and have forgotten to sit at my Master's feet. That is one reason, at least, why my olive tree has only "two or three berries in the top of the uppermost bough".

But look again at verse 10: "Because thou hast not been mindful of the Rock of thy strength . . ." So there has also developed an unspiritually minded *self-sufficiency*. I have been neglectful of prayer. I have foolishly preferred to manage (or *mis*manage) my own affairs. I have forgotten how weak I am, and have imagined that the unsteady little lamb was a strong lion. And now I am like an olive bereft of its berries.

Glance, too, at verse 8; read of "altars" and "images" which those old-time Israelites had made. Can it be that I myself have become *idolatrous*? Have I allowed some friendship or some ambition or some member of the other sex to usurp the place of God in my heart's desire and devotion? If so, then there is judgment against my altars and idols; my olive tree is stripped of all but "two or three berries in the top bough".

What then can we do? See verses 7 and 8: "At that day shall a man *look to his Maker* . . ." When adversity strips our olive tree of all but "two or three berries", it is meant to turn us from our self-made altars and idols back to the true God, our gracious covenant-keeping Jehovah. However unbelievable it seems at times, God could do nothing unkinder than allow us continued prosperity when we are self-willed, wayward, prayerless and backslidden. Adversity must beat the olive tree with hard strokes which leave only "two or three berries". God loves us too wisely to think more of our natural pleasure than of our spiritual profit. Soul of mine, get back to *Him*. Put wrong things right. Throw down those idols. Back to prayer, faith, love, and new consecration. Then shall my olive be laden again!

Tides Versus Winds

"If my people, which are called by my name, shall humble themselves, and pray, and seek my face, and turn from their wicked ways; then will I hear from heaven, and will forgive their sin, and will heal their land."—2 Chron. 7: 14.

THIS is God's striking challenge to His own people. Are not we Christians God's people? Do we not represent the cause of divine truth in the earth? What though the words were first spoken to Israel? Does that diminish their challenge to ourselves? The Hebrews certainly are God's people, chosen in Abraham, and constituted a special divine inheritance among the nations; but in a far profounder, spiritual sense, the blood-bought, Spirit-born people of Christ are God's people, "chosen in Christ before the foundation of the world." "My people . . ." Superlative privilege! Vast responsibility!

Some years ago I spent a holiday near the fringe of a lonely bay on the rugged coast of north east England. Toward sunset one day I went out along by the shore to watch the incoming tide, and became much impressed by the power of the wind as it smote the water with its mighty breath. The weather that day had been fitful, with quickly alternating spells of sunshine and heavy rain. A strong west wind was flinging its rainy gusts down from the Cheviot Hills, which sloped away inland, and as the day wore on it became more boisterous, until by the evening it had become a determined gale, sweeping down full in the face of the incoming tide. As I walked along the inmost reach of the beach, partly sheltered from the wind, I could see, just a little way out, where the wind struck the water; and it seemed as though the waves were forced back by the mighty impact. I learned from a coastman afterwards, that the wind *had* actually retarded the tide to some degree that night. As I looked out across that wind-smitten tide, I found myself comparing it with the present moral and spiritual situation. On the one hand, wherever we go, we seem to see indications that a spiritual revival might break forth at any time, and people seem to be vaguely longing for it; but on the other hand the forces of godlessness seem more rampant and aggressive than ever. The tides of God are flowing in—tides of blessing and glorious revival. The tides of God are breaking on the shores of our national life, and there could be a flood-tide of cleansing and salvation. But there are strong winds of evil beating back the tide! O that the cleansing tide might flood in! What can we do? We must *PRAY*! "Prayer changes things."

The crying need of the hour is for the true people of Christ to seek fresh enduement of the Holy Spirit, and to give themselves to a regular, persevering, intensive ministry of prayer. Prayer is the invisible, determining power which shapes the course and destinies of men and movements—aye even of nations. Many professing Christians know all too little the power of prayer. The prayers of many never break beyond the bounds of their own personal needs, and the little circle of their own interests. There are comparatively few who know anything about engaging in prayer as a *spiritual warfare* for Christ against evil. The writings of Paul reveal how intense was his own prayer-warfare. All the men and women who have wielded great power for Christ on earth have been men and women of prayer. "If my people . . . then will I hear . . . and heal."

Three Reasons Why

"Barnabas and Paul, men that have hazarded their lives (lit: handed themselves over) for the name of our Lord Jesus Christ."—Acts 15:26.

WHEN as guilty sinners we come to Christ for salvation, there are no conditions to fulfil, so long as we truly repent and receive Him; for salvation from eternal ruin is all of grace. But if, having become "a member of Christ, and a child of God, and an inheritor of the kingdom of heaven", you or I would enjoy the fulness of fellowship with Christ, in spiritual life and joy and peace and power and prayer and service, then there *are* conditions which must be fulfilled. In fact there is this one big condition which includes all others: of our own free will we must be entirely *handed over* to Him, after the pattern of Paul and Barnabas—"men who have handed themselves over." Whatever the hazards, we must be "*handed over*"; and there are three big reasons for this.

First, *He cannot fully use us until we are fully His*. Horatio Nelson, whose name shines as the most illustrious of all Britain's naval commanders, had many remarkable episodes in his eventful life. During an engagement with the French, he managed to capture a French man-of-war. The captured officer-in-command, when brought into Nelson's presence, held out his hand as if to congratulate the victor. "No," replied the hero of a hundred fights; "Give me your sword first, and then your hand." The handed-over sword was the token of complete surrender. Our Lord Jesus insists on nothing less; for until we are handed over completely, *self*-will continually frustrates *His* will in our life.

Second, until we are completely handed over *we miss the highest and best*. Nothing else so elevates the mind. Nothing else makes our life so eternally significant. Nothing else gives us such value in service. Nothing else brings such joy or peace or final reward.

Third, our dear Lord is *altogether worthy of our thus handing over completely to Him*. A radiant Christian man who lay slowly dying kept muttering, "Bring . . . bring . . . bring." They brought various things to ease his body, but he shook his head. At last, just before he passed over, he stammered out the full sentence:

"Bring forth the royal diadem,
And crown Him LORD OF ALL."

The good brother had evidently seen one of those death-bed visions of Christ which are sometimes given to the saints to lift their harassed spirits above the struggles which accompany release from the poor, tired body. It is good to pass into heaven exclaiming, "Crown Him Lord of all." It is even better not to wait until then. In that larger life and fuller light of heaven we shall know absolutely how worthy Jesus is to wear the crown of all-transcendent dominion; but can we not see it clearly enough, even here and now, to give Him complete lordship over our lives?

As we have said before, however difficult this entire, life-long hand-over may be to the "flesh" *love* can make it easier. Indeed, it is really a question as to which of the two shall win—love of Christ, or love of self.

Both Sides of the Matter

"Lydia . . . whose heart the Lord opened, that she attended unto the things which were spoken by Paul."—Acts 16: 14.

IN all those spiritual transactions which save and bless people, there are two sides, the divine and the human. We see this in Lydia's conversion. The divine side is: "Whose heart *the Lord opened.*" The human side is: She *attended* unto the things which were spoken by Paul." This is a line of truth well worth pursuing.

As remarked, it is true of *conversion*. We use that word, "conversion" in its good old-fashioned sense as meaning a real turning of heart to the Lord Jesus Christ, in which He is accepted as Saviour and the Holy Spirit imparts a new spiritual life, making a convert a "new creature in Christ Jesus." Glance at our text again: "Lydia . . . whose heart the Lord opened." That was the *divine* aspect of it. God moved upon her heart, so that she became converted. There are those who react strangely to this. They say, "If then our conversion depends on such intervention by God, we ourselves may just as well lie passive. If we are to be saved we shall be saved; if we are not to be saved, we can do nothing about it. Everything depends on God." Our text, however, reminds us of the *human* aspect: "She attended unto the things which were spoken by Paul." There are many whose hearts are moved upon by the Holy Spirit who nevertheless refuse Christ; for God never violates the royalty of the human will. The relationship of divine sovereignty and human freedom in our salvation is a mystery; but one thing is clear: there *is* a human side to it, and there must be a human response. We must "attend", as Lydia did. Our plain duty is to accept Christ as He is offered to us in John 3: 16, 36; 6: 37, and 20: 31.

The same two sides belong to spiritual *assurance*. How many believers there are who, although they are really saved, lack inward assurance of it! How many complain, "I do believe, or try, yet I do not have the joy or peace which others seem to have"! It is because the two sides of assurance are not clearly appreciated. On the divine side there is the clear promise given. On the human side there must be a real resting on it. At my own conversion there was little emotional attestation, but I was counselled to fix my mind on John 3: 36, even though I did not have the faintest inward "experience" of salvation. So I kept resting in the text: "He that believeth on the Son hath everlasting life"—not he who goes to church, says prayers, feels saved, tries to be good; but "he that *believeth*". I kept saying, "Well, you don't *feel* saved; but God says you are, if you *believe.*" As I kept ignoring "feelings" and kept simply believing, oh, the inward assurance came! The Holy Spirit witnessed within me that God's promise was true. After that, although actually I was no more *saved* than before, the "assurance" of it made me so much *happier*.

I meet true believers who, nevertheless, have no *assurance* of salvation. If I ask, "Are you trusting Jesus?" they reply a definite "Yes"; yet if I ask, "Are you saved?" they only answer, "I *hope* so." They think it presumption to say, "I know"; yet they commit the worse presumption of doubting what God has really said. One of Satan's cleverest tricks is to make men think that doubting is a mark of reverence, and faith presumption. Dear doubter, say, "Thank God, now I *know.*" Then you will get the *joy* of salvation.

Reciprocal Aspects

"Lydia . . . whose heart the Lord opened, that she attended unto the things which were spoken by Paul."—Acts 16 : 14.

As we were illustrating from this text yesterday, there are always the two sides—the divine and the human, in all those spiritual transactions by which we are saved or blessed. This is notably applicable to early *discipleship*. We often say that conversion to Christ takes away desire for worldly pleasures; yet does it always? Young converts sometimes ask me how they can overcome the desire for worldly pleasure in which they formerly found diversion. Recently a young man told me that since his conversion he had felt he must give up smoking, but oh, the craving to smoke again was at times almost intolerable; what could he do? Another asked me was there deliverance from unclean *memories* persisting from pre-conversion days. Well, in all such cases, if there is to be deliverance, it should be recognised that there are two sides. On the divine side there is the Scripture promise through which the Holy Spirit works. On the human side there must be complete surrender of the heart to Christ; then a trustful resting on such promises as Philippians 4 : 13, Romans 8 : 2, II Corinthians 12 : 9 or whichever other may fit the case. It is thus that the Holy Spirit finds opportunity to make the promises operative in our experience.

The same is true in Christian *service*. Take, for instance, witness-bearing in difficult circumstances. When I was just a young Christian, I had a repeated urge to speak of Christ to a certain older man whose relationship with me was such that he could have made things unhappy for me if I had annoyed him. I tried to speak to him, but lost my nerve. Then I decided to act on II Corinthians 12 : 9, "My grace is sufficient for thee." Next time we were alone, I whispered that text and prepared to witness. Just as I was about to risk the first word, however, the text seemed suddenly to fail. My pulse raced, I spluttered, and lapsed into ignominious silence. What I suffered! I thought the text had failed! Later, though, I reflected that perhaps the text could not work until I actually spoke to the man. But oh, dare I take such a risk? What if the promise failed *then*? I shall never forget the day I took the risk. There was the same chaotic nervousness, but what did it matter if only the man's soul could be saved? I blurted out the first word. For a second it was like stepping over a precipice and whizzing through space. Then the most joyful calm filled me. As soon as I really *acted* on the promise it proved itself. So is it with every form of Christian service for which we feel unequal: the promises are there (that is the *divine* side); and we must really trust them (that is the *human* side). The two together bring victory.

Again, the same is true of *prayer*. The divine side is the promise to answer; the human side is to ask and believe. All too many seem to think that their praying is unsatisfactory unless they are uplifted *emotionally*. No; prayer is neither validated nor *in*validated by the subjective condition of the one who prays. When human faith lays hold on divine promise, then prayer is "alive" and effectual. Many of us need to rescue our praying from the tyranny of moods. Never mind the emotions! Pray in *faith*. When faith rules with firm sceptre, the emotions soon become co-operative subjects. "Whatsoever ye shall ask in prayer, *believing*, ye shall receive" (Matt. 21 : 22).

"Every place that the sole of your foot shall tread upon, that have I given unto you."—Joshua 1:3.

TODAY, we return again to the truth that in our experiencing of spiritual blessings there are always two sides, the divine and the human. This is seen in the *deeper* blessings of the Christian life.

It is notably so in the blessing of *sanctification*, and for want of perceiving it many have missed the blessing. Our word, "sanctification" comes from the Latin *sanctus* (sacred or apart) and *facio* (I make or set). That is it: *sanctus facio*, "I set apart". Sanctification is set-apart-ness to Christ. When I am completely handed over to Him, I am set apart, or sanctified. As a mental concept, therefore, sanctification is simplicity itself, even though as a spiritual crisis it may be the final point of a protracted or agonising struggle. But there are two sides to it. The human side is this continued set-apart-ness to Christ. The divine side is the possessing and purifying of the yielded believer. When once the soul is fully given over to Christ, then the Holy Spirit begins in a new way to lift it to new victory over sin, new consciousness of Christ, new fellowship with God, new power in prayer, new usefulness in service. To be strictly correct, sanctification itself must be distinguished from these blessings. Sanctification, or set-apart-ness, is that which makes them all possible. It is the human and divine together which result in "the *fulness* of the blessing".

The same is true in the experience of being *filled by the Holy Spirit*. There are the two sides; and it is only in the conjunction of both that the blessing becomes real. On the human side there must be unreserved committal of the whole being, especially of the will, to God; then the undoubting appropriation of the divine promise. Often, in meetings for the deepening of the spiritual life, believers are counselled to "claim" the fulness, or to "reckon" it as already possessed by faith; but despite all the "claiming" and "reckoning", the blessing remains elusive. It is because of defective compliance on the human side. There is absolutely no substitute for unconditional surrender. The impartation of spiritual power is unsafe except under the complete monopoly and wisdom of the Holy Spirit. But when once the glad crisis of entire yielding has taken place, *then* faith can "claim", and find the claim honoured.

A young man was once much impressed by an address on the motto: "*LET GOD*". He cut out the six letters, pasted them on a card, and hung the motto on his bedroom wall. Yet somehow the blessing he sought did not seem to come. Then, one day, he found that the last letter had dropped off, leaving the motto, "*LET GO*". When we really "let go" all hindering things and all rights of self-management, then all the promises are ours, and we find how true is Joshua 1:3, "Every place that the sole of your foot shall tread upon, that have I given unto you."

Now abdicates my vain self-will,
  The sceptre, Lord, is Thine.
Now reign, and with Thy Spirit fill
  This yielded heart of mine.
Thus sanctified, may I possess
The Canaan of true holiness.

Qualities of True Faith

"That which is lacking in your faith."—I Thess. 3 : 10.

THESE words suggest a profitable enquiry into those qualities of mind which accompany a true faith in Christ. It is good to examine our faith, and see whether it is really begetting within us its intended results.

To begin with, true faith in Christ is *restful.* As Hebrews 4 : 3 says, "We which have *believed* do enter into *rest.*" Real believing is resting. A faith which only struggles is undeveloped.

Next, true faith in Christ is *joyful.* Remember I Peter 1 : 8 : "Believing, ye rejoice with joy unspeakable. . . ." How can faith in such a gracious, redeeming, risen, returning Saviour be any other than joyful?

Again, real faith is *hopeful.* Indeed, as Hebrews 11 : 1 says, "Faith is the substance of things hoped for." In Galatians 5 : 5, we have the expression, "hope . . . by faith". Faith and hope are not identical, but they are inseparable. Such faith annihilates pessimism.

Besides this, genuine faith in Christ is *loving.* "Faith . . . worketh by love." (Gal. 5 : 6). "Peace be to the brethren, and *love* with faith" (Eph. 6 : 23). "Good tidings of your faith and *love*" (I Thess. 3 : 6). Trust in a God of love makes faith a reflex vehicle of that love to others.

This leads to a further reflection: Christian faith is *practical.* "Faith without works is dead," says James 2 : 20. "If a brother or sister be destitute, and you say: Depart in peace, be ye warmed and filled; notwithstanding ye give them not those things which are needful; what does that profit?" (15, 16). "Can *that* faith save?" (14).

We must not omit that real faith is *patient.* II Timothy 3 : 10, links faith with "longsuffering", and "*patience*". Hebrews 6 : 12 exhorts us to be "followers of them who through faith and *patience* inherit the promises." Revelation 13 : 10 says, "He that killeth with the sword must be killed with the sword. Here is the *patience and faith* of the saints." Real faith in God cures panic and impatience.

Moreover, faith is *victorious.* "This is the victory that overcometh the world, even our faith" (I Jn. 5 : 4). Let Hebrews 11 tell us again how faith has "subdued kingdoms, wrought righteousness, obtained promises, stopped the mouths of lions"!

Still further, faith is *vocal.* "We believe and therefore *speak*" (II Cor. 4 : 13). Doubt is dumb (Luke 1 : 20) but faith opens the lips in confession (Rom. 10 : 10). Finally, faith should be *ever-growing* (II Cor. 10 : 15; II Thess. 1 : 3) so that we experience the "*full assurance of faith*" (Heb. 10 : 22).

These are tests which we should apply to our faith. Is it restful, joyful, hopeful, loving, practical, patient, victorious, vocal, growing? "Lord, *increase* our faith."

Lord, help my faith to grow,
   And doubt be less and less;
As more of saving truth I know,
   The more may I possess,
Till faith shall every doubt destroy,
And cloudless blessing I enjoy.

A Page from David's Diary

"This poor man cried, and the Lord heard him, and saved him out of all his troubles."—Ps. 34 : 6.

THIS psalm is a page from David's diary of the Lord's dealing with him. As he reviews it he would bear grateful testimony. He would tell it to the men of his own time. He would inscribe it in a scroll to be read by posterity. He would weave it into an ode to be sung by the godly in the house of the Lord. We should continually keep in mind outstanding answers to prayer, and the deliverances God has wrought for us in the past. They should be like evergreens in memory's garden, so that we may be encouraged amid present difficulties to "bless the Lord at all times". How much we miss because we fail to remember, or because we restrain testimony! If the Lord has redeemed us, let us "say so" (Ps. 107 : 2). If He has brought us up from a "horrible pit", let us "say so". To tell another of God's goodness often causes the embers on our own hearth to glow again.

The inscription to this psalm reads: "A Psalm of David, when he changed his behaviour before Abimelech; who drove him away, and he departed." When David fled from Saul, he came to Nob, to Abimelech the priest, who gave the fainting fugitive sustenance from the Lord's table, and supplied him with Goliath's sword. From there David fled to Gath, where, because he feared king Achish, he feigned madness, and was driven away. During those days some of David's doings were far from commendable. He gave way to lying and deception; yet he was in dire straits through no fault of his own, and God responded to his distress signals.

This reminiscent pin-pointing of the psalm not only gives it colour, it shows the fine sense of restraint intermingling with David's exuberant desire to give testimony. He refrains from going into all the smurky details of his sinning. He need not lay them bare to men, seeing he had made full confession to God. Some people go into all manner of unsavoury disclosures. They seem as proud of their sins as old soldiers used to be of sword gashes. That kind of testimony is wrong. It is like undressing oneself in public. It harms rather than edifies, and makes gossip for scandal-mongers. After someone had given such a testimony, a man in the meeting complained that it had put evil thoughts into his mind which were never there before! Christian testimony should be such as becomes "children of light".

Notice our text says, "*This* man cried. . . ." Some dear brethren are always able to relate what God has done for others, but seldom have testimony from their own experience. They live inside quotes commas instead of writing original paragraphs. "This poor man cried, and Jehovah heard him, and saved him out of all his troubles." Is not this the testimony of *all* the saved in Christ? Is it not here and now *your* testimony and *mine*? Will it not be our testimony-song at last in heaven? Lord, keep the song of glad testimony on my lips!

Let me oft recount the story
  Of His mercies all my days,
Till amid celestial glory
  I shall utter loftier praise.
Listen, neighbours, to my voice,
And with this poor man rejoice!

A Poor Man Saved

"This poor man cried, and the Lord heard him, and saved him out of all his troubles."—Ps. 34: 6.

In this excerpt from David there is a cry of need, then a song of joy. Linger at each in turn. First there is the cry of need: "This poor man cried . . ." Notice *to whom* it was uttered. It was to the "LORD". This was no fine prayer, worded to please human ears, as some prayers in the Lord's house are today. Nor, with all respect to present-day mental therapeutists, was it the psychopathic sigh of some introspective hypochondriac seeking subjective relief in the reflex influence of prayer. It was a quick arrow of appeal shot straight toward heaven from the bow of adversity. Twang it went, in a sob, a groan, a cry. Prayer is direct dealing with God. The best prayer is that which most comes to grips with God. The great thing in prayer is to keep the mind fixedly, utterly, on God.

Notice *by whom* this prayer was uttered—a "poor man". David certainly was a poor man just then. He had to beg bread, and to borrow a sword. Poverty, so far as prayer is concerned, is a qualification rather than a barrier. The Lord never says, "That's a shabby coat you are wearing." Being "down at our heels" is no hindrance to getting down on our knees!

Notice *the way* this poor man prayed: he "cried". A cry expresses *intensity*; it is short but urgent. A cry is a verbal *simplicity*; no school was ever needed to teach even babies to cry! A cry indicates *bitterness*; it is the language of pain. Cries are not set to music! A cry is the voice of *importunity*. If it really comes from the depths, it will cry again and again until heard. Oh, friend, if you know not how to pray a set prayer, just *cry* like that "poor man". Cry because *you*, like him, need to be "saved".

But now, besides the cry of need there is a song of joy: "*The Lord heard him.*" The more David reflects, the more praise-inspiring it is. He who reigns in the heaven of heavens, where angels laud, and seraphs adore, stoops to hear the cry of one "poor man". Earnest hearts never pray to a deaf God. Heaven is only deaf when need is dumb. Some medical groups today recommend prayer as having distinct therapeutic value in certain forms of ill-health. We ourselves would gladly acknowledge this subjective "reflex" of prayer; yet it carries a subtle danger. If the meaning of prayer ends in therapeutic reflexes, then its Christian significance is annihilated. Christian praying presupposes a prayer-hearing, prayer-answering God.

Yes, "This poor man cried, and the Lord heard him, and *saved him out of all his troubles.*" That is the kind of prayer which is taught in the Christian Scriptures and proved in Christian experience. Men and women are not going to pray for mere love of the act, if prayer goes no further than subjective reflexes; but if God really hears and saves, then oh, how significant prayer is for God-conscious, sin-burdened, trouble-beset human hearts! Look through the psalm at some of the poor man's troubles: fears for the future (9), shame for the past (5), wants in the present (9), dangers to the body (20), dangers to the soul (22). Now read the text again! All this from a cry—not to a priest, but to *GOD*!

How oft His listening ears
Have heard me weep and pray!
How oft has He dispersed my fears,
And turned my night to day!

"Casting all your care upon Him, for He careth for you."—1 Peter 5: 7.

THIS word of the Holy Spirit through Peter has always been a precious comfort to believers; but, as its position in the structure of the epistle shows, it is meant to become most of all precious to Christians who are on earth during the intensified tribulations at the end of the present age. The epistle runs in three movements. First, from chapter 1: 3 to 2: 10, we have *THE LIVING HOPE*, and what goes with it. Second, from chapter 2: 11 to 4: 11, we have *THE PILGRIM LIFE*, and how to live it. Third, from chapter 4: 12 to the end of the epistle, we have *THE FIERY TRIAL* and how to bear it. The relationship of the Christian life to suffering is prominent all through the epistle; but the final part (almost like an addendum, after the climactic doxology and "Amen" in 4: 11) is about a "fiery trial" which was yet to come, and which the context associates with the second coming of our Lord (4: 12, 13; 5: 1, 4, 10).

Now the words, "Casting all your care upon Him, for He careth for you", occur in chapter 5: 7, in the final section which concerns itself with the "fiery trial" or "great tribulation" at the end of the present age. In these days, therefore, this verse of counsel and comfort lights up with new relevance and reassurance.

What verbal battles are waged today, sometimes in uncharitable spirit, between those who hold the view that members of the true Church will *not* go through the so-called "great tribulation" and those who hold that they *will*! Far more important than the settling of that question is to remember our Lord's word, "By this shall all men know that ye are my disciples, if ye have *love* one to another." In any case, the great thing is that He Himself is really coming. What *if* some of us must go through the "fiery trial"? Will not our ever-present Saviour prove Himself our all-sufficiency? He did not save Shadrach, Meshach, and Abed-nego from the seven-times-heated "burning, fiercy furnace", but He suddenly appeared with them in the flames, and not even the smell of the fire lingered on them afterward. He did not save Daniel from the lion's den, but He companioned him there in angel-form, and "no manner of hurt" was found upon Daniel. He did not spare seraphic Stephen from the pelting stones, but He gave him such a transporting vision of glory as made even martyrdom a luxury.

Unless our inward eyes are impaired by a strange astigmatism, the signs are surely around us today that the present age is nearing its end. What we saw happen in the last two world wars is enough to make us wonder what awesome evils may yet be set loose on earth. But whatever may be coming, we need have no fear. "He never fails." The "fiery trial" has been anticipated, and will be overruled. We may go into the future without alarm. The Holy Spirit Himself breathes divine reassurance through our text—"Casting all your care upon Him, for He careth for you."

It is surprising how many of us are victims of fear, despite our profession of peace in Christ. How easily we are scared by the newspapers, and the things which seem to be coming upon the earth! Yet faith and fear are opposites. Christian, if you are really trusting Jesus, how *can* you fear? Cast all your anxiety upon HIM, for He careth for *you*.

The Cure for Care

"Casting all your care upon Him, for He careth for you."—1 Peter 5 : 7.

THERE are two kinds of care in this text. There is *anxious* care, in the words, "Casting all your care upon Him"; and there is *affectionate* care, in the words, "He careth for you." Over against all our own *anxious* care is our Saviour's never-failing *affectionate* care.

Take the first part of the text: "Casting all your care upon Him." That word, "casting", is in the aorist tense in the Greek, which means *once for all*. In fact, the Greek aorist participle here might well be rendered, "once for all having cast". There is one sense, of course, in which we cannot cast upon Him all the anxieties of days yet to come, for we do not know what a day may bring forth; yet we can say, "Lord, whatever cares may be coming, I cast them all in advance on Thee." Yes, we can do that once for all, if we will; and, oh, what mental relief it brings!

Notice next that we are to cast "*all*" our care upon Him; not only the larger but the lesser; not only the spiritual but the material; not only in general but in particular; not only part of the time but all the time. He Himself invites us to do this.

Look again at that word, "*care*". Perhaps a better translation would be "anxiety". Nowadays there is more than a shade of difference between care and anxiety. None of us can escape cares, but we may be free from anxiety. We cannot hand over our cares to Jesus in the sense of exemption from them; but we can transfer the *weight* of them to Him; so that if we must still carry *them*, He will carry *us*. Weymouth aptly renders the clause, "Throw the whole weight of your anxiety upon Him."

And now take the further clause: "For He careth for you." How persuasively it invites us to lay our anxiety upon Him! Think again how *powerful* He is: "HE [who upholds the very universe] careth for you." Think again how *sympathetic* He is. Instead of "He careth for you", we might render the Greek more idiomatically, "It really matters to Him about you." Think again how *near to us* He is. He is not only with us, He actually indwells us by His Spirit. Think again how *constant* He is. The verb is in the present and continuous tense—"He careth", every day and every hour. Oh, what encouragements these are to us, to roll the burden of our anxiety upon Him!

During the terrible days of the "Indian Mutiny", when the beleaguered refugees in Lucknow were almost starved into surrender to the rebel sepoys, one morning a Scottish girl put her ear to the ground, and then sprang up shouting, "The Campbells are coming!" She had caught the sound of the bagpipes. Soon after, the city was saved. Careworn Christian, put your ear to this text again, and hear the dear Saviour coming to *your* rescue! "Casting all your care upon Him, for He careth for you."

He never fails the soul that trusts in Him;
Tho' disappointments come, and hope burns dim;
  He never fails.
Tho' testings surge like angry seas around,
Tho' trials sore like ambushed foes abound,
Yet this my soul with myriads more has found,
  He never fails; He never fails.

"Thou hast done foolishly."—1 Sam. 13 : 13.

SAUL, the strapping, handsome first king of Israel, had blown the trumpet for war! He had the royal right to do so. He had shown military leadership in a resounding victory over the Ammonites. He was highly popular. Yet now there was a sudden, chilling unresponsiveness; and not without reason. Jonathan, the crown prince, had smitten the garrison of the Philistines, to which the Philistines had immediately replied by assembling 30,000 chariots, 6,000 horsemen, and an immense mass of pedestrian troops. To hack a victory over the Ammonites was one thing; but to face the Philistine war-lords and their well-equipped divisions was another; in fact, it appeared like a mouse challenging a panther. Until well into David's reign, the men of Israel always had a tendency to cower before the might of the warlike Philistines. There was now a slinking away from Saul. Some fled beyond Jordan; others made off to caves in the mountains or in the rocky wilderness. Some of the braver hearts, however, did respond, and gathered to Gilgal, the appointed rendezvous; yet even they followed "trembling". The one hope lay in a mighty intervention by Jehovah, whose prophet, Samuel, was due by set arrangement to join Saul on the seventh day.

The seventh day came, and its earlier hours slipped away, yet no sign of Samuel. Each day Saul's meagre forces had the more dwindled. Now, on the seventh day, he felt there would be utter desertion unless *something* impressive was done. Oh, why did not Samuel come? Had he not promised to come on that seventh day, to offer sacrifice before the people, and to make known the will of Israel's *divine* King whose *viceroy* Saul was? We can understand Saul's dismay and impatience; but oh, had he only realised that he was being tested, and that Samuel was actually coming, just in the nick of time! Saul's obedience to the theocratic principle on which he had accepted the crown was being tested. Alas, he broke down. He lost patience. He looked at things as a sovereign and a soldier instead of as Jehovah's *servant*; then, in sudden quick-temper, he usurped the place of both prophet and priest, saying, "Bring hither a burnt-offering to me, and peace-offerings." Verse 10 says, "As soon as he had made an end of offering the burnt-offering, behold, Samuel came . . ." Verse 13 gives Samuel's verdict: "Thou hast done foolishly; thou hast not kept the command of Jehovah thy God."

Poor Saul! It was a hard test to flesh and blood; yet it was really necessary for he was Israel's first king, and his acts would form precedents for his successors. To one like David, who from the first realised the theocratic conditions of the monarchy and gloried in them, the test would have been far easier; but to the incipient vainglory of Saul it was a sure cut. You and I are intended to exercise a theocratic reigning over our own personalities—not a reigning for self, but for *God*. Oh, that we may learn never to forfeit His blessings and deliverance by disobediently acting in self-will as Saul did! In many a crisis the same test comes to you and me. Have we faith to wait for the promised intervention of God?—or do we reach breaking-point, and act in self-will? Someone asked George Muller, "How do you get guidance?" He replied, "I pray, and wait until light comes." "But what if the light does not come?" "I wait until it *does* come." Waiting is often a bigger test than working.

A Solemn Homily

"Thou hast done foolishly."—1 Sam. 13: 13.

SAUL had indeed "done foolishly" in disobeying the will of God, even though the circumstances were aggravating. The words must have fallen like dull hammer-blows when Samuel now said, "The Lord would have established thy kingdom upon Israel for ever; but now thy kingdom shall not continue." "Thou hast done foolishly." The words suggest a solemn, threefold homily, as follows:

First, *WHY IS IT FOOLISHNESS TO DISOBEY GOD?* Answer: (1) Because His will is highest wisdom. (2) Because His will is for our highest good. (3) Because we miss our life's highest purpose. (4) Because there is no escaping Him.

Second, *WHY DO PEOPLE COMMIT THIS FOOLISHNESS?* Answer: (1) Often through ignorance of His word. (2) Often through pride of the flesh. (3) Often through love of sin. (4) Sometimes through self-important presumption (as Saul).

Third, *HOW MAY WE KNOW THE WILL OF GOD FOR US?* Answer: (1) Through the Holy Scriptures. (2) Through the inward urge of the Holy Spirit. (3) Through the corroboration of outward circumstances. Many years ago, now, the saintly F. B. Meyer was returning to England from a preaching engagement in Northern Ireland. The ship crossed from Belfast to Liverpool; and the landing was at night. As the lights of Liverpool began to sparkle and twinkle away ahead, Dr. Meyer and a few others were standing on deck just near the bridge. The night was very dark; the November air was damp and chilling; the sea looked oily and evil; and as the ship neared the port the myriads of yellow lights along the city front and the adjoining coastline, all making shivering reflections in the greasy-looking water, did not give the homiest of welcomes to Lancashire. But it was the seeming countlessness of the lights which bothered Dr. Meyer, and he called up to the bridge, "Captain, however do you know which way to steer, with that confusing mass of lights in front of you?" The captain called him to come up on the bridge, and then said, "You see, sir, it's really very simple at night. I'll show you how. D'you see that *big* light over there to the left? And d'you see that *other* big light over there to the right of it? And now d'you see that *third* outstanding light further still this way? Well, now, keep your eyes on those three lights, and see what happens." Dr. Meyer did so. Soon the big, outer light on the left gradually moved in until it coincided with the middle one; then, as the boat slowly veered further, that light gradually merged into the third. "There, now," said the boatman, "all I have to do is to see to it that those *three* big lights become *one*; and when those three lights become one, then all I have to do is to go straight forward." Even so, when the Word of Scripture, and the inward urge of the Spirit, and the corroboration of outward circumstances become one—"when those three become one", have no fear; go straight ahead; God's will is clear!

Of course, divine guidance requires that we walk sincerely as Christian believers. "If we walk in the light . . ." (1 Jn. 1: 7). Have you ever tried to direct someone in the dark—someone strange to your district? Guidance which would be easy in daylight is not easy in the dark. Even God cannot guide us clearly if we do not "walk in the light".

"And I, if I be lifted up from the earth, will draw all men unto Me."—Jn. 12 : 32.

THE first verse of this twelfth chapter brings us to the last week of our Lord's public ministry. The air is full of impending crisis. The shadow of tragedy lies athwart the narrative. The admiring crowds are large as ever. The name of Jesus is on all lips. Hosannas, palm branches and royal epithets have glamorised His triumphal entry into the capital; and the thronging enthusiasts are certain that at last His resplendent hour has come. But the lovely Hero of it all is not deceived. He knows what the powers of darkness and their human accomplices are already plotting. He foresees how quickly these applauding but fickle bands of Galilean pilgrims to the Passover will be outweighed and outwitted by the hostile bigots in Jerusalem.

Truly enough His "hour" has come; but He knows that it is to prove the utter opposite of what His hosanna-singers are expecting. Instead of coronation, it is bringing crucifixion. On many a startled ear He now flings the startling paradox, "The hour is come that the Son of Man should be glorified. Verily, verily, I say unto you, Except a seed of wheat fall into the ground and die, it abideth alone; but if it die it bringeth forth much fruit . . . And I, if I be lifted up from the earth, will draw all men unto Me."

This, in fact, was our Lord's very last pronouncement before He finally withdrew from His public teaching; for verse 36 says, "These things spake Jesus, and departed and did hide Himself from them." He never taught publicly again. To an impenitent and unbelieving Jewry the Cross was His last word. Even after His resurrection He never appeared again to the populace.

But oh, how that Cross speaks! It is the most eloquent word in all the vocabulary of God. If *that* does not speak to men's hearts, then they shall remain deaf indeed until the fearful thunder-clap of judgment startles them to hear dread sentence from the Great White Throne.

How wonderful beyond words is that tragic yet magnetic Cross! In it the deadliest sin of fallen man becomes the purest triumph of divine love. Our Lord's towering prediction that by His Cross He would "draw all men" unto Himself is the climax of a remarkable context. In verse 24 see the inescapable *necessity* of the Cross; in verse 27 the unutterable *anguish* of the Cross; in verse 28 the master *principle* of the Cross; in verse 32 the ultimate *triumph* of the Cross.

How these four aspects speak to you and me! Let verse 24 ("Except a corn of wheat die") show us the cure of loneliness and the secret of harvest in the affections of others toward us. Let verse 27 ("Now is My soul troubled") remind us of this again, that everything which really counts really *costs*. Let verse 28 ("Father glorify thy name") teach us the true master-principle for our own lives. And let verse 32 finally convince us of ultimate triumph beyond present tragedy.

O love of God, O sin of man,
  In this dread act your strength is tried;
And victory remains with love,
  For He, our Lord, is crucified!

"Christ, and Him Crucified"

"And I, if I be lifted up from the earth, will draw all men unto Me."—Jn. 12 : 32.

THE very grammar of this towering prediction surely strikes a significant balance which defines the drawing-power of Calvary. Our Lord does not say that either He alone or the Cross alone would constitute the attraction. There is a deliberate dual emphasis when He says, "And *I*, if I be *lifted up*." The Cross itself apart from Christ has no saving power; nor has even the Lord Himself apart from the Cross. Therefore, in the saving sense, neither Christ nor the Cross apart from each other has this drawing-power. But together they are the most wonderful magnet which ever drew the hearts of earth's sin-cursed millions. And herein lie two vastly momentous truths which need strong reassertion today.

First: it is *not Christ apart from the Cross* who draws and saves. Many modern divines have a way of eulogising Jesus without any reference to His death as a substitutionary sacrifice for sin. If they bring in the Cross at all, it is decked with the draperies of a sublimated sentimentalism which obscures its real nature, tragedy and glory. Yet the real power of the Gospel to draw and to save lies in that very Cross which these aesthetic preachers deem to be its most *un*attractive feature. They fondly dream that if they preach His exemplary life without His ignominious death, men will be attracted to Him: but they are wrong. Christ, presented only as supreme Teacher and Ideal, has never drawn the sin-conscious sons of Adam, who are far too fallen to be charmed into holiness by a mere exhibition of moral excellence, however perfect. What men need is not just a beautiful portrait, but a cure for their sin-disease. It is the Christ of Calvary, and He alone, who really saves and really draws.

Second: it is *not the Cross apart from Christ which draws and saves*. Let the public evangelist guard against the easy danger of preaching the Cross as a mere doctrine, or as a sort of detached transaction which in itself can save. There is a cheap evangelistic jargon today which almost sounds like bargaining the Cross off to those who will only "believe" in it and lift up their hands in meetings—as though the Cross by itself were a free entry-permit to heaven, apart from a persevering, life-long faith-union with Christ Himself which sanctifies character and conduct. We are making a true distinction when we say that it is not strictly the Cross which saves us, but *Jesus Himself* who saves us *through* the Cross. And, remember, it is not the mere creature-Christ of the so-called Christian Scientists, the Spiritualists, the Jehovah's Witnesses, and other such unitarian cults, but the Christ who is the Son of God and *God the Son*. It is the deity behind the manhood which makes the Cross an atonement. It is the manhood within the deity which makes it an atonement for *us*, and such a magnet to us. Wonderful Christ! Wonderful Cross!

Still, still He draws; true Man, incarnate God,
Who once the sad, brown earth as Jesus trod,
Until, with pinioned limbs and deep-torn side,
On yonder rough-hewn beam and bar He died.
Yes, still that Cross compels our gaze today;
Sin nailed Him there; yet sin He bears away!

"He beheld the city, and wept over it."—Luke 19: 41.
"His spirit was stirred when he saw the city wholly given to idolatry."—Acts 17: 16.
"I, John, saw the holy city, new Jerusalem, coming down from God out of heaven."—Rev. 21: 2.

HERE in these three verses are three cities. The first is Jerusalem. The second is Athens. The third is the "city whose Builder and Maker is God". Concerning the first of them, we read that Jesus "beheld the city, and *wept* over it". Concerning the second of them, we read that Paul beheld its idolatry and was "*stirred*" by it. Concerning the third, we read that John beheld it and then prayed, "Even so, come, Lord Jesus."

Why did Jesus weep over old-time Jerusalem? The answer is in Luke 13: 34, 35. Mark the process in those verses—"I would . . . ye would not . . . ye shall not." Jesus wept over it because it was a city which *knew the truth but did not want it.* Why was Paul stirred over ancient Athens? The answer is in Acts 17: 22, 23. Paul was stirred so poignantly over old Athens because it was a city which *wanted the truth but did not know it.*

Those two ancient capitals have their counterparts all over our modern world. Jerusalem knew the truth but did not want it. Athens wanted the truth but did not know it. Modern Christendom is full of cities which know the truth but do not want it. The *non*-Christian areas are full of cities which want the truth but do not know it. Jesus "wept" brokenly over the former kind. Paul was "stirred" painfully by the latter. Have you and I tears like those of Jesus, over the cities of Christendom which know the truth but do not want it? Have we a heart-paining compassion for those other cities which want the truth but do not know it?

Think again of those great major towns and super-cities of our Western, industrialised, commercialised, mechanised world. Are you and I ever moved to tears by their hard, metallic rebound against pure, spiritual Christianity? Many years ago now, after a round of visits to the night-time dens and haunts of New York City, Sam Hadley, leader of the famous Water Street Mission, was seen leaning heavily against a lamp-post, as though ill. A friend hurrying back overheard him sobbing, "O God, the sin of this city is breaking my heart!" That same Sam Hadley was used of God, directly and indirectly, to save thousands in that city.

Oh, for more tears! When our tears begin to flow, we begin to *do* something. We begin in a new way to pray, to give, to go, to help, to sacrifice. Somehow we must interpenetrate these cities of ours again with the saving truth of Christ. Often it is far from inviting. Sometimes it is almost frightening; but listen to these lines:

I said, "Let me walk in the field";
  God said, "No, walk in the town";
I said, "There are no flowers there";
  He said, "No flowers, but a crown".

I said, "I shall miss the light,
  And friends will miss me, they say";
He answered, "Choose you tonight
  If I am to miss you or they."

Are We Stirred?

"He beheld the city, and wept over it."—Luke 19: 41.
"His spirit was stirred when he saw the city wholly given to idolatry."—Acts 17: 16.
"I, John, saw the holy city, new Jerusalem, coming down from God out of heaven."—Rev. 21: 2.

THINK again of those cities in "the regions beyond", where thousands, yea millions, are really wanting the truth, but do not know it, and cannot find it. Do I now address some younger person who ought to offer as a messenger to them? Does not the thought of their darkness and futile groping *stir* you, as Paul was "stirred" over Athens long ago? Let these lines of Eva Doerksen speak to you:

If you had been to heathen lands,
Where weary ones with eager hands
Still plead, yet no one understands,
Would you go back? Would you?

If you had seen them in despair,
Beat on the breast, pull out the hair,
While demon powers filled the air,
Would you go back? Would you?

If you had seen the glorious sight,
When heathen people, long in night,
Are brought from darkness into light,
Would you go back? Would you?

Yet still they wait, a weary throng,
They've waited, some, so very long,
When shall despair be turned to song?
I'm going back! Would you?

Do I now address some middle-aged or older person who cannot go out to other lands, but who ought to be praying more, or giving more, or encouraging more, or helping more, towards the evangelising of those cities and peoples? Oh, let the thought of them stir you into compassionate co-operation with those who actually go out there to tell them!

Think now of that third city, "the holy city, New Jerusalem", which John saw "coming down from God out of heaven". Unlike the *old* Jerusalem, which knew the truth but did not want it; and unlike ancient Athens, which wanted the truth but did not know it; that glorious future city is to be one in which all the citizens *know* the truth, and *love* the truth, and are eternally *glorified* by it. It is a city so beautiful that John immediately describes it as "a bride adorned for her husband". Then he hears a great voice out of heaven saying, "Behold the tabernacle of God is with men, and He will dwell with them, and they shall be His people . . . And God shall wipe away all tears from their eyes." Every time we go to our cities of today, to "rescue the perishing", we are anticipatively contributing to the holy and blessed society of that rapturous city of the ultimate future, "whose Builder and Maker is God".

"He was in the world, and the world was made by Him, and the world knew Him not."—Jn. 1 : 10.

This verse expresses undisguised amazement at a world so sin-blinded that it could not recognise its own Creator. It also strikingly epitomises certain vast aspects of the Incarnation. Take its three statements in their logical order: (1) "The world was made by Him." That is the supreme truth about our earth. (2) "He was in the world." That is the supreme fact of past history. (3) "The world knew Him not." That is the supreme tragedy of human depravity.

First, here is *THE SUPREME TRUTH ABOUT OUR EARTH*: "The world was made by Him." This is the supreme cosmic truth because everything else about the earth stems from it. We cannot but be intrigued by the simple audacity of the statement. John does not argue it, or propose its probability; he simply states it as final fact. He *knows* that it is just as true as it is tremendous. This Jesus of Nazareth was God come to earth as Man, by a real human birth; and it was He who, in His pre-incarnate eternality, away back beyond all the geological ages, gave this planet its first separate existence! All sorts of ideas were rife in John's time concerning the earth's origin, including the worn-old evolution theory, which has been re-hashed in our own time as some supposedly new scientific discovery. Over against them all, John sets the simple statement, "The world was made by *Him*."

"The world was made by Him." Then *the origin of this world is creation, not evolution*. It is because we Christians believe this that we have a fundamentally happier view of the universe than evolutionists and atheists. See verse 3, which literally translated reads, "All things through Him came into being; and apart from Him not one thing came into being." A man's view as to the origin of the universe fundamentally affects his whole outlook on human life and destiny. The Christian view of the universe leads to ethical nobility and intelligent optimism. The evolutionary or atheistic view necessarily and provenly leads to moral deterioration and philosophic pessimism.

"The world was made by Him." Then there is *good purpose in the universe, and not just blind chance*. To the atheist, everything which happens is merely fortuitous, accidental, morally inexplicable; and on that theory life is meaningless. Of course, while there are many who *call* themselves athiests, I seriously doubt whether there are any *real* athiests. As Dr. R. A. Torrey used to say, "Men hope by the denial of God's existence to shield themselves from the discomfort of His acknowledged presence." But suppose there *is* real atheism; how sterile, blank, mocking, useless it is,—everything and all of us, on the way *from* nothing *to* nothing! While all the time, the marvellous order and regularity everywhere observable in Nature poses an unanswerable evidence of divine design! With revolt and relief we turn back to John: "The world was made by *Him*," and immediately *every*thing again means *some*thing, and the whole universe grows friendly with good purpose. We are really going somewhere. The universe's centre is not some stellar super-colossus, but a mind of infinite wisdom and a Heart of infinite love—a heart which once was spear-thrust by a world which "knew Him not".

"He was in the world, and the world was made by Him, and the world knew Him not."—Jn. 1: 10.

"THE world was made by Him." Then *Christ is God, and not a creature.* Were we to expunge from the New Testament all those verses which directly assert His deity or tacitly assume it, even then, if the New Testament documents are divinely inspired, we should be obliged to accept His real Godhead in face of such a statement as this: "The *world* was made by Him." Present-day unitarian cults like the so-called Jehovah's Witnesses, or the Christian Scientists, may try to juggle its meaning away in spurious new "explainings", or else unscientifically evade it as merely the fond excitement of John's adoring hero-worship. But there it is, and there it stays: "The world was made by Him." It survives the centuries as one of the cardinal articles of Apostolic Christianity.

But now halt at that other short but vast statement in our text: "He was in the world." That is *THE SUPREME EVENT OF OUR RACE'S HISTORY.* It is the supreme event because all other cosmic unfoldings and consummations, as fore-promised in Scripture prophecy, are the ultimate issue of it.

"He was in the world." This confers upon our race *the highest of all honour.* No wonder that inspired prophets pre-advertised it centuries beforehand! No wonder that in Israel's supernatural religion, priests and sacrifices, tabernacle and ritual, all typically anticipated it! No wonder that troops of angels overleapt heaven's parapets and swept down into earthly visibility on the night when He was born! No wonder that the stars sent a diamond-fingered comet to point down on the strange crib where He lay in His miracle-babyhood!

"He was in the world." This involves our race in *the sublimest of all mysteries.* That the eternal, infinite, ineffable Creator-Spirit, the Divine Being, should become indissolubly united to human creaturehood, and thus henceforth for evermore express to all His worlds and all His creatures the compassionate love of His heart, is surely the incomparable colossus of all mysteries. Must not this indissoluble union of the Creator with His human creature be the mightiest marvel in all the ages-and-ages-long continuity of the whole vast universe? Can you imagine how the apostles felt when, as they companied with Him, they gradually discerned not only *what* He was, i.e. the incarnation of the supernatural, but *who* He was, i.e. "*God* manifest in the flesh"?

"He was in the world." This sets upon our race *the greatest of all values.* Modern astronomy has shrunk our orb into an infinitesimal speck in a universe of staggering vastness filled with constellations of bewildering immensity and countlessness. Can we believe any longer that God "so loved" *this* world, and came to *this* world—even to undergo incarnation and crucifixion as its Saviour? Well, there are two things to remember. (1) To a Creator who is *infinite* there is no such thing as "big" and "little" in *our* way of estimating. (2) God does not love this world for its physical dimensions, but for its *moral value.* One God-conscious human soul, capable of love or hate, fellowship or rebellion, heaven or hell is of more value than Orion and Pleiades and all other merely physical immensities.

"And the world knew Him not."—Jn. 1 : 10.

THIS is the supreme tragedy of human depravity, for it was this which led to the shameful repudiation and humiliation and crucifixion of the incarnate King.

"The world knew Him not." This failure to recognise Him was surely *inexcusable*. He should have been known through the holiness and sublimity of His character. He should have been known through the astonishing miracles which He wrought as credentials of His Messiahship. He should have been known through the supernatural wisdom of His teachings. He should have been known through His spoken claims. He should have been known to Israel's scribes through the correspondence of His birth-place, His life, His deeds, and His death, with Scripture prediction. Yet, alas, they failed to recognise Him.

"The world knew Him not." This failure to recognise Him was also deplorably *significant*. It was due to sin-blindedness. Israel's leaders, and most of the people, were proudly Jehovistic and fiercely Judaistic. They thought that in religious matters they of all the earth's families were the people who *knew*. Job's words perfectly described them, "Doubtless ye are the people, and wisdom shall die with you." Their big, proud hope was the coming of Jehovah's long-promised Messiah. Yet when He came they "knew Him not", because they were sin-blinded. Sin is not only transgression of moral law; it is an hereditarily transmitted disease in the moral nature of our fallen humanity which causes chronic spiritual blindness. When in addition to that, there is jealous pride, selfish ambition, or knowing hypocrisy, how acute is the blindness! Israel's leaders kept asking for "signs", yet all the while clear signs were being given. What they needed was not signs, but *sight*.

"The world knew Him not." This failure to recognise Him had bitterest *consequences*. See the verse following our text: "He came unto His own, and His own received Him not." Israel's sin-blindedness led to the rejection and even the humiliating crucifixion of their non-resisting Messiah-Sinbearer. In sin-inflicted blindness they mocked their very Maker and murdered their benignant heavenly Benefactor. So is it with the spiritual blindness of unbelievers today. They repel and wound their best Friend and only Saviour. In Wales there is a romantic village, Beddgelert, the name of which means "The grave of Gelert". There is a famous legend about this Gelert, which was a dog, the hound of Llewellyn the Great. One day, on returning to his castle, Llewellyn found his child lying dead, and the hound, Gelert, beside it. Llewellyn at once plunged his sword into the poor animal, only to discover too late a huge wolf which had attacked the child, and which the faithful hound had slain. In his blind rage, Llewellyn had killed a faithful friend. In a far more terrible sense, that is what all Christ-rejectors are doing today. In their awful spiritual blindness they are repudiating their truest Friend and Saviour.

"The world knew Him not." What was true *then* is true *now* (1 Cor. 2 : 8; 2 Cor. 4 : 3, 4; 1 Jn. 3 : 1, 2). But, thank God, there is something else true. There were those who *did* recognise Him and receive Him. See verse 12: "To as many as received Him, to them gave He power to become the sons of God . . ."; and He *still* gives "power to become . . ."!

The Great Unveiling

"No man hath seen God at any time; the only-begotten Son, which is in the bosom of the Father, He hath declared Him."—Jn. 1 : 18.

OF ALL mysteries the greatest is God—spiritual, invisible, eternal, infinite, incomprehensible. How ardently have men longed to see Him! But they have longed for the impossible. "No man hath seen God at any time." Long ago, in lonely desert, on Sinai's height, in Solomon's temple, by Chebar's river, God assuredly did at intervals reveal Himself in visible theophanies to patriarchs and prophets; yet those "holy men of old" never saw, and never *could* see God in His essential spiritual being; for in that sense "there shall no man see God and live" (Exod. 33: 20). Now, however, "the only begotten Son which is in the bosom of the Father, He hath declared Him".

Think how deep and distressing was the *need* for such a benignant revelation. It was needed as a *corrective* to fallen man's distortion of original enlightenment. How rapidly human ideas of God deteriorated into ruinous perversions! And since man's concept of God determines his behaviour more than anything else, how disastrous have been the consequences! Better have *no* idea than a *bad* one! The piteous need was that somehow a truer and clearer revelation of God should be given than could ever be conveyed in evanescent theophanies.

But such a revelation was needed, also, as a *counterpart* to man's inborn quest after his Maker. What is it that we really ache to know about God? Is it His awesome attributes—His omnipotence, omniscience, omnipresence? Nay, we long to know what He is like in His *character*. That alone can decide what we are meant to be. God must somehow be unveiled in the living characters of a human life, lived out under the same conditions as those under which I myself am obliged to live. It must be lips like my own which teach me the way of life. It must be eyes like mine through which must shine the light of the divine holiness and love. It must be hands like my own hands which show me what true service is.

Could such a revelation even be thinkable? Marvel of marvels!—Divine wisdom, power and love have contrived the way. In the fulness of time "the only-begotten Son which is in the bosom of the Father, He hath declared Him".

Think how surpassingly wonderful is the *nature* of this revelation. Mark the three superlative features of it in our text. First; see who *brings* it. i.e. "the only-begotten Son". The title always implies His deity. There could no more be a full revelation of God through a merely human or angelic Christ than the mighty Amazon could pour itself through the narrow channel of a streamlet. Second; see *what* He reveals, i.e. He comes from "the bosom of the Father" and therefore reveals the very heart of God. Third see *how* he reveals, i.e. "He hath *declared* Him" (lit. *exegeted*) or brought Him out to view. In all He taught and wrought, in all He said and did, in all He felt and showed; and supremely in His dying, He is translating God to us. He *must* be God, for even God cannot be better. There is nothing higher. And is God like *that*! Then I cannot do without Him. *Now* I understand; I *want* Him. And I may *have* Him, for He who is the Revealer of God is also the Redeemer of men.

Towers, Bulwarks, Palaces

"Walk about Zion, and go round about her; tell the towers thereof. Mark ye well her bulwarks; consider her palaces; that ye may tell it to the generation following. For this God is our God for ever and ever: He will be our guide even unto death."—Ps. 48: 12–14.

OUR King here invites us to perambulate Zion and observe its excellencies! We may well do so, for is not the earthly Zion a symbol of that greater, *spiritual* Zion, the blood-bought Church of the Lamb, in which all true believers have their place? Let us compass Zion, then, and inspect her glory. She is described as having a triple grandeur—"towers" and "bulwarks" and "palaces". In the towers see her *dignity*. In the bulwarks see her *defence*. In the palaces see her *delight*.

First, gaze at the "*towers*"—those transcendent spiritual truths which are the glory of the Christian Church. They are unmatched in the non-Christian religions. See that resplendent tower, the Bible doctrine of the one, eternal, triune God, the God of infinite power and wisdom and love. See those magnificent companion towers, the doctrines of the divine attributes, the divine holiness, sovereignty, grace. See those gleaming Gospel towers, the doctrines of the incarnate Word, salvation by the Cross, justification by imputed righteousness, regeneration and sanctification by the Holy Spirit, and final glorification.

Mark equally well Zion's *bulwarks*. There are the inner *divine* fortifications, and there are the outer *human* ramparts. The *inner* protections are the divine covenant and promises which ensure that this spiritual Zion shall never perish (Zeph. 3: 17; Matt. 16: 18). The *outer* defences are those redeemed and regenerated men and women who champion the cause of Christ, and constitute the true Church on earth. Even if these outer defences should fail, the inner are eternally invulnerable.

And now view Zion's *palaces*. In the spiritual Zion these palaces are *the privileges of the saints*. They are too many to number, and too glorious to be adequately described. "Palaces" that speaks of *beauty*; and in Christ there is provided for us the "beauty of holiness". "Palaces"—that speaks of *riches*; and in Christ God has "blessed us with all spiritual blessings in the heavenlies". "Palaces"—that speaks of *honour*; and in Christ "now are we the sons of God", "joint-heirs with Christ" to eternal glories. "Oh, the palaces! the privileges, the precious promises" which are "yea and amen" to us in Christ! Oh, the privilege of access to the heavenly throne, of fellowship with the Father and the Son, of service for the King of Kings, and of "Christ in you, the hope of glory"!

Read the royal word again. If towers, bulwarks, palaces, speak of dignity, defence, delight, there is also something here which speaks of *duty*; for the injunction runs: "Tell it to the generation following." Yes, we have something to *tell*. (Ps. 107: 2). Our dear King Himself is in Zion. When last did we talk about Him to friends, workmates, neighbours? Am I a parent, or an elderly person?—then am I telling of Him to the "generation following"? Am I preaching to all that "salvation is in Zion"? If so, then more than ever let me exult in the final pledge of the King's word: "*THIS GOD IS OUR GOD FOR EVER AND EVER. HE WILL BE OUR GUIDE EVEN UNTO DEATH.*"

Use or Lose!

"For whosoever hath, to him shall be given . . . but whosoever hath not, from him shall be taken away even that he hath."—Matt. 13 : 12.

OUR Lord here enunciates a principle of such far-reaching seriousness that all of us should consider it carefully. It has a two-way operation. In the one direction it brings multiplied addition: "Whosoever hath to him shall be given . . ." In the other direction it inflicts merciless denudation: "Whosoever hath not, from him shall be taken away even that he hath." Ponder, therefore; "the goodness and the severity" of this principle, the more so because it operates inflexibly in all life, and throughout the universe.

Does the nether operation of this law seem too severe—"Whosoever hath not, from him shall be taken away even that he hath?" Superficially perhaps, it does; yet in the nature of things it is inevitable and unalterable. Take our text in its connection. The disciples ask Jesus, "Why speakest Thou unto them in parables?" Our Lord's reply is: "Because they seeing see not, and hearing they hear not." All the time those fickle people were hearing the plain-spoken teachings of the kingdom without genuinely responding, they were mounting their own guilt, and at the same time destroying their very *capability* to respond. It lessened their guilt somewhat to have the truth now put to them in covert parable, though at the same time it was a penalty brought on themselves by their own self-diminished capacity to "hear". Idle unresponsiveness, neglect, disuse, refusal, inevitably bring their own retribution. What we will not *use*, we thereby *lose*. That is a fundamental principle of all life.

How invariably this law works in the *natural* realm! We cover one of our eyes for six months, and it is seriously weakened. We keep a fractured arm in a sling for eight weeks, and it becomes thinner, weaker, slower. I have seen ascetic "holy men" in India who have held an arm upright for weeks, months, years, until it has become atrophied and gangrenous simply through disuse. There is a white fish in certain American waters which for centuries now has lived nearly a thousand feet below the surface, and although it is found to have eye-organs it is quite blind, apparently through long disuse of its eyes. Similarly, the mole has eyes but is blind. He has kept boring in the dark for so long that Nature has said, "What you will not use, you lose." There is a medical theory that the appendix was originally much larger in the human body than now. Man was at first vegetarian (Gen. 1 : 29). After the fall meat was permitted; and since then, with the increase of concentrated foods, the appendix has fallen into less and less its original use, the digesting of vegetable foods, and has shrunk into an atrophied terminal part of the caecum. The same law operates even in the *mechanical* world, as any motorist or machinist knows. Everywhere this principle is stamped upon life and things: "Use or lose". It is especially true in hearing the Word of God. "Whosoever hath not" (because of idly neglecting or refusing) "from him shall be taken away even that he hath."

To present truth may I respond
With all my heart and mind;
Then ever reach to truth beyond,
And further treasures find.

"For whosoever hath, to him shall be given . . . but whosoever hath not, from him shall be taken away even that he hath."—Matt. 13: 12.

THIS principle, that "whosoever hath, to him shall be given" and "whosoever hath not, from him shall be taken away . . ." is disturbingly illustrated in the parable of the talents (Matt. 25). The servant with five talents trades them into ten. The servant with two talents turns two into four. But the slothful servant with only the one talent buries it, and later reports to his master, "I was afraid, and went and hid thy talent in the earth." The master's denunciation is fearful: "Thou wicked and slothful servant . . . Take the talent from him, and give it unto him which hath ten . . . and cast ye the unprofitable servant into the outer darkness." Yes, there it is, in vivid warning: what we will not use we lose!

Thank God, you and I, as Christian believers, are saved by *grace* from that "outer darkness" of damnation; yet none-the-less the *principle* illustrated in the parable applies to us, both before and after our conversion to Christ. What we will not use we lose. A gloomy-looking man said to me some years ago, "When I was a young man I had a flare for hearing fine preachers. I heard most of the great ones. Often I was stirred into concern about my soul; but I did not want to be troubled beyond the mere intellectual pleasure of hearing fine discourses. Alas, I can no more respond to Gospel preaching now than a marble statue. I *try* to be stirred, but something has gone dead within me. Oh, I envy those who can still really *hear*!" Through long refusal to make inward response, that man had *lost* what he would not use.

Some Christians are always "going to" start *praying* more regularly and for longer seasons, but they put off and off, and then find that even the capacity for praying has left them. Others are always "going to" become individual *soul-winners*, but they keep leaving their talent unused until the very aptitude to witness dies. As one loses pianistic skill by neglect of practice, or precision-strokes on the tennis court through abstention from play, so is it with mental and spiritual aptitudes.

Now all these considerations add up to this: you and I are *responsible* for the powers, aptitudes and opportunities which are ours. That is the purport of our text and of the parable about the buried talent. What we do not use we lose; and what we lose by slothful disuse will rise up in judgment against us hereafter. To bury our talent is not preservation, but mortification! Burial is for the dead, not the living! If we bury the living, however, even the living dies; but it rises up to condemn us, by and by. I had a friend who used to look round his shelves of good books, and say, "Lord may these books never rise in judgment against me." That is a true attitude. Though we are "saved by grace" from ultimate Gehenna, we are responsible as servants to our Lord. What kind of servants does He want? He wants "stewards" who *use* their talents; not mere "caretakers" who *bury* them. Oh, how many talents and gifts have been buried in the grave of a supposed "inferiority complex"! They should never have been buried; for they were buried alive, and have died underground! Some are buried but still alive. What about digging them out and using them again?

Next Door to a Kingdom

"Thou art not far from the kingdom of God."—Mark 12: 34.

THE brief altercation between our Lord and this lawyer who "answered discreetly" is like a cloud-rift on a rainy day, letting a golden sunshaft through to cheer a dismal landscape. The Pharisees had been to Jesus with their hypocritical question about the tribute money. The Sadducees had followed with their nonsensical problem of the woman who supposedly was married to seven brothers, each in turn, and then died childless. True, instead of tripping up the Prince of teachers, both groups had been put to open confusion by His consummate replies; yet their questionings had showed none-the-less sadly that those religionists were far from the kingdom of God. Then came this scribe who clearly discerned that real love to God and to one's neighbour is "more than whole burnt-offerings and sacrifices" (v. 33). It was like the sudden gleaming of a pure gem amid a heap of rubbish; and Jesus said to him, "Thou art not far from the kingdom of God."

We need not here discuss the dispensational aspect of the kingdom of God. Quite apart from that, there is a *spiritual* relevance and a present-day applicability of this incident which we ought not to miss. Our Lord meant that this lawyer was not far from the kingdom in the sense of feeling out wistfully towards its spiritual ideals and moral requirements; which reminds us, of course, that just as truly today there are thousands who, although they are not born-again believers, are "not far" from a true faith in Christ as Saviour.

This scribe of old was representative of many other men who, although they were sick of the dead formulas, narrow bigotries, musty traditionalism, and petty-fogging religious controversies of their day, were nevertheless yearning after a true knowledge of the living God. There are multitudes of men and women like that today. They do not often go to church, but they have far more real religion in them than many superficial church-goers. They fight shy of what they dub, "religion", yet inwardly they are feeling after God, longing to find the secret of a right relationship with Him, sincerely groping after spiritual reality and rest of heart. Thousands of them are looking wistfully towards the organised church, feeling that the church *could* tell them the true way if only it *would*.

Those of us who really know our Lord Jesus as Saviour should have a quick eye and a discerning sympathy for all such. Beware of trying to make them Baptists or Methodists or Presbyterians or any other kind of denominationalists. Keep patient and quiet in talking with them; they are sincere, though cautious and hesitant. You will find, generally, that they prefer direct quotations from Jesus Himself. Show them how Jesus Himself taught that He did not come *merely* to "teach", but that the supreme purpose was His death to redeem and save us (Matt. 20: 28; 26: 28). Show them that while God appreciates all sincere seeking (Acts 10: 35) yet sin is still sin; the best of our fallen human nature is still depraved; and we need a Saviour (Acts 10: 43), and that without faith in Jesus as Saviour it is impossible either to *find* God (Jn. 14: 6) or to please Him (Heb. 11: 6; 1 Jn. 3: 23). Beware of "quick results" or forced decisions. There is need for special care with those who are "not far from the kingdom".

About Trusting and Proving

"Now on whom dost thou trust?"—2 Kgs. 18 : 20.

SUCH was the challenge which the blatant Assyrian field-marshal, Rab-shakeh, flung at the beleagured king Hezekiah, more than two-and-a-half millenniums ago. Little did he guess that before many more sunrises 185,000 of his proud army would be corpses, cut down by an invisible scythe of the Almighty! Hezekiah did not reply to Rab-shakeh, but despite the hopeless-looking circumstances his heart was fixed, trusting in Jehovah (18 : 5). This was his secret of victory.

Even so today, the first mark of the true Christian is reliance on Jehovah-Jesus. We rely on Him exclusively as the *vicarious Sinbearer* through whom we have the salvation of our souls.

But we are to rely on Him continually as our *victorious Champion* through whom we have victory in our daily life. See 2 Chronicles 13 : 18, "The children of Judah prevailed (i.e. against twice their number) *because they relied* upon the Lord God of their fathers." See also chapter 16 : 8, "Were not the Ethiopians and the Lubims a great host with very many chariots and horsemen? yet *because thou didst rely on the Lord*, He delivered them into thine hand." So long as we rely on Him we have victory (Luke 10 : 17, 19; Rom. 5 : 17). Temper, fear, lust, pride, envy, grudging, moodiness, impatience, despondency, worry; over all such we gain victory as we really *rely* on Jesus.

Again, we are to rely on Him as our *vigilant Provider*, who "supplies all our need" (Phil. 4: 19; Ps. 34: 22). He does not always employ ravens to feed His Elijahs, but by one means or another He sustains them if they really rely on Him. We would not eulogise poverty, yet one of its blessings is that it keeps us more directly looking to God, and thus occasions more evidences that our extremities are God's opportunities.

But we are obliged to add a qualifying word. Our relying on God must be marked by three characteristics. First, it must be a *real* relying; not merely pretended or imagined. See Micah 3 : 11, "The heads (of the nation) judge for reward (bribes) and the priests thereof teach for hire, and the prophets thereof divine for money: yet they will *lean upon the Lord*, and say, Is not the Lord among us? None evil can come upon us." That kind of reliance was merely seeming, and God would not regard it (see verse 4).

Second, our relying must be *constant*. Alas, even good king Hezekiah had relapses (2 Chron. 32 : 25). We must guard against such vacillations, and be like the godly man of Psalm 112 : 7: "His heart is *fixed*, trusting in (relying on) Jehovah."

Third, our relying must be *unadmixed*. It must be on our Lord alone. A linsey-wolsey faith dishonours God and leaves its double-minded exerciser self-frustrated. We must learn to say with David, "He *only* is my Rock . . . My soul wait thou *only* upon God. . . . He *only* is my defence" (Ps. 62 : 2, 5, 6). We must see "no man save *Jesus only*".

Stayed upon Jehovah,
  Hearts are fully blest;
Finding, as He promised,
  Perfect peace and rest.

The Wall Shall be Built

"The street shall be built again, and the wall, even in troublous times."—Dan. 9:25.

DANIEL was a captive in a foreign land. His country had been at war, and had lost. His homeland had been trodden beneath the feet of invading armies. A third of the people had been slain by the sword. A third had been scattered to the winds. The remainder had been carried away to exile. The land had been laid waste, and the beloved capital razed to the ground. Daniel's heart was heavy. He prayed for his scattered countrymen. He longed that the wall of Jerusalem might be built up again. It was in response to Daniel's wistful prayer that a heavenly envoy was sent with the message in our text: "The street shall be built again, and the wall, even in troublous times." And the wall *was* built again in troublous times—by Nehemiah.

But there is a wall which *we*, the servants of Christ, are to build; a wall of Christian truth and righteousness and good will among nations; the wall of that city of God among earth's peoples which alone will give mankind protection from international hatred and war. If that wall is to be built at all, it will have to be built in "troublous times". To my own mind, it is a disguised betrayal of our heavenly Captain to argue, "Oh, well, even if things *are* going badly today, it is what the prophetic Word foretells; and anyway Christ is coming back again soon." I myself believe that "the coming of the Lord draweth nigh"; but who will dare to say for certain *just when*? Scripture prediction is infallible, but our interpretation of it is *far* from being so. Second Advent prophecy is so worded that none of us can justifiably find in it any reason for slacking off from fighting the holy war or building the city wall. The wonderful rest which is ours in Christ is that of inward repose, not lazy inactivity. If, presuming that our Lord's return is imminent, we slump into supine star-gazing or jejune lethargy, the Lord can but say to us, "Thou wicked and slothful servant."

Since the twentieth century came in, the very pillars of civilization have been rocked by two global wars. War is always a time when things are pulled down, not only buildings of brick and stone, but moral and spiritual buildings, those ideas and ideals which have been slowly built up in the minds of men and in the life of nations which mean the true progress of civilization. The 1914–18 war pulled a whole lot down; and the breaches were still gaping when the 1939–45 war did even more pulling down, and left vast moral wreckage in its wake. Today there is a large-scale moral breakdown and bigger challenge than ever to the Lord's Nehemiahs. Each one of us, in some way or other, must "arise and build". The Lord has a trowel for every willing hand. Let each one of us pray, "Lord, use even *me* in some way to help in the building of Thy new Jerusalem."

Though Sanballats and Tobiahs
  In their thousands may oppose,
God has still His Nehemiahs
  Who at last repulse all foes.
Oft resisted, ne'er defeated,
  With our trowels let us prod,
Till the city is completed
  By the reigning Christ of God.

"The street shall be built again, and the wall, even in troublous times."—Dan. 9: 25.

So, then, as we were saying yesterday, the wall is to be built, "even in troublous times"—the wall of Christian witness to our generation; the wall of truth and righteousness in human society and among the nations. The more difficult and impracticable it seems, the more bravely must we accept the challenge. Christ, being raised from the dead, dieth no more. He is with us in all our battling and building. We must learn to see an opportunity in every difficulty, not a difficulty in every opportunity!

We should confront the present situation with four dominant reactions. First, we should feel a disturbing *concern*, the same kind of concern about the moral wreckage all around us today as Daniel and Nehemiah felt about the broken-down walls of Jerusalem long ago. Second, we should make godly *resolve* that something shall really be done about it, in whatever smaller or larger degree we have influence. The other day I heard the following satirical definition of certain church conferences: "A conference is a coming together of a number of persons who, as separate individuals, can do nothing, but who collectively can decide that nothing can be done." We need to rescue ourselves from that sort of make-believe building! We should resolve to get something *done*, both individually and collectively. Third, we should exercise sanctified *initiative*, trying to match our methods to new situations. It was complained of the pre-war Chamberlain government in England that it was always "jumping to catch up with the last event". If we are always on the hop after a today which has now become yesterday, we shall destroy in ourselves any bold, courageous, clear-headed planning. Fourth, by much prayer we must bring down the "*enduement of power* from on high", for that is the divine equipment which makes us "more than conquerors through Him that loved us".

Let it be again admitted that two ruinous world-wars have done their deadly havoc of pulling down, and have left us with pitiful wreckage of social morals and marriage ideals. Let it be admitted that the materialist "evolution theory" has done its deadly work in breaking down the sacredness and dignity of human personality. Let it be admitted that the "modernism" of the German-originated "higher critical" schools and of our later "liberal" preachers, has broken down faith in the older view of the Bible as the inerrantly inspired Word of God, and has thus undermined the whole superstructure of Christian ethics. Let it be admitted that the "new psychology" of mere relativity in morals has now grown up as the offspring of world wars and evolutionary philosophy and theological apostasy, and is busy breaking down traditional Christian ideology. Yes, let it all be admitted; the breakdown is grievous. But what then? Must we simply sink down like weeping Jeremiahs amid the wreckage? No! there are "men of Israel" everywhere around us who are ready again to "arise and build". Weepers must become workers! Let each of us resolve again: "What I *can* do, by the grace of God I *will* do." What a heartbreak was that broken-down wall of Jerusalem! How hopeless the rebuilding! Yet he rebuilt it—with many willing helpers. We cannot all be Nehemiahs, but we can all be helpers; and, remember, there is *God*!

"Building Undaunted"!

"The street shall be built again, and the wall, even in troublous times."—Dan. 9 : 25.

LET us bring this wall-building issue right down to a practical, individual application. Each one of us is to grasp a sword and a trowel; the sword to ward off Satan's Tobiahs and Sanballats, and the trowel to build up our own bit of the wall. In a Christian sense, we tackle this in three ways—(1) by doing, (2) by giving, (3) by praying.

First there is to be *doing*. For most of us this readily means to co-operate usefully with a sound, evangelical, local church. A lady said to me, "I like to go and hear the Rev. So-and-So. He gives such a nice, brief, thoughtful address each time." When I asked if he brought people to Christ, or sent his hearers out to win others, she replied, "I'm afraid that's not his line." In far too many churches there is trowel-rattling rather than wall-building. I used to counsel believers, "Stay at your church, even if it *is* unevangelical; perhaps your witness is most needed there." I no longer give that advice. Not only are true believers spiritually starved in such places, they are wasting vital time, and giving financial support which is needed by churches which are loyal to the true faith. Give your support to a soundly evangelical church. If you *are* a member of such a church, do not leave the preacher and officials to do everything. *You* can put your little bricks into the building of the wall. Let the mighty bring their loads of stone or cement if they will; but it is the millions of smaller contributions which expedite the building most effectively. Every time we bring an unconverted person under Gospel preaching, or win a child to Christ, or give out a good tract, or support an evangelical enterprise, we help build the wall "even in troublous times".

But besides "doing", there is to be *giving*. Such giving is never to be an excuse for evading *doing* ! It is a supplement, not a substitute. Giving of our means is real wall-building. The Americans always call their paper money "bills"; the British call theirs "notes". Once, after the famous John Wesley had made an appeal on behalf of some Methodist project, he received a letter quoting Psalm 37 : 21, and enclosing two large bank notes. Wesley replied, "Those are the best 'notes' I have ever seen on that text." With many of us, our giving to the Lord's work is scanty, compared with our spending on other things. Let the younger, especially, take this to heart. We never lose what we give to God. Let the older among us, if we have money to bequeath, make certain that the Lord's work is generously remembered. Making a will never hastens our demise, but it can help us to pass over much more comfortably!

Finally, there must be *praying*. This brings the resources of *God* to our task of building the wall. During the 1939–45 war, when things seemed most hopeless, a copy of the China Inland Mission "Annual Report" came to me. The front cover showed a massive old Chinese gateway, and underneath was the title: "*BUILDING UNDAUNTED*." That must be our spirit, until our reappearing King shall complete the wall-building in millennial splendour. And let us ever remember that our mightiest weapon is prayer. Even when we can "do" nothing, and "give" nothing, we can still use the greatest means of all—*pray*. When we really pray, we really build. Best, however, is when all three go together—doing, giving, praying.

Garlands for Ashes!

"A garland instead of ashes."—Isa. 61 : 3.

I CAN never forget my first visit to the Hawaiian Islands. We arrived at the magic hour when an enchanting, starry night was shyly retiring before the peering eyes of new morning. Amid the rosy flush of dawn a scene of almost fairyland picturesqueness lay before us. As our good ship, *Aorangi*, glided smoothly into the pretty little harbour of Honolulu, the romantic melody of an Hawaiian folk-song floated to us across the scintillating water, played by a flamboyant early-morning band. Lining the water-front were Hawaiians in gay costumes of florid colours, welcoming us, and gently waving garlands of exotic flowers. Word had somehow gone before that we were on board, and to our surprise seven Christian gentlemen were at the wharf to greet us, each of them carrying a garland, or "lei" (as the Hawaiians call it). Then a mortifying experience befell me. According to custom, each of the seven gentlemen put his "lei" round my wife's neck, and kissed her!—leaving me a chagrined spectator, with not a lady to do the same for me!

Besides the happy humour of that gay landing, however, there was something else which fixed the occasion indelibly in my memory. As I saw my dear one, looking so beautiful with those seven floral garlands gracefully adorning her, my mind went back to Isaiah 41 : 1–3 and its wonderful fore-picture of Jesus: "The Spirit of the Lord God is upon Me, because Jehovah hath anointed Me to preach good tidings to the meek. He hath sent Me to bind up the broken-hearted, to proclaim liberty to the captives ... to comfort all that mourn; to give unto them a *garland instead of ashes*; the oil of joy for mourning, the garment of praise for the spirit of heaviness."

Yes, Jesus came as our Saviour, to give "*a garland instead of ashes*". The King James version renders it "beauty for ashes", but strictly the Hebrew word is "a garland". Oh, the ashes of this sin-cursed earth! Ashes are the symbol of sorrow, sadness, grief, bereavement, failure, despair. The garland is a lovely fragrant symbol of joy, gladness, blessing, success, reward. Our gracious Saviour, the Son of God, comes to replace the ashes of earthly sin and sorrow and bitterness with heaven-bestowed garlands of salvation and consolation and blessing. He came to give the garland of hope for the ashes of fear; the garland of love for the ashes of hate; the garland of new promise for the ashes of regret; the garland of divine friendship for the ashes of human loneliness; the garland of joy in God for the ashes of sorrow in sin; the garland of inward healing for the ashes of soul-sickness; the garland of moral victory for the ashes of defeat; the garland of spiritual liberty for the ashes of bondage; the garland of heart's ease for the ashes of unrest; the garland of godly contentment for the ashes of worldly envy; the garland of a worthwhile life for the ashes of godless pleasure.

Like a fuddling miasma, the idea overhangs the minds of many people, that Christianity drapes human life with sombreness. They mistake *churchianity* for Christianity. They equate "Jesus" merely with "religion". It is a deplorable misunderstanding. Jesus came to bedeck human life with garlands—not with funeral wreaths! Let us continually seek to dispel the delusion which beclouds many minds. May they see in you and me that radiant joy which only Jesus gives!

Justification and Forgivness

"A garland instead of ashes."—Isa. 61 : 3.

To continue our pleasant little reminiscence of yesterday, when I saw my dear wife adorned with those seven garlands, or "leis", at Honolulu, I thought especially of *seven* garlands which our Lord Jesus enrings around those who receive Him as Saviour and Sovereign. Let me mention *two* of them here, in this present meditation.

First, He gives the garland of imputed *righteousness* for the ashes of guilt. That word, "guilt", is a legal term. The Bible teaches that as sinners we are "guilty" before God. Besides having inherited a sinful nature as members of Adam's fallen race, we have committed sins of our own—sins too many to count and too deadly to assess. We have to admit, as did Joseph's brothers, "We are verily guilty." Guilt brings condemnation. We are "under condemnation", says God's Word. But this tragic plight of ours is counter-matched by the glorious Gospel doctrine of "justification", or imputed righteousness. The Romans epistle teaches that when Jesus voluntarily became our Sinbearer on the Cross, *our guilt* was imputed, or reckoned, to *Him,* and that now *His righteousness* may be imputed, or reckoned, to *us.* Because of this, Romans 5 : 1 assures us, "Therefore, being *justified* (reckoned righteous before God) *by faith* (which accepts Jesus as Saviour) we have peace with God, through our Lord Jesus Christ." Oh, it is a blessed, soul-saving thing to have this new standing of "justification", before God, and to wear the garland of Christ's imputed righteousness instead of the ashes of our soul-condemning guilt!

Second, Jesus brings us the garland of a heavenly Father's *forgiveness* for the ashes of helpless remorse. What is more wonderful than to find that God our Creator is not only the heavenly Judge who now "justifies" us in Christ, but the heavenly Father who compassionately forgives us for Jesus' sake? His forgiveness is ours when we become "reconciled to God by the death of His Son" (Rom. 5 : 10). There could be no such forgiveness apart from the Cross, for the principles of divine righteousness are involved in the way God deals with sin. Even God must needs find a morally consistent way of exercising forgiveness. The Cross of Christ dealt with that aspect of the human sin-problem once for all. After that Cross, none of the myriad onlooking intelligences in the universe could ever allege that God forgives human sinners at the expense of those moral principles which condition the safety of the universe. Through that Cross there comes to us a full, free, forever forgiveness. Jesus shows us the compassionateness of that forgiveness in the parable of the prodigal son. When the prodigal dragged himself home, covered with the ashes of remorse, he little expected what transpired. The father "had compassion, and ran, and fell on his neck, and kissed him". Oh, it was such a glad, magnanimous, overflowing forgiveness! And Jesus offers to every other penitent heart this garland of forgiveness for the ashes of helpless remorse.

Oh, wonderful heart of the Father above,
For homecoming prodigals, pardoning love!
A full reinstatement as son of the King!
A garland of gladness, a robe and a ring!
Oh, come, ragged prodigal, hasten today;
Forgiveness awaits you; why longer delay?

"A garland instead of ashes."—Isa. 61 : 3.

JESUS offers us the garland of *new spiritual life* for the ashes of spiritual death. Do you know that song about "England's green and pleasant land"? I have roamed far around the world, but I know of no lovelier scene than the countryside of "England's green and pleasant land" on a smiling, sunny day in Spring. Oh, those homey hills, and fresh-budded hedgerows, and dear old winding lanes, and tidy fields all carpeted with rich green! Those of us who were brought up among them can never forget them. They cast a continual spell over one's memory. And every year that lovely miracle of transformation is repeated. Every year Spring comes and enrings the countryside with her garland of new life after the cold, grey ashes of wintry death. And what a silent, eloquent, exquisite parable it always is, of the new spiritual life which regenerates those who receive the Saviour! Jesus garlands us not only with imputed righteousness and a heavenly Father's forgiveness, but with new spiritual springtide in resurrection-union with Himself. By His Spirit He indwells us, and renews us, and transforms us. Did He not say, in John 10 : 10, "I am come that they might have *life* (corresponding to Spring) and that they might have it more abundantly" (corresponding to Summer)? Yes, Jesus brings the garland of new spiritual life after the dull, mournful ashes of deadness toward God; the *new* life of spiritual Spring, the *full* life of spiritual Summer; then, in the golden yet-to-be, the endless glory-harvest of heaven!

But again, Jesus offers us the garland of *joy and peace* instead of the ashes of sin and unrest. Not only does He gladden us by an assurance of peace *toward* God, through His Cross which puts away our sin; but if we really commit ourselves to Him, He gently garlands our hearts with a tranquilizing sense of peace *from* God. The peace of heaven quietly possesses us, and we know that because we are completely His, all is well fundamentally for time and eternity. Friend, is your life like an agitated sea which cannot rest? Is it disturbed by fear, anxiety, temper, wrong desire, passion, envy? Well, we are not exaggerating: Jesus offers you true joy and peace. In John 14 : 27 and 15 : 11 He actually speaks of His own peace and joy indwelling us; and thousands have proved how really He fulfils His word.

Jesus also brings us the garland of *victory and holiness* for the ashes of defeat. There cannot be unclouded joy in any life without mastery over sin and self. We may have money, position, entertainment, and many other gratifications, but if there is defeat there is wretchedness. Oh, how many of us know what it is to sit down amid the ashes of defeat, and weep our eyes out at the abjectness of our slavery! These blurting tongues of ours which seem beyond all power to bridle them! These unruly thoughts of evil which seem incurably innate in our nature! These oft-repeated collapses before temptation! We have cried out with Paul, "Oh, wretched man that I am! who shall deliver me?" Thank God, many of us have learned to say with the disciples of old, "Lord, even the demons are subject unto us through Thy name" (Luke 10 : 17). "Who is he that overcometh the world?" Alexander? Caesar? No; you do not overcome the "world", in a moral sense, by swinging a sword or firing a gun. "Who is he that overcometh? . . . He that believeth [relies on] Jesus, the Son of God" (1 Jn. 5 : 5).

Victory, Resurrection, Heaven!

"A garland instead of ashes."—Isa. 61 : 3.

RECENTLY, at a luncheon group of businessmen, I heard a big, impressive man give his testimony. He had been in prison for larceny, violence, and other felonies, but mostly for drunkenness. He had been an alcoholic. No prison or other institution could cure him. He had been in such a state that even in prison he was kept in solitary separation. Then, one day, a group of Gospel singers visited that prison. He heard a woman testify that Jesus had saved her from alcoholism. There and then he flung himself down and accepted Jesus as his Saviour. In all the years since, he has never touched the cursed drink. His health is restored. His face is radiant. His testimony is vibrant with victory. The only marks of the old wretchedness are the disfigurements where several times he tried to commit suicide. He now goes round telling other drink-slaves the way of victory through Christ. As he gave his testimony, I could see, with my inner eyes, a lovely garland around him—that garland which Jesus gives to those who really trust Him, the garland of victory for the ashes of defeat and shame.

But further, Jesus gives the garland of *resurrection* for the ashes of the grave. Most of us have stood at the opened grave and heard the funereal dirge, "Dust to dust, ashes to ashes", over the body of a loved one. The eyes and lips which smiled their love to us are gone beyond recall. The arms which embraced us no longer move. Oh, bleak, heartless grave, if thou art the final word, what stark futility is all human life and love! But, O grave, thou art not a final blank. Jesus has risen, "bringing life and immortality to light". Boast not thyself against us, O grave, for even these ashes thou shalt not long retain! As for thee, O death, Jesus has transformed thee into sleep. "The trumpet shall sound, and the dead shall be raised incorruptible." In that transfiguring climax, Jesus shall change the ashes of our graves into the fadeless garland of immortality!

Yet again, Jesus gives the garland of *heaven* for the ashes of earth. Many of us, as we reach our later years, sing with new pathos Henry F. Lyte's words, "Change and decay in all around I see." Old friends and old times are gone. What changes! How transitory everything is! Worst of all, amid the unresting flux is unhalting decay. Fairest flowers wilt and wither. Greenest foliage turns sear and yellow. In the end, the worm and the canker win. Youth and maturity decline into grey age. The bouquet of the wedding day becomes the melancholy wreath on a coffin lid. To live only for *this* world leaves nothing but ashes in the end. But for the redeemed in Christ it is the very opposite. To be "absent from the body" is to be "present with the Lord". Instead of spent fires and pathetic ashes there is the unfading garland of eternal glory in the land where the roses never fade, and the sun never sets, and the night never comes, and sickness never invades, and death never divides; the land where, instead of moth and rust and corruption and decay, there are "fountains of living waters" which never run dry, and sinless raptures which never have an end! Oh, this wonderful Jesus—Friend of sinners, Saviour of Souls! "The wages of sin is death," but the garlands which Jesus bestows are forgiveness, and righteousness, and new life, and victory, and holiness, and immortality, and heavenly glory!

Are You Living in the Plan?

"Good works, which God hath before ordained that we should walk in them."—Eph. 2 : 10.

GOD has a plan for each life. This tremendous truth, when firmly grasped, can have a revolutionary effect upon our thinking and living. Every vicissitude becomes transformed by it. Everything that happens to us becomes recognised as a foreseen contribution to the development of the plan.

It is tragically easy to *miss* God's pre-envisaged plan for us. Besides God's original plan for us, there is His *permissive* will. Never for a moment must we think that everything which happens to human beings is *predetermined* by God. There are hyper-Calvinists who teach so; but they are wrong; and if, in saying so bluntly that they are wrong, we sound rather dogmatic, it is because we are unmovably convinced that they are unsound exegetes of the Scriptures, at least in *that* particular doctrine. They confuse foreordination or predestination with *foreknowledge*. God never predetermined sin, or disobedience to His will. Such a thought forever perish! Sin and suffering belong to the lower level of His *permissive* will. All that God permits, however, He foresees, and overrules.

Millions of human beings live outside God's special plan for them, though they are covered by God's permissive and overruling will. There seem to be many professing Christians, too, who know little about being *in*, and living *out*, God's special plan for them. Self-will frustrates its fulfilment. Our individual responsibility is to *get* in it, and *keep* in it.

The way to get in it and keep in it is complete and continual *consecration*. When we thus "abide" in Him, our eyes become gradually opened to the wonderful unfolding of the plan. A deep and settled peace possesses us. We rest in the "good and acceptable and perfect will of God" (Rom. 12 : 2). When we are thus living "according to plan", there may be many incidents but there are no accidents. God makes no mistakes.

Another lesson which we need to learn is, that if we are to live out the plan carefully, then besides consecration to Christ there must be daily *consultation* with Him, for He is the Master of the plan in all its details. We should practise consulting Him about everything, but especially about those things which seem like frustrations or contradictions. In a certain factory with complicated machinery for the making of textile goods, the instructions are, "If your threads get tangled, send for the foreman." One of the workers, a diligent and busy woman, got her threads tangled and tried to disentangle them herself, only making them worse. After that she sent for the foreman. He came and looked, then turned and asked, "Have you been doing this yourself?" She said: "Yes." "Why did you not send for *me* according to instructions?" "I did my best," she rather sullenly replied. Then the foreman quietly rebuked her, "Always remember," he said, "that 'doing your best' is *sending for me*."

Behind our life the Weaver stands
And works His wondrous will;
When yielded to His all-wise hands
We learn His wondrous skill.

Pain May be in the Plan

"Them that suffer according to the will of God."—1 Peter 4: 19.

YESTERDAY we were speaking about God's plan for us as individuals; but now there is a further aspect of the matter which we do well to consider, namely, that *pain* may be a part of the plan.

Pain, suffering, trouble, adversity, temptation, affliction, can exercise a wonderful ministry of spiritual discipline, refinement, and enrichment. Some flowers, as the rose, must be crushed before their full fragrance is released. Some fruit, as the sycamore, must be bruised before it will attain ripeness and sweetness. Some metals, as gold, must be flung into the furnace before they reach full value and purity. The old oak log must be laid on the fire, and the flames encircle it, before its imprisoned music is set free. So is it with the saints. It is true with many of us that we must be laid low before we will look high. We must know God's smiting before we can appreciate His smiling. The Potter must break the vessel before He can make out of the same material a new and beautiful vase. Our hearts must be broken before their richest contents can leak out and flow forth to bless others.

But whenever God sends a trial with one hand, He gives grace with the other. Thus trials become triumphs. Burdens become wings. Affliction, instead of being a bed of thorns and a pathway of nettles, becomes a quilt of roses. The very things which seem to break us are the things which really "make" us. Euroclydon blows its tempests upon us! We shall be dashed in pieces on the rock-bound coast! We shall be strangled in the hidden reef! But nay, we are self-deceived. Lo, God is in the hurricane, and instead of driving us to destruction, it beats the scared mariner into that safest of all harbours, the encircling arms of God's love!

Trials, tribulations, adversity, are frequently our biggest benedictions. They are blessings in disguise; angels dressed in black for a small moment; messengers from Heaven, come to bless us and make us more like the Captain of our salvation, Who Himself was made "perfect through sufferings". The crown of thorns was in the plan for Jesus, but the thorns have given place to diadems! The Cross was the step to the Throne! Let us learn well, that *pain may be part of the plan*! "It is God which worketh in you, both to will and to do His good pleasure" (Phil. 2: 13).

Yes, pain may be in the plan. This has been a sore problem to many a devout Christian heart; yet others, not a few, have testified that their choicest spiritual enrichments came to them on their "Via Dolorosa". Moreover, it is supremely important that we relate this problem of pain to our *ultimate destiny*. Jude 24 tells us that in the coming consummation we Christian believers are to be "presented faultless" before the heavenly Majesty, which means, of course, the entire perfection of our human nature—spirit, soul, body. But although we are all to be thus faultless, or perfect, in our *nature* as human beings, does that mean, also, that we shall all be the same in *character*? No; our nature is what we basically *are*, whereas our character is a quality or blend of qualities which we *develop* from our nature, by our reactions. Pain, suffering, adversity, do something of eternal significance to our *character*, according to the way we react to them.

"Behold also the Ships"

"There go the ships."—Ps. 104: 26.

YES, there go the ships, on the "great and wide sea"; and every one of them is a floating parable. Catch the parallel. The sea is human life. The ships are human beings. The winds and waves are the testings which come to us. The rudder is our free-will or power of choice. The helmsman is the heart behind the will.

"There go the ships." How often we speak of ships as though they were living beings! We use the pronoun, "she". Those of us who have travelled enjoy telling of our favourite ship—what "she" is like, and how "she" behaves when conveying us over the liquid bosom of the swelling main. In some of my many travels I have seen hardy seamen weep with emotion in talking of some beloved ship which they had sailed for years and had come to regard as almost human.

Perhaps that is not so strange, after all. Human beings and ships have much in common. Like the ships, we human beings are meant to fulfil the pre-formed purpose of our Maker and Owner. We have to sail this wide and perilous sea of life with its changeful moods and varying currents. We are meant to sail with a definite purpose and port before us, not just to float like rafts, anywhere or nowhere. We encounter rough weather and fierce storms: we can founder mid-seas, or break to pieces on jagged rocks and hidden reefs. Like ships, we need to be under safe and wise control.

"There go the ships." Yes, and here comes the weather!—placid waters, balmy zephyrs, genial skies, which pleasantly deceive the unwary into thinking that cruel storms could never disturb those latitudes and longitudes; beguiling calms and shimmering smoothness and prosperous stretches which look too innocent to conceal treacherous cross-currents and submerged death-traps which have sent many a seaworthy craft to destruction; stormy head-gales of opposition; fierce blasts of adversity; heavy seas of sorrow; high-speed winds of temptation; tempests of lust; swelling waves of unholy desire; tornadoes of passion; whirlpools of seduction; cyclones of anger; raging storms from the evil one himself which would lash us into despair, recklessness, unbelief and blasphemy. We are no match for it all unless we have Jesus as Captain.

"There go the ships"—those human ships, amid fair weather or foul, and the rudder which turns their course is the *will*, the dangerous, momentous power of human *choice*. A lady traveller who knew little about "putting the helm hard over" and "bouting ship" and steering port or starboard, was alarmed to hear that something had gone wrong with the ship. On accosting the captain she extracted that the rudder was broken. "Well," she said, "I'm glad it's nothing worse than that." Nothing worse than that! Oh, the tragedies which happen when the rudder of human will and choice goes wrong! What smash-ups on merciless rocks!

"There go the ships"—turned hither and thither by the rudder; but behind the rudder is the helmsman at the wheel. How easily we turn or drift into errors and sins which wreck lives and ruin souls! Oh, we need Jesus in control. As the rudder obeys the helmsman, so the helmsman needs his orders from the captain. Jesus is the one sure Captain. Let our prayer this day be: "Jesus, Saviour, pilot me."

"Veiled in Flesh the Godhead See"

"That holy being which shall be born of thee shall be called the Son of God."—Luke 1 : 35.

THE greatest of all thoughts in the human mind is the thought of a Supreme Being, or *GOD*. Whence came this idea, this universal and ineradicable God-awareness of mankind? It seems an inexplicable enigma, if there is no God in reality. The human concept and conviction of the Divine Being comes from God himself.

Man *needs* God, and gropes after Him; for besides life there is fear, and besides reason there is conscience, and besides God-consciousness there is sin-consciousness. Man knows that God is, and that to find Him is the deepest need of our strangely self-contradictory nature. But how shall God be known? Mere man-made religions are at best a hope and a guess. The most specious philosophies can only taper away into doubtful suppositions when they pass from physical phenomena to spiritual mysteries.

The big, deep, acute need is for God to become *self-revealed* to man. But can that be achieved? God is purely spiritual and infinite; man is housed in the physical and is finite. Apparently there was only one adequate way, namely, that God Himself should assume our human nature, astonishing as this may seem, by a real human birth, and become a Member of our race as well as its Creator. This is verily what was effected in the Bethlehem miracle of two millenniums ago. The Son of God became the Son of Man. Whether such a sublime prodigy would have been needed or effected if man had never fallen and become sinful, as taught in the Bible, we do not know, but it seems doubtful. Biblical theology always connects the Incarnation with man's need as a sinner. Fallen man is sin-blinded, alienated from God, lost, and unable to find his way back, and physical death has become a precipice into eternal ruin. The Incarnation was no mere aesthetic condescension of the Godhead; it was a desperate necessity for man's salvation and restoration. Thus, it came to pass that in "the fulness of the time . . . God sent forth His Son". This answers man's heart-cry in three ways.

First, *the Unseen becomes seen.* In the Incarnation God emerges from heavenly hiddenness into earthly visibility. The incomprehensible SOMEONE becomes the approachable, touchable, understandable JESUS. The Eternal Mind breaks into time.

Second, *the Distant becomes near.* See Him at the carpenter's bench: how near God is to us *there*! See Him wearily sitting on the well at Sychar: how near God is to us *there*! See Him weeping at the grave of Lazarus: how near God is to us *there*! See Him on that criminal's crucifixion-stake: how near is God to us and our sin *there*! (2 Cor. 5: 19).

Third, *the Creator becomes the Saviour.* This is the greatest fact of all. He alone could bear the enormity of righteous penalty due to total human sin. Let me quote a poor woman's prayer in the Welsh revival: "Dear Saviour, I thank Thee Thou wast crucified with Thine arms outstretched to show that there is a welcome for everyone. I thank Thee that the old devil was not allowed to tie Thy hands behind Thy back. Nor were they just folded on Thy breast, but outstretched wide to invite the whole world to Thy bosom."

"For this thing I besought the Lord thrice that it might depart from me. And He said unto me: My grace is sufficient for thee. . . ."—2 Cor. 12: 8, 9.

PERHAPS no verse of Scripture has brought more comfort to Christian hearts than this one; and does not the explanation of its pre-eminent appeal largely lie in the fact that it is the record of a personal experience? "He said unto *me*."

"*My grace is sufficient for thee*"—sublime and satisfying answer! How much better than the literal granting of the apostle's request! Had the pleading of those sensitive nerves been literally yielded to, what losers would Paul and ourselves have been! Paul would have lost more power than pain; and how many thoughts that have since inspired patient heroism would never have come to us! Such epistles as Paul's could only have their birth in the travail of trial. Paul's prayer was sincere and intense, but it left the higher spiritual altitudes unscaled. To have the "thorn" removed was poor compared with having its presence sanctified. To have the "messenger of Satan" taken away was poor compared with having him transformed into a "ministering spirit". Paul wanted the thorn away; whereas Christ wanted to show how grapes may be gathered of thorns. God's choicest flowers often bloom on bitter stems.

"*My grace*"—how gloriously the grace of Christ shines from the pages of the New Testament! Gaze at that matchless character. See His perfect grace revealing itself through everything He said and did, giving Him perfect poise in every situation and on all occasions. See how He combines in Himself all the masculine virtues, and all the feminine graces. Gaze at Calvary. See that utter triumph of sheer self-sacrifice! O that life! that death! "We beheld His glory, the glory as of the Only Begotten of the Father, *full of grace* and truth." That grace may be *mine*!

"*My* grace"—who but the absolutely Divine Christ could say this? How empty would the words be from the lips of any but a Christ who is verily God! "*My* grace"—the words involve omnipotence, omnipresence, the possession of all the Divine resources, the perfect knowledge of all human needs, and our Lord's perpetual presence everywhere with His people. For any mere creature to make such a claim—whether worm or archangel makes no essential difference—would be ludicrous.

"*Sufficient*"—the supply has exact correspondence with the need; never too much, never too little, but perfect adequacy; never too soon, never too late, but timed to the tick of the clock and to the beat of the heart. Grace for tomorrow's needs will not come today. Grace for today will not come tomorrow. There is a story comes to us from the old-time martyr days, about a condemned Christian who lay one night in his prison cell knowing that at daybreak he must be burned at the stake. The prospect was terrible. How could he endure the ordeal? He picked up the candle that flickered in his cell, and tried the experiment of holding his little finger in the tiny flame. With a gasp of pain he quickly withdrew it. How could he possibly undergo the torture of his whole body in the flames? Yet at sunrise he went to his death with irrepressible exuberance, and sang with heavenly ecstasy shining from his face. When the real emergency came, sufficient grace was given. So is it always.

The Secret of Joy and Peace

"Joy and peace in believing."—Rom. 15: 13.

It is no mere wishful thinking, but sober truth, that we Christian believers are the only people on earth who have found the secret of real joy and peace. There are many others who *think*, or for the time being *feel*, that they have found the secret in sects or faiths *other* than that of strictly New Testament Christianity; but they are deluded. Of course, there is a certain uplifting or calming influence in adhering to *any* high-aspiring religious sect or philosophy; but what sad collapses and pathetic disillusionments often come later, when those fair-seeming false refuges are tested by the deeper sorrows of human experience, or by the persistent, hereditary perversity of the human heart! What distressful eye-openings of this kind we ourselves have witnessed from time to time!

But this does not happen to those of us who know and trust and love and possess the Lord Jesus as our Saviour. We are "born again" of the Holy Spirit, and "the love of God is shed abroad in our hearts".

We've found a joy in sorrow,
  A secret balm for pain,
A beautiful tomorrow
  Of sunshine after rain:
We've found a branch of healing
  Near every bitter spring,
A whispered promise stealing
  O'er every broken string.

There cannot really be joy or peace of *that* kind in any but a Christian heart; for until the sin-problem has been dealt with, there cannot be a right relation with God; and there is no solution of the individual sin-problem apart from Christ. Only in Him is there atonement for sin, and real reconciliation to God. Only in Him is there the new standing of "justification" before God, and the new birth from above. Only in Him do we have covenant access to the heavenly Throne, and find ourselves "accepted in the Beloved". Only in Him is there the joy which outmatches all sorrow, and the "peace which passes all understanding".

Dear fellow-believer, let us rejoice this day that we have found such "joy and peace in believing". It is better to have this spiritual joy and peace in our hearts than all the material emoluments and embellishments which could ever come our way. These are treasures which will outlive the grave, and outlast the years, and outshine the sunset.

Yes, let us rejoice; but let it be with no such conceit as that of the old-time Pharisees who imagined themselves the objects of an arbitrary divine favouritism. Let us rejoice in grateful humility that in purest grace God has opened our eyes to see, and our minds to know, and our hearts to possess that which we never, never deserved to see and know and possess. And let us this day be prayerfully concerned for those who as yet—millions of them—have never found this "joy and peace in believing", especially those who are deceived by plausible heresies and specious cults. Lord, increase our own "joy and peace in believing". Lord, make us earnest in our prayers for those who still have not found!

"To him that Overcometh . . ."

"To him that overcometh will I grant to sit with Me in My Throne."—Rev. 3: 21.

IN this promise our Lord is referring, of course, to His Messianic throne and His millennial reign. When He comes again, in power and glory, then will He lift His resistless rod over the nations, and unfurl the banner of world-wide empire. The evil one shall be interned in the bottomless abyss. Evil shall be completely subjugated. Righteousness and peace shall be dispensed to the nations. Christ Jesus shall reign upon the Davidic throne which has been promised and covanted to Him. A chastened and renewed Israel will send His messengers of enlightenment and peace throughout the earth. Science and invention, scholarship and art, shall all devote themselves to noblest ends. War shall be done away, and the throne of David's greater Son shall be supreme.

It will be wonderful to live under that reign, yet it will be even more wonderful to reign *with* Him; and this is what Jesus promises. "To him that overcometh will I grant to *sit with Me in My Throne*." What a promise!

But the promise is to "the *overcomer*". Are all believers "overcomers"? Let him think twice who would answer a dogmatic "Yes" to this question. The letters to the seven churches, at least, suggest otherwise to an unprejudiced reader. Our standing in Christ is no artificial position of immunity. As there are degrees of punishment so there are degrees of reward. One is made ruler over ten cities, another over five. "One star differeth from another star in glory."

We have no sympathy with what is known as the "partial" rapture. We do not believe that Christ is coming only for a certain number of His people and that the others will be left on earth when the vials of God's wrath are poured out. We have no sympathy with it because we find no Scripture for it.

Surely 1 Corinthians 15: 51 settles the point, without need for quoting other verses. Mark the distinction made by the double occurrence of the word, "all"—"We shall not *all* sleep, but we shall *all* be changed." And *when* are we "all" to be thus transfigured? Is it at different times, or simultaneously? The next verse tells us: "In a moment, in the twinkling of an eye, *at the last trump*; for the trumpet shall sound, and the dead shall be raised incorruptible, and we shall be changed."

No, we do not believe in a "partial" rapture. We simply cannot conceive of our Lord's coming for only a *part* of His mystic "body" and "bride" and "temple", the Church (for we believe that the metaphor of "bride" refers to the Church, over against some who teach otherwise). When the "fulness" of the Gentiles shall come in, and the elect members of the "body of Christ" are numerically completed, then our Lord will return for His own. As His coming is actually contingent upon that completed inbringing of the elect, can we think that He is coming for only a part of them?

All true believers will be "caught up . . . to meet the Lord in the air". All will have their part in that transfiguring translation. All will share in the millennial reign of David's Greater Son. Yet even that does not mean that there will be no difference of reward among believers. Let our eager prayer ever be that we may be among the "overcomers".

Meaningful Metaphors

"I have fought the good fight. I have finished the course. I have kept the faith."—2 Tim. 4 : 7.

Here is the Christian life in three metaphors—a fight, a race, a trust. It is a *fight*, for there is a foe to quell. It is a *race*, for there is a goal to reach. It is a *trust*, for there is a truth to guard. It is a fight; we must be *brave*. It is a race; we must be *keen*. It is a trust; we must be *true*. It is a fight; we are to be "strong in the Lord". It is a race; we are to "run with patience". It is a trust; we are to be "faithful unto death". It is a fight; and there is a palm of victory for the overcomer. It is a race; and there is the prize of the high calling for those who endure. It is a trust; and there is the Master's "Well done!" for the faithful steward.

Each of these three metaphors is true to fact. Each describes one aspect of the Christian life. Each is in a sense independent; yet all three go together and are necessary to each other. They are a trinity in unity, and we should keep all three well in mind. Predominantly, they tell us that the Christian life demands bravery, perseverance, fidelity. They "sweep the deck" of all loose and lazy notions. There is nothing here of being "carried to the skies on flowery beds of ease"! All these three figures imply godly effort and earnest tenacity. If we let the apostle's own life be our commentary on his words, there is "blood and sweat and toil" in these three metaphors: a fight, a race, a trust.

Possibly this occasions some *perplexity*, especially in younger disciples. Many of us, at our conversion to Christ, thought that the Christian life would be altogether one of peace and heart-rest. Did not Jesus say, "I will give you rest"? Does not the Gospel offer "joy and peace in believing"? Yet here Paul makes the Christian life a fight which is to be fought, a race which is to be run, and a faith which is to be guarded; something demanding an unremitting striving. How are we to reconcile the seeming contradiction? The answer is that there are two kinds of rest. There is the rest which comes *after*; and there is the rest which comes *in*. There is the rest which comes *after* the fight is over; *after* the race is won; *after* the march is ended; *after* the hill is climbed; *after* the goal is reached; *after* the toil is done. And there is that other kind of rest; that inward calm and quiet repose which may be ours in Christ while the fight, the race, the march, the climb, the exertion, and the toil are still in progress. That is rest *in and during* it all, here and now. It is the rest which is ours when we are completely consecrated to Christ.

Strange as this may sound to some ears, in the Christian life it is possible to be at rest while at war!—to be relaxed while on stretch in the race!—to have heart's ease during all the exacting vigil. Indeed, although it sounds strangely paradoxical, it is part of the Christian fight and race and trust to *get* to that place of inward rest, and then *keep* there. That is why Hebrews 4 : 11 says, "Let us *labour* therefore to enter into that *rest*"!

Oh, it is wonderful, this rest in and during the fight and the race and the vigil; but our point of emphasis at the moment is the fact that the Christian life *is* indeed a "fight". Our conversion was our enlistment. Every new blessing is meant to be new ammunition. Dear heavenly Captain, help us to keep fighting sin wherever we find it—especially in ourselves!

"I have fought the good fight . . ."—2 Tim. 4: 7.

THE Christian life is a *fight*. Paul here calls it the "good" fight. In 1 Timothy 6: 12, he defines this good fight as "the good fight of *the faith*". So our fight is the good fight of the Christian faith against *sin*—against sin in its triune expression through the "world" without, and the "flesh" within, and the "devil" behind them both.

Every Christian is called to wage that war. It is not something which another can do in our stead. There is no proxy. Even God cannot fight this moral and spiritual fight for us. We ourselves have to fight it, each one of us, individually. There are immense and blessed things which God has done for us because we could never have done them for ourselves. He has provided atonement for our sin; He has regenerated us by His Holy Spirit; He has given us the Scriptures to guide us; He has sent the ever-abiding Paraclete to teach us; He has written our names in heaven. But there are other things which we must do for ourselves. God will give us grace and strength to do them, but the choice and the act and the purpose and the endeavour must be our own. He will not conquer our temptations for us, if we ourselves do not fight them. He will not give us victory over evil propensities and "fleshly lusts which war against the soul", unless we ourselves contend against them. He cannot fight our battle *instead* of us. As the farmer must co-operate with God if there is to be a harvest, so must it be in our Christian life and warfare. Temper, covetousness, vicious habits, ulterior motives, lure of gossipy exaggeration, selfishness, not to mention other Amalekites firmly pocketed in our fallen human nature—as *soon* as we fight against them, and as *long* as we fight against them, the grace and power of Christ are transported to us; but if we ourselves do not resist them, even our Lord Himself cannot fight the battle in our stead.

I gratefully agree that there *are* certain special exceptions to this. Helpless drunkards have been converted, and the very appetite for drink has been taken out of their nature. The same has happened with inveterate tobacco-smokers, and drug addicts, and lust-fiends. But these must be regarded as particular interventions where the physical system itself had become so uncontrollably inflamed or chronically weakened, that the "good fight" could not even begin without some such initial shock-deliverance. Once saved in Christ, those souls which have formerly known "the depths of Satan" must start fighting the "good fight" like all other believers.

Let us settle it in our minds: so long as we are in this present life we shall be beset by temptation in every conceivable form. The "good fight" is for complete mastery over sin and self and Satan. Thank God, we may *have* that mastery, through the imparted life and grace and power and wisdom of our Lord Jesus. Yet we need always to realize that the imparting of His life and grace and power and wisdom does not do away with our *obligation* to fight the "good fight". We are strengthened by this continual impartation *in order* to fight; and we *must* fight. But be of good cheer, Christian comrade, you may live in continual *victory*; for, "Greater is He that is in you than he that is in the world!"

A Race: A Trust

"I have finished the course; I have kept the faith."—2 Tim. 4: 7.

We are meant to see the Christian life as a *race*. When Paul says, "I have finished the course", he has the stadium and the Olympic racecourse in mind. Catch the significance of the metaphor. A race is more individualistic than a fight. There is a set course or track. When Paul says, "I have finished the course", he means that he has now completed the special track or stretch of ministry set before *him* (see Acts 20: 24).

In that sense, the Christian life is to be viewed as a race, by every Christian believer. There is a special course divinely marked out and set before *each* one of us. To grasp this clearly, transforms life. Each of us is dear to our heavenly Lord. To Him, all mere earthly distinctions between rich and poor, high and low, educated and uneducated, mean nothing. In heaven there will be no such distinctions. The humblest and poorest of us is as dear to Him as the richest and highest. He has a special, individualistic track of service marked out for each of us, whoever and whatever we may be. As in a physical race there is a track, a goal, and a prize, so in this spiritual race there is a track, a goal and a prize. As in a physical race there are spectators, so in this spiritual race there are spectators—some encouraging, some discouraging. As in a physical race the runners discard all hindering weights and hampering indulgences, so in this spiritual race we must "lay aside every weight and the sin which doth so easily beset us" (Heb. 12: 1). As in a physical race the runners concentrate with keen determination to press on, so in this spiritual race *we* must concentrate with keen determination to press on. As in a physical race the runners keep their eye on the winning post and the prize, so must *we* keep our eyes on the goal and the heavenly prize.

But now, in these further words, "I have kept the faith", Paul means us to see the Christian life as a *trust*. In 1 Timothy 6: 20, he writes, "O Timothy, keep that which is committed to thy trust." Actually, the Greek is, "Guard the *deposit*." In 2 Timothy 1: 14 we find, "That good thing which was committed unto thee, keep . . ." But again the Greek is, "Guard the *deposit*." What, then, *is* the "deposit"? 1 Timothy 1: 11 defines it as, "The glorious Gospel of the Blessed God, which was committed to my trust."

Yes, that is the "deposit". Paul was entrusted with it. So was Peter. So was John. So were the other Apostles. Then, by Apostolic hand-down, Timothy was entrusted with it. So was John Mark. So were the Elders. Then the churches were entrusted with it, by which time it was theirs in the written fixity of the New Testament documents. And so it has come down to *us*, in the four Gospels, the Acts, the nine Christian Church Epistles, the four Pastoral Epistles, and the nine Hebrew Christian Epistles. *All* in these twenty-seven oracles is the "Deposit", the "Glorious Gospel". *Nothing* outside them is a part of the "Deposit". These twenty-seven New Covenant testimonies we must "guard". In them is the pure Gospel, which we must declare and defend. This sacred, vital "Deposit" we must guard against the smothering deceptions of Romanism; against the ravening teeth of Modernism or Rationalism; and against the plausible misinterpretations of heretical sects. God keep us faithful to our trust!

"Honour all men. Love the brotherhood. Fear God. Honour the king."—1 Peter 2 : 17.

HERE are four human obligations which at once commend themselves to the Christian conscience. The first two belong together. The second two, also, should always be kept together.

Take the first: "*Honour all men.*" A Christian believer will honour all men in a way which no others can. That is easily explainable. We Christians recognize the stamp of the Creator upon all men, even upon the brow of the demoralised savage. Despite the degradation caused by sin and superstition and Satanic oppression, we believe that fundamentally, in his mental and moral nature, man is made in the image and likeness of God (Gen. 1 : 26). No one who believes the usual evolutionary theory as to the origin of species can hold an equal view of human dignity. Furthermore, we Christians also believe that the incarnate God Himself died on Calvary for all men, as Sin-bearer and Saviour. That puts the highest of all values upon each individual human being. How then can we do other than "honour all men"?

Yet while we Christians "honour all men" it is understandable that in a special sense we should "*love the brotherhood*". Not only are all of us Christian brethren washed from our guilt by the same precious blood, but we are all "born anew" by the same regenerating Holy Spirit. We Christians are not members merely of a "society", or even of a "church"; we are all members of one *family*. There is not a different regenerating spirit in each of us, but the one, same, Holy Spirit, who has given to each of us our new spiritual nature. That is why (whatever subsidiary denominational differences there may be) all of us Christian believers are conscious of a family *affinity* between us. We know each other when we meet. We have the same family nature, disposition, atmosphere, and characteristics. Beneath all outward and superficial diversity of denomination, there is a basic, vital, sympathetic, spiritual unity. When we are in each other's company we know by a deep, heart-to-heart reciprocity that we are "all one in Christ", and that although we are still "*in* the world" we are no longer "*of* the world".

Our Lord Jesus said, "By this shall all men know that ye are my disciples, if ye have love one to another." When we allow the new nature in us to have its way, we *do* love one another, and delight in each other, and sympathize with each other. As members of the Christian "brotherhood" we should guard against those unchristlike attitudes and contentions which disrupt our family fellowship. Though we hold our distinctive views *firmly*, we should never hold them *fiercely*! However grown up we may feel, we are spiritually juvenile when we make cruel rifts in our fellowship, and speak with asperity about each other, on such non-fundamental questions as to whether the Church will go through the so-called "great tribulation" or not. Far more important than any such question is that we should "love the brotherhood". Let us pray daily that we may *do* this. In the first century of our Christian era, the thing which most astonished the enemies of the new faith was the *love* which Christians bore toward each other. Dear Lord, may *we* never allow differences of opinions to degenerate into lack of Christian love.

Greater and Lesser

"Fear God. Honour the king."—1 Peter 2: 17.

THESE two go together. They should always be kept together. What God hath joined, let no man put asunder, for patriotism apart from godliness is a root of many evils. There is a false patriotism arising from racial pride or selfishness; and there is a true patriotism grounded in God's wisdom, which seeks supremely the moral and spiritual wellbeing of one's country. There is a nationalism which is competitive, jealous, fierce, intolerant of others; and there can be a nationalism which is godly, co-operative and contributory to the good of all. The reason why Communism so quickly debased itself into rabid Bolshevism and Russianism was that it is godless. Any idealism which there may originally have been in Communism has long ago given place to scheming Russian imperialism, as all the world knows. There can be no such thing as genuine Communism apart from godliness. One of the most misery-inflicting ironies of our twentieth century is, that so-called "Communism" has proved the most Judas-like plunderer of neighbour-nations ever known. Any kind of patriotism, nationalism, or political loyalty divorced from godliness is a bane and not a blessing.

"Fear God" is linked with "Honour the king" because the fear of God is the one sure safeguard against giving the *wrong* kind of honour to an earthly ruler or leader. No man should ever behave to an earthly king, ruler, dictator, council, president, or civil power, in any way which violates conscience toward God; and no prayerful Christian ever will; he will suffer or even die first. In Europe, during recent times, many hundreds of faithful Christian ministers have been banished to cruel concentration camps and torturous deaths, not because of refusing respect to proper authority, but for refusal to yield a compulsory servitude which compromised conscience toward God. Those nations which banished or murdered them have lived to learn that those *others* who pay homage, either voluntarily or compulsorily at the expense of conscience, *never* add to the real strength of a throne or nation or cause.

Again, "Fear God" is joined to "Honour the king" because godliness alone can supply the true *motive* for patriotism. The Christian man, because he has an earnest devotedness to God, will also have a genuine respect for earthly rulers, knowing that they hold their places only by divine appointment or permission. Even if he cannot always respect the man who fills the office, he will always honour the office which holds the man. When the apostle Peter wrote, "Fear God" and "Honour the king", the man on the throne was Nero, one of the vilest monsters who ever disgraced the crown and sceptre. Those early Jewish Christians were not the only ones who have been so placed. We have heard of a brave old philosopher who once said to his royal master, "As king I adore thee; as man I abhor thee."

As Christians we should always render special loyalty to *upright and godly rulers*, both in the ballot box and in all our behaviour. Godliness never makes violent reactionaries against proper law and order. Of all patriotic, upright citizens, Christians should be the best. Did not our Lord Jesus Himself say, "Render therefore unto Caesar the things which are Caesar's, and unto God the things that are God's"?

The Supreme Possession

"Lay hold on eternal life."—1 Tim. 6: 12.

So wrote Paul to Timothy. Never was sounded advice given by an older man to a younger. Paul knew how glamorous this world can be to a young man. In contrast with the Cains and Nimrods and Lots and Esaus who live only for the life that now is, Paul would have Timothy set his mind on the life eternal. In contrast with the ephemeral pursuits and butterfly life of the worldling, he would have his young friend live for the true and permanent. He says, in effect, "Don't live for the mere *seeming*; lay hold on the *real*."

To "lay hold on eternal life", as our text urges, is in reality laying hold on Christ Himself, for He *is* the eternal life. That is why John speaks of Him as "that Eternal Life which was with the Father and was manifested to us". That is why it is also written, "He that hath the *Son* hath the *life*; he that hath *not* the Son of God hath *not* the life" (1 Jn. 5: 12).

How *urgent*, therefore, it is to "lay hold" on Him! It is well worth letting go all else. High or low, rich or poor, men and women who have never laid hold on Him, the Saviour and the Life, are poverty-stricken paupers. Thousands of them do not think so, but that only makes them the more to be commiserated. In their unregenerate obfuscation they imagine themselves, like the Laodiceans, to be "rich and increased with goods and to have need of nothing". They are too impervious to perceive that they are "wretched and miserable and poor and blind and naked". Sooner or later, when heavy trouble comes, or death stares them in the face, they discover the falsity of their imagined self-sufficiency; or even if they never awaken to their tragic plight in this present life, they lift up their eyes in hades, at last, in destitution beyond remedy.

Laying hold is a metaphor of *faith*. We are to "lay hold" upon Him as a man lays hold on suddenly discovered treasure; or as a man dying of thirst lays hold upon the flask of water which his rescuers bring; or as the drowning man lays hold upon the life-line; or as the ivy lays hold upon the great trunk of the oak tree; or even as the limpet tenaciously lays hold upon rocks or timbers. We are to "lay hold" upon Him by laying hold of His *promise* in the Gospel: "He that believeth on the Son hath everlasting life" (Jn. 3: 36). "Him that cometh to Me, I will in no wise cast out" (Jn. 6: 37); many of us have already laid hold upon Him. We know Whom we have believed. But are we now addressing someone still unsaved? Oh, friend, make haste to "lay hold"! Among the millions who know the Gospel yet remain unsaved, the big majority are those who *want* to "lay hold" on the Saviour, but will not "*let go*" the world. In the end they lose both.

Many people remain unsaved because *faith alone* as the means seems too small or too simple. It is much more impressive to be saved by sacraments, religious merit, laudable character, or union with some imposing church. Years ago a small boat capsized not far above the Niagara Falls. Two men were left struggling against the strong, downward current. A thin rope was flung out, and both managed to grasp it. Then a large log came floating by, and one man let go the rope to grab the log—it looked so much more substantial. Soon log and man were swept over the Falls; but the man who clung to the rope was saved. It is that thin rope of faith which saves; you hold at *this* end, the Saviour pulls at the *other*.

Reclaimed from Satan

"And that they may recover themselves out of the snare of the devil, who are taken captive by him at his will."—2 Tim. 2 : 26.

THIS verse is a halting-point for any thoughtful reader. It indicates that souls ensnared by Satan may be recaptured for the Lord. Unfortunately, that is not easily perceivable in our Authorised Version translation. Indeed, there is a curious contradictoriness about the A.V. rendering; for how could such ensnared souls "recover *themselves*" from Satan, if as the verse later says, they are "taken captive by him" like mere play-things "*at his will*"? That cannot be the meaning, even though the construction in the Greek original is admittedly awkward.

The interpretation swings on that pronoun, "him", in the final clause: "taken captive by *him* at his will". Does that "him" refer to Satan at all? Not if we interpret it in strict keeping with the context. This second chapter is all about aspects of the pastoral vocation. In verse 3 the man of God is a *soldier*. In verse 5 he is an *athlete*. In verse 6 he is a *husbandman*. In verse 15 he is a *workman*. In verse 24 he is a *bondman*. Going with these different metaphors are different aspects of the pastor's ministry. The central thought all through is the "man of God" and his doings.

Look carefully, now, at those last three verses (24–26). In the Greek they are one continuous sentence. The subject is "the servant of the Lord" (24). He is to be "gentle to all, apt to teach, patient; in meekness *instructing* those who oppose" (25) so that by this "instructing" from *him* (i.e. from the Lord's servant) they may "recover from the snare of the devil, having been captured alive by *him* (i.e. by the Lord's servant) unto His (God's) will". That is undoubtedly the force of the text. The Revised Version therefore renders it: "Having been taken captive *by the Lord's servant* unto the will of God." It is startling, illuminating, challenging. Satan's holds may be raided. Ensnared souls may be "taken alive" (as the Greek word means: see Luke 5 : 10) and recaptured from the deceitful enemy! The means of recapture is sound "*instruction*" from the Word.

One of the saddest features of Protestant Christendom today is the wide breakdown in teaching the Word. Instead of constructive indoctrination, in thousands of our denominational churches there is a meagre fifteen or twenty minute discourse on some moral or social or other topic of current interest. This is no petty criticism on our part, but a sincere complaint with a sob in it. The breakdown in sound teaching of the Bible leaves our people the easier prey of error, and in recent years hundreds of thousands have been beguiled away by specious counterfeits. The call to each of us is so to know our Bible that we can "instruct" others. Despite rebuffs from "them that oppose", our words will be used of the Holy Spirit to "recover" others from Satan's snare.

Modern unitarian cults like Christian Science, or Jehovah's Witnesses, do their deadliest proselytizing among persons already religiously connected who know little of the Bible. Those who best know their New Testament are least prone to these new heresies. All of us who know the truth of Salvation according to the New Testament should take pains to "instruct", as opportunity allows, those who are ensnared. Especially should we try to show them the Scripture teaching as to the deity of Christ, and the simplicity of salvation by faith.

"They may recover themselves out of the snare of the devil, having been taken captive by the Lord's servant unto the will of God." —2 Tim. 2 : 26 (Eng. R.V.).

NOTICE that Satan, having first ensnared men from the truth, incites them to "*oppose*" it (verse 25) lest "God may peradventure give unto them repentance to the *acknowledging* of the truth" (25). They commit themselves to a position, or rather to an *opposition*, and then are too proud to admit fault or to retract. Satan uses all manner of strategems to turn souls from the truth: a sieve to "sift" them (Luke 22: 31), "devices" to trick them (2 Cor. 2: 11), "weeds" to "choke" them (Matt. 13: 22), "wiles" to intrigue them (Eph. 6: 11), the roaring of a lion to terrify them (1 Peter 5: 8), the disguise of an angel to deceive them (2 Cor. 11 : 14) and "snares" to entangle them (as in our text).

What is the entanglement indicated in our text? It is entanglement, not in moral evil, but in doctrinal *error*; not of those who never knew the truth, but rather those who have known it and then been tricked into false theories. This is implied in that their desired "recovery" is "repentance to the acknowledging of *the truth*" (25). That word, "recover", is remarkable. Literally, the clause is, "That they may *return to soberness*." A strange intoxication often goes with error. That is probably because it has the excitement of subtle extremism, the lure of seeming novelty, or some pretended superiority of insight.

How easily Satan seems to ensnare people by such errors! One Sunday evening I was preaching on Revelation 3: 20. As I ended my message, I asked, "Who, then, will say 'I will' to Jesus?" Suddenly, from away back under the gallery, a stentorian voice shouted, "I will!" It came like an electric shock on the crowded congregation, but the dear shouter was not aware of committing an impropriety. He was a Communist. He had never been in a church before. He had sneaked in simply because of something he had heard at our open-air meeting. That night he professed conversion, and rejoiced in Jesus. Thereafter, he was at all our services. His presence was a tonic, for he was a bonny man, with a florid, beaming face, and bubbling over with his newfound joy. Later, however, his attendance became irregular. Then, he had an obsession. He had been ensnared by the "Conditional Immortality" group, and was headily inebriated by their theories. A few years later I saw him being wheeled about as a chronic invalid, and having lost his faith altogether. His is a typical case.

There is a sobriety about the *true* Christian faith. We should try to guard young converts against parasite movements which have no real Gospel for the unconverted, but live by preying on those who have already become spiritually minded. Most evangelical book-stores have good publications exposing the falacies of modern extremisms and heterodoxies. We should know them and prayerfully use them. Who knows how many we may rescue thereby from Satan's snares? One of the notable features about the new heresies is their emphasis on propagation by *literature*. Should we not emulate them, and by the same means *counteract* them? We never know what recaptures we may make by handing a well-written booklet to some misguided friend.

Technique of Recapture

"And recover themselves out of the snare of the devil, having been taken captive by the Lord's servant unto the will of God."
—2 Tim. 2 : 26 (Eng. R.V.).

A FENCE at the top of the precipice is far better than an ambulance at the bottom of it. Those of us who are older and more firmly grounded in "the faith once for all delivered to the saints" should always be ready and patiently waiting to guard younger believers from the clever heresies and siren-voiced false Gospels of our day. We should seek to know well the teachings of the Bible, and we should take the trouble to read what able evangelical Bible scholars have written in clarification of the true faith against bewitching modern perversions of it.

But what of those who have already become ensnared into error? Our text speaks about the possibility of their being recaptured "by the Lord's servant". Each one of us may be considered as the Lord's servant in this connection. What then is to be our technique of recapture? Seven requirements are advised in the context: two "don'ts", and five "*do's*".

First, avoid "foolish questions" which get nowhere (23). Keep to the main things. Second, do not "strive", or argue contentiously (24). Better lose our logic than our temper; or we may win an argument but lose a soul. Third, we must be "gentle unto all" (24), even to those who "oppose" or insult us. Often a greater argument than what we say is how we bear being differed from. Fourth, we must be "apt to teach" (24)—which, remember, does not mean merely apt to *talk*! We must be prepared by having carefully compared the teachings of the Word on the subject. This takes time, but it becomes the decisive weapon. Fifth, we must be "patient" (24), forbearing with those who are too bewitched or too headstrong to be easily persuaded by us. Sixth, we must exhibit "meekness" (25). Any semblance of pride in *us* will beget prejudice in *them*. Seventh, there must be a real "instructing" of them from the Word (25), not just a pressing of human opinions upon them.

These constitute our apparatus or technique, according to the context. Our weapon is the Word; but the vital handling of it is in the spirit we show, and the way we behave. Not always, perhaps, is there success; but that is the *way* of success. All too often the approach to those who have become ensnared into error is uninformed and contentious. If with compassionate concern we were to follow the foregoing sevenfold direction, immersing it all in prayer, then the Holy Spirit would have His opportunity through us, and what numerous recaptures for the Lord there might be!

Often I have heard, "Oh, Christians must not argue. You never win souls by arguing." To my own mind, *that* attitude is a pious blunder. C. H. Spurgeon was truer: "No man can be a Christian nowadays without being a controversialist." What are Paul's epistles but arguments? Argument is not argumentativeness! Argument cannot regenerate, but it can remove obstacles. "Instructing" from the Word must often *include* argument. What we need with it is a loving spirit and prayerful dependence on the Holy Spirit. No, do not be put off with the trite old gasp, "Oh, Christians must not argue!" Like Paul, we must be "set for the defence of the Gospel" (Phil. 1: 17). Argument need not be heated; it can be punctuated with courteous smiles—or sympathetic tears.

"Therefore, if any man be in Christ, he is a new creature; old things are passed away; behold, all things are become new."—2 Cor. 5: 17.

To an unconverted person these words might seem like an enthusiastic exaggeration, but those of us who have become regenerated through saving union with Christ can bear witness that there is no exaggeration at all. In a spiritual sense, we are new-created. The old is gone. All is new. If we are asked *how and why* this transforming change-over has come about, we call attention to the first word in our text, the "Therefore", which links the text with its explanatory context.

What, then, does the context tell us? To begin with, we find the "how and why" of this wonderful transition *theologically*. It has come about through union with Christ in His death and resurrection. We are here told four things about the death of Christ. First, verse 14 says, "One died for all", which means that Christ died *representatively*. In His real human being He represented the whole race of Adamic humanity. Second, the Greek preposition translated "for" has the meaning "instead of"; so Christ also died *substitutionarily*. He not only represented all; He took the place of each. Third, and perhaps most arresting of all, we are told that in a judicial sense Christ died *all-inclusively*; for verse 14 says, "If One died for all, then all died in Him" (see R.V.).

In a judicial sense the whole Adam race died when Christ died. "*All* died in Him!" The divine purpose in Christ was not the repairing or reforming of the humanity which had fallen in the first Adam, but the bringing in of a re-generation or new humanity in Christ. The old humanity in the first Adam was no longer on trial or under probation; it had been variously tested and had proved incurably corrupt, sinful, guilty. At Calvary, in a judicial sense, it was put away. "All died in Him."

Fourth, He died *anticipatively*. His crucifixion (which judicially put away the old) anticipated His resurrection (which now originated the new). That is why verse 15 says, "He died for all, that they which live should no longer live unto themselves, but unto Him who died for them *and rose again*." Having now discarded the gross flesh-and-blood body which made Him part of the old Adam creation, He has risen in a still real but superior humanhood, as the Progenitor of a re-creation, a new humanity, "the sons of God". In His glorified manhood and infinite godhead He now sits on the throne of supreme sovereignty, and at the same time re-generatingly communicates Himself to all who now become savingly united to Him. "Therefore" (as our text says) "if any man be in Christ, he is a new creature . . ." The Greek word translated "creature" is *ktisis*, which really means "creation". It is better to read the text: "Therefore, if any man be in Christ, *there is the new creation* . . ." Yes, indeed, *there* is the new "creation", seen in the new "creature". "Old things are passed away; behold, *all things are become new*." Bless the Lord, O my soul! If this is conversion, what a miracle has happened within me!

A wonderful myst'ry has happened in me,
For after long darkness my soul can now see!
My Saviour has banished my death and my night!
My grave has been opened! I live in new light!

New Creatures

"Therefore, if any man be in Christ, he is a new creature; old things are passed away; behold all things are become new."—2 Cor. 5: 17.

THIS is true not only theologically, but *experientially*. All of us who are truly Christ's can give genuine testimony from individual experience that we are "new creatures"; that "old things are passed away", and that "all things are become new".

We have a new spiritual *life* with a Christward pulling-power. We have a new spiritual *nature*, with new faculties of spiritual seeing and hearing and knowing. We have new spiritual *desires*, begotten in us by a fundamental intervention in our personalities. We have a new standing before God, and live in a new fellowship with Him. We have a new relationship toward the Adamic human race; for although bodily we are still members of the old humanity, yet spiritually we are lifted out of it and above it.

Everything now has a new *centre* for us; and that new centre is the Lord Jesus Christ; not the Jesus of history, as such, sublime and indispensable though He is; but the same Jesus (the same yet no longer the same) who is now the Christ of resurrection and ascension; the Christ who now transcends the earthly and temporal; the Christ of the infinities and eternities; the Christ who is lifted to the throne of heaven as the God-appointed Centre of the new creation. As verse 16 says, "Even though we have known Christ after the flesh, yet now we know Him so no more" (E.R.V.).

In this wonderful Christ is the re-generation, the new humanity, the new creation. We view everything now in relation to Him. We do not ask any more what a man is in relation to the old humanity which is already judicially repudiated, and is quickly passing. We do not ask whether he is rich or poor, learned or unlearned, high-born or low, white or any other colour; but is he in regenerating resurrection-union with the risen Christ of the new humanity which is destined to eternal glory?

Yes, indeed, "If any man be in Christ . . . *old things are passed away*"; old ways of viewing things; old ways of estimating people; old standards of value; old ideas of pleasure; old fascinations with things merely material; old earth-bound horizons; old hates, loves, habits, fetters, misunderstandings, prejudices, blindness, darkness and spiritual death. "Old things are passed away." "The darkness is past, and the true light now shineth" (1 Jn. 2: 8). "One thing I know, that, whereas I was blind, now I see" (Jn. 9: 25).

Oh, there is a music in our text which never tires the ears of those who know its meaning. "Wherefore, if any man be in Christ, he is [or, there is] a new creation; old things are passed away; behold, *all things are become new*." The most wonderful thing of all is that we ourselves have become new. We are not self-deceived; the change is too deep and strong and lasting; and we know that the transition-point was our union with Christ when we accepted Him as Saviour.

The outward evidence of this inward miracle is *the way we live*. May we never forget! "How were you converted?" asked a famous preacher. "Strangely enough," replied the applicant, "I was converted in my sleep." "Certainly unusual," commented the preacher; "but we had better see how you behave *when you are awake*."

"Old things are passed away; behold, all things are become new."—2 Cor. 5 : 17.

A FRIEND of mine was brought up in an Irish coastal town which has a busy little port and fishing fleet. When he was a tiny boy his mother often took him along the sea-front, where his special heroes were the coastguards with their big telescopes. His mother bought him a little telescope of his own; then, when the coastguard lifted up his big telescope to look out over the sea, little Arthur would stand by and look through *his* telescope. One day, as he did this, he piped out, "No ships in sight, Mummie". The coastguard bent down and said, "Little man, look through *my* telescope." Young Arthur did so, and then, "Ooh, Mummie, ships! . . . ships! . . . everywhere!" That big telescope transformed everything. So it is, but far more so, with us who have become "new creatures" in Christ. We have seen a new world of spiritual realities which we never saw before through our little telescopes of human reason. "All things are become new!"

We have a new *Bible*. Some of us thought we believed it before, but our supposed believing was like the groping of a blind man in a palace, sensing its beauty but not seeing it. Others of us did *not* believe it before; but now we cannot *help* believing it, for it has "come alive". Grimshaw of Haworth, one of the stars of the early Methodist days in England, was already an ordained minister when he became converted to Christ. The change was both spiritually and intellectually revolutionary. He said that "if God had drawn up the Bible to heaven, and sent him down another, it could not have been newer."

We have a new *Gospel*. The old, old story has become the new, new wonder. The ever-true is the ever-new. It is no longer an oft-repeated tale, too familiar to startle us; it lives and thrills and glows and flames, and perpetually surprises us.

We have a new *church*; no longer a building, a congregation, an organisation, though these have their place; but something seen with *inward* eyes, compared with which the most magnificent cathedral is paltry; something which transcends all visible organisation, and ignores all denominational barriers; something so spiritual that to earth-bound eyes it seems unreal, yet so real to *us* that in comparison all the merely material and visible now seems *un*real. It is the *spiritual* Zion, the "church of the Firstborn" who are "written in heaven"; the bloodwashed, twice-born, Spirit-sealed members of the mystic body and bride and temple of God's dear Son.

We have a new *outlook on life*. We see God in everything, either directly guiding or permissively overruling for our good. There may be many incidents, but there are no accidents. Everything tingles with new significance.

We have a new view of the *Beyond*. As a man leans forward and holds a big, bright lamp in a dark, mysterious room, so our risen Lord has gone before and suddenly lit up the Beyond for us. John Wesley said, "Our people die well." Yes, "in Christ" we even *die* well. "Behold, all things are become new!"

Discipleship Stipulations

"Then said Jesus unto His disciples: If any man will come after Me, let him deny himself, and take up his cross, and follow Me."—Matt. 16: 24.

It can never be said too often that the salvation of our souls is by grace alone on God's part, and by faith alone on ours. Once for all, on the Cross, the incarnate Son of God made atonement for human sin. Once for all He rose from the grave, as our ever-living Saviour. When in simple but sincere trust I open my heart to receive the Saviour He comes in, and thereby I become eternally saved.

But, being thus saved, I am meant to become a *disciple* of Jesus; and such discipleship is far from easy to our human nature in its present condition, in "this present evil world". Yet we dare not argue: "Well, I am eternally saved in Christ, so I need not bother about being His disciple." No, it is by being His disciples that we *prove* ourselves saved. All who have renounced sin and self-righteousness, for the sake of possessing Jesus, *want* to be His disciples. But they all find discipleship hard, because, as the word indicates, it means *discipline.* In today's text our Lord plainly apprises us that discipleship means (1) following Him, (2) self-denial, (3) cross-bearing. This should pull us up sharply, in the light of average Christian profession today.

There is a tendency nowadays to *relax* discipleship. In many Christian sanctuaries the motto is, "Brief, bright, and brotherly." There are sermonettes of fifteen minutes, and Christianettes whose religion costs them nothing but the collection. If there is a meeting between Sundays it is the "Weekly Happy Hour", or the "Pleasant Social Circle", or some other beautifully innocuous rendezvous. The minister must never preach on final retribution, or the "wrath to come". Great doctrines such as free grace, election, predestination, regeneration, sanctification, must all be sacrificed to brevity and brightness, while hungry souls starve for lack of Biblical nourishment. In place of virile Christian challenge there is a laxity which accommodates discipleship to anybody's whims. How often even the more serious among us, when we are inviting outsiders, put the emphasis on, "Oh, you'll have a good time; our church is so comfortable"! Why, that is just the peril with most of us today—a "*comfortable*" religion!

There is *no relaxing* of the conditions according to Christ. *He* never beguiled anybody by a false appeal (Matt. 10: 37–39 etc.). Garibaldi, setting out to liberate Italy, saw some young men at a street corner, and summoned them to enlist. "What do you offer?" they asked. "Offer!" replied Garibaldi; "I offer you hardship, hunger, rags, thirst, sleepless nights, footsores in long marches, privations innumerable, and victory in the noblest cause which ever asked you." Our Lord Jesus is just as clear, as He calls us to self-discipline in a far higher cause (Mark 10: 21, Luke 9: 57–62).

Is there not serious reason, then, to *reconsider* the conditions of Christian discipleship? See what Jesus says about His own words: Matthew 7: 24–27. If so important, what are they? See Matthew 5: 29, 30, 38–42, 44, 6: 19, 20, 7: 12. A man once said to me, "I don't need your church; my religion is the Sermon on the Mount." I asked him, "Do you *live* it?" That is the test.

"To me to live is Christ; and to die is gain."—Phil. 1:21.

AMONG the generality of people, death is considered the greatest of all losses. That is not to be wondered at. The merely natural man lives only for this earth and this life. His pursuits and pleasures and possessions are all things of this present world. At death he must leave them *all*. He has invested nothing in the life beyond. Even if he believes in a life beyond, his ideas of it are vague, and he dies unprepared for it. The last few flickers of his earthly pleasures are smothered in a comfortless grave.

But for the Christian, "to die is *gain*". This is no childish credulity. It is true—unless the Christian faith as a whole is spurious. It is a part of that total Christian truth which is based on irrefutable facts, and guaranteed by supernaturally attested revelation. In 1 Corinthians 3: 21–23, where Paul makes an inventory of the Christian's assets, it is observable that he includes death as one of them.

"To die is gain." This is not an isolated affirmation. It belongs to a context which amplifies it. Notice particularly verse 23: "For I am in a strait betwixt two; having a desire to depart and to be with Christ, which is far better . . ." Ah, *that* is the central fact which makes death gain to the Christian: to depart from this life is to be "with Christ". All other aspects of the gain are subsidiary to that, and are included in it.

"To die is gain" because it means to be "with Christ *consciously*. Away with the thought that at death the soul of the believer passes into stark unconsciousness until the second coming of Christ! What possible "gain" could it have been for Paul to leave his apostolic service for Christ, his world-wide evangelism, his saving of souls, his founding of churches, his fellowship with the brethren, and his heart-to-heart fellowship with Christ, to lie in the black-out of stark oblivion for some long, indeterminate duration? Paul would never have said, "To die is gain", if that had been his expectation! At one time or another we have examined the several arguments of the soul-sleep theorists. They are subtle and tenuous as a spider's web—and as easily broken. For instance, we have seen it argued that in this first chapter of Philippians Paul had *three* choices in mind: (1) "To depart", i.e. from the body into soul-sleep; (2) "And to be with Christ", i.e. at our Lord's eventual return; (3) "nevertheless to abide in the flesh is more needful". But unfortunately for the soul-sleep exegesis, and much to our own comfort, Paul says, "I am in a strait betwixt *two*"—not three!

"To die is gain", for besides being with Christ consciously, it means to be with Him *in heaven*, in that "third heaven" which is "Paradise", and the "Father's house"; where shadows never come, and genial summer never ends; where the roses never fade, and the fruits never decay; where disease never invades and death never divides; where there are no tears and no goodbyes; where there is no sin and no sorrow; no temptation and not a breath of impurity; where all is light and love and sinless ecstasy.

"To die is gain", for besides being consciously with Christ in heaven, it means *release* from earthly troubles; it means *re-union* with other Christian loved ones over yonder; it means *reward* for present service rendered to our Master; and it means *realisation* of all our highest, truest, dearest longings.

A Paradox of the Spiritual Life

"Lest I should be exalted above measure...."—2 Cor. 12: 7.

WEYMOUTH'S rendering of Paul's words in 2 Corinthians 12: 7–9 is: "Lest I should be over-elated there has been sent to me, like the agony of impalement, Satan's angel dealing blow after blow, lest I should be over-elated. Three times have I besought the Lord to rid me of him; but His reply has been 'My grace suffices for you, for (My) power matures in weakness.'"

What depth of agony is here! Think, too, how long-drawn-out it was. See how the chapter begins: "Fourteen years ago . . . caught up to Paradise . . . abundance of revelations . . . lest I should be exalted above measure . . . there was given me a thorn . . ." Fourteen years of long-drawn crucifixion and Satanic buffeting! What is more, it seemed as though the thing must go dragging on to the end of life! "Who is sufficient for these things?" Paul himself tells us.

The risen Lord said to him: "My strength is made perfect in (thy) weakness." The pronoun "My" does not come in some of the manuscripts, but the sense of the passage requires it as clearly as the glory of noonday requires the sun. It is "*My* strength"—the strength of *Jesus*, which is to find its opportunity in Paul's weakness. "*My strength*"—not so much that solitary might which belongs to Christ by original right as the Son of God, as, rather, that saving strength which He Himself acquired when, in the days of His flesh, He laboured and suffered and struggled and bled to become our Saviour. *That* strength is infused into the heart and life of the believer. He who has victoriously undergone all our human experiences shares *His* victory with *us*.

Christ does not strengthen us by a periodic succession of miracles, but by a continuous communication of Himself to us through the Holy Spirit. It is thus that the strength of Christ finds its opportunities in our weakness.

When we are self-sufficient there is no scope for the imparted strength of Christ; but when some such agony as Paul's plunges us into the consciousness of utter destitution and we fling ourselves in helpless prostration at the feet of Christ, then, in our very extremity, Christ finds His opportunity. His strength then has its perfect work within us; and upon the ruins of our self-sufficiency we rise to new life and victory in Christ! It was thus that Paul himself learned the secret of strength in weakness. It was thus that bewildering repulse was turned into riotous triumph, and the apostle pressed forward singing, "Most gladly therefore will I rather glory in my weaknesses, that the power of Christ may rest upon me. Therefore I take pleasure in weaknesses, in reproaches, in necessities, in persecutions, in distresses, for Christ's sake; for when I am weak, then am I strong".

Christian, mark well this double paradox of the spiritual life; in ourselves we are weak even where we are stong; in Christ we are strong even where we are weak. Self-sufficiency is *in*sufficiency. Christ-sufficiency is *all*-sufficiency.

Oh, to be saved from myself, dear Lord;
  Oh, to be lost in Thee!
Oh, that it may be no more "I",
  But Christ who lives in me!

"Who being in the form of God thought it not robbery to be equal with God."—Phil. 2 : 6.

As we read these words we are atmosphered in infinite mystery. We read of One who, "being in the form of God", became in "the likeness of men". That word, "form", here cannot mean shape, for shape belongs to material things, whereas God is purely spiritual. It must mean that He was *like* God; and He could only be so by being of *identical nature.* A man can only be truly like a man by actually being a man. The reason why two human beings are fundamentally alike is that they have the same kind of nature. Our Lord's true likeness with the Father involves His own deity; and this is endorsed by the added word that He "thought it not robbery (i.e. something to be graspingly retained) to be *equal* with God". The stupendous mystery is that this glorious One who was in the "form" of God, and "equal" with God, and therefore absolutely divine, becomes Man.

This fathomless mystery is the most transcendent revelation of the Gospel. The Architect of the Universe walks to me out of His infinity and invisibility, in human form. He looks on me through human eyes; beckons to me with human hands; feels for me with human emotions. Oh, sacred marvel of Bethlehem, Nazareth and Calvary! Before I see God in Jesus, He is unknowably distant in His super-stellar transcendence. He is incomprehensible in His immensity. But in Jesus I see Him; recognise Him; understand Him; and though I still fear Him, I like Him; I *love* Him; I can utterly *trust* Him, and *possess* Him!

This incarnation of God in Christ once for all interprets the idea of a Supreme Being which is found universally in our human constitution. Among the dusky savages of the tropics; among the Laplanders of the frozen arctics; everywhere you find this innate idea of God. Where did it come from? It seems unthinkable that it could be so racially persistent if there were no corresponding Reality. How then can the great Reality behind this human idea of God be expressed to me? All great ideas are elusive until they become expressed in some concrete form. Beauty is a mere abstraction until expressed in some lovely flower. Music is a mere fantasy until some instrument gives it speech. Art is ethereal until embodied in picture or sculpture. Even the idea of love is without significance until it becomes livingly aflame in some holy attachment, or in some life which reveals its reality. Similarly, the idea of God needs an interpretation which will make it realistic to me; and Jesus is the answer (Jn. 1 : 18).

How different it was to *pray* before Jesus came. What picture of God would men try to have as they prayed? They could but think of some awesome, incomprehensible Super-Being utterly beyond all power of human imagination. How different was it with the disciples after our Lord's ascension! When *they* prayed together during those ten days preceding Pentecost, no longer was heaven an indecipherable infinity; their thoughts found focus in the radiant figure of the ascended God-Man.

Whenever we think on this magnificent mystery, are we not "lost in wonder, love, and praise"? Let us remember amid it all that He who was in "the form of God" yet became in "the likeness of men" is here lifted up as the supreme example of self-sacrifice. "Let this mind be in you . . ."

The Message for the Hour

"Emmanuel" . . . "Christ" . . . "Jesus."—Matt. 1 : 23, 16, 21.

THE European nations passed from the nineteenth to the twentieth century inebriated with the exuberance of man-made philosophies, and spell-bound under the wand of that new fairy-godmother, "Science". The watchword was "Upward and Onward", to the utopia which was at last visibly flashing ahead, the consummation which would crown and glorify the evolution of our human species.

But the fond dreams of the nineteenth century about the "march of civilization", and the gradual "extinction of the ape and the tiger" thereby, have dissolved in a shocking eye-opening during this twentieth century. World wars, gluttonous nationalisms, and tyrannical totalitarianisms have exposed a demoniacal sadism and a worse-than-bestial savagery in twentieth-century human nature which out-shame anything ever uncovered in the so-called "primitive barbarians" of antiquity! The "upward march" is now seen by the most casual observer to be a downward one, from whatever viewpoint it may be considered, whether political, moral, or religious. Man without God has once more proved himself a failure, and the ultimate salvation of the race by human brains alone has turned out to be nothing but a shimmering mirage.

All around us today there is disillusionment and unrest of soul. The splitting of the atom has not only unceremoniously introduced a new physical epoch, it has brought a new and intenser attitude of mind. Tomorrow is a bigger doubt than ever. The eleventh-hour clarion to *us*, the Christian minority, is as never before to lift up the Lord Jesus Christ as "*EMMANUEL*", the one complete answer to man's deepest need.

Yes, our Lord Jesus is "Emmanuel", but this first chapter of Matthew also calls Him the *CHRIST*. See verse 16 again: "And Jacob begat Joseph, the husband of Mary, of whom was born Jesus which is called the Christ." That title, "Christ" (Greek: *Christos*), is, of course, the New Testament correspondent of the Old Testament "Messiah" (Hebrew: *Mashiyach*), and both mean "The Anointed One". In Old Testament times there were three classes of public servants who were the subjects of special anointing: the prophet, the priest, the king. Hebrew prophecy foretells of a Messiah who should somehow be all three in one.

In the four Gospels He is the anointed *Prophet*, preaching *to* the people. In the Acts and the Epistles He is the ascended *Priest*, interceding *for* the people. In the Book of Revelation He is the returned *King* reigning *over* the people.

Some golden daybreak in the near future He will break in upon our world again, in overwhelming splendour as World-Emperor, but meanwhile, besides being "Emmanuel" and "Christ", He is "*JESUS*". See verse 21 again: "Thou shalt call His name JESUS, for He shall save His people from their sins." This is best of all. He who is the embodiment of the Deity visibly, and the fulfilment of prophecy historically, is the Saviour of men morally and spiritually and eternally. This is the message for the hour; not the evolution of man, but the incarnation of God; not some pseudo-deliverance by human brains, but real salvation by divine grace; not some wistful "extinction of the ape and the tiger" in man, but a Saviour who really saves men from *sin*!

Looking Backward and Forward

"For unto us a Child is born, unto us a Son is given; and the government shall be upon His shoulder."—Isa. 9: 6.

THOSE inspired Old Testament prophets fore-wrote an amazing variety of guide-facts concerning the coming Messiah, but there was one major feature which they were not given either to know or to tell. Not one of them foresaw or even distantly guessed that there was to be a long time-gap of two thousand years between the fulfilment of the words, "Unto us a Child is born", and the later fulfilment of those other words, "The Government shall be upon His shoulder". Not one of them knew that there were to be *two* comings of the one Messiah. Not one of them perceived that there was to be this present "Church" age intervening between His shouldering of the Sin-bearer's cross and His shouldering of universal government. That was an undivulged secret of the divine counsels (Eph. 3: 5, 9, 1 Peter 1: 10, 11).

So, then, let us once again look back and *marvel at His incarnation.* One of the most fascinating lines of study in the Old Testament is the progressive development of prophecy concerning the Messiah-Saviour. Away back in Eden we find God promising that the "seed" of the woman should "bruise the head" of the serpent (Gen. 3: 15). Later, God says to Abraham, "In *thy* seed shall all the nations of the earth be blessed" (Gen. 22: 18). Next we find Jacob foretelling that "the sceptre shall not depart from *Judah* . . . until Shiloh come" (Gen. 49: 10). Again, later, God pledges to David, "I will set up thy seed after thee . . . and I will establish the throne of his kingdom for ever" (2 Sam. 7: 12, 13). Still later the prophet Micah declares: "Out of *thee* (Bethlehem of Judah) shall He come forth that is to be Ruler in Israel, whose goings forth have been from of old, from everlasting" (Mic. 5: 2). Then to this the inspired Isaiah adds: "Behold, the virgin shall conceive, and bear a Son, and shall call his name, Immanuel" (Isa. 7: 14). Thus it was revealed to Adam of which *race* He should come; then to Abraham of which *nation*; then to Jacob of which *tribe*; then to David of which *family*; then to Micah of which *place.* Then to Isaiah of which *woman.* And at last it happened: "Unto us a Child is born; unto us a Son is given"! That the eternal Son could *ever* be born into our humanity must remain sheer mystery; yet thus to be "born" was a necessity if He was to become our Kinsman-Redeemer. He was really "born". He became really human. In the mysterious transition, however, His eternal divinity did not, *could not,* sustain any depletion. His two natures, divine and human, were not intermixed to form a compound making Him neither fully God nor fully man, a sort of demi-god and super-man. No! There were two natures, but the personality was one. Well may we marvel.

But we must look forward and *marvel at His coming world-dominion.* Christmas is not only a commemoration; it is a prophecy! "The government shall be upon His shoulder"! It will really happen—and soon! Look again at the prophet's words. It is to be a real, visible throne and kingdom on earth—"*the throne of David.*" He is to reign in full title as "Wonderful Counsellor; Mighty God; Everlasting Father; Prince of Peace". The characteristics of His global empire are to be "peace", "judgment", "justice". And the perpetuity of His reign is to be "from henceforth even unto the ages"! Yes, it will really happen!

The Wondrous Expedition

"For the Son of Man is come to seek and to save that which was lost."—Luke 19: 10.

FROM time to time remarkable expeditions have been organised by different men in different places for different purposes; but the most wonderful expedition ever heard of was the coming of the very Son of God from heaven to this sin-blighted world, to seek and to save the lost. The spectacular expeditions of Xerxes and Alexander the Great; the expedition of Christopher Columbus to the mystery-land beyond the unpredictable Atlantic; the ill-fated Shackleton expedition to the Arctic Pole; the daring and elaborate expeditions to conquer the topmost battlements of Mount Everest—what are all of these, compared with that super-expedition of which the Gospel tells us?

Reflect again that it was none less than God the Son Himself who came from those sinless heights of heaven to this shadow-enveloped world below, came from the very throne of the universe to that depthless Cross of Calvary, to seek and to save us. Yes, it was really He; but read the text again: He calls Himself the "Son of Man". That is the title which He most frequently used of Himself, and it is immense with significance. Its appropriation by Him is at once His assumption of Messiahship, for it links back to the Daniel prophecies concerning that "Son of Man" who is the predestined crowned Head of imperishable world-empire (Dan. 7: 13, 14, etc.).

But now, see the *persons* to whom He came. When our Lord said, "For the Son of Man is come to seek and to save that which was lost", He was referring particularly to Zacchaeus, the newly converted taxman; but that word, "lost", describes the unregenerate condition of us all, as members of Adam's fallen race. The religious leaders of old-time Jewry, who sneered that Jesus was gone to be a friend of tax-men and vulgar transgressors, were just as truly "lost" themselves, had they but realised it, despite their elaborate religiosity. In fact, they were lost in deadlier degree, because their self-righteousness deadened them to their need of salvation, whereas the tax-agents and public degenerates whom they despised were stricken with sin-consciousness, and were therefore nearer to repentance.

There are millions of people today, most of them persons of religious upbringing, who scout the suggestion that they are lost. Such a notion stings their pride, and annoys them in their self-confident opinions. The reason they do not see their need of salvation is that they compare themselves with other human beings instead of viewing themselves in the light of God's Word. Sin is a matter of our condition before *God*. It is not a question whether we are more religious than other human sinners. The awful truth is that because sin has become innate in the race, the human heart itself has become *alienated* from God; and it is this which constitutes our lost condition. It is when sickness lays men low, or when emergencies face them with dire realities, or when the hour of death stalks them down, that they wake up in sudden consternation to their lost condition. What fools we are to ignore the Word of God!—for besides exposing our *malady* it also reveals the *remedy*, and besides showing us our *need* of salvation it also shows us the *way* of salvation.

"Lost"! Who? How?

"For the Son of Man is come to seek and to save that which was lost."—Luke 19: 10.

LET the breezy unconcern and jaunty sarcasms of Christ-rejecting worldlings be what they may, apart from Christ they are lost souls. That word "lost", usually excites pity or alarm or grief. Even a lost dog gains our ready pity. A lost child stirs us up to deep concern. If we hear that a ship has been lost with all on board, or that lives have been lost in a mine disaster, instantly we feel alarm and grief. Yet what are the greatest physical losses compared with the loss of the *soul*? Think what it means to be a lost soul.

It means *lost to fellowship with God*. Does someone exclaim, "Why, fellowship with God is something far removed from most people's minds"? Well, could anything more sadly prove their lost condition? Is it not surprisingly strange that human beings should shiftily evade all thought of the very One who gives them life, who sustains them, gives them the breath they breathe, and the light in which they see, and the food which they eat? Is it not stranger still that men in general prefer any philosophic or scientific theory to the Bible, whether pantheistic, fatalistic or evolutionary, so long as it assures them that God does not even exist? How strange we should think it if growing children who had been well fed, well clothed, well cared-for in every way, and surrounded by sympathetic parental love, should all the while be shiftily evading their parents, and at the very earliest opportunity hive away from them and push them entirely out of thought! Yet that is how human beings in general treat the great heavenly Parent; and does it not indicate strangest alienation?

But it also means *lost to life's highest purpose*. Did God allow any of us to be born without some special purpose in view? Has God endowed our nature with intellect, conscience, and free will, only to leave us as wisps of meaningless consciousness blown about by blind chance? "No," say the birds of the heaven and the stars of the sky. "No," says the whole of the well-ordered universe. "No," says the written Word of God; there is a purpose for each of us as truly as for Jeremiah (Jer. 1: 5). But sin has driven a deep, wide wedge between God's will and man's; so that instead of finding heart-satisfying consummation of our human personalities, we spend ourselves on the merely temporal, and then die saying, "Vanity of vanities; all is vanity!" Life has no real purpose apart from God. To be "lost" is therefore to be lost to life's highest purpose.

It also means to be *lost to life's purest joys*. It is difficult for worldly-minded people to think this, especially the younger among them; but that is simply because there is one part of their nature torpid, atrophied, dead. It is difficult for the sensual and voluptuous to think that the pleasures of the mind are more enjoyable than those of the body; yet the poet, the philosopher, the intellectual, will tell them that mere animal indulgences are crude compared with mental pleasures. And the prayerful Christian knows that even mental pleasures are far below the pure *spiritual* joys which are ours in Christ. Oh, the sad, sad tragedy, "Lost"!—lost to fellowship with God; lost to life's highest purpose; lost to life's purest joys; and lost to all these for ever! May we who know the Saviour do all we can to arouse them, and bring them to the Saviour!

To Seek and to Save

"For the Son of Man is come to seek and to save that which was lost."—Luke 19: 10.

In our reflection yesterday we spoke about that sad, sad word, "lost". The saddest tragedy of all is that to be finally lost is to be *lost to the eternal glory of heaven*. Heaven is the home of the holy, the city of the sinless, the paradise of the pure, the temple of the untarnished, the inheritance of the redeemed, the Summer-land of the sanctified. Its very atmosphere is holy love. Its pure bliss is that of sinless fellowship with God. Nothing that defiles shall ever enter. There are only the two classes among its shining hosts—the angels who have *never* sinned, and sinners who have been *saved* from sin through the Redeemer's precious blood. Yet there are unconverted people who think they will enter heaven at last, when they die. Silly, blind, mocking delusion! Even if they *could* enter that ineffable glory, heaven would be hell to them. For sinful, unsaved, uncleansed human sinners to dwell in the burning rays of that utter holiness would be like the torture of diseased eyes exposed to the blaze of a tropical sun. No, no; the unsaved can never enter into that heaven of sinless, never-ending rapture. To be "lost" is to be lost to that for ever.

Most terrible of all, to be "lost" is to be *lost in the interminable damnation of Gehenna*, where the gnawing worm never dies and the tormenting flame is never quenched. It is not a bit of use shutting our eyes to what the Word of God says about this. It does not help, to start wresting Scripture phraseology into meaning everlasting annihilation or complete obliteration of personality. There are *some* passages, at least, which clearly indicate ageless continuity of conscious penalty (Matt. 25: 41, 46; Rev. 20: 10 with 15, etc.). Oh, the unutterable awfulness of thus being "lost"!

We turn with relief to those other words in our text: "For the Son of Man is come *to seek and to save* . . ." It was the knowledge of what it means for a soul to be lost which brought the Son of God from heaven's glories to that stark, brutal, ugly, yet glorious Cross on Calvary.

He came to "seek" and *He still seeks*. In former times, when a child was lost in a British town or city, a "Crier" used to go through the streets, ringing a bell, and calling out in a doleful voice such words as, "Lost, lost, a lost child; five years of age, blue eyes, light hair; lost child!" Oh, thank God, the great Seeker from heaven has come to the streets and cities of our world, ringing the bell of the best tidings which ever resounded on human ears. He comes seeking the lost ones because He loves them. He comes seeking them with an eager intensity outmatching that of any man or woman seeking a lost diamond, and with a tenderer compassion even than that of anxious parents seeking a lost child.

He came to "save", and *he still saves*. Next time He comes, it will be as King and Judge, but now, in this age of grace, He is the seeking Saviour. When Napoleon envisaged a military campaign in Italy, his generals pronounced any attempt to cross the Alps suicidal. Napoleon exclaimed, "There shall be no Alps!"—and the great road was built through the Simplon Pass. So the great Seeker from heaven breaks through all obstacles to save us—to save us from sins mountainous as the Alps, numberless as the stars, and black as night.

"Keep in memory what I have preached unto you."—I Cor. 15: 2.

MEMORY! What a world in a word! What rapture can be in it! —and what torture! According to one of the poets, memory was given us that we might have Summer's roses right through Winter; but sometimes it retains only the stinging thorns of blooms which have perished for ever.

Memory! Who shall say the full word about it? There is not a more wonderful faculty in the human mind. Aristotle aptly called it "the scribe of the soul". Without it, thought would be incoherent and chaotic. It is the most amazing cupboard ever devised; and oh, how important a matter is what we store away in it!

Memory! What a valuable ally it can be to the Christian! How useful a comrade when it leaps to our rescue, in some emergency, with the promises or warnings of God's holy Book! During one of the Ulster religious revivals last century, a godless old farm-labourer, sitting by a hedgerow, was suddenly convicted of sin, and savingly converted to Christ, when his memory unexpectedly resurrected part of a Gospel sermon which he had heard seventy years earlier! And how often does memory bring loveliest consolations from Holy Writ to Christian believers in times of special need! And how memory blesses us by its retention of much that we read in good literature, or hear preached in God's house, or see in the example of godly persons! Eusebius tells how a Christian whose eyes were burned out in the Diocletian persecution was able to repeat page after page of Scripture from memory. Of another it was said that he had so memorised the Scriptures that his soul was "a library for Christ".

Memory! What a ministry it can have, if we use it wisely! That is why the Scriptures repeatedly exhort us to "*remember*".

There is much to be said for memorising the *wording* of Scripture. But we should also stock the mind with Scripture by continual reading, allowing its truths to sink in, even where we cannot remember all the wording. Its purifying and fortifying power is beyond estimation.

"Keep in memory what I have preached." What was it, in gist, that he had preached? It was *salvation in Christ*; and his epistles show that the salvation which he preached was threefold. There is one sense in which salvation is *instantaneous;* for at the very moment when we accept Christ, our sins are pardoned, our guilt is washed away, and we are justified through the merits of Calvary's sinless Sin-bearer. But in another sense salvation is *progressive*; for when we thus receive the Saviour the Holy Spirit implants a new spiritual life and nature within us, and there is to be growth in spiritual power, understanding, usefulness and Christlikeness. Finally, at the return of Christ, salvation in its *consummative* aspect is to give us sinless hearts, perfected powers, immortal bodies, and "faultlessness" before the Majesty on high.

Such is salvation in its three, clear *tenses*—past, present, future. And such is salvation in its three main *senses*—justification, sanctification, glorification. And such is salvation in its three distinct aspects—the judicial, the spiritual, the ultimate. In its judicial aspect it is *instantaneous*. In its experiential aspect it is *progressive*. In its consummative aspect it is *all-perfecting*.

What and Why and How

"Keep in memory what I have preached unto you."—1 Cor. 15:2.

First, then, *what* would Paul have us "keep in memory"? See verse 1: "The Gospel which I preached unto you." He had now been preaching that same glorious Gospel for a quarter of a century. He never veered away, for he had received the historical facts of it direct from eye-witnesses, and the spiritual truths of it direct from God, as he says in verse 3: "I delivered unto you . . . that which *I also received*." He had taught them both the rich spiritual provisions and the high moral challenges of the Gospel. He would have them keep all these in memory, and keep on proving their dynamic power in daily living. It is a great thing when a Christian minister can look back over the years, and say as Paul did, "Keep in memory what I have preached unto you." When the at-one-time famous preacher, Rowland Hill, was becoming an old man, he leaned over his pulpit one Sunday and said, "I hear of some folk who complain that poor old Rowland Hill wanders from his *subject*. I call you to bear witness that he has never wandered from his *object*."

Some years ago I was in a crowded service where a minister was saying farewell after a long pastorate. He said: "Have I not always upheld this Book as verily the Word of God? Like a dutiful watchman have I not warned the careless, and implored the unsaved to 'flee from the wrath to come'? Have I not subordinated all other pulpit considerations to that of preaching salvation the more plainly? Have I not taught young disciples the separated life, and endeavoured to build them up in the doctrines of grace? Have I not sought to lead believers into that lovely Canaan where we really 'possess our possessions' in Christ? From my watchtower have I not discerned 'the signs of the times' and proclaimed from 'the sure word of prophecy', 'Behold the Bridegroom cometh!'? Have I not gloried to present Christ in His fourfold all-sufficiency as Saviour, Sanctifier, Healer of mind and body, and soon-returning King?" Oh, these are the things to "keep in memory"!

But second, *why* should we "keep in memory" these things? Paul tells us: "Keep in memory what I have preached unto you, by which also *ye are saved*." Oh, what a reason for remembering! Was Paul anxious to be remembered merely for his own sake? No, the master-passion of the true Christian preacher is to fill his hearers' minds with the Saviour, for thereby they become *saved*. Gospel preaching is a life-and-death business.

And now, just a completive word on *how* to remember. We all know that memory can be much helped by the *will*. Notice again how Paul says, "*Keep in memory* . . ."—indicating that there can be the will to do so. As a matter of fact, the word "memory" here does not occur in the Greek, though it is implied; but the word translated as "keep" is a quite forceful verb which the Revised Version well renders as "hold fast".

Hold fast the Word! If you hold *it*, it will hold *you!* Let the Word of God be your guide, and it will be your *guard*. Let it be your *law*, and it will be your *light*. Let it be your *treasure*, and it will be your *triumph*. Above all else, focus the gaze of your heart on the ever-living, ever-loving, everlasting Christ Himself; for He is the sum and substance of the Written Word, even as He is the heart and glory of the Gospel.

Those Sad Refusals

"How often would I . . . and ye would not!"—Luke 13: 34.

We have reached the last week of November. The end of another year is drawing upon us. We are reminded again of the stealthy elusiveness with which time slips away from us. Perhaps, also, as we review the expiring year, some of us feel discomfort in that we have fallen far below our shining ideals of twelve months ago. Why is it that we so often suffer this discomfort at year-end? The other day, as I was reflecting on this, there came one of those moments of vivid clarification in which we suddenly see everything in a new way, or discern with startling clearness the total harmony of things. I seemed to see, in silhouette sharpness, that for many of us who mean so well yet fail so sadly, the essence of what we call "sin" is not so much the *committing* of something unworthy as a *refusing* of something high and heavenly.

As we now look back, does not our discomfort arise mainly from an awareness of having selfishly *refused* something of supreme value which might have been ours? Blossoms of promise have left only bitter stalks without fruit. Rosebuds have fallen away without blooming, and left only sharp thorns which jag our conscience. There lurks within us a conviction that somehow it is all due to our own *refusal* of what might have been. Probe this a bit more deeply. Most of us have thought that the core of sin is rebellion. May it not be that sin is something far more pathetic than rebellion? Before the Son of God died as our Saviour, sin could well be exposed as a rebellious breaking of God's *law*; but since Calvary the essence of sin is *refusal* which wounds God's *heart*. In line with this, as we now look back over the past year, is it not a realisation of *refusal* on our part which creates our sense of blameworthiness?

This sin of refusal works itself out in three directions: (1) toward ourselves, (2) toward others, (3) toward God. Consider it in relation to *our own selves*. There is in each of us a higher nature and a lower; the spiritual and the animal. Breathed upon by the Spirit of God, the higher part is constantly alluring us to those higher ideals and choices which make life truly noble. That higher nature is in all men; but in those of us who have become regenerated through union with Christ it is vitally accentuated. Through the mystery of a spiritual rebirth within us, we have become "partakers of the divine nature". Our eyes have been opened to see in Christ the divine ideal of humanhood incarnated in its loveliest form and appeal. And the new nature within us continually appeals for our response to Him. With us believers, therefore, the "sin which doth so easily beset us" is not now so much the perpetration of an evil action, as a selfish *refusal* to that heaven-born voice within us which is all the while alluring us to higher things in Christ. Oh, that we had not so often refused! Our refusal of *Him* has been, in reality, a refusal of our own highest *self-realisation*. But, oh, what might be, even yet, if from now onwards our lives were to be lived *responding*! Our patient Lord looks on us, and says, "How often would I . . . and ye would not!" But He also says, "Thou art . . . thou shalt be . . ." Yes, if there is response to Him, He can yet make us all we long to be.

"Today, if Ye will Hear"

"How often would I . . . and ye would not!"—Luke 13 : 34.

A DISTURBING sense of sin and blame comes to different people in different ways; but to those of us who know Christian truth it most often comes as a conviction of having *refused* that to which we should have responded. We may know that we have done what is wrong, and may be fearful of the consequences; or we may try to fool ourselves that the wrong was not *very* wrong; but the keen sense of sin comes when we see our behaviour as a *refusal* of that which is highest, loveliest, truest. A man who used to be a drunkard and wife-beater told me that the hell of remorse which he used to endure after his outbreaks was a burning, shaming sense of having violently *refused* all the highest and noblest. It used to look out at him through the frightened, appealing eyes of his felled wife, recalling the gentle, manly vows of the wedding morning, until at last it broke him in utter contrition.

This reminds us that our refusal of the highest often expresses itself in our behaviour toward *others*. In a spiritual sense the kingdom of heaven comes appealing to us again and again through others who need our help, or to whom we may show kindness. It looks out at us, and beckons us through a thousand seeming trivialities daily. In reality the seeming trivialities are appeals, allurements, priceless opportunities to "receive the kingdom" and to "walk with the King". As we now look back, what tragic refusals we see! Some of them seemed such tiny incidents at the time, that no one else has ever given them a thought since; but they stand out to *us* because we now see them as what they really were—*refusals* to the King who beckoned us through other persons.

Such refusals register deeply in us, even from childhood. We are made that way. Some time ago, I chanced on a little book in which the author tells the following incident of his childhood. "I was lagging behind my nurse on a walk in my own native west country in Spring, when three children ran out of a cottage garden, holding in their hands small branches of sycamore from which they had stripped all but the young, bronze-coloured leaves at the top. These branches they offered to me. I can see them still offering them as if they were performing a rite, and they smiled as they offered them. But I looked at them and ran after my nurse without saying a word. When I turned back to look at them again, they were still standing in the road, holding the branches out as if they had been disappointed." Well, that was all; yet the author's comment after years of manhood, is that the "refusal" which he childishly indulged that day "still makes me feel guilty far more than many evil things I have done since".

Yes, underneath trivialities there is often deep meaning for us. The "kingdom" beckons to us through the hands and eyes and needs of others every day we live; but alas all too often there is selfish refusal. Later, when the fugitive moment has gone for ever, we realise—often with a guilty start—that it was the King himself who beckoned to us through the opportunity, and then withdrew with sadness on His dear face. How we have disappointed Him! Yet deep in our hearts, we love Him more than anyone else on earth or in heaven. Master, give me quicker perception, and readier responsiveness.

Refusing the Highest

"How often would I . . . and ye would not!"—Luke 13:34.

WHEN our Lord was on earth, He was all the while trying to show us that there is a higher life everywhere appealing to us, but being refused. The parable of the good Samaritan illustrates this. Lying in the roadway is the robbed and wounded man. A priest comes by, and sees him, but refuses to help. Then a Levite passes by in similar refusal. Next a Samaritan comes by, and sees that the half-dead victim is a Jew, one of the nation detested by Samaritans, yet he immediately responds with a compassion overleaping racial animosities. The priest and the Levite, notwithstanding their religious profession, *refused* the appeal of that higher, bigger, diviner realm which is everywhere around and appealing to us; but the Samaritan responded despite obstacles of racial antipathy. The priest and the Levite saved themselves much inconvenience, but they also refused "the kingdom" and missed the divinest joy we can know on earth. We have the same thing in the parable of the sheep and the goats: "Inasmuch as ye did it not to one of the least of these, ye did it not unto Me." The tragic, damning feature is not active committing of evil, but selfish *refusal* of the higher, which at last is exposed as refusal of Christ Himself.

Well, there it is: in a mystical sense the "kingdom of heaven" is everywhere around us, beckoning, appealing, in daily incidents, situations, opportunities. As we have said before, it is our sense of having *refused* what "might have been" which casts such gloomy self-reproach over us as we look back. We have allowed the evil to keep us from the good; the good to keep us from the better; the better to keep us from the best. We have allowed selfish refusals to keep us from richest self-fulfilment and mystic communion with "the King in His beauty". We must drag out these innate attitudes of refusal. Our psycho-analysts do not speak of sin, but they insist that the worst enemies to peace of mind lurk in the sub-conscious, and that we must drag them up to conscious exposures if we are to conquer them. Is not that nearly Plato's dictum of "the lie in the soul"?

We should guard against becoming introverts or morbidly introspective, but an occasional crisis of dragging these sub-conscious refusals to light is a wholesome necessity. Drag the skulking Agags of pride, snobbery, fear, prejudice, green envy and ugly grudge to the light, and hack them in pieces! These are the hidden scoundrels which keep tricking us into refusing the meek, lowly, brave, noble, generous, lovely, Christlike life which we know we ought to live. Thank God, there is blood-bought absolution from all the accumulated culpability of the past; and if we will fling wide the portals of our inner life to the risen Lord Jesus, He will work gracious miracles in our nature, so that the shining ideal may indeed become the daily actual.

A man of the city, I scurried around,
For joy ever greedy—a joy never found;
Till once, on an impulse, denying my greed,
I suffered to help a poor fellow in need.
Lo, all of a sudden—a rapturous glow,
The purest of joy that a human can know!

The Saddest Refusal of All

"How often would I . . . and ye would not!"—Luke 13 : 34.

LOOK once again at the sad words of our text. The saddest of all refusals is a direct refusal of the divine love which came down to this earth in the person of the meek and lowly Jesus.

Love came down at Christmas,
Love all lovely; Love divine.

Yes, "Love came down at Christmas." Love walked and talked with us, up and down the lanes of Galilee and Judæa. Love grieved and bled and broke its heart in agonising expiation for us, on Calvary! In Jesus, the incarnate Son of God, the divine love has clothed itself in visible sublimity. "The Word became flesh, and dwelt among us; and we beheld His glory . . . full of grace and truth." In Jesus, God looks on us through human eyes, beckons to us with human hands, calls to us through human lips, walks toward us with human feet over life's troubled sea, sympathises with us through human susceptibilities, and feels after us with a divine love which now beats through a human heart!

God's thoughts are love, and Jesus is
The loving voice they find.
His life lights up the vast abyss
Of the eternal Mind.

Who can sound the deeps of that fathomless sob, "Oh, Jerusalem, Jerusalem . . . how often would I have gathered thy children together as a hen gathers her brood under her wings, *and ye would not!*" Yet even that sad refusal was not as ungrateful as the refusal of many a heart today; for when Jesus wept over Jerusalem He had not yet gone to the crowning expression of divine love on Calvary. As we have said before, to those of us who live on *this* side of Calvary, the greatest sin is no longer that of transgressing the commanding *law* sent down through the venerable Moses, but the refusing of the redeeming *love* poured out through the crucified Saviour. Through the Cross, not only does salvation from eternal Gehenna come to believers, but there draws near to us in its sublimest, tenderest, most appealing way, the kingdom of heaven, the kingdom of love, the kingdom of Jesus. How can men refuse? Yet they do! And then, what? They know they cannot be neutral, so they build false little kingdoms of their own—little kingdoms of intellectuality, personal superiority, religion, philosophy, pleasure, angry resentment. Or they drive *conscious* refusal of Christ down into the vaults of the *sub*-conscious, thinking it will die in the dark; and then, when they gradually become insensitive to Christ, they think it a sign of strength, when all the time it is the weakness of a mind cowering away from reality; a chronic mental *state* of cowardly refusal brought on by successive *acts* of refusal. It is a morbid thickening of the mind's "outer skin", not protecting it, but cutting it off from the one true kingdom of light and health. Let us say a big, eager "*YES*" to Jesus, now and always!

"Christ died, yea rather, is risen again, who is even at the right hand of God, who also maketh intercession for us."—Rom. 8 : 34.

THE old Israelite tabernacle consisted of a covered sanctuary enclosed in a large oblong outer court. The one and only ingress to the latter was at its eastern end; and the first object inside it was the altar of sacrifice. That altar was made of stout wood overlaid with brass. It was exactly square, each of its four sides measuring five cubits, that is, approximately seven feet six inches. According to divinely ordained pattern, at each of the four corners there was an ornamental projection called a horn. Ornamental to some degree those four horns of the altar certainly were, but they had a more than merely ornamental purpose. They were horns of *refuge*. When an Israelite was in danger from one who sought his life, he could flee to the tabernacle and lay hold on the horns of the altar, knowing that as long as he stayed there, his pursuer dare not touch him (see 1 Kgs. 1 : 50).

As we near the end of another year, are there some of us who are dogged by rueful regrets, sleuth-hounded by condemning memories, pursued by an accusing conscience, and longing to find some place of refuge? Or could it be that I now address someone who has never found refuge from that awful slayer, *Sin*? Does a sense of guilt track you down like a pursuer with drawn knife? Does the assassin, Fear, chase you, making you to know that to die in your present state is to be a lost soul? Or is it that evil habits, like bandits, overpower you? Oh, let me point you to the horns of the altar. See them in our text: *Horn one:* "Christ died." *Horn two:* "Yea rather, is risen again." *Horn three:* "Who is at the right hand of God." *Horn four:* "Who maketh intercession for us."

If conscience, like a pursuer with drawn knife, is hounding you down, and you know yourself to be a guilty sinner, a perishing soul, lay hold on that first horn: "*Christ died*"! In His atoning death there is forgiveness of sin, and cleansing from guilt. Or if you are relentlessly run down by temptations and evil influences which you cannot overcome, lay hold on that second horn: "*Yea rather, is risen again*"; for He who conquered death can overcome your strongest enemies. Or if you are footpadded by shadowy fears of troubles coming upon you, grasp firmly that third horn, "*Who is even at the right hand of God*"—in control of everything which concerns you. Or are you afraid that your salvation will fail? You believe on Jesus, but you lack assurance and are overtaken by stealthy doubts? Then lay hold upon that fourth horn: "*Who also maketh intercession for us.*" Let go all self-suggested weapons. Your pursuers are too strong for you. Flee to the horns of the altar! None dare touch you there; you are safe (see verses 38, 39).

Those altar horns show us what an *all-complete* Saviour Jesus is. Had He died but not risen, then even though there were a dearly-bought forgiveness, there would be no conqueror's power to guard us. Had He risen but not ascended, there would be only a partial deliverance, because He would not be in absolute control. Had He ascended without interceding, there could be no access to God as our Father, for we are still sinners, though forgiven. Blessed be His Name, He died, and He rose, and He ascended to the very throne of God, and He "ever liveth to make intercession".

The Text of Texts

"He gave His only-begotten Son."—Jn. 3: 16.

We have reached December. Christmas draws near again, with all its tender associations and mighty meaning. Over against the saddening spectacle of our war-scarred, sin-strangled, twentieth-century world, let us reflect again, with simple-hearted gratitude, on the wonder of wonders, in the text of texts, John 3: 16.

"He gave His only-begotten Son." The measure of love is always its willingness to give; its capacity for sacrifice. If we would measure the love of God, we must measure it by Calvary. Someone has thus written of love:

Love ever gives, forgives, outlives;
And ever stands with open hands;
And while it lives it gives;
For while it gives it lives;
And this is Love's prerogative—
To give—and give—and give.

This is certainly true of the love of God. It is revealed in its giving, and is thus seen to be beyond all measure. We can never know the costliness of Calvary to God, nor can we ever measure the love that lay behind it. All we can do is to fall back on that elastic particle, "so": "God *so* loved . . . that He gave His only-begotten Son."

This we know: such is the oneness of the Father and the Son, that, in giving the Son, the Father gave Himself; for "God was *in* Christ, reconciling the world unto Himself" (2 Cor. 5: 19). The Lord Jesus is not merely an agent through whom God sends the message that He loves us. He is God Himself actually come to earth loving us. He does not merely declare or expound the love of God: He *is* the love of God incarnate.

What adverbs we may unite with that particle "so"! "God *so* loved" —so fully, so freely, so sublimely. But when we proceed to the counterpart of that particle "so", in the words, "that He gave His only-begotten Son", and when we reflect on the mysterious fact that the Father gave up the eternal Son, not only to the fathomless woe of Calvary, but to the incorporating of our human nature itself into His divine being, by a real human birth, so that He is now the Son of Man for evermore, as well as God the Son, we can only exclaim, "God loved so *unutterably* . . ." Language indeed breaks down. We are lost in wonder, love and praise.

Yes, Christmas draws near again. In our thinking of it, we must never isolate Bethlehem from Golgotha, or the Cradle from the Cross. Apart from the Incarnation there never *could* have been the Atonement; and apart from the Atonement there never *would* have been the Incarnation; and apart from the infinite love of God there neither could nor would have been either. Orion and Pleiades may be wonderful to us, in their flaming magnificence and immensity; but the greatest thing we know about the Creator is just this: "God so loved . . . that He gave His only-begotten Son."

"He gave His only-begotten Son."—Jn. 3: 16.

UNDOUBTEDLY there is in these words an allusion to Abraham's offering up of Isaac. There is a similar allusion to Abraham, in Romans 8: 32, where Paul says: "He that spared not His own Son, but delivered Him up for us all, how shall He not with Him also freely give us all things?"

The patriarch Abraham is an appealing type of the heavenly Father. We see this in the following eight ways. (1) In the uniqueness of his love for Isaac. The unique circumstances connected with the promise and birth of Isaac made him the object of Abraham's special love; so that he was with special emphasis "Isaac whom thou lovest".

(2) In the costliness of his sacrifice. How this is brought out in the words: "Take now thy son, thine only Isaac, whom thou lovest . . . and offer him." How costly indeed it must have been to Abraham, to sacrifice the son of his old age, in whom all his own hopes and all the divine promises were centred!

(3) In his readiness to make the sacrifice. Not a demur on Abraham's part is recorded, though the strange request must have contradicted all he knew about God.

(4) In his preparation and foresight. See Abraham several days in advance of the anticipated ordeal, preparing the requisites for the offering, and then, on the third day, lifting up his eyes and seeing the place "afar off". So was Calvary seen "afar off", and divinely prepared-for, long in advance.

(5) In his intense suffering. How glad would Abraham have been to give anything, even his own life, rather than his precious Isaac! His suffering was dual: there was the suffering of his own heart in its loss, and, at the same time, a sympathetic suffering with Isaac. So it was with the divine Father, at Calvary.

(6) In that his sacrifice revealed his heart. It revealed the heart of Abraham as nothing else did or could. Supremely, it revealed his love to God (Gen. 22: 12). In fact, it is the supreme thing we know about him. So is Calvary the supreme unveiling of the heart of God. "*Herein* is love, not that we loved God, but that He loved us, and sent His Son to be the propitiation for our sins."

(7) In that his sacrifice was in response to a call. It was the voice of God which called Abraham to make that supreme sacrifice (Gen. 22: 1, 2). There was a divine necessity in it. Abraham could not have been led to the highest height of faith and fellowship, or have given absolutely decisive evidence of love to God, apart from it. Even so, the heavenly Father's giving of the Only-Begotten was in response to a call—the call of human need.

(8) In that his sacrifice had wonderfully beneficent results. In the end, as we know, Abraham did not need actually to sacrifice Isaac. God did not desire that. But so far as Abraham's faith was concerned, the deed was as good as done; and, in Genesis 22: 15–18, comes the assurance that in consequence should "all nations of the earth be blessed". Even so, and measurelessly more, is it with the beneficent results of the heavenly Father's yielding up of the only-begotten Son. See Revelation 7: 9–17.

The Wonder of Wonders

"He gave His only-begotten Son."—Jn. 3: 16.

THAT word "gave" has in it the force of "gave *up*". As an old commentator says, God not only gave His Son *to* the world, but *for* it. That meant the birth in the cattle-shed at Bethlehem, the struggle with poverty at Nazareth, the carpenter's bench, the being "tempted in all points like as we are", the suffering of reproach and the being "acquainted with grief", the shame and the spitting, the purple robe and the crown of thorns, the iron spikes and the deadly spear, the awful darkness, and the "tasting of death". Oh, there is titanic meaning in Paul's words, "He *spared not* His own Son." Was ever a gift like the Saviour given? He leaves the bosom of the eternal Father, and comes to the bosom of an earthly mother. The Son of God becomes the Son of Mary. The Infinite becomes an infant. He who holds the world in His arms is held in the arms of a frail woman. He whose garment is space, whose house is the universe, whose chariots are the clouds, and whose diadems are the stars, is wrapped in swaddling bands, and laid in a manger. He leaves the palace-beautiful of heaven, for the stable, and the work-bench, and the having "not where to lay His head". He lays aside His celestial insignia, for the peasant dress and the purple robe. He puts aside His sceptre of universal sovereignty, for the reed of mock royalty in Pilate's hall. He leaves the throne of heaven, for the Cross outside the city wall. He who is the Prince of life bows His head in death. He who is without sin becomes the Sinbearer. The Christ of God becomes the Crucified. He who is the Father's delight becomes the God-forsaken. He who lit the stars lies in the dust. He comes, He toils, He hungers and thirsts, He weeps, He suffers, He bleeds and dies!—for God so loved the world that He "gave up" His only-begotten Son.

Oh, how different is God's giving from men's! In all too many instances, men's giving is for self-advantage; their giving is a subtle form of getting; but God gives out of pure beneficence. Men's giving can only be to a certain extent: but God's is without limit. Men's giving is usually in response to urgent cries for help: but God gives to those who neither realise their need nor appreciate His gift. Men's giving is usually to friends: but God gives His gift of gifts to those who are alienated and rebellious; for, as the Scriptures declare, "God died for us"; and "In due time Christ died for the *ungodly*", and again "When we were *enemies* we were reconciled to God by the death of His Son" (Rom. 5: 8; 6:10). At the wonder of such redeeming giving, Edward Young breaks forth:

A pardon bought with blood! with blood divine!
With blood divine of Him I made my foe!—
My species up in arms! not one exempt!
Yet for the foulest of the foul He dies,
As if our race were held of highest rank,
And Godhead dearer as more kind to man!
Oh, what a scale of miracles is here!
Its lowest round high planted in the skies;
Its towering summit lost beyond the thought
    Of man or angel.

All Gifts in One

"He gave His only-begotten Son."—Jn. 3 : 16.

In giving Christ, God gives us all things *in* Him. Do we need forgiveness? God does not offer us forgiveness as a thing by itself. If we would receive a heavenly Father's forgiveness for all our sins, we must receive Jesus Christ Himself, for God's forgiveness comes to us in *Him*. Do we seek cleansing? Peace with God? The assurance of salvation? The gift of eternal life? Power to overcome evil habit and strong temptation? Courage to confess the Saviour before men? Spiritual equipment for service? Fellowship with God? Joy and comfort and hope? A mansion in the Father's house, and an inheritance among them that are sanctified? Not one of these great blessings is given to us as a thing by itself. They are all included in the one comprehensive gift of the only-begotten Son.

Oh, friend, if you are seeking pardon, cleansing, peace, power, assurance, eternal life, joy, comfort, hope, and a blessed hereafter, do not seek them merely as a list of things which you feel you need. See in Jesus all that poor sinners can ever need for their present and everlasting well-being. God has freely given all things to us in Him. Receive *Him*! To possess Him is to possess a full salvation.

"He *gave* His only-begotten Son." Ponder the words once more. They tell us that Christ is a *gift*. What is our normal response to a gift? Do we *pay* for it? Do we *work* for it? Do we *beg* for it? Do we *wait* for it? No. We just *take* it; and it is ours. If, then, Jesus is God's gift to us, our proper response is simply and gratefully to *receive* Him; and it is by doing this that we become saved.

What a sad thing it is that millions of people treat God's gift with an unintelligent artificiality such as they would never display toward any other precious gift! Although, in clear language, the old Book tells us that the Saviour is "the gift of God", and that He may be savingly received by the simplest, men and women try to *pay* for salvation by supposed merit of character, or they try to *earn* it by supposed good works and so-called Christian service, or they *pray* and *wait* and *weep* for it through days of anxious concern about their souls. What folly, what tragedy, what stupidity it all is! Oh, let us simply, gratefully, undoubtingly receive God's gift at once! To use a word which is often on the lips of Gospel preachers, let us "appropriate" the Saviour by faith; for our text says "that whosoever *believeth* on Him should not perish, but *have*". To believe is to have; for believing is receiving. If a friend offers me a valuable gift, how do I show him that I really believe he is giving it to me? Why, of course, by simply and gratefully taking it. If I should start profusely thanking my friend, or wordily praising him for his kindness, or carefully explaining that his gift is exactly what I am needing, or assuring him that it will be most useful—if I should do all these things most volubly, and yet not take the proffered gift, my friend would either say or think: "Well, in spite of all his thanking and praising and explaining and assuring, he does not honestly believe that I am really giving him this thing, or he would *take* it." Yes, taking is the evidence of believing. This is made quite clear by that verse in the first chapter of John—"As many as *RECEIVED* Him, to them gave He power to become the sons of God, even to them that *BELIEVE* on His name." So simple? Yes!

The Road to Bethlehem

"Glory to God in the highest; and on earth peace, good will toward men."—Luke 2 : 14.

WE are in the Christmas month again. Soon the festive season will be upon us. The bells of Bethlehem will peal out once more their message of "Peace on earth; good will to men". As their gentle music falls again on human ears, what will men and women be thinking? There are millions, alas, even in so-called Christian countries, to whom those Christmas chimes will signify nothing of vital spiritual significance, nothing beyond the pleasant symbolism of an annual festivity. But there are others, too, all over the world, who will think deeply again. They will ponder again the profound mystery of divine love which Christmas memorialises.

But the thing which most of all will strike the minds of thoughtful people again this Christmas is the ironic contrast between those appealing chimes of "Peace on earth, good will to men", and the present state of the world, with its seething rivalries and ill-will, its international suspicions and crooked diplomacies, its bitter factions and frictions, its war-hauntedness and disturbing fears. The supreme irony is that although the cure for all the world's ills lies wrapped up in the swaddling bands of that little Babe of Bethlehem, the nations will not have it, and are still seeking vain cures elsewhere.

Away back in the Book of Ruth, we are told of a certain man of Bethlehem, named Elimelech, and his wife, Naomi, who went away from Bethlehem to seek better fare in the alien land of Moab. The name *Elimelech* means "My God is my King"; and *Naomi* means "pleasantness" or "favour".

This Elimelech and his wife Naomi leave for Moab. They take with them their two sons, *Mahlon*, whose name means "joy" or "song", and *Chilion*, whose name means "ornament" or "perfectness". These four leave Bethlehem, which means "House of Bread" (*Beyth*=house; *lechem*= bread), and they go to Moab. But in Moab, Elimelech ("God is my King") dies; so do Mahlon ("song") and Chilion ("perfectness"). After ten tragic years Naomi returns to Bethlehem, saying, "Call me not Naomi; call me *Marah* (bitter)".

Is not that an advance type-picture telling the sad story of men and nations in relation to Bethlehem? The great crying need is for leaders and peoples to get back to Bethlehem. Sometime we shall *have* to get back there, however hard and humbling we have made the way for ourselves. We shall have to get back there even if we have to be *driven* there by the agonies which we bring upon ourselves.

All this was brought to my mind afresh by some lines from the pen of a dear old friend of mine, the late Rev. W. T. Macgregor of Edinburgh.

> It's a long, hard road back to Bethlehem,
>   And many have lost the way;
> War trumpets outsound the angels' song,
>   The wise men have gone astray:
> But the face of the sky shows the star of morn
>   Still pointing to where our Lord was born.

The Way to Peace on Earth

"Glory to God in the highest; and on earth peace, good will toward men."—Luke 2 : 14.

Oh, how the nations of today need to hush their clashing clamour and listen again to those Bethlehem angels! The millions of broken hearts and homes which linger on as the dreary legacy of world-wars are due to the refusal of men and nations to crown the Jesus Christ of Bethlehem and Calvary and Easter morning as Lord of their lives. If the great Christian denominations in Christendom had kept true to the real Jesus Christ of the New Testament, how different might the so-called Christian nations have been today! And if the governments of the so-called Christian nations had spent a millionth part on sending out Christian missionaries as they have prodigally expended on armaments and wars, how different would have been the first half of the twentieth century and the world-picture today! These are not just pathetic platitudes; they are tragic truths; yet the fact is that even to this hour, even after the self-inflicted agonies of two monster world-wars, our leaders and peoples will not have it.

Doubtless, when the angels trooped down into the night skies around Bethlehem, they did not pay too much attention to the order of the clauses in their rapturous chorus of praises; yet we cannot but be struck by the fact that "Glory to God in the highest" comes before "Peace on earth, good will toward men". There never will be "peace on earth" until there is first "Glory to God in the highest". This has been said a million times, but it has fallen on deaf ears, and needs saying again with a loud voice. Perhaps some of the nations and their peoples are more inclined to listen to it after the happenings of the past fifty years. Do we detect a wistful yearning in some recent public speeches?

And, of course, it has a direct application to each individual human being. Each of us should endeavour to bring this "Glory to God in the highest" into our commercial and industrial and social life wherever we may live and work. Some time ago, in a certain church, two sermons were being preached at the same time—one by the minister, the other by a stained-glass window. Thousands, at one time or another, had admired that window with its large-lettered wording, "GLORY TO GOD IN THE HIGHEST"; but now, owing to a temporary defect, one of the letters was obscured, so that the message of the window was, "GLORY TO GOD IN THE HIGH ST". Yes, let the businessmen of every city learn that if there is to be peace, goodwill, prosperity on earth, there must be glory to God in the High Street, on Main Avenue, and in Central Market.

Is it not time that both collectively and individually we went back again to Bethlehem, yea, rather, to the dear Lord who there was born into our world to save us?

It's a long, hard road back to Bethlehem,
  Yet, there's hope when hearts are torn.
And eyes look up to that Lamb of God
  Who for man's redemption was born;
And the signs of the times seem growing clear
  That the day of our world's rebirth draws near.

The Christ Who Fulfils

"I am not come to destroy, but to fulfil."—Matt. 5: 17.

ALWAYS, as Christmastide draws on, we think of the Christ who came to our world on that long-ago day in Bethlehem; but there are all too few who ponder *why* He came. Have you ever picked out those verses in which our Lord Himself declares why He came? They are full of mighty meaning. Here is one of them: "I am not come to destroy, but to fulfil." Besides its specific contextual meaning, it suggests a majestic train of thought which we can profitably touch upon here, even though we cannot follow it right through.

Our Lord Jesus is the fulfilment of *prophecy*. The apostle John makes a remarkable little comment in his account of the crucifixion. "After this, Jesus knowing that all things were now accomplished, *that the Scripture might be fulfilled*, saith, I thirst." What a sudden flash of revealing light that comment throws for us upon the mind of Jesus as He suffered, suspended there, on that cross! His omniscient mind roved back through the prophecies of the Old Testament Scriptures while He hung there. He reviewed them, and knew that all the predictive descriptions of His death were now fulfilled, with one exception. Away back in Psalm 22: 15, it we pre-written, "My tongue cleaveth to my jaws"; therefore, "*that the Scripture might be fulfilled*", Jesus now cried, "I thirst"!

But if our Lord was the fulfilment of prophecy at His *first* coming, He will be completely so in His future *second* coming. All the spectacular "kingdom" prophecies await fulfilment then, and He will certainly fulfil them as World Emperor. That first instalment of fulfilments, when He came as Sin-bearer nineteen centuries ago, is the proof and pledge that all the *remaining* prophecies will be fulfilled with a like certitude. Already He has come to us as *Prophet*; and now He intercedes for us as *Priest*; but it still remains for Him to return as *King*, and thus to finalise the three-fold fulfilment of Messianic prophecy.

Consider further that Christ is the fulfilment of *history*. Look into that Bethlehem manger again. See those chubby, dimpled little hands: one day they shall wield the sceptre of global dominion. Read history apart from that little Babe, and it becomes a muddle without a meaning, a fitful tragedy without a final triumph, a strange story without moral significance, an enigma without a solution. Sunny patches, golden streaks, snatches of Summer; touches of bright colour, there certainly are, here and there; but taking history in its broad lines, it is a "ghastly tale", the record of human sinning and suffering and struggling and dying.

Look down the centuries: see the successive heaps of ruins. One after another, civilizations have collapsed, cultural systems have petered out, and ambitious aspirations have perished. Our own grandiose, commercialised, twentieth-century civilization is now in huge dread of atomic annihilation. Must the pathetic alternation of rise and fall, glory and shame, life and death, go on and on in never-ending indeterminateness? Or must it end in the final mockery of titanic self-obliteration? Is there *no* stable throne? Is there *no* king who never dies? Is there *no* conqueror of evil and death? Is there *no* predetermined high goal of history? There is; for the Babe of Bethlehem who died as the Sin-bearer on Calvary has risen and ascended, and is soon returning to our earth as World-Ruler.

"I am not come to destroy, but to fulfil."—Matt. 5: 17.

YES, as we were saying yesterday, the soon-coming Christ of millennial world-rule is the God-given answer to the big question-mark which hangs over tomorrow.

Going back to the days before the first of the two World Wars, some of us can remember how glibly and confidently scientists and educationalists used to talk about the "ascent of man". It was a pleasant fashion and a fond daydream. But man's history is not the upward movement which our biologists saw it to be through Darwin's spectacles. Not only have the two World Wars given a shocking exposure of educated demon-possession, and revealed a bestiality in man lower than anything Charles Darwin ever saw in Tierra Del Fuego, but our archæologists have now shown us, through the spade of the excavator and the skill of the decipherer, that instead of human history being an "*ascent* of man", it is a *descent*.

For instance, instead of *monotheism* being a gradual evolution from a primitive polytheism, as evolution-minded modernists have assured us, it is now revealed that the further we dig back into antiquity, so the clearer do the indications become that the various polytheisms were subsequent degenerations of an original pure monotheism. Instead of ascending, man has been descending; and instead of really advancing, man has been retrograding. Why, even politically, what is the crazy modern clamour for the totalitarian State but an infantile drop-back from hard-won democratic adulthood in communal self-management to kindergarten irresponsibility again, in which a few do all the thinking for the immature many?

The intervention of God in human history at the first coming of our Lord Jesus Christ put a mighty check on the downward momentum. Let the historian tell you the moral quagmire into which the civilized world had sunk two thousand years ago. Only God Himself knows what our corrupt race would have been by now, if still continuing, had not that mighty intervention taken place. Today, the downward pace is accelerated again. Great nations, and men in their millions, are refusing the true King, and saying, "We will not have this man to reign over us."

Many of us can remember how it was often asked, sometimes resentfully, and sometimes ruefully, during the Second World War, "Why does not God intervene?" Yet the question might just as pertinently be extended to the whole drama of human history. From the beginning until now there has been sin, hate, war, suffering, death. Sin did not enter as a tiny molecule and then slowly develop; it leapt into the world full-grown when Cain murdered Abel. "Why does not God intervene?" The mighty fact is that God *has* intervened; and His intervention is *CHRIST*.

For two thousand years a silent Heaven has been a sore problem to men; but this is the "age of grace" in which God's silence is His patient waiting upon the response of men to what He has already spoken in Christ. But this age is well-nigh spent. Heaven is about to break silence again. The God who spoke yesterday, and is silent today, speaks again on the dawning morrow. Christ is the "Word", the speech of God; and His return is due. In Him is the goal of history. In the words of Tennyson, His global, endless reign is "the one divine event to which the whole creation moves".

Fulfilment of Destiny

"I am not come to destroy but to fulfil."—Matt. 5: 17.

CHRIST is not only the fulfilment of prophecy and history; He is the fulfilment of *destiny*, both national and individual. Jehovah's covenant nation, Israel, is the premier object-lesson. Freed from a generations-long servitude in Egypt, the twelve tribes were gathered below Sinai, and welded into a theocracy, with the high destiny of a teaching priesthood among the nations. But Israel more and more fouled the covenant, and grieved "the Angel of His presence" (Isa. 63: 9, 10) who was none other than the pre-incarnate Christ, until the nation was distintegrated in the Assyrian and Babylonian captivities. A "Remnant" was later restored, which developed through four centuries into the Palestinian Jewry to whom Jesus came as Messiah. Instead of recognition there was repudiation and crucifixion. The cry was, "His blood be on us and on our children!" (Matt. 27: 25). It has been on them ever since. But soon now they shall "look upon Him whom they pierced, and shall mourn for Him." Then Israel shall at last find fulfilment of its high destiny.

Modern America may well reflect. Four hundred years ago the Pilgrim Fathers emigrated to North America with an open Bible and the Gospel of Christ; and among the nations today North America leads the van. Four hundred years ago the Spanish priests took the priestcraft of Romanism to *South* America; and we know the result. All the best blessings of its democracy the U.S.A. owes to Christ. Its God-given leadership will last as long, and *only* as long as Christ is honoured.

How did Britain become "*Great* Britain", mistress of the most far-flung empire of history? Queen Victoria held up a Bible, and said, "This Book is the secret of England's greatness." It was Britain's godliness rather than military power which frustrated Napoleon. On August 15th, 1804, at Boulogne, Napoleon inspected his great army for the "Descent upon England". They only awaited "a favourable wind", so he said, to "put the Imperial Eagle on the Tower of London". That very year the British and Foreign Bible Society was founded in London! A year later Napoleon wrote to one of his admirals, "If you make me master of the Pas-de-Calais for the mere space of three days, I will put an end to the destinies of England." Just before the Battle of Trafalgar the British Admiral Nelson was found praying. The boastful Napoleon died a British prisoner. Latterly, however, Britain has wandered from Christ. German-originated religious rationalism has destroyed faith in the Bible; wealth of empire and lure of Mammon have caused leaders and people to "imagine a vain thing". Two ghastly wars have weakened Britain; overseas credits, prestige and influence have dwindled; the empire has shrunk.

France has expunged the word, "God", from all her government documents. As the Nazi attack developed in 1940, the Roman Catholic *Universe* of June 21, said, "The great Church of the Madeleine was packed all day—packed to the doors. And continually the cry went up: 'Our Lady of Lourdes, save France! St. Genevieve, save France! St. Joan of Arc, save France!'" The prayers were to the wrong persons. France fell. The one Saviour was left out! Oh, let the nations learn: *IN CHRIST ALONE IS THE FULFILMENT OF HIGH DESTINY!*

Thanks be to God!

"Thanks be unto God for His unspeakable gift."—2 Cor. 9: 15.

AMONG the seasons of the year, Christmas is distinctively that of gift-making. To my own thinking, the exchanging of gifts has reached a point where it is overdone; though the original idea behind it is beautiful. It derives, of course, from the fact that Christmas celebrates God's unspeakable gift, even Christ to be the Saviour of men. If only people had their minds gratefully absorbed with *that* supreme and divine gift, in the sending and receiving of their Christmas presents, what a hallowing ministry the season would have! We have so spoiled the annual observance, however, by competitive buying and selling, rushing and straining, that many people cannot see Christ for Christmas. They forget the Saviour in the "season". Their thoughts are more on the table in the dining room than on the stable in David's town. They cannot hear the singing of the angels for the voices on the radio. They miss the stellar vision, the wondrous guiding star, in watching television and its Christmas programme stars.

Thank God, there *are* those, not a few, up and down the land, to whom Christmas still means what it was originally intended to mean; and I rejoice to think that you who read these lines are responding with renewed sensitiveness to the sacred mystery and heavenly love-light of the Christmas festival. Let us be looking heavenwards with the eyes of our hearts, and saying again with the apostle, "*Thanks be unto God for His unspeakable gift*"!

It is well worth noting where these words occur. They do *not* occur in a passage dealing with the person of Christ, or the wonder of the Cross, or the joy of redemption, or the love of the heavenly Father. No, they come after a passage dealing with money matters, that is, a collection on behalf of poor and afflicted Christian believers in Judæa. That fact alone speaks to us. Paul's mind was so full of Christ that whatever subject he was thinking or speaking about, he somehow found it leading to Christ. Wherever he began, he was sure to end there. You see it again and again in his writings. It is a characteristic which all Christians should covet to acquire. When he appeals for generous giving, he immediately breaks out with, "For ye know the grace of our Lord Jesus Christ, that though He was rich, yet for your sakes He became poor, that ye through His poverty might become rich" (8: 9), and when he eulogises generosity he cannot help exclaiming, "Thanks be unto God for His unspeakable gift!"

Oh, if we loved Jesus as Paul did, we should *speak* of Him as Paul did. If we are not wanting to be often talking of Him, we are symptomatic of backsliddenness in heart. It is sadly enigmatical, the way some seemingly sincere believers can go through all the gaieties of the Christmas season with scarce a mention of Him to friends or relatives. So far as we ourselves are concerned, let us make much of Him *this* Christmas. It will give all our social joys a sweeter and richer quality.

Not even God a greater gift could give,
Nor heav'n itself a dearer boon impart;
When Jesus came, and died that I might live,
God gave without reserve His very heart.

Language Breaks Down

"Thanks be unto God for His unspeakable gift."—2 Cor. 9: 15.

"*Unspeakable.*" It is well to appreciate that Paul picked this adjective with care. He did not use it with the glibness which often characterises our use of adjectives today. Of all parts of speech, the adjective and the adverb are the most abused in modern conversation; and our school-teachers seem as bad as other transgressors! Only the other day a lady teacher told me that she was "*terribly* pleased" about something; and another said she was "*awfully* happy" about it! That dainty little new hat is "*marvellous*", when in reality it is only rather pretty. We often use the word, "unspeakable", in the same extravagant way; but that is not how Paul uses it in our text. It is the one adjective which fits. In the utter sense, Christ is God's "*unspeakable*" gift.

In these days we need to make war against gross exaggerations. There never was a time when superlatives were so splashed about as today. During election time in Britain, as Mr. Churchill was approaching a certain town, a loud speaker was blaring, "Here comes Winnie—watch the third car—the greatest man on earth—the greatest statesman in the world." Just about the same time, Pravda was saying of Stalin, "He stands on a pinnacle never reached before. He is the greatest general of all nations"; and Moscow radio was shouting him round as "the greatest military genius of all time", who "saved freedom and the world"!

There is nothing of such gaudy salesmanship when the New Testament writers resort to superlatives. I can well imagine Paul pausing and pondering before he selected the adjective, "unspeakable", for this is the only place in the New Testament where it occurs. It is not one of his common words. It is a "special", and he carefully picks it. This is a gift of such infinite glory that language breaks down. Christ, as the Father's gift, is a sheer divine wonder. He is the supreme superlative. He is utterly "*unspeakable*".

And why? For three reasons. First, because of who He was. Second, because of what He did. Third, because of the *results* from what He did. He has brought us forgiveness for our sins, reconciliation with God, justification through imputed righteousness, cleansing from guilt, new spiritual life, restored sonship in the family of God, the pledge of immortality and eternal glory!

Oh, the "unspeakableness" of such a gift! What food is to the starving, what water is to the thirsting, what liberation is to the slave, what riches are to the poverty-stricken, what relief is to the beleaguered, what release is to the condemned prisoner, what healing is to the diseased and dying, all that and much more is Jesus Christ, the Son of God and Saviour of men. "Thanks be unto God for His *unspeakable* gift"! Language breaks down.

It is most wonderful to learn
  Such love to me, so free, so sure;
But sadly strange that I return
  A love so faltering and poor.
Yet, Lord, I want to love Thee more;
  Renew the flame within my heart,
To love Thee wholly, and adore,
  Until I see Thee as Thou art.

"I hate this place."

The FAR SIDE

August

29

TUESDAY

"Thanks be unto God for His unspeakable gift."—2 Cor. 9: 15.

SEE here the great *Giver*. This truth, that Christ is a gift of God is one of the most cardinal and far-reaching in the New Testament. We only need to reflect for a moment to realise this.

If Christ is the "gift" of God, then see the Father's *love*. By forgetting that Christ is a gift, many have slipped into the error of supposing that the First Person of the divine Triunity is a frowning Judge whose whole thought toward us is implacably severe, whereas His fundamental attitude toward us is that of fatherhood and compassion. He certainly is also moral Governor, and righteous Judge, and awful as well as sublime in His utter holiness; but all this is equally true of the Son and of the Holy Spirit. Indeed, the Father has "committed all judgment to the Son" (Jn. 5: 22) and for the very sake of righteousness has ordained that the Saviour of the race shall also be the race's Judge. Let it never be forgotten that the great bosom of the heavenly Father abounds with compassion toward us, and that Christ is *His* redeeming gift to us.

Further, if Christ is the "gift" of God, then see the Father's *grace*. Remember, a gift is something given utterly apart from obligation. Man has no claim on God in this connection. Indeed, sinners have no right to *expect* such a gift. God's "unspeakable" gift is all the *more* "unspeakable" because it is altogether unmerited and undeserved. The Father's giving of the Son was an expression of purest grace.

Still further, if Christ is the "gift" of God, then see the Father's *concern*. If He would allow the Beloved of His bosom to suffer the shameful humiliation and gory agony and depthless woe of Calvary, then how great must be His concern to save us! and how awful must it be to perish in that ages-long Gehenna from which God would fain save us! The very fact that God "spared not His own Son, but delivered Him up for us all" (Rom. 8: 32) should awaken a corresponding concern in ourselves—concern for our own salvation, and the salvation of others.

Finally, if Christ is the "gift" of God, then He is meant to be eagerly, immediately, and gratefully *received*. Thank God, it is possible to receive Him, here and now. If we have not already received Him as Saviour, we may at once do so, simply by a sincere welcoming of Him into the heart.

But, on the other hand, if He is the "gift" of God, He may also be *refused*. A gift is never something forced upon the intended receiver, or it ceases to be a gift in the real sense of the word. Not even in giving salvation will God violate the responsible freedom of the human will. None of those who finally perish will be able to allege that salvation was not made free enough. Nay, it is a "*gift*"! Those who have known the Gospel, yet perish in the "outer darkness" beyond the grave, will do so by refusing God's free gift; for to spurn this amazing gift of divine love is far greater and graver sin than to break God's law or even to rebel against His rule.

One thing is obviously true: only those who have received the "gift" can really give "thanks" for it. No others can sing the carols this Christmas with real understanding or loving gratitude to the heavenly Father. Oh, that you and I, having received and proved the Saviour, may sing more feelingly than ever, this Christmas, "Thanks be unto God for His unspeakable gift"!

Come, and Behold Him

"They shall call His name Emmanuel . . . God with us."—Matt. 1 : 23.

"THE Word became flesh." "Emmanuel . . . God with us." "A Saviour . . . Christ the Lord." What mysterious splendour flashes from these New Testament phrases which the Christmas season underlines! How surely the annual commemoration provokes new wonder in grateful Christian hearts! How eloquent indeed it is to all who have "ears to hear"! In the super-miracle of the Incarnation, our very Creator, Preserver, Judge, becomes our Kinsman, Sinbearer, Redeemer! Of all miracles and mysteries this is the most staggering. Reflect again on some of its profound and precious relevances.

Think what sacredness it gives to *motherhood*. The eternal Son of God, brighter than the brightest of the morning stars, holier than the holiest of the flaming seraphs, lovelier than the loveliest of the anointed cherubs in the paradise of God, enters our race by a real human birth. If He was to become really one with us, so as really to represent us and redeem us, a real human birth was a *necessity*. It was also necessary that He should be born of a *virgin*. It was impossible that He should have a human father; for a Christ with a human father could not possibly have been the eternal Son of God. Yet He must not be born even of the virgin until she has become a *married* woman, lest His incarnation should ever seem to countenance unmarried parenthood. How wonderfully then the Incarnation honours and sanctifies womanhood, wedlock, parenthood, childhood, and especially motherhood!

Again, what dignity it confers on *human nature*! Years ago, Professor Dana of Yale raised the question as to whether some new and more noble order of beings might yet appear on earth and outrank man, as man now outranks the lower animals. Professor Agassiz partly answered this from a scientific point of view by observing that in the lowest vertebrates the spinal column is horizontal; in the next higher species it is oblique; while in man it has reached perpendicularity. A well-known geologist argued that man must be the highest order of being which will ever stand on earth, because he crowns the long series of animal creations, the fossils of which lie embedded in the successive geological strata as we ascend from the fire-rocks to the alluvium on which we now live. To my own mind, neither of these arguments seems conclusive. But what *does* settle it conclusively that there will never be a higher order than man is the *incarnation of Christ*. Our very Creator has taken our nature upon Himself. This stamps our human constitution (apart from its present degeneration in sin) as of highest dignity, never to take second rank by the creation of a superior order, even though the earth should roll through its orbit ten million million years to come; for it is *inconceivable* that God would create a species outranking that to which the eternal Son is now united for ever. It is the more inconceivable because when our risen Lord ascended, He carried to heaven our humanity in a far more glorious form than had been given to it even in unfallen Adam. The One who now shares the throne of universal government with the eternal Father is One who wears the form of man! And in the ultimate consummation, all His redeemed people will be presented before that same throne as lovely replicas of *that* Man! And He is "Jesus Christ, the same yesterday, and today, and *for ever*".

"They shall call call His name Emmanuel . . . God with us"—Matt. 1 : 23."

LINGER again by Bethlehem's manger. Only to those who linger reverently does it confide its deepest meanings and loveliest inspirations. To hurried callers it tells little. Indeed, even the politest hurry is an impertinence here in this cattle-shed which Emmanuel's infant majesty transforms into the sublimest of palaces. That transfigured outhouse demands adoration, not merely a hurried annual patronage at Christmas. What! are we so engrossed in the merchandise and merriment of the yearly commemoration that our Saviour is obscured by the very season which ostensibly honours Him? Oh, strangest mockery! While eastern sages travel miles and months to spread their rich devotion at His cradle, shall we who know so much more clearly the Babe's divine identity spare only intermittent snatches of our time? Nay, this all-transcendent marvel of the Incarnation calls for undistracted *contemplation.*

Following up our yesterday's meditation on it, think again what promise it brings into *human history*. Would anyone seriously deny that the history of the human race, from the earliest records onwards, is stranger and sadder than the most pathetic fiction ever fabricated? Oh, this tragic tale of sin and suffering, war and woe, evil-sowing and evil-reaping! Will the sinister lines *never* be ironed out? A troubled poet asks,

Shall crime bring crime for ever,
  Strength aiding still the strong?
Is it Thy will, O Father,
  That man should toil for wrong?

And then with pathetic bravery the poet answers his own question:

No! say Thy mountains; No! Thy skies;
  Man's clouded sun shall brightly rise,
And songs ascend instead of sighs.

But is the poet's sanguine deduction anything more than desperate optimism? *Do* the mountains and the skies guarantee any such eventual utopia? My own eyes do not always so interpret them. The one and only real pledge of an ultimate golden daybreak is *the fact of Christ*; His birth into our race; His espousal of our cause; His repulsing of our foe; His substitutionary atonement; His resurrection from death—with Satan, the grave, and Hades subdued beneath Him; and, crowningly, the promise of His second coming to our earth as global Administrator. *That* is Heaven's sure token of earth's bright morrow. "Unto us a Child is born; unto us a Son is given; and the government shall be upon His shoulders." Already He sits on the throne of universal sovereignty in heaven. His kingdom rules over all. The mystery of permitted evil on earth has thereby assumed a new aspect and has almost run its course. The usurper shall be finally banished, and the now rebellious territory shall rest in warless, tearless quietude beneath His sceptre. It shall certainly be so, for He has really *risen*; and He really *reigns*, and He will really *return.*

The Wonderful News

"Unto you is born a Saviour . . ."—Luke 2: 11.

AND now, finally, think again what wonderful hope the Incarnation brings to us as *sinful human individuals.* Said the announcing angel to Joseph, "Thou shalt call His name Jesus, for He shall *SAVE* His people from their sins". Soon afterwards the angels were singing over the fields of Bethlehem, "Unto you is born this day a *SAVIOUR* which is Christ the Lord". His very name defines Him as a Saviour. His very birth was that He might *become* our Saviour.

No lesser explanation of His incarnation is adequate. He did not *need* to become incarnate for any *other* reason. Theological philosophers have theorised that quite apart from the grim fact of human sin, God would have become incarnate, because (as they aver) it is inconceivable that He should have remained forever invisible and unrevealed. But why, then, in all His eternal continuity did not God assume such permanent visibility at some point long before the Bethlehem miracle? And why, in thus becoming linked for ever to visible creaturehood, did God choose *this* astronomically infinitesimal little planet, and this short-lasting Adam race of ours? Why did He not assume permanent visibility in some *other* way? And why did He need to endure that ugly, awful Cross on Golgotha?

We are far wiser to keep to the forthright testimony of the Scriptures: "Thou shalt call His name Jesus, for He shall *save* . . . " "Unto you is born this day a *Saviour* . . ."

We are foolish when we try to explain the Incarnation on *other* grounds; and we are equally foolish when we try to "explain away" the fact of human *sin.* We have listened to the evolutionists telling us that sin, so-called, is but an animalistic barbarity from which evolving humanity is gradually freeing itself—until two world wars of cultured, scientific brutality laughed the pathetic nonsense out of court. We have listened to aesthetic psychologists and humanistic poets telling us in technical or decorative phraseology that sin is not really the evil thing which it used to be thought—while all the time conscience, *conscience, CONSCIENCE,* that solemn sentinel within us which neither evolution nor any of your humanistic philosophies has ever satisfactorily explained, keeps on telling us with unsilenceable authority that sin is indeed SIN.

Our wisdom is to accept the united witness of human nature and divine Scripture: we are *sinners*; and there is a *Saviour.* Sin is man's tragedy. Jesus is God's answer. "God so loved the world that He gave His only-begotten Son"—gave Him to become one *with* us through His holy incarnation at Bethlehem; gave Him to become one *of* us, so that He might offer up from *within* humanity, and on our behalf, a perfectly sinless life, a perfectly obedient will, and an infinitely meritorious atonement on the Cross.

Oh what a Gospel this brings to us needy human sinners! Listen to the angels again: "Unto *you* is born this day a Saviour." Yes, "unto *you*". Let us each make it individual, and say, "Unto *me* is born this day a *Saviour*". He is no longer the Babe of Bethlehem. He is no longer the Boy of Nazareth. He is no longer the young Prophet of Galilee. He is no longer on the Cross or in the grave. He is the living and ever-contemporary Saviour who this minute stands at the heart's door of every unconverted person, saying: "Behold, I stand at the door and knock."

"This is a faithful saying, and worthy of all acceptation, that Christ Jesus came into the world to save sinners. . . ."—1 Tim. 1: 15.

CHRISTMAS comes round again. Let us suppose ourselves unexpectedly called upon to give a Christmas address to a crowd of unconverted persons who know little about the Gospel. Let us select our text, and prepare our address, you and I together. Could we choose a better text than the one here cited?

What title shall we give our address? Remember, a title should always focalise the main subject or idea of a text or discourse. In this instance, if we stick strictly to our text, the title can scarcely be other than the simple yet tremendous one, "*A SAVIOUR FOR SINNERS*".

Next, what about drawing up an homiletical outline, so that our address is methodical and orderly? Well, again, if we keep close to our text, it will have to be something like this: (1) Here is a most wonderful kind of salvation—a salvation for "sinners". (2) Here is a most wonderful kind of Saviour—"Christ Jesus *came* into the world". (3) Here is a most wonderful message, which is "worthy of all acceptation".

Many a one, of course, with far quicker brains, would think of expressing it in much more ornate or catching phraseology; but the three main constituents are those which we have indicated.

First, then, here is a most wonderful kind of salvation—a *salvation for sinners*. It is not just a salvation from poverty, or from sickness, or from war, or from ignorance, or from bad government. For the greater part of their life, many people think that *those* are the things from which we most need to be saved; but eventually they come to see differently. They perceive at last that there is a deadlier evil which lies behind all others and is their originating cause, an evil which the Bible calls "sin"; yes, *sin*, not in the modern high-faluting psychological sense, but in the plain, stark, old-fashioned Bible sense of the word. We are living in a disillusioned age. The dreams of humanitarian poets, and the fond fancies of evolutionist philosophers, with which our twentieth century dawned, have been mocked by world wars of such staggering vastness and educated vileness that the brave notion of a future man-made utopia has become inane. The world is in a state of social and political upheaval. Society has been shaken to its foundations. And behind all our twentieth-century brutalities, calamities and agonies is *sin*. Yet the world is still vainly pinning its hope on the big reformer, the big businessman, the big diplomat, the big combine, or the dictator-wizard, when all the time what it really needs is a Saviour, *the* Saviour, whose name is JESUS. He alone can save individuals from sin, and nations from corruption, and the world from atomic self-destruction.

It is comic, tragic, pathetic, how thinking people will bluff and shuffle and pretend that this is not so, when all the time, deep down in their hearts, they know that it *is* so. Sometimes it takes a spurt of candidness on the part of some newspaper editorial to express it. The other day we came across this: "The materialism born of the industrial revolution, and which has found its apogee in the terrible conception of the totalitarian State, has brought neither inward peace nor outward security. Never did we more need the Christian message of a *SAVIOUR*." That, from a modern newspaper editor! Any why not? Nothing could be truer.

A Faithful Saying

"This is a faithful saying, and worthy of all acceptation, that Christ Jesus came into the world to save sinners. . . ."—1 Tim. 1 : 15.

YES, the great need is for a Saviour to save *sinners*. But then sinners are ugly; sinners are rebels; sinners are undeserving of divine benevolence. In the moral sense, sin is loathsome leprosy. In the legal sense, sin is treason against divine law and government. What is more, millions of this world's sinners do not even *want* to be saved, so long as they may "enjoy the pleasures of sin for a season". Sinners need not only pardon for *sins*, but deliverance from innate *sin*—from that perverse inward twist and unclean condition of their inherited nature. Sinners need not only saving in time, but in the after-death state which seems to have neither horizon nor terminus. They need saving from judgment and damnation and that awful hell which is Gehenna.

But who can do all that for us? Well, look at the text again, and see the most wonderful Saviour ever heard of: "*Christ Jesus* came into the world." That title, "Christ", immediately links Him back to the Old Testament. He is the "Christ", or "Messiah", or "Anointed One", projected in Hebrew prophecy, the One "whose goings forth have been from of old, even from everlasting"; the One whose name is "Wonderful Counsellor, Mighty God, Father of Eternity, Prince of Peace"; the One predestined to be "Ruler in Israel", and a "Saviour" unto the "ends of the earth".

His precious name, "Jesus", is the equivalent of the Old Testament name "Joshua", and means "Saviour". He might have been given a more resplendent, high-sounding name for saviourhood: but no, the instruction of the angel to Mary (Luke 1 : 31), and then to Joseph (Matt. 1 : 21), was that they should call His name "Jesus", a name which was as common then as "William" is today, and which therefore makes Him one with the commonest of us ordinary folk. Oh, what music there is in the angel's words, "Thou shalt call His name JESUS".

Notice again that word, "came", in our text: "Christ Jesus *came* into the world." He was not merely born; He "*came*", which means that He came into our life and into our world from a pre-existent life and a heavenly world outside our own. His birth at Bethlehem was not His personal origination. Before He became the Son of Mary He was already the Son of God. Before the world itself had a beginning, the Eternal Son had His being. With that first little baby-breath of Bethlehem's chilly night air, the King of Ages had come from beyond the stars to dwell with us as our blood-relative! He who gave the stars and suns their flash and flame became the miracle-babe of the virgin!

Our text is noticeably specific: "Christ Jesus came *into the world*." Yes, He knowingly, voluntarily, compassionately came to the ugly, to the rebels, to the rude refusals of those who needed Him but hatefully spurned Him. He came *right into* our world, to live our life, to share our lot, to feel our woe, to show us the love of God, to bear our sin, and to make atonement for it all! Moreover, when He came into our world, our *kosmos*, our mankind, He came to stay as One of us for ever. He is still "Jesus", and He still "saves His people from their sins". His manhood was no mere transitory identification with us, which He has now discarded. His manhood and saviourhood are for ever; and He *saves* for ever all who accept Him.

"This is a faithful saying, and worthy of all acceptation, that Christ Jesus came into the world to save sinners."—1 Tim. 1 : 15.

Is all this really true? Yes, for it is a "*faithful* saying"; it is completely true and trustworthy. Perhaps not all the sayings which floated around among Christians in the early days were models of accuracy and succinctness; but *this* one was. It was true in every syllable, and was therefore "worthy of all acceptation". It was true *then*, and it is true *now*.

Away back in 1934, the following incident was narrated in a British magazine. The young Prince Edward, heir to the throne, was visiting a small hospital where thirty-six hopelessly injured and disfigured veterans of the First World War were tended. He stopped at each cot, shook hands with each veteran, and spoke words of encouragement. He was then conducted to the exit, but he observed, "I understood you had thirty-six patients here; I have seen only twenty-nine." The head nurse explained that the other seven were so shockingly disfigured that for the sake of his own feelings he had not been taken to see them. The prince insisted that he must see them, and he stayed long enough to thank each soldier for the great sacrifice he had made, and to assure each that it should never be forgotten. Then he turned to the nurse again, "But I've seen *six* men. Where is the *seventh*?" He was informed that no one was allowed to see *him*. Blind, maimed, dismembered, the most hideously disfigured of them all, he was isolated in a room which he would never leave alive. "Please do not ask to see *him*," the nurse pleaded. The prince, however, could not be dissuaded, and the nurse reluctantly led him into the darkened room. The royal visitor stood there, with white face and drawn lips, looking down at what had once been a fine man but was now a horror. Then the tears broke out, and with lovely impulse the prince bent down and reverently kissed the cheeks of the broken hero.

There is one who has stooped far, far lower, to kiss a far, far worse ugliness—not the physical disfigurement of a broken hero whose brokenness called forth reverent gratitude, but the leprous, evil ugliness of corrupt sinners and hard rebels against infinite love! Oh, there never was a story to equal it! Calvary is the gracious, compassionate, redeeming kiss of the condescending Prince of Heaven upon these sinful hearts of ours. "Christ Jesus came into the world to save *sinners*"! Is not *that* "worthy of all acceptation"? —and if we refuse it, is not our refusal the most *un*worthy behaviour we could indulge? Friend, you may receive this best and biggest and dearest of all Christmas gifts right here and now. Years ago, a workman high up on the huge glass roof of the famous Crystal Palace, London, England, took his mid-day break for lunch, and was eating it, high up there, when a curious thing happened. For weeks he had been in deep concern about his soul, and wanted to be saved. Suddenly, and apparently from nowhere, a sonorous voice rang out, "This is a faithful saying, and worthy of all acceptation, that Christ Jesus came into the world to save sinners"! To that solitary man up there, it was the voice of God direct from heaven. He lay full length on the roof, accepted Christ into his heart, and became saved. The fact was that the great Victorian preacher, C. H. Spurgeon, had gone into the Crystal Palace, to test his voice for a meeting there! Ring it out again this Christmas: "worthy of all acceptation".

The "Child" and the Son"

"For unto us a child is born; unto us a son is given."—Isa. 9:6.

JEWISH exegetes are agreed that these words and their context are Messianic. In line with this, evangelical expositors unanimously concur that the reference is to our Lord Jesus. The duality and precision of the wording have often been pointed out. He is the "Child"; and He is the "Son". As the "Child" He is "*born*". As the "Son" He is "*given*". These are the dual aspects of His humanity and deity.

"Unto us a Child is born." Oh, the *mystery* of it! The eternal Son of God entered our human life by a real birth. He did not merely occupy a human body. That would not have been incarnation; for then He would have been only a Doketic Christ, with a manhood seeming, but not real. He could easily have created a fully-developed human body and indwelt it; but that would not have made him really one with us, for it would not have given Him a human *nature*. When our Lord entered this life of ours there was an assumption of our entire human nature, spiritual, psychical, physical.

His becoming Man did not mean that He ceased to be God. His humanity did not negate His divinity. Nor were His two natures, the divine and the human, so blended as to form out of the two a compound, making Him neither fully God nor truly Man, a sort of super-man and demi-god. Nor was His personality in two parts—half human and half divine. There were the two natures, but the personality was one indivisible unity: He was God the Son. In Him, by a real human birth, God has become inseparably linked to our humanity. It is staggering.

"Unto us a Son is given." Oh, the boundless *love* which gave Him! Who the Son is, the prophecy depicts in startling terms: "Wonderful Counsellor, Mighty God, Everlasting Father, Prince of Peace." Despite the exegetical jugglery of present-day unitarian heresies, can these titles mean anything less than real deity? Even if they stood *alone* they are pretty convincing; but when taken with all the other pronouncements of Old and New Testaments concerning Him, there can be no doubt in any unbiased mind. The "Son" is co-eternal and co-equal with the Father. Take away the deity of our Lord Jesus, and you take away the glory of the Incarnation at once. It is the divine glory of the One who was "born" which makes the birth so mysterious, so stupendous!

"*Unto us* . . ." Yes, it is "unto us" that the Child is born and the Son is given. It is "to the Jew first, and also to the Gentile". Was not Ruth a Gentile? Yet did she not come into the Messianic line as the wife of Boaz, thereby becoming a fore-mother of our Lord Himself? Thus the Gentiles owe Him to the Hebrews; and the Hebrews owe Him to the Gentiles; and both owe Him to God, even the Father.

During the First World War a little boy was walking out with his father one night. Each home which had given a son to the war displayed a small silver star in the front window. When the houses were left behind, the little boy looked up at the dark sky. There was no moon, and all but one of the stars had forgotten to shine. There it was, just one bright star. The little boy went very quiet, then asked, "Daddy, did *God* give a Son, too?"

Raison d'etre

"Even as the Son of Man came not to be ministered unto, but to minister, and to give His life a ransom for many."—Matt. 20: 28.

No two persons react to anything in exactly the same way. The famous Herbert Spencer, in his argument for the mere relativity of knowledge, remarked that no two persons ever see the same rainbow. The same is emphatically true of the human reaction to Christmas. What an endless diversity of responses it evokes, both intellectually and emotionally, among the millions who live in our so-called Christendom! Choose any ten persons at random; ask each of them to write the meaning of the Christmas season in fifty words; and you will be surprised at the variety of their replies. How many vague, wrong, uninformed, or pathetically inadequate ideas of Christmas float around! Yet the truth enshrined in the annual Christmas commemoration is the most basic and vital in our Christian religion. It is the original protoplasm from which every other distinguishingly Christian truth evolves. Nothing is more important than to grasp the real meaning of Christmas.

So, then, look again at our oft-quoted text and see in it, first, *the one explanation of Christmas which really matters*. This is the explanation of Christ Himself. A few Christmases ago, I happened to be free from preaching appointments, so I took leisured opportunity to read and hear what others were saying about Christmas. Some thought this, and some thought that, and others thought something else. There was not only happy variety, there was serious variance. To one, Christmas was a symbol of intangible aspirations. To another, it was an idealistic enshrinement of motherhood and family life. To another it was "the most significant domestic festival in the Church's calendar". But when I turned back again to our Lord's own explanation, this is what I found: "The Son of Man came not to be ministered unto, but to minister, and to give His life a ransom for many." If *any*one knows "the reason why", *He* does. His is the one explanation of Christmas which really matters.

This immediately leads to the further thought that here we have *the one explanation of Christmas which is really adequate*. In view of our Lord's words, it is intolerably inadequate to offer some beautifully-worded yet merely aesthetic explanation of Christmas. Our Lord's incarnation was not merely idealistic; it was *redemptive*, as the text says. That first baby breath in the outhouse at Bethlehem was the first step of the incarnated Deity toward the awful yet glorious Cross on Calvary. Mark it well: He came to "give His life" as a "ransom for many".

Once again, in our text we see *the one explanation of Christmas which really safeguards it*. Separate Christmas Day from Good Friday, and Christmas is doomed—doomed to decay into a merely sentimental or superstitious or sensuous "eat-drink-and-be-merry" festivity of December. Bethlehem and Golgotha, the Manger and the Cross, the birth and the death, must always be seen together, if the real Christmas is to survive with all its profound inspirations; for "the Son of Man came not to be ministered unto, but to minister; and to give His life a ransom for many". Yes, we must always see that Manger in the light of that Cross.

The Manger and the Cross

"Even as the Son of Man came not to be ministered unto, but to minister, and to give His life a ransom for many."—Matt. 20:28.

LET us stand before these words of our Lord again this Christmas, and marvel at the *divine wonder* which they express. I sometimes fear that the capability of wondering is becoming sadly perverted in modern man. We are so occupied with wondering at little things which are only *seemingly* big, that we do not marvel any more at the things which are *really* big. We are so in the way of marvelling at clever new gadgets in the latest automaticity of automobiles that we are losing our marvel at the sunrise and the procession of the seasons. We are so kept marvelling at aeroplanes whizzing through skies at supersonic speeds, guided missiles prophetically screaming from continent to continent, outer-atmosphere rockets, projected space-ships, and other inventions of these days, that we are losing both the appetite and the aptitude to marvel at the *really* big things, the things which are spiritual and divine. We think ourselves wonderful twentieth-century-ites, when in fact it may be that we are fast becoming metallic-minded mechanics, or mere children again, too busy playing with exciting toys to have an adult sense of marvel at what is *really* marvellous.

This very minute I have picked up a pretty Christmas card in which the brief, ornate message is, "Greetings and best wishes for the holiday season." That card represents the big tragedy: Christmas for millions is just "the holiday season". Are we losing the sense of marvel at the Christmas miracle? Why, this is the most stupendous and astonishing wonder which could ever engross the human mind—that the eternal, infinite Creator of the universe should enter our human life, and assume our human nature, by being born as a baby of a human mother!

So far as we know, time, in the sense of days, weeks, months, years, decades, centuries, millenniums, began only some six thousand years ago. To our human review, what mighty developments have occurred in that long unrolling of time! To our little, day-at-a-time existence, what a vast sweep six thousand years seem! Yet what *is* "time" but a very temporary concept? It is a purely temporary way of making continuity intelligible to tiny, finite man. The earth itself is much older than time, the modern concensus of scientific opinion dating it as some three thousand million years old. Yet what are three million million years compared with eternity? Earth and time are a mere infinitesimal parenthesis. Oh, that word "eternity"—without beginning, without ending. Yet, at that first Christmas, it was the Eternal who became born of a human mother, to become our Kinsman-Representative and vicarious Sin-bearer!

Oh, wondrous mystery,
  That Thou, Eternal One,
Shouldst enter human history
  As Mary's lowly Son!

Each baby sigh and breath
  Proclaims Thee now my kin;
Oh, perfect life! Oh, Calvary death!
  Atonement for my sin!

"The shepherds said one to another, Let us now go even unto Bethlehem, and see this thing which is come to pass."—Luke 2 : 15.

THREE days from now, we shall be celebrating again that most wonderful mystery of divine love, the coming of the Son of God into our human life, as the Son of Mary. It is the tenderest of all the Christian festivals. May we observe it with happiness of the right kind, with softened hearts and prayerful praise. As the wistful pealing of the Bethlehem bells is wafted to us again over the miles and down the centuries, let us pray that the meaning and message of Christmas may break upon human hearts this year as never before.

Let us also turn to the Scripture again. Turn to Luke 2 : 8–20. We are told five things about shepherds—their resolve, their reward, their report, their return, their rejoicing.

First, note their *resolve*, "Let us now go even unto Bethlehem." It was marked by the right qualities. They resolved to go at the right time—"Now"; and to the right place—"Bethlehem"; and for the right purpose—"to see this thing"; and in the right spirit—to make the most of the heavenly visitation. So should we, too, make the most of whatever means God is pleased to use in our own case. He may not send contingents of angels; but He has sent the Holy Spirit to urge and guide. The angels were soon gone; the Holy Spirit abides.

Second, note their *reward*. Verse 16 says, "They came . . . and found . . ." And what a rewarding find! They were the first mortals, apart from Mary and Joseph, to see the incarnate Christ! Perhaps they came at some risk to their sheep. We may safely leave earthly cares with God when we are really following a divine direction. What rewards there are to those who respond to the word of God as the shepherds did!

Now note their *report*. See verses 17, 18. There are three observable features, (1) it was widespread—they "made known abroad", (2) it was true to fact—"the saying which was told them", (3) it was impressive—"all they that heard it wondered". And dare we ourselves hold our peace, who know Jesus as our Saviour?

See now their *return*. Verse 20 says, "And the shepherds returned." Does this cause mild surprise? Do we think that after such an experience they would not wish any more to return to their ordinary work? Here is an important lesson; Most of us must return to so-called "secular" work; and we are meant to return to it in such a way as to glorify it because of the vision of Christ which we now carry in our minds.

Finally, see their *rejoicing*—"The shepherds returned glorifying God." Their rejoicing did not call attention to their own privilege. It was full of Christ, to the glory of God. Here is a true example. Let us, too, rejoice in our dear Saviour in such a way as keeps men's eyes on HIM, to the glory of God, who so loved the world that He gave His only-begotten Son, that whosoever believeth on Him "should not perish, but have everlasting life". Nowadays, Christmas festivities are often such as to make social adjustment problematical for true Christian believers. It is an irony. Yet there need be no frigid aloofness, any more than compromise. Let there be eager participation, but always in suchwise that "in all things *HE* might have the pre-eminence".

Hope for the Nations

"Now the God of hope fill you with all joy and peace in believing, that ye may abound in hope. . . ."—Rom. 15: 13.

THE Assyrians, Babylonians, Phœnicians, Egyptians, Persians, Greeks, and Romans had their "gods many and lords many"; gods of war, gods of industry, gods of agriculture, gods of cities, gods of towns, and various others; but in all their galaxy of gods they never had one who was called, or ever *could* be called a "god of hope". That is scarcely surprising, however, for in that ancient world hope had become a despised delusion, long enough before our Lord was born in Bethlehem. The fact is, there is *no* real hope for this sin-cursed human world of ours apart from the true God, the God of Israel, the "God and Father of our Lord Jesus Christ", the God of Christmas.

No book ever heard of calls God by such sympathetic and attractive names as the New Testament. He is the "God of all comfort"; the "God of compassion"; the "God of consolation"; the "God of patience"; the "God of peace"; the "God of grace"; the "God of glory"; and (one of the most appealing) the "God of *hope*". But on what grounds does the New Testament use such endearing titles of the infinite deity? And why do we ourselves, today, dare to address Him by such names? It is all because of what happened nineteen hundred years ago in that stable at Bethlehem, and afterward on the cross of Calvary.

And why in our text is God called the "God of *hope*"? The answer is in the preceding verse: "Esaias (i.e. the Book of Isaiah) saith: There shall be a root of Jesse, and He that shall rise to reign over the Gentiles; in Him shall the Gentiles (or nations) *hope*" (verse 12). "Now the God of (this) *hope* fill you with all joy and peace in believing, that ye may abound in *hope* (especially in *this* hope of the Lord's coming Messianic reign) through the power of the Holy Spirit" (verse 13). So, then, God is the "God of hope" because in "the fulness of the time" the eternal Son was born of a human mother, born in Bethlehem on that first Christmas day; born as the "root" or offspring of the house of David; born to be the Saviour, not only of Israel, but of all the Gentile peoples as well. "In Him shall the Gentiles (or nations) hope."

So, then, in Him is *hope for the nations*. Can we not see it more clearly today than ever? The atom has been split. Incalculable weapons of destruction have emerged. Fearful risks and tensions, with frightful possibilities of racial self-extinguishment, cover tomorrow with an ominous question-mark. Is there hope in science or philosophy or in any of the non-Christian religions, or anywhere else? The one true hope for the nations is the promised return of David's Greater Son, our Lord Jesus, as universal Sovereign. "In *Him* shall the nations hope."

Soon after the splitting of the atom, and the opening up of this new atomic epoch, Sir Winston Churchill said, "The one hope of this twentieth century is a return to the teaching of Jesus Christ." Yes, Jesus is the one true hope in *that* sense, i.e. ethically and spiritually; but He is also the one true hope in a further sense: He is soon coming back to this earth in the splendour of His *second* advent, as universal Ruler. Then shall tyrannies and misrule be done away. Then shall the meek inherit the earth; and peace cover the earth. "Even so, come, Lord Jesus."

Hope for the Individual

"Now the God of hope fill you with all joy and peace in believing, that ye may abound in hope. . . ."—Rom. 15:13.

TARRY at this favourite verse again: "Now the God of hope fill *you* (i.e. each of you, all of you, as believers) with all joy and peace in believing, that ye (as Christian individuals) may abound in hope." This is a lovely picture of what our Christian experience should be: fulness of "joy", fulness of "peace", and abounding in "hope". Notice that it is "joy and peace in *believing*"; but in believing what? See verse 12 again: "In Him (Christ) shall the Gentiles hope." This "believing" is a believing in the Lord Jesus Christ as the one great hope of human individuals.

Think again what a marvel is the Incarnation. At all ordinary births a new personality is brought into existence. When a little babe is born, there is not only the tiny body; there is a new human personality which absolutely did not exist before. Where there was a sheer blank there is now a new mind, a new being, a living, thinking, human entity. But this was *not* the case when Jesus was born in Bethlehem. In that supernormal conception and birth an already existing divine Person actually assumed our human nature, both physically and mentally.

The Roman Catholics have a crude title for Mary which is as repugnant to *us* as it seems morbidly gratifying to *them*. We shudder every time we hear it: "Mary, the *Mother of God*." Mary was *not* the mother of God, and as for ourselves we respect her far too highly ever to inflict such a blasphemous obloquy upon her. She was not even the mother of His essential manhood, much less of His eternal godhead. He did not inherit His *mind* from Mary. It was of the *physical* part that she became mother. Our Lord's manhood had no father; His godhead has no mother. What happened away back in Bethlehem was that the pre-existent Son of God took our human nature to Himself, and entered our human family by the process of a supernatural conception and a truly natural birth. On that long-ago Christmas day the Son of God became humanly one with us. In His stainless life He became our accepted Representative. In His Calvary death He became our vicarious Sin-bearer and Saviour. In His resurrection and ascension He flooded man's dark sky with the sunrise of glorious new *hope*.

In Him is *hope for the sin-distressed*. See the three spiritual benefits denoted in our text: "joy", "peace", "hope". In Him is the joy of a heavenly Father's forgiveness. In Him is the peace of a new standing in imputed righteousness before the heavenly Judge. In Him is the hope of a heavenly destiny by and by.

In Him, too, is *hope for the sin-defeated*. See that other phrase in our text: "through the *power* of the Holy Spirit". So also there is *hope for the sad and desolate*. The divine sympathy and understanding now come to us through a human heart, even that of the "meek and lowly" Jesus.

Christmas is here;
The bells ring *hope*
To millions of souls
Who in darkness grope.

Christmas is here;
The bells ring *joy*.
World-empire is wrapped
In that baby-boy.

The Great Day

"For unto you is born this day in the city of David a Saviour which is Christ the Lord."—Luke 2:11.

"A SAVIOUR"!—everything in this announcement of the angels gathers round that precious word. Seven amplifying features are supplied: first, who He is; then how, when, where, why, and to whom He came; and what feelings His coming should evoke.

First, see *Who* it was who came: "Christ the Lord." He is the long-predicted, long-expected Messiah, the God-appointed and God-anointed One who should fulfil the promises of the Abrahamic and Davidic covenants, and in whom the long-cherished national aspirations should fructify into actual realisation. And He is none less than "the Lord", that is, Jehovah (for the Greek word, *Kurios*, translated as "Lord", was the Septuagint equivalent of the Hebrew "Jehovah"). That title, "Christ the Lord", would startle those shepherds beyond measure; and in like manner should it still affect you and me.

Second, see *how* He came: "Unto you is *born* . . . a Saviour." How this sanctifies human motherhood—let us remember its sanctity today. How it honours womanhood!—in contrast with non-Christian religions and present-day tendencies. What dignity it confers on our race—for it links God Himself indissolubly with it. How irrefutably it proves the real manhood of Christ! If He was "born" then He is truly human as well as eternally divine. He spans the gulf between God and man. Think of it: God the Son was humanly "born". Oh, the mystery!

Third, see *where* He was born. It was "in the city of David". What historical connections Bethlehem had for those shepherds. It was there that Jacob's beloved Rachel died, giving him that last pledge of her affection, little Benjamin. It was there that the gentle Ruth gleaned in the fields, and became the wife of noble Boaz. It was the city of Joab, Abishai, and others among the mighty. But above all, it was *David's* city. It was there that David was born; and there, amid the nearby hills and gorges, that he learned to sling his stones and play his harp and sing his psalms. And it was David's Messiah-Successor for whom all were waiting.

Fourth, remember *when* He was born. It was "this day". How gladdening that was to the shepherds! How condemning it is to *us*! "This day" was two thousand years ago, yet still there are millions who have never even heard.

Fifth, see again *why* He was born. "Unto you is born . . . a *SAVIOUR*." Do you think the angels would have come with such ecstatic alacrity to announce the birth of a philosopher, a statesman, a warrior, a reformer? Nay, nothing could have brought them trooping over the parapets of glory but the titanic tidings of a *SAVIOUR* from sin and death and hell.

Sixth, observe *unto whom* He came. The word runs, "Unto *you* is born a Saviour," that is, "unto you shepherds; unto you people of Israel; but especially unto you human beings as distinct from us angels."

Seventh, note what *feelings* should be ours in reaction to the joyous tidings. The first word in our text is "For", which connects it at once with the foregoing verse, where we have, "*Fear not*", and "*great joy*". May our own hearts find peace and joy in believing the glad message.

"God . . . hath spoken in His Son."—Heb. 1: 1, 2.

ONE of the worthwhile features in the observing of sacred seasons is that it causes many minds to concentrate simultaneously on the same big truth. However much Christmas may be abused by godless worldlings, it brings home to Christian hearts around the globe, all at the same time, that wonderful event which is the *first* of all strictly Christian facts, the incarnation of the Divine Son.

In these days the tendency in Christmas observation is to become pleasantly sentimental but undoctrinal. Sentiment is wholesome when moored to sound doctrine, but it is gullible and evanescent when it drifts *away* from doctrine. There is urgent need today to re-emboss the season with sound Christmas *teaching*; and with this in mind we turn again to the first two chapters of Hebrews,.

First, He comes as divine *REVEALER*. See chapter 1: 1. In contradistinction to all merely human messengers, He is the "Son", who is the full and final speech of the Self-revealing God. He is divine revelation incarnate and consummate. Not that we have yet *grasped* all this ultimate divine word; but everything in Him is revelatorily full and final. In this supreme articulation of God to man there is yet to be the eloquence of the Second Advent. See verse 6, in which the word, "again.", should be the third word, not the second; "And when *again* (i.e. in the future) He bringeth the First-Begotten into the habitable world, He saith: Let all the angels of God worship Him." The eternal Creator-Spirit has found permanent full-manifestation "in the face of Jesus Christ". The yearning Father-heart of the Deity has found eternal full-utterance in "the Word become flesh".

But second, our Lord Jesus comes as divine *RESCUER*. See 1: 3; 2: 3, 9, 10, and especially 2: 14, 15, where we find that the Eternal Son "took flesh and blood" for the twofold purpose of destroying the devil and rescuing us human beings. Note carefully that He came to "destroy him that had the power of death". It was Satan who brought sin and death into the human race. It is an awing thought that because of this, Satan wielded the power of death, and held millions of the departed as his prisoners in hades. But the sinless Christ of God, having voluntarily undergone dissolution of soul and body through crucifixion, "went and preached to the spirits in prison", proclaiming to them that *He* was now Lord of that domain—even as He says to John in Revelation 1: 18, "*I* have the keys of hell (hades) and of death (the grave)."

Third, He comes as the divine *RESTORER*. See 2: 5–10. Originally, God "put all things in subjection" under man; but in the first Adam man lost his crown and sceptre; so that now we "see *not* all things put under him". But we *do* "see Jesus (the *new* Man) crowned with glory and honour", as the Progenitor of a new humanity; the pledge of a coming new age; and the great Restorer who "brings many sons into glory"! Even people who never read the Bible realise that this atomic epoch is heading up to some global super-crisis. A new age is soon to break! See 2: 5, "Unto the angels God hath not subjected the age to come." Nor will it be under Kremlin or United Nations or Vatican mastery. It will be the first thousand-year earth-phase of an endless Christocracy.

"Emmanuel . . . God With Us"

"They shall call His name Emmanuel . . ."—Matt. 1 : 23.

IN the first chapter of Matthew there are three names used of the wonder child born at Bethlehem; in verse 23, "Emmanuel"; in verse 16, "Christ"; in verse 21, "Jesus". These three express the essential mystery and meaning and message of the Incarnation.

"*EMMANUEL.*" Verse 23 reads, "They shall call His name Emmanuel which being interpreted is, *God with us.*" If our Lord Jesus is only a creature, as certain modern unitarian sects aver, then, even though He may now be the most exalted of all creatures, there is really nothing in the Christmas story to command the utter astonishment of the human intellect; for the Creator and the creature are still infinitely apart. But if, as our texts says, He is "Emmanuel—*God* with us", then (let everlasting amazement be ours!) there is a union of the Creator with the creature. Once you grant that the awful Power within and behind phenomena has parted the veil and appeared in fashion as Man, then the proper reaction is that nothing else matters except in relation to this all-eclipsing event. This union of the Divine and the human necessarily dwarfs all other facts and concerns. Indeed, all other phenomena, knowledge, events and concerns must now be viewed in the light of it; for it not only dwarfs all others, it illumines and changes them all, whether natural, social, political, racial, or individual. All other appearances which have held the gaze of admiration, including all the trophies of art, philosophy, and science, are burned, as it were, in the unique white light of *this* super-fact. That is to say, it is the *continual surprise* from which the mind never recovers, so long as the mind is awake and real, and not torpid with unthinking acquiescence.

"*EMMANUEL.*" This is the miracle-of-miracles, the meaning-of-meanings, which should rivet the attention of so-called Christendom today as never before. It is the fundamental interpretation of things, compared with which the splitting of the atom is merely an infinitesimal incident. As the angels of heaven look down upon this earthly scene, surely their biggest marvel must be the *absence* of human marvel at this eternal surprise that Infinity has clothed itself with our humanity. It has been truly said that our local regimes and revolutions are temporary surface things compared with the possibilities open to us under One who is the "appointed Heir of all things." If the Son of Man be the predecreed corner-stone of the long human story, it is inept to build on any other foundation. Everything that men need is in Him, in whom are all the treasures of wisdom.

Today the nations of Christendom long for deliverance from international strife and the threat of global chaos through atomic war. It can be found in HIM. Today millions everywhere long for release from "the deadening dulness and secular prose of the ant-hill existence". The answer is in HIM. But the cleverest brains of our little epoch are straining, eye-wearied, after electrons and protons; and the churches are wonderfully busy with merely secondary things. The Lord Jesus Christ, EMMANUEL, He is the "Door of Hope" to the badly needed "New Order". In our time, all tributary questions and secondary controversies should be given a rest, for the sake of concentration upon this master-idea, the gathering together in one of "all things which are in heaven and which are on earth, even in Him" (Eph. 1 : 10).

A Yuletide Flashback

"And the government shall be upon His shoulders."—Isa. 9: 6.

In turning over some old leaves recently, I came across a short article which I wrote for Christmas 1944, while the Second World War was still raging. This is how it began:

"Christmas has come round again, with all its tender associations and reminders; but for the sixth year in succession, Christmas has found the nations locked in a deadly monster-war; and war is the blatant repudiation of all that Christmas represents. Christmas incarnated Love; war expresses hate. Christmas breathes peace; war is murderous strife. Christmas immortalises humility; war exalts callous tyranny. Christmas glorifies gentleness; war unleashes gloating brutality.

"Such are the weapons of war in this age of science, and so interrelated have all five continents now become, that each new war is bigger and ghastlier than its predecessor. God is allowing the nations to drive themselves through their own costly folly to an agonising ultimate where they will cry out of very anguish for Christ Himself to assume world government. It will be a choice between racial self-annihilation through prostituted science, and global unification under the millennial sceptre of the Lord Jesus. That time, indeed, is all but upon us. The one, big, lovely sunshaft through the storm-clouds of this present World War is this great Christmas prophecy of long ago: "The government shall be upon *His* shoulders."

"There will be many sad homes this Christmas, and comparatively few homes where the family is complete. Perhaps many of us are feeling far from inclined to enter into Christmas rejoicings in the usual way. Yet if I may say so, without being thought unsympathetic, we *must* rejoice, despite everything. It is a *duty*. We owe it to *God*. For, remember, though wars grow worse and worse, though malicious men and fuming fiends work viler and viler wickedness, it is the message of Christmas and the manger of the Christ-Child which are to win in the end. Tears of today *will* be wiped away tomorrow. We must read the story of Bethlehem in the light of Easter morning. Jesus rose; and His resurrection is the divine pre-attestation that He shall yet rule the world as King and Judge (Acts 17: 31).

"Therefore, whatever our sorrows may be this Christmas, let us enter gratefully into the joys of the sacred celebration. Let us enter the season, not only retrospectively and commemoratively—looking back, that is, to what happened nineteen hundred years ago, but prospectively and anticipatively, looking onward to that compensating consummation which will yet come to us and to our suffering world, as the final repercussion of that long-ago nativity. Let us see this year's Christmas as one more link in the now almost-completed chain of years between that manger which *was*, and that royal daybreak which is *yet to be*."

Well, that Second World War is now a nightmare of the past. The world still rolls on. The years slip away. Sin and suffering, sighs and tears, hate-filled rivalries and haunting fear of atomic super-war linger with us. But over against all that, the big, unmistakeable signs now appear—too clearly for us to be deceived, that the longed-for reappearing of our Lord is "at hand" when "the government shall be upon His shoulder", and all the earth shall sing the song of the Bethlehem angels. Yes, we *MUST* rejoice this Christmas, for *HIS* sake!

"I Remember, I Remember"

"I do remember my faults this day."—Gen. 41 : 9.

REMEMBRANCE days are frequent nowadays. Many, alas, are connected with wars; but again and again we are asked to pause and remember. The soul, too, should have remembrance days. If we paused more often, to remember and review, what improvements might be ours!

There is no time when reflection on the past seems more congruous than year-end. In the commercial world, it is the time when accounts are finalised, balances drawn, inventories made, and a general review is taken. We cannot deal with the soul in just the same way as a business house, yet there are real parallels.

Year-end is on us. Are we too busy to halt for unhurried reviewing of the past? How foolish we are! We are denying the soul (made for eternal destiny) what any trader gives to a mere business of earth and time. Look back over the bygone months. How do you feel? Are there no thorns of conscience to make memory bleed with regret? Are the past months so strewn with golden deeds that you feel only complacence? Or are there ugly ghosts which you would fain smother in deep oblivion? Can you say with the psalmist, "I have refrained my feet from every evil way"? Or must you say with Pharaoh's butler, "I do remember my faults this day"?

Look again at that butler's *memory*. First, he remembered that he had *forgotten*! (read the incident). Forgetting what we ought to remember, and remembering what we ought to forget, is a common fault. We forget vows, answers to prayer, blessings both common and uncommon. Should we not amend this?

Again, that butler's fault was one of *omission*. It was a promise he had omitted to fulfil. It was a kindness he had omitted to repay. It was a humanitarian obligation he had omitted to discharge. Sometimes such faults of omission disclose our sinfulness even more than active transgressions (Jas. 4: 17).

Further, the fault which he remembered was essentially *personal*. He had omitted to do something which only he himself could do, for one who had been grievously wronged. Are there such things which you and I ought to have done—and which now will *never* be done, because *we* failed?

But see now that butler's *conscience*. "I do remember *my* faults"—not other people's! "*This day*"—after a lapse of two years! "My *faults*"—the one reminded him of the many! Thank God, he not only remembered and regretted, he confessed, and resolved to put wrongs right.

At a large school the final classes had been held before year-end vacation. Some bolder boys started a fire in the quad. Soon all the scholars gathered round. Suddenly all faces paled. The headmaster walked towards them, with the big "black book" which recorded misdeeds. Amid tense silence he said, "This is year-end. In this black book are things which many would like blotted out. I now fling it into the fire, that we may all start the new year with not a line against us." Amid cheers he then cast it into the fire! Thank God, we may all start the new year with all our guilt cleansed away. See 1 John 1: 7, "The blood of Jesus Christ, His Son, cleanseth us from *all* sin." See Ephesians 1: 7, "In whom we have . . . the forgiveness of sins, *according to the riches of His grace.*"

The Important Left-Overs

"Gather up the fragments which remain, that nothing be lost."—Jn. 6 : 12.

OUR Lord here teaches a vital lesson by what seems almost a humorous incongruity. What! does He who can multiply five barley cakes and two small fishes to feed thousands request conservation of the "fragments"? He does; and He thereby teaches us not to presume on miraculous interventions. If God sends us an overplus and we waste a part, He may *not* intervene to supply us the *next* time we are in need. "Gather up the fragments which remain." Do not despise economy amid plenty, or the little amid the big. It was while Ruth gleaned fragments in the harvest field that the biggest thing in her life happened. It was because the little American boy cared for his nickels and dimes that he is now a wealthy businessman giving thousands a year to overseas missions.

We are near the end of another year. What of the "fragments" which remain? Are some of us so eager to experiment with the *new* year that we discount the fragments of the old? We err. The new year is always much affected by the way we use the last fragments of the old. We cannot waste *them* and then suddenly be "in the Spirit" as the new year glides in. Let me mention three ways in which, at year's end, we should "gather up the fragments which remain, that nothing be lost".

We should gather up the fragments of *the old year's last moments*. Have you not noticed, it is when we near the end of an event or period that we count the moments? When we think ahead about a *new* year, we tend to think of it in its totality as a *year*; but at year's *end* we realize accentuatedly how the years build themselves up and then silently fall way in fugitive, unrecallable, inexorable *moments*, and that it is our use of those elusive moments which determines the character and outcome of the whole. It is handed down that the first Queen Elizabeth of England cried from her death-bed, "Thirty thousand pounds for another ten minutes of time!" When we are losing the last few moments we know their value. It was when Abram thought he was losing Sarah that he suddenly said, "Behold now, I know that thou art a fair woman to look upon" (Gen. 12 : 11). It was when David came to his last moments that conscience confronted him with wrongs left unrighted (1 Kings 2 : 5–9). There is a significant little participle clause in Ephesians 5 : 16, "Redeeming the time." More literally, it is, "Buying up the opportunity". I never come to year-end without recalling Horatius Bonar's lines,

> Fill up the hours with what will last;
> Buy up the moments as they go.
> The life above, when this is past,
> Is the ripe fruit of life below.

What! are we too cumbered with "cares of this world", or with "eating and drinking", to get alone with God in prayer? Then how *can* the new year be what we long for it to be? One day, the ungathered fragments of this year-end may be gathered up in testimony against us!

More About Those "Fragments"

"Gather up the fragments which remain, that nothing be lost."—Jn. 6: 12.

As we draw near the end of another December, ought we not to "gather up the fragments" of *the old year's aspirations*? Think back; recall how brave and sanguine were our resolves at the beginning of the year which is now ebbing out. Have all those idealistic intentions been realised? Does the very question seem grimly humorous as we now regret pathetic failures or ironic frustrations? Well, remember that the past year would have been measurelessly worse if we had started *without* those high aims. Moreover, if we cannot exult in victorious fulfilments, the *longings* still remain, like precious "fragments" which our Lord can make into "twelve baskets" of blessing for us in the coming twelve months. Gather up the fragments of those unfulfilled resolves and aspirings. Do you not recognise that those very yearnings which linger on within you are the comforting evidence that the Holy Spirit is still tenderly ministering within you, causing you still to "hunger and thirst" after higher things, even though the old year is sadly tip-toeing away with such a poor record? Yes, gather up those remaining aspirations, and turn them now into new prayers. Remember, you are dealing with a *sympathetic* Christ. He forgives the past, and offers new enablement for the new year. He can turn even twelve baskets of regrets into twelve baskets of new promise.

But again, we should "gather up the fragments" of *the old year's lessons*. Have not the past twelve months taught us again that the simpler our life, the richer and more restful it is?—that when we neglect prayer the meaning goes out of things, and even success does not satisfy?—that a babbling brook is always shallow, and a life of cumbered rush is superficial? Have we not learned again that our adversities are God's opportunities, and that Jesus never fails us if we really trust Him? Have we not found even if in only snatchy experiments, that when we live according to Philippians 4: 6, 7, it all comes true?—"Be anxious for nothing, but in everything by prayer and supplication with thanksgiving let your requests be made known unto God; and the peace of God which passeth all understanding shall guard your hearts and minds in Christ Jesus." Nearly four thousand years ago, uncle Laban said to nephew Jacob, "I have learned by experience . . ." Experience is the greatest of teachers, but his fees are heavy. Shall the lessons of experience during the past year be left idly ungathered? Ought we not to gather them to fill twelve baskets of wisdom for the coming year?

Then again, there are the "fragments" of *the old year's last opportunities*; opportunities of putting things right with our heavenly Father; with our dearest Friend and Master, the Lord Jesus; and with the ever-present, ever-patient, ever-gracious Holy Spirit; opportunities of putting wrong things right between ourselves and other human beings; opportunities of Christian witness ere another year is gone for ever.

Best of all, there are those precious "fragments", *the divine promises*. Someone has counted 3,300 of them in the Bible. They are all "Yea and Amen" to us in Christ. Gather them up! Then tread confidently into the new year, with "twelve baskets" full of wonderful reassurance!

INDEX OF TEXTS